GREAT WRITERS STU

20th-CENTURY
POETRY

GREAT WRITERS STUDENT LIBRARY

1. The Beginnings to 1558
2. The Renaissance Excluding Drama
3. Renaissance Drama
4. Restoration and 18th-Century Prose and Poetry
   Excluding Drama and the Novel
5. Restoration and 18th-Century Drama
6. The Romantic Period Excluding the Novel
7. The Victorian Period Excluding the Novel
8. The Novel to 1900
9. 20th-Century Poetry
10. 20th-Century Fiction
11. 20th-Century Drama
12. American Literature to 1900
13. 20th-Century American Literature
14. Commonwealth Literature

Editor: James Vinson
Associate Editor: D. L. Kirkpatrick

GREAT WRITERS STUDENT LIBRARY

20th-CENTURY
POETRY

INTRODUCTION BY
STAN SMITH

First published 1983 by
THE MACMILLAN PRESS LTD
London and Basingstoke
Associated Companies throughout the world

ISBN 0 333 28329 5   hard cover edition

ISBN 0 333 28330 9   paperback edition

Printed in Hong Kong

CONTENTS

EDITOR'S NOTE   page vii

INTRODUCTION   1

20th-CENTURY POETRY   33

NOTES ON CONTRIBUTORS   517

EDITOR'S NOTE

The entry for each writer consists of a biography, a complete list of his published books, a selected list of published bibliographies and critical studies on the writer, and a signed critical essay on his work.

In the biographies, details of education, military service, and marriage(s) are generally given before the usual chronological summary of the life of the writer; awards and honours are given last.

The Publications section is meant to include all book publications, though as a rule broadsheets, single sermons and lectures, minor pamphlets, exhibition catalogues, etc. are omitted. Under the heading Collections, we have listed the most recent collections of the complete works and those of individual genres (verse, plays, novels, stories, and letters); only those collections which have some editorial authority and were issued after the writer's death are listed; on-going editions are indicated by a dash after the date of publication; often a general selection from the writer's works or a selection from the works in the individual genres listed above is included.

Titles are given in modern spelling, though the essayists were allowed to use original spelling for titles and quotations; often the titles are "short." The date given is that of the first book publication, which often followed the first periodical or anthology publication by some time; we have listed the actual year of publication, often different from that given on the title-page. No attempt has been made to indicate which works were published anonymously or pseudonymously, or which works of fiction were published in more than one volume. We have listed plays which were produced but not published, but only since 1700; librettos and musical plays are listed along with the other plays; no attempt has been made to list lost or unverified plays. Reprints of books (including facsimile editions) and revivals of plays are not listed unless a revision or change of title is involved. The most recent edited version of individual works is included if it supersedes the collected edition cited.

In the essays, short references to critical remarks refer to items cited in the Publications section or in the Reading List. Introductions, memoirs, editorial matter, etc. in works cited in the Publications section are not repeated in the Reading List.

INTRODUCTION

1. The Origins of Modernism

"On or about December 1910," Virginia Woolf observed in a famous phrase, "human nature changed." E. M. Forster, writing immediately after the Great War, offered a more conventional assessment, remarking that "the world broke up" in 1914. Forster's is the interpretation which has stayed with us, calling up those long sunny afternoons of Georgian tranquillity, plunged into sudden darkness by the eruption of continental war. It is a satisfying and a convenient myth, but it will not hold up to scrutiny, as George Dangerfield showed many years ago in his authoritative work, *The Strange Death of Liberal England*.

Britain on the accession of George V in May 1910 was already riddled with social conflict. In Ireland, a resurgent nationalist movement had provoked a virulent and equally militant Unionism. The formation of the Labour Party, and the rapid spread of socialist and particularly syndicalist ideas in the trade unions, resulted in a sharpening of class antagonisms that issued, as inflation crept up in the second half of the decade, in increasingly bitter strikes, demonstrations and even riots in the most concentratedly proletarian parts of the country: South Wales, Glasgow, the London Docks. A general strike seems to have been planned for the very month that war was declared in 1914. Militant suffragettes had begun to organize and act in ways which, to respectable minds, resembled those of the more unruly elements in the "lower orders." 1910 saw a major constitutional crisis in that most venerable of institutions, Parliament, with two elections called in one year to contest the right of the House of Lords to block financial legislation (Lloyd George's "People's Budget").

Externally, too, crisis after crisis pointed to an inevitable confrontation at some point between Britain and Germany, the waning and the ascendant industrial and commercial powers. Charles Doughty's epics *The Cliffs* (1909) and *The Clouds* (1912) envisaged a German invasion of Britain by dirigible; and traditional poets such as Newbolt, Noyes, and William Watson were warning that the British who, in the words of the latter, "stretch one hand to Huron's bearded pines,/ And one on Kashmir's snowy shoulder lay," should not rest complacently on past glories. Forster's own *Howards End*, published in 1910, contains many symptoms of this unease, focused in the image of the "goblin footfalls" which advance and then recede during the playing of Beethoven's Fifth Symphony, threatening, like the "unthinkable" lower orders, to break down the bastions of civilized order.

The pre-War spirit has been perhaps irrevocably identified with those poets published in Edward Marsh's *Georgian Poetry* between 1912 and 1922, which sold tens of thousands of copies. Much has been written about who, precisely, the "Georgians" were. The truth is that, like all anthologies, Marsh's brought together the most diverse talents: Robert Graves and D. H. Lawrence, Rupert Brooke and Isaac Rosenberg, among others. Edward Thomas, who has often been numbered among the Georgians, though he never published there, was quite certain that they belonged to a generation considerably younger than himself. Reviewing the first volume in the *Daily Chronicle* in January 1913, he caught their mood with his usual acuity. Chesterton, W. H. Davies, T. Sturge Moore, he wrote, were all writing as they had under Victoria and Edward. To Gordon Bottomley, Masefield, and Wilfrid Gibson there was a new "accession of power":

> These three, together with Messrs. Abercrombie, Brooke, Lawrence, Sargant and Stephens, have most of the Georgian tone, and would alone give a scientific critic material for defining that tone. Messrs. Brooke, Lawrence and Sargant are, as it were, the core of the group. [There is] much beauty, strength, and mystery, and some magic – much aspiration, less defiance, no revolt – and it brings out ... the modern love of the simple and primitive, as seen in children, peasants, savages, early men, animals, and Nature in general....

This primarily "narrative or meditative verse" might superficially have something in common with Thomas's own poetry, which he had not yet even started to write, or with the remarkable narrative monologues and dialogues of Robert Frost's *North of Boston* (1914), hailed as "revolutionary" by Thomas, in a subsequent review, "because they lack the exaggeration of rhetoric." In reality, as F. R. Leavis wrote magisterially of Thomas in *New Bearings in English Poetry* (1932), both these poets reveal "a representative modern sensibility," with a "negativeness [which] has nothing in common with the vacuity of the Georgians" but "records the modern disintegration, the sense of directionlessness" with fidelity and precision.

Robert Graves, disowning his own poetic infancy, was to write in 1927 of Georgianism as "a poetry which could be praised rather for what it was not than for what it was ..., principally concerned with Nature and love and leisure and old age and childhood and animals and sleep and similar uncontroversial subjects" (*A Survey of Modernist Poetry*). It is interesting to compare this dismissal with the more immediate, and more immediately partisan, review D. H. Lawrence gave to the first volume, in John Middleton Murry's ostensibly avant-garde little magazine, *Rhythm*, in 1913:

> This collection is like a big breath taken when we are waking up after a night of oppressive dreams. The nihilists, the intellectual, hopeless people – Ibsen, Flaubert, Thomas Hardy – represent the dream we are waking from. It was a dream of demolition. Nothing was, but was nothing.
>
> But we are awake again, our lungs are full of new air, our eyes of morning. The first song is nearly a cry, fear and the pain of remembrance sharpening away the pure music. And that is this book.

In 1913, Hardy had not yet published the great elegies for his wife, "Poems of 1912–13," which were to appear in *Satires of Circumstance* (1914) and were to consolidate for many subsequent critics his claim to greatness. Nevertheless, there was enough evidence to make Lawrence's claim, even polemically, ludicrously disproportionate. What Lawrence read into the Georgian movement was his own apocalyptic yearnings, so much a part of the atmosphere of "Modernism" but, ironically, originating in the nebulous, world-weary vapidities of the "fin de siècle" Decadence, in Dowson and Symons, et al., which, rather than the tough, solid, down-to-earth pessimism of Hardy, was to have the profoundest influence on the early poetry of Yeats, Pound, and Lawrence himself.

1909 had seen the publication of Ezra Pound's *Personae*, a text which moves graciously between the cadences of a fin-de-siècle medievalism of villonaud and sestina and a new, characteristically faltering utterance that nevertheless speaks with consummate authority, and, as Edward Thomas remarked in a perceptive review, "holds us steadily in his own pure, grave, passionate world" (*The English Review*, June 1909). It also saw, according to F. S. Flint, writing its "History" in *The Egoist* in May 1915, the founding of "Imagism." In a sense one of the most short-lived "movements" in English poetry (Flint's "History" is a conscious irony), Imagism has nevertheless had long-term and profound effects on the development of Modernism. Its aim, according to Flint, was to replace the current, post-Victorian sententiousness "by pure *vers libre*; by the Japanese *tanka* and *hakai* ... by poems like T. E. Hulme's 'Autumn' and so on," with "absolutely accurate presentation and no verbiage."

A more compelling example today would be Pound's remarkable two-line poem from *Lustra* (1916), "In a Station of the Metro":

> The apparition of these faces in the crowd;
> Petals on a wet, black bough.

As the poems in this volume make clear, in form and content, both the *Greek Anthology* and classical Chinese poetry were contributory influences, the latter seen largely through the medium of Ernest Fenollosa's essay on "The Chinese Written Character as a Medium for Poetry," which Pound had spent the winter of 1914–15 preparing for publication. Fenollosa had argued that the Chinese ideogram presented an integrated and unitary image of a whole action, with a vivid and pictorial immediacy. Pound found here confirmation of his own definition of the Image, in "A Few Don'ts," first published in *Poetry* (March 1913): "An 'Image' is that which presents an intellectual and emotional complex in an instant of time."

As a movement, "Imagism" was no more than the brief encounter of a few like minds; but the Image lived on. By 1914 Pound, ever the devourer of new ideas, could assimilate it to Wyndham Lewis's "vortex" in the columns of the latter's little magazine, *Blast* (which Pound described to Joyce as "a new Futurist, Cubist, Imagiste Quarterly").

The definition was repeated in "As for Imagisme" in *The New Age* (January 1915): "the Image is more than an idea. It is a vortex or cluster of fused ideas and is endowed with energy." But perhaps the most forceful definition, which looks forward to the sculptural and architectonic leitmotivs of *The Cantos*, and the principle of their dynamic construction, can be found in his 1916 *Memoir* for his sculptor friend Gaudier-Brzeska, an early casualty of the War: "The image ... is a radiant node or cluster; it is ... a VORTEX, from which, and through which, and into which, ideas are constantly rushing."

In Pound's case, then, the major break with tradition preceded the War, though the energies whirling in the European vortex no doubt gave a new brutal intensity to his art, as it did to that of Wyndham Lewis, the Futurists, and the Expressionists.

The same change had taken place in Yeats's poetry, which in 1910, with the publication of *The Green Helmet*, had moved decisively away from the languors and world-weariness of the Celtic Twilight, and entered into a new and contentious engagement with the actual faction-ridden world of literary and political Dublin. The Yeats who wrote the essays "The Autumn of the Body" (1898) and "The Symbolism of Poetry" (1900) had found in Arthur Symons's account of French Symbolism, collected as *The Symbolist Movement in Literature* (1899), an endorsement of all his own deepest beliefs. The first spoke of an art which should be hieratic, esoteric, spiritualized, millennial, with "faint outlines and faint energies ... dreaming of things to come," "at a crowning crisis of the world" engaged in "an ever more arduous search for an almost disembodied ecstasy." The second concluded with an emphatic vision of this future poetry:

> With this change of substance, this return to imagination, this understanding that the laws of art, which are the hidden laws of the world, can alone bind the imagination, would come a change of style, and we would cast out of serious poetry those energetic rhythms, as of a man running, which are the invention of the will with its eyes always on something to be done or undone; and we would seek out those wavering, meditative, organic rhythms, which are the embodiment of the imagination, that neither desires nor hates, because it has done with time, and only wishes to gaze upon some reality, some beauty; nor would it be any longer possible for anybody to deny the importance of form, in all its kinds, for although you can expound an opinion, or describe a thing, when your words are not quite well chosen, you cannot give a body to something that moves beyond the senses, unless your words are as subtle, as complex, as full of mysterious life, as the body of a flower or of a woman.

Yeats never really abandoned any of the attitudes and moods evinced here; but they were taken up into a new and dramatic synthesis after 1910. Symons's book was reissued in revised form in 1908, and it seemed to say new things to a new generation and a new historical conjuncture. Maurice Maeterlinck is the presence behind poems such as Yeats's "He Gives His Beloved Certain Rhymes" in *The Wind among the Reeds* (1899):

> You need but lift a pearl-pale hand,
> And bind up your long hair and sigh;
> And all men's hearts must burn and beat;
> And candle-like foam on the dim sand,
> And stars climbing the dew-dropping sky,
> Live but to light your passing feet.

It is Jules Laforgue who stands behind the energetic rhythms of "To a Poet, Who Would Have Me Praise Certain Bad Poets, Imitators of His and Mine," in *The Green Helmet*:

> You say, as I have often given tongue
> In praise of what another's said or sung,
> 'Twere politic to do the like by these;
> But was there ever dog that praised his fleas?

In such a world, it may be that, as he says, "The fascination of what's difficult/Has dried the sap out of my veins, and rent/Spontaneous joy and natural content/Out of my heart"; but the struggle has also brought a new, masculine vigour. "Will" was to be a key concept in Yeats's thinking hereafter, entering into innumerable combinations with "imagination" and "energy." In these poems, "organic rhythms" are no longer bodiless, though they are certainly subtle and complex; but the subtlety has put on flesh. Determined to "wither into the truth," Yeats was in fact preparing the ground for that remarkable blossoming of his talent which was to transform him into a major poet.

Though T. S. Eliot's first volume of poems, *Prufrock and Other Observations*, was not published until 1917 (when E. M. Forster, ensconced in Alexandria, pronounced it the best poetry to come out of the War), he began writing them in 1909, shortly after the reading of Symons's book prompted him to buy Laforgue's poems for himself. The influence is apparent everywhere in this volume. Forster praised *Prufrock* because it "sang of people who were ineffectual and weak" and was "innocent of public spirit." What Symons called "an art of the nerves," with all its sly romantic irony and oblique, self-deprecating arrogance, was to provide Eliot with the model he needed.

"The Love Song of J. Alfred Prufrock" (completed in 1911) is about a song which never crosses the lips of its putative "author," as he warily circles round the prospect of daring to "Disturb the universe." Diffident, self-conscious, but ultimately untouchable in his supercilious detachment, Prufrock can never be caught "sprawling on a pin" by the gaze of others, despite his bald spot and his anxious self-questioning, any more than his author can be, lurking behind the coyly untranslated epigraph from Dante which reminds us, with a nudge, that *he* can't be held responsible for anything his character says. Both poet and Prufrock always have "a face to meet the faces that you meet." Describing T. S. Eliot, in the title of his seminal study, as *The Invisible Poet* (1959), Hugh Kenner underlines this doubly ironic distancing which leaves the poet, like the young man of "Portrait of a Lady," "invulnerable," with "no Achilles' heel," at the very moment that his disgraceful self-extricating strategies are seen through, vanishing in a Cheshire cat smile at the end of the poem. Like Dedalus's artist in *A Portrait of the Artist as a Young Man* (1916), he stands behind his work, "like the God of creation, invisible, paring his fingernails." From Laforgue, in fact, Modernism derived one of the most potent elements in its witches' brew: irony.

In his famous essay on "The Metaphysical Poets" in 1921, Eliot suggests that Laforgue and Tristan Corbière "are nearer to the 'school of Donne' than any modern English poet." Donne had already been acknowledged, along with Webster, in "Whispers of Immortality," and the presence of a whole range of 17th-century poets and dramatists is apparent throughout the whole of his second collection. Herbert Grierson's Oxford English Texts edition of Donne had appeared in 1912, and certainly seems to have had an influence on Yeats's *Responsibilities* (1914). But Yeats never made the large claims for Donne which Eliot makes in this essay, using him as the linchpin in an argument about an imputed "dissociation of sensibility" which set in about the middle of the 17th century, "from which we have never recovered." Eliot's myth of cultural decline was to become a major item in the intellectual and even political armoury of the next half-century.

Something "had happened to the mind of England" between Donne and the time of Tennyson and Browning, he suggests. The latter "do not feel their thought as immediately as the odour of a rose." "A thought to Donne was an experience; it modified his sensibility." The ordinary man's experience is "chaotic, irregular, fragmentary"; the "perfectly equipped" poet, however, "is constantly amalgamating disparate experience": for him, falling in love, reading Spinoza, the noise of his typewriter and the smell of cooking "are always forming new wholes" in his mind. "Wit," the "metaphysical conceit," are the product of such a fusion: the 17th-century poets "possessed a mechanism of sensibility which could devour any kind of experience." The modern poet has lost this, but if he is to match the "great variety and complexity" of modern civilization, he "must be *difficult* ..., must become more and more comprehensive, more allusive, more indirect, in order to force, to dislocate if necessary, language into his meaning." (In the wrenched syntax and linguistic torsions of Gerard Manley Hopkins's poetry, not published until 1918, another model of complexity was added to the modern repertoire.)

A very complex negotiation is going on here, in which Eliot is shifting his ground as he thinks; but underneath the surface contradictions, an argument of considerable ideological force is emerging, which was to be taken up with as much rapidity as *The Waste Land* (1922) was seized upon as an authoritative statement on the modern world. What they both have in common is revealed in the poem's sudden shifts of register, rifts in sense, and ironic juxtapositions of sordid present and past richness, beauty and dignity: a myth of rupture and loss. But more than this, the degenerate present can perhaps be redeemed by some cataclysmic occurrence: language can be "dislocated," "forced" into meaning; the vision of collapsing cities in "What the Thunder Said" can be redeemed by some masterful, fateful act of "controlling hands," "set[ting] my lands in order."

Eliot is hesitant enough at the end of *The Waste Land* to present this merely as a question: "Shall I at least set my lands in order?" In an essay in *The Egoist* in 1918 he had been a little more insistent on the elite role of the writer to transform sensibility and thereby to change society:

> What we want is to disturb and alarm the public.... To point out that every generation, every turn of time when the work of four of five men who count has reached middle age, is a *crisis*. Also that the intelligence of a nation must go on developing, or it will deteriorate.... That the forces of deterioration are a large crawling mass, and the forces of development half a dozen men.

Examples could be multiplied from Yeats, Pound, Lawrence, Wyndham Lewis: they all boil down to the same thing. Democracy is the source of linguistic corruption, and therefore of social decay. Order can by restored only by purifying the dialect of the tribe, by cleansing the culture in a "refining fire," in the turbulent vortex, for, as Lawrence says: "The breath of life is in the sharp winds of change mingled with the breath of destruction."

Lawrence in his letters is quite clear that the Great War is itself some purgatorial apocalypse, in which the old husk of an amorphous, superficial civilization will be blown away. Rupert Brooke could proclaim "Now God be praised who has matched us with his hour!" and even Edward Thomas welcomed the War as a "witch's cauldron" from which a phoenix England would arise, serene and beautiful. But of course, as the poetry of such combatants as Wilfred Owen and Isaac Rosenberg shows, these sentiments soon wore off in the trenches, and a deeper, darker mood formed, of frustration, anger, futility.

For many, whether combatants or not, peace brought not renewal and regeneration but a continued stagnation, this time in a world in which many of the old landmarks had been levelled by continuous bombardment. It is this, perhaps, which sets the final seal on Modernism: its identification with a reactionary radicalism. Wyndham Lewis and Yeats both admired Fascism, or rather, what they imagined to be its aesthetic ruthlessness; Lawrence, in *The Plumed Serpent* (1926), sees a blood-and-soil ideology as the only answer for the split soul of modern man. And as for Pound: Mussolini's "continuing artistic and political revolution," he wrote, had the "material and immediate effect" of "grain, swamp-drainage, restorations, and I am ready to add off my own bat, AN AWAKENED INTELLIGENCE in the nation and a new LANGUAGE in the Chamber" (*Jefferson and/or Mussolini*, 1935).

All the forms of the "modern," post-War consciousness were there in the years that preceded it, but in suspension, uncrystallized. What the Great War did, so to speak, was to mobilize, to regiment them into that new configuration Forster was later to characterize, somewhat bathetically, as "an age in which sensitive people could not feel comfortable, and were driven to seek inner compensation." Paul Fussell's comprehensive study, *The Great War and Modern Memory*, has demonstrated the ways in which the traumatic shock of the War led to major redefinitions of common experience, infiltrating even the ordinary vocabulary of polite and demotic speech, bringing about a seismic shift in the way we explain ourselves. Both he and Robert Wohl, in *The Generation of 1914*, point out how the memoirs of the survivors of that War, mainly published during the late 1920's, helped to shape, as a historic myth, subsequent perceptions of it, particularly in terms of a rhetoric of betrayal, in which a "lost" or "sacrificed" generation were thrown away by the "old men" of a senile culture. In a sense, this radical critique of the pre-War peace is the equally sentimental obverse of that myth of prelapsarian calm shattered by an irrational and insurgent history.

Wohl argues that the whole idea of perceiving men in *generations*, that word which in its complex meanings is so central, for example, to Yeats's poetry, could not have been effected, as an intellectual system, without the experience of the Great War. Here for the first time, as Robert Graves in *Goodbye to All That* (1929) or Siegfried Sassoon in *Memoirs of a Foxhunting Man* (1928) record, young boys fresh from public school were brought into close contact, in the atrocious conditions of trench warfare, with working-men from suburb, slum, and village of whom they had previously had little experience. A generational loyalty which cut across class and, sometimes, national allegiances was to become a major shaping force in European politics for the next 30 years, less remarkably so in English that in German or Italian society, where it became a potent weapon in the armoury of National Socialist and Fascist demagogues on the one hand, and Communists on the other. Neverthless it provided one current in that radical Modernist culture which, in the 1920's, embraced a Nietzschean revolutionary nihilism, and, in the 1930's, led another generation of public-school poets to rush to the defence of the Spanish Republic. The step from Wilfred Owen's latently homosexual "Strange Meeting" in dream with "the enemy you killed, my friend" to W. H. Auden's "Fumbled and unsatisfactory embrace before hurting" in "Spain 1937" is not a large one.

Ezra Pound is probably the first major poet to have expressed this post-War mood of generational revolt, in *Hugh Selwyn Mauberley* (1920), in an indictment which ominously links cultural degeneracy with the spread of that "usury" which, in *The Cantos*, is unequivocally blamed upon the Jews:

> Died some, pro patria, non "dulce," non "et decor" ...
> walked eye-deep in hell
> believing in old men's lies, then unbelieving
> came home, home to a lie,
> home to many deceits;
> home to old lies and new infamy;
> usury age-old and age-thick
> and liars in public places.

Daring as never before, wastage as never before.
Young blood and high blood,
fair cheeks and fine bodies....

There died a myriad,
And of the best, among them,
For an old bitch gone in the teeth,
For a botched civilization....

Such phrase-mongering, less beautifully cadenced, was to become a familiar part of anti-semitic propaganda in Europe, "justifying," for example, the assassination in 1922 of Walter Rathenau, the Jewish Minister for Reparations and then Foreign Minister in the post-Versailles German government. Pound's own admiration for Mussolini's bully-boys was expressed as support for youthful vigour against decrepit age. The echoes of *Mauberley* which can be heard in Eliot's "Gerontion" (1920; the name means "little old man") suggest a subterranean link between the scabrous image of "the jew [who] squats on my window sill, the owner" and the picture of a shell-shocked Europe wandering aimless in a "wilderness of mirrors" that recalls the Hall of Mirrors at Versailles, where the Peace Treaty was signed:

After such knowledge, what forgiveness? Think now
History has many cunning passages, contrived corridors
And issues, deceives with whispering ambitions,
Guides us by vanities.

The conviction that the world is chaotic and irrational, that there is no pattern to history, and that structure has to be externally imposed upon an incoherent flux, is a recurring tenet of the movement which established itself as "Modernism." T. S. Eliot gave this belief its classic formulation in his comments (in *The Dial*, November 1923) on Joyce's *Ulysses* (1922), where the wanderings of a modern Jew in the Dublin of 1904 are organized by narrative analogy with the events of *The Odyssey*:

In using the myth, in manipulating a continuous parallel between contemporaneity and antiquity, Mr. Joyce is pursuing a method which others must pursue after him.... It is simply a way of controlling, of ordering, of giving a shape and a significance to the immense panorama of futility and anarchy which is contemporary history. It is a method already adumbrated by Mr. Yeats, and of the need for which I believe Mr. Yeats to have been the first contemporary to be conscious. It is, I seriously believe, a step toward making the modern world possible in art.

Eliot does not acknowledge, since it does not square with his obvious disdain for "the modern world," the extent to which *Ulysses* is structured by more fundamental, everyday routines, such as work, meals, lovemaking, and all the busy repetitions and assumed continuities which constitute the modern city. (It is only when there is a momentary power-cut, for example, that men become aware that electric circuits link all the city's trams; similarly, when Bloom fills the kettle to make a cup of tea, the text launches into a marvellous rhapsody on democracy and the modern water-supply system.) Eliot does stress, however, the importance of recent psychoanalytic and anthropological investigations of myth: "Psychology (such as it is, and whether our reaction to it be comic or serious), ethnology and *The Golden Bough* have concurred to make possible what was impossible even a few years ago. Instead of narrative method, we may now use the mythical method."

It was a method Eliot himself had recently used in *The Waste Land*, and Pound was to make the organizing principle of *The Cantos*, begun about this time, but continually transformed in the years to come by the overlaying of new mythic patterns on the original formula of a descent into

Hell which linked Orpheus, Odysseus, Aeneas, Virgil, and Dante, the poets and heroes of an accumulating cultural palimpsest.

As Eliot indicates in the notes to *The Wast Land*, "Not only the title, but the plan and a good deal of the incidental symbolism of the poem" were suggested by Jessie L. Weston's book on the Grail Legend, *From Ritual to Romance* (1920), together with the two volumes *Adonis, Attis, Osiris* of Sir James Frazer's *Golden Bough* (1890–1915), particularly in "certain references to vegetation ceremonies." Unlike the essay on Joyce, however, the notes contain no overt reference (comic or serious) to the writings of Freud and Jung, which he evidently studied in Geneva while convalescing (and possibly receiving psychiatric treatment) after a nervous breakdown which is the personal substratum of the poem, surfacing in lines such as "By the waters of Leman I sat down and wept." For if *The Waste Land*, in its desolation, incoherence, and futility, alludes at one level to the consequences of the Great War "and the present decay of eastern Europe" (by which he can only mean the Bolshevik revolution and the civil war currently raging in Russia), at another it expresses the collapse of a mind overwhelmed by a personal sense of failure and impotence.

Jessie Weston argued that the Christian myth of the dying god, and the Grail legends founded upon it, both embody much more ancient fertility rituals, in which a dead soil can by nourished to new life only by the ritual shedding of blood. *The Golden Bough* had traced similar patterns on a global scale which ranged from classical myths to those of the Pacific islands. For the Tiresias who is the suffering consciousness of the poem, transfixed in bisexual and yet sexless passivity and voyeurism, too intellectual and abstract a knowledge of the human, the sexual, mystery has brought spiritual death. In *The Birth of Tragedy* (1872), the German philosopher Friedrich Nietzsche had used the Tiresias of Euripides's play *The Bacchae* as the figure of modern, rootless, and cerebral consciousness, which could be redeemed only through rediscovery of the orgiastic Dionysian principle. Nietzsche saw in Wagner's music the first sign that such a new spirit was stirring in Europe, and he quotes the same passages from *Tristan und Isolde* that Eliot uses in *The Waste Land*. The renewal that this poem sees as the outcome of finding the Holy Grail comes from self-sacrificial immersion in a new dispensation in which flesh and spirit, Dionysus and Christ, are reconciled. "Death by water" (and water is everywhere associated with music) is in reality a baptismal rebirth through loss of self, a surrender of the self-conscious ego like that prescribed by psychoanalysis. The personal breakdown, and the enormous blood-letting of the First World War, are then both seen as harbingers of a coming apocalypse.

Yeats had registered the same expectations, in poems such as "The Second Coming" (1921), taking sinister apocalyptic delight in the loosing of "the blood-dimmed tide" of "mere anarchy" in which "The ceremony of innocence is drowned." In the contemporary disorders of Europe, from Irish to Russian civil wars, lie the signs that a "rough beast, its hour come round at last/ Slouches towards Bethlehem to be born." If he remains ambivalent here, as in "Meditations in Time of Civil War" (1923), as that tide laps his own doorstep, the Nietzschean joy in destructive renewal is strong. In the elaborate mythological schema *A Vision* (1925), in which Yeats tried to codify his philosophy, he offers a gloss on the line which ends section III of "Meditations" – "Juno's peacock screamed" – which makes it clear that this ambivalence, the struggle between Apollonian order and Dionysian energy, is the essence of the modern mind, the joyous core of the modern "tragedy":

A civilization is a struggle to keep self-control, and in this it is like some great tragic person, some Niobe who must display an almost superhuman will or the cry will not touch our sympathy. The loss of control over thought comes towards the end; first the sinking in upon the moral being, then the last surrender, the irrational cry, revelation – the scream of Juno's peacock.

Like Eliot, Yeats saw in his own time "Phantoms of Hatred and of the Heart's Fullness and of the Coming Emptiness," but he took more overt delight in "The half-read wisdom of daemonic images." He saw too, as in "Nineteen Hundred and Nineteen," that "Many ingenious lovely things are gone/That seemed sheer miracle to the multitude," and found in that multitude, with its heterogeneity, its "levelling, rancorous, rational sort of mind," the mind of "Whiggery" and democracy, with all its "casual comedy," the true culprit. In the aristocratic values of ancient Celtic Ireland, or medieval Japan, and of Lady Gregory and her Ascendancy peers, and in the passionate extremism of men of action such as Major Robert Gregory, artists such as John Synge and beautiful women like Maud Gonne, he found embodied an antithetical principle, which embraced and was fulfilled by tragedy: "We begin to live when we have conceived life as tragedy," he said elsewhere, striking a characteristic pose. Such fine aesthetic contempt for the commonplace could easily lead him to naive flirtation with the Irish fascists, O'Duffy's Blueshirts, in the 1930's, for whom he even wrote marching songs, and to the closing lines of "A Bronze Head" (*Last Poems*, 1939), which raged against "this foul world in its decline and fall":

> Ancestral pearls all pitched into a sty,
> Heroic reverie mocked by clown and knave,
> And wondered what was left for massacre to save.

There is a sense, however, in which Yeats's political posturings were as imaginary as those spirit voices who supposedly dictated *A Vision* to him through the medium of his wife, merely there to give him "metaphors for poetry."

2. The Hollow Men: Self, Society, and Belief

In his "General Introduction for My Work" (1937) Yeats wrote that "A poet writes always of his personal life, in his finest work out of its tragedy"; but "he never speaks directly as to someone at the breakfast table, there is always a phantasmagoria." In Yeats's case, the "phantasmagoria" involved the assumption of a "mask," an "antithetical self," at odds with his "internal nature." This is one of the most recurring elements in Modernist ideology, apparent, too, in Pound's idea of the *persona* (literally, "mask"), and finding its most cogent expression in Eliot's 1919 essay in *The Egoist*, "Tradition and the Individual Talent," which sets out his "Impersonal theory of poetry."

Poetry, he says, "is not a turning loose of emotion, but an escape from emotion; ... not the expression of personality, but an escape from personality." A poem is an "expression of *significant* emotion, emotion which has its life in the poem and not in the history of the poet" ("significant" here means "signifying," *made of signs*). It is "an experience different in kind from any experience not of art," what, in another essay of the same year, "Hamlet and His Problems" (in *The Athenaeum*), he called an "objective correlative": an *objective* organization of signs such that it will produce, in the reader, a particular, and unique *subjective* experience. The poet's mind is simply a "receptacle," a "catalyst," synthesizing disparate materials into this new, *signifying* whole. Effectively to achieve this, the "individual talent" of the poet must submit itself to a living "tradition" which is the synchronic co-presence, in his mind, of "the whole of the literature of Europe from Homer," which "has a simultaneous existence and composes a simultaneous order." "The existing monuments form an ideal order among themselves," which is then "modified by the introduction of the new ... work of art."

In its insistence upon the *objective* status of the text, independent of its maker, this is wholly salutary, and was to be elaborated and codified, through the work of the "New Critics," into the conventional wisdom of the academic study of literature. The poetry of Wallace Stevens recurrently adverts to and embodies the theory, in poems as diverse as "Peter Quince at the Clavier" (*Harmonium*, 1923), "The Man with the Blue Guitar" (1937), and "The Planet on the Table" (*Collected Poems*, 1954).

When, however, Eliot asserts that "The progress of an artist is a continual self-sacrifice, a continual extinction of personality," the disavowal has a distinctly personal resonance, something that seems to issue directly from "the man who suffers." This is the man who, in *The Waste Land*, was to speak of "The awful daring of a moment's surrender/Which an age of prudence cannot retract"; who, after his conversion to Christianity in 1927, was to "proffer [his] deeds to oblivion, and [his] love/To the posterity of the desert" (*Ash-Wednesday*, 1930); and who, in "Coriolan" (1931), was to cry in the solitary desolation of his soul: "RESIGN RESIGN RESIGN."

Writing in the Introduction to *The Oxford Book of Modern Verse* in 1936, Yeats looked back to the profound changes in consciousness at the turn of the century, of which the most far-reaching, possibly, was the concept of consciousness itself. Henri Bergson in *Creative Evolution* (translated 1911) and William James in *The Principles of Psychology* (1890) had demonstrated the essential fluidity of consciousness – the latter in a famous metaphor which was to become part of the common stock of ideas in 20th-century literature:

> Consciousness, then, does not appear to itself chopped up in bits.... It is nothing jointed; it flows. A "river" or "stream" are the metaphors by which it is most naturally described. In talking of it hereafter, let us call it the stream of thought, of consciousness, or of subjective life.

For Yeats, however, such a recognition was more dearly bought:

> Change has come suddenly, the despair of my friends in the 'nineties part of its preparation. Nature, steel-bound or stone-built in the nineteenth century, became a flux where man drowned or swam; the moment had come for some poet to cry "the flux is in my own mind."

In Pound's *Cantos* Yeats discerned "a poetry, a philosophy, where the individual is nothing, ... objects without contour ..., human experience no longer shut into brief lives, cut off into this place and that place." The figure of Proteus presides over *The Cantos*, and the motif of metamorphosis is a crucial organizing principle, as it is, too, in *The Waste Land*; Eliot in fact refers the reader to Ovid's *Metamorphoses* for the account of Tiresias.

Right at the centre of Eliot's poetry is the tension between two ideas of the self: that of consciousness as a rigid hollow container for subjective events, and that of it as a shifting, flowing, amorphous stream. In an essay in *The Monist* on the Idealist philosophy of F. H. Bradley (on whom he prepared a Harvard graduate thesis), Eliot discussed at length Bradley's idea of the self as an extrapolation from events, like the objects of the world itself, which are "admitted fictions," "intellectual constructions." The self is "an ideal and largely practical construction, one's own self as much as others.... The self is a construction in space and time. It is an object among others, a self among others, and could not exist save in a common world."

If the individual is no more than an abstraction from the flux of being (as Fenollosa saw nouns as no more than "cross-sections cut through actions"), then identity itself becomes problematic, a nexus of possibilities, constantly shifting and redefining itself. D. H. Lawrence spoke of this new idea of the self in a letter to Edward Garnett in 1914, dismissing "the old stable ego of the character" in favour of "another ego according to whose action the individual is unrecognizable, and passes through, as it were, allotropic states which it needs a deeper sense than any that we are used to exercise, to discover are states of the same single radically unchanged element."

The word "ego" here suggests the presence of the psychoanalytic theories of Freud and Jung, for whom the conscious ego is no more than the iceberg tip peering out from the individual or collective unconscious. In a review Lawrence spells out this new philosophy as one which dissolves individuality:

> Man, and the animals, and the flowers, all live within a strange and forever surging chaos. The chaos which we have got used to we call a cosmos. The unspeakable inner chaos of which we are composed we call consciousness, and mind, and even civilization. But it is, ultimately, chaos, lit up by visions, or not lit up by visions.

Man, he says, makes "a house of apparent form and stability, fixity" which he puts like "an umbrella between himself and the everlasting whirl." The poet's function is to "show the desire for chaos, and the fear of chaos," when that umbrella becomes an oppressive, suffocating vault – to force man to admit himself "part of the vast and potent living chaos."

Unlike Eliot, Lawrence has little sympathy for the "ideal construction" we interpose between ourselves and this chaos, as he affirms in *Studies in Classic American Literature* (1922): "The ideal self! Oh, but I have a strange and fugitive self shut out and howling like a wolf or a coyote under the ideal windows. See his red eyes in the dark? This is the self who is coming into his own." The apocalyptic note extends to what, in the same book, he calls his "creed": "That I am I. That my soul is a dark forest. That my known self will never be more than a little clearing in the forest. That gods, strange gods, come forth from the forest into the clearing of my known self, and then go back. That I must have the courage to let them come and go." Here, in brief, is one of the major preoccupations of the two decades that follow.

Stephen Spender, for example, in his autobiography *World Within World* (1951) recalls that, as an undergraduate at Oxford in the 1930's, "Lawrence seemed to challenge my own existence, my mind and body.... This lack of confidence in the quality of my own nature was reinforced later by Communism." Marx, Freud, Lawrence: an intellectual Molotov cocktail, threatening to blow apart the unitary self. For if Freud suggested that the conscious ego was no more than a puppet of infantile traumas, repressed into the unconscious (what Spender called "some hidden thought/Which my parents did forget," and Auden "drowned parental voices"), Marx questioned the construction of that ego on larger, historical grounds. Consciousness was merely a secretion of class identity, as Spender noted:

> The Marxist challenge ... made me think out for myself the position of the freedom of the individual. It became extremely important to answer the question – was my sense of my own individuality simply an expression of the class interest which I, unknowingly and instinctively in everything I thought and wrote and did, represented? If this was so, must I accept the argument that to alter my position I must make myself its exact opposite – a function of the proletariat?

C. Day Lewis likewise wrote of consciousness in "In Me Two Worlds" as "This lighted ring of sense where clinch/Heir and ancestor," making his "senses' darkened fields/A theatre of war" – a class war, between his bourgeois inheritance and proletarian longings. Liberalism is no longer sufficient, as "The Conflict" records, significantly, calling up Great War scenarios:

> Yet living here,
> As one between two massive powers I live
> Whom neutrality cannot save....
>
> Move then with new desires,
> For where we used to build and love
> Is no man's land, and only ghosts can live
> Between two fires.

Day Lewis, in his autobiography, *The Buried Day* (1960), spoke of the indeterminate identity to which such iron commitments were, briefly, an answer: "but how shadowy you feel, how much at the mercy of the insubstantial present, knowing there are so many thousands of days, so many layers of past selves buried within you, yet seldom able to recover one article of the hoard intact!" Spender's cry *Forward from Liberalism* (1937) seemed realistic enough at the time; just as Auden's powerful evocation of liberal guilt, "A Summer Night" (*Look, Stranger!*, 1936), set nostalgically in the walled garden of a country house, seemed no more than a simple admission of complicity and remorse:

> ... we
> Whom hunger does not move,
> From garden where we feel secure
> Look up and with a sigh endure
> The tyrannies of love:

And gentle, do not care to know,
Where Poland draws her eastern bow,
What violence is done,
Nor ask what doubtful act allows
Our freedom in this English house,
Our picnics in the sun....

But the apocalyptic vision which follows calls up familiar echoes:

Soon, through the dykes of our content
The crumpling flood will force a rent
And, taller than a tree,
Hold sudden death before our eyes....

Spender's study of modern literature, *The Destructive Element*, had appeared in 1935. The title is from the injunction in Conrad's *Heart of Darkness* (1902): "In the destructive element immerse. That is the way." Eliot had used Conrad's novel as source of both epigraph and imagery for "The Hollow Men" (1925); in *The Waste Land*, too, a river journey, cannibalism, and other features of the novel are set against "the heart of light, the silence" of spiritual revelation; and death by water is the necessary prelude to salvation for the hollow men of the modern world. In *The Destructive Element* Spender constructs an elaborate and impressive mosaic, from Conrad, James, Eliot, Lawrence, etc., which points to one end: that the only way forward for the death-obsessed bourgeois consciousness is to sink its separateness in "the destructive element," the revolutionary flood which will in any case overwhelm it, and thus, perhaps, be reborn. It is not surprising, then, that he should see in *Ash-Wednesday* an exploration of the unconscious like that found in Auden's verse. Nor is it surprising that, the hectic in the blood cooled by the experience of actual politics and war, Auden should follow Eliot into the Anglican church. For that subordination of the self to a power beyond it which Auden's generation originally sought in Communism could equally be supplied by the "privileged moments" of religious revelation, those "moments in and out of time" of which Eliot wrote so movingly in *Four Quartets* (1943), where the soul, submitting itself to God, or music, or the "pattern/Of timeless moments" which is English history (or "Tradition"), can both find and lose itself, "in a lifetime's death in love/Ardour and selflessness and self-surrender."

Only in the work of Dylan Thomas, in a handful of poems, does this demolition of the old self successfully outlive the 1930's. For all the stridency of the neo-romantics and "The New Apocalypse" school of the 1940's, founded by Henry Treece, apocalypse, surrealism, anarchism, the unconscious, rapidly lost ground in English poetry. Dylan Thomas himself is most effective in those poems where the breathless spilling of images works to create an almost traditional effect: the Trahernian vision of childhood in "Fern Hill," the moving address to his dying father, "Do not go gentle into that good night," or the "Refusal to Mourn ..." with its concentrated evocation of first and last things in responding to the death of a child in the Blitz. But Dylan Thomas's early death, compounding those of Sidney Keyes, Keith Douglas, and Alun Lewis in war, left a gap that was not filled by the survivors.

One survivor from the 1930's who was to have an influence in the post-war period was the fourth party to that composite thirties beast, MacSpaunday: Louis MacNeice. In "An Eclogue for Christmas" (1933), MacNeice chronicles the metamorphoses through which the modern psyche has passed, matched by the rapid transformations of artistic fashions, and points toward the preoccupation with the mundane, "particular life," which was to characterize the poetry of reconstruction of the 1950's:

I who was Harlequin in the childhood of the century,
Posed by Picasso beside an endless opaque sea,
Have seen myself sifted and splintered in broken facets,
Tentative pencillings, endless liabilities, no assets,

> Without reference to this particular life.
> And so it has gone on; I have not been allowed to be
> Myself in flesh or face, but abstracting and dissecting me
> They have made of me pure form, a symbol or a pastiche,
> Stylised profile, anything but soul and flesh....

There is a prophetic pointer here to the exasperation of Kingsley Amis and Philip Larkin, in D. J. Enright's anthology *Poets of the 1950's*, inveighing against "poems about philosophers or paintings or novelists or art galleries or mythology or foreign cities or other poems" and the ideas of "'tradition' or a common myth-kitty or casual allusions in poems to other poems or poets."

The poets of the 1950's, loosely congregated around an indefinite core that came to be known as "The Movement," turned their backs on the Modernist tradition alluded to so snidely here, and set about reconstructing (with vaguely new, social-democratic, welfare-state trappings) the old liberal-conservative idea of the self, of the "English" poetic tradition, temporarily "eclipsed" by Modernism: Hardy, Edward Thomas, and even, in the case of Philip Larkin at least, the soured lyricism of A. E. Housman.

Fifties poetry is that of the meritocratic spirit, deeply intimidated by the Cold War deadlock, yet finding in individual self-construction a kind of destiny, like Thom Gunn's motor-cyclists in the *locus classicus* of the period, "On the Move": "The self-defined, astride the created will." Gunn can claim "I am condemned to be/An individual" as if identity were an easy and inescapable given. At the same time, he espouses a simplifed version of French existentialism which saw identity as merely a "pose" (a recurring word) assumed against chaos. The most lucid exposition of this moral stance is contained in "To Yvor Winters," which, praising the older poet for his conservative's "Defence of Reason," warns:

> Denial of the discriminating brain
> Brings the neurotic vision and the vein
> Of necromancy....

Donald Davie's "Rejoinder to a Critic" explains the distrust of emotion which underlies the careful pentameters, regular stanzas, and rhymes of this largely academic poetry:

> You may be right: "How can I dare to feel?"
> May be the only question I can pose....
> "Alas, alas, who's injured by my love?"
> And recent history answers: half Japan!
> Not love, but hate? Well both are versions of
> The "feeling" that you dare me to.... Be dumb!
> Appear concerned only to make it scan!
> How dare we now be anything but numb?

Philip Larkin, in an exceptional and bountiful poem such as "Wedding Wind," might concede the "all-generous waters" of passion, the "bodying forth ... by joy" of love. But his characteristic mood is that of the title poem of *The Less Deceived* (1955), a sad little meditation on the girl victim of a Victorian rape, or of "Mr. Bleaney," with its dreary vision of life as a slow decline to death, pointless and trivial. Perpetually middle-aged, he concludes in "Send No Money": "What does it prove? Sod all." Yet the little lyric insurrections of his poetry, like those strange stirrings of rebellious energy in the early poetry of Ted Hughes, usually embodied in animals or veiled as dream, represent a last-ditch resistance against the inertia of a one-dimensional, end-stopped world.

Most of these poets have developed in new directions, under the stimulus of inner and outer changes. In his introduction to the anthology *The New Poetry* in 1962, A. Alvarez spoke of their need to go "beyond the gentility principle." In an almost equally widely discussed essay in 1961,

"Poetry Today" (in *The Modern Age*, edited by Boris Ford), Charles Tomlinson lamented the turning away of English poetry from the great heritage of Modernism, into "a self-congratulatory parochialism." It remains the case that, in what Robert Lowell called "the tranquillized fifties," Modernism had gone elsewhere, to America. Thom Gunn, for one, followed it. It was an increasingly common pattern.

3.   In the American Grain

Ezra Pound left America in 1906, turning his back on a philistine continent whose "crudity is an exceeding great stench." He was only to return, in disgrace, almost in manacles, in 1945, to stand trial for making wartime broadcasts over Rome Radio in support of Mussolini and Fascism, broadcasts of such anti-semitic virulence that even now, reading the transcripts in David Heymann's book, *Ezra Pound: The Last Rower*, one is astounded that such scatological banality could issue from the same pen that wrote the delicate poems of *Cathay*. He was swiftly certified unfit to plead and consigned to St. Elizabeth's mental asylum, in Washington, to be released only in 1958.

T. S. Eliot's destiny was rather more condign. Leaving America in the 1910's to study at the Sorbonne, in Munich, and at Oxford, he became a teacher, senior bank clerk, and then editor and director with the London publishers Faber. In 1927 he became a naturalized Englishman, and the same year was received into the Church of England. By the mid-1920's, as founding editor of the prestigious "little magazine" *The Criterion*, he had become a respectable figure on the English literary scene, and in his publishing capacity acted *in loco parentis* for successive generations of young and unknown poets. Auden, one of his most significant protégés, was to reverse the pattern perpetuated by Eliot and Pound, by emigrating in 1938 to the United States, where he took out citizenship in 1946. Like Eliot, though, he became a practising Anglican.

The reversal of the pattern is a significant one, in which the whole matter of adoptive countries seems bound up intimately with the question of belief. Writing (possibly with some causticness about Eliot's naturalization) in *The New York Herald* in 1927, Pound picked out the salient feature of this process, and its larger significance for English culture:

> the language is now in the keeping of the Irish (Yeats and Joyce); apart from Yeats, since the death of Hardy, poetry is being written by Americans. All the developments in English verse since 1910 are due almost wholly to Americans. In fact, there is no longer any reason to call it English verse, and there is no present reason to think of England at all.

The centre of gravity of "English" literature had shifted decisively in the inter-war years. No longer was it assumed that the natural destination of the American poet was Europe. Individual writers such as Sylvia Plath and Robert Lowell would continue to spend long periods in England. But the overall pull was in the opposite direction. Not only could the United States offer large audiences and fees and plush university positions for visiting poets, but its own indigenous tradition had also superseded "English" as the mainstream of modern poetry. Ironically, this displacement of England from the centre of "English" literature had been effected, at one level at least, by two renegade Americans. But what, on a larger scale, Eliot and Pound expressed was the extraordinary exuberance and vitality of a culture which, at the beginning of the 20th century, found itself on the threshold of world power, and which, in the years that followed, has emerged to unchallenged political, economic, and cultural hegemony in all spheres of western life.

Wallace Stevens is the laureate of this ascendancy. Whereas Pound struggled to break the pentameter, Stevens uses it with an ease, fluency, and power that recalls Wordsworth. But he gives new colour, resonance, and suppleness to the blank verse form, as he revives and transforms Wordsworth's concept of the Imagination. For Stevens, "an isolated fact, cut loose from the universe, has no significance"; it is endowed with value by the human context within which it is articulated. Reality is "the supreme fiction," humanly evolved and transformed by the collective imaginings of the men and women who constitute it; and "The world is the only thing fit to think about." "Things as they are" are changed on the "blue guitar" of art and mind. In his poetry, the self seeks masterful authority over the diversity of the external world, subjecting it all to the cool imperium of his mind through the power of a syntax which establishes new and vivid relations between things, making them pliable to a "blessed rage for order." Stevens's linguistic idealism cancels history, as an external and contingent force, by taking everything up into the synchronicity of the imagination, as Eliot had attempted, in his theory of "tradition and the individual talent," to overcome the gulf between subject and object, mind and its cultural imbrication. "The Idea of Order at Key West" presents this exercise of mastery over the world through the innocuous image of a girl singing by the sea-shore. But it makes large claims, claims that the very assurance of tone ensures will not have to be cashed:

> It was her voice that made
> The sky acutest at its vanishing.
> She measured to the hour its solitude.
> She was the single artificer of the world
> In which she sang. And when she sang, the sea,
> Whatever self it had, became the self
> That was her song, for she was the maker.

This is not an activity confined to art and perception. Men also transform the world through their labours, through the patterns they create in their day-to-day activities. The lights of the town and the fishing boats, with night-fall,

> Mastered the night and portioned out the sea,
> Fixing emblazoned zones and fiery poles,
> Arranging, deepening, enchanting night.

The sheer vastness and energy of the American continent, however, has presented its poets with a massive dilemma, acutely summed up by Saul Bellow's remarks in the novel *Humboldt's Gift* (1975) on the fictitious poet Von Humboldt Fleisher, a man who has turned into a spiritual derelict, finally virtually drinking himself to death. Generally thought to be modelled on Bellow's friend Delmore Schwartz, but with facets which recall John Berryman – yet one more poetic suicide in that long tradition which extends from Hart Crane to Sylvia Plath – Humboldt is clearly intended to represent a characteristic side of the American poetic character:

> The noble idea of being an American poet certainly made Humboldt feel at times like a card, a boy, a comic, a fool.... Maybe America didn't need art and inner miracles. It had so many outer ones. The USA was a big operation, very big. The more *it*, the less *we*. So Humboldt behaved like an eccentric and a comic subject. But occasionally there was a break in his eccentricity when he stopped and thought.... I could see that Humboldt was pondering what to do between *then* and *now*, between birth and death, to satisfy certain great questions. Such brooding didn't make him any saner.

The desperate clowning on the high wire, one step away from disaster, is certainly there in Schwartz's poetry, as even the title of his 1951 volume, *Vaudeville for a Princess*, indicates. In "The Heavy Bear Who Goes with Me" he speaks of the "strutting show-off" of the body (who is nevertheless "terrified") as "A stupid clown of the spirit's motive." In Berryman's *77 Dream Songs* (1964), as in *His Toy, His Dream, His Rest* (1968), the self is split between an intent, serious, and depressive character called Henry and an unnamed "friend" who addresses him with the mordant wit of the minstrel-show burnt-cork "nigger" as "Mr. Bones," passing sarcastic comment on all his thoughts and acts, and sometimes, as in "April Fool's Day; or, St. Mary of Egypt," on the very title of the poem in which they appear ("– Thass a funny title, Mr. Bones").

By and large, the American poet has faced Bellow's "great questions" in one of two ways, each of them containing the possibility of eccentricity and breakdown: either, in Philip Rahv's terms, as a "paleface" or a "redskin." It is not surprising that the two poets who stand, at the beginning of this century, as the tutelary or totemic spirits of the American tradition, should correspond to the two halves of this opposition: Emily Dickinson and Walt Whitman, symbolically, perhaps, a spinster and a homosexual.

Whitman sought to encompass the vastness of America within the panoramic and promiscuous plenitude of his democratic imagination, proclaiming "I am large, I contain multitudes," and reeling off, in poem after poem, enormous cumulative catalogues of American sights and sounds. The characteristic pattern is of an imperious appropriation of reality by the expansive subject:

> There was a child went forth every day,
> And the first object he looked upon, that object he became,
> And that object became part of him for the day....

The rest of the poem is merely a list of the various things the child saw, loosely held in sequence by a series of "Ands," and vaguely in apposition to the subject of the poem's concluding sentence: "These became part of that child." There is no fusion of the heterogeneous materials; they remain isolated perceptions, connected only by the consciousness of the observer. There is no attempt to establish a logical network of relations between the things themselves, that might be reflected in a forward narrative movement. Nouns stand in splendid isolation in Whitman's poetry, passively waiting to be plucked by the omnivorous subjectivity of the poet/consumer, as in "Sparkles from a Wheel":

> The blab of the pave, tires of carts, sluff of boot-soles, talk
>   of the promenaders,
> The heavy omnibus, the driver with his interrogating thumb, the
>   clank of the shod horses on the granite floor,
> The snow-sleighs, clinking, shouted jokes, pelts of snowballs....

Theodore Roethke, a poet who attempted Whitman's expansiveness but knew also the value of the contracted, lyric concentration of Emily Dickinson, spoke of the recurring need for such a procedure in American poetry, in *Conversations on the Craft of Poetry* (1961):

> There are areas of experience in modern life that simply cannot be rendered by either the formal lyric or straight prose. We need the catalogue in our time. We need the eye close to the object, the poem about the single incident – the animal, the child. We must permit poetry to extend consciousness as far, as deeply, as particularly as it can, to recapture, in Stanley Kunitz' phrase, "what it has lost to some extent to prose."

Eliot and Pound, of course, both have their debts to Whitman; "Dry Salvages," in *Four Quartets*, is a testimony to this, while Pound's wide-ranging, discursive, episodic narratives in *The Cantos* are also in this particular American grain. But the strand in Modernist poetry which has followed on from Whitman most clearly is that which, in the manner of William Carlos Williams, has extended consciousness by concentrating on the particular incident, explored with all the apparent casualness of a mind improvising upon experience. It was this which, in his 1925 book of essays, Williams identified as archetypally *In the American Grain*.

The most striking quality Williams derives from Whitman is his rare optimism: Williams delights in the sheer multiplicity of the world, the play of light, movement and calm, his reiterated conviction, which owes something to Imagism, that there are "no ideas but in things," and his confidence that there is nothing in the world of things which is unamenable to poetry. In *Paterson* (1946–63) he attempted, like many other poets, to write the American epic, forging homologies between the central character and the New Jersey city in which he lives and with which he shares the name of the title. The stasis of rock and the ever-changing, perpetually-the-same flow of water over the falls becomes Williams's model of the world of experience. But it is in the little vignettes of everyday life that he excels, as in Book Two, "Sunday in the Park":

Outside
            outside myself
                        there is a world,
he rumbled, subject to my incursions
– a world
            (to me) at rest,
which I approach
concretely –
            The scene's the Park
            upon the rock,
            female to the city
– upon whose body Paterson instructs his thoughts
(concretely)
                        – late spring,
            a Sunday afternoon!
– and goes by the footpath to the cliff (counting:
the proof)
            himself among the others,
– treads there the same stones
on which their feet slip as they climb,
paced by their dogs!
laughing, calling to each other –
            Wait for me!

Williams's typographic lay-out here catches the real drama and shifting excitements of this peopled world, and the changing pace of the mind as it moves among its objects. E. E. Cummings, in a rather different poetry which nevertheless derives some of its chirpy insouciance from the redskin tradition, had also employed the gratuitous possibilities offered by the typewriter to add a new dimension to the poem, while at the same time calling attention to the text as an act not just of thought but of physical, printed characters. Cummings's poetry is largely set up for the eye. Williams's certainly relies for its effect on pacing the eye's movement over the page, but there is always in his verse a sense too of the freshness, the spontaneity of the spoken voice, at times cadenced almost into song, yet never losing its immediacy and the presence of an actual, tangible world.

Charles Olson, in an important manifesto on "Projective Verse" in *Poetry New York* (1950), set out the key elements of this poetic, taking it back through Williams to Pound and "The revolution of the ear, 1910, the trochee's heave" which broke the dominance of the pentameter in English verse, and what he calls the "closed" forms associated with it.

"Open" verse, he says, is "composition by field," in which "ONE PERCEPTION MUST IMMEDIATELY AND DIRECTLY LEAD TO A FURTHER PERCEPTION," and the poem enacts, follows, through syllable and line, the movements of the breath, "the breathing of the man who writes." In the work of Olson and Robert Creeley, Denise Levertov and Robert Duncan, among others, Pound's and Williams's innovations have been carried over as a major strand of the tradition that descends from Whitman. It is a strand more lasting than that associated with the "Beats," Jack Kerouac, Gregory Corso, and Allen Ginsberg, though the latter's "Supermarket in California" is a moving evocation of that "dear father, graybeard, lonely old courage-teacher," as he might appear now, among the appurtenances of a modern, unlovely America.

The "line of wit" which originates in Emily Dickinson's sharply etched cameos of the sequestered life, with their wicked, off-hand ironies, was to establish the "paleface" as for many years the undisputed master of the American mainstream. This was largely because the transvaluation of values effected by Eliot's and Pound's critical work fairly rapidly became incorporated into the canon of that new and increasingly central discipline, the university teaching of English.

John Crowe Ransom, teaching English in the 1920's at Vanderbilt University in Tennessee, founded, together with the younger poets Allen Tate and Robert Penn Warren, the "Fugitive" group of Southern writers, gathered around the journal *The Fugitive*, which they co-edited from 1922 to 1925. Ransom went on to become editor of the influential *Kenyon Review*, 1937–59, Tate the editor of *Sewanee Review*, 1944–46, Warren of *Southern Review*, 1935–42. This convergence of academia and Modernism through a university-based review reinforced those elements in Modernism which placed stress on textual objectivity, tradition, irony, intelligence, allusiveness, and complexity.

The same process was happening in England, in rather more complicated ways. At Cambridge, I. A. Richards had instituted courses in the close reading of poetry which stressed both the technical and linguistic complexity of the text and its psychological affectivity, as a polysemic coding of experience. The conclusions of this work were published in *The Meaning of Meaning* (1923), *Principles of Literary Criticism* (1924), *Science and Poetry* (1926), and *Practical Criticism* (1929). One of his most brilliant undergraduates, William Empson, impressed by Laura Riding's and Robert Graves's demonstration of the semantic ambiguities of a Shakespeare sonnet in *A Survey of Modernist Poetry* (1927), developed this into a full-fledged practical methodology which was published, in 1930, as *Seven Types of Ambiguity*, followed in 1935 by *Some Versions of Pastoral*, and in 1951 by *The Structure of Complex Words*. Another Cambridge don and colleague of Richards, F. R. Leavis, founded in 1932 the journal *Scrutiny*, which was to have a complicated and prickly relationship with academia until its demise in 1953. 1932 saw, also, the publication of Leavis's *New Bearings in English Poetry*, which had as its purpose the propagation of those "new bearings" offered to English poetry by Eliot and Pound. This is not the place to go into the complex history of the movement that emerged from *Scrutiny*: Francis Mulhern's monumental history, *The Moment of "Scrutiny"* (1979) has done this at length. Suffice it to say that by 1936, the reorientation which the Modernists had set out to effect seemed by and large to have been completed, at least as far as a perceptive cultural cicerone such as Leavis was concerned:

> The work has been done, the re-orientation effected: the heresies of ten years ago are orthodoxy. Mr Eliot's achievement is matter for academic evaluation, his poetry is accepted, and his early observations on the Metaphysicals and on Marvell provide currency for university lectures and undergraduate exercises. His own projected book on the School of Donne has come to seem to him unnecessary, and certainly in the last ten years much industry has been devoted to applying and expanding his hints.

In the period after the Second World War, the practice of poetry had become increasingly bound up with a university career: the poet was also usually a critic and teacher – either a career-academic or a writer-in-residence. This professionalization of literature was reflected in the burgeoning of literary journals which had a clear academic base, unlike those vastly influential but small-circulation "little magazines" in which Modernism had first made its appearance and come to maturity.

In post-1945 conditions, an increasingly academic poetry, of high intelligence and great polish, flourished in the American universities. Ransom's own volumes, particularly *Chills and Fever* (1924) and *Two Gentlemen in Bonds* (1927), largely written in the early years of the decade, were a major influence. The combination of Laforgue's "romantic irony," sustaining while apparently subverting strong emotion, and of Hopkins's and Donne's grotesque metaphors is apparent for example in "Winter Remembered," which without these superadditions would be a rather melodramatic and traditional love poem. With them, the melodrama becomes an integral part of the overall effect:

> Dear love, these fingers that had known your touch,
> And tied our separate forces first together,
> Were ten poor idiot fingers not worth much,
> Ten frozen parsnips hanging in the weather.

In the work of Tate and Warren, of Randall Jarrell, Karl Shapiro, Richard Eberhart, Howard Nemerov, and Richard Wilbur, is repeated the same urbane, balanced tone, modulating through outrageous collocations of allusion and metaphoric flights of fancy, without losing control, and articulating them all within a Marvellian assurance of rhyme, metre, and stanza. Ransom's book *The New Criticism* (1941) even provided the name for the critical procedures by which this and all poetry could subsequently be assessed, by academics such as Cleanth Brooks and W. K. Wimsatt, authors of the significantly titled *The Well-Wrought Urn* (1947) and *The Verbal Icon* (1954).

Of this rich concoction of language, the ebullient verbal rhodomontade of Hart Crane's attempt to write the American epic in *The Bridge* (1930) was another obvious progenitor. But there was always too much disturbance in Crane, too little control over an emotion that threatened to get out of hand, like the putative suicide of "To Brooklyn Bridge":

> Out of some subway scuttle, cell or loft
> A bedlamite speeds to the parapets,
> Tilting there momently, shrill shirt ballooning,
> A jest falls from the speechless caravan....

Robert Lowell has many things in common with Crane, not least his attempt, in *Notebook* (1970) and *History* (1973) to write, if not an epic, then a *long* poem that would combine individual and collective experience in a way which spoke to the condition of contemporary America. Lowell himself has registered, in his interview with A. Alvarez in *The Review* (August 1963), his debt to "the Southern group of poets," the habit "of analysing poems to see how they're put together," the "great emphasis on craftsmanship" that about 1950 "was prevailing everywhere in America," with "poets trained that way, writing in the style, writing rather complicated, difficult, laboured poems." But even in his earliest poetry there is a shrill edge of unease that points beyond capable professionalism to the manic heights of "To Brooklyn Bridge." In a symposium on his poem "Skunk Hour" in 1964, Lowell explained the origins of the conversion that was to produce the new, open style of *Life Studies* (1959). He had been giving readings in California in "the era and setting of Allen Ginsberg." He began to feel his style was "distant, symbol-ridden and wilfully difficult": "I felt my old poems hid what they were really about, and many times offered a stiff, humorless and even impenetrable surface ..., like prehistoric monsters dragged down into the bog and death by their ponderous armor." Lowell's subsequent poetry was, in fact, a major struggle to overcome the central oppositions of the American poetic tradition. He came close to first-order greatness in *History*, an unrhymed sonnet sequence in which the individual continually finds himself asking improbable and unanswerable or stunningly answered questions of his own experience, and of the history of the world, in ways which emphasize the actual seamlessness of the imaginarily distinct planes of "public" and "private" on which we live. He asks, for example, how many pounds Hannibal weighed; he repeats the question of the young boy Marcus Cato of the homicidal despot Sulla, "Why hasn't someone killed him?" "At Canterbury," we're told, "a guilty pilgrim may ask/'Have I the right to my imagination?' " Climbing the scaffold in "Vision," in a sequence haunted by Robespierre and the Terror, he asks "What does having my life behind me mean?"

In the "Program of the Boston Arts Festival" in 1960, the year after *Life Studies*, Lowell wrote of the antithetical traditions into which American poetry was divided:

> Our modern American poetry has a snarl on its hands.... Two poetries are now competing, a cooked and a raw. The cooked, marvellously expert, often seems laboriously concocted to be tasted and digested by a graduate seminar. The raw, huge

blood-dripping gobbets of unseasoned experience are dished up for midnight listeners. There is a poetry that can only be studied, and a poetry that can only be declaimed, a poetry of pedantry, and a poetry of scandal.

Lowell's poetic career is in fact a demonstration that such antinomies can be overcome, and that it is possible for the poet to ask, and answer, "certain great questions," about "what to do between *then* and *now*, between birth and death." But perhaps it is now only in the "big operation" of modern America that such a confrontation is possible, in the English language.

4. Poetry and Nationality

> Out of Ireland have we come.
> Great hatred, little room
> Maimed us from the start.
> I carry from my mother's womb
> A fanatic heart.

Such was Yeats's famous comment on the Irish situation, in "Remorse for Intemperate Speech" in 1931. The Irish poet's conflict has always been one of allegiances. The heritage of nationalism has made it difficult for him to resolve the contrary pulls of parochiality and cosmopolitanism; his own anomalous place in a divided culture has often driven him either to despair of and renounce his country, or to sink his talents in immediate concerns.

Yeats, although of Anglo-Irish Protestant and (slightly faded) Ascendancy stock, early espoused the cause of Nationalism. His first, fin-de-siecle poetry attempted, in volumes such as *The Wanderings of Oisin*, *The Countess Kathleen* and *In the Seven Woods* (poems, he informed his readers, "Chiefly of the Irish Heroic Age") to recover what he called the "ancient idealism" of the Celtic race, polluted by too close a contact with the money-grubbing, vulgar, democratic materialism of the Anglo-Saxons. Under the influence of Maud Gonne, he found himself increasingly drawn to the insurrectionary nationalism of the Fenians, and his masterly poem "Easter 1916" is a powerful, if equivocal, evocation of the mood that produced the Easter Uprising, written after defeat had transformed the participants to martyrs and shifted the national consciousness irrevocably in favour of complete independence. Yet one of the few major speeches he made in the Irish Senate (elevation to which led to threats against his life from the extreme Sinn Fein opposed to Partition) was on the vexed subject of divorce, in which he proclaimed himself, as a Protestant, the scion of a proud race, a claim repeated in section III of "The Tower":

> The pride of a people that were
> Bound neither to Cause nor to State,
> Neither to slaves that were spat on,
> Nor to the tyrants that spat,
> The people of Burke and of Grattan
> That gave, though free to refuse....

Responsibilities had already delineated this alternative patrimony for Irish nationalism, calling up the shades of Edward Fitzgerald, Robert Emmet, Wolfe Tone, and Parnell as Protestant leaders of the independence movement, to be set against the venality, the "fumbling wits, the obscure spite/Of our old Paudeen in his shop," fumbling in the greasy till and adding the halfpence to the pence, prayer to shivering prayer. In his poems on his friend John Synge and the Irish public who jeered *The Playboy of the Western World* off the stage of the Abbey Theatre, he sounded a recurring note of contempt for the Catholic petty-bourgeoisie who were the backbone of Nationalism, whose "new ill-breeding," he inveighed in *Dramatis Personae*, "may in a few years destroy all that has given Ireland a distinguished name in the world." Such people he saw to be as much a cause of the Irish paralysis as the English occupying power:

The root of it all is that the political class in Ireland – the lower-middle class from whom the patriotic associations have drawn their journalists and their leaders for the last ten years – have suffered through the cultivation of hatred as the one energy of their movement, a deprivation which is the intellectual equivalent to a certain surgical operation. Hence the shrillness of their voices. They contemplate all creative power as the eunuchs contemplate Don Juan as he passes through Hell on the white horse.

Against such parochial banality Yeats could only set, throughout his work, that great 18th-century tradition of Tory magnanimity represented by Bishop Berkeley, "the first to say the world is a vision," Edmund Burke, "with his conviction that all states not grown slowly like a forest tree are tyrannies," Swift, "with his love of perfect nature," and Goldsmith, with "his delight in the particulars of common life," all of whom "found in England the opposite that made their thought mad or stung it into expression." The latter-day representatives of such a tradition Yeats found among the "rich man's flowering lawns" of the great ancestral houses such as Lady Gregory's Coole Park, peopling the Norman tower he attempted to renovate for himself at Thoor Ballylee, and in the fantasy vision of a West of Ireland where peasant, poet, and aristocrat lived together in timeless rural community, described most beautifully in the calm majestic prose of "The Galway Plains": "There is still in truth upon these great level plains a people, a community bound together by imaginative possessions, by stories and poems which have grown out of its own life, and by a past of great passions which can still waken the heart to imaginative action."

But at this point, a perennial problem for Yeats crops up. "Does not the greatest poetry always require a people to listen to it?" he asks. England, he goes on, a city-dominated culture, has a mob, but not a people. The poet always prefers a community where the perfected minds express the people; the people are a great river, and where a people has died, a nation is about to die. This was in 1903. At the end of his life, in "A General Introduction for My Work" (1937), he returned to the theme. The poets of the Young Ireland movement of the 19th century "were not separated individual men; they spoke or tried to speak out of a people to a people; behind them stretched the generations." As a young man he had admired them for this, and tried to emulate them. But he had discovered that "the common and its befitting language is the research of a lifetime and when found may lack popular recognition."

In *Dramatis Personae* his remedy had been desperate: the creation by the poet of "a secondary or interior personality created out of the tradition of myself," an anti-self which takes the heterogeneity of Ireland, as he said in a letter to AE (George Russell) in 1898, and absorbs it, makes it harmonious, making him "the poet of a people, the poet of a new insurrection." In "The Fisherman" (1919) Yeats reiterated his desire "To write for my own race/ And the reality." But the poem ends by admitting that his audience is an imaginary one, "A man who does not exist,/ A man who is but a dream"; and though, with his characteristic panache, the poem ends on a speculative note of triumph, it is difficult not to feel the desperation here. In 1930, he saw in Augustus John's portrait of him "Anglo-Irish solitude, a solitude I have made for myself, an outlawed solitude." Yeats's failure to make himself the poet of a people was an exemplary one, which has continued to perplex the modern writer, in a variety of contexts.

There is little that is original in Yeats's ideas; they have been the stock-in-trade of Romanticism at least since Wordsworth's Preface to *Lyrical Ballads*. But the extraordinary vividness, the felt reality, of Yeats's pastoral vision, coming at that moment of heightened national consciousness that accompanied secession, ensured that he bequeathed to his successors a poetic mould it has been difficult to relinquish.

Louis MacNeice is a case in point. The son of an Ulster Church of Ireland minister who preached Irish unity to a fiercely Loyalist flock, he soon learnt to negotiate with a deliberate but concerned scepticism what he called the condition of being "spiritually hyphenated without knowing it" which is the usual lot of the Anglo-Irish Protestant, "brought up to think myself Irish, without question or qualification," yet distrusted by both communities and belonging to neither. Significantly, MacNeice had to tear apart that peculiar combination of pastoral and realism that Yeats had forged. Many of his poems are allegories, parables, or fables, frequently cast in the mode of eclogue or classical myth. Yet by pointedly calling attention to the literariness of the device, MacNeice manages to comment on the contemporary scene without losing himself in its enormity. He evokes the craggy, refractory reality of things through a species of apparently casual reportage which focusses democratically on "All this debris of day-to-day experience," the "Importunate real world of wife, boss, dun, clients." In *Autumn Journal* (1939) he achieved a masterly compendium of a world on the brink of war, yet locked in the quotidian, seen through the marginal, self-deprecating, essentially private gaze of one who can hardly believe he is witness to such world-shattering events. Even in his personal lyrics, though, MacNeice reproduces the familiar dilemma, guiltily aware that "When all is told/We cannot beg for pardon."

The world of phenomena for MacNeice is founded in a terrifying emptiness – silence, absence, death. Beneath the film of appearances there are murderous depths. In this, perhaps, he reproduced unwittingly the ambiguous attitudes of his father, explaining his reluctance to visit the Republic whose creation he had welcomed: "How can you mix with people who might be murderers without you knowing it?"

The Yeatsian pastoral tradition is handled less circumspectly by a poet such as Padraic Fallon, who worked for most of his life as a customs official in Wexford, and knew the parochial hinterland, not as a legendary or mythic terrain, but as one transfixed in lethargy, where men "must endure the wide stare of things," a world "Unhinged now from giant epics," yet occasionally shot through with miracle. Patrick Kavanagh's long poem *The Great Hunger* (1942) attempted an even more ambitious refutation of Yeats's bucolic vision, presenting the harsh, bitter history of rural Ireland in its consequences for one individual, the farmer Patrick Maguire, goaded by mother and Catholic Church into a twisted, sterile virginity which becomes the figure of a larger, national paralysis. Austin Clarke, too, beginning as a conscientious imitator of Yeats in his "Heroic" phase, developed into a fierce critic of Catholic Ireland, his passionate anti-clericalism driving him, in his later poetry, to that mixture of vitriol and sensuality which is a feature of Yeats's "Crazy Jane" poems. Clarke's Ireland is specifically urban, the squalid, decaying life of Dublin's shabby gentility, in churches, tenements, and beer parlours, yet it is depicted with a vivacity and zest, and a rich range of verbal techniques culled from both ancient Irish poetry and the European tradition, which make his characteristic mood one of delight in the everyday mixed with vigorous anger. Thomas Kinsella, in a poem such as *Nightwalker* (1967), explores the same ambivalent world, "Mindful of the/shambles of the day/But mindful," too, "Of will that gropes for/structure," angry at the betrayals and venalities that have come with a meretricious "independence."

Recent years have seen the emergence of a new and powerful strain of poetry from Ulster, in two different but often interwoven keys. Less interesting, in many ways, is that which looks back to MacNeice as its mentor. This poetry moves between parable and a decent, mundane realism, performs its civic duties equitably, and has all the urbane virtues of good prose; its closest links are with the writers of the "Movement." If, at times, it speaks with the tone of a shell-shocked Georgianism, or protestant sobriety and wit, nevertheless, in the hands of writers such as Derek Mahon and Michael Longley, it can register some of the anxieties and urgencies that inform the work of that other tradition, drawing largely on a Catholic, rural background, most sharply focussed in the work of Seamus Heaney and John Montague.

Heaney uses Stephen Dedalus's reflections on the English Jesuit convert, in *Portrait of the Artist*, as an epigraph in one of his volumes: "My soul frets in the shadow of his language." He is preoccupied by this relation between the individual speaker and the language he inherits, which he sees everywhere embedding a past of imperial domination, and the destruction of a native culture. In "Whatever you say, say nothing," for example, the wry Irishism of the title indicates a real dilemma. In a land "Of open minds as open as a trap," one's accent and even one's name can give away cultural and ethnic loyalties: "Norman, Ken and Sidney signalled Prod/And Seamus (call me Sean) was sure-fire Pape." In another poem, he writes of being stopped at a night-time roadblock, not knowing who the men are, and fearful that giving his name may betray him to murder, or at least intimidation. Complicity, in all its forms, is a key term in his moral vocabulary.

In many of his poems, he uses the image of the language as a rich peat bog of latent meanings, waiting to be kindled into new fire, but also treacherous and potentially deadly. His own poetry is full of elusive and recondite allusions to earlier poets – not only Yeats, for example, but many of those, such as Spenser, Ralegh, and Marvell, who had a hand in the oppression of Ireland. For Heaney, history is defeat. Starting out from a tough bucolic vision recalling the early Ted Hughes, he has moved away from the dangerous, entrapping bog of Irish identity, where the self is so easily caught up in the gratuitous violations and atrocities recorded in *North* (1975), the deadly serious and infantile game of terror, into a larger field, where the mind has room to contemplate the horrors it has passed through.

John Montague assumes a similarly wary stance to the "Irish dimension"; but in *The Rough Field* (1972) he explores the centuries-old history of Irish fratricidal misery with a sharp and compassionate eye. In his recent *The Dead Kingdom* he moves beyond the mythic explanations of the current Troubles in Ulster which had animated *A Slow Dance* (1975) to a clearer historical analysis. The Irish writer, he says, is tempted to romanticize the conflict as a legendary, primordial feud (just as Yeats imagined the Celtic hero Cuchulain at the side of Padraic Pearse in the Dublin Post Office during the uprising). But it is really "wise imperial policy/hurling the small peoples/against each other." The poem concludes with a pithy overlaying of literary and historical moments, where the cadence of Yeats's self-appointed epitaph ("*Cast a cold eye/On life, on death./Horseman, pass by!*") is reproduced in the quite different injunction now inscribed in the hillside above his grave:

> Do pale horsemen still
>   ride the wintry dawn?
> Above Yeats's tomb
>   large letters stain
> Ben Bulben's side:
>   *Britons, go home!*

The play between text and ghost-cadence sums up, in miniature, a predicament Yeats defined and, in defining, passed on to his heirs. It is perhaps precisely the tension between the two pulls, of history and art, which has made for the richness and resonance of Irish poetry in this century. As G. J. Watson argues persuasively in his study, *Irish Identity and the Literary Revival*:

> For all [the Irish writer's] sense of separate identity, always, lurking somewhere near the surface, is a painful sense of insecurity deriving ultimately from the sense of a lost identity, a broken tradition, and a knowledge that an alien identity has been, however reluctantly, more than half-embraced.

By comparison, the poetry of Wales and Scotland has lacked this nationalist dimension, despite the fact that, in Hugh MacDiarmid at least, Scottish literature found a figure of international stature who simultaneously propounded a doctrine of national independence, and set about a largely successful programme for reviving, or inventing, a national literary language, Lallans, based on the historic speech of literate Lowland Scots. Important poets such as Sorley Maclean and Iain Crichton Smith have continued to write in Scots Gaelic, the latter translating the works of both, and also contributing a large body of poetry in English which, like that of MacDiarmid, derives its nourishment from the literature of Modernism (particularly Wallace Stevens) while its roots are firmly planted in the Scottish landscape and experience. MacDiarmid's work has much in common, for all its avowed anti-English sentiments and its Stalinist attitudinizings, with the work of such English regional Modernists as Basil Bunting, whose *Briggflatts* (1966) is rooted in his native northeast of England, but derives its poetic forms and attitudes from the Poundian making-new of language. Geoffrey Hill, in *Mercian Hymns* (1971), attempts a cognate recovery of Saxon history through a remaking of the linguistic forms by which men experience themselves, while *King Log* (1968) reverts to the middle ages as a means of penetrating the opacities of personal and national life. Such attempts to explore the roots of English culture through contemplating some of the more arcane and murky moments of its history are to be distinguished from the explicitly *local* emphasis revealed in, say, Ted Hughes's recent poetry, *Moortown* and *Remains of Elmet*, which by and large replace historic understanding by a timeless and finally subjective symbolism.

Such a temptation is there too in the work of R. S. Thomas, which too readily transfigures the individuals of a Welsh hill-farming community into the prototypes of a Christian myth of endurance, fallenness, and redemption, where Romantic populism merges with a Yeatsian apocalyptic strain, in a vision of "stark naturalness" which is pre-eminently literary in origin. Whereas Dylan Thomas is only contingently a Welsh poet, R. S. Thomas is at his best when he registers the tension not only between the parochial culture of the Welsh valleys and his other-wordly commitments as a minister, but between both and his astute eye for the English, metropolitan audience for his poetry, whose touristic attitudes towards Wales his poetry negotiates with irony and reserve, as in "The Welsh Hill Country":

> Too far for you to see
> The fluke and the foot-rot and the fat maggot
> Gnawing the skin from the small bones,
> The sheep are grazing at Bwlch-y-Fedwen,
> Arranged romantically in the usual manner
> On a bleak background of bald stone.

Thomas is aware of the "sham ghosts" investing such a landscape. In many ways, he shares with that quintessentially regional English poet Philip Larkin a distrust of the fashions and fads of the capital, its shallow and ephemeral enthusiasms, together with the rather self-indulgent and at times mawkish melancholy that since Housman's *Shropshire Lad* (1896) has always been associated by rather academic poets with the idiocies of provincial life. A poem such as Larkin's "Whitsun Weddings" is a consummate expression of a mind that is only really at ease moving between the equally uncongenial seductions of London and the provinces, beginning "That Whitsun, I was late getting away" (with its idiomatic ambivalence), and quickening, after all the vulgar and recurring specificities of wedding-party after wedding-party at every station on the way, only as the train approaches London, improbably invested with a harvest-festival fecundity, "Its postal districts packed like squares of wheat," to end:

> And as the tightened brakes took hold, there swelled
> A sense of falling, like an arrow-shower
> Sent out of sight, somewhere becoming rain.

English poetry has tended to find in the mythology of place a substitute for other, failing systems of belief. Hardy, perhaps, is the foremost exponent of such a resort. Elsewhere, however, understanding the spirit of a locale, getting on good terms with its *genius loci*, has been the precondition of establishing a genuine collective and individual identity.

Any attempt to generalize about the vast amount of poetry in English now issuing from the Commonwealth would be foolhardy. The "Commonwealth" itself is a rather nebulous concept, comprising the old Dominions, Canada, Australia, and New Zealand, where the mother-tongue has always been more or less standard English, such intermediate zones as the West Indies, where a patois growing out of a slave culture has given specific political and emotional inflexions to the language, and the diverse regions of Africa and the Indian sub-continent, where English was initially an administrative language, but has now inserted itself to varying degrees into the consciousness of the indigenous ruling class. Nevertheless, certain recurring features may be discerned, of which the most obvious, arising from the one experience all these countries have in common, is the whole question of nationhood and national identity. In the case of the older, "white" Commonwealth, this is primarily a matter of breaking free from the dominance of the mother-culture, of shedding the inferiority complexes of a settler mentality, with all its feelings of marginality and expatriation, and founding a genuinely autochthonous literary tradition.

Kenneth Slessor's long poem "Five Visions of Captain Cook" reflects, for example, on how Cook, unlike Tasman and Bougainville, chose to sail "into the devil's mouth," and "So men write poems in Australia." A similar sense of historical gratuitousness lies behind Geoffrey Dutton's poem about visiting the childhood home in Suffolk of the founder of Adelaide, which ruefully admits: "We owe to strangers the earth in which we've grown." Allen Curnow's "Landfall in Unknown Seas" turns the 300th anniversary of Tasman's discovery of New Zealand into a complex parable of spiritual voyaging, in which "the nameless waters of the world" are given to history, the fabulous turned into the everyday, at "the world's end where wonders cease" – the very point at which the restless spirit has to begin. His fellow-countryman Charles Doyle draws a similar analogy in "Misgivings of Mercator," as does James McAuley in "Terra Australis," inviting the reader to "Voyage within you, on the fabled ocean." Christopher Brennan, one of Australia's earliest poets, describes in "The Wanderer" the cultural rootlessness of her first generations, "driven everywhere from a clinging home." More obliquely, A. D. Hope's "The Death of the Bird" refers to the same condition. Summoned by a speck on the map, the bird migrates to a new home, only to experience there an "exiled love," "ghosts that haunt the heart's possession." It is in migration alone that she is real, for "Going away she is also coming home," while in each resting place she is "Single and frail, uncertain of her place." Death is the last migration.

Australian poetry seems particularly fraught with this sense not only of the transience of the self but of the many transits and transitions through which it passes, what Brennan refers to as the experience of the "threshold." Judith Wright's "Child with a Dead Animal" responds to this, seeing "the creature changed to thing, kindness to dread," and concluding that it is precisely this experience which marks us Man, "whose very earth is made/of light's encounter with its answering shade." Rosemary Dobson also considers thresholds, as with the man raised from the dead, "who once had caught/A wink, a glimpse, of Paradise"; while a poem about a jack-in-a-box turns it into a symbol of a perennial condition which nevertheless has a strong local resonance, speaking for

> All lowly Jacks shut up in boxes,
> Composed of odds and ends of wood,
> Who have such brief, amended chances
> To see the world and find it good.

The same underlying sense of the enclosure and isolation of the island continent, and yet of its comforting seclusion, gives a specifically Australian inflection to Douglas Stewart's "Silkworms," which begins: "All their lives in a box!" but proceeds to balance the pulls of the beyond and of the habitual:

> They stir, they think they will go. Then they remember
> It was forbidden, forbidden, ever to go out....
> Still the night calls them to unimaginable bliss
> But there is terror around them, the vast, the abyss.
>
> And here is the tribe that they know, in their known place,
> They are gentle and kind together, they are safe for ever....

A poem such as Stewart's "Rock Carving," however, touches a note which has become increasingly urgent in Australian poetry, as in that of the other Old Dominions: the contact of the sophisticated western psyche with the vestiges and survivors of the aboriginal culture, in a way which reinforces the felt transience of individual and collective life.

This confrontation is particularly strong in the poetry of Canada, which, as the oldest dominion, has had longest to shake off the shackles of its colonial heritage. Indeed, in post-war Canadian poetry, one feels much more the pressure of other cultural, political, and economic relations: of dependence, on its more powerful neighbour, the United States, and of dominance, over its own, internal "colony," Quebec. The split personality of a country which is on the one hand sympathetic to the non-aligned, dependent nations of the Third World and on the other deeply involved in the North Atlantic Alliance, a major power in the Western, industrialized camp, is not simply confined to its foreign policy. It can be found, for example, in poems such as Earle Birney's "Letter to a Cuzco Priest." The priest, through his sermon preached against a government which is only "an armed front for Fifty Families" and U.S. economic interests, is the unwitting author of a peasant demonstration which ends in troops shooting down the Indians. But the priest, Birney says, is not guilty: "the guilt begins/in the other pulpits and all the places/where no one will say your words." Pointedly, Birney repeats them. A poem such as "Meeting of Strangers" indicates the limits of this guilt. The poet, "White man tourist surrogate" in Trinidad, is nevertheless "not guilty enough to be skewered in the guts for it" by a threatening native; but the final racy, joky exchange redeems something from the encounter.

Similar anxieties and remorse are explored in many recent poems through the theme of the Canadian wilderness, and the men and animals supplanted in the founding of a "New World." Margaret Atwood, for example, in "The Settlers," counts the cost of enclosing a terrain which is both the continent and the "civilized" mind, "made/less than immense/by networks of/roads and grids and fences." Margaret Avison, in "Voluptuaries and Others," contemplates the price paid for the banalities by which we map out history, making it a "comprehended" and "containing space"; while her "New Year's Poem" celebrates the "Gentle and just pleasure/It is, being human, to have won from space/This unchill, habitable interior." In many of these poets, comments upon the landscape are also observations about a *paysage intérieur* felt to be intimately linked with it.

"We wear our features to suit the landscape" says the Pakistani poet Taufiq Rafat; and from the "tumultuous landscape" of Blanche Baughan's New Zealand to Derek Walcott's St. Lucia the preoccupation recurs, though few poets have the self-critical awareness evinced in the latter's "Postcard":

> Schizophrenic, wrenched by two styles,
> One a hack's prose, I earn
> My exile. I trudge this sickle beach for miles.
>
> Tan, burn
> To slough off
> This love of landscape that's self-love.
> To change your language you must change your life.

Some of the best Commonwealth poetry arises from the complex tensions where two or more cultures intersect, in a language and an identity shot through with the inequities of history. Both Walcott and the Barbadian Edward Brathwaite, for example, look not only towards the European literary tradition their words evoke, but also, with varying degrees of scepticism and fascination, to the West African origins and the Creole soil of their experience. In "The Emigrants" Brathwaite considers Columbus's Arcadian dream, and sets beside it the bitter reality of plunder, slavery, and genocide. He can reach no final answer to the questions raised by this brutal history:

> What did this journey mean, this
> New world mean: dis-
> Covery? Or a return to terrors
> He had sailed from, known before?

In a poem such as "South," however, he can juxtapose "the strength of that turbulent soil" from which he sprang with the insights gained from travel, in a language which, evoking T. S. Eliot, itself points to cosmopolitan allegiances. "The Spade," its very title bracketing with irony the white man's perception, settles delicately on a negro ("Gentleman or gigolo or/Both") stepping his way among the follies of the Boulevard St. Michel, "With this nonchalance/Of shoulder/And this urbane head," playing his own game and playing it hard. A similar insight invests Dom Moraes's vision of the lonely drinkers in "One of Us"; while the Audenish rhythms and attitudes of his "From Tibet" add an urgency – that of unseen war, the Chinese invasion – to the tourist's posture, only to be subverted by a self-conscious, self-dismissive gesture full of literary echoes:

> Like cinders the red flowers
> Brush fire across my sleeve.
> I shall remount and leave
> Taking no backward look,
> And then collect these hours
> In a travel book.

The predicament of the cultural emigré, writing in a language not his own, recurs again and again in the poetry of the "new" Commonwealth, in Zulfikar Ghose's "One Chooses a Language" as in R. Parthasarathy's "Unfinished Biography":

> There is something to be said for exile:
> You learn roots are deep. That language
> Is a tree, loses colour
> Under another sky....

Independence in such countries was achieved by an alliance of the national bourgeoisie and the popular classes, largely urban. Yet the very pre-condition of founding a national culture lay in re-appropriating those rural, largely peasant forms and traditions overshadowed by the westernized culture of the educated elites of the towns. As A. N. Forde of Grenada observes:

> Building a culture for ourselves ...,
> Fondly we search for *regionalia*
> In our poetry to fool the world
> That we are sprung from foam.

The word "*regionalia*" itself, with its Latin origins, calls up complex imperial ironies. A central problem for the new nation-states of the Third World is focussed here. In many of these countries, besides being the language of the literary intelligentsia, English is the only mode of communication that transcends regional and tribal divisions, and the only means of reaching that larger, international audience on whom the new nation wishes to make an impression. In the Indian sub-continent, English has had time to enter the bloodstream of the culture, and to provide the same kind of literary *lingua franca* earlier offered by Persian. In Africa, however, the strain is more noticeable. Either the poet, like John Pepper Clark, is so steeped in the English tradition that he writes as an outpost of that culture; or, like his fellow Nigerians Gabriel Okara and Christopher Okigbo, he moves uncertainly between that fortified position and the culture of the villages, struggling to synthesize an indigenous and yet up-to-date literature from the disparate materials to hand: physical landscape, local history, myth, inherited rituals, folk traditions, linked by an at-times somewhat sentimental Romantic primitivism about the "Interior."

African poetry has not yet fully thrown off the myths about "The Dark Continent" fabricated in the heyday of imperialism by such diverse figures as Conrad, Rider Haggard, and the early-modern artists who discovered the masks and statuettes of Benin and the Congo. Christopher Okigbo, in "Lament of the Drums," attempts a rather more sophisticated montage of European and African traditions, linking an elegy for an imprisoned Nigerian politician with the death of Aeneas's helmsman Palinurus and Ishtar's lament for Tammuz. It is an ambitious poem, which summons up echoes of Eliot and other modern poets, and employs Eliot's technique of juxtaposing, overlaying, and counterpointing contrasted styles and registers, to suggest the unassimilated relations of the many voices that jostle in the sensibility of the modern African poet.

Two lines from Okara's "Song Without Words" sum up this abiding problem. Again, Eliot is the presiding voice:

> So think of me as a shadow
> flitting from extreme to extreme.

In Africa more than anywhere else, perhaps, the predicament of "The Hollow Men," announced with a raffish allusion to Conrad's African *Heart of Darkness* at the beginning of the Modernist era as the defining condition of that modernity, survives as a genuine cultural and personal dilemma.

READING LIST

1. Bibliographies, handbooks, etc.

Tate, Allen, *Recent American Poetry and Poetic Criticism: A Selected List of References*, 1943.

Tate, Allen, *Sixty America Poets 1896–1944*, 1945; revised edition, edited by Kenton Kilmer, 1954.

Arms, George, and Joseph M. Kuntz, *Poetry Explication*, 1950; revised edition by Kuntz, 1962.

Shapiro, Karl, *A Bibliography of Modern Prosody*, 1948.

Spender, Stephen, and Donald Hall, *The Concise Encyclopaedia of English and American Poets and Poetry*, 1963; revised edition, 1970.

Press, John, *A Map of Modern English Verse*, 1969.

Murphy, Rosalie, and James Vinson, editors, *Contemporary Poets of the English Language*, 1970; revised edition, edited by Vinson and D. L. Kirkpatrick, 1975, 1980.

2. General histories

Clarke, Austin, *Poetry in Modern Ireland*, 1951; revised edition, 1962.

Deutsch, Babette, *Poetry in Our Time*, 1952; revised edition, 1963.

Fraser, G. S., *The Modern Writer and His World*, 1953; revised edition, 1968, 1972.

Press, John, *A Map of Modern English Verse*, 1969

Sisson, C. H., *English Poetry 1900–50*, 1971.

Bradbury, Malcolm, *The Social Context of Modern English Literature*, 1971.

Rexroth, Kenneth, *American Poetry in the Twentieth Century*, 1971.

Perkins, David, *A History of Modern Poetry: From the 1890's to the High Modernist Mode*, 1976.

McAuley, James, *A Map of Australian Verse*, 1976.

Thwaite, Anthony, *Twentieth-Century English Poetry*, 1976.

3. Themes, topics, short periods, etc.

Riding, Laura, and Robert Graves, *A Survey of Modernist Poetry*, 1927.

Wilson, Edmund, *Axel's Castle: A Study in the Imaginative Literature of 1870–1930*, 1931.

Leavis, F. R., *New Bearings in English Poetry*, 1932; revised edition, 1950.

Brooks, Cleanth, *Modern Poetry and the Tradition*, 1939.

Daiches, David, *Poetry and the Modern World*, 1940.

Scarfe, Francis, *Auden and After: The Liberation of Poetry 1930–41*, 1942.

Lindsay, Maurice, *The Scottish Renaissance*, 1948.

O'Connor, William Van, *Sense and Sensibility in Modern Poetry*, 1948.

Pinto, V. de Sola, *Crisis in English Poetry 1880–1914*, 1951.

Coffman, S. K., *Imagism: A Chapter for the History of Modern Poetry*, 1951.

Durrell, Lawrence, *Key to Modern Poetry*, 1952; as *A Key to Modern British Poetry*, 1952.

Blackmur, R. P., *Language as Gesture: Essays in Poetry*, 1952; shortened edition, as *Form and Value in Modern Poetry*, 1952.

Davie, Donald, *Articulate Energy: An Enquiry into the Syntax of English Poetry*, 1955.

Kermode, Frank, *Romantic Image*, 1957.

Moore, Geoffrey, *Poetry To-day*, 1958.

Alvarez, A., *The Shaping Spirit: Studies in Modern English and American Poets*, 1958; as *Stewards of Excellence*, 1958.

Winters, Yvor, *On Modern Poets*, 1959.

Fraser, G. S., *Vision and Rhetoric: Studies in Modern Poetry*, 1959.

Rosenthal, M. L., *The Modern Poets: An Introduction*, 1960.

Currey, R. N., *Poets of the 1939-45 War*, 1960.

Beach, Joseph Warren, *Obsessive Images: Symbolism in Poetry of the 1930's and 1940's*, 1960.

Fairchild, H. N., *Religious Trends in English Poetry*, vol. 5: *1880-1920*, 1961; vol. 6: *1920-65*, 1968.

Parkinson, Thomas, editor, *A Casebook on the Beat*, 1961.

Pratt, J. C., *The Meaning of Modern Poetry*, 1962.

Smith, A. J. M., editor, *Masks of Poetry: Canadian Critics on Canadian Verse*, 1962.

Spender, Stephen, *The Struggle of the Modern*, 1963.

Press, John, *Rule and Energy: Trends in British Poetry since the Second World War*, 1963.

Phillips, Robert, *The Confessional Poets*, 1963.

Stead, C. K., *The New Poetic: Yeats to Eliot*, 1964.

Johnson, J. H., *English Poetry of the First World War*, 1964.

Scully, James, editor, *Modern Poetics*, 1965; as *Modern Poets on Modern Poetry*, 1966.

Mills, Ralph J., Jr., *Contemporary American Poetry*, 1965.

Ross, R. H., *The Georgian Revolt 1910-22: Rise and Fall of a Poetic Ideal*, 1965.

Bergonzi, Bernard, *Heroes' Twilight: A Study of the Literature of the Great War*, 1965.

Smithyman, Kendrick, *A Way of Saying: A Study of New Zealand Poetry*, 1965.

Orr, Peter, editor, *The Poet Speaks: Interviews with Contemporary Poets*, 1966.

Rosenthal, M. L., *The New Poets: American and British Poetry since World War II*, 1967.

Baxter, James K., *Aspects of Poetry in New Zealand*, 1967.

Elliott, Brian, *The Landscape of Australian Poetry*, 1967.

Hollander, John, editor, *Modern Poetry: Essays in Criticism*, 1968.

Hamilton, Ian, editor, *The Modern Poet: Essays from The Review*, 1968.

Hamburger, Michael, *The Truth of Poetry: Tensions in Modern Poetry from Baudelaire to the 1960's*, 1969.

Maxwell, D. E. S., *Poets of the Thirties*, 1969.

Howard, Richard, *Alone with America: Essays on the Art of Poetry in the United States since 1950*, 1969.

Spears, Monroe K., *Dionysus and the City: Modernism in Twentieth-Century Poetry*, 1970.

McAuley, James, *The Personal Element in Australian Poetry*, 1970.

Kenner, Hugh, *The Pound Era*, 1972.

Schmidt, Michael, and Grevel Lindop, editors, *British Poetry since 1960: A Critical Survey*, 1972.

Armstrong, Isobel, *The Poetic Vision: Signposts and Landmarks in Poetry*, 1973.

Shaw, Robert, editor, *American Poetry since 1960*, 1973.

Allen, Donald, and Warren Tallman, *The Poetics of the New American Poetry*, 1973.

Sutton, Walter, *American Free Verse: The Modern Revolution in Poetry*, 1973.

Pondrom, Cyrena N., *The Road from Paris: French Influence on English Poetry 1900-20*, 1974.

Brown, Terence, *Northern Voices: Poets from Ulster*, 1975.

Tolley, A. T., *The Poetry of the Thirties*, 1975.

Harmer, J. B., *Victory in Limbo: Imagism 1908-17*, 1975.

Martin, Graham, and P. N. Furbank, editors, *Twentieth-Century Poetry: Critical Essays and Documents*, 1975.

Dunn, Douglas, editor, *Two Decades of Irish Writing: A Critical Survey*, 1976.

Scannell, Vernon, *Not Without Glory: Poets of the Second World War*, 1976.

Gregson, J. M., *Poetry of the First World War*, 1976.

Partridge, A. C., *The Language of Modern Poetry: Yeats, Eliot, Auden*, 1976.
Simon, Myron, *The Georgian Poetic*, 1976.
Tate, Allen, *Memories and Essays*, 1976.
Hynes, Samuel, *The Auden Generation: Literature and Politics in England in the 1930's*, 1976.
Homberger, Eric, *The Art of the Real: Poetry in England and America since 1939*, 1977.
Bergonzi, Bernard, *Reading the Thirties*, 1977.
Fraser, G. S., *Essays on 20th-Century Poets*, 1977.
Schmidt, Michael, *An Introduction to 50 Modern British Poets*, 1979.
Morrison, Blake, *The Movement*, 1980.
Barker, Francis, and others, editors, *1936*, 2 vols., 1980.

4. Anthologies of primary material

Smith, A. J. M., editor, *The Book of Canadian Poetry*, 1943; revised edition, 1948, 1957.
Aiken, Conrad, editor, *Twentieth-Century American Foetry*, 1944; revised edition, 1963.
Wright, Judith, editor, *A Book of Australian Verse*, 1956; revised edition, 1968.
Chapman, R., and J. Bennett, editors, *An Anthology of New Zealand Verse*, 1956.
Hall, Donald, Robert Pack, and Louis Simpson, editors, *New Poets of England and America*, 1957; second selection, edited by Hall and Pack, 1962.
Butler, Guy, editor, *A Book of South African Verse*, 1959.
Smith, A. J. M., editor, *The Oxford Book of Canadian Verse: In English and French*, 1960; revised edition, 1965.
Curnow, Allen, editor, *The Penguin Book of New Zealand Verse*, 1960.
Allen, Donald, editor, *The New American Poetry 1945–1960*, 1960.
Plath, Sylvia, editor, *American Poetry Now: A Selection of the Best Poems by Modern American Writers*, 1961.
Sanders, Gerald De Witt, John Herbert Nelson, and M. L. Rosenthal, editors, *Chief Modern Poets of England and America*, 1962; revised edition, 1970.
Hall, Donald, editor, *Contemporary American Poetry*, 1962; revised edition, 1972.
Alvarez, A., editor, *The New Poetry*, 1962; revised edition, 1966.
Reeves, James, editor, *Georgian Poetry*, 1962.
Allott, Kenneth, editor, *The Penguin Book of Contemporary Verse 1918–1960*, 1962.
Moore, Geoffrey, and Ulli Beier, editors, *Modern Poetry from Africa*, 1963; revised edition, 1968.
Brinnin, John Malcolm, and Bill Reid, editors, *Twentieth Century Poetry: American and British*, 1963; revised edition, 1970.
Wilston, M. T., editor, *Poetry of Midcentury 1940–1960* [Canadian verse], 1964.
Doyle, Charles, editor, *Recent Poetry in New Zealand*, 1965.
Heath-Stubbs, John, and David Wright, editors, *The Faber Book of Twentieth Century Verse*, revised edition, 1965.
Figueroa, John, editor, *Caribbean Voices: An Anthology of West Indian Poetry*, 2 vols., 1966–70.
Smith, A. J. M., editor, *Modern Canadian Verse: In English and French*, 1967.
Cope, Jack, and Uys Krige, editors, *The Penguin Book of South African Verse*, 1968.
Lal, P., editor, *Modern Indian Poetry in English*, 1969.
Strand, Mark, editor, *The Contemporary American Poets*, 1969.
Williams, John Stuart, and Meic Stephens, editors, *The Lilting House: An Anthology of Anglo-Welsh Poetry 1917–1967*, 1969.
O'Sullivan, Vincent, editor, *An Anthology of Twentieth Century New Zealand Poetry*, 1970.
Lucie-Smith, Edward, editor, *British Poetry since 1945*, 1970.
MacCaig, Norman, and Alexander Scott, editors, *Contemporary Scottish Poetry*, 1970.
Montague, John, editor, *The Faber Book of Irish Verse*, 1970.
Ramchand, Kenneth, and C. Gray, editors, *West Indian Poetry*, 1971.
Salkey, Andrew, editor, *Breaklight: An Anthology of Caribbean Poetry*, 1971.

Randall, Dudley, editor, *The Black Poets: A New Anthology*, 1971.
Heseltine, H., editor, *The Penguin Book of Australian Verse*, 1972.
Nandy, Pritish, editor, *Indian Poetry in English 1947–1972*, 1972.
Larkin, Philip, editor, *The Oxford Book of Twentieth Century English Verse*, 1973.
Ellmann, Richard, and Robert O'Clair, editors, *The Norton Anthology of Modern Poetry*, 1973.
Bradbury, Malcolm, and James McFarlane, editors, *Modernism*, 1976.
Bold, Alan, editor, *Cambridge Book of English Verse 1939–1975*, 1976.
Moore, Geoffrey, editor, *The Penguin Book of American Verse*, 1977.
Harmon, Maurice, editor, *Irish Poetry after Yeats: Seven Poets*, 1979.
Enright, D. J., editor, *The Oxford Book of Contemporary Verse 1945–1980*, 1980.

ABERCROMBIE, Lascelles. English. Born in Ashton-upon-Mersey, Cheshire, 9 January 1881. Educated at Malvern College; University of Manchester, 1900–02. Married Catherine Gwatkin in 1909; three sons, one daughter. Reporter, Liverpool *Daily Courier*, 1908–10; free-lance journalist and reviewer, 1910–15; Inspector of Munitions, Liverpool, 1915–18. Lecturer in Poetry, University of Liverpool, 1919–22; Professor of English Literature, University of Leeds, 1922–29; Hildred Carlile Professor of English, Bedford College, University of London, 1929–35; Goldsmith Reader in English, Merton College, Oxford, 1935–38. Clark Lecturer, Trinity College, Cambridge, 1923; Ballard Matthews Lecturer, University College, Bangor, 1924; Leslie Stephen Lecturer, Cambridge, 1929; Lecturer in Fine Arts, Queen's University of Belfast, 1931; Turnbull Lecturer, Johns Hopkins University, Baltimore, 1935; Gregynog Lecturer, University College, Aberystwyth, 1938. M.A.: University of Liverpool; Oxford University; D.Lit.: Queen's University of Belfast; Litt.D.: University of Manchester; Cambridge University. Member of the British Academy, 1937. *Died 27 October 1938.*

PUBLICATIONS

Verse

    Interludes and Poems. 1908.
    Mary and the Bramble. 1910.
    Emblems of Love, Designed in Several Discourses. 1912.
    Twelve Idyls and Other Poems. 1928.
    The Poems. 1930.
    Lyrics and Unfinished Poems. 1940.
    Vision and Love. 1966.

Plays

    The Sale of Saint Thomas, act 1. 1911; complete version, 1930.
    Deborah (produced 1964). 1913.
    The Adder (produced 1913). In *Four Short Plays,* 1922.
    The End of the World (produced 1914). In *Four Short Plays,* 1922.
    The Staircase (produced 1920). In *Four Short Plays,* 1922.
    Four Short Plays (includes *The Adder, The Staircase, The End of the World, The Deserter*). 1922.
    Phoenix (produced 1924). 1923.

Other

    Thomas Hardy: A Critical Study. 1912.
    Speculative Dialogues. 1913.
    Poetry and Contemporary Speech. 1914.
    The Epic. 1914.
    An Essay Towards a Theory of Art. 1922.
    Principles of English Prosody. 1923.
    Communication Versus Expression in Art. 1923.
    Stratford-upon-Avon: A Report on Future Development, with Patrick Abercrombie. 1923.

The Theory of Poetry. 1924.
The Idea of Great Poetry (lectures). 1925.
Romanticism. 1925.
Drowsie Frightened Steeds. 1928.
Poetry: Its Music and Meaning. 1932.
Principles of Literary Criticism. 1932.
The Art of Wordsworth, edited by R. Abercrombie. 1952.
A Personal Note. 1974.

Editor, *New English Poems: A Miscellany.* 1931.

Bibliography: *A Bibliography and Notes on the Works of Abercrombie* by Jeffrey Cooper, 1928.

Reading List: *Abercrombie* by Oliver Elton, 1939.

*   *   *

T. S. Eliot reviewing the latest Georgian anthology in 1918 remarked disparagingly that "the Georgians caress everything they touch," and he called the prevailing tone "minor-Keatsian." Although Lascelles Abercrombie was a leading member of this group, his poetry is neither lyrical nor sensuous. For the most part he is a philosophical poet dealing with abstract ideas in closely-packed, complex, and often turgid style. His fundamental belief, set out in his poems and the pseudo-philosophical book *Speculative Dialogues,* is that life is a striving towards a perfect consciousness, producing an "ecstasy" or "exultation" which is the manifestation of God. In "Soul and Body," for example, Soul tells Body that he is seeking a passion beyond that which Body can give, and in "The Eternal Wedding" the poet says,

> Now all life's loveliness and power we have
> Dissolved in this one moment, and our burning
> Carries all shining upward, till in us
> Life is not life, but the desire of God,
> Himself desiring and himself accepting.

Many of the poems, called Dramatic Interludes, are set out in dramatic form, though they were not intended for staging, but he also wrote a number of verse plays which were produced. They are flawed like many of his poems by an over-inflated style. Frequently the Interludes and the plays reveal characters coming to self-knowledge or a realisation that their past actions have been caused by motives of which they were unaware: St. Thomas (in *The Sale of Saint Thomas*) is forced by the Noble Stranger to see that his waverings are the result of his lack of faith; Judith, in the poem of that name, realises "How a mere bragging was my purity," and how her defilement by Holofernes has brought her new perfection of virginity; the woman in "Blind," who has tramped the roads with her blind son seeking the man who had betrayed her many years before, finds, when her son has killed the man, that her search was not for vengeance, but for her lost love – "it was I who was blind." Paradoxical, enigmatic, or unexpected endings are common in Abercrombie's poetry and often they can seem merely contrived.

There is also at times an unnecessary dwelling on violence and horror, as, for example, in "The Olympians," *The Sale of Saint Thomas,* and *The End of the World.* More disturbingly there is often too a sense of some mysterious fear or evil waiting to pounce; so even in the by and large joyful "Marriage Song" the God of Marriages is accompanied by "the black, ravenous and gaunt" "wild hound Fear," "All frenzied fire the head – /The hunger of its mouth a hollow crimson flame/The hatred in its eyes a blaze/Fierce and green."

In spite of being only the second living poet to have his collected poems published by the Oxford University Press, Abercrombie felt his poems represented a sense of "unrealised ambition," and after the War he devoted most of his time to criticism, particularly aesthetic theory in which he was greatly influenced by Croce. His theorising is sometimes rather simplistic, but the discussions of such topics as Romanticism and Wordsworth are stimulating and acute.

—David Astle

AIKEN, Conrad (Potter). American. Born in Savannah, Georgia, 5 August 1889. Educated at Middlesex School, Concord, Massachusetts; Harvard University, Cambridge, Massachusetts (President, *Harvard Advocate*), 1907–12, A.B. 1912. Married 1) Jessie McDonald in 1912 (divorced, 1929), one son, two daughters; 2) Clarice Lorenz, 1930 (divorced, 1937); 3) Mary Hoover, 1937. Contributing Editor, *The Dial*, New York, 1916–19; American Correspondent, *Athenaeum*, London, 1919–25, and *London Mercury*, 1921–22; London Correspondent, *The New Yorker*, 1933–36. Instructor, Harvard University, 1927–28. Fellow, 1948, and Consultant in Poetry, 1950–52, Library of Congress, Washington, D.C. Recipient: Pulitzer Prize, 1930; Shelley Memorial Prize, 1930; Guggenheim Fellowship, 1934; Bryher Award, 1952; National Book Award, 1954; Bollingen Prize, 1956; Academy of American Poets Fellowship, 1957; National Institute of Arts and Letters Gold Medal, 1958; Huntington Hartford Foundation Award, 1961; Brandeis University Creative Arts Award, 1966; National Medal for Literature, 1969. Member, American Academy of Arts and Letters, 1957. *Died 17 August 1973.*

PUBLICATIONS

Collections

   Selected Letters, edited by Joseph Killorin.   1978.

Verse

   Earth Triumphant and Other Tales in Verse.   1914.
   The Jig of Forslin: A Symphony.   1916.
   Turns and Movies and Other Tales in Verse.   1916.
   Nocturne of Remembered Spring and Other Poems.   1917.
   The Charnal Rose, Senlin: A Biography, and Other Poems.   1918.
   The House of Dust: A Symphony.   1920.
   Punch: The Immortal Liar.   1921.
   The Pilgrimage of Festus.   1923.
   Priapus and the Pool and Other Poems.   1925.
   (Poems), edited by Louis Untermeyer.   1927.
   Prelude.   1929.
   Selected Poems.   1929.

John Deth, A Metaphysical Legend, and Other Poems.   1930.
Preludes for Memnon.   1931.
The Coming Forth by Day of Osiris Jones.   1931.
Landscape West of Eden.   1934.
Time in the Rock: Preludes to Definition.   1936.
And in the Human Heart.   1940.
Brownstone Eclogues and Other Poems.   1942.
The Soldier.   1944.
The Kid.   1947.
The Divine Pilgrim.   1949.
Skylight One: Fifteen Poems.   1949.
Collected Poems.   1953.
A Letter from Li Po and Other Poems.   1955.
The Flute Player.   1956.
Sheepfold Hill: 15 Poems.   1958.
Selected Poems.   1961.
The Morning Song of Lord Zero: Poems Old and New.   1963.
A Seizure of Limericks.   1964.
Thee.   1967.
The Clerk's Journal: An Undergraduate Poem, Together with a Brief Memoir of Dean LeBaron Russell Briggs, T. S. Eliot, and Harvard, in 1911.   1971.
Collected Poems 1916–1970.   1971.

Play

Mr. Arcularis (produced 1949).   1957.

Fiction

Bring! Bring! and Other Stories.   1925.
Blue Voyage.   1927.
Costumes by Eros.   1928.
Gehenna.   1930.
Great Circle.   1933.
Among the Lost People (stories).   1934.
King Coffin.   1935.
A Heart for the Gods of Mexico.   1939.
Conversation; or, Pilgrims' Progress.   1940; as *The Conversation*, 1948.
The Short Stories.   1950.
The Collected Short Stories.   1960.
The Collected Novels.   1964.

Other

Scepticisms: Notes on Contemporary Poetry.   1919.
Ushant: An Essay (autobiography).   1952.
A Reviewer's ABC: Collected Criticism from 1916 to the Present, edited by Rufus A. Blanshard.   1958; as *Collected Criticism*, 1968.
Cats and Bats and Things with Wings (juvenile).   1965.
Tom, Sue, and the Clock (juvenile).   1966.

Editor, *Modern American Poets.* 1922; as *Twentieth Century American Poetry,* 1944; revised edition, 1963.
Editor, *Selected Poems of Emily Dickinson.* 1924.
Editor, *American Poetry, 1671–1928: A Comprehensive Anthology.* 1929; as *A Comprehensive Anthology of American Poetry,* 1944.
Editor, with William Rose Benét, *An Anthology of Famous English and American Poetry.* 1945.

Reading List: *Aiken: A Life of His Art* by Jay Martin, 1962; *Aiken* by Frederick J. Hoffman, 1962; *Aiken* by Reuel Denney, 1964.

*   *   *

Characteristically, Conrad Aiken himself raises the essential critical problem in a note he wrote in 1917: "It is difficult to place Conrad Aiken in the poetic firmament, so difficult that one sometimes wonders whether he deserves a place there at all" (*Collected Criticism*). The problem is further complicated by the fact that Aiken was not only a poet, but also a respected novelist and critic. The list of his admirers is persuasive: R. P. Blackmur, Allen Tate, Malcolm Lowry all find in him one of the central voices of his age. Yet to the contemporary reader such claims are likely to seem excessive.

About the scope of his ambition there can be no doubt. Five long, complicated novels; many lengthy poetic sequences, or "symphonies," dealing with themes as varied, and as large, as the history of America (*The Kid*), the importance of his Puritan heritage ("Mayflower"), the problems of the self encountering the realities of love and death (*Preludes for Memnon* and *The Coming Forth by Day of Osiris Jones*): all testify to the courageous attempt to convey a rich, complex life in a wide-ranging, always technically experimental, art.

The centre of this art lies in the difficultly maintained balance between aesthetic purity and formal perfection on the one hand, and the menacing chaos of terrifying experience on the other. It is tempting to relate this to Aiken's very early experience as a child when he discovered the bodies of his parents after a mutual suicide pact: this moment is placed at the centre of his long autobiographical essay *Ushant*. This deeply buried memory may also have encouraged Aiken's passionate interest in Freud. The five novels show this interest everywhere: the hero of *Blue Voyage*, Demarest, is on a voyage of self-discovery through journey, quest, and dream. This novel, like *Great Circle* – which Freud himself admired – is an elaborate metaphor for the author's psychic search, the exploration of his own consciousness. At their best, the novels find a language for disturbing, hidden states of the psyche: the combination of thriller form and psychoanalytic imagery in *King Coffin* is uniquely memorable. But too often the novels slip into vagueness and imprecision. As Frederick J. Hoffman has observed, their separate parts fail *quite* to cohere. The lack of adequate characterisation, and the over-literariness of the enterprise, are at odds with our valid expectations of prose fiction. It is significant, then, that Aiken's "autobiography," *Ushant*, should seem to so many of his critics his finest achievement in prose. Here, Aiken as writer, and his literary friends, including Eliot and Pound, are at the centre of a "fictionalised" account of the author's life. Apart from its other intrinsic interests, this quite extraordinary, unclassifiable work is justified, almost alone, by the majestic sweep and lyrical seductiveness of Aiken's rhetoric.

It is this majestic rhetoric that one also recognises in the poetry: Malcolm Lowry referred to Aiken as "the truest and most direct descendant of our own great Elizabethans" (*Wake, 11,* 1952). This quality is immediately apparent in *Preludes for Memnon*:

> What dignity can death bestow on us,
> Who kiss beneath a street lamp, or hold hands
> Half hidden in a taxi, or replete
> With coffee, figs and Barsac make our way
> To a dark bedroom in a wormworn house?

The combination here of the common and quotidian – street lamp, taxi, coffee – with noble, "Elizabethan" cadences, is the characteristic Aiken manner. It is a manner that frequently skirts parody and pastiche, but equally often rises to a rich, solemn verbal music. In poem after poem in his enormous output, Aiken sustains a long, flowing musical line, celebrating, as in "Landscape West of Eden," the capacity of language to order the chaos of the unaccomodated self. What one misses, however, in too much of this poetry, and what contributes to a certain lack of *energy* in the verse, is any intense verbal particularity, or, often, the sense of real feeling significantly expressed. In *Time in the Rock*, one of his most ambitious pieces, there is little sense of any real pressure or urgency behind the words; they have a tendency, as it were, to slip off the edge of the page as we read; nothing seems to make it all *cohere*.

His more objective, "dramatic" poems, like *The Kid* and "Mayflower," with their incorporation of historical and legendary material and their evocations of New England landscape and geography, are perhaps more valuable, in the end, than his lyrical self-communings. The contemporary reader is also likely to be more drawn to the lighter side of Aiken: in a poem like "Blues for Ruby Matrix" the rhetoric remains, but allied now to a delightful sexiness and tenderness.

Whatever the mode, however, there is always in Aiken, even if only residually, that sense of horror, of terror, and of death – "The sombre note that gives the chord its power," as he puts it in "Palimpsest" – that gives the best poetry its capacity to hurt and wound us. When, in *Preludes for Memnon*, he defines the role of the poet, Aiken finds a definition that takes full note of this fundamental ground-bass of his own work: the poet is one who

> by imagination [apes]
> God, the supreme poet of despair ...
> Knowing the rank intolerable taste of death,
> And walking dead on the still living earth.

—Neil Corcoran

AMMONS, A(rchie) R(andolph). American. Born in Whiteville, North Carolina, 18 February 1926. Educated at Wake Forest College, North Carolina, B.A. 1949; University of California, Berkeley, 1950–52. Served in the United States Naval Reserve, 1944–46. Married Phyllis Plumbo in 1949; one child. Principal, Hatteras Elementary School, North Carolina, 1949–50; Executive Vice-President, Friedrich and Dimmock Inc., Mellville, New Jersey, 1952–62. Since 1964, Member of the Faculty, Associate Professor, 1969–71, since 1971, Professor of English, and since 1973, Goldwin Smith Professor of English, Cornell University, Ithaca, New York. Visiting Professor, Wake Forest University, 1974–75. Poetry Editor, *Nation*, New York, 1963. Recipient: Bread Loaf Writers Conference Scholarship, 1961; Guggenheim Fellowship, 1966; American Academy of Arts and Letters Travelling Fellowship, 1967; National Endowment for the Arts grant, 1969; National Book Award, 1973; Bollingen Prize, 1975; National Institute of Arts and Letters award, 1977. D.Litt.: Wake Forest University, 1972; University of North Carolina, Chapel Hill, 1973. Lives in Ithaca, New York.

Verse

> Ommateum, with Doxology.   1955.
> Expressions of Sea Level.   1964.
> Corsons Inlet.   1965.
> Tape for the Turn of the Year.   1965.
> Northfield Poems.   1966.
> Selected Poems.   1968.
> Uplands.   1970.
> Briefings: Poems Small and Easy.   1971.
> Collected Poems 1951–1971.   1972.
> Sphere: The Form of a Motion.   1974.
> Diversifications.   1975.
> The Snow Poems.   1977.
> The Selected Poems 1951–1977.   1977.

Reading List: "Ammons Issue" of Diacritics, 1974.

* * *

A.R. Ammons is one of the most prolific poets of his generation, amassing to date some dozen books of verse that have won him the National Book Award in 1973, for his Collected Poems 1951–1971, and the Bollingen Award for Sphere: The Form of a Motion. The earliest poems, searching boldly for a center of self from which to project his persona, achieve their best effect from his recklessly strewn imagery and the pressure of his imagination to find the edges and furthest barriers of experience. The excellent Selected Poems of 1968, a winnowing of all the early work, dramatizes this search with varied, often profoundly moving language.

Ammons's attention ranges from intricately detailed portraits of the landscape of upper New York state, to travels throughout the southwestern United States, and memories of his childhood growing up on a farm in North Carolina, where he is fresh and original as a lyric poet. His reminiscence of the partly mute woman who raised him as a child, "Nelly Myers," is a minor classic of the modern elegy, with its lilting rhythms and its quiet, loving tribute to her wisdom and imperfections.

Much of Ammons's poetry depends upon a texture of rapid, rambling speech that precipitates a poem within its often lush formations. The edge of his poem is not silence but the banter and commentary in which it lies embedded. This pointedly risky strategy of creating a lyric can, when it is not in control, produce tracts and harangues that run tediously on devoid of any poetry. When inspired, however, the language gives way to a charged form of words partly submerged in the verbal undergrowth. His poems are like forms half perceived lying in high grass.

His verbal felicity has, however, occasioned more dry commentary than inspired lyricism. In an experiment with writing on adding machine tape, which imposed a narrow frame on the poet, Ammons wrote a seemingly endless discourse on the minutiae of his life during the winter of 1964–65, published as Tape for the Turn of the Year. As a professor teaching at Cornell University and living in Ithaca, New York, the persona lacks adventure and change, and the poet's journal suffers from the uneventful pace of his days. In succeeding volumes, Northfield Poems and Uplands, the style is noticeably more clipped and abrupt, approaching Imagist concision. The poet is clearly inspired by natural phenomena, particularly in the latter volume where his attention to mountain scenery is keenly alert. In Briefings he continues to experiment with short, sudden articulations of feeling and momentary perceptions. But in

Sphere the style changes again into a long sequential discourse patterned by sections of four triplets where language is only partly sculpted. *The Snow Poems* returns to the mode of shorter poems and is a large collection devoted to the poet's favourite landscape, the snow-laden terrain of the northeast.

Throughout this large canon, Ammons continues to search for a final center of self irreducible of ambiguity. In his natural landscapes he has sought the recesses of the mystery of his own nature. But in chronicling his middle years and the details of his life from day to day, he provides the fullest account of the frustrations and triumphs of the middle class American reluctant to accept his professional life as the whole of his existence.

—Paul Christensen

ASHBERY, John (Lawrence). American. Born in Rochester, New York, 28 July 1927. Educated at Deerfield Academy, Massachusetts; Harvard University, Cambridge, Massachusetts (Member of the Editorial Board, *The Harvard Advocate*), B.A. in English 1949; Columbia University, New York, M.A. in English 1951; New York University, 1957–58. Copywriter, Oxford University Press, New York, 1951–54, and McGraw-Hill Book Company, New York, 1954–55. Art Critic, European Edition of the *New York Herald Tribune*, Paris, 1960–65, and *Art International*, Lugano, Switzerland, 1961–64; Editor, *Locus Solus* magazine, Lans-en-Vercors, France, 1960–62; Editor, *Art and Literature*, Paris, 1963–64; Paris Correspondent, 1964–65, and Executive Editor, 1965–72, *Art News*, New York. Since 1974, Professor of English, Brooklyn College of the City University of New York. Since 1976, Poetry Editor, *Partisan Review*, New Brunswick, New Jersey. Recipient: Fulbright Fellowship, 1955, 1956; Yale Series of Younger Poets Award, 1956; Poets Foundation grant, 1960, 1964; Ingram Merrill Foundation grant, 1962, 1972; Guggenheim Fellowship, 1967, 1973; National Endowment for the Arts grant, 1968, 1969; National Institute of Arts and Letters award, 1969; Shelley Memorial Award, 1973; Modern Poetry Association Frank O'Hara Prize, 1974; National Book Critics Circle Award, 1976; Pulitzer Prize, 1976; National Book Award, 1976. Lives in New York City.

PUBLICATIONS

Verse

Turandot and Other Poems. 1953.
Some Trees. 1956.
The Poems. 1960.
The Tennis Court Oath. 1962.
Rivers and Mountains. 1966.
Selected Poems. 1967.
Sunrise in Suburbia. 1968.
Three Madrigals. 1968.
Fragment. 1969.
The Double Dream of Spring. 1970.
The New Spirit. 1970.

Three Poems.   1972.
The Vermont Notebook, with Joe Brainard.   1975.
Fragment, Clepsydre, Poèmes Francais.   1975.
Self-Portrait in a Convex Mirror.   1975.
Houseboat Days.   1977.

Plays

The Heroes (produced 1952).   In *Three Plays,* 1978.
The Compromise (produced 1956).   In *Three Plays,* 1978.
Three Plays (includes *The Heroes, The Compromise, The Philosopher*).   1978.

Fiction

A Nest of Ninnies, with James Schuyler.   1969.

Other

Editor, with others, *American Literary Anthology 1.*   1968.
Editor, *Penguin Modern Poets 24.*   1973.
Editor, *Muck Arbour,* by Bruce Marcus.   1974.

Translator, *Melville,* by Jean-Jacques Mayoux.   1960.
Translator, *Alberto Giacometti,* by Jacques Dupin.   1963.

Bibliography: *Ashbery: A Comprehensive Bibliography Including the Art Criticism, and with Selected Notes from Unpublished Material* by David K. S. Kermani, 1976.

Reading List: *Alone with America* by Richard Howard, 1969; *American Free Verse: The Modern Revolution in Poetry* by Walter Sutton, 1973; "Ashbery: The Charity of Hard Moments" by Harold Bloom, in *Salmagundi,* Spring-Summer 1973.

*   *   *

John Ashbery was originally associated with the New York school of poets, whose central figure is Frank O'Hara, and whose poetic style is noted for its painterly emphasis on setting, luxurious detailing, and leisurely meditative argument. This group closely identified itself with the abstract expressionist painters and with the Museum of Modern Art; some of these poets wrote for *Art News*. Ashbery was directly connected with all three spheres, and from the painters learned a curious collage-like style of poetry made of bits and pieces of lyric phrasing. This mode of speech, lacking transition between leaps of thought and reflection, early marked Ashbery as difficult, if not impenetrable. As he remarked in a later poem,

> I know that I braid too much my own
> Snapped-off perceptions of things as they come to me.
> They are private and always will be.

The root of Ashbery's lyric style may be traced back to the Symbolists, and to the allusive poems of T. S. Eliot, whose echo is frequently heard in Ashbery's work. At his best, Ashbery can give uncanny immediacy to his language; his stance of uncertainty before life draws him to the appearance of the phenomenal world which he contemplates in a delicate, sinewy language.

Some Trees is Ashbery's first work of note, and contains one of his most anthologized poems, "The Instruction Manual." His second major book of poems, *The Tennis Court Oath*, in particular emphasizes the style of pastiche. Beginning with *Rivers and Mountains*, Ashbery introduced his specialty, the long discursive meditation running to many pages in which the effort is made to piece together the fragments of experience into a sensible whole. "The Skaters" makes up half of the book. The meditative style is pursued most fully in *Three Poems*, prose poems that are linked like the moments of dialectical reason, in which the speaker struggles to reveal the metaphysical and spiritual basis of his existence.

Much of the poetry of these books is suffused with a restrained melancholy. Ashbery is articulating the post-existential awareness, in which existence is an accepted but utterly unknowable dimension. That stance is succinctly phrased in "Poems in Three Parts":

> One must bear in mind one thing.
> It isn't necessary to know what that thing is.
> All things are palpable, none are known.

No faith or hope can fully support the speaker, and he is recurrently plunged into self-analysis to discover the purpose of his life. *Self-Portrait in a Convex Mirror* continues this self-analysis and metaphysical exploration, particularly in the brilliant long title poem and in "Grand Galop." In his recent books, there is a perceptible effort to take up subjects beyond the self, but the poems are still deeply absorbed with the absence of a philosophical and religious context in which to value or understand life. Ashbery's innovative and sophisticated humor is clear in *The Double Dream of Spring*, particularly in such surreal high jinks as his "Variations, Calypso and Fugue on a Theme of Ella Wheeler Wilcox."

—Paul Christensen

ATWOOD, Margaret (Eleanor). Canadian. Born in Ottawa, Ontario, 18 November 1939. Educated at Victoria College, University of Toronto, B.A. 1961; Radcliffe College, Cambridge, Massachusetts, A.M. 1962; Harvard University, Cambridge, Massachusetts. Lecturer in English, University of British Columbia, Vancouver, 1964–65; Instructor in English, Sir George Williams University, Montreal, 1967–68. Recipient: E. J. Pratt Medal, 1961; President's Medal, University of Western Ontario, 1966; Governor-General's Award, 1967; Centennial Commission prize, 1967. Lives in Ontario.

PUBLICATIONS

Verse

Double Persephone. 1961.
The Circle Game. 1964; revised edition, 1966.
Talismans for Children. 1965.
Kaleidoscopes: Baroque. 1965.

Speeches for Doctor Frankenstein.   1966.
The Animals in That Country.   1968.
Five Modern Canadian Poets, with others, edited by Eli Mandel.   1970.
The Journals of Susanna Moodie: Poems.   1970.
Procedures for Underground.   1970.
Power Politics.   1971.
You Are Happy.   1974.
Selected Poems.   1976.

Fiction

The Edible Woman.   1969.
Surfacing.   1972.
Lady Oracle.   1976.

Other

Survival: A Thematic Guide to Canadian Literature.   1972.

Reading List: "The Poetry of Atwood" by John Wilson Foster, in *Canadian Literature* Autumn 1977.

*   *   *

Margaret Atwood's poetry succeeds not by masterly technique or style but by a peculiar and highly individual force of content, by exciting transformations whereby the identities of Canadian pioneers, of forest animals, Indians, the wilderness, women, and Canada itself conduct strange traffic with one another. These identities flesh out in multiple guise the root formula of Atwood's poetry. In most of her work, Atwood concerns herself with the self's inhabitation of spaces and forms, and the metamorphoses entailed therein. In her world, extinction and obsolescence are illusory, for life is a constant process of re-formation. Metaphor, simile, and personification in her verse might therefore just as easily be explained in terms of zoomorphism, anthropomorphism, and totemism as in terms of poetic convention. The self is eternally divided in its attitude to the forms and spaces it inhabits, simultaneously needing, fearing, desiring, and despising them. Hence the paranoid and schizophrenic motifs of the poetry.

Atwood's many Canadian admirers regard her as being deeply involved, at a time of cultural resurgence in Canada, with the problematic identity of her country, and to an extent this is true. As though aware of belonging to a minority culture on the North American continent, Atwood has in her poetry, particularly *The Circle Game, The Animals in That Country, Procedures for Underground,* and, above all, *The Journals of Susanna Moodie,* re-enacted her pioneer ancestors' experience in early Canada. But the metaphoric possibilities of pioneering are what interest Atwood.

Animals, for example, abound in her poetry as they did in the world of the pioneer, but they frequently embody the timeless dreads of the poet and her speakers. They are also the heraldic and mythic animals of the red men whom the settlers confronted and who still pre-empt white Canadians. The wilderness still beckons and forbids Canadians, as the novel *Surfacing* and the poetry demonstrate; it represents the interior and dangerous landscape of the mind as well as the primordiality to which all must in the end revert, as the briefly resurrected Susanna Moodie explains: "at the last/judgement we will all be trees."

Atwood's verse transformation of Mrs. Moodie's nineteenth-century pioneer journals (e.g.,

Roughing It in the Bush) is her finest volume of poetry, and offers pioneering as one extended metaphor for contemporary women's questioning of the traditional roles laid down by men for them to play. *Power Politics* explores sexual identity and relationships by means of the different metaphor of politics. Yet another and more original metaphor is the Circe episode of the *Odyssey* in the "Circe/Mud Poems" sequence of *You Are Happy*, in which the themes of pioneering, Canada and womanhood are connected.

Atwood is a prolific poet and novelist (occasionally hasty, one might feel) who seems, like her speakers, both to desire and fear escape from form. Her verse avoids rhyme and merely flirts with stanzaic pattern. Her basic unit is not the line (sense is fractured into an abundance of short lines) but the insight, and this in turn relies on the terse shock of metaphor. Yet the bones of older forms show appropriately through, to provide an uneasy counterpoint to her themes.

—John Wilson Foster

AUDEN, W(ystan) H(ugh).   American.   Born in York, England, 21 February 1907; emigrated to the United States in 1938; naturalized, 1946. Educated at St. Edmund's School, Grayshott, Surrey; Gresham's School, Holt, Norfolk; Christ Church, Oxford (exhibitioner), 1925–28. Served with the Strategic Bombing Survey of the United States Army in Germany during World War II. Married Erika Mann in 1935. Schoolmaster, Larchfield Academy, Helensburgh, Scotland, and Downs School, Colwall, near Malvern, Worcestershire, 1930–35. Co-Founder of the Group Theatre, 1932; worked with the G.P.O. Film Unit, 1935. Travelled extensively in the 1930's, in Europe, Iceland, and China. Taught at St. Mark's School, Southborough, Massachusetts, 1939–40; American Writers League School, 1939; New School for Social Research, New York, 1940–41, 1946–47; University of Michigan, Ann Arbor, 1941–42; Swarthmore College, Pennsylvania, 1942–45; Bryn Mawr College, Pennsylvania, 1943–45; Bennington College, Vermont, 1946; Barnard College, New York, 1947; Neilson Research Professor, Smith College, Northampton, Massachusetts, 1953; Professor of Poetry, Oxford University, 1956–61. Editor, Yale Series of Younger Poets, 1947–62. Member of the Editorial Board, *Decision* magazine, 1940–41, and *Delos* magazine, 1968; The Readers' Subscription book club, 1951–59, and The Mid-Century Book Club, 1959–62. Recipient: King's Gold Medal for Poetry, 1936; Guggenheim Fellowship, 1942; American Academy of Arts and Letters Award of Merit Medal, 1945, Gold Medal, 1968; Pulitzer Prize, 1948; Bollingen Prize, 1954; National Book Award, 1956; Feltrinelli Prize, 1957; Guinness Award, 1959; Poetry Society of America's Droutskoy Gold Medal, 1959; National Endowment for the Arts grant, 1966; National Book Committee's National Medal for Literature, 1967. D.Litt.: Swarthmore College, 1964. Member, American Academy of Arts and Letters, 1954; Honorary Student, Christ Church, 1962, and in residence, 1972–73. *Died 28 September 1973.*

PUBLICATIONS

Collections

Collected Poems, edited by Edward Mendelson.   1976.

Verse

Poems. 1928.
Poems. 1930; revised edition, 1933.
The Orators: An English Study. 1932; revised edition, 1934, 1966.
Poems (includes *The Orators* and *The Dance of Death*) 1934.
Look, Stranger! 1936; as *On This Island,* 1937.
Spain. 1937.
Letters from Iceland, with Louis MacNeice. 1937.
Selected Poems. 1938.
Journey to a War (verse sections), with Christopher Isherwood. 1939; revised edition, 1973.
Another Time: Poems (includes *Spain*). 1940.
Some Poems. 1940.
The Double Man. 1941; as *New Year Letter,* 1941.
Three Songs for St. Cecilia's Day. 1941.
For the Time Being. 1944.
The Collected Poetry. 1945.
The Age of Anxiety: A Baroque Eclogue (produced 1954). 1947.
Collected Shorter Poems 1930–1944. 1950.
Nones. 1951.
The Shield of Achilles. 1955.
The Old Man's Road. 1956.
Reflections on a Forest. 1957.
Auden: A Selection by the Author. 1958; as *Selected Poetry,* 1959.
Homage to Clio. 1960.
Auden: A Selection, edited by Richard Hoggart. 1961.
Elegy for J. F. K., music by Igor Stravinsky. 1964.
About the House. 1965.
The Twelve, music by William Walton. 1966.
Marginalia. 1966.
Collected Shorter Poems, 1927–1957. 1966.
Selected Poems. 1968.
Collected Longer Poems. 1968.
A New Year Greeting, with *The Dance of the Solids,* by John Updike. 1969.
City Without Walls and Other Poems. 1969.
Academic Graffiti. 1971.
Epistle to a Godson and Other Poems. 1972.
Auden/Moore: Poems and Lithographs, edited by John Russell. 1974.
Poems, lithographs by Henry Moore, edited by Vera Lindsay. 1974.
Thank You, Fog: Last Poems. 1974.

Plays

The Dance of Death (produced 1934; as *Come Out into the Sun,* produced 1935). 1933.
The Dog Beneath the Skin; or, Where Is Francis?, with Christopher Isherwood (produced 1936; revised version, produced 1947). 1935.
No More Peace! A Thoughtful Comedy, with Edward Crankshaw, from the play by Ernst Toller (produced 1936). 1937.
The Ascent of F6, with Christopher Isherwood (produced 1937). 1936; revised edition. 1937.
On the Frontier, with Christopher Isherwood (produced 1938). 1938.

The Dark Valley (broadcast, 1940). In *Best Broadcasts of 1939–40*, edited by Max Wylie, 1940.

Paul Bunyan, music by Benjamin Britten (produced 1941). 1976.

The Duchess of Malfi, music by Benjamin Britten, from the play by John Webster (produced 1946).

The Knights of the Round Table, from the work by Jean Cocteau (broadcast, 1951; produced 1954). In *The Infernal Machine and Other Plays*, by Jean Cocteau, 1964.

The Rake's Progress, with Chester Kallman, music by Igor Stravinsky (produced 1951). 1951.

Delia; or, A Masque of Night, with Chester Kallman (libretto), in *Botteghe Oscure XII*. 1953.

The Punch Revue (lyrics only) (produced 1955).

The Magic Flute, with Chester Kallman, from the libretto by Schikaneder and Giesecke, music by Mozart (televised, 1956). 1956.

The Play of Daniel (narration only) (produced 1958). Editor, with Noah Greenberg, 1959.

The Seven Deadly Sins of the Lower Middle Class, with Chester Kallman, from the work by Brecht, music by Kurt Weill (produced 1959). In *Tulane Drama Review*, September 1961.

Don Giovanni, with Chester Kallman, from the libretto by Lorenzo da Ponte, music by Mozart (televised, 1960). 1961.

The Caucasian Chalk Circle (lyrics only), with James and Tania Stern, from the play by Brecht (produced 1962). In *Plays*, by Brecht, 1960.

Elegy for Young Lovers, with Chester Kallman, music by Hans Werner Henze (produced 1961). 1961.

Arcifanfarlo, King of Fools; or, It's Always Too Late to Learn, with Chester Kallman, from the libretto by Goldoni, music by Dittersdorf (produced 1965).

Die Bassariden (The Bassarids), with Chester Kallman, music by Hans Werner Henze (produced 1966). 1966.

Moralities: Three Scenic Plays from Fables by Aesop, music by Hans Werner Henze. 1969.

The Ballad of Barnaby, music by Wykeham Rise School Students realized by Charles Turner (produced 1970).

Love's Labour's Lost, with Chester Kallman, music by Nicholas Nabokov, from the play by Shakespeare (produced 1973).

The Entertainment of the Senses, with Chester Kallman, music by John Gardner (produced 1974). In *Thank You, Fog*, 1974.

The Rise and Fall of the City of Mahagonny, with Chester Kallman, from the opera by Brecht. 1976.

Screenplays (documentaries, in verse): *Night Mail*, 1936; *Coal Face*, 1936; *The Londoners*, 1938.

Radio Writing: *Hadrian's Wall*, 1937 (UK); *The Dark Valley*, 1940 (USA); *The Rocking-Horse Winner*, with James Stern, from the story by D. H. Lawrence, 1941 (USA); *The Knights of the Round Table*, from a work by Jean Cocteau, 1951 (UK).

Television Writing (with Chester Kallman): *The Magic Flute*, 1956 (USA); *Don Giovanni*, 1960 (USA).

Other

Education Today – and Tomorrow, with T. C. Worsley. 1939.

The Intent of the Critic, with others, edited by Donald A. Stauffer. 1941.

Poets at Work: Essays Based on the Modern Poetry Collection at the Lockwood Memorial Library, University of Buffalo, with others, edited by Charles D. Abbott. 1948.
The Enchafèd Flood; or, The Romantic Iconography of the Sea. 1950.
The Dyer's Hand and Other Essays. 1962.
Selected Essays. 1964.
Secondary Worlds. 1968.
A Certain World: A Commonplace Book. 1970.
Forewords and Afterwords (essays), edited by Edward Mendelson. 1973.
The English Auden: Poems, Essays, and Dramatic Writings, 1927–1939, edited by Edward Mendelson. 1977.

Editor, with Charles Plumb, *Oxford Poetry 1926.* 1926.
Editor, with C. Day Lewis, *Oxford Poetry 1927.* 1927.
Editor, with John Garrett, *The Poet's Tongue: An Anthology.* 2 vols., 1935.
Editor, *The Oxford Book of Light Verse.* 1938.
Editor, *A Selection from the Poems of Alfred, Lord Tennyson.* 1944; as *Tennyson: An Introduction and a Selection,* 1946.
Editor, *The American Scene, Together with Three Essays from "Portraits of Places,"* by Henry James. 1946.
Editor, *Slick But Not Streamlined: Poems and Short Pieces,* by John Betjeman. 1947.
Editor, *The Portable Greek Reader.* 1948.
Editor, with Norman Holmes Pearson, *Poets of the English Language.* 5 vols., 1950.
Editor, *Selected Prose and Poetry,* by Edgar Allan Poe. 1950; revised edition, 1955.
Editor, *The Living Thoughts of Kierkegaard.* 1952; as *Kierkegaard,* 1955.
Editor, with Marianne Moore and Karl Shapiro, *Riverside Poetry 1953: Poems by Students in Colleges and Universities in New York City.* 1953.
Editor, with Chester Kallman and Noah Greenberg, *An Elizabethan Song Book: Lute Songs, Madrigals, and Rounds.* 1955.
Editor, *The Faber Book of Modern American Verse.* 1956; as *The Criterion Book of Modern American Verse,* 1956.
Editor, *Selected Writings of Sydney Smith.* 1956.
Editor, *Van Gogh: A Self-Portrait: Letters Revealing His Life as a Painter.* 1961.
Editor, with Louis Kronenberger, *The Viking Book of Aphorisms: A Personal Selection.* 1962; as *The Faber Book of Aphorisms,* 1964.
Editor, *A Choice of de la Mare's Verse.* 1963.
Editor, *The Pied Piper and Other Fairy Tales,* by Joseph Jacobs. 1963.
Editor, *Selected Poems,* by Louis MacNeice. 1964.
Editor, with John Lawlor, *To Nevill Coghill from Friends.* 1966.
Editor, *Selected Poetry and Prose,* by Byron. 1966.
Editor, *Nineteenth Century British Minor Poets.* 1966; as *Nineteenth Century Minor Poets,* 1967.
Editor, *G. K. Chesterton: A Selection from His Non-Fiction Prose.* 1970.
Editor, *A Choice of Dryden's Verse.* 1973.
Editor, *George Herbert.* 1973.
Editor, *Selected Songs of Thomas Campion.* 1974.

Translator, with Elizabeth Mayer, *Italian Journey 1786–1788,* by Goethe. 1962.
Translator, with Leif Sjöberg, *Markings,* by Dag Hammarskjöld. 1964.
Translator, with Paul B. Taylor, *Völupsá: The Song of the Sybil,* with an Icelandic Text edited by Peter H. Salus and Paul B. Taylor. 1968.
Translator, *The Elder Edda: A Selection.* 1969.
Translator, with Elizabeth Mayer and Louise Bogan, *The Sorrows of Young Werther, and Novella,* by Goethe. 1971.
Translator, with Leif Sjöberg, *Evening Land/Aftonland,* by Pär Lagerkvist. 1975.

Bibliography: *Auden: A Bibliography 1924–1969* by Barry C. Bloomfield and Edward Mendelson, 1972.

Reading List: *The Poetry of Auden: The Disenchanted Island* by Monroe K. Spears, 1963, and *Auden: A Collection of Critical Essays* edited by Spears, 1964; *Auden's Poetry* by Justin Replogle, 1969; *Changes of Heart: A Study of the Poetry of Auden* by Gerald Nelson, 1969; *A Reader's Guide to Auden* by John Fuller, 1970; *Auden* by Dennis Davison, 1970; *The Later Auden* by George W. Bahlke, 1970; *Auden as a Social Poet* by Frederick H. Buell, 1973; *Man's Place: An Essay on Auden* by Richard Johnson, 1973; *Auden: A Tribute* edited by Stephen Spender, 1975.

*   *   *

One of the most recurrent features of W. H. Auden's poetry is the *paysage moralisé* (an early poem is actually called this) in which the landscape becomes the emblematic topography of a spiritual condition. Auden, whose earliest reading was in geology and mining and who first thought of becoming an engineer, has always believed that the way we locate ourselves in space, in a specific lanscape we alter and adapt to, both determines and reveals our moral being, our sense of personal destiny and collective responsibility. Thus, in those fine "Horatian" *Bucolics* from the 1950's he can playfully link our neuroses with our choice of locale, as in "Mountains" –

> And it is curious how often in steep places
>   You meet someone short who frowns,
> A type you catch beheading daisies with a stick

– or prescribe the curative powers of "Lakes" (which always recall the "amniotic mere" of the womb): "Moraine, pot, oxbow, glint, sink, crater, piedmont, dimple ...?/Just reeling off their names is ever so comfy." While in "Plains" he can express his aversion to those flats "where all elsewheres are equal," "nothing points," and the tax-collector's writ is unchallengeable ("where roads run level,/How swift to the point of protest strides the crown./It hangs, it flogs, it fines, it goes"). "In Praise of Limestone" (1948) sets the tone for much of this later work, making a limestone landscape symbol of both our yearning for stability and our actual transience, beginning

> If it form the one landscape that we, the inconstant ones,
>   Are consistently homesick for, this is chiefly
> Because it dissolves in water

and ending with a wistful confession:

> Dear, I know nothing of
> Either, but when I try to imagine a faultless love
>   Or the life to come, what I hear is the murmur
> Of underground streams, what I see is a limestone landscape.

The tone is more relaxed in these post-war poems, but the technique is the same as that employed in those poems of quest, pursuit, and flight which dominate his earlier writings, poems whose terrain is best described by Caliban in *The Sea and the Mirror,* that extended commentary in verse and prose on Shakespeare's *Tempest* which enables Auden to dramatize his views on the relation between life and art. Caliban, spokesman of the carnal and material, of "history," speaks with sympathy of the spirit Ariel's obligation to deliver us from "the terrible mess that this particularized life, which we have so futilely attempted to tidy, sullenly insists on leaving behind," translating "all the phenomena of an empirically ordinary world" into "elements in an allegorical landscape":

a nightmare which has all the wealth of exciting action and all the emotional poverty of an adventure story for boys, a state of perpetual emergency and everlasting improvisation where all is need and change.

Certainly, John Buchan seems as much an influence as Marx or Nietzsche on those early poems in which the young, proud inheritor finds himself unexpectedly turned into an outsider, as in "The Watershed," "frustrate and vexed" in face of an abandoned, derelict landscape racked by depression and unemployment, "already comatose,/Yet sparsely living"; one who "must migrate" ("Missing") to become a leader, turn into a "trained spy" ("The Secret Agent"), and, ("Our Hunting Fathers") "hunger, work illegally,/And be anonymous" in a world of suspicion, insecurity and betrayal, as "all the while/Conjectures on our maps grow stranger/And threaten danger" ("No Change of Place"). The Auden of these early poems, walking a dangerous tightrope between "Always" and "Never" ("Between Adventure") saw his personal anxieties bodied forth in the world at large, and found a refuge for his public-school hauteur and élitism in a communism which rationalized his contempt for an age of mediocrity, impotence and defeat. In "Family Ghosts," for example, he sees "the assaulted city" surrounded by "the watchfires of a stronger army," and it isn't possible to decide whether this is a personal allegory of love or a political poem which looks towards class-struggle as release from the "Massive and taciturn years, the Age of Ice." Christopher Isherwood, Auden's collaborator in the verse-plays *The Dog Beneath the Skin, The Ascent of F6,* and *On the Frontier,* wrote of him in these terms in 1937, speaking of Auden's love for the Norse sagas: "The saga world is a schoolboy world, with its feuds, its practical jokes, its dark threats conveyed in puns and riddles and understatements"; in *Paid on Both Sides,* Auden's early, expressionist charade, he adds, "the two worlds are so inextricably confused that it is impossible to say whether the characters are really epic heroes or only members of a school O.T.C." Stephen Spender, also one of Auden's "Gang" during this period, has written of the "schoolboy ruthlessness" and latent fascism of *The Orators,* and the once-popular plays in which Auden and Isherwood tried to explore the contemporary crisis in the terms of Ruritanian allegory, knockabout, and morality-play which rob it of all urgency, are dismissed by Spender as virtuoso exercises, "a hash of the revolutionary and pacifist thought of the 1930s, reduced to their least convincing terms," which "provide considerable evidence that one aspect of the 1930s was a rackety exploitation of literary fashions."

Letter to Lord Byron perhaps best sums up the ambivalence of Auden's mood in the 1930's. Written is a skilful pastiche of Byron's own insouciant rhythms and rhymes, it expresses an aristocratic, Byronic disdain for the cant and hypocrisy of the "well-to-do" Home Counties, with their bland, self-deceiving smugness, against which Auden sets the urgencies of a more desolate world:

> To those who live in Warrington or Wigan,
> It's not a white lie, it's a whacking big 'un.

> There on the old historic battlefield,
>   The cold ferocity of human wills,
> The scars of struggle are as yet unhealed;
>   Slattern the tenements on sombre hills,
>   And gaunt in valleys the square-windowed mills
> That since the Georgian house, in my conjecture
> Remain our finest native architecture.

Yet that shift in the last couplet from moral outrage to sober aesthetic appreciation, together with the easy abstraction and the typecast imagery, reveals Auden's basic remoteness from his subject; indeed, a stanza later he can confess openly to his twentieth-century delight in that landscape: "Tramlines and slagheaps, pieces of machinery,/That was, and still is, my ideal scenery."

"Journey to Iceland" (1936) explains the rationale of Auden's travelogues: "North means to all *Reject*"; but such rejection also brought with it a new perspective that extended his control of his material and made possible a larger, clearer vision, revealed in that mythic conspectus of human evolution "Sonnets from China," originally included in the travel book *Journey to a War*. After the claustrophobic, cryptic, furtive atmosphere of the earlier poems, Auden here perfected the new straightforwardness already evinced in "Spain 1937," where "the menacing shapes of our fever/Are precise and alive." Significantly, the latter's explicit commitment to communism led a censorious later Auden to excise it from the canon (those patriarchal, castrating imagos, the Censor and the Scissor Man, have made themselves felt again and again in his poetic career). His reasons are interesting. Of the last stanza of "Spain" –

> The stars are dead. The animals will not look.
> We are left alone with our day, and the time is short, and
> > History to the defeated
> May say alas but cannot help or pardon

– he has said: "To say this is to equate goodness with success. It would have been bad enough if I had ever held this wicked doctrine, but that I should have stated it simply because it sounded to me rhetorically effective is quite inexcusable." But what the poem in fact stresses is the openness of human choice and the tragic discrepancy between history and morality (success may involve "The conscious acceptance of guilt in the necessary murder"), between – in Pascal's terms – Nature and Justice. There is nothing here which belies Auden's later conversion to Kierkegaard's Christian existentialism: the belief that man is responsible for his acts, and must make his leap of faith in fear and trembling, knowing that it may be a wrong and corrosive choice. That faith is best expressed in *For the Time Being*, a "Christmas Oratorio" which recreates the Christian myth in contemporary terms (casting Herod, for example, as a well-intentioned liberal statesman whose massacre of the innocents is for the public good). History is now for Auden seen in the perspective of eternity:

> To those who have seen
> The Child, however dimly, however incredulously
> The Time Being is, in a sense, the most trying time of all.
> For the innocent children who whispered so excitedly
> Outside the locked door where they knew the presents to be
> Grew up when it opened. Now, recollecting that moment
> We can repress the joy, but the guilt remains conscious.

For Auden, who had originally identified with "Voltaire at Ferney" (1939), perennial oedipal rebel –

> Cajoling, scolding, scheming, cleverest of them all,
> He'd led the other children in a holy war
> Against the infamous grownups

– this "growing up" expressed, in terms of traditional theology, his final transfer of allegiance from the Son to the Father, effected, ironically enough, through the advent of that Child to a world at war. The transfer can be seen occurring in his fine poem "In Memory of Sigmund Freud" (1939), where that liberating discoverer of the unconscious is seen both as wide-eyed child and benevolent father who

> showed us what evil is, not, as we thought,
> deeds that must be punished, but our lack of faith,
> > our dishonest mood of denial,
> the concupiscence of the oppressor.

The same affirmation animates "In Memory of Ernst Toller," acknowledging the great gift of both Freud and Marx to human self-understanding: the disclosure of those unconscious determinations of our identity – whether biological or socio-economic, each shaping the other – which constrain our existential freedom only when unrecognized:

> We are lived by powers we pretend to understand:
> They arrange our loves; it is they who direct at the end
> The enemy bullet, the sickness, or even our hand.
>
> It is their tomorrow hangs over the earth of the living
> And all that we wish for our friends: but existence is believing
> We know for whom we mourn and who is grieving.

For the later, Anglican, Auden, finally expatriate in an alien and yet familiar America, acknowledgment of our guilt is the ground of freedom. Rosetta, one of the four "displaced persons" lining a wartime bar in New York in *The Age of Anxiety,* at a time when "Many have perished, more will," daydreams of

> one of those landscapes familiar to all readers of English
> detective stories, those lovely innocent countrysides
> inhabited by charming eccentrics with independent means
> and amusing hobbies to whom, until the sudden intrusion
> of a horrid corpse onto the tennis court or into the greenhouse,
> work and law and guilt are just literary words.

As the 1936 poem "Detective Story" and the essay "The Guilty Vicarage" make clear, this landscape is Auden's own peculiar version of the myth of the Fall: to live in history is to accept complicity, and to accept complicity is the beginning of grace: "But time is always guilty. Someone must pay for/Our loss of happiness, our happiness itself." Each of the "travellers through time" of *The Age of Anxiety* sets out "in quest of his own/Absconded self yet scared to find it" (for it will turn out to be the culprit). In *New Year Letter* Auden resolves, in his own person, to accept responsibility for his fallen condition. History is the middle way, that Purgatory where, "Consenting parties to our lives," we may "win/Truth out of Time. In Time we sin./But Time is sin and can forgive"; in Time too we learn "To what conditions we must bow/In building the Just City now." But the world remains one in which "Aloneness is man's real condition."

What underlies all Auden's poetry, in fact, early and late, is this tension between aristocratic disdain and a humble and, at times, humiliating love for the things of this world. It is there in his love poetry, whether in the early and beautiful "Lullaby" ("Lay your sleeping head, my love,/Human on my faithless arm") or the innocuous narcissism of the last poem in his *Collected Poems* (1976), also called "A Lullaby" – "now you fondle/your almost feminine flesh/with mettled satisfaction" – but with its last line, "Sleep, Big Baby, sleep your fill," almost an epitaph. The explicit homosexual lust of "Three Posthumous Poems" that translation of *Eros* into *Agape,* of sensual into spiritual love, was no more difficult for Auden than it was for the Sufi poets. His perennial movement between renouncing and embracing, *askesis* and indulgence, is embodied in his very language, which at once delights in the rich multiplicity of an abundant world and yet keeps it at bay with a deliberate, distancing artificiality that defamiliarizes the accustomed, or calls attention to the medium itself through nonce-words and neologisms, arcane or archaic usages, portentous polysyllables cut short by sudden racy slang, magpie gauds and macaronics. By turns demotic and hieratic, shifting peremptorily in rhythm, tone, and register, skittish, hoydenish, and haughty, polyglot and jargonish, ruminative and aphoristic, shocking and coy, Auden's language corresponds in its variety to a frame of mind, to that master of disguises (Sherlock Holmes was always a hero) his poems expose from first to last. If his later poetry is more domestic and muted, full of thanksgivings and valedictions, elegies and reminiscences, it can still rise to pyrotechnic heroisms of language. But perhaps the best of these later volumes is *Homage to Clio,* a series of poems dedicated to Auden's first and last love, the matronly Muse of History:

> Madonna of silences, to whom we turn
>
> When we have lost control, your eyes, Clio, into which
>   We look for recognition after
> We have been found out....
>   I have seen
> Your photo, I think, in the papers, nursing
> A baby or mourning a corpse: each time
>
> You had nothing to say and did not, one could see,
>   Observe where you were, Muse of the unique
> Historical fact, defending with silence
>   Some world of your beholding....

With this one poem alone Auden could establish his claim to be a serious and a major poet, fulfilling that specifically human vocation, the ability "with a rhythm or a rhyme" to "Assume ... responsibility for time."

—Stan Smith

AVISON, Margaret (Kirkland). Canadian. Born in Galt, Ontario, 23 April 1918. Educated at the University of Toronto, B.A. 1940. Recipient: Guggenheim Fellowship, 1956; Governor-General's Award, 1961. Lives in Toronto.

PUBLICATIONS

Verse

> *Winter Sun.*   1960.
> *The Dumbfounding.*   1966.

Other

> *The Research Compendium,* with Albert Rose.   1964.

Reading List: *Avison* by E. H. Redekop, 1970.

*   *   *

Throughout her life, Margaret Avison has been concerned with the nature of imaginative perception. She writes of the transcendental nature of reality, about the ability of the "optic heart" to see beyond the surfaces of things. Like many Canadian poets, she has a strong sense of the physical landscape, of earth, rock, water, of city streets and buildings which support or overwhelm man, but a close, often undefinable and dangerous, relationship links man to the world in which he lives. In many of the shorter poems of her first book, *Winter Sun,* she depicts, with acuteness and compassion, the modern city, sometimes in extraordinary vignettes, sometimes in sequences of brief scenes or images. Strange and sudden interlockings of external and internal landscapes occur; her landscape becomes multiple, an everywhere inhabited by the mind of the poet, an always in which past and present collide.

Avison believes that the forms of language, words themselves, are threatened by our inability to see things freshly. So the "deciphering heart" must take the confusion in speech between the ancient and the new and resolve it into a new imaginative order. She does this in her own language, crossing the often rigid boundaries between our newest technologies and our lagging perceptions of history, between the secular and sacred imaginations, between given poetic forms and new structures of words. In her longer poems, she moves freely back and forth between centuries and places, creating pieces of a jigsaw world which the reader must put together. The reader, in fact, must behave much like her persona of the artist, "at once Hansel and Gretel," plunging into the forests and seas of the imagination, for her diction is terse and economical, sometimes arcane, her syntax often convoluted, and her images always dense.

In the context of other contemporary poetry, some of Avison's most remarkable poems are the explicitly Christian poems in *The Dumbfounding.* Here she writes in the traditions of Donne, Herbert, and Hopkins, drawing ideas and sometimes language from each, and creating poems that are deeply personal expressions of the poet's relation to God. Many of them, although at first sight somewhat remote from the poems in *Winter Sun,* are about ways of perceiving reality, spiritual exercises of the optic heart. In poem after poem, she imagines the vision of rebirth, the moment when, like her swimmer, man recognizes the existence of the whirlpool and enters the black pit, or when Christ transcends the defining lines drawn by man. The recognition of this moment of love is for her "the dumbfounding." In a poem arising out of the first landing by man on the moon, she continues to express this "now" as the moment beyond the technical data of the moon mission – that epiphanic, dumbfounding perception of reality.

Avison's poems are both immediately recognizable and profoundly strange, because her perspectives of common, ordinary things are always unexpected. She communicates in all her poetry a strong sense of historical continuity, but the contemporary world of dams, TV, space flight, napalm, and fission is always at hand, waiting for the encounter with imagination, waiting for judgment.

—E. H. Redekop

BARKER, George (Granville). English. Born in Loughton, Essex, 26 February 1913. Educated at Marlborough Road School, Chelsea, London; Regent Street Polytechnic, London. Married Elspeth Langlands in 1964; has several children. Lived in the United States, 1940–43, and in Rome, 1960–65. Professor of English Literature, Imperial Tohoku

University, Sendai, Japan, 1939–41; Visiting Professor, State University of New York at Buffalo, 1965–66; Arts Fellow, York University, 1966–67; Visiting Professor, University of Wisconsin, Madison, 1971–72, and Florida International University, 1974. Recipient: Royal Society of Literature bursary, 1950; Guinness Prize, 1962; Borestone Mountain Poetry Prize, 1967; Arts Council bursary, 1968. Lives in Norfolk.

PUBLICATIONS

Verse

Thirty Preliminary Poems.   1933.
Poems.   1935.
Calamiterror.   1937.
Elegy on Spain.   1939.
Lament and Triumph.   1940.
Selected Poems.   1941.
Sacred and Secular Elegies.   1943.
Eros in Dogma.   1944.
Love Poems.   1947.
The True Confession of George Barker.   1950; augmented edition.   1964.
News of the World.   1950.
A Vision of Beasts and Gods.   1954.
Collected Poems, 1930–1955.   1957.
The View from a Blind I.   1962.
Collected Poems 1930–1965.   1965.
Dreams of a Summer Night.   1966.
The Golden Chains.   1968.
At Thurgarton Church.   1969.
Runes and Rhymes and Tunes and Chimes (for children).   1969.
To Aylsham Fair (for children).   1970.
The Alphabetical Zoo (for children).   1970.
Poems of Places and People.   1971.
III Hallucination Poems.   1972.
In Memory of David Archer.   1973.
Dialogues etc.   1976.

Plays

Two Plays (includes The Seraphina and In the Shade of the Old Apple Tree).   1958.

Radio Plays: The Seraphina, 1956; Oriel O'Hanlon (published as In the Shade of the Old Apple Tree), 1957.

Fiction

Alanna Autumnal.   1933.
Janus (includes The Documents of Death and The Bacchant).   1935.
The Dead Seagull.   1950.

Other

Essays.   1970.

Editor, *Idylls of the King and a Selection of Poems,* by Tennyson.   1961.

Reading List: *Barker* by Martha Fodaski, 1969; *Homage to Barker on His 60th Birthday* edited by John Heath-Stubbs and Martin Green, 1973.

*   *   *

In the 1930's, critics had tended to think of the young George Barker as ranking, in his vivid and bewildering use of images, with Dylan Thomas and, in his awareness of the destructive effect of social privation ("It was hard cash I needed at my roots"), with Auden and what was sometimes called Auden's "school." Nobody compared him, as in his off-hand vividness he might have been compared, with Louis MacNeice. As he grew older, it became harder to range him with anybody else, and by the 1950's he was in a sense a very isolated writer, critically speaking. The 1950's saw the publication of his most personal long poem, *The True Confession of George Barker,* a poem both blasphemous and obscene in a Villonesque way, and yet, like Villon's poems, obviously the work of a born Roman Catholic. He had become the last *poète maudit,* the last conscious bohemian. In fact, when Faber, his publishers, brought out his *Collected Poems, 1930–1955,* they left out the poem, against his wishes.

By 1973, on his sixtieth birthday, that omission was generally ignored, but the event brought forth a very distinguished *festschrift,* many of the contributors to which were either unknown to or not on speaking terms with each other; but they were all united in admiration of a desperately honest and unduly neglected poet. Barker has puzzled critics because he combines a comic wit and a polished impropriety with a lyrical simplicity and an ability to express the inner agony of the obdurate Catholic sinner. All these themes can be found in the contortedly powerful prose of his partly autobiographical novel, *The Dead Seagull.* Barker is technically a very uneven poet, his feelings too often at the mercy of a facile rhetoric, but his best work will last.

—G. S. Fraser

BAUGHAN, Blanche (Edith).   New Zealander.   Born in Putney, London, in 1870; emigrated to New Zealand, 1900. Educated at Brighton High School, Sussex; Royal Holloway College, University of London, B.A. Social worker, prominent in penal reform: Honorary Secretary, and Vice-President, 1928, Howard League for Penal Reform. *Died in August 1958.*

PUBLICATIONS

Verse

Verses. 1898.
Reuben and Other Poems. 1903.
Shingle-Short and Other Verses. 1908.
Hope. 1916(?).
Poems from the Port Hills. 1923.

Other

The Finest Walk in the World (on the Milford Track). 1909; revised edition, 1926.
Snow Kings of the Southern Alps. 1910.
Uncanny Country: The Thermal Country of New Zealand. 1911.
Brown Bread from a Colonial Oven, Being Sketches of Up-Country Life in New Zealand. 1912.
Forest and Ice. 1913.
A River of Pictures and Peace (on Wanganui River). 1913.
The Summit Road: Its Scenery, Botany, and Geology, with Leonard Cockayne and Robert Speight. 1914.
Studies in New Zealand Scenery. 1916; revised edition, as *Glimpses of New Zealand Scenery,* 1922.
Akaroa. 1919.
Arthur's Pass and Otira Gorge. 1925.
Mt. Egmont. 1929.
People in Prison, with F. A. de la Mare. 1936.

*　　*　　*

Blanche Baughan's essential writing is in *Reuben and Other Poems, Shingle-Short and Other Verses,* and her by no means negligible prose sketches (rather of people, like her verse, than places) *Brown Bread from a Colonial Oven.* Her "gift" died after illness in 1910 – "I did not desert it, it deserted me." Through nearly six decades following she became a pioneer of prison reform and was involved with Indian thought. Of one anthologised poem in *Shingle-Short,* New Zealand's leading poet, an uncompromising critic, Allen Curnow, writes: "But nothing about this time compares with Blanche Baughan's 'A Bush Section,' written within a few years of her arrival in 1900. No earlier New Zealand poem exhibits such unabashed truth to its subject....It is the best New Zealand poem before Mason and how different in kind!" Here is its "burned-off" landscape:

> ... the opposite rampart of ridges
> Bristles against the sky, all the tawny, tumultuous landscape
> Is stuck, and prickled, and spiked with standing black and grey splinters....

Its child protagonist is: "Here, to this rough and raw prospect, these black-blocks of Being assign'd –" and so:

> Standing, small and alone:
> Bright Promise on Poverty's threshold!
> What art thou? Where hast thou come from?
> How far, how far! wilt thou go?

"Reuben" masters Wordsworthian blank verse and Crabbe-like realism; other poems in that book echo, say, Christina Rossetti or are increasingly colloquial ("The Old Place"); some use cantering dactyls and fourteeners reminiscent of Australiana.

With some unevenness *Shingle-Short* shows her full strength. The title character is mentally handicapped; outcasts and isolates (compare Patrick White's *The Burnt Ones*) recur; yet (as in *Brown Bread*) a dominant theme is the prevailing colonial work ethic. Her chief mode is dramatic monologue; tone, language, topics are for the most part sophisticatedly demotic; generally these pages may recall Browning, the Christina Rossetti of "Goblin Market," or numerous analogues in comparable North America, say, Lanier or James Whitcomb Riley (as *Brown Bread* may suggest Sarah Orne Jewett). "Maui's Fish" is a stunning free verse rendering of that legend. "The Paddock" is a long "cantata" in many styles and voices, a patch-work quilt most authentically colonial (her titles are revealing!) on colonial dilemmas of youth and age and place; a Maori component is, again, in rhetorical free verse; there are passages of brilliance in this unjustly neglected work.

In *Brown Bread* a "foreigner" expostulates: "Oh you live so bad, you do live so bad!" Our author comments: "Art comes at all times scantly to the back-blocks; and with what hope can Literature appeal to brains exhausted already by the exhaustion of the body?" Miss Baughan's contemporaries – Satchell in fiction, Jessie Mackay in poetry – lack either her single-minded *esthetic* commitment or ability, yet she has been "out of step" both with her own and later generations. In breadth and consistency of technical achievement, and in themes and strategies alike, Miss Baughan both far surpasses her predecessors and has no peer until the generations of R. A. K. Mason and Robin Hyde. The new ground on which she stands is precisely that where Maui's envious elders slither and fall, the ground, slippery and changing, of truth to emergent New Zealand consciousness.

—Peter Alcock

BAXTER, James K(eir). New Zealander. Born in Dunedin, 29 June 1926; son of the writer Archibald Baxter. Educated at Quaker schools in New Zealand and England; Otago University, Dunedin; Victoria University, Wellington, B.A. 1952. Married Jacqueline Sturm in 1948; two children. Worked as a labourer, journalist, and school-teacher. Editor, *Numbers* magazine, Wellington, 1954–60. Spent 5 months in India studying school publications, 1958; started commune in Jerusalem (a Maori community on the Wanganui River), 1969. Recipient: Unesco grant, 1958; Robert Burns Fellowship, Otago University, 1966, 1967. *Died 22 October 1972.*

PUBLICATIONS

Verse

Beyond the Palisade: Poems. 1944.
Blow, Wind of Fruitfulness. 1948.
Hart Crane. 1948.
Rapunzel: A Fantasia for Six Voices. 1948.
Charm for Hilary. 1949.

Poems Unpleasant, with Louis Johnson and Anton Vogt.   1952.
The Fallen House: Poems.   1953.
Lament for Barney Flanagan.   1954.
Traveller's Litany.   1955.
The Night Shift: Poems of Aspects of Love, with others.   1957.
The Iron Breadboard: Studies in New Zealand Writing (verse parodies).   1957.
In Fires of No Return: Poems.   1958.
Chosen Poems, 1958.   1958.
Ballad of Calvary Street.   1960.
Howrah Bridge and Other Poems.   1961.
Poems.   1964.
Pig Island Letters.   1966.
A Death Song for M. Mouldybroke.   1967.
A Small Ode on Mixed Flatting: Elicited by the Decision of the Otago University Authorities to Forbid This Practice among Students.   1967.
The Lion Skin: Poems.   1967.
A Bucket of Blood for a Dollar: A Conversation Between Uncle Sam and the Rt. Hon. Keith Holyoake, Prime Minister of New Zealand.   1968.
The Rock Woman: Selected Poems.   1969.
Ballad of the Stonegut Sugar Works.   1969.
Jerusalem Sonnets: Poems for Colin Durning.   1970.
The Junkies and the Fuzz.   1970.
Jerusalem Daybook (poetry and prose journal).   1971.
Jerusalem Blues (2).   1971.
Autumn Testament (poetry and prose journal).   1972.
Four God Songs.   1972.
Letter to Peter Olds.   1972.
Runes.   1973.
The Labyrinth: Some Uncollected Poems, 1944–1972.   1974.
The Bone Chanter: Unpublished Poems 1945–1972.   1977.
The Holy Life and Death of Concrete Grady: Various Uncollected and Unpublished Poems, edited by J. E. Weir.   1977.

Plays

Jack Winter's Dream (broadcast 1958).   In *The Wide Open Cage and Jack Winter's Dream*, 1959.
The Wide Open Cage (produced 1959).   In *The Wide Open Cage and Jack Winter's Dream*, 1959.
The Wide Open Cage and Jack Winter's Dream: Two Plays.   1959.
The Spots of the Leopard (produced 1963).
The Band Rotunda (produced 1967).   In *The Devil and Mr. Mulcahy and The Band Rotunda*, 1971.
The Sore-Footed Man, based on *Philoctetes* by Euripides (produced 1967).   In *The Sore-Footed Man and The Temptations of Oedipus*, 1971.
The Bureaucrat (produced 1967).
The Devil and Mr. Mulcahy (produced 1967).   In *The Devil and Mr. Mulcahy and The Band Rotunda*, 1971.
Mr. O'Dwyer's Dancing Party (produced 1968).
The Day Flanagan Died (produced 1969).
The Temptations of Oedipus (produced 1970).   In *The Sore-Footed Man and The Temptations of Oedipus*, 1971.
The Devil and Mr Mulcahy and The Band Rotunda.   1971.

The Sore-Footed Man and The Temptations of Oedipus. 1971.

Radio Play: *Jack Winter's Dream,* 1958.

Other

    Recent Trends in New Zealand Poetry. 1951.
    The Fire and the Anvil: Notes on Modern Poetry. 1955; revised edition, 1960.
    Oil (primary school bulletin). 1957.
    The Coaster (primary school bulletin). 1959.
    The Trawler (primary school bulletin). 1961.
    New Zealand in Colour, photographs by Kenneth and Jean Bigwood. 1961.
    The Old Earth Closet: A Tribute to Regional Poetry. 1965.
    Aspects of Poetry in New Zealand. 1967.
    The Man on the Horse (lectures). 1967.
    The Flowering Cross: Pastoral Articles. 1969.
    The Six Faces of Love: Lenten Lectures. 1972.
    A Walking Stick for an Old Man. 1972.

Reading List: *The Poetry of Baxter* by J. E. Weir, 1970; *Baxter* by Charles Doyle, 1976; *Baxter* by Vincent O'Sullivan, 1976.

*   *   *

At his best one of the finest English-language poets of the past thirty years, James K. Baxter is the one New Zealand poet of undeniable international reputation. Although he died in his mid-forties, his literary career lasted for over thirty years. Its fruits were many volumes of poems, a number of plays, works of literary commentary or criticism, essays on religious topics, and a small amount of fiction (he was a fine exponent of the parable).

With publication of his first book, *Beyond the Palisade,* when he was eighteen, Baxter at once became a figure of note in New Zealand letters. Within a few years, he already occupied a central position in the literary scene, so that his booklet, *Recent Trends in New Zealand Poetry,* a beautifully condensed commentary, was from the first accepted as authoritative. Alongside his literary reputation, Baxter quickly began to build one as a maverick and a bohemian. When, late in the 1940's, he moved to Wellington and began his long friendship and collaboration with Louis Johnson, they became the focus of the "romantic" element in New Zealand writing, which found its centre in Wellington for the next dozen years or so.

Throughout the 1950's Baxter produced a prolific variety of poems, plays, stories, and criticism, work which ranged from makeshift to brilliant. With Johnson and Charles Doyle (and, latterly, others) he edited the characteristically erratic periodical *Numbers,* then the only alternative to the few "establishment" periodicals such as *Landfall.*

1958 was a crucial moment in Baxter's career. Until then, his adult life had been a strange compound of Christian concern and rip-roaring bohemianism. That year he stayed for a long spell in the Trappist monastery at Kopua, Hawke's Bay, and was converted to Roman Catholicism. At the same time, his superb collection *In Fires of No Return* drew upon the work of his whole career to that point. *Howrah Bridge and Other Poems* followed in 1961 and was composed of new poems plus fine pieces ranging back to the 1940's; but Baxter's talent as a poet for a time seemed to lose focus. It was typical of Baxter that he made little or no effort to become known outside his own country; untypical as he was, he was very deeply a New Zealander, though anguished at his country's unspiritual puritanism.

After a low-energy period, Baxter's career gathered momentum again when he was awarded a Burns Fellowship at the University of Otago. Writing in the *Dominion* on 23

October 1965, Louis Johnson suggested that "the Burns scholarship may well mark a turning-point in his career" and this proved to be the case in remarkable ways. First, it produced what many consider to be Baxter's best verse collection, *Pig Island Letters*, a book in which he learned from, and transcended, the unlikely twin influences of Lawrence Durrell and Robert Lowell. Besides the critical-autobiographical pieces of *The Man on the Horse* and *Aspects of New Zealand Poetry*, those years in Dunedin witnessed the flowering of Baxter's career as a playwright. During 1967 and 1968, Patric Carey at the Globe Theatre produced seven Baxter plays, including all the most important. Although secondary to the poetry, those plays make it a reasonable claim that, besides being the country's foremost poet, Baxter is the most productive and interesting New Zealand playwright up to the present.

The Dunedin years also led him more deeply into religious and social concerns. After a period of catechetical work in the city, he went into solitude for some months at Jerusalem (Hiruharama), a tiny religious settlement on the Wanganui River. Later he founded a commune there for troubled youths and social drop-outs, and he was also the moving spirit in setting up doss-houses in both Auckland and Wellington. These ventures, pursued in a Franciscan spirit, including a vow of poverty, took much of his energy, but the commitment also carried over into his vocation as a poet and this period witnessed a further remarkable shift in the development of his writing, especially in the Jerusalem writings, *Jerusalem Sonnets*, *Jerusalem Daybook*, and *Autumn Testament*. He developed a very personal "sonnet" form, in fluid pentameter couplets, and, particularly in *Jerusalem Daybook*, made effective use of an amalgam of prose and verse. Baxter was also important in his community as a man. His best poems have a natural incandescence which partly derives from his being permeated from boyhood with the finest poetry of the British tradition, but which also comes from a human commitment based on religion. New Zealand is a relatively successful social welfare state, secular in spirit. Baxter, notably, brought to it a strong religious consciousness. A literary talent with a touch of genius was deepened and strengthened by the religious element in his character. That this did not escape the notice of his fellow-countrymen is evident from the crowds which thronged to his funeral and memorial services. Baxter's legacy to his country is a double one, a substantial amount of first-rate writing, especially poems, and the example of a man able to carry the spiritual life as far as it can go.

—Charles Doyle

BELLOC, (Joseph) Hilaire (Pierre). British. Born in St. Cloud, near Paris, France, 27 July 1870; naturalized British subject, 1902. Educated at the Oratory School, Edgbaston; Balliol College, Oxford (Brackenbury History Scholar), 1892–95, B.A. (honours) in history 1895. Served in the 10th Battery of the 8th Regiment of Artillery of the French Army, 1891. Married Elodie Agnes Hogan in 1896 (died, 1914); three sons, two daughters. Journalist: Editor, with A. H. Pollen, *Paternoster Review*, 1890–91; Literary Editor, *Morning Post*, 1906–09; Editor, with Maurice Baring, *North Street Gazette*, 1910; Editor, with others, *Eye-Witness*, 1911–12; Editor, *G. K.'s Weekly*, 1936–38; columnist ("A Wanderer's Notebook"), *Sunday Times*, 1938–53. Liberal Member of Parliament for South Salford, 1906–10. Head of the English Department, East London College. LL.D.: University of Glasgow, 1902. Knight Commander with Star, Order of St. Gregory the Great, 1934. *Died 16 July 1953.*

Collections

The Verse, edited by W. N. Roughead.   1954; as *Complete Verse*, 1970.
Selected Essays, edited by J. B. Morton.   1958.
Belloc: A Biographical Anthology, edited by Herbert Van Thal and Jane Soames
    Nickerson.   1970.

Verse

Verses and Sonnets.   1896.
The Bad Child's Book of Beasts.   1896.
More Beasts (for Worse Children).   1897.
The Modern Traveller.   1898.
A Moral Alphabet.   1899.
*Cautionary Tales for Children: Designed for the Admonition of Children Between the
    Ages of Eight and Fourteen Years.*   1907.
Verses.   1910.
More Peers.   1911.
Sonnets and Verse.   1923; revised edition, 1938; as *Collected Verse*, 1958.
New Cautionary Tales.   1930.
The Praise of Wine: An Heroic Poem.   1931.
Ladies and Gentlemen: For Adults Only and Mature at That.   1932.
Cautionary Verses: The Collected Humorous Poems.   1939.
Songs of the South Country.   1951.

Play

The Candour of Maturity (produced 1912).

Fiction

Emmanuel Burden, Merchant.   1904.
Mr. Clutterbuck's Election.   1908.
A Change in the Cabinet.   1909.
Pongo and the Bull.   1910.
The Girondin.   1911.
The Green Overcoat.   1912.
The Mercy of Allah.   1922.
Mr. Petre.   1925.
The Emerald of Catherine the Great.   1926.
The Haunted House.   1927.
But Soft – We Are Observed! 1928; as *Shadowed!*,   1929.
Belinda: A Tale of Affection in Youth and Age.   1928.
The Missing Masterpiece.   1929.
The Man Who Made Gold.   1930.
The Postmaster-General.   1932.
The Hedge and the Horse.   1936.

Other

Danton: A Study. 1899.

Lambkin's Remains. 1900.

Paris. 1900.

Robespierre: A Study. 1901.

The Path to Rome. 1902.

The Aftermath: or, Gleanings from a Busy Life, Called upon the Outer Cover, for Purposes of Sale, Caliban's Guide to Letters. 1903

The Great Inquiry (Only Authorised Version) Faithfully Reported. 1903.

The Old Road. 1904.

Avril, Being Essays on the Poetry of the French Renaissance. 1904.

An Open Letter on the Decay of Faith. 1906.

Esto Perpetua: Algerian Studies and Impressions. 1906.

Sussex Painted by Wilfrid Ball. 1906; revised edition, as *The County of Sussex,* 1936.

Hills and the Sea. 1906.

The Historic Thames. 1907.

The Eye-Witness (incidents in history). 1908.

On Nothing and Kindred Subjects. 1908.

An Examination of Socialism. 1908; as *The Alternative,* 1947.

The Pyrenees. 1909.

On Everything. 1909.

Marie Antoinette. 1909.

The Church and Socialism. 1910.

The Ferrer Case. 1910.

The International. 1910.

On Anything. 1910.

On Something. 1910.

The Party System, with Cecil Chesterton. 1911.

Socialism and the Servile State (debate with J. Ramsay Macdonald). 1911.

First and Last. 1911.

The French Revolution. 1911.

British Battles. 6 vols., 1911–13; revised edition, as *Six British Battles,* 1931.

The Four Men: A Farrago. 1912.

The River of London. 1912.

Warfare in England. 1912.

The Servile State. 1912.

This and That and the Other. 1912.

The Stane Street: A Monograph. 1913.

The Book of the Bayeux Tapestry, Presenting the Complete Work in a Series of Colour Facsimiles. 1914.

Anti-Catholic History: How It Is Written. 1914.

Three Essays. 1914.

The History of England from the First Invasion by the Romans to the Accession of King George the Fifth (volume 11 only). 1915.

A General Sketch of the European War: The First and *Second Phase.* 2 vols., 1915–16: as *The Elements of the Great War.* 2 vols., 1915–16.

A Picked Company, Being a Selection from the Writings of Hilaire Belloc, edited by E. V. Lucas. 1915.

High Lights of the French Revolution. 1915.

The Two Maps of Europe and Some Other Aspects of the Great War. 1915.

Land and Water Map of the War and How to Use It. 1915.

At the Sign of the Lion and Other Essays. 1916.

The Last Days of the French Monarchy. 1916.

The Second Year of the War.   1916.
The Free Press.   1918.
Religion and Civil Liberty.   1918.
The Catholic Church and the Principle of Private Property.   1920.
The House of Commons and Monarchy.   1920.
Europe and the Faith.   1920.
Pascal's Provincial Letters.   1921.
Catholic Social Reform Versus Socialism.   1922.
The Jews.   1922.
The Contrast.   1923.
The Road.   1923.
On (essays).   1923.
Economics for Helen.   1924; as *Economics for Young People,* 1925.
The Political Effort.   1924.
The Campaign of 1812 and the Retreat from Moscow.   1924; as *Napoleon's Campaign of 1812 and the Retreat from Moscow,* 1926.
The Cruise of the "Nona".   1925.
England and the Faith.   1925.
A History of England.   4 vols., 1925–31.
Miniatures of French History.   1925.
The Highway and Its Vehicles. edited by Geoffrey Holme.   1926.
Short Talks with the Dead and Others.   1926.
Mrs. Markham's New History of England. Being an Introduction for Young People to the Current History and Institutions of Our Times.   1926.
A Companion to Mr. Wells's "Outline of History."   1926.
Mr. Belloc Still Objects to Mr. Wells's "Outline of History."   1926.
The Catholic Church and History.   1926.
Selected Works.   9 vols., 1927.
Towns of Destiny.   1927: as *Many Cities,* 1928.
Oliver Cromwell.   1927.
James the Second.   1928.
How the Reformation Happened.   1928.
A Conversation with an Angel and Other Essays.   1928.
Joan of Arc.   1929.
Survivals and New Arrivals.   1929.
Richelieu.   1929.
Wolsey.   1930.
A Pamphlet, July 27th, 1930.   1930; as *World Conflict,* 1951.
A Conversation with a Cat and Others (essays).   1931.
Cranmer.   1931; as *Cranmer, Archbishop of Canterbury, 1533–1556.*   1931.
Essays of a Catholic Layman in England.   1931: as *Essays of a Catholic,* 1931.
How We Got the Bible.   1932.
Napoleon.   1932.
The Question and the Answer.   1932.
The Tactics and Strategy of the Great Duke of Marlborough.   1933.
William the Conqueror.   1933.
Becket.   1933.
Charles the First, King of England.   1933.
Cromwell.   1934.
A Shorter History of England.   1934.
Milton.   1935.
Hilaire Belloc (humorous writings), edited by E. V. Knox.   1935.
An Essay on the Restoration of Property.   1936: as *The Restoration of Property,* 1936.
Selected Essays, edited by John Edward Dineen.   1936.

The Battle Ground (on Syria). 1936.

Characters of the Reformation. 1936.

The Crusade: The World's Debate. 1937: as *The Crusades: The World's Debate.* 1937.

The Crisis of Our Civilization. 1937; as *The Crisis of Civilization,* 1937.

An Essay on the Nature of Contemporary England. 1937.

The Issue. 1937.

The Great Heresies. 1938.

Monarchy: A Study of Louis XIV. 1938; as *Louis XIV,* 1938.

Stories, Essays, and Poems. 1938.

The Case of Dr. Coulton. 1938.

Return to the Baltic. 1938.

Charles II: The Last Rally. 1939: as *The Last Rally: A Story of Charles II,* 1940.

The Test Is Poland. 1939.

On Sailing the Sea: A Collection of the Seagoing Writings of Belloc. edited by W. N. Roughead. 1939.

The Catholic and the War. 1940.

On the Place of G. K. Chesterton in English Letters. 1940.

The Silence of the Sea and Other Essays. 1940.

Places. 1941.

Elizabethan Commentary. 1942: as *Elizabeth: Creature of Circumstance.* 1942.

Selected Essays. 1948.

Hilaire Belloc: An Anthology of His Prose and Verse. edited by W. N. Roughead. 1951.

One Thing and Another: A Miscellany from His Uncollected Essays. edited by Patrick Cahill. 1955.

Essays. edited by Anthony Forster. 1955.

Letters from Belloc. edited by Robert Speaight. 1958.

Advice. 1960.

Editor, *Extracts from the Diaries and Letters of Hubert Howard.* 1899.

Editor, *The Footpath Way: An Anthology for Walkers.* 1911.

Editor, *Travel Notes on a Holiday Tour in France,* by James Murray Allison. 1931.

Translator. *The Romance of Tristan and Iseult.* by J. Bedier. 1903.

Translator. *The Principles of War.* by Marshal Foch. 1918.

Translator. *Precepts and Judgments.* by Marshal Foch. 1919.

Bibliography: *The English First Editions of Belloc* by Patrick Cahill, 1953.

Reading List: *Belloc* by Renée Haynes, 1953, revised edition, 1958; *Belloc, No Alienated Man: A Study in Christian Integration* by Frederick Wilhelmsen. 1954; *Belloc: A Memoir* by J. B. Morton, 1955; *The Young Belloc* by Marie Belloc Lowndes, 1956; *Testimony to Belloc* by E. and R. Jebb, 1956; *The Life of Belloc* by Robert Speaight, 1957.

*　　*　　*

Hilaire Belloc's career as crusading man-of-letters puts to shame by its polish, energy, and range any subsequent English propagandists for a radically Catholic point of view in politics and history. His many polemical works of historical biography, his essays and tracts, form a kind of armed column of anti-modern opinions, now passed well below the horizon of active readership, except perhaps among the Knights of Malta. He was anti-Drefusard, anti-socialist, and anti-Protestant, and the residue of feelings left us by the Second World War debars him from modern democratic sympathies. Yet the glitter and the rumour of his passage live on, perhaps most readably (among his serious works) in *The Servile State*, *Robespierre*, *Napoleon*, and *Cromwell*. As these titles suggest, he was also a radical, a rebel, a republican, and a revolutionary, and his history, always very personal and actual, has the vividness of the memoirs of a combatant.

His years as a Liberal M.P. (1906–1910), which went into his later political novels, left him with a disglish propagandists for a radically Catholic point of view in politics and history. His many polemical works of historical biography, his essays and tracts, form a kind of armed column of anti-modern opinions, now passed well below the horizon of active readership, except perhaps among the Knights of Malta. He was anti-Drefusard, anti-socialist, and anti-Protestant, and the residue of feelings left us by the Second World War debars him from modern democratic sympathies. Yet the glitter and the rumour of his passage live on, perhaps most readably (among his serious works) in *The Servile State*, *Robespierre*, *Napoleon*, and *Cromwell*. As these titles suggest, he was also a radical, a rebel, a republican, and a revolutionary, and his history, always very personal and actual, has the vividness of the memoirs of a combatant.

His years as a Liberal M.P. (1906–1910), which went into his later political novels, left him with a distaste for British political life, best represented by his epigram "On a General Election":

> The accursed power which stands on Privilege
> (And goes with Women, and Champagne and Bridge)
> Broke – and Democracy resumed her reign:
> (Which goes with Bridge, and Women and Champagne).

His great ally in journalism, radicalism, Romanism, and light verse, G. K. Chesterton, had more humour and an Englishness which made his crusading acceptable. Belloc was half-French and had been to Balliol, and his combination of clarity, wit, rhetoric, and sentiment made him a dangerously unpredictable figure to the English: he had principles and liked to win arguments. "Europe is the Faith, and the Faith is Europe" was one of his battle-cries; and by Europe he meant France, just as by England he meant Oxford. He admired Napoleon, was against the Boer War, and did not feel that "Judas was a tolerable chap."

Much of his distinct personality and charm remain in his travel books, especially *The Path to Rome*, partly autobiographical. His lucid prose was sometimes brazened in his tendentious later works, and his English set into a Gallic mannerism which now seems dated.

Belloc was fatally skilful in too many fields at a time when the press could support a versatile pen – or "a free lance" – the age of his opponents Shaw and Wells, as later of John Buchan and Ronald Knox, also Balliol man. There is a consciousness of waste in his verse – one thinks of Milton's "that one talent which is death to hide," a phrase Belloc would have admired. He thought of himself as a poet *manqué*. His serious verse strikes sentimental attitudes with style and he is still best loved for his light verse, especially the *Cautionary Tales*. Here his gifts found a minor triumph:

> Augustus Horne was nobly born,
> He held the human race in scorn.
> He lived with all his sisters where
> His father lived, in Berkeley Square.

—M. J. Alexander

BENÉT, Stephen Vincent.   American.   Born in Bethlehem, Pennsylvania, 22 July 1898; brother of the poet William Rose Benét, *q.v.* Educated at Summerville Academy; Yale University, New Haven, Connecticut (Chairman, *Yale Literary Magazine*, 1919), A.B. 1919, M.A. 1920; the Sorbonne, Paris. Married Rosemary Carr in 1921; one son, two daughters. During the Depression and war years became an active lecturer and radio propagandist for the liberal cause. Editor, Yale Series of Younger Poets. Recipient: Poetry Society of America Prize, 1921; Guggenheim Fellowship, 1926; Pulitzer Prize, 1929, 1944; O. Henry Award, 1932, 1937, 1940; Shelley Memorial Award, 1933; National Institute of Arts and Letters Gold Medal, 1943. D.Litt.: Middlebury College, Vermont, 1936. Vice-President, National Institute of Arts and Letters. *Died 13 March 1943.*

PUBLICATIONS

Collections

Selected Poetry and Prose, edited by Basil Davenport.   1960.
Selected Letters, edited by Charles A. Fenton.   1960.

Verse

The Drug-Shop; or, Endymion in Edmonstoun.   1917.
Young Adventure.   1918.
Heavens and Earth.   1920.
The Ballad of William Sycamore 1790–1880.   1923.
King David.   1923.
Tiger Joy.   1925.
John Brown's Body.   1928.
Ballads and Poems 1915–1930.   1931.
A Book of Americans, with Rosemary Benét.   1933.
Burning City.   1936.
The Ballad of the Duke's Mercy.   1939.
Nightmare at Noon.   1940.
Listen to the People: Independence Day 1941.   1941.
Western Star.   1943.
The Last Circle: Stories and Poems.   1946.

Plays

Five Men and Pompey: A Series of Dramatic Portraits.   1915.
The Headless Horseman, music by Douglas Moore (broadcast 1937).   1937.
The Devil and Daniel Webster, music by Douglas Moore, from the story by Benét (produced 1938).   1939.
Elementals (broadcast 1940–41). In *Best Broadcasts of 1940–41,* edited by Max Wylie, 1942.
Freedom's a Hard Bought Thing (broadcast 1941).   In *The Free Company Presents,* edited by James Boyd, 1941.
Nightmare at Noon, in *The Treasury Star Parade,* edited by William A. Bacher.   1942.
A Child Is Born (broadcast 1942).   1942.
They Burned the Books (broadcast 1942).   1942.

All That Money Can Buy (screenplay), with Dan Totheroh, in *Twenty Best Film Plays*, edited by John Gassner and Dudley Nichols. 1943.
We Stand United and Other Radio Scripts (includes *A Child Is Born, The Undefended Border, Dear Adolf, Listen to the People, Thanksgiving Day – 1941, They Burned the Books, A Time to Reap, Toward the Century of Modern Man, Your Army*). 1945.

Screenplays: *Cheers for Miss Bishop*, with Adelaide Heilbron and Sheridan Gibney, 1941; *All That Money Can Buy*, with Dan Totheroh, 1941.

Radio Plays: *The Headless Horseman*, 1937; *The Undefended Border*, 1940; *We Stand United*, 1940; *Elementals*, 1940–41; *Listen to the People*, 1941; *Thanksgiving Day – 1941*, 1941; *Freedom's a Hard Bought Thing*, 1941; *Nightmare at Noon; A Child Is Born*, 1942; *Dear Adolf*, 1942; *They Burned the Books*, 1942; *A Time to Reap*, 1942; *Toward the Century of Modern Man*, 1942; *Your Army*, 1944.

Fiction

The Beginning of Wisdom. 1921.
Young People's Pride. 1922.
Jean Huguenot. 1923.
Spanish Bayonet. 1926.
The Barefoot Saint (stories). 1929.
The Litter of Rose Leaves (stories). 1930.
James Shore's Daughter. 1934.
Thirteen O'Clock: Stories of Several Worlds. 1937.
The Devil and Daniel Webster. 1937.
Johnny Pye and the Fool-Killer (stories). 1938.
Tales Before Midnight. 1939.
Short Stories: A Selection. 1942.
O'Halloran's Luck and Other Short Stories. 1944.

Other

A Summons to the Free. 1941.
Selected Works. 2 vols., 1942.
America. 1944.
Benét on Writing: A Great Writer's Letter of Advice to a Young Beginner, edited by George Abbe. 1964.

Editor, with others, *The Yale Book of Student Verse 1910–1919*. 1919.

Bibliography: "Benét: A Bibliography" by Gladys Louise Maddocks, in *Bulletin of Bibliography 20*, 1951–52.

Reading List: *Benét* by William Rose Benét, 1943; *Benét: The Life and Times of an American Man of Letters* by Charles A. Fenton, 1958; *Benét* by Parry Stroud, 1962.

*   *   *

Stephen Vincent Benét occupies a curiously equivocal position in American letters. One of America's best known and rewarded poets and storytellers, he has at the same time been virtually ignored in academic discussions of major 20th-century writers, and seldom anthologized. In light of the greater critical success enjoyed by his student friends at Yale – Thornton Wilder, Archibald MacLeish, and Philip Barry, themselves often unremarked among "major" writers – Benét's reputation seems thin indeed.

Benét's permanent place in the history of American fiction is nevertheless assured by the fact that among his many volumes of prose and verse there are several minor classics that are widely read and admired. His early light and ironic verse, such as "For City Spring" and "Evening and Morning," and such frolicking ballads as "Captain Kidd," "Thomas Jefferson," "The Mountain Whippoorwill," and "The Ballad of William Sycamore" are highly regarded. His long narrative poem about the Civil War, *John Brown's Body*, dramatized by Charles Laughton in 1953 and called by Henry Steele Commager "not only the best poem about the Civil War, and the best narrative, but also the best history," won Benét his first Pulitzer Prize. Benét's best known short story, "The Devil and Daniel Webster," which combines the author's flare for fantasy and old folktale traditions, shares an equally prominent place in the tall-tale genre of American story-telling. Finally, *Western Star*, another long narrative poem about the heroic pioneering of America, begun in 1934 and incomplete at his death, won for Benét a second Pulitzer prize in 1944.

Among the notes for the continuation of *Western Star* found after Benét's death, the following quatrain was saved:

> Now for my country that it still may live,
> All that I have, all that I am I'll give.
> It is not much beside the gift of the brave
> And yet accept it since tis all I have.

What Benét had – an unbounded, 19th-century faith in the promises of American democracy, and an expansive, Whitmanesque love for what seemed the nation's special attributes, diversity, amplitude, self-sufficiency, frankness, innocence – he poured into every poem, story, and novel he wrote. He praised New York as the communal achievement of the spirit of man, and America because there every man could most freely become what God meant him to be. "Out of your fever and your moving on," he said in the "Prelude" to *Western Star*, "Americans, Americans, Americans … I make my song."

Both in sentiment and in style, Benét's work attempts to embody the very democratic virtues it is about. Like Sandburg, Hart Crane, and Vachel Lindsay, he uses the zesty tempos, conversational rhythms, and laconic vernacular to capture the spirit of greatness in the strength and simplicity of the nation's common people. In his book of fifty-six verses about famous American men and women, great and small, *A Book of Americans*, Benét says of the greatest and humblest of American native sons:

> Lincoln was a long man
> He liked out of doors.
> He liked the wind blowing
> And the talk in country stores.

Just as *John Brown's Body* projects Benét's sensitive feeling for half a dozen countrysides, racial strains, and political attitudes, so this book stands in praise of the nation's heroic ability to reconcile its opposites among that "varied lot" who "each by deed and speech/Adorned our history."

Despite the warmth, genuineness, and impish charm with which Benét celebrates the country's democratic potential, his failure to win wider critical respectability is clearly attributable to the fact that his breadth of sympathy and deep-rooted patriotism seem parochial and old-fashioned to today's audiences, and that even his best work, viewed along side the more realistic and richly inventive fiction of such contemporaries as Crane, Joyce, Proust, and Eliot, appears lacking in depth, subtlety, and originality. The pastoral rebellion of the earth against machines, against the "Age of Steam," which pervades so many of his poems, and his use of conventional verse forms and technical devices that have made him dear to school teachers, seem, in the words of one critic, "all too clear and all too facile." It is significant that Benét's writing has been praised more for its lively evocation of American history than for its aesthetic value.

—Lawrence R. Broer

BENÉT, William Rose.   American.   Born in New York City, 2 February 1886; brother of the poet Stephen Vincent Benét, *q.v.* Educated at Albany Academy, New York; Yale University, New Haven, Connecticut (Chairman, *Yale Courant*; Editor, *Yale Record*). Served in the United States Army Air Force in Europe, 1918: Second Lieutenant. Married 1) Teresa Frances Thompson in 1921 (died), one son, two daughters; 2) the poet Elinor Wylie, *q.v.*, in 1923 (died, 1928); 3) Lora Baxter; 4) the writer Marjorie Flack in 1943. Journalist: Reader, 1911–14, and Assistant Editor, 1914–18, *Century* magazine; Assistant Editor, *Nation's Business*, 1918–19; Associate Editor, *New York Evening Post* "Literary Review," 1920–24; Founder, with Christopher Morley, 1924, Associate Editor, 1924–29, and Contributing Editor after 1929, *Saturday Evening Post*; Editor, Brewer and Warren, publishers, 1929–30. Recipient: Pulitzer Prize, 1942. Secretary, National Institute of Arts and Letters. *Died 4 May 1950.*

PUBLICATIONS

Verse

> *Merchants from Cathay.*   1913.
> *The Falconer of God and Other Poems.*   1914.
> *The Great White Wall.*   1916.
> *The Burglar of the Zodiac and Other Poems.*   1918.
> *Perpetual Light: A Memorial.*   1919.
> *Moons of Grandeur.*   1920.
> *Man Possessed: Selected Poems.*   1927.
> *Sagacity.*   1929.
> *Rip Tide: A Novel in Verse.*   1932.
> *Starry Harness.*   1933.
> *Golden Fleece.*   1935.
> *Harlem and Other Poems.*   1935.
> *A Baker's Dozen of Emblems.*   1935.
> *With Wings as Eagles: Poems and Ballads of the Air.*   1940.
> *The Dust Which Is God: A Novel in Verse.*   1941.
> *Adolphus; or, The Adopted Dolphin and the Pirate's Daughter* (juvenile), with Marjorie
>   Flack.   1941.
> *Day of Deliverance.*   1944.
> *The Stairway of Surprise.*   1947.
> *Timothy's Angels* (juvenile). 1947.

Poetry Package, with Christopher Morley.   1949.
The Spirit of the Scene.   1951.

Play

Day's End, in *The Best One-Act Plays of 1939,* edited by Margaret Mayorga.   1939.

Fiction

The First Person Singular.   1922.

Other

Saturday Papers: Essays, with Henry Seidel Canby and Amy Loveman.   1921.
The Flying King of Kurio (juvenile).   1926.
Wild Goslings: A Selection of Fugitive Pieces.   1927.
Stephen Vincent Benét: My Brother Steve.   1943.

Editor, *Poems for Youth: An American Anthology.*   1925.
Editor, with John Drinkwater and Henry Seidel Canby, *Twentieth-Century Poetry.*   1929.
Editor, *Collected Poems, Collected Prose,* by Elinor Wylie.   2 vols., 1932–33.
Editor, *Fifty Poets: An American Auto-Anthology.*   1933.
Editor, *Guide to Daily Reading.*   1934.
Editor, *The Pocket University.*   13 vols., 1934.
Editor, with others, *Adventures in English Literature.*   1936.
Editor, *Mother Goose: A Comprehensive Collection of the Rhymes.*   1936.
Editor, *From Robert to Elizabeth Barrett Browning* (letters).   1936.
Editor, with Norman Holmes Pearson, *The Oxford Anthology of American Literature.*   1938.
Editor, with Adolph Gillis, *Poems for Modern Youth.*   1938.
Editor, *Supplement to Great Poems of the English Language,* edited by Wallace Alvin Briggs.   1941.
Editor, with Conrad Aiken, *An Anthology of Famous English and American Poetry.*   1945.
Editor, with Norman Cousins, *The Poetry of Freedom.*   1945.
Editor, *The Reader's Encyclopedia.*   1948.

Translator, with Teresa Frances, *The East I Know,* by Paul Claudel.   1914.

*   *   *

William Rose Benét has perhaps been more remarked upon in recent American literary history as the "older brother" of the writer Stephen Vincent Benét, and as husband of the poet Elinor Wylie, than as an accomplished poet in his own right. Serious attention to his verse has also been diverted by his prominence as a reviewer, critic, and anthologist, and by his numerous activities as a promoter of the arts. But despite this dispersion of energies, Benét managed to publish many volumes of verse whose value has not properly been acknowledged.

The obvious unevenness of Benét's creative output is hinted at by the fact that Rolfe Humphries rates him no better than a mere "journeyman of letters," while Marguerite

Wilkinson says he was a "builder [whose] strongest rhythms have the certitude of an arch...." Certainly Benét's weakest poems are unapologetically romantic and lacking in intensity. When he announces his poetic intentions in his most celebrated work, *The Dust Which Is God*, as "I will be plain at least," he does more than alert us to what he hopes will be a poetic voice free of bombast and ornamentation; unwittingly, he indicts a good number of poems whose over-statedness results in an absence of colour or emotional vitality. "Throw wide/The gates of the heart," he counsels in his poem "Study of Man," "Taking your part/In percipient life ... Ever extend/Your boundaries, and be/Inwardly free!"

Such direct statement issues from the poet's almost passionate reverence for the freedom and dignity of man, and for the ample spirit of God and nature, which he finds so abundantly manifest in his native America, as in "Men on Strike":

> The Country of the Free! Yes, a great land.
> Thank God that I have known it East to West
> And North to South, and still I love it best
> Of all the various world the seas command.

From the point of view of the wise primitivist, Benét celebrates the democratic virtues of common men, and envisions portents of disaster in the encroachments of the machine age. In "The Stricken Average," he writes:

> Little of brilliance did they write or say.
> They bore the battle of living, and were gay.
> Little of wealth or fame they left behind.
> They were merely honorable, brave, and kind.

He yearns for that "pristine creation/Unsullied by our civilization," ("Young Girl") whose elemental harmonies are forever threatened by factories, corporations, "towers of glass and steel" ("Shadow of the Mountain Man").

Such romantic attitudes were bound to lessen the appeal of Benét's work in an age whose best literary efforts were in direct opposition to such simple and sentimental verse. Yet there are indisputable qualities in Benét's best work, perhaps most forcibly realized in *The Dust Which Is God*, which in 1942 won him a Pulitzer Prize. An autobiographical verse narrative, it demonstrates a remarkable range of interests and intellect, and admirable versatility in the use of changing forms and rhythms to capture the diverse and sprawling nature of his subject – the birth and growth of the country, which he treats as synonymous with his own life. The poetry here reveals a lively and sophisticated grasp of cultural ideas, and often achieves a rich synthesis of opposites: classical and modern, noble and banal, holy and sensual, lyrical and prosaic. At their best, these "vignette illustrations" project for us a poetic talent of greater potential stature than that of the author's more celebrated brother – more original, more sensuous, and more varied and universal in scope.

—Lawrence R. Broer

BENNETT, Louise. Jamaican.   Educated at primary and secondary schools in Jamaica; Royal Academy of Dramatic Art, London (British Council Scholarship). Worked with the BBC (West Indies Section) as resident artist, 1945–46, 1950–53, and with repertory companies in Coventry, Huddersfield, and Amersham. Returned to Jamaica, 1955: Drama

Specialist with the Jamaica Social Welfare Commission, 1955–60; Lecturer in drama and Jamaican folklore, Extra-Mural Department, University of the West Indies, Kingston, 1959–61. Represented Jamaica at the Royal Commonwealth Arts Festival in Britain, 1965. Has lectured in the United States and the United Kingdom on Jamaican music and folklore. Recipient: Silver Musgrave Medal, Institute of Jamaica. M.B.E. (Member, Order of the British Empire). Lives in Jamaica.

PUBLICATIONS

Verse

> *Dialect Verses.*   1940.
> *Jamaican Dialect Verses.*   1942; expanded version,   1951.
> *Jamaican Humour in Dialect.*   1943.
> *Miss Lulu Sez.*   1948.
> *Anancy Stories and Dialect Verse,* with others.   1950.
> *Laugh with Louise: A Potpourri of Jamaican Folklore, Stories, Songs, Verses.*   1960.
> *Jamaica Labrish.*   1966.

Reading List: Introduction by Rex Nettlefold to *Jamaica Labrish,* 1966.

*   *   *

Afters years of popularity Louise Bennett is now attracting the attention of the critic and scholarly researcher. This belated attention is partly in response to Bennett's formidable merits as a poet, but it also reflects the current interest in Afro-Caribbean folk arts (music, songs, dances, folktales) – not simply as sources for writers and folklorists, but more importantly as significant art forms in their own right. And as a poet whose art has always been based on oral performance and rooted in Jamaican folk idioms, Bennett fully exploits the potentiality of folk arts in the Caribbean. Indeed her themes repeatedly emphasize both the oral nature of her poetry and her own role as a performer. Moreover her language and the loquacious characters in her poems dramatize the political, emotional, and cultural significance of the spoken word among Jamaica's poor and unlettered classes.

Conversely her unlettered but robust folk often ridicule the literate middle-class world of the printed word, not because they reject literacy and middle-class values as such, but because Bennett questions the tendency, in some quarters, to elevate the European values inherent in standard English literacy at the expense of the experience represented by the folk idiom and its Afro-Caribbean cultural milieu. For that cultural milieu results from a complex cultural synthesis of African, European, and New World sources which is in danger of being ignored or minimized by a narrowly literate value system. Bennett's techniques (particularly her choice of language and the oral nature of her poetry) are therefore integral to her vision as an artist. These techniques enable her to immerse her audience in the experience of the folk, affirming in the process that that experience is central rather than peripheral to a Jamaican (and West Indian) consciousness.

This cultural immersion is aided by another Bennett technique: she never allows her authorial voice to obtrude upon the theme of any work, and this is a constant in her work, notwithstanding the authoritarian, even overbearing, voice which discourses on a variety of topics in her poetry. The voice we hear belongs to the persona of the moment, whether it is a politician, a trades unionist, a loyal Black colonial, or a spirited anti-colonialist. And on the whole her poetry relies upon the unfettered self-description of her characters rather than upon some comprehensive definition or overview by the author herself. Hence although Bennett the poet says nothing directly about the status and experience of women, her work represents the most thorough exploration of the woman's experience in the Caribbean. Nearly all of her poems are presented through the eyes – and energetic voices – of women, and in the process they reveal a wide variety of women's attitudes towards men, themselves, and society as a whole. In their vocal self-expressiveness Bennett's women emerge as a rather diverse lot – militant, conventional, strong, or weak. They are therefore representations of Bennett's special kind of poetic truth – a relentless realism that confronts her audience with society and its people as they are and as they express their diverse selves in their oral modes.

—Lloyd W. Brown

BERRYMAN, John. American. Born in McAlester, Oklahoma, 25 October 1914. Educated at South Kent School, Connecticut; Columbia University, New York, A.B. 1936 (Phi Beta Kappa); Clare College, Cambridge (Kellett Fellow, 1936–37; Oldham Shakespeare Scholar, 1937), B.A. 1938; Princeton University, New Jersey (Creative Writing Fellow), 1943–44. Married 1) Eileen Patricia Mulligan in 1942 (divorced, 1953); 2) Ann Levine in 1956 (divorced, 1959); 3) Kathleen Donahue in 1961; three children. Instructor in English, Wayne State University, Detroit, 1939, and Princeton University, 1940–43; Briggs-Copeland Instructor in English Composition, Harvard University, Cambridge, Massachusetts, 1945–49; Lecturer in English, University of Washington, Seattle, 1950; Elliston Lecturer in Poetry, University of Cincinnati, 1951–52; Member of the English Department, rising to the rank of Professor, University of Minnesota, Minneapolis, 1954–72. Recipient: Rockefeller grant, 1944, 1946; Shelley Memorial Award, 1949; National Institute of Arts and Letters grant, 1950; Hodder Fellowship, Princeton University, 1950; Guggenheim Fellowship, 1952, 1966; Harriet Monroe Award, 1957; Brandeis University Creative Arts Award, 1959; Loines Award, 1964; Pulitzer Prize, 1965; Academy of American Poets Fellowship, 1966; National Endowment for the Arts grant, 1967; Bollingen Prize, 1968; National Book Award, 1969. D.Let.: Drake University, Des Moines, Iowa, 1971. Member, National Institute of Arts and Letters, American Academy of Arts and Sciences, and Academy of American Poets. *Died* (by suicide) *7 January 1972.*

PUBLICATIONS

Verse

Five Young American Poets, with others.   1940.
Poems.   1942.
The Dispossessed.   1948.
Homage to Mistress Bradstreet.   1956; as *Homage to Mistress Bradstreet and Other Poems,* 1959.
His Thought Made Pockets and the Plane Buckt.   1958.
77 Dream Songs.   1964.
Berryman's Sonnets.   1967.
Short Poems.   1967.

His Toy, His Dream, His Rest: 308 Dream Songs.   1968.
The Dream Songs.   1969.
Love and Fame.   1970; revised edition, 1972.
Selected Poems 1938–1968.   1972.
Delusions, Etc.   1972.
Henry's Fate and Other Poems, edited by John Haffenden.   1977.

Fiction

Recovery.   1973.

Other

Stephen Crane (biography).   1950.
The Freedom of the Poet (miscellany).   1976.

Editor, with Ralph Ross and Allen Tate, *The Arts of Reading* (anthology).   1960.
Editor, *The Unfortunate Traveller; or, The Life of Jack Wilton,* by Thomas Nashe.   1960.

Bibliography: *Berryman: A Descriptive Bibliography* by Ernest C. Stefanik, Jr., 1974; *Berryman: A Reference Guide* by Gary Q. Arpin, 1976.

Reading List: *Berryman* by William J. Martz, 1969; *Berryman* by James M. Linebarger, 1974; *The Poetry of Berryman* by Gary Q. Arpin, 1977; *Berryman: An Introduction to the Poetry* by Joel Conarroe, 1977.

*   *   *

John Berryman spent his childhood on a farm in Oklahoma under the sombre and difficult aegis of a father whose improvidence finally led to his suicide, an event which haunted and disturbed the poet for the rest of his life. From these dark beginnings, he leapt into the brighter world of his education, first at a private school in Connecticut, and then at Columbia University, where his immense energies and brilliance were manifested. A scholarship to Cambridge University led to his studies in Shakespeare and the English Renaissance, the stylistic exuberance of which was to influence his own discordant, richly embellished mode of verse. At Princeton University, he began a frenzied pace of writing that led to his first full-length collection of short poems, *The Dispossessed.* He had also completed much of the cycle of poems later published as *Berryman's Sonnets.* In both volumes Berryman is a mature craftsman of traditional forms and meters, which he renewed with his energetic speech.

Berryman's major work begins with *Homage to Mistress Bradstreet,* which includes poems from *The Dispossessed.* The title poem, a sequence of 57 eight-line stanzas, evokes the life and hardships of this American poet through an original strategy of merging the narrator's voice with his subject's, in which all the details of her sickness, frailty, and harsh family life are rendered with powerful immediacy. The poet's speech slips into the Colonial tongue and out again into a flinty modern colloquialism with masterful control. Berryman etches the character of Bradstreet and holds her up as an instance of the artist's eternal struggle against adversity:

Headstones stagger under great draughts of time
after heads pass out, and their world must reel
speechless, blind in the end
about its chilling star: thrift tuft,
whin cushion – nothing. Already with the wounded flying
dark air fills, I am a closet of secrets dying,
races murder, foxholes hold men,
reactor piles wage slow upon the wet brain rime.

Included in *Homage* is the series "The Nervous Songs," where he again inhabits other strained minds and articulates their emotions. They are important, however, chiefly for their form; each poem is cast in three six-line stanzas, the form employed throughout his greatest work, *The Dream Songs*.

The persona of the *Dream Songs* is variously referred to as Henry, Pussy-Cat, and Mr. Bones, and the poems evoke his daily inner life as he struggles through the routines of teaching, drying-out from chronic alcoholism, and writing ambitious books of poems. His deepest dilemma is with his own identity, which fits him in the middle of every extreme of life: he is middle-aged, of the middle-class, and of middling talent. Against all these middlings he struggles to find an edge, by occasionally daubing burnt cork on his face, by heavy drinking, and by hard working, but each time falls back into the slough of his middleness depressed and exhausted:

He lay in the middle of the world, and twicht.
More Sparine for Pelides,
human (half) & down here as he is,
with probably insulting mail to open
and certainly unworthy words to hear
and his unforgivable memory.

Or again, "Henry felt baffled, in the middle of the thing," which is a refrain of his efforts and sufferings.

The desire to transcend his undefined existence wears down into defeat in later sections of this sequence, until "Henry hates the world. What the world to Henry/did will not bear thought." The despair deepens into rejection: "This world is gradually becoming a place/ where I do not care to be any more." He broods upon death in all its forms and nightmare possibilities, including the frequent lamentations for other poets who have died recently, and who seem to share his dark view of the world:

I'm cross with God who has wrecked this generation.
First he seized Ted [Roethke], then Richard [Blackmur], Randall [Jarrell], and now
                                                                    Delmore [Schwartz].

In between he gorged on Sylvia Plath.
That was a first rate haul. He left alive
fools I could number like a kitchen knife
but Lowell he did not touch.

In a later, grimmer juncture of the *Songs*, Henry remarks bitterly, "The world grows more disgusting dawn by dawn." The poems then take up a plot of sorts with a residence in Ireland, followed by a return to the United States and the long attempt to recover from alcoholism, a turn that also involves Henry in religious conversion.

The whole work, including the posthumous additions, *Henry's Fate*, amounts to a vast mosaic of pieces of Henry's life and character, without transforming such pieces into a unified vision. The work is discordant throughout, in its language and in its jagged progression of themes and motifs. It is essentially a long and despairing examination of a poet's alienation from the post-war world, in which his brilliance and cultural inheritance appear to have no place or value. The grave, devoted artist founders and ultimately destroys himself, lamenting throughout the cursed and crooked fate of his fellow poets. This tragedy is lifted above self-pity and sentimentality by the essential good character of Henry, whose complicated interiors give us a Hamlet for this age.

Berryman's later works, *Love and Fame, Delusions, Etc.*, and the novel *Recovery*, turn away from the *Dream Songs* to treat more directly of the poet's life. *Love and Fame* is unabashed autobiography of the poet's education and rise to prominence, delivered in a flat, narrative style unlike his earlier verse. In *Delusions, Etc.* his religious turning is expressed in a section of liturgical poems where Berryman is again the effortless master of sonorous lyrics. *Recovery*, unfinished at the poet's death, exposes the torment of the alcoholic and eloquently pleads for understanding of this disease from which the poet suffered much of his life.

—Paul Christensen

BETHELL, Mary Ursula. New Zealander. Born in Surrey, England, 6 October 1874. Educated in England and New Zealand; studied music and painting. Social worker in London and Scotland, 1898–1902; returned to New Zealand permanently in 1919, and settled in Canterbury. *Died 15 January 1945.*

PUBLICATIONS

Verse

From a Garden in the Antipodes. 1929.
The Glad Returning and Other Poems. 1932.
The Haunted Gallery and Other Poems. 1932.
Time and Place. 1936.
Day and Night: Poems 1924–1934. 1939.
Collected Poems. 1950.

Reading List: *Bethell* by M. M. Holcroft, 1975.

*   *   *

Almost all of Mary Ursula Bethell's verse was written (though not published) during a single period of sustained creative activity from 1924 to 1934, between her fiftieth and sixtieth years. Her late flowering began when, after a lifetime spent moving back and forth between England (where she was born) and New Zealand (where she had spent her childhood), she finally settled permanently in New Zealand. With her beloved companion Effie Pollen she moved into a house on the Cashmere Hills overlooking the city of Christchurch, with the Pacific coast of the South Island curving away to the north and east and the Canterbury plains stretching away to the mountains of the Southern Alps in the north and west, as described in "Southerly Sunday":

The great south wind has covered with cloud the whole of the river-plain,
soft white ocean of foaming mist, blotting out, billowing

fast to the east, where Pacific main surges on vaster bed.
But here, on the hills, south wind unvapoured encounters the sunshine,
lacing and interlocking, the invisible effervescence
you almost hear, and the laughter of light and air at play overhead.

Seabirds fly free; see the sharp flash of their underwings!
and high lifted up to the north, the mountains, the mighty, the white ones
rising sheer from the cloudy sea, light-crowned, established.

Her productive phase ended when Miss Pollen died in 1934 and the house and garden on the hills was vacated. Little was added to her work in the last decade of her life beyond a sequence of annual anniversary poems, written to commemorate the friend whom she considered the "only begetter" of her verse.

Her first book, *From a Garden in the Antipodes*, consists of brief, unpretentious, apparently mundane but deceptively simple poems recording the trivia of a gardener's chores and observations through the seasonal cycle from one autumn to another. Digging, planting, weeding, planning, watching shrubs and plants sprout and bloom, reporting changes in the weather and the view – such is the substance of these modest, prosaic but delightful verses. Beyond the simple surface, however, are wider implications, as suggested by the phrase "garden of exile, garden of my pilgrimage" from an unpublished poem. Ursula Bethell felt herself to be a transplanted Englishwoman for whom her garden (and her poetry which she tends to identify with it) was both a reminder of her exile and a compensation for it. To some degree she stands for all New Zealanders, colonists all, gardening the antipodes. The garden is also her pilgrimage, her way to God. She was a deeply religious woman, and her garden poems were her means of localising the transcendent truths of her religion, though the religious meaning is seldom pointed directly as it is almost invariably in her later volumes.

In *Time and Place* and *Day and Night* the symbolism is more explicit and the message more manifestly Christian. The final stanza of "Southerly Sunday," for example, points the religious meaning of the preceding landscape description (quoted above):

This sparkling day is the Lord's day. Let us be glad and rejoice in it;
for he cometh, he cometh to judge and redeem his beautiful universe,
and holds in his hands all worlds, all men, the quick and the dead.

Time and Place is organised according to the sequence of the seasons, *Day and Night* according to the diurnal cycle, thereby underlining the theme of death and resurrection which is central to her work. The religious poems tend on the whole to be less spontaneous than the garden poems, and are occasionally overwrought both emotionally and technically. When the natural occasion, however, is sufficiently realised to sustain the supernatural meanings attributed to it, Ursula Bethell achieves poems of considerable beauty and force.

—Peter Simpson

BETJEMAN, Sir John. English. Born in Highgate, London, in 1906. Educated at Marlborough; Magdalen College, Oxford. Served as Press Attaché, Dublin, 1941–42; in the

Admiralty, London, 1943. Married the author Penelope Valentine Hester in 1933; one son and one daughter. Book Reviewer, *Daily Herald*, London; radio and television broadcaster. Columnist ("City and Suburban"), *Spectator*, London, 1954–58. Founder, Victorian Society; Member, Royal Fine Art Commission; Governor, Pusey House (Church of England). Recipient: Heinemann Award, 1949; Foyle Poetry Prize, 1955, 1959; Loines Award, 1956; Duff Cooper Memorial Prize, 1958; Queen's Gold Medal for Poetry, 1960. LL.D.: Aberdeen University; D.Litt.: Oxford, Reading, and Birmingham universities. Honorary Fellow, Keble College, Oxford, 1972. Companion of Literature, Royal Society of Literature, 1968. Honorary Associate, Royal Institute of British Architects; Honorary Member, American Academy of Arts and Letters, 1973. C.B.E. (Commander, Order of the British Empire), 1960; knighted, 1969. Poet Laureate since 1972. Lives in London.

PUBLICATIONS

Verse

Mount Zion; or, In Touch with the Infinite. 1931.
Continual Dew: A Little Book of Bourgeois Verse. 1937.
Sir John Piers. 1938.
Old Lights for New Chancels: Verses Topographical and Amatory. 1940.
New Bats in Old Belfries. 1945.
Slick But Not Streamlined: Poems and Short Pieces, edited by W. H. Auden. 1947.
Selected Poems, edited by John Sparrow. 1948.
A Few Late Chrysanthemums. 1954.
Poems in the Porch. 1954.
Collected Poems, edited by the Earl of Birkenhead. 1958; revised edition, 1962, 1972.
(Poems). 1958.
Summoned by Bells (verse autobiography). 1960.
A Ring of Bells, edited by Irene Slade. 1962.
High and Low. 1966.
Six Betjeman Songs, music by Mervyn Horder. 1967.
A Nip in the Air. 1974.
Betjeman in Miniature: A Selection of Short Poems. 1976.
Metro-land: Selected Verses from His Commentary for the Film. 1977.

Plays

Television Documentaries: *The Stained Glass at Fairford,* 1955; *Pity about the Abbey,* with Stewart Farver, 1965; *Metro-land,* 1973; *A Passion for Churches,* 1974; *Vicar of This Parish* (on Francis Kilvert), 1976.

Other

Ghastly Good Taste; or, A Depressing Story of the Rise and Fall of English Architecture. 1933; revised edititon, 1970.
Devon. 1936.
An Oxford University Chest: Comprising a Description of the Present State of the Town and University of Oxford, with an Itinerary Arranged Alphabetically. 1938.
Vintage London. 1942.

English Cities and Small Towns. 1943.

John Piper. 1944.

Murray's Buckinghamshire Architectural Guide, with John Piper. 1948.

Murray's Berkshire Architectural Guide, with John Piper. 1949.

Murray's Shropshire Architectural Guide, with John Piper. 1951.

First and Last Loves (essay on architecture). 1952.

Collins Guide to English Parish Churches, Including the Isle of Man. 1958; as *An American's Guide to English Parish Churches,* 1959; revised edition, as *Collins Pocket Guide to English Parish Churches,* 2 vols., 1968.

Ground Plan to Skyline. 1960.

English Churches, with Basil Clarke. 1964.

Cornwall. 1964.

The City of London Churches. 1965.

London's Historic Railway Stations. 1972.

A Pictorial History of English Architecture. 1972.

West Country Churches. 1973.

A Plea for Holy Trinity Church. 1974.

Archie and the Strict Baptists (juvenile). 1977.

Editor, *Cornwall Illustrated: In a Series of Views of Castles, Seats of the Nobility, Mines, Picturesque Scenery, Towns, Public Buildings, Churches, Antiquities, Etc.* 1934.

Editor, *A Pickwick Portrait Gallery, from the Pens of Divers Admirers.* 1936.

Editor, *Selected Poems,* by Sir Henry Newbolt. 1940.

Editor, with Geoffrey Taylor, *English, Scottish, and Welsh Landscape, 1700–ca. 1860* (verse anthology). 1944.

Editor, with Geoffrey Taylor, *English Love Poems.* 1957.

Editor, *Altar and Pew: Church of England Verses.* 1959.

Editor, with Sir Charles Tennyson, *A Hundred Sonnets,* by Charles Tennyson Turner. 1960.

Editor, with Winifred Hindley, *A Wealth of Poetry.* 1963.

Editor, *Victorian and Edwardian London from Old Photographs.* 1968.

Editor, with J. S. Gray, *Victorian and Edwardian Brighton from Old Photographs.* 1972.

Editor, with A. L. Rowse, *Victorian and Edwardian Cornwall from Old Photographs.* 1974.

Editor, *A Selection of Poems,* by John Masefield. 1978.

Bibliography: *Betjeman: A Bibliography of Writings by and about Him* by Margaret L. Stapleton, 1974.

Reading List: *Betjeman: A Study* by Derek Stanford, 1961; *Ronald Firbank and Betjeman* by Jocelyn Brooke, 1962; *Betjeman* by John Press, 1974.

* * *

Had anybody prophesied in 1936 that John Betjeman would become an immensely popular figure on television, the most financially successful living poet, a Knight, and the successor to Cecil Day Lewis as Poet Laureate, his forecast would have seemed ludicrously far-fetched. For Betjeman was known in the mid 1930's only as the author of a volume of poems, *Mount Zion,* published in 1931 by a friend who owned a small printing firm, and of a book on architecture with the somewhat frivolous title, *Ghastly Good Taste.* Betjeman describes *Mount Zion* in the dedication as a "precious hyper-sophisticated book," and its sub-title, *In Touch with the Infinite,* taken in conjunction with some of the poems, bears out the promise or the threat of the dedication. "Competition," one of the nine poems from *Mount Zion* omitted from Betjeman's *Collected Poems*, contains some lines that exude what casual readers still regard as the quintessence of Betjeman's poetry, a half-mocking, half-affectionate celebration of Victorian piety and Victorian architecture:

> The Gothic is bursting over the way
> With Evangelical Song,
> For the pinnacled Wesley Memorial Church
> Is over a hundred strong.

Betjeman has continued over the years to write about architecture and to delight mass audiences on TV with his guided tours of city and suburban buildings in Britain and Australia. Anybody who takes the trouble to read his architectural writings, from *Ghastly Good Taste* onwards, will discover that he is no mere antiquary bent on preserving anything that is quaint or amusing but, on the contrary, a serious historian of English architecture.

W. H. Auden, who dedicated *The Age of Anxiety* to Betjeman, wrote a preface to his choice of Betjeman's verse and prose, *Slick But Not Streamlined*. He stressed the importance of *topophilia* in Betjeman's poetry, taking up a remark made by Betjeman in his preface to *Old Lights for New Chancels*: "I see no harm in trying to describe overbuilt Surrey in verse. But when I do so I am not being satirical but topographical." He has continued to write such poems throughout his career, but they are only one of the several kinds of verse that he has made peculiarly his own. His satirical poems are among his weakest, and what has been called his *New Statesman* competition verse is even less rewarding. Yet anthologists continue to reprint "Slough," "In Westminster Abbey," and "How to Get On in Society," even though Betjeman himself has remarked that "they now seem to me merely comic verse and competent magazine writing, topical and tiresome."

His exploration of "Betjeman country" in poems such as "Pot Pourri from a Surrey Garden" (a title cribbed from a late Victorian book by a high-born lady) is a more original and more serious achievement. Through those landscapes with figures there stalk such formidable Amazons as Pam, that "great big mountainous sports girl," and a young woman apostrophised in "The Olympic Girl" as "Fair tigress of the tennis courts." Yet his topographical poems are most moving when precise observation is fused with irony tempered by compassion. "Middlesex" begins by portraying "Fair Elaine the bobby-soxer,/ Fresh-complexioned with Innoxa," but it broadens into a lament for the enormous hayfields of the Middlesex countryside obliterated by Elaine's suburban world, and concludes with an evocation of the Carrara-covered cemeteries where the Victorian dead repose, "Long in Kensal Green and Highgate silent under soot and stone."

In the late 1940's a new theme – the sea, linked with memories of childhood – entered Betjeman's poetry, at much the same time as he embarked on his first attempts at blank verse, "Sunday Afternoon Service in St. Enodoc Church, Cornwall" and "North Coast Recollections." He handles blank verse with considerable skill in those poems, in his long autobiographical poem, *Summoned by Bells*, and in a few other pieces, notably in the valediction, "On Leaving Wantage 1972," from *A Nip in the Air*.

Betjeman, however, is one of those poets who enjoy the challenge presented by rhyming schemes and metrical patterns. He tells us that, with him, a poem begins when some recollection "hammers inside the head," that "a line or a phrase suggests itself," and that the next step is "the selection of a metre. I am a traditionalist in metres and have made few experiments. The rhythms of Tennyson, Crabbe, Hawker, Dowson, Hardy, James Elroy Flecker, Moore and Hymns A & M are generally buzzing about in my brain and I choose one from these which seems to me to suit the theme." To that list we may add the names of Frederick Locker-Lampson, Father Prout, Dibdin, William Allingham, Longfellow, and Newbolt. The chances are that the more intricate the pattern the more accomplished the poem. Examples that come to mind are "Pot Pourri from a Surrey Garden," "Henley-on-Thames," "Middlesex," "Ireland with Emily," and "I. M. Walter Ramsden."

Some of Betjeman's most powerful and memorable poems are inspired by the contemplation of death, recollections of childhood, memories of lust, the spectacle of change and decay, the longing for eternal peace in the presence of God. When two or more of those elements are commingled in a poem they yield a potent brew. "Late-Flowering Lust" dwells on the image of two skeletons:

> Dark sockets look on emptiness
> Which once was loving-eyed,
> The mouth that opens for a kiss
> Has got no tongue inside.

"N.W.5 & N.6" evokes Betjeman's childhood fears awakened by a nursery-maid's talk of damnation as church bells rang out in the evening sky, infecting the child with

> her fear
> And guilt at endlessness. I caught them too,
> Hating to think of sphere succeeding sphere
> Into eternity and God's dread will.
> I caught her terror then. I have it still.

In "Felixstowe or The Last of Her Order" the only survivor of an order founded in 1894 avows her faith: "Safe from the surging of the lonely sea/My heart finds rest, my heart finds rest in Thee." Many of Betjeman's finest poems derive their energy from the tension between faith and despair.

—John Press

BIRNEY, Earle. Canadian. Born in Calgary, Alberta, 13 May 1904. Educated at the University of British Columbia, Vancouver, B.A. 1926; University of Toronto, M.A. 1927, Ph.D. 1936; University of California, Berkeley, 1927–30; Queen Mary College, London, 1934–35. Served in the Canadian Army, in the reserves, 1940–41, and on active duty, 1942–45; Major-in-Charge, Personnel Selection, Belgium and Holland, 1944–45. Married Esther Bull in 1940; one child. Instructor in English, University of Utah, Salt Lake City, 1930–34; Lecturer, later Assistant Professor of English, University of Toronto, 1936–42; Supervisor, European Foreign Language Broadcasts, Radio Canada, Montreal, 1945–46; Professor of Medieval English Literature, 1946–63, and Professor and Chairman of the Department of Creative Writing, 1963–65, University of British Columbia; Writer-in-Residence, University of Toronto, 1965–67, and University of Waterloo, Ontario, 1967–68; Regents Professor in Creative Writing, University of California at Irvine, 1968. Since 1968, free-lance writer and lecturer. Literary Editor, *Canadian Forum*, Toronto, 1936–40; Editor, *Canadian Poetry Magazine*, Edmonton, 1946–48; Editor, *Prism International*, Vancouver, 1964–65; Advisory Editor, *New: American and Canadian Poetry*, Trumansburg, New York, 1966–70. Recipient: Governor-General's Award, 1943, 1946; Stephen Leacock Medal, 1950; Borestone Mountain Poetry Award, 1951; Canadian Government Overseas Fellowship, 1953, Service Medal, 1970; Lorne Pierce Medal, 1953; President's Medal, University of Western Ontario, 1954; Nuffield Fellowship, 1958; Canada Council Senior Arts Grant, 1962, 1974, Medal, 1968, Special Fellowship, 1968, and Travel Grant, 1971, 1974. LL.D.: University of Alberta, Edmonton, 1965. Fellow, Royal Society of Canada, 1954. Lives in Toronto.

PUBLICATIONS

Verse

> David and Other Poems. 1942.
> Now Is the Time. 1945.
> Strait of Anian: Selected Poems. 1948.
> Trial of a City and Other Verse. 1952.
> Ice Cod Bell or Stone. 1962.
> Near False Creek Mouth. 1964.
> Selected Poems 1940–1966. 1966.
> Memory No Servant. 1968.
> Poems. 1969.
> Pnomes, Jukollages and Other Stunzas. 1969.
> Rag and Bone Shop. 1971.
> Five Modern Canadian Poets, with others, edited by Eli Mandel. 1970.
> Four Parts Sand: Concrete Poems, with others. 1972.
> Bear on the Delhi Road. 1973.
> What's So Big about Green? 1973.
> Collected Poems. 2 vols., 1974.

Play

> The Damnation of Vancouver: A Comedy in Seven Episodes (broadcast, 1952). In Trial of a City, 1952; revised version (produced 1957), in Selected Poems, 1966.

Radio Play: The Damnation of Vancouver, 1952.

Fiction

> Turvey: A Military Picaresque. 1949.
> Down the Long Table. 1955.

Other

> The Creative Writer. 1966.
> The Cow Jumped over the Moon: The Writing and Reading of Poetry. 1972.

Editor, Twentieth Century Canadian Poetry. 1953.
Editor, Record of Service in the Second World War. 1955.
Editor, with others, New Voices. 1956.
Editor, with Margerie Lowry, Selected Poems of Malcoim Lowry. 1962.
Editor, with Margerie Lowry, Lunar Caustic, by Malcolm Lowry. 1963.

Bibliography: in West Coast Review, October 1970.

Reading List: Birney by Richard Robillard, 1971; Birney by Frank Davey, 1971; Birney edited by Bruce Nesbitt, 1974.

*   *   *

Earle Birney is almost certainly the most distinguished of living Canadian poets. Even in his earliest verse we can see his essential poetic qualifications, a gift for cut and graven detail, a flowing empathy, and a natural rhythm in which the breathing meets the sense to produce an evolving, living line. Impressive miniatures of these powers are "Slug in Woods" and "Aluroid."

Landscape is a traditional theme in Canadian poetry, a fact which is hardly surprising in a country so physically overwhelming and so variously beautiful as Canada, where even today life is intimately harnessed to the rhythms of the climate and the seasons. Some of the most notable members of Birney's Canadian scene are "Atlantic Door," "Maritime Faces," "Dusk on the Bay," "Hands," "North of Superior," "Ellesmere Land, I," "North Star West," "The Ebb Begins from Dream," "Winter Saturday," "Holiday in the Foothills," "Bushed," "Images in Place of Logging." "David," an energetic narrative poem about climbing, and reminiscent of those "action" poems of the 1930's in England, is less successfully realised, perhaps spoilt by moralising, as is another well-known poem, "November Walk by False Creek Mouth." But the successful poems of this kind compose a poetic geography of Canada, defining its bone, frame, moods, and treacheries. Birney evokes in each of these poems of landscape the natural world in process: the verbs are continuous, there is a sense of stirring molecular activity implicit in the stoniest, harshest landscape, the mountains are weathering, the rooms lighting, the dampness steams. At the same time, something enduring in the country matches something stubborn in the poet. Birney's sensibility has, indeed, a hard and cobbled quality, a strength which does not forbid sensitivity and delicate registration but which sustains and toughens them. It is a note which we find in that slim, perfectly articulated poem, "Ellesmere Land, I."

What is clear from these poems and many others is a central fact of human existence for Birney: that man exists in a state of stoic detachment from the supporting earth, from his neighbours, from everything. In the candid and occasionally tetchy preface to his *Selected Poems 1940–1966* he explains that the poems are not so much efforts to bridge the gap as recognitions of the fact:

> That I go on so stubbornly to publish my incantations, in a world which may not last long enough to read them, and has shown little need for them so far, might be construed as mere vanity, or again as proof that the outer me is as abnormally compulsive as the inner. I prefer to believe, rather, that my poems are the best proof I can print of my humanness, signals out of the loneliness into which all of us are born and in which we die, affirmations of kinship with the other wayfarers....

Just so: and man is joined to man not by his effort, and its necessary failure, to cross over to his neighbour or his lover, but by the acknowledgment of a common predicament.

Buoyant and balanced: this phrase aptly describes his work at large. About its buoyancy one can say that the poet's natural sense of rhythm, itself the development of a profound human instinct, has been educated over fifty years of severe professional practice to such a pitch of intuitive taste, as to be utterly responsive to the needs of the poetry, and completely clean of any involuntarily deposited sludge or accidental silt. The medium has become an instrument. The same is true of the self. By unremitting application, by the most disinterested discipline, Birney's nature has been scraped and scrubbed free of affectation, presupposition, prejudice, so that it appears in the poetry of these last years in its authentically individual, true, worn state.

Buoyancy, not bounce, the product of discipline and a certain ease and confidence of character, itself the hard-won consequence of a life spent in the service of poetry and the mind, enables Birney in his poems, particularly in those of travel, to see a situation squarely with no distorting squint of preconception, without the patronage of self-indulgent pity or defensive guiltiness. He deals with it solely out of his own resources and purely on its own merits. There is, then, a balance or proportion between subject and object, a wholeness and unity in the former recognising the fullness and complexity of the latter. A Birney poem is never just the evocation of a scene. It always has an intellectual and moral structure. In all his poems of place, place itself aspires to support, or even to be, an event.

—William Walsh

BISHOP, Elizabeth. American. Born in Worcester, Massachusetts, 8 February 1911. Educated at Vassar College, Poughkeepsie, New York, A.B. 1934. Lived in Brazil for 16 years. Consultant in Poetry, Library of Congress, Washington, D.C., 1949–50. Poet-in-Residence, University of Washington, Seattle, 1966, 1973. Since 1970, Lecturer in English, Harvard University, Cambridge, Massachusetts. Recipient: Guggenheim Fellowship, 1947; National Institute of Arts and Letters grant, 1951; Shelley Memorial Award, 1953; Pulitzer Prize, 1956; Amy Lowell Traveling Fellowship, 1957; Chapelbrook Fellowship, 1962; Academy of American Poets Fellowship, 1964; Rockefeller Fellowship, 1967; Ingram Merrill Foundation grant, 1969; National Book Award, 1970; Harriet Monroe Prize, 1974. LL.D.: Smith College, Northampton, Massachusetts, 1968; Rutgers University, New Brunswick, New Jersey, 1972; Brown University, Providence, Rhode Island, 1972. Chancellor, Academy of American Poets, 1966; Member, American Academy of Arts and Letters, 1976. Order of Rio Branco (Brazil), 1971.

PUBLICATIONS

Verse

North and South. 1946.
Poems: North and South – A Cold Spring. 1955.
Poems. 1956.
Questions of Travel. 1965.
Selected Poems. 1967.
The Ballad of the Burglar of Babylon (juvenile). 1968.
The Complete Poems. 1969.
Geography III. 1977.

Other

Brazil, with the Editors of Life. 1962.

Editor and Translator, Anthology of Contemporary Brazilian Poetry, vol. 1. 1972.

Translator, The Diary of Helena Morley. 1957.

Reading List: Bishop by Anne Stevenson, 1966.

*   *   *

Elizabeth Bishop's autobiographical "In the Village," a story which moves towards poetry and was included at the center of *Questions of Travel*, shows how the sounds and sights and textures of a Nova Scotia village enable a child to come to terms with the sound of the scream which signified her mother's madness and, ultimately, with human isolation, loss, mortality; the child's capacity for meticulous attention serves not merely as a method of escaping from intolerable pain, but also as an opening from the prison of the self and its wounds to a rejoicing in both human creativity and the things and events of an ordinary day. The story, with its nod of homage to Chekhov, provides an accurate anticipation of the peculiar virtues of Elizabeth Bishop's poetry: her fantastic powers of observation, her impeccable ear, and her precise and often haunting sense of tone.

Her first volume, *North and South*, was a rigorous selection from earlier work. Although some of its poems are set in New York or Paris or New England or have no localized geographical setting, a number of the best ones are firmly placed in Nova Scotia or Florida. *A Cold Spring* continued the emphasis on place: a farm in Maryland, Nova Scotia again, Washington, D.C., Key West and New York, and, with "Arrival at Santos," Brazil, which was to be her home for a number of years. The poems in *Questions of Travel* are divided into two groups: "Brazil" and "Elsewhere." (Another result of her residence in Brazil was her beautiful translation of *The Diary of Helena Morley*.) *The Complete Poems* included new original poems set in Brazil as well as translation from Carlos Drummond de Andrade and João Cabral de Melo Neto.

The title and some of the directions of *Geography III* were anticipated in the final line of "The Map," the first poem in her first volume: "More delicate than the historian's are the map-maker's colors." The map-maker (not the tourist) who comes truly to know differing peoples and their places for himself can see with fresh and multiple perspectives, and his discriminations may well be finer than the historian's if his powers of observation are intense, his sympathies wide, his moral judgments delicate, and his imagination that of a poet.

Miss Bishop's geography is also of the imagination and the soul. Her poems treat their readers with unusual consideration. With the beginning of each poem we know that we *are* somewhere interesting (whether in a real or a surreal or a dream world), and we hear immediately a recognizable human voice: the poems make absorbing sense on a simple or naturalistic level. She is interested in, and asks our respectful attention for, everything that she puts into her poems; ultimate and "large" significances come only (and naturally) out of our experience of the whole.

The consideration is real, and one of its chief instruments is an unusual purity of diction. On a number of occasions one may be surprised to discover an image or detail or even a quoted phrase from the poetry of George Herbert. She found Herbert's example thoroughly congruent with one of the things she admired most about modernist poetry of the early twentieth century: the rejection of familiar public rhetoric and the consciously poetic for a language closer to that of a conversation between literate friends. Miss Bishop has consistently sustained her own high version of that standard: no inversions and no inflations, no Ciceronian periods, no elevated "poetic diction." Her indebtedness to Marianne Moore's imaginative precision is handsomely acknowledged in "Invitation to Miss Marianne Moore" (the poem also owes something to Pablo Neruda). Her uses of other writers are markedly individual: her few epigrams are from Bunyan, Hopkins, and Sir Kenneth Clark; the poignant "Crusoe in England" owes as much to Charles Darwin as to Defoe.

Also like Herbert, Miss Bishop seems to have sought a unique form for almost every poem. Her range extends from prose poems such as "Rainy Season; Sub-Tropics" and "12 O'Clock News" through relatively "free" and blank verse and unrhymed Horatian forms to strict quatrains and elaborately "counter-pointed" stanzas, a double sonnet ("The Prodigal," one of her best poems), sestinas and a villanelle, including along the way the lengthening triplets of "Roosters," derived from Crashaw's "Wishes to his (supposed) Mistress," "Visits to St. Elizabeths," modelled on "The House that Jack Built," a true ballad, "The Burglar of Babylon," and the songs that she wrote for Billie Holiday. Whatever the forms, they provide opportunities rather than limitations, and their art is self-effacing: the lines of "Sestina" end with the words *house, grandmother, child, stove, almanac,* and *tears.* Her use of assonance and slant-rhymes and variable line-lengths and rhyme patterns promises a useful freedom. Her example suggested to Robert Lowell the "way of breaking through the shell of my old manner" indicated by "Skunk Hour."

Miss Bishop has remained remarkably independent of schools or movements, religious, political, or literary. One modern practice that has proved fruitful for her is that of the collage, in which the artist discovers his subject and his form in ordinary or unexpected materials and objects. ("Objects and Apparitions," Bishop's translation of Octavio Paz's poem for Joseph Cornell, suggests the relation between collage and all art – as do her poems on the pictures of her great-uncle George.) Although the fictional speakers of her poems are often moving or witty (the Trollope of the Journals, a Brazilian friend in "Manuelzinho," Crusoe, a giant snail, a very small alien who reports on the writer's desk as a foreign landscape – all remarkable observers), in most of the poems the poet speaks in a voice recognizably her own. That the poems remain deeply personal rather than confessional may owe something to how firmly they are rooted in the "found": "Trouvée" in the flattened white hen on West 4th Street, "The Man-Moth" in a newspaper misprint for *mammoth,* "The Burglar of Babylon" in the fact that on the hills of Rio the rich and poor live their melodramas and lives within sight and sound of each other, "The Moose" in the Nova Scotia busride, "In the Waiting Room" in the events of late afternoon, "the fifth/of February, 1918." Almost every poem of Elizabeth Bishop's represents a human discovery both of the world and of an angle of vision. It is only superficially paradoxical that such creative novelty returns us, like "The Prodigal," to a familiar place and life: "But it took him a long time/finally to make his mind up to go home."

—Joseph H. Summers

BISHOP, John Peale. American. Born in Charles Town, West Virginia, 21 May 1892. Educated at high school in Hagerstown, Maryland; Mercersburg Academy, Pennsylvania; Princeton University, New Jersey, 1913–17 (Managing Editor, *Nassau Literary Magazine*), Litt.B. 1917 (Phi Beta Kappa). Served in the United States Army Infantry, 1917–19: First Lieutenant; Director of the Publications Program, 1941–42, and Special Consultant, 1943, Office of the Coordinator of Inter-American Affairs, Washington, D.C. Married Margaret Grosvenor Hutchins in 1922; three sons. Managing Editor, *Vanity Fair,* New York, 1920–22; free-lance writer from 1922; lived in Paris and Sorrento, 1922–24, New York, 1924–26, France, 1927–33, Louisiana and Connecticut, 1933–37, and in South Chatham, Massachusetts, 1937–44. *Died 4 April 1944.*

PUBLICATIONS

Collections

Collected Poems, edited by Allen Tate. 1948; *Selected Poems,* 1960.
Collected Essays, edited by Edmund Wilson. 1948.

Verse

> *Green Fruit.* 1917.
> *The Undertaker's Garland* (poems and stories), with Edmund Wilson.   1922.
> *Now with His Love.* 1933.
> *Minute Particulars.* 1935.
> *Selected Poems.* 1941.

Fiction

> *Many Thousands Gone* (stories).   1931.
> *Act of Darkness.* 1935.

Other

> Editor, with Allen Tate, *American Harvest: Twenty Years of Creative Writing in the United States.* 1942.

Bibliography: "Bishop: A Checklist" by J. Max Patrick and Robert W. Stallman, in *Princeton University Library Chronicle 7,* 1946.

Reading List: *A Southern Vanguard: The Bishop Memorial Volume* edited by Allen Tate, 1947; "The Achievement of Bishop" by Joseph Frank, in *The Widening Gyre,* 1963; *Bishop* by Robert L. White, 1966; "Bishop and the Other Thirties" by Leslie Fiedler, in *Commentary 43,* 1967; "Bishop" by Allen Tate, in *Essays of Four Decades,* 1968.

*   *   *

John Peale Bishop seems to owe his posthumous reputation to Allen Tate and Edmund Wilson, whose editing of the *Collected Poems* and *Collected Essays* in 1948 brought his most important work to the attention of a small audience. These books have long been out of print, but he continues to attract critics as different as Joseph Frank and Leslie Fiedler, and no account of American literary life between the two World Wars is complete without his name. He was at Princeton with Wilson and F. Scott Fitzgerald and consequently has associations with the milieu popularized by Fitzgerald's early novels; indeed he is the original for a character in *This Side of Paradise.* During the 1930's, especially after his return to America, he was thought of as a Southerner, partly because of his friendship with Tate. His two works of prose fiction are set in the "lost" part of West Virginia where he spent his boyhood and certainly have something in common with the Southern tradition of Faulkner, Caroline Gordon, and the others.

Bishop, however, must be thought of mainly as a poet, and it is the verse of his last decade that is most impressive. His regional allegiances count for very little here, though his residence on Cape Cod after 1938 was surely responsible for such late poems as "A Subject of Sea Change" and the group called "The Statues." These meditations on the sea and the destiny of civilizations carry forward the strongly pictorial qualities of such earlier poems as "The Return." Eventually one should see Bishop as an American poet who is descended from a great tradition of European humanism, and his criticism of the American scene is conducted from this point of view. One of his finest poems, "The Burning Wheel," sets the American pioneers beside the figure of Aeneas:

They, too, the stalwart conquerors of space,
Each on his shoulders wore a wise delirium
Of memory and age: ghostly embrace
Of fathers slanted toward a western tomb.

A hundred and a hundred years they stayed
Aloft, until they were as light as autumn
Shells of locusts. Where then were they laid?
And in what wilderness oblivion?

This refined yet deeply felt humanism is perhaps not characteristic of American writers, and Bishop was a writer on a small scale, but his best work in poetry and criticism survives very well.

—Ashley Brown

BLUNDEN, Edmund (Charles).   English.   Born in London, 1 November 1896. Educated at Cleave's Grammar School, Yalding, Kent; Christ's Hospital; Queen's College, Oxford, M.A. Served with The Southdowns, Royal Sussex Regiment, in France and Belgium, 1916–19: Military Cross; Staff Member, Oxford University Senior Training Corps, 1940–44. Married Claire Margaret Poynting in 1945; four daughters. Professor of English Literature, University of Tokyo, 1924–27; Fellow and Tutor in English Literature, Merton College, Oxford, 1931–43; Member, U.K. Liaison Mission, Tokyo, 1948–50; Professor of English Literature, 1953–64, and Emeritus Professor, 1964–74, University of Hong Kong. Clark Lecturer, Cambridge University, 1932; Professor of Poetry, Oxford University, 1966–68. Recipient: Hawthornden Prize, 1922; Royal Society of Literature Benson Medal, 1932; Queen's Gold Medal for Poetry, 1956; Corporation of London Midsummer Prize, 1970. Litt.D.: Leeds and Leicester universities. Companion of Literature, Royal Society of Literature: Member, Japan Academy. C.B.E. (Commander, Order of the British Empire), 1951; Order of the Rising Sun, 3rd class (Japan), 1963. *Died 20 January 1974.*

PUBLICATIONS

Collections

Verse

Poems, 1913 and 1914.   1914.
Poems, Translated from the French, July 1913-January 1914.   1914.
The Barn, with Certain Other Poems.   1916.

Three Poems.   1916.
The Harbingers.   1916.
Pastorals: A Book of Verses.   1916.
The Waggoner and Other Poems.   1920.
The Shepherd and Other Poems of Peace and War.   1922.
Dead Letters: Poems.   1922.
To Nature: New Poems.   1923.
Masks of Time: A New Collection of Poems, Principally Meditative.   1925.
English Poems.   1925.
Retreat.   1928.
Japanese Garland.   1928.
Near and Far: New Poems   1929.
The Poems 1914–1930.   1930.
A Summer's Fancy.   1930.
To Themis: Poems on Famous Trials, and Other Pieces.   1931.
Halfway House: A Miscellany of New Poems.   1932.
Choice or Chance: New Poems.   1934.
An Elegy and Other Poems.   1937.
On Several Occasions, by a Fellow of Merton College.   1938.
Poems 1930–1940.   1940.
Shells by a Stream: New Poems.   1944.
After the Bombing and Other Short Poems.   1949.
Eastward: A Selection of Verses Original and Translated.   1949.
Records of Friendship: Occasional and Epistolary Poems, edited by T. Nakayama.   1950.
Poems of Many Years.   1957.
A Hong Kong House: Poems 1951–1961.   1962.
Eleven Poems.   1965.
Poems on Japan, Hitherto Uncollected and Mostly Unprinted, edited by T. Saito.   1967.
The Midnight Skaters: Poems for Young Readers, edited by C. Day Lewis.   1968.

Play

The Dede of Pittie: Dramatic Scenes Reflecting the History of Christ's Hospital and Offered in Celebration of the Quatercentenary (produced 1953).   1953.

Fiction

We'll Shift Our Ground; or, Two on a Tour, with Sylvia Norman.   1933.

Other

The Appreciation of Literary Prose.   1921.
The Bonadventure: A Random Journal of an Atlantic Holiday.   1922.
Christ's Hospital: A Retrospect.   1923.
More Footnotes to Literary History: Essays on Keats and Clare.   1926.
On the Poems of Henry Vaughan: Characteristics and Imitations, with His Principal Latin Poems Carefully Translated into English Verse.   1927.
Lectures in English Literature.   1927; revised edition, 1952.
Undertones of War.   1928.
Leigh Hunt's "Examiner" Examined.   1928.

Leigh Hunt: A Biography.   1930; as *Leigh Hunt and His Circle,* 1930.
De Bello Germanico: A Fragment of Trench History.   1930.
Votive Tablets: Studies Chiefly Appreciative of English Authors and Books (includes verse).   1931.
Fall In, Ghosts: An Essay on a Battalion Reunion.   1932.
The Face of England, in a Series of Occasional Sketches.   1932.
The Mind's Eye: Essays.   1934.
Keats's Publisher: A Memoir of John Taylor 1781–1864.   1936.
English Villages.   1941.
Thomas Hardy.   1941.
Cricket Country.   1944.
Shelley: A Life Story.   1946.
Shakespeare to Hardy: Short Studies of Characteristic English Authors.   1948.
Two Lectures on English Literature.   1948.
Sons of Light: A Series of Lectures on English Writers.   1949.
Addresses on General Subjects Connected with English Literature.   1949.
Poetry and Science and Other Lectures.   1949.
Favourite Studies in English Literature.   1950.
Blunden: A Selection of His Poetry and Prose, edited by Kenneth Hopkins.   1950.
Influential Books.   1950.
Reprinted Papers, Partly Concerning Some English Romantic Poets.   1950.
Chaucer to "B.V.," with an Additional Paper on Herman Melville.   1950.
Hamlet and Other Studies.   1950.
A Wanderer in Japan: Sketches and Reflections in Prose and Verse (bilingual edition).   1950.
John Keats.   1950; revised edition, 1954, 1966.
Sketches and Reflections.   1951.
Essayists in the Romantic Period, edited by I. Nishizaki.   1952.
Charles Lamb.   1954; revised edition, 1964.
War Poets 1914–1918.   1958; revised edition, 1964.
Three Young Poets: Critical Sketches of Byron, Shelley, and Keats.   1959.
A Wessex Worthy: Thomas Russell.   1960.
A Corscambe Inhabitant.   1963.
William Crowe 1745–1829.   1963.
Guest of Thomas Hardy.   1964.
A Brief Guide to the Great Church of the Holy Trinity, Long Melford.   1965.
John Clare: Beginner's Luck.   1972.
A Tribute to Walter de la Mare, with Leonard Clark.   1974.

Editor, with Alan Porter, *Poems Chiefly from Manuscript,* by John Clare.   1920.
Editor, *Madrigals and Chronicles, Being Newly Found Poems,* by John Clare.   1924.
Editor, *A Song to David and Other Poems,* by Christopher Smart.   1924.
Editor, *Shelley and Keats as They Struck Their Contemporaries.*   1925.
Editor, with B. Brady, *Selected Poems,* by Bret Harte.   1926.
Editor, *A Hundred English Poems from the Elizabethan Age to the Victorian.*   1927.
Editor, *The Autobiography of Leigh Hunt.*   1928.
Editor, *Last Essays of Elia,* by Charles Lamb,   1929.
Editor, *The Poems of William Collins.*   1929.
Editor, with others, *The War 1914–1918: A Booklist.*   1930.
Editor, *Great Short Stories of the War.*   1930.
Editor, *Sketches in the Life of John Clare Written by Himself.*   1931.
Editor, *The Poems of Wilfrid Owen.*   1931.
Editor, with E. L. Griggs, *Coleridge: Studies by Several Hands on the Hundredth Anniversary of His Death.*   1934.

Editor, *Charles Lamb: His Life Recorded by His Contemporaries.*   1934.
Editor, *Return to Husbandry: An Annotated List of Books Dealing with the History,
    Philosophy, and Craftsmanship of Rural England.*   1943.
Editor, *Hymns for the Amusement of Children,* by Christopher Smart.   1947.
Editor, *Shelley's Defence of Poetry.*   1948.
Editor, with others, *The Christ's Hospital Book.*   1953.
Editor, *Poems, Principally Selected from Unpublished Manuscripts,* by Ivor
    Gurney.   1954.
Editor, *Selected Poems of Shelley.*   1954.
Editor, *Selected Poems of Keats.*   1955.
Editor, *Selected Poems of Tennyson.*   1960.
Editor, with Bernard Mellor, *Wayside Poems of the Early Seventeenth Century.*   1963;
    Early Eighteenth Century, 1964; *Wayside Sonnets 1750–1850,* 1970.

Translator, *Lee Lan Flies the Dragon Kite,* by R. Herrmanns.   1962.

Bibliography: *A Bibliography of Blunden* by B. J. Kirkpatrick, 1978.

Reading List: "The Poetry of Blunden" by Margaret Willy, in *English 11,* 1957; *Blunden* by
A. M. Hardie, 1958; *Heroes' Twilight: A Study of the Literature of the Great War* by Bernard
Bergonzi, 1965; *The Poetry of Blunden* by Michael Thorpe, 1971.

*   *   *

One of the most eloquent and versatile writers of this century, and – because of his
generosity to other writers, to scholars, and to students – one of the most influential, Edmund
Blunden has nevertheless been too often condemned by literary historians and anthologists to
an unenviably restricted fame as a First World War poet who happened to survive for a half-
a-century after the war of which he wrote, and as a Georgian who had the misfortune to
outlive both the utility and the respectability of the movement to which he is said to have
belonged.

Blunden was in truth a poet of the countryside and a poet of war; it is the conjunction of
these two attributes which gives his poetry and his prose-work *Undertones of War* their
especial quality, and sets his work above the range of conventional ruralist writing. He was
nineteen when he went to the Western Front. His countryman's delight in the fecundity of
his own Sussex informed his sorrow as he watched the destruction of Flanders:

> I have seen a green country, useful to the race,
> Knocked silly with guns and mines, its villages vanished,
> Even the last rat and kestrel banished –
> God bless us all, this was peculiar grace.

For him the guns were never silenced; over fifty years the bombardment of mind and spirit
continued. Destruction, waste, futility: these caused him pain but above the discords he
found beauty and beyond the grief he discovered optimism.

"Haunted ever by war's agony" he remained for the rest of his days within the fraternity of
soldiers. It was just one of the communities to which he gave his loyalty and his literary
service. There were others, in Japan and Hong Kong, where he taught and is revered and
perhaps above all, his old school, Christ's Hospital. No author in the whole history of English
letters has paid such generous attention to the place of his education as did Blunden to
Christ's Hospital. Not only did he write a full-length history and several poems and essays
about the school, but he also produced sensitive books on Lamb and Leigh Hunt, two of his
predecessors as Christ's Hospital authors, and was at work on a biography of Coleridge, "the

greatest of our Bluecoat clan," when the last illness ended his life. His sturdy support for that fine poet of the Second War, Keith Douglas, was by his own account inspired in part by responsibility for one of his pupils at Merton College, Oxford, in part by respect for Douglas's gifts as poet and as soldier, but not least because Douglas was yet another Christ's Hospital product.

Wide-ranging and prolific exercise as a literary journalist, the most literate of all books about cricket, *Cricket Country*, editions of Clare, a biography of Shelley, innumerable introductions contributed to other men's books, a range of correspondence such as is rare in our times (and all of it in an exquisite calligraphy) – and still there is more to say about Blunden, for it was he who first presented the poems of Wilfred Owen to the public. But the evidence exists that what would have pleased him most in his long, varied and distinguished career is that two of the finest and most sensitive books about the Second World War, Keith Douglas's *Alamein to Zem Zem* and Douglas Grant's *The Fuel of the Fire*, were by authors who had served their literary apprenticeship under the author of *Undertones of War*.

—J. E. Morpurgo

BLY, Robert (Elwood).   American.   Born in Madison, Minnesota, 23 December 1926. Educated at St. Olaf College, Northfield, Minnesota, 1946–47; Harvard University, Cambridge, Massachusetts, B.A. (magna cum laude) 1950; University of Iowa, Iowa City, M.A. 1956. Served in the United States Navy, 1944–46. Married Carolyn McLean in 1955; four children. Since 1958, Founding-Editor, *The Fifties* magazine (later *The Sixties* and *The Seventies*) and The Fifties Press (later The Sixties and The Seventies Press), Madison, Minnesota. Recipient: Fulbright Fellowship, 1956; Amy Lowell Traveling Fellowship, 1964; Guggenheim Fellowship, 1964, 1972; National Institute of Arts and Letters grant, 1965; Rockefeller Fellowship, 1967; National Book Award, 1968. Lives in Madison, Minnesota.

PUBLICATIONS

Verse

Silence in the Snowy Fields.   1962.
The Lion's Tail and Eyes: Poems Written Out of Laziness and Silence, with James Wright and William Duffy.   1962.
The Light Around the Body.   1967.
Chrysanthemums.   1967.
Ducks.   1968.
The Morning Glory: Another Thing That Will Never Be My Friend: Twelve Prose Poems.   1969; revised edition, 1970.
The Teeth-Mother Naked at Last.   1970.
Poems for Tennessee, with William Stafford and William Matthews.   1971.
Jumping Out of Bed.   1973.
Sleepers Joining Hands.   1973.
Point Reyes Poems.   1974.
The Hockey Poem.   1974.
Old Man Rubbing His Eyes.   1975.
This Body Is Made of Camphor and Gopherwood.   1977.

Other

Editor, with David Ray, *A Poetry Reading Against the Vietnam War*.   1966.
Editor, *The Sea and the Honeycomb: A Book of Tiny Poems*.   1966.
Editor, *Forty Poems Touching on Recent American History*.   1970.
Editor, *Selected Poems*, by David Ignatow.   1975.
Editor, *Leaping Poetry: An Idea with Poems and Translations*.   1975.

Translator, *Reptiles and Amphibians of the World*, by Hans Hvass.   1960.
Translator, with James Wright, *Twenty Poems of Georg Trakl*.   1961.
Translator, *The Story of Gösta Berling*, by Selma Lagerlöf.   1962.
Translator, with James Wright and John Knoepfle, *Twenty Poems of César Vallejo*.   1962.
Translator, with Eric Sellin and Thomas Buckman, *Three Poems*, by Thomas Tranströmer.   1966.
Translator, *Hunger*, by Knut Hamsun.   1967.
Translator, with Christina Paulston, *I Do Best Alone at Night*, by Gunnar Ekelöf.   1967.
Translator, with Christina Paulston, *Late Arrival on Earth: Selected Poems of Gunnar Ekelöf*.   1967.
Translator, with others, *Selected Poems* by Yvan Goll.   1968.
Translator, with James Wright, *Twenty Poems of Pablo Neruda*.   1968.
Translator, *Forty Poems of Juan Ramón Jiménez*.   1969.
Translator, *Ten Poems*, by Issa Kobayashi.   1969.
Translator, with James Wright and John Knoepfle, *Neruda and Vallejo: Selected Poems*.   1971.
Translator, *Twenty Poems of Tomas Tranströmer*.   1971.
Translator, *The Fish in the Sea Is Not Thirsty: Versions of Kabir*.   1971.
Translator, *Night Vision*, by Tomas Tranströmer.   1971.
Translator, *Lorca and Jiménez: Selected Poems*.   1973.
Translator, *Basho*.   1974.
Translator, *Ten Sonnets to Orpheus*, by Rilke.   1974.
Translator, *Friends, You Drank Some Darkness: Three Swedish Poets, Henry Martinson, Gunnar Ekelöf, Tomas Tranströmer*.   1975.
Translator, *Try to Live to See This: Versions of Kabir*.   1976.
Translator, *The Kabir Book*.   1977.
Translator, *The Voices*, by Rilke.   1977.

Bibliography: "Bly Checklist" by Sandy Dorbin, in *Schist 1*, Fall 1973.

Reading List: *Alone with America* by Richard Howard, 1969; "Bly Alive in Darkness" by Anthony Libby, in *Iowa Review*, Summer 1972.

*   *   *

The spirited presence of Robert Bly is felt throughout the realms of modern poetry and literary criticism; he emerged from the early 1960's as one of the more stubbornly independent and critical poets of his generation, bold to state his positions against war and commercial monopoly, spread of federal government, and crassness in literature wherever a forum was open to him. He was a dominating spokesman for the anti-war circles during the course of the Vietnam War, staging readings around the United States and compiling (with David Ray) the extraordinary poetic protests in the anthology, *A Poetry Reading Against the Vietnam War*. Throughout his career, he has been a cranky but refreshing influence on American thought and culture for the very grandeur of his positions and the force he has given to his artistic individuality.

Although his output of poetry has been relatively small in an era of prolific poets, his books follow a distinctive course of deepening conviction and widening of conceptions. *Silence in the Snowy Fields*, his first book, is a slender collection of smooth, mildly surreal evocations of his life in Minnesota and of the landscape, with its harsh winters and huddled townships. Bly's brief poems animate natural settings with a secret, wilful life-force, as in this final stanza from "Snowfall in the Afternoon":

> The barn is full of corn, and moving toward us now,
> Like a hulk blown toward us in a storm at sea:
> All the sailors on deck have been blind for many years.

Silence in the Snowy Fields has an immediacy of the poet's personal life that reflects the inward shift of poetry during the late 1950's and early 1960's, a direction that Bly then actively retreated from, claiming poetry deserved a larger frame of experience than the poet's own circumstances and private dilemmas.

The Light Around the Body moves into the political and social arena, with poems against corporate power and profiteering, presidential politics, and the Vietnam War. Here the poems are charged with greater flight of imagination and a more intensely surreal mode of discourse. The poems wildly juxtapose the familiar with the bizarre, in "A Dream of Suffocation" − "Accountants hover over the earth like helicopters,/Dropping bits of paper engraved with Hegel's name" − and "War and Silence" −

> Filaments of death grow out.
> The sheriff cuts off his black legs
> And nails them to a tree

To explain his poetic and to give it context, Bly edited a volume of poems entitled *Leaping Poetry* in which he argued that consciousness had now expanded to a new faculty of the brain where spiritual and supralogical awareness is stored. His commentary is wonderfully speculative and vivid, but bluffly assertive of its premise. Building on this provocative thesis, he commented in an essay, "I Came Out of the Mother Naked," part of his volume *Sleepers Joining Hands*, that society is now returning to a matriarchal order, where sensuousness of thought and synthetic reason are replacing the patriarchal emphasis on rationality and analytic thinking. *The Kabir Book*, Bly's translations of the 15th-century Indian poet, are an effort to present the work of a figure who both "leaps" in his poetry and illustrates the kind of thinking Bly has argued for recently.

Bly continues to read poetry on the university circuit and to translate Scandinavian literature as his livelihood, but even in these facets of his life he has rooted his new convictions. His readings are now made dramatic with masks, singing, and extemporaneous lectures on the new mind he feels is emerging throughout the West.

—Paul Christensen

BOGAN, Louise. American. Born in Livermore Falls, Maine, 11 August 1897. Educated at Mount St. Mary's Academy, Manchester, New Hampshire, 1907–09; Girls' Latin School, Boston, 1910–15; Boston University, 1915–16. Married 1) Curt Alexander, 1916 (died, 1920), one daughter; 2) Raymond Holden in 1925 (divorced, 1937). Poetry Editor of *The New Yorker*, 1931–70. Visiting Professor, University of Washington, Seattle, 1948; University of

Chicago, 1949; University of Arkansas, 1952; Salzburg Seminar in American Studies, 1958; Brandeis University, Waltham, Massachusetts, 1964–65. Recipient: Guggenheim Fellowship, 1933, 1937; Harriet Monroe Poetry Award, 1948; National Institute of Arts and Letters grant, 1951; Bollingen Prize, 1955; Academy of American Poets Fellowship, 1959; Brandeis University Creative Arts Award, 1961; National Endowment for the Arts grant, 1967. Library of Congress Chair in Poetry, 1945–46. L.H.D.: Western College for Women, Oxford, Ohio, 1956; Litt.D.: Colby College, Waterville, Maine, 1960. Member, American Academy of Arts and Letters. *Died 4 February 1970.*

PUBLICATIONS

Collections

What the Woman Lived: Selected Letters 1920–1970, edited by Ruth Limmer.   1973.

Verse

Body of This Death.   1923.
Dark Summer.   1929.
The Sleeping Fury.   1937.
Poems and New Poems.   1941.
Collected Poems 1923–1953.   1954.
The Blue Estuaries: Poems 1923–1968.   1968.

Other

Works in the Humanities Published in Great Britain 1939–1946: A Select List.   1950.
Achievement in American Poetry 1900–1950.   1951.
Selected Criticism: Prose, Poetry.   1955.
A Poet's Alphabet: Reflections on the Literary Art and Vocation, edited by Robert Phelps and Ruth Limmer.   1970.

Editor, with William Jay Smith, *The Golden Journey: Poems for Young People.*   1965.

Translator, with W. H. Auden and Elizabeth Mayer, *The Sorrows of Young Werther, and Novella,* by Goethe.   1971.

Reading List: "Bogan and Léonie Adams" by Elder Olson, in *Chicago Review 8,* Fall 1954.

*   *   *

Louise Bogan's collected poems, *The Blue Estuaries,* make up a slender volume that brings together work published from 1923 to 1968. She rarely wrote poems longer than a page, and all her earlier published books are brief and cut to the bone. She was a relentless reviser of her work and a slow, cautious craftsman who refused publishers' urgings to increase her output.

Although she was keenly aware of the revolutions in poetic technique throughout her life, her poems adhered to rhyme and set meter and treated the themes of love, regret, death, memory, landscape meditation in subtly alliterative language. Her style shows the influence of Emily Dickinson and perhaps the wit of Metaphysical poetry, but the essential charm of her best work is the quiet, feminine perception she expresses in her strict, tightly framed forms, as in "Second Song," an early poem:

> I said out of sleeping:
> Passion, farewell.
> Take from my keeping
> Bauble and shell.
>
> Black salt, black provender.
> Tender your store
> To a new pensioner,
> To me no more.

Although she relaxes into a certain lyric frankness of feeling in her later work, her style of spare restraint remains consistent throughout her work. In several of her poems a more strident feminine consciousness flares, as in "Women," with its sardonic portrayal of woman caught in her stereotype of the put-upon mate:

> Their love is an eager meaninglessness
> Too tense, or too lax.
>
> They hear in every whisper that speaks to them
> A shout and a cry.
> As like as not, when they take life over their door-sills
> They should let it go by.

Bogan regarded the poem as a deliberate and highly worked distillation of thought, and was perhaps too strict with her own imagination. The fire and wit of her mind are muted in most of her poetry but luxuriously displayed in her brilliant correspondence, collected in *What the Woman Lived*, where her sarcasm and acute critical nature are shared with a circle of notable literary figures of her time, including Edmund Wilson, Morton Dauwen Zabel, Rolfe Humphries, and Theodore Roethke.

Like her poetry, her critical writing eschewed partisanship and fashion in favor of a classical standard of moderation, balance, and form. As the poetry critic for *The New Yorker*, she was well known for her honest and abrasive judgments of the work of even her close friends, and her essays of these years, published in *A Poet's Alphabet*, endure in their accuracy and acumen. A brief treatise on modern poetry, *Achievement in American Poetry 1900–1950*, though merely a sketch of the main trends of these years, argues a provocative thesis that female poets of the late 19th century were chiefly responsible for revitalizing poetry with their sensuous, daring imaginations.

—Paul Christensen

BRATHWAITE, Edward. Barbadian. Born in Bridgetown, Barbados, 11 May 1930. Educated at Harrison College, Barbados; Pembroke College, Cambridge (Barbados Scholar), 1950–54, B.A. (honours) in history 1953, Cert. Ed. 1954; University of Sussex, Brighton, 1965–68, D.Phil. 1968. Married Doris Monica Welcome in 1960; one son. Education Officer,

Ministry of Education, Ghana, 1955–62; Tutor, University of the West Indies Extra Mural Department, St. Lucia, 1962–63. Lecturer, 1963–72, and since 1972 Senior Lecturer in History, University of the West Indies, Kingston. Plebiscite Officer in the Trans-Volta Togoland, United Nations, 1956–57. Founding Secretary, Caribbean Artists Movement, 1966. Since 1970, Editor, *Savacou* magazine, Mona. Recipient: Arts Council of Great Britain bursary, 1967; Camden Arts Festival prize, London, 1967; Cholmondeley Award, 1970; Guggenheim Fellowship, 1972; City of Nairobi Fellowship, 1972; Bussa Award, 1973. Lives in Kingston, Jamaica.

PUBLICATIONS

Verse

Rights of Passage. 1967; *Masks,* 1968; *Islands,* 1969; combined version, as *The Arrivants,* 1973.
Other Exiles. 1975.
Mother Poem. 1977.

Plays

Four Plays for Primary Schools (produced 1961–62). 1964.
Odale's Choice (produced 1962). 1967.

Other

The People Who Came, 1–3 (textbooks). 3 vols., 1968–72.
Folk Culture of the Slaves in Jamaica. 1970.
The Development of Creole Society in Jamaica. 1971.
Caribbean Man in Space and Time. 1974.
Contradictory Omens: Cultural Diversity and Integration in the Caribbean. 1974.

Editor, *Iouanaloa: Recent Writing from St. Lucia.* 1963.

Bibliography: in *Savacou Bibliographical Series 2,* 1973.

*   *   *

Edward Brathwaite has emerged as one of the major writers in contemporary West Indian literature. His trilogy *Rights of Passage, Masks,* and *Islands* (reprinted as *The Arrivants*) is an epic of sorts on Black West Indian history and culture. Much of his present reputation rests on that trilogy, although he has published other poetry, and his scholarly writing has established him as a West Indian historian. Paradoxically, however, Brathwaite's reputation as a poet-historian of the "Black diaspora" sometimes has the effect of minimizing rather than illuminating his full achievements as a poet. The point is not, of course, that the themes of Black ethnicity are themselves insignificant. Indeed the opposite is the truth, a truth that needs to be repeatedly emphasized in light of the fact that ethnic and national consciousness has historically been an underdeveloped aspect of West Indian life. And, accordingly, writers like Brathwaite have had a significant impact on their Caribbean readership because their ethnic themes appeal to a cultural consciousness that has only assumed mass proportions since the achievement of nationhood. Brathwaite's appeal as an ethnic poet is in itself an interesting reflection on the belated nature of the ethnic awakening.

Indeed, the intensity with which Brathwaite has been received in some quarters has tended to limit perception and analysis of his less obtrusive but crucial emphasis on the complex texture of West Indian history and identity. That texture reflects the distinctive intermingling of African, European, and American elements that is characteristic of West Indian society. For like the equally distinguished Derek Walcott (St. Lucia) with whom he is more often contrasted than compared, Brathwaite really perceives and describes the West Indies as a synthesis of diverse cultural traditions. *Islands*, for example, reflects the contributions of Western religion and literature, just as much as the symbols of Akan culture pervade the language and vision of *Masks*. And on the whole the techniques and themes of the trilogy are an example as well as explication of this Afro-Caribbean diversity.

There is also a danger of approaching Brathwaite, in strictly thematic terms, as a compiler of historical statements about the West Indian experience rather than as a complex artist whose crucial cultural themes are interwoven with a sophisticated awareness of the nature of his own art as poet. In fact his poetry is not only socially descriptive but also introspective in that it explores the function of the poetic imagination itself and by extension the implications of the artist's identity. The quest themes of the trilogy are illustrative here. In one sense they reinforce a sense of cultural and historical continuities, or movements, as we move with Brathwaite's composite cultural archetypes from the Caribbean to North America and back (*Rights of Passage*), to West Africa (*Masks*) and back to the Caribbean (*Islands*). But in another sense this cultural quest is an allegory, dramatizing the nature and function of the artist's imagination: art is a journey through time and space, analogous to and at the same time inseparable from memory itself – the memory of the poet as individual artist, the imaginative memory of all artists like himself (the Black musician, for example) and the collective memory of the poet's people as it is manifested in their songs, dances, and other folk art forms. Moreover, as an act of memory the artistic imagination imitates the cycles of time itself, imitating and exemplifying the manner in which the mind simultaneously anticipates the future and recreates the past in the present: the Akan sounds of welcome in *Masks*, for example, greet the West Indian visitor returning to West African roots but they simultaneously evoke the earlier, unsuspecting offer of hospitality to the seventeenth-century slavetrader. Brathwaite is therefore a poet-historian both on the basis of his vision of cultural history and in light of the manner in which his poetic imagination imitates perceived patterns of time and history.

—Lloyd W. Brown

BRENNAN, Christopher (John). Australian. Born in Sydney, New South Wales, 1 November 1870. Educated at Riverview School, Sydney; University of Sydney, M.A. 1892; studied philosophy and classics at the University of Berlin (travelling scholarship), 1892–94. Married Anna Elizabeth Werth in 1897 (divorced, 1925); two sons. Assistant Librarian, rising to Chief Cataloguer, Sydney Public Library, 1897–1908; joined the Modern Languages Department, University of Sydney, 1908: Lecturer in French and German, 1908–1920; Associate Professor of German and Comparative Literature, 1920–25; schoolteacher, 1926–32. Recipient: Commonwealth Literary Fund pension. *Died 7 October 1932.*

PUBLICATIONS

Collections

The Verse, The Prose, edited by A. R. Chisholm and J. J. Quinn.   2 vols., 1960–62.

Verse

XVIII Poems, Being the First Collection of Verse and Prose.   1897.
XXI Poems (1893–1897): Towards the Source.   1897.
Poems 1913.   1914.
A Chant of Doom and Other Verses.   1918.
Twenty-Three Poems.   1928.

Play

A Mask, with John Le Gay Brereton, Jr. (produced 1913).   1913.

Other

Editor, with G. G. Nicholson, *Passages for Translation into French and German.*   1914.

Bibliography: *Brennan: A Comprehensive Bibliography* by Walter Stone and Hugh
Anderson, 1959.

Reading List: *Brennan* by H. M. Green, 1939; *Brennan: The Man and His Poetry,* 1946, and
A Study of Brennan's "A Forest of Night," 1970, both by A. R. Chisholm; *New Perspectives
on Brennan's Poetry* by G. A. Wilkes, 1952; *Brennan* by James McAuley, 1973.

*   *   *

Christopher Brennan, a legend still in Australian literature, belonged, like Herman Melville
in *Clarel* and Walter Pater in *Marius the Epicurean* to that numerous company of 19th-
century writers who, finding belief too difficult, found unbelief even more difficult, and so
embarked on an impossible quest for certainties. Writing of the doctrine of correspondences,
Brennan said in an essay on Nineteenth Century Literature (1904): "What spiritual fact needs
is corroboration, and of corroboration it can never have enough." His verse traces the inner
history of an unremitting search, as elusive as the alchemists' dream, for corroboration, for
intellectual confirmation of faith.

Brennan was a devout Catholic, of Irish parentage, who as a young university student
abandoned his intention to become a priest and became estranged from the practice of his
faith. This loss of commitment is likely to have affected him more deeply than he admitted,
and it is possible he tried to internalize his vocation, first as a philosopher, then as a poet,
seeking a religion without a personal god. Keats's *Endymion* seems to have initiated him into
the poet's perennial quest, and it is possible that he came into contact with esoteric ideas
before he left Sydney, perhaps by reading Maitland's novels, or by associating with
Spiritualists, or through hints in Pater. When he arrived in Berlin and became aware of the
French Symbolist movement, he found Mallarmé's theory and practice of poetry immensely
congenial to him, though the cast of his mind and his style in prose and verse belong much

more to the German tradition than to the French. As a technician Brennan is indeed a mosaic of the Victorians, and, through the Victorians, an inheritor of Miltonic eloquence. His chief affinities, he said later in life, were Mallarmé and Coventry Patmore! More important, Brennan was above all a scholar-poet; he was indeed one of Australia's most brilliant classical scholars, whose theories about the manuscripts of Aeschylus attracted the attention of Jowett, and have since been vindicated. On this foundation and on that of a wide knowledge of German, Italian and French, he pursued his studies in German theosophy, Jewish mysticism, and Eastern gnosticism, while his personal and professional life began to crumble around him, and in the end he returned, with enriched understanding of the common human predicament, to the simple pieties of his youth, "*naturaliter Christiana*." In an essay on Mallarmé he spoke of throwing the mystics overboard and returning to the visible world: "Our daily bread, if we are satisfied with it, will prove richer than we thought."

Brennan's reputation rests principally on *Poems 1913*, though "Fifteen Poems," circulated in typescript and published after his death as "The Burden of Tyre," is of great interest in foreshadowing the complexities of his Eden symbol, to be fully explored in the main work.

Brennan is the one Australian poet who practised what Arnold would have recognised as "the grand style," and, though it was going out of fashion when he wrote and is quite obsolete now, it could be argued that no other would have served his theme quite so well, even though it lays him open to charges of using archaic poetic diction, occasional Victorian lushness or Pre-Raphaelite sweetness, and syntactically convoluted paragraphs.

It is divided into five sections or "movements," for if, as has been claimed, *Poems 1913* is a *livre composé*, it is so in a musical rather than a purely literary sense. "Towards the Source" is the first step on the journey towards the innermost self, through the agency of love and marriage. Though, as in the poems as a whole, the autobiographical element is strong, it would be unwise to ignore esoteric interpretations of "nuptial exchanges," especially in view of the alchemical references scattered throughout. "The Forest of Night" is the most sustained and powerful attempt to penetrate to the depths of the unconscious, and the brooding and majestic figure of Lilith, "mournful until we find her fair," is one of the most compelling symbols in modern English verse of the mysterious, terrible, yet fascinating womb of becoming, of the Void in which all possibilities wait for being, where "gods and stars and songs and souls of men/are the sparse jewels in her scattered hair." The third movement, "The Wanderer," returns us to the conscious world with its ever-present conflict between social and individual man, between the longing for security and the urge to explore, symbolised in contrasting images of window and hearth, of winds and sea. Questing is accepted as an end in itself, necessary to continuing life, and courage is its moral imperative. The two final sections, "Pauca Mea" and "Epilogues," in turn agonised and defiant, culminate not in capitulation, but in the quiet wisdom of "1908," which offers staff and scrip for the journey. In spite of Brennan's deep involvement with the French symbolists and the legacy of Hegel and Novalis, it is conceivable that he drew his theories of poetry from earlier sources, from Augustine's "Rhetoric of Silence," for example, with its vision of the world as a divine poem which man had to learn, while in the flesh, to read, in the expectation of encountering its meaning in the spirit, face to face. The notion of the "grand man" may also have come to him, not from Swedenborg, but more directly from Origen.

As a poet, Brennan is still, as he was in his lifetime, isolated from the main tradition of Australian poetry. His is the work of a man struggling with a great internal solitude, and in it he accuses not only himself, but his society and his civilisation of a "total dereliction from the human path, the human dream" and sees mankind, perhaps, as a fellow-poet saw him: "a star in exile, unconstellated at the south," alienated from his true self as the image of God.

—Dorothy Green

BROOKE, Rupert (Chawner). English. Born in Rugby, Warwickshire, 3 August 1887. Educated at Hillbrow School; Rugby School, 1901–06; King's College, Cambridge, 1906. Served in the Artists' Rifles and the Royal Naval Division, 1914–15: Sub-Lieutenant. Wrote travel letters from the U.S.A. and the South Seas for the *Westminster Gazette*, London, 1913. *Died 23 April 1915.*

PUBLICATIONS

Collections

Poetical Works, edited by Geoffrey Keynes. 1946.
The Prose, edited by Christopher Hassall. 1956.
The Letters, edited by Geoffrey Keynes. 1968.
A Reappraisal and Selection, edited by Timothy Rogers. 1971.

Verse

Poems. 1911.
1914 and Other Poems. 1915.
Collected Poems. 1915; revised edition, 1918, 1928; as *Complete Poems*, 1932.
Selected Poems. 1917.

Play

Lithuania (produced 1915). 1915.

Other

John Webster and the Elizabethan Drama. 1916.
Letters from America. 1916.
Fragments Now First Collected, edited by R. M. G. Potter. 1925.
Democracy and the Arts. 1946.

Bibliography: *A Bibliography of the Works of Brooke* by Geoffrey Keynes, 1954, revised edition, 1964.

Reading List: *Brooke: A Biography* by Christopher Hassall, 1964; *The Handsomest Young Man in England: Rupert Brooke: A Biographical Essay* by Michael Hastings, 1967.

* * *

When Rupert Brooke died in 1915, he was twenty-seven years old and at the height of his fame and popularity. Henry James wrote of his death: "If there was a stupid and hideous disfigurement of life or outrage to beauty left for our awful conditions to perpetrate, these things have now been supremely achieved and no other brutal blow in the private sphere can better them for making one just stare through one's tears"; and D. H. Lawrence commented: "Bright Phoebus smote him down. It was all in the saga." His apotheosis was achieved then and rests now on the legend of his physical beauty and the passionate and patriotic sonnets which he wrote on the outbreak of war. These poems of 1914 proclaim the value of sacrifice and suffering over the "little emptiness" and selfishness of everyday life. Their appeal and the appeal of such arguments have been diminished by the slaughter which Brooke never saw, and which informs the now better-known poetry of Sassoon, Owen, and Rosenberg.

The contemporary enthusiasm for and equally excessive later reaction against the war sonnets have tended to obscure the considerable achievement of Brooke's other work in poetry and prose. The graceful and ironic earlier love sonnets, like "Oh! Death will find me, long before I tire/Of watching you," deserve to be better known, as do Brooke's more realistic experiments. The twin sonnets "Menelaus and Helen," for example, picture their dramatic reunion as Troy burns, and then the unsung "Long, connubial years." He grows deaf and she becomes a scold: "So Menelaus nagged; and Helen cried;/And Paris slept on by Scamander side." "The Old Vicarage, Grantchester" – Brooke's best-known poem, apart from "The Soldier" – indicates the elegance and wit of which he was capable:

> And in that garden, black and white,
> Creep whispers through the grass all night;
> And spectral dance, before the dawn,
> A hundred Vicars down the lawn;
> Curates, long dust, will come and go
> On lissom, clerical, printless toe;
> And off between the boughs is seen
> The sly shade of a Rural Dean...

This witty facility with poetic diction and the rhyming couplet is seen to good advantage elsewhere in Brooke's verse, as in "Heaven," where the fish hope for an aquatic Paradise and the poet smiles at the shapes taken by such faith:

> But somewhere, beyond Space and Time,
> Is wetter water, slimier slime!
> And there (they trust) there swimmeth One
> Who swam ere rivers were begun,
> Immense, of fishy form and mind,
> Squamous, omnipotent, and kind;
> And under that Almighty Fin,
> The littlest fish may enter in.

He succeeds easily in this whimsically witty and very English vein, but there are signs of a wider range of interest and a less silvery style, which render suspect the too common deployment of Brooke as a gilded foil to later and grimmer war poets.

—M. J. Alexander

BROOKS, Gwendolyn. American. Born in Topeka, Kansas, 17 June 1917. Educated at Wilson Junior College, Chicago, graduated 1936. Married Henry L. Blakely in 1939; one son, one daughter. Publicity Director, National Association for the Advancement of Colored People Youth Council, Chicago, in the 1930's. Taught at Northeastern Illinois State College, Chicago, Columbia College, Chicago, Elmhurst College, Illinois, and the University of

Wisconsin, Madison; Distinguished Professor of the Arts, City College of the City University of New York, 1971. Editor, *The Black Position* magazine; Member, Illinois Arts Council. Recipient: Guggenheim Fellowship, 1946, 1947; National Institute of Arts and Letters grant, 1946; Pulitzer Prize, 1950; Friends of Literature Award, 1964; Monsen Award, 1964; Anisfield-Wolf Award, 1968; Black Academy Award, 1971; Shelley Memorial Award, 1976. L.H.D.: Columbia College, 1964; D. Litt.: Lake Forest College, Illinois, 1965; Brown University, Providence, Rhode Island, 1974. Poet Laureate of Illinois, 1969. Member, National Institute of Arts and Letters, 1976. Lives in Chicago.

PUBLICATIONS

Verse

A Street in Bronzeville.   1945.
Annie Allen.   1949.
Bronzeville Boys and Girls.   1956.
The Bean Eaters (verse for children).   1960.
Selected Poems.   1963.
In the Time of Detachment, In the Time of Cold.   1965.
In the Mecca.   1968.
For Illinois 1968: A Sesquicentennial Poem.   1968.
Riot.   1969.
Family Pictures.   1970.
Aloneness.   1971.
Beckonings.   1975.

Fiction

Maud Martha.   1953.

Other

A Portion of That Field, with others.   1967.
The World of Gwendolyn Brooks (miscellany).   1971.
Report from Part One: An Autobiography.   1972.
The Tiger Who Wore White Gloves; or, You Are What You Are (juvenile).   1974.

Editor, *A Broadside Treasury.*   1971.
Editor, *Jump Bad: A New Chicago Anthology.*   1971.

*   *   *

Gwendolyn Brooks solves the critical question of whether to judge black poetry in America by standards different from those applied to white poetry: she simply writes so powerfully and universally out of the black American milieu that the question does not arise. Her poems may sometimes be bitter, angry, or threatening, but always they are poems and never mere propaganda. She may personally feel caught between racial allegiance and the need for social action on the one hand and purer and higher art on the other, but in her work the distinction dissolves.

Indeed, *In the Mecca*, published in 1968, and especially the poems published since, reflect the conversion from deep racial pride to a harsher militancy that she experienced under the tutelage of a group of young blacks at a meeting at Fisk University in 1967. Thus she speaks in "Young Africans" (from *Family Pictures*) of "our black revival, our black vinegar,/our hands and our hot blood," and warns in the acerbic *Riot*, "Cabot! John! You are a desperate man,/and the desperate die expensively today." But nearly always she finds the tight poetic structure, the *things* in which to embody the idea, so that the reader comes away with that sense of surprise and delight at the insight – in addition to any other emotion – that means that the work was a poem, and that the poem was a fine one.

Gwendolyn Brooks has devoted much of her time since the late 1960's to helping young black Americans, and especially writers. But she speaks out of the American consciousness and to the American conscience, and it is the color-blind America that has rightly given her a Pulitzer Prize, the Poet Laureateship of the State of Illinois, and other testaments to her great lyrical voice.

—Alan R. Shucard

BROWN, Sterling (Allen).   American.   Born in Washington, D.C., 1 May 1901. Educated at public schools in Washington, D.C.; Williams College, Williamstown, Massachusetts, A.B. 1925 (Phi Beta Kappa); Harvard University, Cambridge, Massachusetts, A.M. 1930. Married Daisy Turnbull in 1919. Teacher, Virginia Seminary and College, Lynchburg, 1923–26, Lincoln University, Jefferson City, Missouri, 1926–28, and Fisk University, Nashville, Tennessee, 1929. Since 1929, Professor of English, Howard University, Washington, D.C. Visiting Professor, New York University, New School for Social Research, New York, Sarah Lawrence College, Bronxville, New York, and Vassar College, Poughkeepsie, New York. Literary Editor, *Opportunity* magazine, in the 1930's; Editor of *Negro Affairs* for the Federal Writers' Project, 1936–39. Recipient: Guggenheim Fellowship, 1937. Lives in Washington, D.C.

PUBLICATIONS

Verse

> *Southern Road.* 1932.
> *The Last Ride of Wild Bill and Eleven Narrative Poems.* 1975.

Other

> *Outline for the Study of the Poetry of American Negroes* (study guide for James Weldon Johnson's *The Book of American Negro Poetry*). 1931.
> *The Negro in American Fiction.* 1937.
> *Negro Poetry and Drama.* 1937.

> Editor, with Arthur P. Davis and Ulysses Lee, *The Negro Caravan.* 1941.

*   *   *

Essentially a traditional song-maker and story teller, Sterling Brown has witnessed cross-currents of American literature, and chooses in his poetry to depict blacks and the clash of their roles with those of whites in the variegated society of the American South, particularly in the time caught between two world wars.

His poetry has been collected in anthologies as early as James Weldon Johnson's *The Book of American Negro Poetry* (1922), and, like Johnson himself and Langston Hughes, he set about disrupting the patently false and banal image of the docile American Negro with his charming *patois*, artificially stylized and mimicked by the whites in the minstrel shows still popular in the 1920's and 1930's. Johnson says in his preface of Hughes and Brown that they "*do* use a dialect, but it is not the dialect of the comic minstrel tradition or the sentimental plantation tradition; it is the common, racy, living, authentic speech of the Negro in certain phases of real life."

Brown uses original Afro-American ballads such as "Casey Jones," "John Henry," and "Staggolee" as counterpoint for his modern ones, but the portent of his ironic wit should not be underestimated, for it is actually a tool to shape an ironic, infernal vision of American life as Hades: "The Place was Dixie I took for Hell," says Slim in "Slim in Hell." The American Negro is heralded not as Black Orpheus but as modern tragic hero Mose, a leader of *all* people while futilely attempting to save his own: "A soft song, filled with a misery/Older than Mose will be." In "Sharecropper" he is broken as Christ was broken; his landlord "shot him in the side" to put him out of his misery; he is lost and wild as Odysseus in "Odyssey of a Big Boy"; and found again:

> Man wanta live
> Man want find himself
> Man gotta learn
> How to go it alone.

Though minimal in quantity, Brown's poetry is epic in conception; his ballad, blues, and jazz forms are the vehicles for creative insight into themes of American life.

—Carol Lee Saffioti

BUNTING, Basil. English. Born in Scotswood on Tyne, Northumberland, 1 March 1900. Educated at Ackworth School; Leighton Park School; London School of Economics. Jailed as a conscientious objector during World War 1. Married 1) Marian Culver in 1930; 2) Sima Alladadian in 1948; two children. Assistant Editor, *Transatlantic Review*, Paris, in the 1920's; Music Critic, *The Outlook*, London; lived in Italy and the United States in the 1930's; Persian Correspondent for *The Times*, London, after World War II; Sub-Editor, Newcastle *Morning Chronicle*, for 12 years. Taught at the University of California, Santa Barbara; Poetry Fellow, universities of Durham and Newcastle, 1968–70; taught at the universities of British Columbia, Vancouver; Binghamton, New York; and Victoria, British Columbia. Since 1972, President, the Poetry Society, London; since 1973, President, Northern Arts. Recipient: Arts Council bursary, 1966. D. Litt.: University of Newcastle, 1971. Lives in Northumberland.

PUBLICATION

Verse

> Redimiculum Matellarum. 1930.
> Poems 1950. 1950.
> Loquitur. 1965.
> The Spoils. 1965.
> Ode II/2. 1965.
> First Book of Odes. 1966.
> Briggflatts. 1966.
> Two Poems. 1967.
> What the Chairman Told Tom. 1967.
> Collected Poems. 1968.
> Descant on Rawley's Madrigal (Conversations with Jonathan Williams). 1968.
> Collected Poems. 1978.

Other

> Editor, Selected Poems, by Joseph Skipsey. 1976.

Bibliography: Bunting: A Bibliography of Works and Criticism by Roger Guedalla, 1973.

Reading List: "Bunting Issue" of Agenda 4, 1966.

*   *   *

Until the mid-1960's Basil Bunting was almost completely neglected in England, although he had established an enthusiastic and discriminating group of admirers in America, including some of the leading Beat and Black Mountain poets. This was partly because most of his literary connections were with American poets, notably Ezra Pound and Louis Zukofsky. The critical euphoria at the time of his "re-discovery" in the later 1960's, which presented him as an overlooked genius almost comparable to Hopkins, has now given way to a more balanced view of him as a distinguished but minor poet; Bunting himself has always insisted on his minor status.

In the 1920's and 1930's Bunting came into contact with many of the leading literary figures of the time, including Yeats, Eliot, Lawrence, Ford Madox Ford, Tzara, Williams, and Hemingway, as well as Pound and Zukofsky, both of whom exerted a powerful influence on his earlier work, although he maintains that a fellow-northerner, Wordsworth, is the most important literary force behind his poetry. Of the English poets who emerged during the inter-war years, Bunting is probably the one most in tune with American modernism, and his work exhibits many characteristics of early Pound and Eliot, such as musical free verse, a wealth of literary and mythological allusions, and the satiric use of parody and irony. During the 1930's Bunting eschewed the political and propagandist poetry of many of his English contemporaries, although, as someone who had been imprisoned during World War I as a conscientious objector, he could not be accused of being an aesthete without any social commitment or political views. Eliot eventually decided against publishing Bunting among the Faber poets in 1951 because he was "too Poundian." Poundian as his poems of the 1920's and 1930's are, they reveal some of the best qualities of Pound: meticulous craftsmanship, an acute ear for the music of words, and a freedom from the stultifying conventions of much English, as opposed to American, poetry of the time. And poems like "Villon," "Chomei at

Toyama," and many of the odes are not simply derivative. Bunting's own voice can be heard clearly not only in his well-known dialect ballad "The Complaint of the Morpethshire Farmer," but also in such delicate and well-wrought lyrics as "Southwind, tell her what" and "A thrush in the syringa sings."

Bunting was a music critic in the 1920's and he has always adhered to the Symbolist view that poetry should aspire to the condition of music, and insists on its aural nature. For him, a poem on the page is incomplete; it exists fully only when read aloud: to experience poetry is to hear it. He has collected all but one of his longer poems under the heading "Sonatas" and his work contains numerous references to music. But it is in his masterpiece, *Briggflatts*, a spiritual and Symbolist "autobiography" written after a long period of silence, that he brings his preoccupation with the music of poetry to full flower. Its rich assonantal and alliterative textures and its concentrated pithiness of expression, recalling Anglo-Saxon poetry as well as Hopkins, are the culmination of his efforts to produce pure poetry, but the structure of the entire work is itself musical, in the way that Eliot's *Four Quartets* are. Like each of the *Quartets*, to which it is indebted, *Briggflatts* is in five sections or "movements," as Bunting calls them, although it also contains a short coda, and the analogy to musical form is pursued throughout. One reason for the success and individuality of *Briggflatts* is that Bunting draws more heavily than in any other poem on his own north-country heritage, which he greatly values. He is intent on defining himself in terms of his cultural origins, and the poem relates the present to a tradition descending from the ancient kingdom of Northumbria. Compared with his two poetic masters, Wordsworth and Pound, Bunting appears as a poet decidedly limited in range and scope, but, within the fairly narrow confines within which he has chosen to work, his poetry is exquisitely written, and *Briggflatts* is likely to remain one of the outstanding English poems from the second half of this century.

—Peter Lewis

BUTLER, (Frederick) Guy. South African.   Born in Cradock, Cape Province, 21 January 1918. Educated at a local high school; Rhodes University, Grahamstown, M.A. 1939; Brasenose College, Oxford, M.A. 1947. Served during World War II in the Middle East, Italy, and the United Kingdom. Married Jean Murray Satchwell in 1940; three sons, one daughter. Lecturer in English, University of the Witwatersrand, Johannesburg, 1948–50. Since 1952, Professor of English, Rhodes University, Grahamstown. Editor, with Ruth Harnett, *New Coin* poetry quarterly, Grahamstown. D.Litt.: University of Natal, Durban, 1968. Lives in Grahamstown.

PUBLICATIONS

Verse

Stranger to Europe.   1952; augmented edition, 1960.
South of the Zambezi: Poems from South Africa.   1966.
On First Seeing Florence.   1968.
Selected Poems.   1975.
Ballads and Songs.   1977.

Plays

The Dam (produced 1953).   1953.
The Dove Returns (produced 1956).   1956.
Take Root or Die (produced 1966).   1970.
Cape Charade (produced 1968). ˙ 1968.

Other

An Aspect of Tragedy.   1953.
The Republic of the Arts.   1964.

Editor, A Book of South African Verse.   1959.
Editor, When Boys Were Men.   1969.
Editor, The 1820 Settlers.   1974.

*   *   *

When Guy Butler was serving as a soldier in Italy he carried his paintings with him in a shell-case, hoping to return to his native South Africa with a pictorial record of his European experiences. His poems and plays reflect a life-long attempt to contrast what Europe and Africa mean to him. In "Cape Coloured Batman" Butler finds himself on the "terraced groves of Tuscany," contemplating the pathetic fusion of Europe and Africa in the shape of the despised half-caste. But in "Servant Girl" he is aware of his distance from true African culture:

> [She is] singing a song which seems more integral
> With rain-rinsed sky and sandstone hill
> Than any cadence wrung
> From my taut tongue.

Butler's descriptive talent enables him to present sympathetically the African ritualistic killing of an ox, or, in "Isibongo of Matiwane," a legendary warrior:

> Matiwane, royal, wearing the blood-red feathers of the lourie,
> his eyes red, red his lips from drinking the blood of strong men,
> moves over the earth with the speed of a startled gnu.

Sometimes, as in "The Underdogs," Butler is sharply satirical about White South Africa:

> "Lord, save the shining Christian culture
> Of White South Africa!" Then squat
> Heroically behind clean Vickers guns
> Jabbering death in our innocent hands.

But a more characterisitc attitude is the positive desire, as expressed in the long poem, "Home Thoughts," to "civilize my semi-barbarous land" by the meeting and mating of European clarity (Apollo) and African primitive instinct (Black Dionysus).

Guy Butler's range is wide. He can recount family anecdotes in a simple, but moving, manner; recall poignantly the ironies of war; or paint for us his Cradock Mountains in lines both detailed and lyrical. Varied though his style is, it is always verbally inventive (a train whistle "drove a long spear through/The unexpecting stillness") and rich with a painter's vision. It can adapt itself to many poetic strands – social satire, elegy, narrative, or religious meditation. His stylistic flexibility succeeds outstandingly in the long poem *On First Seeing Florence*, a masterly evocation of personal experiences leading to profound metaphysical intuitions.

His major plays, *The Dam* and *The Dove Returns*, are verse dramas on South African themes. *The Dam* is an anguished, but not despairing, symbolic play about personal destinies within a multi-racial society, written in a verse which modulates remarkably from colloquial idiom to impassioned utterance.

Guy Butler's achievement, in poems and plays, has been to look profoundly and honestly at South African life today, and to write about it with sensitive clarity in an original style which avoids eccentricities.

—Dennis Davison

CAMPBELL, Alistair (Te Ariki).   New Zealander.   Born in Rarotonga, Cook Islands, 25 June 1925; emigrated to New Zealand in 1933. Educated at Otago Boys' High School, Dunedin; Victoria University of Wellington, B.A. in Latin and English. Married 1) the poet Fleur Adcock (divorced), two sons; 2) Meg Anderson in 1958, three children. Editor, Department of Education School Publications Branch, Wellington, 1955–72. Since 1972, Senior Editor, New Zealand Council for Educational Research, Wellington. Lives in Wellington.

PUBLICATIONS

Verse

   Mine Eyes Dazzle: Poems 1947–49.   1950; revised edition, 1951, 1956.
   Sanctuary of Spirits.   1963.
   Wild Honey.   1964.
   Blue Rain.   1967.
   Drinking Horn.   1971.
   Walk the Black Path.   1971.
   Kapiti: Selected Poems, 1947–71.   1972.
   Dreams, Yellow Lions.   1975.

Plays

   When the Bough Breaks (produced 1970).   1970.

   Radio Plays: *The Homecoming; The Proprietor; The Suicide; The Wairau Incident.*

   Television Documentaries: *Island of Spirits,* 1973; *Like You I'm Trapped,* 1975.

Other

The Fruit Farm (juvenile). 1953.
The Happy Summer (juvenile). 1961.
New Zealand: A Book for Children. 1967.
Maori Legends. 1969.

Reading List: essay by James Bertram, in *Comment*, January–February 1965; "Campbell's *Mine Eyes Dazzle*: An Anatomy of Success" by David Gunby, in *Landfall*, March 1969; "Campbell's *Sanctuary of Spirits*: The Historical and Cultural Context" by F. M. McKay, in *Landfall*, June 1978.

*   *   *

Alistair Campbell's first book, *Mine Eyes Dazzle*, laid out as his territory the natural world. The descriptions of nature are notable for an animism which gives them a primitive strength and which is perhaps to be accounted for by Campbell's part-Polynesian background. The volume announced him as a Romantic poet who had learnt much from Yeats, though Campbell's concern has always been to explore feeling rather than ideas. His Romanticism is deepened by an empathy with Maori culture in which the spoken arts are highly poetical and a good deal of imagery is drawn from nature. One of the best of these early poems is "The Elegy," in memory of a fellow-student killed while climbing in the Southern Alps. As James K. Baxter wrote, in this poem "mountain, gorge, tree, and river become protagonists in the drama." The mysterious poem "The Return," peopled by strange figures on a beach, "Plant gods, tree gods, gods of the middle world," for some readers expresses a kind of race memory of the early Polynesian migrations.

The vividness of Campbell's evocation of the landscape is matched by the strong physicality of his love poetry, with its truly pagan delight in youth and beauty. Campbell's poetry is rooted in this world and he is the least metaphysical of New Zealand poets.

Sanctuary of Spirits is a lyrical sequence based on the history of the great pre-colonial Maori fighting-chief Te Rauparaha. To his theme Campbell brought a realism made possible by his capacity to enter into the actualities of an oral culture and to acclimatise the style of Maori oratory into English verse. The allusive method of the sequence allowed Campbell to compress into a brief compass the rich and complex history of the chief who has been called the Maori Napoleon. Success with Maori themes has evaded most previous New Zealand poets; by showing how they might be handled Campbell has reclaimed a valuable territory for New Zealand poetry.

Campbell's early poems were written in tight forms inherited from Yeats. More recently he has loosened his style. This has allowed him to develop the talent for creating moods he demonstrated in earlier poems like "At a Fishing Settlement" and "Hut Near Desolated Pines," where every detail establishes that feeling of sadness and loneliness which Campbell's verse often conveys. He is not a prolific poet, but he has established himself as one of the best lyric writers New Zealand has produced.

—F. M. McKay

CAMPBELL, (Ignatius) Roy (Dunnachie). South African. Born in Durban, 2 October 1901. Educated at Durban High School; Oxford University. Served with the British Army in

Africa, 1942–44. Married Mary Margaret Garman in 1922; two daughters. Spent most of his adult life in Provence, Spain, and Portugal. Editor, with William Plomer, *Voorslag*, 1926–27; Member, Literary Advisory Board, BBC, London, 1945–49. Recipient: Foyle Prize, 1952. Fellow, Royal Society of Literature, 1947; Member, Society of Provençal Poets, 1954. *Died 22 April 1957.*

PUBLICATIONS

Collections

Selected Poetry, edited by J. M. Lalley. 1968.

Verse

The Flaming Terrapin. 1924.
The Wayzgoose: A South African Satire. 1928.
Adamastor: Poems. 1930.
Poems. 1930.
The Georgiad: A Satirical Fantasy in Verse. 1931.
Pomegranates. 1932.
Flowering Reeds. 1933.
Mithraic Emblems. 1936.
Flowering Rifle: A Poem from the Battlefield of Spain. 1939.
Sons of the Mistral. 1941.
Talking Bronco. 1946.
Collected Poems. 3 vols., 1949–60.

Other

The History of a Rejected Address, with Satire and Fiction by Wyndham Lewis. 1930.
Burns. 1932.
Taurine Provence: The Philosophy, Technique, and Religion of the Bullfighter. 1932.
Wyndham Lewis: An Essay. 1932.
Broken Record: Reminiscences. 1934.
Light on a Dark Horse: An Autobiography 1901–1935. 1951.
Lorca: An Appreciation of His Poetry. 1952.
The Mamba's Precipice (juvenile). 1953.
Portugal. 1957.

Translator, Three Plays, by Helge Krog. 1934.
Translator, The Poems of St. John of the Cross. 1951.
Translator, Poems of Baudelaire. 1952.
Translator, Cousin Bazilio, by Eça de Queiroz. 1953.
Translator, The City and the Mountains, by Eça de Queiroz. 1955.
Translator, The Trickster of Seville and His Guest of Stone, by Tirso de Molina, Life Is a
    Dream, by Calderón, The Siege of Numantia, by Cervantes, and Fuente Ovejuna, by
    Lope de Vega, in The Classic Theatre, edited by Eric Bentley. 1959.
Translator, Nostalgia: A Collection of Poems, by J. Paco d'Arcos. 1960.
Translator, The Surgeon of His Honour, by Calderón. 1960.

Reading List: *Campbell* by David Wright, 1961, revised edition, 1971; *Lyric and Polemic: The Literary Personality of Campbell* by Rowland Smith, 1972; "Campbell: Outsider on the Right" by Bernard Bergonzi, in *The Turn of a Century*, 1973.

*　　*　　*

Roy Campbell was in every sense an outsider. He grew up in South Africa, in an idyllic pre-industrial world, and was familiar from his early childhood with boats and horses. As a very young man he came to England and began to establish himself as a poet, but he had little in common with the English literary world which he later lampooned in his long satirical poem *The Georgiad*. He returned to South Africa for some years in the 1920's and found himself equally at odds with the literary life of his own country, which he duly satirized in *The Wayzgoose*. Eventually Campbell came back to Europe, and spent the rest of his life – apart from the years during and just after the Second World War – in Provence, Spain, and Portugal. He reached his maximum alienation from other writers during the Spanish Civil War, when, a convert to Catholicism, he became an ardent supporter of General Franco's cause – the only poet of any stature in the English-speaking world to do so. He expressed his convictions, and his hatred for conventional left-wing attitudes, in a third long satirical poem, *Flowering Rifle*. During the Second World War Campbell somewhat rehabilitated himself with liberal opinion by serving in the British Army. Throughout his life Campbell saw himself as a man of action rather than an intellectual, and during the thirties he lived among cattlemen and fishermen in Provence and Spain and despised the sedentary life of men of letters. But for all his anti-intellectual, "plain man" pose, Campbell was in fact a cultured man of wide reading in several languages: the third volume of his *Collected Poems* is made up of translations from French, Spanish, Portuguese, and Latin.

As a poet Campbell was not in any clear English tradition. He wrote exclusively formal verse, in stanzas and couplets, and was immensely fluent, so that many of his poems, whether lyrics or satires, are diffuse and repetitive. His literary antecedents were in some ways un-English: he admired and imitated French poets, like Baudelaire, Rimbaud, and Valéry, and from those sources he acquired a characteristically rhetorical lyricism that is assertive rather then subtle. Yet in some of his lyrical poems, such as "The Zulu Girl," "Mass at Dawn," "Horses on the Camargue," "Autumn," and "Choosing a Mast," Campbell could write with delicacy as well as force. The *tour de force* of his earliest poetry is *The Flaming Terrapin*, a long poem in couplets which celebrates in exuberant and colourful verse a mythical beast, a giant tortoise that towed Noah's Ark during the flood. This poem shows a capacity for mythopoeic inventiveness that did not often recur in Campbell's later work, though we find it in a more severe and chastened form in the sequence called "Mithraic Frieze," published in 1936. Another early poem, "Tristan da Cunha," provides an instance of Campbell's image of himself as a lonely and misunderstood figure. He once saw the isolated island in the South Atlantic when sailing from South Africa, and in the poem he uses it as a symbol for himself as an aloof, Byronic figure, contemptuous of modern mass society. The present-day reader may have difficulty in responding to the more assertively rhetorical side of Campbell's poetry, though his lyrical quality is unmistakable. The satire has inevitably dated, though passages of *The Georgiad* are still vigorously comic and enjoyable. *Flowering Rifle*, though, is now best regarded as an over-extended footnote to the history of the Spanish Civil War rather than a living poem. "Mithraic Frieze" reflects Campbell's interest in the ancient Roman Mithraic religion, which he tried to interpret in a Catholic fashion. These poems are unlike most of Campbell's other work in that they are elliptical and compressed and allusive rather than extended and assertive; they present a group of enigmatic emblems and are poetically very effective in a symbolist way. They may prove in the long run to be the most enduring poetry that Campbell wrote.

After the outbreak of the Spanish Civil War Campbell declined in power as a poet; he became increasingly repetitive and crude in his invective. But in his verse translations he revealed himself as still capable of expressing a wide range of feeling, and some of them have a remarkable sensitivity, notably those from the mystical poetry of St. John of the Cross. Campbell remains an outsider in modern English literature: too idiosyncratic to be easily assimilated, and too gifted and rewarding to be ignored.

—Bernard Bergonzi

CLARK, John Pepper. Nigerian.   Born in Kiagbolo, 6 April 1935. Educated at Warri Government College, Ughelli, 1948–54; University of Ibadan, 1955–60, B. A. (honours) in English 1960; Princeton University, New Jersey (Parvin Fellowship), 1962–63; University of Ibadan (Institute of African Studies Research Fellowship, 1961–64). Married; has one daughter. Nigerian Government Information Officer, 1960–61; Head of Features and Editorial Writer, *Daily Express*, Lagos, 1961–62. Founding Editor, *The Horn* magazine, Ibadan. Since 1964, Member of the English Department, and currently Professor of English, University of Lagos. Founding Member, Society of Nigerian Authors. Lives in Lagos.

PUBLICATIONS

Verse

  Poems.   1962.
  A Reed in the Tide: A Selecton of Poems.   1965.
  Casualties: Poems 1966–1968.   1970.

Plays

  Song of a Goat (produced 1961).   1961.
  Three Plays: Song of a Goat, The Raft, The Masquerade.   1964.
  The Masquerade (produced 1965).   In *Three Plays,* 1964.
  The Raft (broadcast 1966).   In *Three Plays,* 1964.
  Ozidi.   1966.

  Screenplays (documentaries): *The Ozidi of Atazi; The Ghost Town.*

  Radio Play: *The Raft,* 1966.

Other

  America, Their America   1964.
  Example of Shakespeare: Critical Essays on African Literature.   1970.

*   *   *

John Pepper Clark says about himself in the introduction to *A Reed in the Tide* that he is "a cultural mulatto." In this way he draws attention to the fact that his outlook is the result of a synthesis of two different cultures, the traditional Nigerian and the modern Western. This is reflected in his authorship which deals with traditional Ijaw myths as well as the modern American way of life which he criticizes from the point of view of an outsider, bringing an African sensibility to bear on the excesses of modern society. On the other hand his choice of the English language is deliberate, born of the desire to reach as many people as possible.

Clark is playwright, poet and prose writer. *Three Plays* contains *Song of a Goat, The Masquerade,* and *The Raft.* The first two plays deal with the tragic events that befall a family in the Niger river delta as a result of an initial crime against the gods. The plays move with a relentless inevitability towards final death and destruction, and the prevailing atmosphere of doom as well as a dramatic use of a chorus show Clark's debt to classical Greek drama. The subject matter, however, is firmly rooted in traditional tales from the Niger delta. *The Raft* is about a group of fishermen set adrift on a raft on the Niger drawing towards their final destruction in the whirlpools at the mouth of the river. The play explores the psychology of the fishermen, but it is also capable of an allegorical interpretation dealing with the Biafran war and Nigerian unity. In *Ozidi* Clark returns to the traditional Ijaw myth. *Ozidi* is based on an Ijaw saga, which took seven days to tell and was accompanied by music and mime. In all the plays the language is very poetic and imaginative, rich in metaphors which are often surprisingly fresh and which show Clark's ability as a poet.

A Reed in the Tide is a collection of occasional poems, varied in aspect and theme (visual images, moral reflections, myths), written in free verse, often deliberately echoing Dylan Thomas or W. H. Auden. The poem "Night Rain," describing a heavy tropical downpour in the wet and swampy Niger delta stands out as an excellent example of successful nature poetry about exotic places.

Casualties deals with the Biafran war. Clark was very close to the events and had an inside knowledge which is denied the ordinary reader, and the collection is therefore heavily glossed and cannot be read without an intimate knowledge of the movements of the war.

As a prose writer Clark has chosen "straight reporting" as his medium for his criticism of America in *America, Their America.* The criticism is flamboyant and often idiosyncratic.

From his writings Clark emerges as a person with strong beliefs, tempered with a compassion and tenderness which appear mainly in his poetry.

—Kirsten Holst Petersen

CLARKE, Austin. Irish. Born in Dublin, 9 May 1896. Educated at Belvedere College, Dublin; University College, Dublin, M.A. Married Nora Walker; three sons. Lecturer in English, University College, Dublin, 1917–21; book reviewer in London, 1923–37, also Assistant Editor, *Argosy*, London, 1929; returned to Ireland as free-lance reviewer and broadcaster, 1937. Founding Member, 1932, and President, 1952–54, Irish Academy of Letters; President, Irish P.E.N., 1939–42, 1946–49. Chairman, Dublin Verse Speaking Society, and Lyric Theatre Company; Literary Adviser, Radio Eireann. Recipient: Tailteann Games National Award, 1932; Denis Devlin Memorial Award, 1964; Arts Council Special Poetry Prize, 1964; Irish Academy of Letters Gregory Medal, 1968. D. Litt.: Trinity College, Dublin, 1966. *Died 19 March 1974.*

PUBLICATIONS

Collections

Collected Poems, edited by Liam Miller.   1974.
Selected Poems, edited by Thomas Kinsella.   1976.

Verse

The Vengeance of Fionn.   1917.
The Fires of Baäl.   1921.
The Sword of the West.   1921.
The Cattledrive in Connaught and Other Poems.   1925.
Pilgrimage and Other Poems.   1929.
The Collected Poems.   1936.
Night and Morning.   1938.
The Straying Student.   1944.
Ancient Lights: Poems and Satires.   1955.
Too Great a Vine: Poems and Satires.   1957.
The Horse-Eaters: Poems and Satires.   1960.
Collected Later Poems.   1961.
Forget-Me-Not.   1962.
Flight to Africa and Other Poems.   1963.
Poems: A Selection, with Tony Connor and Charles Tomlinson.   1964.
Mnemosyne Lay in Dust.   1966.
Old-Fashioned Pilgrimage and Other Poems.   1967.
The Echo at Coole and Other Poems.   1968.
A Sermon on Swift and Other Poems.   1968.
Orphide.   1970.
Tiresias: A Poem.   1971.

Plays

The Son of Learning (produced 1927).   1927.
The Flame (produced 1932).   1930.
Sister Eucharia (produced 1941).   1939.
Black Fast (produced 1941).   1941.
As the Crow Flies (broadcast 1942).   1943.
The Kiss, from a play by Théodore de Banville (produced 1942).   In *The Viscount of Blarney and Other Plot*, 1944.
The Plot Is Ready (produced 1943).   In *The Viscount of Blarney and Other Plays*, 1944.
The Viscount of Blarney (produced 1944).   In *The Viscount of Blarney and Other Plays*, 1944.
The Viscount of Blarney and Other Plays.   1944.
The Second Kiss (produced 1946).   1946.
The Plot Succeeds (produced 1950).   1950.
The Moment Next to Nothing (produced 1958).   1953.
Collected Plays.   1963.
The Student from Salamanca (produced 1966).   In *Two Interludes*, 1968.
Two Interludes Adapted from Cervantes: The Student from Salamanca, and The Silent Lover.   1968.

The Impuritans. 1973.
The Third Kiss. 1976.

Other plays: *Liberty Lane; St Patrick's Purgatory.*

Fiction

The Bright Temptations: A Romance. 1932.
The Singing-Men at Cashel. 1936.
The Sun Dances at Easter: A Romance. 1952.

Other

First Visit to England and Other Memories. 1945.
Poetry in Modern Ireland. 1951; revised edition, 1962.
Twice round the Black Church: Early Memories of Ireland and England. 1962.
A Penny in the Clouds: More Memories of Ireland and England. 1968.
The Celtic Twilight and the Nineties. 1969.

Editor, *The Poems of Joseph Campbell.* 1963.

Reading List: *A Tribute to Clarke on His Seventieth Birthday* edited by John Montague and Liam Miller, 1966 (includes bibliography by Miller); *Clarke: His Life and Works* by Susan Halpern, 1974.

*   *   *

Austin Clarke began his literary career in the manner of a Celtic Revival poet, with a number of epic narratives drawn from Irish material. In this he was affected by the work of W. B. Yeats, Standish O'Grady, Samuel Ferguson, and many others poets and scholars who had responded before him to the Irish heritage of myth and saga. He soon developed a more individual response: where Yeats presented a dichotomy between the pagan, aristocratic world of Cuchulain and the democratic present, Clarke dramatised a contrast between the medieval, Christian past and the dogmatic, Catholic present. For him the religious question was central and in his poems, plays, and prose romances the problem of the individual Catholic conscience became part of Irish literature. The conflict is between repressive Church teachings and natural instincts. Clarke's response to the Gaelic past also included the adaptation of various forms of Gaelic prosody to poetry in English; his experiments in prosody, and in the uses of rhyme and assonance, are an important aspect of his poetry.

Clarke's setting for his three prose romances, for many of his verse plays, and for much of the poetry of his middle period is the Celtic-Romanesque period in Ireland that lasted from the introduction of Christianity in the fifth century to the coming of monastic reform at the end of the twelfth. It was a time in which Irish art flourished in the illumination of manuscripts, the making of ornaments, and the building of the round towers and celtic crosses, a time when the country was largely independent of the Roman church and experienced much literary activity. Clarke's work celebrates this period, and he also uses it as a framework of reference through which to comment on his own time. In his work after 1955, he had a renewal of power, producing several books of poetry in which he is both satirical observer of the contemporary scene, warm recorder of his own life, and, finally, the cheerful sensualist in a number of narrative poems based on Irish and classical myth.

Like Joyce, whom he resembles in many ways, Clarke drew strength from his acceptance of things as he found them. Drawn initially to the remote past in the manner of the early Yeats, he later faced up to his personal problems, making poems out of his anguish of conscience, and accepted then the realities of Irish life in the modern period. This ability to appropriate the minutiae of Irish life is based on his characteristic ability to write with precision about sensuous details. Through his long career he has revitalized many aspects of the Irish past, with the result that he is a central figure in Irish poetry.

—Maurice Harmon

COLUM, Padraic.   Irish.   Born in Longford, 8 December 1881. Educated at the National School, Sandycove, County Dublin. Married the writer Mary Maguire. Worked as a clerk in a railway office, Dublin, until 1904; associated with Lady Gregory and Yeats at the beginning of the Irish Theatre movement, 1902; Founder, 1911, with James Stephens and Thomas MacDonagh, *Irish Review*, Dublin: Editor, 1912–13. Settled in the United States, living in New York and Connecticut after 1939. President, James Joyce Society, New York. Recipient: Academy of American Poets Fellowship, 1952; Irish Academy of Letters Gregory Medal, 1953; Catholic Library Association Regina Medal, 1961. Member, Irish Academy of Letters, and National Institute of Arts and Letters (U.S.). *Died 11 January 1972.*

PUBLICATIONS

Verse

    Heather Ale.   1907.
    Wild Earth.   1907; revised edition, as *Wild Earth and Other Poems,* 1916.
    Dramatic Legends and Other Poems.   1922.
    The Way of the Cross: Devotions on the Progress of Our Lord Jesus Christ from the Judgement Hall to Calvary.   1926.
    Creatures.   1927.
    Old Pastures.   1930.
    Poems.   1932; revised edition, as *Collected Poems,* 1953.
    The Story of Lowry Maen.   1937.
    Flower Pieces: New Poems.   1938.
    The Jackdaw.   1939.
    Ten Poems.   1952.
    The Vegetable Kingdom.   1954.
    Irish Elegies.   1958; revised edition, 1961.
    The Poet's Circuits: Collected Poems of Ireland.   1960.
    Images of Departure.   1969.

Plays

    The Children of Lir, and *Brian Boru,* in *Irish Independent,* 1902.
    The Kingdom of the Young (produced 1902).   In *United Irishman,* 1903.

The Foleys, and *Eoghan's Wife,* in *United Irishman,* 1903.

The Saxon Shillin' (produced 1903).   Edited by Robert G. Hogan and J. F. Kilroy, in *Lost Plays of the Irish,* 1970.

The Fiddler's House (as *Broken Soil,* produced 1903; revised version, as *The Fiddler's House,* produced 1907).   1907.

The Land (produced 1905).   1905.

The Miracle of the Corn: A Miracle Play (produced 1908).   In *Studies,* 1907.

Thomas Muskerry (produced 1910).   1910.

The Destruction of the Hostel (juvenile; produced 1910).

The Desert.   1912; as *Mogu the Wanderer; or, The Desert: A Fantastic Comedy,* 1917; as *Mogu of the Desert* (produced 1931).

The Betrayal (produced 1913).   N.d.

The Grasshopper, with F. E. Washburn-Freund, from a play by Count Keyserling (produced 1917).

Balloon (produced ?).   1929.

The Show-Booth, from a play by Alexander Blok (produced 1948).

Moytura: A Play for Dancers.   1963.

The Challengers: Monasterboice, Glendalough, Cloughoughter (produced 1966).

The Road round Ireland, with Basil Burwell, from works by Colum (produced 1967; as *Carricknabauna,* produced 1967).

Fiction

Castle Conquer.   1923.

Three Men.   1930.

The Flying Swans.   1957.

Other

Studies (miscellany).   1907.

My Irish Year.   1912.

A Boy in Eirinn (juvenile).   1913.

The Irish Rebellion of 1916 and Its Martyrs: Erin's Tragic Easter, with other, edited by Maurice Joy.   1916.

The King of Ireland's Son (juvenile).   1916.

The Boy Who Knew What the Birds Said (juvenile).   1918.

The Adventures of Odysseus and the Tale of Troy (juvenile).   1918; as *The Children's Homer,* 1946.

The Girl Who Sat by the Ashes (juvenile).   1919.

The Children of Odin: A Book of Northern Myths (juvenile).   1920.

The Boy Apprenticed to an Enchanter (juvenile).   1920.

The Golden Fleece and the Heroes Who Lived Before Achilles (juvenile).   1921.

The Children Who Followed the Piper (juvenile).   1922.

The Six Who Were Left in a Shoe (juvenile).   1923.

Tales and Legends of Hawaii: At the Gateways of the Day and *The Bright Islands* (juvenile).   2 vols., 1924–25; as *Legends of Hawaii,* 1937.

The Island of the Mighty, Being the Hero Stories of Celtic Britain Retold from the Mabinogion (juvenile).   1924.

The Peep-Show Man (juvenile).   1924.

The Voyagers, Being Legends and Romances of Atlantic Discovery (juvenile).   1925.

The Forge in the Forest (juvenile).   1925.

The Road round Ireland.   1926.

The Fountain of Youth: Stories to Be Told (juvenile).   1927.
Orpheus: Myths of the World (juvenile).   1930; as *Myths of the Old World,* n.d.
Cross Roads in Ireland.   1930.
Ella Young: An Appreciation.   1931.
A Half-Day's Ride; or, Estates in Corsica.   1932.
The Big Tree of Bunlahy: Stories of My Own Countryside (juvenile).   1933.
The White Sparrow (juvenile).   1935; as *Sparrow Alone,* 1975.
The Legend of Saint Columba.   1935.
Where the Winds Never Blew and the Cocks Never Crew (juvenile).   1940.
The Frenzied Prince, Being Heroic Stories of Ancient Ireland (juvenile).   1943.
Our Friend James Joyce, with Mary Colum.   1958.
Arthur Griffith.   1959; as *Ourselves Alone! The Story of Arthur Griffith and the Irish Free State,* 1959.
Story Telling Old and New.   1961.
The Stone of Victory and Other Tales (juvenile).   1966.

Editor, *Oliver Goldsmith.*   1913.
Editor, *Broad-Sheet Ballads, Being a Collection of Irish Popular Songs.*   1913.
Editor, with Joseph Harrington O'Brien, *Poems of the Irish Revolutionary Brotherhood.*   1916; revised edition, 1916.
Editor, *Gulliver's Travels* (juvenile edition), by Swift.   1917.
Editor, *An Anthology of Irish Verse.*   1922; revised edition, 1948.
Editor, *The Arabian Nights, Tales of Wonder and Magnificence* (juvenile).   1953.
Editor, *A Treasury of Irish Folklore: The Stories, Traditions, Legends, Humor, Wisdom, Ballads, and Songs of the Irish People.*   1954; revised edition, 1962, 1967.
Editor, with Margaret Freeman Cabell, *Between Friends: Letter of James Branch Cabell and Others.*   1962.
Editor, *The Poems of Samuel Ferguson.*   1963.
Editor, *Roofs of Gold: Poems to Read Aloud.*   1964.

Reading List: "Colum: The Peasant Nation" by Richard J. Loftus, in *Nationalism in Modern Anglo-Irish Poetry,* 1964; *Colum: A Biographical-Critical Introduction* by Zack R. Bowen, 1970.

*   *   *

Padraic Colum's poetry which, in a long career of writing fiction, drama, biography, and children's literature, is his chief claim to remembrance, is rooted in a realistic sense of Irish rural life. It is this direct knowledge of the rural scene which distinguishes his work from much of the poetry of the Irish literary revival with which his name was first associated. Of a younger generation than W. B. Yeats, Lady Gregory and George Russell, his background and upbringing were Catholic rather than Protestant. This he felt allowed his poetry a more truly national flavour than could be achieved by poets with their roots in the Irish Protestant Ascendancy. His poetic philosophy is most clearly expressed in his poem "The Poet":

> But close to the ground are reared
> The wings that have widest sway,
> And the birds that sing best in the wood ...
> Were reared with breasts to the clay.

His best work, much of it contained in his volume *Wild Earth,* is a simple, lyrical celebration of the properties and personages of the Irish rural scene mediated in a verse redolent of national and religious pieties. The Gaelic folk-poem, the broadsheet ballad are the poetic modes to which Colum's poems pay their respects, and his most compelling work combines traditional simplicity of metaphor with a dramatic objectivity of tone. The colours, movements, and textures of Irish life are caught in this volume, as in his later collection *The Poet's Circuits: Collected Poems of Ireland*, with a realism that is only occasionally marred by sentimental provincialism and quaint pastoral feeling. At his best, as in his justly famed ballad (based on traditional materials) "She moved through the fair," Colum's work merits praise for its moments of lyric universality. In L. A. G. Strong's words "the work of Padraic Colum, which presents us with poetic experience in its most innocent, naked form, embarrasses criticism. Often there are no allusions, no symbols, only the simplest images, nothing but the singing tone and the thing itself."

—Terence Brown

CRANE, (Harold) Hart. American. Born in Garrettsville, Ohio, 21 July 1899; spent his childhood in Cleveland. Educated in local schools. Assistant Editor, *The Pagan*, 1918; worked in a shipyard in Cleveland, and as a reporter in New York, 1918; Advertising Solicitor, *The Little Review*, 1919; worked for his father in a drug store in Akron, Ohio, 1919–20, and in a Cleveland warehouse, 1920; worked in Washington, D. C. briefly, 1920, and in Cleveland, 1920–21; Copywriter, Cleveland advertising agencies, 1922–23; moved to New York, 1923: clerk, then copywriter, in an advertising agency, 1923; clerk in a publishing firm, 1924–25; patronized by Otto Kahn, 1925; travelled in Europe, 1928, Mexico, 1931–32. Recipient: Guggenheim Fellowship, 1931. Drowned himself on the voyage back from Mexico. *Died 27 April 1932.*

PUBLICATIONS

Collections

    Letters 1916–1932, edited by Brom Weber. 1952.
    Complete Poems and Selected Letters and Prose, edited by Brom Weber. 1966.

Verse

    White Buildings: Poems. 1926.
    The Bridge. 1930.
    Ten Unpublished Poems. 1972.

Other

    Twenty-One Letters to George Bryan, edited by Joseph Katz and others. 1968.
    Letters of Crane and His Family, edited by Thomas S. W. Lewis. 1974.
    Crane and Yvor Winters: Their Literary Correspondence, edited by Thomas Parkinson. 1978.

Bibliography: *Crane: A Descriptive Bibliography* by Joseph Schwartz and Robert C. Schweik, 1972.

Reading List: *Crane: A Biographical and Critical Study* by Brom Weber, 1948; *Crane: An Introduction and Interpretation*, 1963, and *Smithereened Apart: A Critique of Crane*, 1977, both by Samuel Hazo; *Crane* by Vincent Quinn, 1963; *Crane* by Monroe K. Spears, 1965; *The Poetry of Crane* by R. W. B. Lewis, 1967; *The Crane Voyages* by Hunce Voelcker, 1967; *Crane: An Introduction to the Poetry* by Herbert A. Leibowitz, 1968; *Voyager: A Life of Crane* by John Unterecker, 1969; *Crane: The Patterns of His Poetry* by M. D. Uroff, 1974; *Crane's The Bridge: A Description of Its Life* by Richard P. Sugg, 1977.

*   *   *

As with some other American writers, it is difficult to give a final and objective estimate of Hart Crane's place as a poet. He is important, on more than one count, for what he set out to do, but critics have differed widely as to his actual achievement. Furthermore, there is the legend, as we may call it, of his life. We are presented with the picture of a man driven by compulsive and self-destructive urges, both alcoholic and sexual, culminating in a spectacular suicide. Hart Crane himself identified with such doomed and outcast figures as Christopher Marlowe and Arthur Rimbaud, and it is easy to make him into the romantic scapegoat of American civilisation. On the other hand, a critic like Ivor Winters can too readily move from a moral disapproval of the undisciplined life to a total dismissal of the work.

The Bridge is Crane's longest and clearly his most important poem. In form it is modelled on Eliot's *The Waste Land*, and it is generally agreed that Crane intended his own poem as a kind of riposte, giving a positive rather than a negative view of the modern metropolitan city. In *The Waste Land*, and in Joyce's *Ulysses*, the protaganist moves about the city – London or Dublin – which becomes a symbolic landscape, crowded with mythical and heroic archetypes. Past splendours contrast with modern squalor. *The Bridge* follows the same plan. The setting is New York. The protagonist wakes in the morning, passes over Brooklyn Bridge, wanders about the city and returns in the evening by the subway under the River Hudson. Hart Crane tries to create a mythology for America out of scraps of literature, history, and tradition. Columbus, Rip Van Winkle and the Wright brothers appear, as well as Whitman, Poe, Emily Dickinson, and Isadora Duncan. In the section entitled "Powhatan's Daughter" Pocahontas represents the American earth itself and its Red Indian past: "Lie to us. Dance us back our tribal dawn." In "The Tunnel," through the suffocating atmosphere of a rush hour subway, Crane encounters the ghost of Edgar Allan Poe:

> And why do I often meet your visage here,
> Your eyes like agate lanterns – on and on
> Below the toothpaste and the dandruff ads?
> – And did their riding eyes right through your side,
> And did their eyes like unwashed platters ride?
> And Death, aloft, – gigantically down
> Probing through you – toward me, O evermore!

In this remarkable passage, Crane shows that he is aware that the American dream of materialistic, technological progress has its reverse side of neurotic nightmare, and that Poe represents this nightmare. But it is Brooklyn Bridge itself which is the unifying symbol of the poem. The bridge unites the two halves of the city, and by the railroad that it carries unites the city with the country and thus its present with its past. As a feat of engineering it denotes human achievement, and in its clean functional beauty the union of aesthetics and technics.

We may thus consider Crane, as does Harold Bloom, as standing in the succession of Romantic, myth making, and visionary poets. He is one of the explorers of what Charles Williams called "the Image of the City." But as an urban poet he differs sharply from his

British and American successors of the 1930's in that his poetry is almost devoid of social and political comment. He has indeed been reproached by left-wing critics for his unreflecting celebration of the American capitalist system. Indeed, the sudden collapse of that system in the Slump was one of the factors contributing to his despair and his suicide.

Crane may also be considered, at least in part, as the most notable representative in the English speaking world of the Futurist movement of the 1920's. The term "Futurism" was coined by the Italian Marinetti, a figure more notable for self-publicity than literary genius. But his claim that art should celebrate the achievements and imitate the rhythms of a machine civilisation influenced poets better than himself. These included Apollinaire in France and Mayakovsky in Russia. The latter, like Crane, found his new faith inadequate to sustain him and ended in suicide. But Crane, as we have seen, did not regard the traditions of the past as irrelevant. He suffered, however, from a certain paucity in his own cultural background: it really does seem that he thought the phrase "Panus angelicus" which he quotes in the "Cape Hatteras" section of *The Bridge* meant "angelic Pan" and could be applied to Walt Whitman. And some may feel that the only religious tradition he seems to have been acquainted with, his mother's Christian Science, lacked a richness compared with the theological currents which fertilised the work of Eliot and Joyce.

Although Whitman's popularist rhetoric represents one of Crane's stances, his free verse is not in the least Whitmanesque. Like that of Eliot, it is based on an extension of principles already found in the blank verse of Shakespeare's contemporaries. But while Eliot's is founded upon that of Webster and his generation, that of Crane is to be related to the practice of Marlowe, with its strongly stressed iambic rhythm and its terminal pause. As in Marlowe there is an element of bombast in Crane, and a certain degree of rhythmical monotony. At his best he sweeps us along by the sheer energy of his writing, in spite of the frequent difficulty of grasping the exact sense of what he is saying. Crane is undeniably often very obscure. But his much quoted letter to Harriet Monroe, defending his poem "At Melville's Tomb," shows that he was very much intellectually in control. The poem consists in fact of a series of compressed conceits, rather different from the extended metaphysical conceits of Donne and his school. At times it is difficult to translate these into completely logical terms. These lines (from "Voyages") are difficult – "In all the argosy of your bright hair, I dreamed/Nothing so flagless as this piracy" – yet their haunting quality is manifest. As a visual poet Crane is remote from Pound and the Imagists; instead of a clear pictorial impression of a scene or object we get a kind of kaleidoscope of sense impressions. His style might best be described as manneristic, and in this respect his affinities are less with his contemporaries and immediate predecessors than with certain poets who came into prominence a decade later, such as George Barker and Dylan Thomas. Crane has indeed been claimed as an influence on the latter poet, but this is difficult to determine.

When Crane moved from the early short poems of *White Buildings* to the elaborately planned *The Bridge* he was attempting to encompass something in the nature of an epic style. What he in fact achieved might more properly be described as quasi-Pindaric or dithyrambic lyric. This dithyrambic quality is even more marked in "For the Marriage of Faustus and Helen." This sequence of three poems continues some of the themes of *The Bridge*. Faustus's evocation of the shade of Helen is, of course, one of the most memorable moments in Marlowe's *Doctor Faustus*; and Marlowe, as we have seen, was one of Crane's heroes. The marriage of Faust and Helen, in the second part of Goethe's *Faust*, was a symbol of the union of the modern and the antique spirits. Crane may have taken his cue from this, since the theme of these three poems is the union of American technological civilization with the traditional idea of beauty. Crane here forces language almost to the breaking point as he strives to evoke Helen first from a vision of the metropolitan city, second (it would seem) from a scene of jazz revelry at the summit of a skyscraper, and third from the airman's conquest of distance:

> Capped arbiter of beauty in this street
> That narrows darkly into motor dawn, –

You, here beside me, delicate ambassador
Of intricate slain numbers that arise
In whispers, naked of steel;
                                                    religious gunman!
Who faithfully, yourself, will fall too soon,
And in other ways than as the wind settles
On the sixteen thrifty bridges of the city:
Let us unbind our throats of fear and pity.

In contrast to this, the series of poems entitled "Voyages" represent Crane's return to a purer and more personal lyricism. These may in the end constitute his most enduring, though not his most ambitious achievement. In these poems Crane imagines himself united with one of his lovers, a merchant seaman, as he voyages through imaginary seascapes. The verse of these poems has a new kind of music, and they are less rhetorically accentuated. Hart Crane now uses enjambment with effect, especially a characteristic trick of ending a line with a grammatically unimportant word as in the second line of the following quotation:

O minstrel galleons of Carib fire,
Bequeath us to no earthly shore until
Is answered in the vortex of our grave
The seal's wide spindrift gaze toward paradise.

Crane's final days were spent in Mexico. He had gone there on a grant from the Guggenheim Foundation, with a project to compose a long poem on the Spanish Conquest of Mexico. This historical theme, almost too highly charged with imaginative potential, has more than once proved a trap for poets. What Hart Crane might have made of it we can only conjecture. In fact his Mexican days were a disaster, and, before he committed suicide by drowning on his return voyage to the U.S.A., he knew that he had no work on the project to show and in the light of the changed economic situation it was unlikely his grant would be renewed. Nevertheless, some of the last poems, such as "The Idiot" and "Bacardi Spreads the Eagle's Wings," give a compassionate view of the poor and outcast which hints at a grasp of reality previously somewhat wanting in Hart Crane's poetry.

—John Heath-Stubbs

CREELEY, Robert (White). American. Born in Arlington, Massachusetts, 21 May 1926. Educated at Holderness School, Plymouth, New Hampshire; Harvard University, Cambridge, Massachusetts, 1943–46; Black Mountain College, North Carolina, B.A. 1955; University of New Mexico, M.A. 1960. Served with the American Field Service in India and Burma, 1944–45. Married 1) Ann McKinnon in 1946 (divorced, 1955), two sons, one daughter; 2) Bobbie Louise Hall in 1957, three daughters. Taught on a finca in Guatemala for two years; Instructor, Black Mountain College, Spring 1954, Fall 1955; Visiting Lecturer, 1961–62, and Lecturer, 1963–66, 1968–69, University of New Mexico; Lecturer, University of British Columbia, Vancouver, 1962–63. Visiting Professor, 1966–67, and since 1967 Professor of English, State University of New York at Buffalo. Visiting Professor of Creative Writing, San Francisco State College, 1970–71. Operated the Divers Press, Palma, Majorca, 1953–55; Editor, *Black Mountain Review*, North Carolina, 1954–57, and associated with *Wake, Golden Goose, Origin, Fragmente, Vou, Contact, CIV/n,* and *Merlin* magazines in the early 1950's, and other magazines subsequently. Recipient: D. H. Lawrence Fellowship, 1960; Guggenheim Fellowship, 1964, 1971; Rockefeller Fellowship, 1965. Lives in Bolinas, California.

PUBLICATIONS

Verse

Le Fou. 1952.
The Kind of Act of. 1953.
The Immoral Proposition. 1953.
A Snarling Garland of Xmas Verses. 1954.
All That Is Lovely in Men. 1955.
Ferrini and Others, with others. 1955.
If You. 1956.
The Whip. 1957.
A Form of Women. 1959.
For Love: Poems 1950–1960. 1962.
Words. 1965.
About Women. 1966.
Poems 1950–1965. 1966.
A Sight. 1967.
Words. 1967.
Robert Creeley Reads (with recording). 1967.
The Finger. 1968.
5 Numbers. 1968.
The Charm: Early and Uncollected Poems. 1968.
Numbers. 1968.
Divisions and Other Early Poems. 1968.
Pieces. 1968.
Hero. 1969.
A Wall. 1969.
Mary's Fancy. 1970.
In London. 1970.
The Finger: Poems 1966–1969. 1970.
As Now It Would Be Snow. 1970.
America. 1970.
Christmas: May 10, 1970. 1970.
St. Martin's. 1971.
Sea. 1971.
1.2.3.4.5.6.7.8.9.0. 1971.
A Day Book (includes prose). 1972.
For My Mother. 1973.
Kitchen. 1973.
Sitting Here. 1974.
Thirty Things. 1974.
Selected Poems. 1976.
Away. 1976.
Hello – A Journal February 23-May 3, 1976. 1978.

Play

   Listen (produced 1972).   1972.

Fiction

   The Gold Diggers.   1954.
   The Island.   1963.
   Mister Blue.   1964.
   The Gold Diggers and Other Stories.   1965.
   Mabel.   1976.
   Presences.   1976.

Other

   An American Sense (essay).   1965(?).
   Contexts of Poetry.   1968.
   A Quick Graph: Collected Notes and Essays.   1970.
   A Day Book.   1970.
   A Sense of Measure (essays).   1973.
   Contexts of Poetry: Interviews 1961–1971, edited by Donald Allen.   1973.

   Editor, *Mayan Letters,* by Charles Olson.   1953.
   Editor, with Donald Allen, *New American Story.*   1965.
   Editor, *Selected Writings,* by Charles Olson.   1966.
   Editor, with Donald Allen, *The New Writing in the U.S.A.*   1967.
   Editor, *Whitman.*   1973.

Bibliography: *Creeley: An Inventory 1945–1970* by Mary Novik,   1974.

Reading List: *Three Essays on Creeley* by Warren Tallman, 1973; *Measures: Creeley's Poetry* by Ann Mandel, 1974; *Creeley's Poetry: A Critical Introduction* by Cynthia Edelberg, 1978.

*   *   *

   In his 1967 Berlin lecture, "I'm Given to Write Poems," Robert Creeley acknowledged his indebtedness to William Carlos Williams for teaching him the use of an American speech in poetry and for the emotional perception he has achieved, as well as his debt to Charles Olson for "the *freedom* I have as a poet." This freedom lies not in the lyric itself, which is tightly restrained from committing verbal excess, but in the flow of the thought which ranges freely over a complex psychological interior. Creeley's best poems contain remarkable articulation of shades and hues of mood, often achieved by the subtle word play of the discourse. The poems, brief seizures of attention, are a chronicle of his two marriages, in which the self undergoes remorseless scrutiny and analysis. The larger canon of these miniature self-portraits reveals a life of emotional isolation as a man attempts both to possess and submit to women who are repelled by his profound vulnerability.
   The early poems, collected in *For Love: Poems 1950–1960*, are intensely formal in their compactness and closure. Many tend toward epigram in their brevity and pithy advice. A typical instance is "The Warning":

>   For Love – I would
>   split open your head and put
>   a candle in
>   behind the eyes.
>
>   Love is dead in us
>   if we forget
>   the virtue of an amulet
>   and quick surprise.

But the best of the short poems define the self from an oblique but penetrating angle of insight, as in the three couplets of "The End":

>   When I know what people think of me
>   I am plunged into my loneliness. The grey
>
>   hat bought earlier sickens.
>   I have no purpose no longer distinguishable.
>
>   A feeling like being choked
>   enters my throat.

Creeley's marital theme is expressed in the majority of poems in *For Love*, but "The Whip," "A Form of Women," "The Way," "A Marriage," and "Ballad of the Despairing Husband" capture its dilemmas with deep poignance. Other poems in this large collection depict the female as not only a sexual partner, but as a force or element to sustain male consciousness. "The Door," among the longest and most ambitious of these poems, explores the female in her divine and archetypal aspect.

In recent years, Creeley has dissolved the formalism of his verse in order to create verse fields in book-length serial compositions, in the manner of Charles Olson and Robert Duncan. He has abandoned the structural neatness of his earlier verse, but the more fluid compositions of *Words, Pieces,* and *A Day Book* tend to be lax and to include much trivial detail of his daily life.

His prose work follows the themes of his verse. The novel *The Island* deals with his marriage to his first wife. Creeley's prose is unique in modern fiction: his use of detail is extraordinarily delicate and precise, producing an uncanny perceptiveness in his narrators. Self-absorption in *The Island* is all the more compelling as the narrator dismantles his own thinking process to inspect the deterioration jealousy causes in him. Although a highly provocative writer of prose, his poetry has had a more pervasive influence.

In his criticism *A Quick Graph*, and in interviews, collected in *Contexts of Poetry*, he has proved an astute chronicler of modern poetry, particularly on the work and influence of Charles Olson, with whom he launched the movement now known as Black Mountain poetry.

—Paul Christensen

CULLEN, Countée. American. Born Countée L. Porter in New York City, 30 May 1903; adopted by Reverend and Mrs. Cullen, 1918. Educated at De Witt Clinton High School, New

York; New York University, B.A. 1925 (Phi Beta Kappa); Harvard University, Cambridge, Massachusetts, M.A. in English 1926. Married 1) Yolande Du Bois in 1928 (divorced, 1930); 2) Ida Mae Roberson in 1940. Assistant Editor, *Opportunity*, magazine of the National Urban League, 1927; French teacher, Frederick Douglass Junior High School, New York, 1934–46. Recipient: Guggenheim Fellowship, 1929. *Died 9 January 1946.*

PUBLICATIONS

Collections

　　On These I Stand: An Anthology of the Best Poems of Cullen.   1947.

Verse

　　Color.   1925.
　　Copper Sun.   1927.
　　The Ballad of the Brown Girl: An Old Ballad Retold.   1927.
　　The Black Christ and Other Poems.   1929.
　　The Medea and Some Poems.   1935.
　　The Lost Zoo (A Rhyme for the Young, But Not Too Young).   1940.

Plays

　　St. Louis Woman, with Arna Bontemps (produced 1946).
　　The Third Fourth of July, with Owen Dodson, in *Theatre Arts,* August 1946.

Fiction

　　One Way to Heaven.   1932.
　　My Lives and How I Lost Them (juvenile).   1942.

Other

　　Editor, *Caroling Dusk: An Anthology of Verse by Negro Poets.*   1927.

Bibliography: *Cullen: A Bio-Bibliography of Cullen* by Margaret Perry,   1971.

Reading List: *Roots of Negro Racial Consciousness: Three Harlem Renaissance Authors* by Stephen H. Bronz, 1964; *Cullen and the Negro Renaissance* by Blanche E. Ferguson, 1966; *In a Minor Chord* (on Cullen, Hurston, and Toomer) by Darwin T. Turner, 1971; *A Many-Colored Coat of Dreams: The Poetry of Cullen* by Houston A. Baker, Jr., 1974.

*　　*　　*

　　Countée Cullen, a Negro American, was a lyricist who found his inspiration among the 19th-century Romantic poets, especially John Keats. As Cullen himself said in 1928, "good poetry is a lofty thought beautifully expressed" (*St. Louis Argus*, 3 February 1928). Even though Cullen wrote poetry that was racially inspired, he was, first of all, a poet consciously in search of beauty.

Cullen was described frequently as being the least race-conscious among the early modern Negro poets who achieved fame in the 1920's during the period labelled "The Harlem Renaissance." Cullen suffered in his efforts to pay homage to Beauty and his race, and critics were divided about the effect of this conflict of universal vs. black experience (few then, including Cullen, speculated on aesthetic value from a strictly black point of view). When Cullen's first book, *Color*, appeared, one reviewer wrote, "Countée Cullen is a supreme master of Beauty" (*International Book Review*, March 1926). What a reader of Cullen's poetry must understand, however, is that Cullen was trying to place all of his poetry on the same level of achievement, rather than have his "racial" poetry (e.g., "Heritage," "Shroud of Color") judged by one set of standards and his "non-racial" poetry (e.g., "Wisdom Cometh with the Years," "To John Keats, Poet. At Spring Time") judged upon another, more universal, academic set.

As a black man, Cullen was not insensitive to the genre of music and sound indigenous to black Africa. The influence on Cullen's poetry, in most cases, is extremely subtle. Indeed, there is an interesting combination of black sensuousness and Romantic language in such lines as "Her walk is like the replica/Of some barbaric dance/Wherein the soul of Africa/Is winged with arrogance" ("A Song of Praise"). In his poetry, Cullen was consistently absorbed by the themes of love (both its joy and sorrow), beauty, and the evanescence of life as well as racial sorrow and racial problems; and he also revealed a romantic evocation of the African heritage he shared with his fellow poets in Harlem.

In his one novel, *One Way to Heaven*, Cullen displayed a deft skill at characterization and symbolism. His novel was, in Cullen's words, a "two-toned picture" of the upper and lower classes of blacks in Harlem during the 1920's.

Countée Cullen never achieved the heights many felt he was destined to reach when the reading public was exposed to his famous poem "Heritage" in March 1925. But he may have been restrained by the poignant last lines of this particular poem – "Yet do I marvel at this curious thing/To make a poet black and bid him sing!"

—Margaret Perry

CUMMINGS, E(dward) E(stlin). American. Born in Cambridge, Massachusetts, 14 October 1894. Educated at a private school in Cambridge; Cambridge High and Latin School; Harvard University, Cambridge, 1911–16 (Co-Founder, Harvard Poetry Society, 1915), B.A. (magna cum laude), 1915, M.A. 1916. Served in the Norton Harjes Ambulance Corps, 1917; prisoner of war, 1917–18. Married 1) Marion Morehouse; 2) Anne Barton. Worked at P. F. Collier and Company, mail order books, New York, 1916–17; lived in Paris, 1921–23; writer for *Vanity Fair*, New York, 1925–27. Artist: paintings included several times in group shows at the Society of Independent Artists, Paris; one-man shows include Painters and Sculptors Gallery, New York, 1932; American British Art Center, New York, 1944, 1949; Rochester Memorial Art Gallery, New York, 1945, 1950, 1954, 1957. Charles Eliot Norton Professor of Poetry, Harvard University, 1952–53. Recipient: Guggenheim Fellowship, 1933; Shelley Memorial Award, 1945; Academy of American Poets Fellowship, 1950; Harriet Monroe Poetry Award, 1950; National Book Award, 1955; Bollingen Prize, 1958. *Died 3 September 1962.*

Publications

Collections

Three Plays and a Ballet, edited by George Firmage.   1967.
Complete Poems.   1968.
Poems 1905–1962, edited by George Firmage.   1973.

Verse

Tulips and Chimneys.   1923; complete edition, 1937; edited by George Firmage, 1976.
Puella Mea.   1923.
XLI.   1925.
&.   1925.
Is 5.   1926.
Christmas Tree.   1928.
(No Title).   1930.
VV (Viva: Seventy New Poems).   1931.
No Thanks.   1935; edited by George Firmage, 1978.
1/20 (One Over Twenty).   1936.
Collected Poems.   1938.
Fifty Poems.   1940.
1 × 1.   1944.
Xaipe.   1950.
Poems 1923–1954.   1954.
95 Poems.   1958.
100 Selected Poems.   1959.
Selected Poems 1923–1958.   1960.
73 Poems.   1963.

Plays

Him.   1927.
Tom: A Ballet.   1935.
Anthropos; or, The Future of Art.   1945.
Santa Claus: A Morality.   1946.

Fiction

The Enormous Room.   1922; edited by George Firmage, 1978.

Other

CIOPW (drawings and paintings).   1931.
Eimi (travel).   1933.
i: Six Nonlectures.   1953.
Cummings: A Miscellany, edited by George Firmage.   1958; revised edition, 1965.
Adventures in Verse, photographs by Marion Morehouse.   1962.
Fairy Tales (juvenile).   1965.

Selected Letters, edited by F. W. Dupee and George Stade.   1969.

Translator, *The Red Front,* by Louis Aragon.   1933.

Bibliography: *Cummings: A Bibliography* by George Firmage, 1960.

Reading List: *The Magic-Maker: Cummings* by Charles Norman, 1958, revised edition, 1964; *Cummings: The Art of His Poetry,* 1960, and *Cummings: The Growth of a Writer,* 1964, both by Norman Friedman; *Cummings and the Critics* edited by Stanley V. Baum, 1962; *Cummings* by Barry Marks, 1964; *The Poetry and Prose of Cummings* by Robert E. Wegner, 1965; *Cummings* by Eve Triem, 1969; *Cummings: A Collection of Critical Essays* edited by Norman Friedman, 1972; *Cummings: A Remembrance of Miracles* by Bethany K. Dumas, 1973.

*   *   *

Edward Estlin Cummings, better known in lower case as e. e. cummings, is a major poet of the modern period, who grew up in a comfortable, liberal household in Cambridge, Massachusetts, where ingenuity was energetically cultivated. The neighborhood of the Irving Street home was populated by Harvard faculty; his father had taught at Harvard before becoming a Unitarian minister of considerable renown in Boston. Cummings's parents had been introduced to each other by the distinguished psychologist William James, also a neighbor. Summers were spent on the family farm in New Hampshire, where the young Cummings spent his hours musing in a study his father had built him; another was situated in a tree behind their Cambridge house. Both father and mother encouraged the gifted youth to paint and write, and, by their excessive indulgence, perhaps nurtured his diffident character. At Harvard, Cummings distinguished himself and graduated with honors in Greek and English studies, and delivered a commencement address entitled "The New Art," his survey of Cubism, new music, the writings of Gertrude Stein and Amy Lowell, all of which he defended with insight and daring before his proper Bostonian audience. It was an early declaration of Cummings's bold taste and artistic direction.

At Harvard, Cummings wrote and published poems in the undergraduate reviews, but most of them were conventional and uninspired, except for a brief collection of poems issued in a privately printed anthology, *Eight Harvard Poets* (1917). After a brief stint of work in a mail-order publishing house, the first and only regular employment in his career, Cummings quit and volunteered for service in the Norton Harjes Ambulance Corps in France. Soon after he and a friend, William Slater Brown, were interrogated by security police regarding Brown's correspondence with a German professor at Columbia University, and both were incarcerated in a French concentration camp. Cummings was freed after three months, but only after his father had written to President Wilson requesting special attention to his son's internment. From that experience, Cummings wrote *The Enormous Room,* a World War I classic, at the insistence of his father who viewed the incident as a sinister act of an ally. The long autobiographical account sparkles with reportorial details, insight, and comic invention, and asserts a theme of anti-authoritarianism throughout.

Cummings submitted his first book of poems to the publisher of *The Enormous Room,* Boni, but was refused there and at other houses. The large manuscript, entitled *Tulips and Chimneys,* contained 152 poems ranging from a long, rambling epithalamion and other derivative exercises to short, pithy works of explosive energy and significant innovation. As a last resort, Cummings's old classmate John Dos Passos found a publisher for a shortened version of 60 poems in 1923. Two years later 41 more poems were issued as *XLI,* and Cummings printed the remaining poems with some additions in *&.* In 1937, the original manuscript was issued in its entirety under its first title and now stands as one of the great classics of Modernist poetry.

For lyric energy, imagination, and verve, few books of poems compare with it. Even Cummings's later books do not have the vigor of this first work. Among the poems in the collection are "All in green went my love riding," "In Just," "O sweet spontaneous," "Buffalo Bill's/defunct." The work is astounding for its variety of voice, tone, technique, and theme, and the content ranges widely from outrageous satire to jazzy lyrics, from naive rhymes to sexually explicit portraits. Cummings caught the irreverent, slapdash tonality of the jazz age in his sprawling, sensuous lyrics. The old decorums were exploded and replaced by a humor Cummings had absorbed from vaudeville shows, burlesque houses, and music halls of the day.

But there is more to these experiments than we might suspect. The young Cummings was fascinated with the asyntactic language of Stein and the grotesque, paralogical imagery of Amy Lowell, and in the dismantled shapes of Cubist paintings, all of which seemed to liberate the artist from traditional logic. The new art made spontaneous perception the basis of expression. This was equally the force of jazz itself: the soloist departed from the melodic pattern to perform his own spontaneous variations according to his mood. Cummings attacked the conventional lyric with the lesson of these other arts. He took the formal lyric apart and redistributed each of its components: punctuation becomes a series of arbitrary signals he sometimes uses even as words. The function of nouns, pronouns, adverbs, and adjectives could all be interchanged in verbal flights. The barrel shape of the standard lyric could simply be blown open, as though the staves had all been unhooped. Language drips, spills, dribbles, runs over the frame in one of Cummings's Cubist-style poems. The genius in the experiment is that Cummings caught upon a series of innovations that seemed to Americanize the European-born lyric poem: in his irreverent care, the poem had become a display of verbal energy and exuberance, a vehicle of melting-pot humor and extravagance, a youthfully arrogant jazz variation of an old standard form. The modern lyric has continued to sprawl whimsically down the page ever since Cummings first scattered it in *Tulips and Chimneys*.

Cummings's innovations in other forms and media are less sure and significant, but he is nonetheless a refreshing influence. In the play form, he was drawn to over-subtle psychological comedy, as in *Him*, but he was far ahead of his time in his absurdist dialogue and surreal sets and costumes. Cummings was also a prolific graphic artist who worked in most media. Some of this work was published in *CIOPW*. Cummings strained the immediacy of prose with his massive account of a visit to Russia entitled *Eimi*, in which he assails the Marxist state and the regimented condition of Soviet citizens. The book offended the American left at home, which dominated the publishing field during the first years of the depression, and for several years Cummings published little work. A volume entitled *No Thanks*, the title directed at publishers who had rejected the manuscript, appeared in 1935, followed three years later by his first *Collected Poems*.

The many books of poems that succeeded *Tulips and Chimneys* sustained the nervous energy of his first experiments, but Cummings did not advance in new techniques so much as refine and consolidate his discoveries from the first book. As Norman Friedman points out, Cummings experimented with different aspects of his style in the years after 1923. In the 1930's, in *VV (ViVa)* and *No Thanks*, Cummings sought the limits of typographical experiment, extending to the curious strategy known as *tmesis*, or, the breaking up and mingling of words to achieve intense immediacy. The dismantled language of his poems focused attention on the individual word and its component letters, and often gave expressiveness to the word through its spatial arrangement. A famous poem of his later years, "l(a," is an arrangement of letters that plummet abruptly down the page, emblematic of a falling leaf and of autumn.

Over the span of his career, Cummings moved slowly away from the simple delight in love, in the seasons, in nature and simplicity, to more urgent and didactic poems that finally came to preach the virtues of naive existence, as in *Xaipe* and *95 Poems*. His argument against science, with he sometimes equated with "death," may have turned him too much against the modern world and toward pastoral themes. As a result, he is a poet of a large canon of work that is marked by much repetition of theme and perspective, but his status as a major poet is secure; one has only to "look" at an anthology of new poems to see his pervasive influence.

—Paul Christensen

CURNOW, Allen. New Zealander. Born in Timaru, 17 June 1911. Educated at Christchurch Boys High School, 1924–28; University of New Zealand, Canterbury, 1929–30, and Auckland, 1931–38, B.A. 1938; St. John's College (Anglican theological), Auckland, 1931–33. Married 1) Elizabeth J. LeCren in 1936; 2) Jenifer Mary Tole in 1965; three children. Cadet Journalist, *Sun*, Christchurch, 1929–30; Reporter and Sub-Editor, 1935–48, and Drama Critic, 1945–47, *The Press*, Christchurch; Member of the News and Sub-Editorial Staff, *News Chronicle*, London, 1949. Lecturer, 1951–53, Senior Lecturer, 1954–66, and since 1967 Associate Professor of English, University of Auckland. Recipient: New Zealand State Literary Fund travel award, 1949; Carnegie grant, 1950; New Zealand University Research Committee grant, 1957, 1966; Jessie Mackay Memorial Prize, 1957, 1962; Institute of Contemporary Arts Fellowship, Washington, D.C., 1961; Whittall Fund award, Library of Congress, 1966; New Zealand Poetry Award, 1975. Litt.D.: University of New Zealand, Auckland, 1966; University of Canterbury, Christchurch, 1975. Lives in Auckland.

PUBLICATIONS

Verse

Valley of Decision. 1933.
Another Argo, with Denis Glover and A. R. D. Fairburn. 1935.
Three Poems. 1935.
Enemies: Poems 1934–1936. 1937.
Not in Narrow Seas. 1939.
Recent Poems, with others. 1941.
Island and Time. 1941.
Verses, 1941–1942. 1942.
Sailing or Drowning. 1943.
Jack Without Magic. 1946.
At Dead Low Water, and Sonnets. 1949.
Poems 1947–1957. 1957.
A Small Room with Large Windows: Selected Poems. 1962.
Whim Wham Land. 1967.
Trees, Effigies, Moving Objects: A Sequence of 18 Poems. 1972.
An Abominable Temper and Other Poems. 1973.
Collected Poems 1933–1973. 1974.

Plays

The Axe: A Verse Tragedy (produced 1948).   1949.
Moon Section (produced 1959).
The Overseas Expert (broadcast 1961).   In Four Plays, 1972.
Doctor Pom (produced 1964).
The Duke's Miracle (broadcast 1967).   In Four Plays, 1972.
Resident of Nowhere (broadcast 1969).   In Four Plays, 1972.
Four Plays (includes The Axe, The Overseas Expert, The Duke's Miracle, Resident of
    Nowhere).   1972.

Radio Plays: The Overseas Expert, 1961; The Duke's Miracle, 1967; Resident of
Nowhere, 1969.

Other

Editor, A Book of New Zealand Verse, 1923–1945.   1945; revised edition, 1951.
Editor, The Penguin Book of New Zealand Verse.   1960.

Reading List: "Curnow's Poetry (Notes Towards a Criticism)" by C. K. Stead, in Landfall,
March 1963; "Curnow's The Axe" by A. Krishna Sarma, in The Achievement of Christopher
Fry and Other Essays, 1970.

*   *   *

Allen Curnow is the New Zealand poet who has been most closely associated with the
pursuit, common to all emergent societies, of a national identity. His sense of the complex
possibilities of language as personality, individual and national, made him one of the
outstanding poets of his time and place.

Self-scrutiny and a sense of identity are urgent, perhaps primary, objectives in any small
and isolated community where Allen Tate's sense of the word regionalism may be applied.
Curnow's major subject has been what he called the imaginative discovery of New Zealand,
and his most "major" poetry came in the years when he led the search. His later poetry,
technically even more accomplished, is characterised by a search for what Kendrick
Smithyman (in an essay in Essays on New Zealand Literature, edited by Wystan Curnow,
1962) called the "true voice of feeling."

Smithyman's own favoured definition for poetry, a way of saying, is perhaps too limiting a
term for Curnow. Consistently doctrinaire, though courteously argumentative rather than
abrasive, he is always conscious of the isolation not only of his country but of the poet
himself in the community generally indifferent or even hostile to the linguistic and moral
aspects of aesthetics which the poet is the first to record. His life and his poetry show him
consistently rejecting the ivory tower and the easy assumption that poets write only for other
poets. For many years in fact, he wrote a weekly verse column for an Auckland newspaper,
commenting on current events, and he has written verse broadsheets attacking local
philistinism. Curnow's efforts to activate his ideas in the community appear on a different
level in his plays, but it is perhaps best to consider them as complex, well-articulated
presentations of themes accessible in his poems.

Island and Time, At Dead Low Water, and A Small Room with Large Windows are his best
collections of verse. They include highly wrought meditative poems, mostly short, in a voice
that sounds mannered without being idiosyncratic or exhibitionistic. No single poem can be
taken as representative of a poetic career as long as Curnow's or of an oeuvre in which every
poem is a carefully achieved entity, but the verbal precision and concentration are well

demonstrated by the opening lines of "The Eye Is More or Less Satisfied with Seeing" (from *Poems 1949–57*):

> Wholehearted he can't move
> From where he is, nor love
>
> Wholehearted that place,
> Indigene janus-face,
>
> Half mocking half,
> Neither caring to laugh.
>
> Does true or false sun rise?
> Do both half eyes tell lies?

Curnow's voice is uniquely his own. Stylistic and other debts do show up in his poetry, but he never seems imitative. Such influences as do show themselves indicate a firmly eclectic collector's instinct. He has Eliot's concern for tradition and for a literate Europeanism. More conspicuously though, in view of his efforts towards an imaginative discovery of his region's identity, his work does show graftings from American poetry of the 1930's and 1940's, especially the poets of the American South.

C. K. Stead has made the point that the perspectives in Curnow's poems are simultaneously physical, local realities and moral, intellectual, and emotional landscapes. Imaginative self-discovery integrates the two. That kind of concern uses poetic devices as it absorbs influences, without attitudinising, without falling into a single idiom as many poets more ready with words than Curnow have done. His grappling with words and realities alike is slow, earnest, and scrupulous. Curnow is one of the three or four life-size – to use his own term – writers New Zealand has produced.

—Andrew Gurr

DAVIDSON, Donald (Grady). American. Born in Campbellsville, Tennessee, 18 August 1893. Educated at Branham and Hughes School, 1905–09; Vanderbilt University, Nashville, B.A. 1917, M.A. 1922. Served in the 324th Infantry, 81st Division, of the United States Army, in France, 1917–19: First Lieutenant. Married Theresa Sherrer in 1918; one daughter. Teacher in schools in Cedar Hill and Mooresville, Tennessee, 1910–14, and Pulaski, Tennessee, 1916–17, and at Kentucky Wesleyan College, Winchester, 1919–20; Instructor in English, 1920, Professor, 1927–64, and Professor Emeritus, 1964–68, Vanderbilt University; also, Member of the Faculty, Bread Loaf School of English, Middlebuty College, Vermont, Summers 1931–68. Co-Founder, *Fugitive* magazine, Nashville, 1922; Literary Editor and Columnist ("Spyglass"), *Nashville Tennessean*, 1924–30. Member, Advisory Board, *Modern Age* and *The Intercollegiate Review*. Chairman, Tennessee Federation for Constitutional Government, 1955–59. Litt.D.: Cumberland University, 1946; Washington and Lee University, Lexington, Virginia, 1948; L.H.D.: Middlebury College, 1965. *Died 25 April 1968.*

PUBLICATIONS

Verse

> *Avalon,* with *Armageddon* by John Crowe Ransom and *A Fragment* by William
>   Alexander Percy.   1923.
> *An Outland Piper.*   1924.
> *The Tall Men.*   1927.
> *Lee in the Mountains and Other Poems.*   1938.
> *The Long Street.*   1961.
> *Poems 1922–1961.*   1966.

Play

> *Singin' Billy,* music by Charles Faulkner Bryan (produced 1952).

Other

> *The Attack on Leviathan: Regionalism and Nationalism in the United States.*   1938.
> *American Composition and Rhetoric.*   1939; revised edition, with Ivar Lou Myhr, 1947,
>   1959.
> *The Tennessee.*   2 vols., 1946–48.
> *Twenty Lessons in Reading and Writing Prose.*   1955.
> *Still Rebels, Still Yankees, and Other Essays.*   1957.
> *Southern Writers in the Modern World.*   1958.
> *Concise American Composition and Rhetoric.*   1964.
> *The Spyglass: Views and Reviews 1924–1930,* edited by John T. Fain. 1963.
> *It Happened to Them: Character Studies of New Testament Men and Women.*   1965.
> *The Literary Correspondence of Davidson and Allen Tate,* edited by John T. Fain and T.
>   D. Young.   1974.
>
> Editor, *British Poetry of the Eighteen-Nineties.*   1937.
> Editor, with Sidney E. Glenn, *Readings for Composition.*   1942; revised edition, 1957.
> Editor, *Selected Essays and Other Writings of John Donald Wade.*   1966.

Reading List: *The Fugitive Group,* 1957, and *The Southern Critics,* 1971, both by Louise
Cowan; *The Fugitive Poets* edited by William Pratt, 1965; *Davidson: An Essay and a
Bibliography* by T. D. Young and M. Thomas Inge, 1965; *Davidson* by T. D. Young, 1971.

*   *   *

An original member of the group of poets who published *The Fugitive,* Davidson
published some of his first poems in that journal. From 1924 to 1930 he was literary editor of
the *Nashville Tennessean* and produced what one critic has called the "best literary page ever
published in the South." He contributed to both agrarian symposia, *I'll Take My Stand* (1930)
and *Who Owns America?* (1938), and is widely known and respected as poet, essayist, editor,
historian, and critic.

As poet Davidson's reputation must stand on *The Tall Men,* "Lee in the Mountains"
(1934), and a half dozen poems from *The Long Street. The Tall Men,* a book-length narrative,
is organized around a young man's search for a meaningful tradition, a heritage of heroism

and humanism. The exploration of Davidson's protagonist, a modern southern American, is not a vague, nostalgic meandering into a far distant past. Instead, his excruciating self-analysis is an attempt "to name and set apart from time/One sudden face" and to understand his present situation by discovering how he is related to the history and history makers of his own section of the country. He finally becomes aware not only of his traditional heritage but of the forces that would destroy it. "Lee in the Mountains," Davidson's most widely anthologized poem, presents Davidson's art at its best. In its epic dignity, its purity of form, its dramatic presentation of theme, it demonstrates as no other poem of his does the totality of his vision and the range of his imagination. The force and clarity of his presentation in this and many other of his poems give him a place almost unique among the poets of his generation. For Davidson, however, prose was the dominant means of expression throughout his career. As literary critic and social and political philosopher he offered cogent and convincing arguments in a prose that was lucid, smooth, and supple. As a prose stylist Davidson has few peers in contemporary American literature.

—T. D. Young

DAVIE, Donald (Alfred). English. Born in Barnsley, Yorkshire, 17 July, 1922. Educated at Barnsley Holgate Grammar School; St. Catharine's College, Cambridge, B.A. 1947, M.A. 1949, Ph.D. 1951. Served in the Royal Navy, 1941–46. Married Doreen John in 1945; two sons, one daughter. Lecturer in English, 1950–57, and Fellow of Trinity College, 1954–57, University of Dublin; Visiting Professor, University of California at Santa Barbara, 1957–58; Lecturer in English, 1958–64, and Fellow of Gonville and Caius College, 1959–64, Cambridge University; Professor of English, 1964–68, Dean of Comparative Studies, 1964, and Pro-Vice-Chancellor, 1965–68, University of Essex, Wivenhoe, Colchester; Visiting Professor, Grinnell College, Iowa, 1965; Leo S. Bing Professor of English and American Literature, University of Southern California, Los Angeles, 1968–69. Since 1969, Professor of English, and since 1974 Olive H. Palmer Professor of the Humanities, Stanford University, California. British Council Lecturer, Budapest, 1961; Elliston Lecturer, University of Cincinnati, 1963. Recipient: Guggenheim Fellowship, 1973. Honarary Fellow, St. Catharine's College, Cambridge, 1973; Fellow, American Academy of Arts and Sciences, 1973. Lives in Stanford, California.

PUBLICATIONS

Verse

(Poems). 1954.
Brides of Reason. 1955.
A Winter Talent and Other Poems. 1957.
The Forests of Lithuania, from a poem by Adam Mickiewicz. 1959.
A Sequence for Francis Parkman. 1961.
New and Selected Poems. 1961.
Events and Wisdoms: Poems 1957–1963. 1964.
Poems. 1969.

Essex Poems 1963–1967.   1969.
Six Epistles to Eva Hesse.   1970.
Collected Poems, 1950–1970.   1972.
The Shires: Poems.   1974.
In the Stopping Train.   1977.

Other

Purity of Diction in English Verse.   1952.
Articulate Energy: An Enquiry into the Syntax of English Poetry.   1955.
The Heyday of Sir Walter Scott.   1961.
The Language of Science and the Language of Literature, 1700–1740.   1963.
Ezra Pound: Poet as Sculptor.   1964.
Thomas Hardy and British Poetry.   1972.
Poetry in Translation.   1975.
Ezra Pound.   1976.
The Poet in the Imaginary Museum: Essays of Two Decades, edited by Barry
Alpert.   1976.

Editor, *The Victims of Whiggery,* by George Loveless.   1946.
Editor, *The Late Augustans: Longer Poems of the Later Eighteenth Century.*   1958.
Editor, *Poems: Poetry Supplement.*   1960.
Editor, *Poetics Poetyka.*   1961.
Editor, *Selected Poems of Wordsworth.*   1962.
Editor, *Russian Literature and Modern English Fiction: A Collection of Critical
Essays.*   1965.
Editor, with Angela Livingstone, *Pasternak.*   1969.
Editor, *Augustan Lyric.*   1974.
Editor, *The Collected Poems of Elizabeth Daryush.*   1975.

Translator, *The Poems of Dr. Zhivago,* by Pasternak.   1965.

Reading List: essay by Calvin Bedient, in *Iowa Review,* 1971; "A Breakthrough into
Spaciousness" by Donald Greene, in *Queen's Quarterly,* 1973.

*   *   *

In one of his early poems, "Homage to William Cowper," Donald Davie describes himself
as "A pasticheur of late-Augustan styles"; and many of the poems in his early collections
Brides of Reason and *A Winter Talent* display certain qualities associated with English poets
of the mid-18th century – decorum, elegance, and wit. Moreover, his critical work *Purity of
Diction in English Verse* can be read not merely as a study of the principles of purity in diction
but also as an apology for the young poets of the 1950's whose verse appeared in Robert
Conquest's anthology *New Lines* (1956).

Yet some of the poems in *A Winter Talent* suggest that Davie had already moved away
from the confines of the late-Augustan tradition. In "Dream Forest," for example, he names
as types of ideal virtue Brutus, Pushkin, and Strindberg: "Classic, romantic, realist,/These I
have set up." His admiration for Ezra Pound and his discovery of Pasternak have been partly
responsible for the increasing richness and complexity of his later poems. His departure for
Stanford University, where he succeeded to the chair formerly held by Yvor Winters (much
revered by Davie as a poet and a critic), added still more complexity. Yet he has never
forgotten his native roots: *The Shires* is made up entirely of descriptions of and reflections on

the English counties; and his recent volume *In the Stopping Train* ends with a poem about going back to the Yorkshire town of Barnsley where he was born.

Davie is probably the finest critic of his generation, his most important critical works, apart from *Purity of Diction*, being *Articulate Energy, Ezra Pound: Poet as Sculptor*, and *Thomas Hardy and British Poetry*. The title of his collected essays in literary criticism, *The Poet in the Imaginary Museum*, indicates his attitude towards poetry. He is an extremely learned man: it is right, he believes, that poets should be learned, since poetry is a product of the intellect and of the imagination fused into unity by the poetic faculty.

His poetry has always been noteworthy for its technical inventiveness, and he has consistently sought to enlarge the range of his sensibility. His finest poems are those in which his emotional and lyrical powers are allowed to attain their full strength unimpeded by cautious reservations and self-questionings. Davie is an impressive, immensely gifted writer whose creative powers show no signs of slackening.

—John Press

DAVIES, W(illiam) H(enry).   Welsh.   Born in Newport, Monmouthshire, 3 July 1871. Educated at local schools; worked for an ironmonger; apprenticed to a picture framer and gilder, 1886–91. Married Helen Payne in 1923. Travelled across America, tramping, 1893–99 (lost a leg jumping from a freight train in Ontario, 1899); lived in London, 1899–1906, Sevenoaks, Kent, 1906–14, London, 1914–22, and East Grinstead, Sussex, 1922; in Gloucestershire after 1931. Recipient: Royal Literary Fund grant, 1911. D.Litt.: University of Wales, 1926. Granted Civil List pension, 1919. *Died 26 September 1940.*

PUBLICATIONS

Collections

   The Essential Davies, edited by Brian Waters.   1951.
   Complete Poems, edited by Daniel George.   1963.

Verse

   The Soul's Destroyer and Other Poems.   1905.
   New Poems.   1906; revised edition, 1922.
   Nature Poems and Others.   1908.
   Farewell to Poesy and Other Pieces.   1910.
   Songs of Joy and Others.   1911.
   Foliage: Various Poems.   1913; revised edition, 1922.
   The Bird of Paradise and Other Poems.   1914.
   Child Lovers and Other Poems.   1916.
   Collected Poems.   1916; *Second Series,* 1923; revised edition, 1928.
   Forty New Poems.   1918.
   Raptures: A Book of Poems.   1918.

The Song of Life and Other Poems.   1920.
The Captive Lion and Other Poems.   1921.
The Hour of Magic and Other Poems.   1922.
Selected Poems.   1923.
Secrets.   1924.
A Poet's Alphabet.   1925.
The Song of Love.   1926.
A Poet's Calendar.   1927.
Forty-Nine Poems, edited by Jacynth Parsons.   1928.
Selected Poems, edited by Edward Garnett.   1928.
Ambition and Other Poems.   1929.
Poems 1930–31.   1932.
The Lovers' Song-Book.   1933.
The Poems: A Complete Collection.   1934; revised edition, 1940, 1943.
Love Poems.   1935.
The Birth of Song: Poems 1935–36.   1936.
The Loneliest Mountain and Other Poems.   1939.
Common Joys and Other Poems.   1941.

Play

True Travellers: A Tramp's Opera.   1923.

Fiction

A Weak Woman.   1911.
Dancing Mad.   1927.

Other

The Autobiography of a Super-Tramp.   1908.
Beggars.   1909.
The True Traveller.   1912.
Nature.   1914.
A Poet's Pilgrimage.   1918.
Later Days.   1925.
The Adventures of Johnny Walker, Tramp.   1926.
My Birds.   1933.
My Garden.   1933.

Editor, *Shorter Lyrics of the Twentieth Century 1900–1922.*   1922.
Editor, *Poetical Works,* by Burns.   1925.
Editor, *Jewels of Song: An Anthology of Short Poems.*   1930.

Reading List: *Davies* by Thomas Moult, 1934; *Davies: A Critical Biography* by Richard J. Stonesifer, 1963; *Davies* by Lawrence W. Hockey, 1971.

*   *   *

W. H. Davies is still thought of by many people as a poet who composed verses about kingfishers, cuckoos, and rainbows, and when critical taste turned against the rural verses of the Georgians Davies was often dismissed as a sentimental poet who took refuge from the world in an idealized countryside. He was, in fact, a tough little Welshman who had experienced at first hand urban squalor, dosshouses, slums, and rural poverty. It is true that he wrote lyrics about the birds and beasts that inhabited a countryside more beautiful and less spoiled than it is now, and some of these poems retain their charm because they are notable for exact observation as well as for lyrical grace. But Davies was also a poet who drew upon his knowledge of what it was like to be a vagabond, and who got into his poems something of the harshness and realism that characterized his prose reminiscences, *The Autobiography of a Super-Tramp.*

Arthur Waugh (the father of Evelyn Waugh), who regarded the Georgians as rather unpleasant, clever young men who wrote coarse poems, described Davies's "The Bird of Paradise" as a piece of "sheer ugliness." It is one of Davies's best poems, an unsentimental description of a prostitute's deathbed. "The Inquest," a poem put into the mouth of a juryman, describes the inquest into the death of a four-month-old illegitimate child. It is a grim little piece, presenting us with a horribly accurate picture of the corpse:

> One eye, that had a yellow lid,
> Was shut – so was the mouth, that smiled;
> The left eye open, shining bright –
> It seemed a knowing little child.

In poems such as this Davies attained a memorable strength and truthfulness that will keep his best work alive for a long while.

—John Press

DAY LEWIS, C(ecil). British. Born in Ballintubber, Ireland, 27 April 1904. Educated at Sherborne School, Dorset; Wadham College, Oxford, M.A. Served as an Editor in the Ministry of Information, London, 1941–46. Married 1) Constance Mary King in 1928 (divorced, 1951), two sons; 2) Jill Balcon in 1951, one son, one daughter. Assistant Master, Summerfields School, Oxford, 1927–28; Teacher, Larchfield, Helensburgh, 1928–30, and Cheltenham College, 1930–35; Professor of Poetry, Oxford University, 1951–56; Norton Professor of Poetry, Harvard University, Cambridge, Massachusetts, 1964–65. Clark Lecturer, 1946, and Sidgwick Lecturer, 1956, Cambridge University; Warton Lecturer, British Academy, London, 1951; Byron Lecturer, University of Nottingham, 1952; Chancellor Dunning Lecturer, Queen's University, Kingston, Ontario, 1954; Compton Lecturer, University of Hull, Yorkshire, 1968. Director, Chatto and Windus Ltd., publishers, London, 1954–72. Member, Arts Council of Great Britain, 1962–67. D.Litt.: University of Exeter, 1965; University of Hull, 1969; Litt.D.: Trinity College, Dublin, 1968. Honorary Fellow, Wadham College, Oxford, 1968. Fellow, 1944, Vice-President, 1958, and Companion of Literature, 1964, Royal Society of Literature; Honorary Member, American Academy of Arts and Letters, 1966; Member, Irish Academy of Letters, 1968. C.B.E. (Commander, Order of the British Empire), 1950. Poet Laureate, 1968 until his death. *Died 22 May 1972.*

PUBLICATIONS

Collections

The Poems, 1925–1972, edited by Ian Parsons.   1977.

Verse

Beechen Vigil and Other Poems.   1925.
Country Comets.   1928.
Transitional Poem.   1929.
From Feathers to Iron.   1931.
The Magnetic Mountain.   1933.
Collected Poems, 1929–1933.   1935; with *A Hope for Poetry*, 1935.
A Time to Dance and Other Poems.   1935.
Noah and the Waters.   1936.
A Time to Dance, Noah and the Waters and Other Poems, with an Essay, Revolution in Writing.   1936.
Overtures to Death and Other Poems.   1938.
Poems in Wartime.   1940.
Selected Poems.   1940.
Word over All.   1943.
(Poems).   1943.
Short Is the Time: Poems, 1936–43 (includes *Overtures to Death and Word over All*).   1945.
Poems, 1943–1947.   1948.
Collected Poems, 1929–1936.   1948.
Selected Poems.   1951; revised edition, 1957, 1969, 1974.
An Italian Visit.   1953.
Collected Poems.   1954.
The Newborn: D.M.B., 29th April, 1957.   1957.
Pegasus and Other Poems.   1957.
The Gate and Other Poems.   1962.
Requiem for the Living.   1964.
On Not Saying Anything.   1964.
A Marriage Song for Albert and Barbara.   1965.
The Room and Other Poems.   1965.
Day Lewis: Selections from His Poetry, edited by Patric Dickinson.   1967.
Selected Poems.   1967.
The Abbey That Refused to Die: A Poem.   1967.
The Whispering Roots.   1970; as *The Whispering Roots and Other Poems*,   1970.

Fiction

The Friendly Tree.   1936.
Starting Point.   1937.
Child of Misfortune.   1939.

Fiction (as Nicholas Blake)

A Question of Proof.   1935.

Thou Shell of Death.   1936; as *Shell of Death,* 1936.
There's Trouble Brewing.   1937.
The Beast Must Die.   1938.
The Smiler with the Knife.   1939.
Malice in Wonderland.   1940; as *Summer Camp Mystery,* 1940.
The Case of the Abominable Snowman.   1941; as *Corpse in the Snowman,* 1941.
Minute for Murder.   1947.
Head of a Traveller.   1949.
The Dreadful Hollow.   1953.
The Whisper in the Gloom.   1954.
A Tangled Web.   1956; as *Death and Daisy Bland,* 1960.
End of Chapter.   1957.
A Penknife in My Heart.   1958.
The Widow's Cruise.   1959.
The Worm of Death.   1961.
The Deadly Joker.   1963.
The Sad Variety.   1964.
The Morning after Death.   1966.
The Private Wound.   1968.

Other

Dick Willoughby (juvenile).   1933.
A Hope for Poetry.   1934.
Revolution in Writing.   1935.
Imagination and Thinking, with L. Susan Stebbing.   1936.
We're Not Going to Do Nothing: A Reply to Mr. Aldous Huxley's Pamphlet "What Are You Going to Do about It?"   1936.
Poetry for You: A Book for Boys and Girls on the Enjoyment of Poetry.   1944.
The Poetic Image.   1947.
Enjoying Poetry: A Reader's Guide.   1947.
The Colloquial Element in English Poetry.   1947.
The Otterbury Incident (juvenile).   1948.
The Poet's Task.   1951.
The Grand Manner.   1962.
The Lyrical Poetry of Thomas Hardy.   1953.
Notable Images of Virtue: Emily Brontë, George Meredith, W. B. Yeats.   1954.
The Poet's Way of Knowledge.   1957.
The Buried Day (autobiography).   1960.
The Lyric Impulse.   1965.
Thomas Hardy, with R. A. Scott-James.   1965.
A Need for Poetry?   1968.

Editor, with W. H. Auden, *Oxford Poetry 1927.*   1927.
Editor, with John Lehmann and T. A. Jackson, *A Writer in Arms,* by Ralph Fox.   1937.
Editor, *The Mind in Chains: Socialism and the Cultural Revolution.*   1937.
Editor, *The Echoing Green: An Anthology of Verse.*   3 vols., 1937.
Editor, with Charles Fenby, *Anatomy of Oxford: An Anthology.*   1938.
Editor, with L. A. G. Strong, *A New Anthology of Modern Verse, 1920–1940.*   1941.
Editor, with others, *Orion: A Miscellany 2–3.*   2 vols., 1945–46.
Editor, *The Golden Treasury of the Best Songs and Lyrical Poems in the English Language,* by Francis Turner Palgrave.   1954.

Editor, with John Lehmann, *The Chatto Book of Modern Poetry, 1915–1955.* 1956.
Editor, with Kathleen Nott and Thomas Blackburn, *New Poems 1957.* 1957.
Editor, *A Book of English Lyrics.* 1961; as *English Lyric Poems, 1500–1900,* 1961.
Editor, *The Collected Poems of Wilfred Owen.* 1963; revised edition, 1964.
Editor, *The Midnight Skaters: Poems for Young Readers,* by Edmund Blunden.   1968.
Editor, *The Poems of Robert Browning.* 1969.
Editor, *A Choice of Keats's Verse.* 1971.
Editor, *Crabbe.* 1973.

Translator, *The Georgics of Virgil.* 1940.
Translator, *The Graveyard by the Sea,* by Paul Valéry. 1947.
Translator, *The Aeneid of Virgil.* 1952.
Translator, *The Eclogues of Virgil.* 1963; with *The Georgics,* 1964.
Translator, with Mátyás Sárközi, *The Tomtit in the Rain: Traditional Hungarian Rhymes,* by Erzsi Gazdas. 1971.

Bibliography: *Day Lewis, The Poet Laureate: A Bibliography* by Geoffrey Handley-Taylor and Timothy d'Arch Smith, 1968.

Reading List: *Day Lewis* by Clifford Dyment, 1955, revised edition, 1963; *Spender, MacNeice, Day Lewis: A Critical Essay,* by Derek Stanford, 1969; *Day Lewis* by Joseph N. Riddel, 1971; *"The Angry Young Men" of the Thirties* by Elton E. Smith, 1975.

*   *   *

C. Day Lewis, radical Marxist in his youth, yet the successor of John Masefield as Poet Laureate in 1968, died in the home of his friend Kingsley Amis, one of the Angry Young Men of the 1950's. He had been schoolmaster, writer of detective fiction under the pseudonym Nicholas Blake, and lecturer on poetry at Cambridge, Oxford, and Harvard. His charmed decade was the proletarian 1930's when, along with Auden, Spender, and MacNeice, he made a poetic diagnosis of what was wrong with England. Exploring the roots of disease in the past, he rode a light-engine backwards amid rusting iron-works and worked-out mines (*Transitional Poem*). Four years later he played the role of a Socialist Christ, calling Britons to leave all that moribund past, join hands in brotherhood, and make pilgrimage together to the economic heaven of *The Magnetic Mountain.* Four years later still, he was insisting that liberal individualism had lost its chance (*Starting Point*); the encrusted conditions of the life of modern man required radical breakthrough (*Overtures to Death*).

A constitutional dualist, he was always torn between absolute and particular beauty (*Beechen Vigil*), idea and actuality. Although he wrote less about politics than Spender or Auden, he was convinced that a poet in the 1930's must be a propagandist for a new and better world (*A Hope for Poetry*). But he had to keep convincing himself that socialism was the only ideology that offered any hope (*A Time to Dance*). Even in his prayer for his unborn child, he recognizes the two options of complete, unquestioning conformity and total rebellion which needs no props from public opinion (*From Feathers to Iron*).

After having begun with a stirring call to revolution, and holding out the vision of a new and nobler race of men, the capitalistic confrontation of World War II made him reluctantly aware that it was too late to warn, too early to hope (*Word over All*).

Increasingly he turned back to a neo-Georgian verse and the practical expediencies of detective fiction, remuneratively received by the reading public, and to academic lectureships in England and the United States. Undoubtedly the clearest singing voice of the Auden

Group, he managed to unite traditional prosody to radical thought. When the radical element lost its strident message, the lyric voice continued as the special gift of the rebel who became Laureate.

—Elton E. Smith

---

de la MARE, Walter. English. Born in Charlton, Kent, 25 April 1873. Educated at St. Paul's Cathedral Choristers' School, London (Founder, *The Choristers Journal*, 1889). Married Constance Elfrida Ingpen in 1899 (died, 1943); two sons, two daughters. Clerk, Anglo-American Oil Company, 1890–1908. Reviewer for *The Times* and *The Westminster Gazette*, London. Recipient: Polignac Prize, 1911; Black Memorial Prize, for fiction, 1922; Library Association Carnegie Medal, for children's book, 1948; Foyle Poetry Prize, 1954. D.Litt.: Oxford, Cambridge, Bristol, and London universities; LL.D.: University of St. Andrews. Honorary Fellow, Keble College, Oxford. Granted Civil List pension, 1908; Companion of Honour, 1948; Order of Merit, 1953. *Died 22 June 1956.*

PUBLICATIONS

Collections

de la Mare: A Selection from His Writings, edited by Kenneth Hopkins.   1956.
The Complete Poems, edited by Leonard Clark and others.   1969.

Verse

Poems.   1906.
The Listeners and Other Poems.   1912.
The Old Men.   1913.
The Sunken Garden and Other Poems.   1917.
Motley and Other Poems.   1918.
Flora.   1919.
Poems 1901 to 1918.   2 vols., 1920.
The Veil and Other Poems.   1921.
Thus Her Tale: A Poem.   1923.
A Ballad of Christmas.   1924.
The Hostage.   1925.
St. Andrews, with Rudyard Kipling.   1926.
Selected Poems.   1927.
Stuff and Nonsense and So On.   1927; revised edition, 1946.
The Captive and Other Poems.   1928.
The Sunken Garden and Other Verses.   1931.
Two Poems.   1931.
The Fleeting and Other Poems.   1933.
Poems 1919 to 1934.   1935.

Poems.   1937.
Memory and Other Poems.   1938.
Two Poems, with Arthur Rogers.   1938.
Collected Poems.   1941.
Time Passes and Other Poems, edited by Anne Ridler.   1942.
The Burning-Glass and Other Poems, Including The Traveller.   1945.
The Burning-Glass and Other Poems.   1945.
The Traveller.   1946.
Two Poems: Pride, The Truth of Things.   1946.
Inward Companion: Poems.   1950.
Winged Chariot.   1951.
Winged Chariot and Other Poems.   1951.
O Lovely England and Other Poems.   1953.
Selected Poems, edited by R. N. Green-Armytage.   1954.
The Morrow.   1955.
Envoi.   1965.

Play

Crossings: A Fairy Play (juvenile), music by C. Armstrong Gibbs (produced
     1919).   1921.

Fiction

*Henry Brocken: His Travels and Adventures in the Rich, Strange, Scarce-Imaginable
     Regions of Romance.*   1904.
The Return.   1910; revised edition, 1922.
Memoirs of a Midget.   1921.
Lispet, Lispett, and Vaine.   1923.
The Riddle and Other Stories.   1923; as *The Riddle and Other Tales,* 1923.
Ding Dong Bell.   1924.
Two Tales: The Green-Room, The Connoisseur.   1925.
The Connoisseur and Other Stories.   1926.
At First Sight.   1928.
On the Edge: Short Stories.   1930.
Seven Short Stories.   1931.
A Froward Child.   1934.
The Nap and Other Stories.   1936.
The Wind Blows Over.   1936.
The Picnic and Other Stories.   1941.
Best Stories.   1942.
The Collected Tales, edited by Edward Wagenknecht.   1950.
A Beginning and Other Stories.   1955.
Ghost Stories.   1956.

Other

Songs of Childhood (juvenile).   1902.
M. E. Coleridge: An Appreciation.   1907.
The Three Mulla-Mulgars (juvenile).   1910; as *The Three Royal Monkeys; or The Three
     Mulla-Mulgars,*   1935.

A Child's Day: A Book of Rhymes (juvenile).   1912.
Peacock Pie: A Book of Rhymes (juvenile).   1913.
Story and Rhyme: A Selection (juvenile).   1921.
Down-Adown-Derry: A Book of Fairy Poems (juvenile).   1922.
Broomsticks and Other Tales (juvenile).   1925.
Miss Jemima (juvenile).   1925.
Old Joe (juvenile).   1927.
Told Again: Traditional Tales (juvenile).   1927; as *Tales Told Again*, 1959.
Some Women Novelists of the 'Seventies.   1929.
Stories from the Bible (juvenile).   1929.
Desert Islands and Robinson Crusoe.   1930; revised edition, 1932.
Poems for Children.   1930.
The Dutch Cheese and the Lovely Myfanwy (juvenile).   1931.
The Early Novels of Wilkie Collins.   1932.
Lewis Carroll.   1932.
The Lord Fish and Other Tales (juvenile).   1933.
*Early One Morning in the Spring: Chapters on Children and on Childhood as It Is
    Revealed in Particular in Early Memories and Early Writings.*   1935.
This Year, Next Year (juvenile).   1937.
Arthur Thompson: A Memoir.   1938.
An Introduction to Everyman.   1938.
Stories, Essays, and Poems, edited by M. M. Bozman.   1938.
Animal Stories, Chosen, Arranged, and in Some Part Re-Written (juvenile).   1939.
Pleasures and Speculations.   1940.
Bells and Grass: A Book of Rhymes (juvenile).   1941.
The Old Lion and Other Stories (juvenile).   1942.
The Magic Jacket and Other Stories (juvenile).   1943.
Collected Rhymes and Verses (juvenile).   1944; as *Rhymes and Verses: Collected Poems
    for Children,* 1947.
The Scarecrow and Other Stories (juvenile).   1945.
The Dutch Cheese and Other Stories (juvenile).   1946.
Collected Stories for Children.   1947.
Selected Stories and Verses (juvenile), edited by Eleanor Graham.   1952.
Private View (essays).   1953.
A Penny a Day (juvenile).   1960.
Poems (juvenile), edited by Eleanor Graham.   1962.

Editor, *Come Hither: A Collection of Rhymes and Poems for the Young of All
    Ages.*   1923.
Editor, with Thomas Quayle, *Readings: Traditional Tales Told by the Author*
    (juvenile).   5 vols., 1926–28.
Editor, *Poems,* by Christina Rossetti.   1930.
Editor, *The Eighteen-Eighties: Essays by Fellows of the Royal Society of
    Literature.*   1930.
Editor, *Tom Tiddler's Ground: A Book of Poetry for the Junior and Middle Schools.*   3
    vols., 1931.
Editor, *Old Rhymes and New, Chosen for Use in Schools.*   2 vols., 1932.
Editor, *Behold, This Dreamer! Of Reverie, Night, Sleep, Dream, Love-Dreams,
    Nightmare, Death, The Unconscious, The Imagination, Divination, The Artist, and
    Kindred Subjects* (anthology).   1939.
Editor, *Love.*   1943.

Reading List: *de la Mare: An Exploration* by John Atkins, 1947; *de la Mare: A Study of His
Poetry* by H. C. Duffin, 1949; *de la Mare* by Kenneth Hopkins, 1953; *de la Mare* by Leonard

Clark, 1960; *de la Mare* by D. R. McCrosson, 1966; *L'Oeuvre de de la Mare: Une Aventure Spirituelle* by Luce Bonnerot, 1969 (includes bibliography).

*   *   *

"The lovely in life is the familiar," declared Walter de la Mare, "and only the lovelier for continuing strange." Those lines crystallize the poet's renewing sense of wonder in the most apparently ordinary sights and sounds of every day. Through his perception of the miracle shining out from the accepted commonplace, tiny and transient things may mirror, and often illuminate, the nature of the tremendous and timeless: "noonday's immensity ... in a bead of dew," the answer to "a lifetime's mysteries" discovered in a flower or fragment of moss.

The prevalence of the word "strange," with its evocative associates "ghost," "phantom," "haunt," infuse de la Mare's work with its unique, pervasive quality of "otherness." For much of the time his imagination inhabits a twilit borderland between dream and waking. His ubiquitous, enigmatic Strangers, Wanderers, Travellers seem to personify an irresistible compulsion to explore the shadowy regions of fantasy – "the spell of far Arabia" – beckoning just across the frontiers of the visible, known world.

De la Mare's fiction, with its recurring theme of an exile's return, contains like his poems elusive presences by no means always benign. The stories *The Return*, "Seaton's Aunt," and *Memoirs of a Midget* and such sinister poems as "The Feckless Dinner Party," "Good Company," and "Fear" vividly communicate de la Mare's sense of macabre and malignant influences at work. And yet, he affirms, "There is a radiant core of rapture/None but the fearful know"; and his conviction of the potency of evil is equalled by a firm faith in its antithesis. His reverence for innocence is memorably embodied in his portraits of the children in "Pollie," "A Child Asleep," "Tom's Angel," and many other poems; above all, perhaps, in the stubbornly persistent questioner of "Reserved," posing such a disconcerting challenge to adult materialism.

Like Vaughan, Traherne, Blake, and Wordsworth, de la Mare believes that man in his early years is closer than at any other time to understanding the truth of things; and that never again can he recapture the world-without-end contentment of the small boy by the river in "A Sunday." Yet in his own immediacy of response, he himself retains a child's-eye freshness of vision, and brings to it the wisdom and enrichment, rather than the disillusion or cynicism, of maturity. Proof of his rare sympathy with the very young is the perennial popularity of the rhymes and verses in *Peacock Pie*, *Stuff and Nonsense*, and *Bells and Grass*, with their individual blend of fantasy and fun so spellbinding to the imagination of childhood.

The concluding lines of "All That's Past" enshrine two very characteristic de la Mare themes: "Silence and sleep like fields/Of amaranth lie." Listening intently with the ear of spirit rather than sense, in such poems as "Music Unheard," "Unheard Melodies," and "The Sunken Garden," de la Mare finds that echo-haunted "music men call silence here" more pregnant than the most seductive sound. Sleep, for him, holds a similar enchantment, and appears in a variety of guises: from the mother discovered by the wondering child in "The Sleeper" to the shepherd Nod and his "blind old sheepdog, Slumber-Soon." De la Mare has devoted an anthology, *Behold, This Dreamer!*, to "All the enchanted realm of dream/That burgeons out of night"; and the recurrence of the words "dream" and "dreamer" throughout his poems epitomizes his preoccupation with the imagination's adventures once it has slipped free of the curbing reins of consciousness.

Time, in many of de la Mare's poems, is the "quiet enemy" relentless in pursuit and destruction. With a "poppied hand" it steals youth's simplicity and innocence, robs women of their beauty ("beauty vanishes; beauty passes,/However rare, rare it be"), and takes away into death those most deeply loved. Such losses are inconsolably mourned in the poignant lament of "Alone," with its refrain "Alas, my loved one is gone,/I am alone:/It is winter"; the two poems entitled "The Ghost"; and "Autumn," which ends on a dying fall of grief, "Silence where hope was." The plangency of the word "forlorn," in that poem, echoes through many more to express not only regret for time's thefts and human transience, but a sense of man's exile from Eden. He alone among created things is burdened by doubt and inner division, vain subtleties of thought and questioning of the "riddle of life .../An endless war twixt contrarieties." In such moods, the joys of earth are no more than echoes, and shadows, of that lost imperishable delight: "Betrayed and fugitive, I still must roam/A world where sin, and beauty, whisper of home."

As de la Mare grew older, he became increasingly preoccupied, in poems like "The Last Chapter," "Anatomy," "The Death-Dream," and "Even in the Grave," with the ultimate mystery as the subject of endless speculation and surmise. Here the most frequent note is the sadness, revealed at the end of his fine and moving "A Portrait," of "A foolish, fond old man, his bedtime nigh," who "scarce can bear it when the sun goes in." "A Farewell" ("When I lie where shades of darkness") also expresses his reluctance to leave the world it so memorably celebrates – "whose wonder," he confesses, "Was the very proof of me." Yet that poem is also a positive and triumphant affirmation that his love of earth, as that of others before him has done, will intensify and perpetuate its beauty for future generations.

—Margaret Willy

DICKEY, James (Lafayette). American. Born in Atlanta, Georgia, 2 February 1923. Educated at Clemson College, South Carolina, 1942; Vanderbilt University, Nashville, Tennessee, B.A. (magna cum laude) 1949 (Phi Beta Kappa), M.A. 1950. Served in the United States Army Air Force during World War II, and in the Air Force during the Korean War. Married 1) Maxine Syerson in 1948 (died, 1976), two sons; 2) Deborah Dobson in 1976. Taught at Rice University, Houston, 1950, 1952–54, and University of Florida, Gainesville, 1955–56; Poet-in-Residence, Reed College, Portland, Oregon, 1963–64, San Fernando Valley State College, Northridge, California, 1964–66, and the University of Wisconsin, Madison, 1966. Consultant in Poetry, Library of Congress, Washington, D.C., 1966–68. Since 1969, Professor of English and Writer-in-Residence, University of South Carolina. Recipient: Vachel Lindsay Prize, 1959; Longview Foundation Award, 1960; Guggenheim Fellowship, 1961; Melville Cane Award, 1966; National Book Award, 1966; National Institute of Arts and Letters grant, 1966. Lives in South Carolina.

PUBLICATIONS

Verse

Into the Stone and Other Poems.   1960.
Drowning with Others.   1962.
Helmets.   1964.
Two Poems of the Air.   1964.
Buckdancer's Choice.   1965.
Poems 1957–1967.   1967.
The Achievement of James Dickey: A Comprehensive Selection of His Poems, edited by
    Laurence Lieberman.   1968.
The Eye-Beaters, Blood, Victory, Madness, Buckhead, and Mercy.   1970.
The Zodiac.   1976.

Plays

Screenplay: *Deliverance*, 1972.

Television Play: *The Call of the Wild*, from the novel by Jack London, 1976.

Fiction

Deliverance.   1970.

Other

The Suspect in Poetry.   1964.
A Private Brinksmanship.   1965.
Spinning the Crystal Ball: Some Guesses at the Future of American Poetry.   1967.
Babel to Byzantium: Poets and Poetry Now.   1968.
Self-Interviews, edited by Barbara and James Reiss.   1970.
Sorties (essays).   1971.
Exchanges ..., *Being in the Form of a Dialogue with Joseph Trumbull Stickney.*   1971.
Jericho: The South Beheld.   1974.
God's Images: The Bible − A New Vision.   1977.
Tucky the Hunter (juvenile).   1978.

Translator, *Stolen Apples*, by Evgenii Evtushenko.   1971.

Bibliography: *Dickey, The Critic as Poet: An Annotated Bibliography* by Eileen Glancy, 1971; *Dickey: A Checklist* by Franklin Ashley, 1972.

Reading List: *Dickey: The Expansive Imagination* edited by Richard J. Calhoun, 1973.

*   *   *

James Dickey emerged as an important American poet and as a still underrated literary critic through an astonishing period of creative productivity from 1957 to 1967. He was regarded so much as a poet without imitators and without specific social or political concerns that his important contributions to post-modernism, both as poet and critic, were not adequately recognized. But Dickey should be seen as a post-modernist romantic − because of his desire to make imaginative contact with natural forces which have been lost to modern man, because of his romantic faith in the power of his imagination, and because of the expansive, affirmative character of most of his poems.

Dickey has always violated the modernist practice of impersonality in poetry, for there has always been a close correspondence between the chronology of his poems and his life. In his earliest poems he drew from such autobiographical data as the death (before Dickey was born) of his brother Eugene and his experiences as a fighter pilot in two destructive wars, as well as from his love for hunting, archery, and the southern landscape. Many of these poems feature encounters leading to vividly imagined exchanges of identity between the living and the dead, between men and "unthinking" nature, for the purpose of understanding through the imagination what reason alone cannot comprehend.

Dickey early declared himself as an affirmative poet, with an acknowledged affinity for the poetry of his friend and mentor, Theodore Roethke; but his affirmations were from the knowing perspective of a grateful survivor of two wars. His poems have always portrayed those who were *not* survivors and affirmed the risk inherent in an exchange of identity. In his later poems, especially in *The Eye-Beaters*, Dickey's persona is a middle-aged survivor of the destructive forces of nature. In addition, Dickey has exhibited a fascination with fantasy, with what he has called his "country surrealism," blurring distinctions between reality and dreams, or even hallucinations. His intention has been to produce a poetry that releases the unconscious and the irrational, with results that are both life affirmative and life threatening.

Two poems that might serve as transitions from his earlier to his later themes are "Power and Light" and "Falling," both from *Poems 1957–1967*. There is a shift of emphasis from a celebration of "more life" through the imaginative comprehension of nature to the necessity of confronting destructive forces and of finding spiritual resources for that confrontation. Dickey's formal interests have likewise shifted from regular towards more irregular forms, from the directness of "the simple declarative sentence" to the intimations of open and "big forms," and to such devices a split space punctuation within lines – effective in a tour de force like "Falling," but less effective in more recent poems.

Dickey is by birth and residence a southern poet, with academic credentials from the stronghold of agrarianism, Vanderbilt University. Yet he makes it clear that he is no "latter-day Agrarian." Still, like John Crowe Ransom, who feared the loss of "the world's body," and Allen Tate, who feared the loss of "complete knowledge" of man and his universe in an era dominated by science, Dickey has his own version of agrarian fears of technology and urbanization. He is "much more interested in a man's relationship to the God-made world, or the universe made, than to the man-made.... The relationship of the human being to the great natural cycles of birth and death, the seasons, the growing up of seasons out of dead leaves, the generations of animals and of men, all on the heraldic wheel of existence is very beautiful to me" (*Self-Interviews*).

In the 1970's Dickey's production of poetry has lessened with a developing interest in the novel, television and movie scripts, and a form of literary criticism, the self-interview. His successful novel, *Deliverance*, shares with his poetry a concern with the cycle of entry into "unthinking nature," followed by a return to the world, perhaps having become while in nature "another thing." The return to the human realm is just as important as the entry into the natural. He has most recently been engaged in writing prose-poem celebrations of the southern landscape (*Jericho*), and poetic "imitations" of the poems of a drunken, Dutch sailor-poet of the 1940's (*The Zodiac*) and of the King James version of the Bible (*God's Images*).

—Richard J. Calhoun

DOBSON, Rosemary (de Brissac).   Australian.   Born in Sydney, New South Wales, 18 June 1920; grand-daughter of the poet Austin Dobson. Educated at Frensham, Mittagong, New South Wales; University of Sydney; studied art. Married A. T. Bolton in 1951; one daughter, two sons. Recipient: Myer Award, 1966. Lives in Canberra.

PUBLICATIONS

Verse

In a Convex Mirror.   1944.
The Ship of Ice and Other Poems.   1948.

Child with a Cockatoo and Other Poems. 1955.
(Poems). 1963.
Cock Crow: Poems. 1965.
Rosemary Dobson Reads from Her Own Work (with recording). 1970.
Collected Poems. 1973.
Greek Coins. 1977.

Other

Focus on Ray Crooke. 1971.

Editor, *Australia, Land of Colour, Through the Eyes of Australian Painters.* 1962.
Editor, *Songs for All Seasons: 100 Poems for Young People.* 1967.

Reading List: "Dobson: A Portrait in a Mirror" by A. D. Hope, in *Quadrant*, July–August 1972; "The Poetry of Dobson" by James McAuley, in *Australian Literary Studies*, May 1973.

*   *   *

A detachment in Rosemary Dobson's poetry, a high-bred reserve, as well as a reticence in publishing it, has tended to cause her work to be overlooked by the general public. Its fine craftsmanship, its formal elegance, its lack of obvious emotional appeal are not to the taste of this technicolour age. It is true that in the early poems in *In a Convex Mirror* one can perhaps detect here and there a genuine inhibitedness, a fear of feeling, in "Foreshore," "The Dove," or "The Rider." The very title of the book suggests remoteness and detachment: a convex mirror causes objects to look smaller and farther away than they are, though it sharpens their outlines and gives them a curious, brilliant patina. This sheen is characteristic of the work as a whole, and lends a certain distinction to the poems independent of their general success. The poems written in the 1940's, like so many Australian poems of that period, were concerned with the metaphysics of time but it is not certain that the author was merely following a fashion. She is the granddaughter of the Victorian poet and essayist Austin Dobson, and it may have been his poem "The Paradox of Time" which first interested her in the notion of time standing still while humanity moves on. This idea attracts her to great pictures, for example, about which she has written so often and so acutely: their power to hold a given moment forever, as well as their power to lift the commonplace to an other-worldly dimension. Her fullest treatment of the time theme is the long dramatic poem "The Ship of Ice," the title-poem in a book which also contains the masterly sequence "The Devil and the Angel," a series of sharp, dramatic, Browningesque sketches in which lyricism, wit, and humour combine to convey a metaphysical idea. In these poems, the Devil and the Archangel Michael meet various figures who are about to die to invite them to make a final decision on which direction they wish to take – to Heaven or to Hell. The poems point up not only the difference between the two angels, but the subtle similarities between them, especially in the last poems where we find them subject to flattery from a poet. One of the most interesting is the encounter with a scarecrow in a summer field, who refuses to choose at all. He prefers life as an inanimate object in a world of natural objects to eternal, spiritual life – ironic praise of the visible world.

Child with a Cockatoo contains many poems about paintings, including the beautiful "The Bystander" and "Detail from an Annunciation by Crivelli." More traditional in form than Auden's they are, like his "Musée des Beaux Arts," points of departure for individual meditations. More of the poems in this volume, however, are concerned with personal experience, especially the experience of motherhood. One, "Cock Crow," conveys poignantly the difficulties of being at once daughter, mother, and poet. Some pieces are influenced by medieval ballads and have an eerie, legendary, magical quality entirely their own, for example, the haunting "The Stepdaughter":

> She went to the well for water,
> More beautiful than morning,
> Than sweet, clear running water
> And humble as the day.
> She fetched for her sister
> And carried for her mother,
> And the flame on the hearth-stone
> Spoke to her "Stay."

This book contains a few poems which herald Rosemary Dobson's interest in Greek themes. *Greek Coins*, which she has also illustrated, is inspired by J. G. Frazer's and Peter Levi's translations of Pausanias's *Guide to Greece*. These four-line "coin-sized" poems are as exquisitely evocative as epigrams from the *Greek Anthology* itself.

—Dorothy Green

DOOLITTLE, Hilda ("H. D."). American. Born in Bethlehem, Pennsylvania, 10 September 1886. Educated at Gordon School, and Friends' Central School, 1902–04, both in Philadelphia; Bryn Mawr College, Pennsylvania, 1904–06. Married the writer Richard Aldington in 1913 (divorced, 1937); one daughter. Lived in Europe after 1911. Closely associated with the Imagist movement after 1913: took over editorship of *Egoist* magazine from her husband, 1916–17. Recipient: Brandeis University Creative Arts Award, 1959; American Academy of Arts and Letters Award of Merit Medal, 1960. *Died 28 September 1961.*

PUBLICATIONS

Verse

> *Sea Garden.* 1916.
> *Choruses from the Iphigenia in Aulis by Euripides.* 1916.
> *The Tribute, and Circe.* 1917.
> *Choruses from the Iphigenia in Aulis and the Hippolytus by Euripides.* 1919.
> *Hymen.* 1921.
> *Helidora and Other Poems.* 1924.
> *Collected Poems.* 1925.
> *The Usual Star.* 1928.
> *Red Roses for Bronze.* 1929; revised edition, 1931.
> *What Do I Love.* 1943(?).
> *The Walls Do Not Fall.* 1944.

Tribute to the Angels.   1945.
The Flowering of the Rod.   1946.
By Avon River.   1949.
Selected Poems.   1957.
Helen in Egypt.   1961.
Hermetic Definition.   1972.

Plays

Hippolytus Temporizes.   1927.
Ion, by Euripides.   1937.

Fiction

Palimpsest.   1926, revised edition, 1968.
Hedylus.   1928.
Kora and Ka.   1930.
Nights.   1935.
The Hedgehog (juvenile).   1936.
Bid Me to Live: A Madrigal.   1960.

Other

Tribute to Freud, with Unpublished Letters by Freud to the Author.   1956, revised
edition, 1974.

Reading List: *The Classical World of H. D.* by Thomas Burnett Swann, 1962; *Doolittle – H.
D.* by Vincent Quinn, 1967; "Doolittle Issue" of *Contemporary Literature 10,* 1969.

*   *   *

Hilda Doolittle, whose works were published under the initials H. D., was an American
poet of considerable significance. Her work itself is precise, careful, sharp, and compressed; it
gives one the sense that the poet is excluding much more than she expresses. Natural objects
(e.g., "Oread," "Pear Tree") are presented in lines that are free of conventional poetic
rhythms and that are yet as carefully shaped as a piece of Greek statuary. So the immediate
pleasure of much of H. D.'s work is a response to an object that is created by a few carefully
chosen phrases: phrases that exist in the presence of easy and facile language that has been
excluded. As painters say, the "negative space" – the area around a represented object – is as
important as the object itself.

Miss Doolittle's work has an air of being isolated, of being simply her considered and
purified record of what has stirred her senses and her emotions: the natural world with, for
human context, the ancient Greek world as Miss Doolittle remembers it. Birds fly through air
that is radiantly Greek, love intensifies its expression in the presence of Helen and Lais, and
the mysteries of life and death bring into view satyrs and not Christian saints.

But Miss Doolittle's work did not actually proceed in isolation; she was closely associated
with the Imagist movement from 1913 onwards. Ezra Pound, John Gould Fletcher, Amy
Lowell, and others thought of their poetic effort as a realization of Walt Whitman's demand
for new words that would bring poetry closer to the object it was "rendering" and free poetic
expression from the abstractions and the overt moral purposes which had made much

nineteenth-century poetry vague and imprecise. Poetry – and this was a main drive of Imagist theory – was a medium in which could appear the poet's direct apprehension of physical entities and the poet's immediate reaction to those entities. In pursuit of object and emotion, the poet should be free to discard both conventional rhythms and shop-worn poetic diction. Much of Miss Doolittle's poetry achieves these aims. Thus, the emotion in many a poem is coerced, to be recreated in the mind of the reader, by the carefully selected physical details – details which pass before the reader following a syntax that is simple and uninvolved and expressed in words that are familiar and unmysterious. But the poems, in the long run, are not free of general impressions or even abstractions although they state very few. The impressions and abstractions must vary from reader to reader, but they concern the beneficence that reaches the human mind through the senses; it is a beneficence unsullied by ancient dogma and more recent social purpose. Poets like Shelley and Tennyson did not hesitate to offer "gospels." If there is some sort of message in much of Miss Doolittle's work, it is very nearly fused with the external world she duplicates.

A modification of these effects appears in a late work like *The Walls Do Not Fall*. This work, using the techniques of the writer's previous verse, moves beyond the innocent and "natural" invocations of Greek health – health which is also of the physical world. But the destructions of World War II make the Greek health an insufficient corrective to modern chaos. *The Walls Do Not Fall* becomes quite specific about the sources of human health. Those sources find expression not only in halcyon flight and the play of light on the Aegean Sea. They can be traced in the essence of all great religions, and it is particularly the work of Egyptian gods that allows us to see the physical world achieving completion in myths and rituals. In such a body of faith as the Egyptian are myth and "Vision" coming into a focus of great human relevance. H. D. sees the Egyptian Amen and the later "Christos" as identical. They and other august entities are the symbols if not the ultimate élan of the eternal cycles of excellence and health which modern insanity – in its pursuit of power and inferior sorts of knowledge – has ignored.

This concluding attitude in the work of H. D. may strike some readers as going beyond the confines of the early Imagism. The attitude can also be regarded as an effort to defend and exploit the initial stance of Imagist simplicity and directness. These are opposing judgments. At any rate, in her late work Miss Doolittle's implications intensify and complicate themselves. But the modes of expression do not change. Perhaps their persistence indicates an essential continuity in the entire body of Miss Doolittle's poetry.

—Harold H. Watts

DOUGLAS, Keith (Castellain). English. Born in Tunbridge Wells, Kent, 24 January 1920. Educated at Edgeborough School, Guildford, Surrey, 1926–31; Christ's Hospital, Sussex, 1931–38; Merton College, Oxford, 1938–40. Served in the 2nd Derbyshire Yeomanry, British Army, in the Middle East, 1940–44; killed in action in the Normandy invasion. *Died 9 June 1944.*

PUBLICATIONS

Collections

The Collected Poems, edited by John Waller and G. S. Fraser. 1951; revised edition, 1966.

Selected Poems, edited by Ted Hughes.   1964.
Complete Poems, edited by Desmond Graham.   1978.

Verse

Selected Poems, with John Hall and Norman Nicholson.   1943.

Other

Alamein to Zem Zem.   1946; edited by John Waller, G. S. Fraser, and John Hall, 1966.

Editor, with A. M. Hardie, *Augury: An Oxford Miscellany of Verse and Prose.*   1940.

Reading List: "Douglas: A Poet of the Second World War" by G. S. Fraser, in *Proceedings of the British Academy 42,* 1956; *Douglas: A Biography* by Desmond Graham, 1974.

*   *   *

Although his work was admired on its first (posthumous) publication, it was only in the 1960's that Keith Douglas was widely and variously hailed as the finest war poet of his time, the best poet of his generation, the most talented British poet since Auden. His new champions were poets – Hughes, Hill, Silkin, Tomlinson, Hamburger – who saw in his work an object lesson for the poetry of their own time.

The centre of Douglas's art lies in what Geoffrey Hill, linking Douglas with Isaac Rosenberg, has called "a fearlessness of the imagination ... the willingness to lay the mind completely open to experience" (*Stand,* 1964–65). Most intense in his poems and ink sketches of the desert war, this quality of mind was present from the start of a remarkably precocious writing life. Technically accomplished from the age of fourteen, published in *New Verse* while a school-boy, widely published at Oxford and in the Middle East, but fitting neither the coteries nor the fashions of his period, Douglas rapidly assimilated Auden, Yeats and Eliot, Shakespeare and Donne, translated Rimbaud and Horace, read Rilke in German. In a trenchant letter of August 1943 (in *Complete Poems*) he described his progress in terms of a conflict between lyric and cynic. The one early established a fluency of metaphor and sureness of cadence; the other tested his harmonies with the scepticism of intelligence and the abrasiveness of speech. Before experience of battle his style had already clarified into a more metaphysical manner, and his war poems sharpen this focus, looking through appearances and expressing what he finds, in a verse which "combines a colloquial prose readiness with poetic breadth" (Ted Hughes), as in "How to Kill":

> Now in my dial of glass appears
> the soldier who is going to die.
> He smiles, and moves about in ways
> his mother knows, habits of his.
> The wires touch his face: I cry
> NOW. Death, like a familiar, hears
>
> and look, has made a man of dust
> of a man of flesh. This sorcery
> I do. Being damned, I am amused
> to see the centre of love diffused
> and the waves of love travel into vacancy.
> How easy it is to make a ghost.

For Douglas the desert battlefield is "an altered planet" of which the dead are the "true inheritors," a "looking-glass world" where "a man with no head/has a packet of chocolate and a souvenir of Tripoli." It surprises his curiosity, showing fools to be truly heroes, pity to be useless, killing to be pleasing, cynicism to give way to love. He observes honestly, seeking meanings, patterns, employing detachment as a means of contact, a way in which passionate care for consequences can function undeterred. At once assured and unnerving, Douglas looks into war just as, at six, terrified of an injection, he had fixed his gaze on the needle, stared as it entered his arm.

—Desmond Graham

DUGGAN, Eileen (May). New Zealander. Born in Tua Marina, 21 May 1894. Educated at Marlborough Girls' High School; Victoria University College, M.A. (honours) in history 1918. Teacher, Dannevirke High School, St. Patrick's College; Lecturer in History, Victoria University College. Recipient: Royal Society of Literature Honarary Fellowship, 1943. O.B.E. (Officer, Order of the British Empire). *Died in 1972.*

PUBLICATIONS

Verse

Poems. 1921.
New Zealand Bird Songs. 1929.
Poems. 1937.
New Zealand Poems. 1940.
More Poems. 1951.

Other

Editor, *Letters from the North Solomons,* by Emmet McHardy. 1935.

Reading List: *Duggan* by F. M. McKay, 1977.

*   *   *

Eileen Duggan was the first New Zealand poet to establish an international reputation. Her background – the daughter of Irish immigrants and a childhood coloured by tales of famine, rack rents, and evictions – gives her verse its direction. She came to see that the restlessness of exile, experienced through identification with the dispossessed Irish, could be resolved only in New Zealand. This realisation is the basis of her search for a national identity, later a preoccupation of the poets of the 1930's. Her nationalism is apparent in her themes, imagery, and turns of expression. The landscape, in particular that of the Marlborough province, is closely observed and memorably expressed in many lines. In a poem such as "The Tides Run up the Wairau" personal emotion is firmly located in New Zealand. Duggan's interest in Maori themes is part of her nationalism, and she is a pioneer in marrying Maori words and phrases to the natural movement of English verse.

The sense of disinheritance experienced in New Zealand by Katherine Mansfield, Robin Hyde, and others of Duggan's generation took in her case a second and a deeper channel in a ceaseless and growing aspiration for the divine. Her religious faith is grounded in our humanity; "the mystic is no refuge if it forsake the human." "Contrast" presents through the images of the shepherds and the magi the rational and the intuitive approach to belief. In the many poems that explore the dark ways of providence, Duggan's faith is that of the shepherds who instinctively abandon themselves to the incomprehensible mystery of divine love.

The best of her early poems have the qualities of good Georgian verse, simplicity, warmth, and moral innocence. They have, too, clarity, technical skill, and appreciation of the countryside, the unnoticed, and the ordinary. Notable among her early verse is folk-poetry such as the ballad "The Bushfeller" and a striking evocation of childhood, "Twilight." Her later work goes beyond her Georgian origins to find an individual expression in an alert, imaginative, and deeply thoughtful poetry. In her final volume her verse has a greater reach and concentration. Her imagination is possessed by a cosmic vision forced on her by the events of World War II, which like many others she saw as threatening the collapse of civilisation. The didactic nature of many of these poems comes from her diagnosis that bewilderment was the real danger of the time, and that when mankind is bewildered it can be "baffled or hectored to its spiritual ruin." In a time of disillusionment, even despair, she wrote optimistic poetry whose characteristic utterance is affirmation.

—F. M. McKay

DUNCAN, Robert (Edward).   American.   Born in Oakland, California, 7 January 1919. Educated at the University of California, Berkeley, 1936–38, 1948–50. Editor, *The Experimental Review*, Berkeley, 1938–40, and *The Berkeley Miscellany*, 1948–49. Lived in Majorca, 1955–56; taught at Black Mountain College, North Carolina, 1956; Assistant Director of the Poetry Center (Ford grant), 1956–57, and Lecturer in the Poetry Workshop, 1965, San Francisco State College. Recipient: Guggenheim Fellowship, 1963; National Endowment for the Arts grant, 1966 (two grants). Lives in San Fransisco.

PUBLICATIONS

Verse

Heavenly City, Earthly City.   1947.
Poems 1948–1949.   1950.
Medieval Scenes.   1950.
Caesar's Gate: Poems 1949–1950.   1955; revised edition, 1972.
Letters.   1958.
Selected Poems.   1959.
The Opening of the Field.   1960.

Roots and Branches: Poems. 1964.
Writing, Writing: A Composition Book of Madison 1953, Stein Imitations. 1964.
A Book of Resemblances: Poems 1950–1953. 1966.
Of the War: Passages 22–27. 1966.
The Years As Catches: First Poems 1939–1946. 1966.
Fragments of a Disordered Devotion. 1966.
Epilogos. 1967.
Bending the Bow. 1968.
Names of People. 1968.
The First Decade: Selected Poems 1940–1950. 1968.
Derivations: Selected Poems 1950–1956. 1968.
Play Time, Pseudo Stein, 1942: A Story, and A Fairy Play. 1969.
Achilles' Song. 1969.
Poetic Disturbances. 1970.
Tribunals: Passages 31–35. 1970.
Ground Work No. 1. 1971.
In Memoriam Wallace Stevens. 1972.
Poems from the Margins of Thom Gunn's "Moly." 1972.
A Seventeenth Century Suite in Homage to the Metaphysical Genius in English Poetry 1590–1690. 1973.
An Ode and Arcadia, with Jack Spicer. 1974.
Dante. 1974.

Plays

Faust Foutu (produced 1955). 1958; complete edition, as *Faust Foutu: An Entertainment in Four Parts,* 1960.
Medea at Kolchis: The Maiden Head (produced 1956). 1965.

Other

The Artist's View. 1952.
On Poetry (radio interview with Eugene Vance). 1964.
As Testimony: The Poem and the Scene. 1964.
The Sweetness and Greatness of Dante's "Divine Comedy," 1265–1965. 1965.
Six Prose Pieces. 1966.
The Cat and the Blackbird (juvenile). 1967.
The Truth and Life of Myth: An Essay in Essential Autobiography. 1968.
65 Drawings: A Selection of 65 Drawings from One Drawing-Book: 1952–1956. 1970.
An Interview with George Bowering and Robert Hogg, April 19, 1969. 1971.

Reading List: Robert Duncan Issue of *Origin*, June 1963, of *Audit 4*, 1967, and of *Maps 6*, 1974; *Godawful Streets of Man* by Warren Tallman, 1976.

*   *   *

The poet, Robert Duncan has said, is akin to the paranoiac: everything seems to belong to the plot. Raised in a Theosophist environment, in much of his work Duncan seeks, like the paranoiac but without his fear, for something that does *not* belong to the coherent cosmic plot. Duncan, therefore (as he expounds it most clearly in the sections of the incomplete "The H. D. Book"), lives in a world in which "things strive to speak," where the poet seeks to read "the language of things," where "the poet must attend not to what he means to say but to what what he says means" (*Caterpillar 7*). The poet is, then, subject not to "inspiration" so much as he is to "possession," where he may be had by an idea, and poetry is – in Duncan's language – an Office: the text the poet writes is part of a larger text: the Poem, and the office of poet is subsumed in the larger Office, of Poet.

It is thus perhaps to be expected that Duncan, of all poets associated with Black Mountain College and with post-Modernism, should be the American writer most closely associated with the great tradition of English poetry and of mystical poetry, while at the same time he is the one who seems most consistently and perversely to be at odds with the traditions and conventions of English poetry. Such apparent perversity arises in part from Duncan's insistence, drawn from Heraclitus that "an unapparent connexion is stronger than an apparent": it derives also, in part, from "the strongest drive of my life, that things have not come to the conclusions I saw around me, and this involved the conclusions that I saw shaping in my own thought and actions" (*Caterpillar 8/9*). Thus "A Poem Beginning with a Line by Pindar" (1958) is a combination of traditional devices, forms, and sources with the unexpected and unconventional. The synecdoche of "the light foot *hears*," quoted from Pindar's First Pythian Ode, involves the breaking of things "normal" in the language; this in turn suggests a range of possible meanings for "*light* foot." The poem, an extended meditation and discovery on – among other things – the notion of Adulthood, proposes a world in which the Real is found, not in a landscape, but "in an obscurity" – hidden, that is to say, from normal, familiar, conventional (or mortal) sight. In two essays central to his work, "Ideas of the Meaning of Form" (*Kulchur 4*) and "Man's Fulfillment in Order and Strife" (*Caterpillar 8/9*), Duncan insists that "to the conventional mind" form is "what can be imposed," and, in all of his writing, conventional syntax and language are a part of conventional form, and man is a creature of language. In section Two of the "Pindar" poem the language, individual words and syllables, breaks down, loses its articulation, becomes almost nonsense. The breakdown is triggered by the word "stroke" which – initially of a brush, painting, or of a pen, writing – becomes a medical stroke (Eisenhower's?), and the poem, which at that point seems to be struggling to a halt, moves into a firm political rhetoric which reveals adulthood as a condition of nations as well as of individuals, and the condition itself as a process. Reading the poem, we witness the testimony of the poet discovering the world as it reveals itself to him through language. Meaning, in such poems as this, is to be found in the play of possible meanings, rather than in the conventionally ordered exposition of rational or reasonable thought. Duncan's insistence "not to reach a conclusion but to keep our exposure to what we do not know" has led to *Passages*, a series of rhetorical poems which, resting on the Julian motto "The even is bounded, but the uneven is without bounds," explores all possible voices as its testimony to What Is.

—Peter Quartermain

DUTTON, Geoffrey (Piers Henry). Australian. Born in Anlaby, South Australia, 2 August 1922. Educated at Geelong Grammar School, Victoria, 1932–39; University of Adelaide, 1940–41; Magdalen College, Oxford, 1946–49, B.A. 1949. Served in the Royal Australian Air Force, 1941–45: Flight Lieutenant. Married Ninette Trott in 1944; three sons, one daughter. Senior Lecturer in English, University of Adelaide, 1954–62; Visiting Lecturer in Australian Literature, University of Leeds (Commonwealth Fellow), 1960; Visiting Professor of English, Kansas State University, Manhattan, 1962. Editor, Penguin Australia, Melbourne, 1961–65. Since 1965, Editorial Director, Sun Books, Melbourne. Co-Founder,

Australian Letters, Adelaide, 1957, and *Australian Book Review*, Kensington Park, 1962. Member, Australian Council for the Arts, 1968–70, and Commonwealth Literary Fund Advisory Board, 1972–73; Member, Australian Literature Board, 1972–74. Lives in South Australia.

PUBLICATIONS

Verse

Nightflight and Sunrise. 1945.
Antipodes in Shoes. 1955.
Flowers and Fury. 1963.
On My Island: Poems for Children. 1967.
Poems Soft and Loud. 1968.
Findings and Keepings: Selected Poems 1940–70. 1970.
New Poems to 1972. 1972.

Fiction

The Mortal and the Marble. 1950.
Andy. 1968.
Tamara. 1970.
Queen Emma of the South Seas. 1976.

Other

A Long Way South (travel). 1953.
Africa in Black and White. 1956.
States of the Union (travel). 1958.
Founder of a City: The Life of William Light. 1960.
Patrick White. 1961.
Walt Whitman. 1961.
Paintings of S. T. Gill. 1962.
Russell Drysdale (art criticism). 1962.
Tisi and the Yabby (juvenile). 1965.
Seal Bay (juvenile). 1966.
The Hero as Murderer: The Life of Edward John Eyre, Australian Explorer and Governor of Jamaica, 1815–1901. 1967.
Tisi and the Pageant (juvenile). 1968.
Australia's Censorship Crisis. 1970.
Australia's Last Explorer: Ernest Giles. 1970.
Australia since the Camera: 1901–14. 1971.
From Federation to War. 1972.
White on Black: The Australian Aborigine Portrayed in Art. 1974.

Editor, *The Literature of Australia*. 1964; revised edition, 1976.
Editor, *Australia and the Monarchy*. 1966.
Editor, *Modern Australian Writing*. 1966.
Editor, with Max Harris, *The Vital Decade: 10 Years of Australian Art and Letters*. 1968.

Editor, with Max Harris, *Sir Henry Bjelke, Don Baby, and Friends.*   1971.

Translator, with Igor Mezhakoff-Koriakin, *Bratsk Station,* by Yevgeny Yevtushenko.   1966.

Translator, with Igor Mazhakoff-Koriakin, *Fever,* by Bella Akhmadulina.   1968.

Translator, with Eleanor Jackman, *Kazan University and Other New Poems,* by Yevgeny Yevtushenko.   1973.

*   *   *

Wartime air-force experience has had a seminal effect on Geoffrey Dutton's poetry – not so much in subject matter as in its lasting synthesis into a perspective of aerial vision: the lone pilot among the clouds pondering the meaning of existence, the freshness and intensity of his perceptions of the world below enriched by a grateful return to base. Thus we find in Dutton's work a rare marriage of delicate observation and abstract discourse. Expectations of breath-taking vistas, or what he wryly calls "high octane/illusions of freedom," are thwarted by the apocalyptic vision of his early work: "the end uncertain and the past dissolved," "the future groping and the memory slain." Many of his poems give the impression of being specifically addressed, for in the face of this uncertainty, hope lies in the discovery of a meaningful realationship.

The threat of solitude haunts his poetry. "Abandoned Airstrip" poses the attractions of a dingo's freedom against innate fears of isolation: "Lacking lions and wars, our country bred/ In us a fear of loneliness instead." Love and affection, an obvious counterforce, are accordingly given considerable attention, and the wide range of treatments testifies to the variety found in his work. In "Night Fishing" the elaboration of a conceit in a manner reminiscent of the Metaphysicals climaxes with the duality of analogy fused into images of profound tranquillity, the lovers

> Exposed in their ghostly nakedness ...
> Welcome or terrible as they share
> In and around her in his arms the sea.

At the other extreme, the sustained treatment of love manifest in the day-to-day occurrences of a living relationship recalls Williams, particularly in the reverence towards flowers and the disarming fidelity of "Let's risk being obvious in happiness" – complexity is not an end in itself.

Dutton's talent for evocation is well seen in the travel poetry: an English landscape sheltering from industrialization; the "dark centre" of the Danube; a derelict aerodrome in France, when a skylark mockingly alights on a rotting disembowelled aircraft whose "shattered instruments measure the speed of rust"; and the outstanding poem sequence "A Russian Journey" which subtly exposes the blurred vision of conditioning meeting reality – austerity is not compensated by "Remembering the blood that tyranny wrings."

A study of Whitman inspired in the 1960's what Dutton has called "a more complex human response to my own country." Though there is evidence of Whitman's dramatic soliloquizing and a new sense of responsibility brought about by the re-orientation ("Land, that I love, lying all open to me ... I will protect you, I have promised that"), the catalogue is for the most part avoided – there are other ways of conveying vastness. By stressing the elemental in all his descriptions, Dutton can be both comprehensive and express a sense of unity in the imposing massiveness of his subject: "And the winter sun is filling all the ranges/With the blue smoke of the flameless fires of light."

Yet travel has given his Whitmanesque bravura a Jamesian awareness of cultural ambiguity, a "torrent of comparative values" that is also explored in greater detail in the novels (increasingly occupying his attention). Critical of the British legacy, he nevertheless concedes "No style grows out of nothingness"; and, while resenting the "shrivelled sacred umbilical cord" from Mother England, he links it to the bestially mature "hairy bellies" of the uncivilised colonists. Dutton sees Australia's innocent potentiality in the young; their ignorance leads him to treasure "the gift of suffering" and those insights peculiar to the travelling sensibility of a cultural and continental aviator, a heightened awareness with which to seek out contentment in the poetry.

—Garth Clucas

EBERHART, Richard (Ghormley). Born in Austin, Minnesota, 5 April 1904. Educated at the University of Minnesota, Minneapolis, 1922–23; Dartmouth College, Hanover, New Hampshire, B.A. 1926; St. John's College, Cambridge, B.A. 1929, M.A. 1933; Harvard University, Cambridge, Massachusetts, 1932–33. Served in the United States Naval Reserve, 1942–46: Lieutenant Commander. Married Helen Butcher in 1941; has two children. Worked as floorwalker, and as deckboy on tramp ships; tutor to the son of King Prajadhipok of Siam, 1930–31; English Teacher, St. Mark's School, Southboro, Massachusetts, 1933–41, and Cambridge School, Kendal Green, Massachusetts, 1941–42; Assistant Manager to the Vice-President, Butcher Polish Company, Boston, 1946–52 (Honorary Vice-President, 1952, and Member of the Board of Directors, 1958); Visiting Professor, University of Washington, Seattle, 1952–53, 1967, 1972; Professor of English, University of Connecticut, Storrs, 1953–54; Visiting Professor, Wheaton College, Norton, Massachusetts, 1954–55; Resident Fellow and Gauss Lecturer, Princeton University, New Jersey, 1955–56; Distinguished Visiting Professor, University of Florida, Gainesville, Winters 1974, 1977, 1978. Professor of English and Poet-in-Residence, 1956–68, Class of 1925 Professor, 1968–70 and since 1970 Professor Emeritus, Dartmouth College. Elliston Lecturer, University of Cincinnati, 1961. Founder, 1950, and First President, Poets' Theatre, Cambridge, Massachusetts; Member, 1955, and since 1964, Director, Yaddo Corporation; Member, Advisory Committee on the Arts, John F. Kennedy Memorial Theatre, Washington, D.C. Consultant in Poetry, 1959–61, and Honorary Consultant in American Letters, 1963–69, Library of Congress, Washington, D.C. Recipient: New England Poetry Club Golden Rose, 1950; Shelley Memorial Award, 1952; Harriet Monroe Poetry Award, 1955; National Institute of Arts and Letters grant, 1955; Bollingen Prize, 1962; Pulitzer Prize, 1966; Academy of American Poets Fellowship, 1969; National Book Award, 1977. D.Litt.: Dartmouth College, 1954; Skidmore College, Saratoga, New York, 1966; College of Wooster, Ohio, 1969; Colgate University, Hamilton, New York, 1974. Since 1972, Honorary President, Poetry Society of America. Member, National Institute of Arts and Letters, 1960, and American Academy of Arts and Sciences, 1967. Lives in New Hampshire.

PUBLICATIONS

Verse

> *A Bravery of Earth.* 1930.
> *Reading the Spirit.* 1936.
> *Song and Idea.* 1940.
> *Poems, New and Selected.* 1944.

Burr Oaks. 1947.
Brotherhood of Men. 1949.
An Herb Basket. 1950.
Selected Poems. 1951.
Undercliff: Poems 1946–1953. 1953.
Great Praises. 1957.
The Oak: A Poem. 1957.
Collected Poems 1930–1960, Including 51 New Poems. 1960.
The Quarry: New Poems. 1964.
The Vastness and Indifference of the World. 1965.
Fishing for Snakes. 1965.
Selected Poems 1930–1965. 1965.
Thirty One Sonnets. 1967.
Shifts of Being: Poems. 1968.
The Achievement of Richard Eberhart: A Comprehensive Selection of His Poems, edited
    by Bernard F. Engle. 1968.
Three Poems. 1968.
Fields of Grace. 1972.
Two Poems. 1975.
Collected Poems 1930–1976. 1976.
Selected Poems. 1978.

Plays

The Apparition (produced 1951). In *Collected Verse Plays,* 1962.
The Visionary Farms (produced 1952). In *Collected Verse Plays,* 1962.
Triptych (produced 1955). In *Collected Verse Plays,* 1962.
The Mad Musician, and Devils and Angels (produced 1962). In *Collected Verse Plays,*
    1962.
Collected Verse Plays (includes *Preamble I* and *II*). 1962.
The Bride from Mantua, from a play by Lope de Vega (produced 1964).

Other

Editor, with Selden Rodman, *War and the Poet: An Anthology of Poetry Expressing
    Man's Attitude to War from Ancient Times to the Present.* 1945.
Editor, *Dartmouth Poems.* 12 vols., 1958–71.

Reading List: *Eberhart* by Ralph J. Mills, Jr., 1966; *Eberhart: The Progress of an American
Poet* by Joel H. Roache, 1971; *Eberhart* by Bernard F. Engle, 1972.

*   *   *

Even Richard Eberhart's most ardent admirers admit the striking unevenness of his work
– stirring and exquisite poems published with others marred by sentimentality, pedantic
diction, and banal abstractions. That his work might indeed be so uneven derives from
Eberhart's vision of what poetry is, as well as his method of composition: "Poetry is
dynamic, Protean," he writes. "In the rigors of composition ... the poet's mind is a filament,
informed with the irrational vitality of energy as it was discovered in our time in quantum
mechanics. The quanta may shoot off any way." Eberhart rewrites little. His is an

inspirational poetry; through it, he discovers life's significances. "You breathe in maybe God," and at those moments, "the poet writes with a whole clarity."

Unlike many of his contemporaries during the 1930's Eberhart never worked for the hard, spare line; he created no personae. He wrote a personal poetry, much in the vein of the Romantics, especially Blake, Wordsworth, and Whitman, a poetry concerned with understanding and transcending concrete experience. Regardless of the inevitable problems such an aesthetic might invite, there remains a large body of inspired and original verse wherein Eberhart is able to "aggravate" perception into life. Eberhart's best work results from his success in transforming keenly felt sense perceptions, through the language of the experience itself, into meaning – moral, metaphysical, mystical, even religious. His most significant work retains the urgency and radiance of the felt experience, as it simultaneously transforms it into the significant; Eberhart is epiphanic much like Gerard Manley Hopkins. "The poet," he states, "makes the world anew; something grows out of the old, which he locks in words."

In Eberhart's first volume, *A Bravery of Earth* he writes about the three types of "awareness" one must accomplish in order to gai maturity – mortality, mentality, and men's actions. These goals have been reflected tl oughout Eberhart's career. However, particular subjects have also persisted – the poet's sheer wonder in nature, the fierce exhilaration inspired by "lyric" and "lovely" nature, within which is "God" "incarnate," as in "This Fevers Me":

> This fevers me, this sun on green,
> On grass glowing, this young spring.
> The secret hallowing is come,
> Regenerate sudden incarnation,
> Mystery made visible
> In growth, yet subtly veiled in all,
> Ununderstandable in grass,
> In flowers, and in the human heart,
> This lyric mortal loveliness,
> The earth breathing, and the sun.

Such an intimate involvement with physical nature, nevertheless, involves the poet in its cycles of growth and decay, and Eberhart, always aware of his own mortality, searches for intimations of immortality. Some of his poems address death as a creative force, in its recurrent cycles:

> When I can hold a stone within my hand
> And feel time make it sand and soil, and see
> The roots of living things grow in this land,
> Pushing between my fingers flower and tree,
> Then I shall be as wise as death,
> For death has done this and he will
> Do this to me, and blow this breath
> To fire my clay, when I am still.

Eberhart's compassion extends toward all living things which share a common fate. In a poem like "For a Lamb," after describing the lamb as "putrid," "on the slant hill," and "propped with daisies," the poet speaks of the fundamental continuity of life in nature:

> Where's the lamb? whose tender plaint
> Said all for the mute breezes.
> Say he's in the wind somewhere,
> Say, there's a lamb in the daisies.

"The Groundhog," one of Eberhart's best known poems, evokes another sort of wild, extravagant transcendence in the face of physical decay. The poet now experiences an exhilaration not through an awareness of nature's eternal, recurrent cycles, but rather through his creative articulation of the fact of decay. Returning year after year to the dead groundhog, he wishes for its absorption within nature's processes, but instead he witnesses its transformation from simple decay – "I saw a groundhog lying dead./Dead lay he" – to something artistically beautiful, its few bones "bleaching in the sunlight/Beautiful as architecture." He moves from a sense of "naked frailty" to "strange love," "a fever," a "passion of the blood." Elsewhere Eberhart has said: "Poetry is a spell against death," and he concludes "The Groundhog" with:

> I stood there in the whirling summer,
> My hand capped a withered heart,
> And thought of China and of Greece,
> Of Alexander in his tent;
> Of Montaigne and his tower,
> Of Saint Theresa in her wild lament.

Eberhart comes to identify with the mighty figures of the past who transcended the ravages of time through the very energy of their creative living, and through the legacy of historical memory and art. The poet has transcended through the creation of his poem.

Eberhart writes about a variety of experiences associated with death. In "Imagining How It Would Be to Be Dead" and "When Golden Flies upon My Carcass Come," he tries to apprehend his own death. Death may also be the moment of revelation and transcendence, of "worldless Ecstasy/Of mystery." But death may also be "merely death" – "This is a very ordinary experience./A name may be glorious but death is death" ("I Walked over the Grave of Henry James"). In "The Cancer Cells," he expresses an aesthetic glee in the artistic design of malignant cells: "They looked like art itself .../I think Leonardo would have in his disinterest/enjoyed them precisely with a sharp pencil."

Poems like "If I Could Only Live at the Pitch That Is Near Madness" represent another theme through Eberhart's poetry – his desire to retain the intensity of childhood, "the incomparable light," "when everything is as it was in my childhood/Violent, vivid, and of infinite possibility." But Eberhart accepts, indeed embraces, the "moral answer," that awareness that one cannot leave the world of men and maturity; and, as he returns "into a realm of complexity," there is a sense of new wonder and exaltation, as of joyful paternity, in his acceptance of the responsibilities of adulthood. One must not just feel experience; one must understand and articulate it.

Also recurrent are the variety of images of man's fallen state, his cruelty to his fellow man, the varieties of human suffering that grow out of social, political, and family strife. One is under obligation, implies Eberhart in his famous "Am I My Neighbor's Keeper?," to care for his fellow man. Perhaps best known among this group is his "The Fury of Aerial Bombardment," one of his many poems concerned with the inhumanity of war, where the poet ultimately wonders what sort of God would permit the barbarism of war: "You would feel that after so many centuries/God would give man to relent."

Throughout his fifty years of writing, Eberhart has emphasized the importance of man's creating a credo, a transcending vision, through personal and concrete experience. As intensely aware of man's existential condition as many of his contemporaries, Eberhart focuses on life and its creative possibilities. (In his acceptance speech of the National Book Award 1977, he lamented the suicides of some of his contemporaries and said, "Poets should not die for poetry but live for it.") Eberhart has focused upon concrete and everyday experience as the avenue toward transcendence, even if just momentary. For him, words, poetry itself, leads to "joy" and "ecstasy": "The only triumph is some elegance of style."

But each man is a poet, in a sense, for each man is, in his everyday life, the creator of any meaning his life will have. Each man must "make ... [his] own myth." Nature remains benignly indifferent. As James Cotter expressed it, in reviewing Eberhart's *Collected Poems 1930–1976* (*America*, 18 September 1976), the owl's cry tells man nothing unless one goes "somewhere beyond realism," and learns to "listen to the tune of the spiritual. Nature does not love or heed us. We are the lovers of nature."

—Lois Gordon

ELIOT, T(homas) S(tearns).   English.   Born in St. Louis, Missouri, U.S.A., 26 September 1888; naturalized, 1927. Educated at Smith Academy, St. Louis, 1898–1905; Milton Academy, Massachusetts, 1905–06; Harvard University, Cambridge, Massachusetts (Editor, *Harvard Advocate*, 1909–10; Sheldon Fellowship, for study in Munich, 1914), 1906–10, 1911–14, B.A. 1909, M.A. 1910; the Sorbonne, Paris, 1910–11; Merton College, Oxford, 1914–15. Married 1) Vivienne Haigh-Wood in 1915 (died, 1947); 2) Esmé Valerie Fletcher, 1957. Teacher, High Wycombe Grammar School, Buckinghamshire, and Highgate School, London, 1915–17; Clerk, Lloyds Bank, London, 1917–25; Editor, later Director, Faber and Gwyer, later Faber and Faber, publishers, London, 1926–65. Assistant Editor, *The Egoist*, London, 1917–19; Founding Editor, *The Criterion*, London, 1922–39. Clark Lecturer, Trinity College, Cambridge, 1926; Charles Eliot Norton Professor of Poetry, Harvard University, 1932–33; Page-Barbour Lecturer, University of Virginia, Charlottesville, 1933; Theodore Spencer Memorial Lecturer, Harvard University, 1950. President, Classical Association, 1941, Virgil Society, 1943, and Books Across the Sea, 1943–46. Resident, Institute for Advanced Study, Princeton University, New Jersey, 1950; Honorary Fellow, Merton College, Oxford, and Magdalene College, Cambridge. Recipient: Nobel Prize for Literature, 1948; New York Drama Critics Circle Award, 1950; Hanseatic Goethe Prize, 1954; Dante Gold Medal, Florence, 1959; Order of Merit, Bonn, 1959; American Academy of Arts and Sciences Emerson-Thoreau Medal, 1960. Litt.D.: Columbia University, New York, 1933; Cambridge University, 1938; University of Bristol, 1938; University of Leeds, 1939; Harvard University, 1947; Princeton University, 1947; Yale University, New Haven, Connecticut, 1947; Washington University, St. Louis, 1953; University of Rome, 1958; University of Sheffield, 1959; LL.D.: University of Edinburgh, 1937; University of St. Andrews, 1953; D.Litt.: Oxford University, 1948; D.Lit.: University of London, 1950; Docteur-ès-Lettres, University of Aix-Marseille, 1959; University of Rennes, 1959; D.Phil.: University of Munich, 1959. Officer, Legion of Honor; Honorary Member, American Academy of Arts and Letters; Foreign Member, Accademia dei Lincei, Rome, and Akademie der Schönen Künste. Order of Merit, 1948. *Died 4 January 1965.*

PUBLICATIONS

Collections

Selected Prose, edited by Frank Kermode.   1975.

Verse

Prufrock and Other Observations. 1917.

Poems. 1919.

Ara Vos Prec. 1920; as *Poems*, 1920.

The Waste Land. 1922; *A Facsimile and Transcripts of the Original Drafts Including the Annotations of Ezra Pound*, edited by Valerie Eliot, 1971.

Poems 1909–1925. 1925.

Ash-Wednesday. 1930.

Sweeney Agonistes: Fragments of an Aristophanic Melodrama. 1932.

Collected Poems 1909–1935. 1936.

Old Possum's Book of Practical Cats. 1939.

The Waste Land and Other Poems. 1940.

East Coker. 1940.

Later Poems 1925–1935. 1941.

The Dry Salvages. 1941.

Little Gidding. 1942.

Four Quartets. 1943.

A Practical Possum. 1947.

Selected Poems. 1948.

The Undergraduate Poems of T. S. Eliot. 1949.

Poems Written in Early Youth, edited by John Hayward. 1950.

Collected Poems 1909–1962. 1963.

Plays

The Rock: A Pageant Play (produced 1934). 1934.

Murder in the Cathedral (produced 1935). 1935; revised version, as *The Film of Murder in the Cathedral*, 1952.

The Family Reunion (produced 1939). 1939.

The Cocktail Party (produced 1949). 1950; revised edition, 1950.

The Confidential Clerk (produced 1953). 1954.

The Elder Statesman (produced 1958). 1959.

Collected Plays: Murder in the Cathedral, The Family Reunion, The Cocktail Party, The Confidential Clerk, The Elder Statesman. 1962; as *The Complete Plays*, 1969.

Other

Ezra Pound: His Metric and Poetry. 1917.

The Sacred Wood: Essays on Poetry and Criticism. 1920.

Homage to John Dryden: Three Essays on Poetry in the Seventeenth Century. 1924.

For Lancelot Andrewes: Essays on Style and Order. 1928.

Dante. 1929.

Thoughts after Lambeth. 1931.

Selected Essays 1917–1932. 1932; revised edition, 1950.

John Dryden: The Poet, The Dramatist, The Critic. 1932.

The Use of Poetry and the Use of Criticism: Studies in the Relation of Criticism to Poetry in England. 1933.

After Strange Gods: A Primer of Modern Heresy. 1934.

Elizabethan Essays. 1934; as *Elizabethan Dramatists*, 1963.

Essays Ancient and Modern. 1936.

The Idea of a Christian Society. 1939.

Points of View, edited by John Hayward.   1941.

Reunion by Destruction: Reflections on a Scheme for Church Unity in South India Addressed to the Laity.   1943.

Notes Towards the Definition of Culture.   1948.

The Complete Poems and Plays.   1952.

Selected Prose, edited by John Hayward.   1953.

On Poetry and Poets.   1957.

George Herbert.   1962.

Knowledge and Experience in the Philosophy of F. H. Bradley (doctoral dissertation).   1964.

To Criticize the Critic and Other Writings.   1965.

The Literary Criticism of Eliot: New Essays, edited by David Newton de-Molina.   1977.

Editor, *Selected Poems,* by Ezra Pound.   1928; revised edition, 1949.

Editor, *A Choice of Kipling's Verse.*   1941.

Editor, *Introducing James Joyce.*   1942.

Editor, *Literary Essays of Ezra Pound.*   1954.

Editor, *The Criterion 1922–1939.*   18 vols., 1967.

Translator, *Anabasis: A Poem* by St.-John Perse.   1930; revised edition, 1938, 1949, 1959.

Bibliography: *Eliot: A Bibliography* by Donald Gallup, 1952, revised edition, 1969; *The Merrill Checklist of Eliot* by B. Gunter, 1970.

Reading List: *The Achievement of Eliot: An Essay on the Nature of Poetry* by F. O. Matthiessen, 1935, revised edition, 1947, with additional material by C. L. Barber, 1958; *Four Quartets Rehearsed* by R. Preston, 1946; *Eliot: The Design of His Poetry* by Elizabeth Drew, 1949; *The Art of Eliot* by Helen Gardner, 1949; *The Poetry of Eliot* by D. E. S. Maxwell, 1952; *Eliot's Poetry and Plays: A Study in Sources and Meaning* by Grover Smith, 1956, revised edition, 1975; *The Invisible Poet: Eliot* by Hugh Kenner 1959; *Eliot: A Collection of Critical Essays* edited by Hugh Kenner, 1962; *Eliot's Dramatic Theory and Practice* by Carol H. Smith, 1963; *Eliot* by Northrop Frye, 1963; *Eliot: Movements and Patterns* by Leonard Unger, 1966; *Eliot* by Bernard Bergonzi, 1972; *Eliot in His Time: Essays on the Occasion of the Fiftieth Anniversary of The Waste Land* edited by A. Walton Litz, 1973; *Eliot: The Longer Poems* by Derek Traversi, 1976.

*   *   *

T. S. Eliot's influence was predominant in English poetry in the period between the two World Wars. His first small volume of poems, *Prufrock and Other Observations* appeared in 1917. The title is significant. Eliot's earliest verse is composed of *observations,* detached, ironic, and alternately disillusioned and nostalgic in tone. The prevailing influence is that of French poetry, and in particular of Jules Laforgue; the mood is one of reaction against the comfortable certainties of "Georgian" poetry, the projection of a world which presented itself to the poet and his generation as disconcerting, uncertain, and very possibly heading for destruction.

The longest poem in the volume, "The Love Song of J. Alfred Prufrock," shows these qualities, but goes beyond them. The speaker is a kind of modern Hamlet, a man who after a life passed in devotion to the trivial has awakened to a sense of his own futility and to that of the world around him. He feels that some decisive act of commitment is needed to break the meaningless flow of events which his life offers. The question, however, is whether he really dares to reverse the entire course of his existence by a decision the nature of which eludes him:

> And indeed there will be time
> To wonder, "Do I dare?" and, "Do I dare?"
> Time to turn back and descend the stair,
> With a bald spot in the middle of my hair ...
> Do I dare
> Disturb the universe?

The answer, for Prufrock, is negative. Dominated by his fear of life, misunderstood when he tries to express his sense of a possible revelation, Prufrock concludes "No! I am not Prince Hamlet, nor was meant to be," refuses to accept the role which life for a moment seemed to have thrust upon him, and returns to the stagnation which his vision of reality imposes.

After a second small volume, published in 1919, which shows, more especially in its most impressive poem, "Gerontion," a notable deepening into tragedy, the publication in 1922 of *The Waste Land* burst upon its readers with the effect of a literary revolution. Many of its first readers found the poem arid and incomprehensible, though it was in fact neither. The poet tells us that he is working through "a heap of broken images." He does this because it is a world of dissociated fragments that he is describing; but his aim, like that of any artist, is not merely an evocation of chaos. The poem is built on the interweaving of two great themes: the broken pieces of the present, as it presents itself to a disillusioned contemporary understanding, and the significant continuity of tradition. These two strains begin apart, like two separate themes in a musical composition, but the poem is animated by the hope, the *method*, that at the end they will converge into some kind of unity. Some critics, reading it in the light of Eliot's later development, have tried to find in the poem a specifically "religious" content, which however is not there. At best, there is a suggestion at the close that such a content, were it available, might provide a way out of the "waste land" situation, that the life-giving rain *may* be on the point of relieving the intolerable drought; but the poet cannot honestly propose such a resolution and the step which might have affirmed it is never rendered actual.

For some years after 1922, Eliot wrote little poetry and the greater part of his effort went into critical prose, much of it published in *The Criterion*, the literary quarterly which he edited until 1939. Eliot's criticism, which profoundly affected the literary taste of his generation, contributed to the revaluation of certain writers – the lesser Elizabethan dramatists, Donne, Marvell, Dryden – and, more controversially, to the depreciation of others, such as Milton (concerning whom, however, Eliot later modified his views) and some of the Romantic poets. It was the work of a poet whose interest in other writers was largely conditioned by the search for solutions to the problems raised by his own art; and, as such, it was marked by the idiosyncracies which constitute at once its strength and its limitation.

In 1928, in his preface to the collection of essays *For Lancelot Andrewes*, Eliot declared himself Anglo-Catholic in religion, royalist in politics, classicist in literature: a typically enigmatic statement which indicated the direction he was to give to the work of his later years. 1930 saw the publication of *Ash-Wednesday*, his first considerable poem of explicitly Christian inspiration: a work at once religious in content and modern in inspiration, personal yet without concession to sentiment. The main theme is an acceptance of conversion as a necessary and irretrievable act. The answer to the question posed by Prufrock – "Do I dare/ Disturb the universe?" – is seen, in the translation of the first line of the Italian poet Guido Cavalcanti's ballad, "Because I do not hope to turn again," as an embarkation, dangerous but decisive, upon the adventure of faith.

The consequences of this development were explored in the last and in some respects the most ambitious of Eliot's poetic efforts: the sequence of poems initiated in 1935 and finally published, in 1943, under the title of *Four Quartets*. The series opens, in *Burnt Norton*, with an exploration of the *possible* significance of certain moments which seem to penetrate, briefly and elusively, a reality beyond that of normal temporal experience. "To be conscious," the poem suggests, "is not to be in time": only to balance that possibility with the counter-assertion that "Only through time time is conquered." The first step towards an understanding of the problems raised in the *Quartets* is a recognition that time, though inseparable from our human experience, is not the whole of it. If we consider time as an ultimate reality, our spiritual intuitions are turned into an illusion: whereas if we seek to deny the reality of time, our experience becomes impossible. The two elements – the temporal and the timeless – need to be woven together in an embracing pattern of experience which is, in fact, the end to which the entire sequence points.

The later "quartets" build upon this provisional foundation in the light of the poet's experience as artist and human being. The impulse to create in words reflects another, still more fundamental, impulse which prompts men to seek *form*, coherence, and meaning in the broken intuitions which their experience offers them. The nature of the search is such that it can never be complete in time. The true value of our actions only begins to emerge when we abstract ourselves from the temporal sequence – "time before and time after" – in which they were realized; and the final sense of our experience only reveals itself when the pattern is completed, at the moment of death. This moment, indeed, is not properly speaking a single final point, but a reality which covers the whole course of our existence.

These reflections lead the poet, in the last two poems of the series, *The Dry Salvages* and *Little Gidding*, to acceptance and even to a certain optimism. The end of the journey becomes the key to its beginning, and this in turn an invitation to confidence: "Not fare well,/But fare forward, voyagers." The doctrine of detachment explored in the second poem, *East Coker*, becomes an "expanding" one of "love beyond desire." The conclusion stresses the continuity between the "birth" and "death" which are simultaneously present in each moment, in each individual life, and in the history of the human race. It is true, as the closing section of *Little Gidding* puts it, that "we die with the dying"; but it is equally true, as they also go on to say, that "we are born with the dead." We die, in other words, as part of the tragedy which the fact of our humanity implies, but we are born again when, having understood the temporal process in its true light, we are ready to accept our present position within a still-living and continually unfolding tradition.

Eliot's poetic output was relatively small and intensely concentrated: a fact which at once confirms its value and constitutes, in some sense, a limiting factor. It should be mentioned that in his later years he devoted himself to the writing of verse plays, in an attempt to create a contemporary mode of poetic drama. The earlier plays, *Murder in the Cathedral* and *The Family Reunion*, which are also the best, take up the themes which were being explored at the same time in his poetry and develop them in ways that are often interesting. *The Cocktail Party*, though still a skilful work, shows some decline in conception and execution, and the later plays – *The Confidential Clerk* and *The Elder Statesman* – can safely be said to add little to Eliot's achievement.

—Derek A. Traversi

EMPSON, William   English.   Born in Yokefleet, East Yorkshire, 27 September 1906. Educated at Winchester College; Magdalene College, Cambridge, B.A. in mathematics 1929, M.A. 1935. Married Hester Henrietta Crouse in 1941; two children. Held Chair of English Literature, Bunrika Daigaku University, Tokyo, 1931–34; Professor of English Literature,

1937–39, and Professor, Western Languages Department, 1947–53, Peking National University; Professor of English, University of Sheffield, 1953–71, now Emeritus. Worked in the Monitoring Department, 1940–41, and as Chinese Editor, Far Eastern Department, 1941–46, BBC, London. Visiting Fellow, Kenyon College, Gambier, Ohio, Summers 1948, 1950, 1954; Visiting Professor, University of Toronto, 1973–74, and Pennsylvania State University, University Park, 1974–75. Litt.D.: University of East Anglia, Norwich, 1968; University of Bristol, 1971; University of Sheffield, 1974. Lives in London.

PUBLICATIONS

Verse

Letter IV.   1929.
Poems.   1935.
The Gathering Storm.   1940.
Collected Poems.   1949; revised edition, 1961.

Other

Seven Types of Ambiguity: A Study of Its Effects on English Verse.   1930; revised edition, 1947, 1953, 1955, 1963.
Some Versions of Pastoral.   1935; as English Pastoral Poetry, 1938.
Shakespeare Survey, with George Garrett.   1937.
The Structure of Complex Words.   1951.
Milton's God.   1961; revised edition, 1965.

Editor, The Outlook of Science, by J. B. S. Haldane.   1935.
Editor, Science and Well-Being, by J. B. S. Haldane.   1935.
Editor, Shakespeare's Poems.   1969.
Editor, with David Pirie, Coleridge's Verse: A Selection.   1972.

Reading List: Empson by J. H. Wills, Jr., 1969; Modern Heroism: Essays on D. H. Lawrence, Empson, and Tolkien, by Roger Sale, 1973; Empson: The Man and His Work edited by Roma Gill, 1974 (includes bibliography by Moira Megaw); Empson and the Philosophy of Literary Criticism by Christopher Norris, 1978.

*   *   *

"How extravagantly romantic he is, and how he has to cover it up!" This remark, in a private letter by the American poetess and critic Anne Stevenson, suggests the peculiar fascination of William Empson's poems, and why a whole group of young English poets, fleeing from the romanticism of Dylan Thomas, imitated from about 1953 onwards the verse forms (villanelle and terza rima with a last hanging line) of his second volume, The Gathering Storm, and were ready to accept the label "Empsonians." The difference was, as Edwin Muir shrewdly pointed out, that Empson's bluff, dry, and off-hand manner was a way of controlling and half-concealing, half-revealing an inner agony, whereas there was not such evidence that his young admirers and imitators had suffered much, or would ever be capable of suffering. Of his two volumes, the first, Poems, is the more difficult in its manner (making a great deal of use, like Donne, of references to the science of his time), but the simpler in its themes, broadly the non-responsiveness of love and the absence of God. The second, *The Gathering Storm*, dealt with the social and political situation, and the emotions it aroused, just before the Second World War.

Empson is probably, in *Seven Types of Ambiguity*, *Some Versions of Pastoral*, *The Structure of Complex Words*, and *Milton's God*, very much more widely influential in his work as a theoretical critic than as a poet. The theory of ambiguity is that double meanings in poetry are not muddles but represent a true doubt in the poet's mind. The pastoral form, in Empson's usage, is not a poem about shepherds but any literary mode of representing a complex social situation in terms of a simpler mode of life. A complex word is a word like "native" or "honest" whose positive meaning is good or neutral but which we use only about our inferiors. The book on Milton is a vivid diatribe against the Christian idea of God as represented by Milton (of course, by no means orthodoxly, since he seems to be a tritheist rather than a trinitarian, and the Son appears to be of like rather than one substance with the Father). The best answer to it is that Milton, by incliniation or instinct, is no more a Christian than Empson. The general influence of these critical books, though silent, has been pervasive. They are part of the furniture of any good English or American critic's mind.

—G. S. Fraser

FAIRBURN, A(rthur) R(ex) D(ugard).   New Zealander.   Born in Auckland, 2 February 1904. Educated at Parnell Primary School, Auckland; Auckland Grammar School, 1918–20. Served in the New Zealand Army, 1943. Married Jocelyn Mays in 1931; one son, three daughters. Clerk, New Zealand Insurance Company, Auckland, 1920–26; Labourer, free-lance writer, and part-time teacher, 1926–30; came to London, 1930, and lived in Wiltshire, 1931–32; Spokesman for the radical writers of the Phoenix group, Auckland, 1932–33; held various relief jobs in New Zealand, 1932–34; Assistant Secretary, and Editor of *Farming First* magazine, Auckland Farmer's Union, 1934–42; radio scriptwriter, Auckland, 1943–46; produced and designed fabrics, 1946–47; Tutor in English, 1947–54, and Lecturer, Elam School of Fine Arts, 1954–57, Auckland University College. *Died 25 March 1957.*

PUBLICATIONS

Collections

   Collected Poems, edited by Denis Glover.   1966.
   The Woman Problem and Other Prose, edited by Denis Glover and Geoffrey
      Fairburn.   1967.

Verse

   He Shall Not Rise.   1930.
   The County.   1931.
   Another Argo, with Allen Curnow and Denis Glover.   1935.
   Dominion.   1938.
   Recent Poems, with others,   1941.

Poems 1929–1941.   1943.
The Rakehelly Man and Other Verses.   1946.
Three Poems.   1952.
Strange Rendezvous: Poems 1929–1941, with Additions.   1953.
The Disadvantages of Being Dead and Other Sharp Verses, edited by Denis
    Glover.   1958.
Poetry Harbinger, with Denis Glover.   1958.

Fiction

*The Sky Is a Limpet (A Pollytickle Parrotty), also Four (4) Stories, or Moral
    Feebles.*   1939.

Other

A Discussion on Communism Between Fairburn and S. W. Scott.   1936.
Who Said Red Ruin?   1938.
Hands Off the Tom Tom.   1944.
We New Zealanders: An Informal Essay.   1944.
How to Ride a Bicycle in Seventeen Lovely Colours.   1947.
Crisis in the Wine Industry.   1948.
R. M. S. Rangitoto.   1949.

Bibliography: *Fairburn: A Bibliography* by Olive Johnson, 1958.

Reading List: *Fairburn* by W. S. Broughton, 1968.

*   *   *

A. R. D. Fairburn's poetic development may be seen as a paradigm for the New Zealand writers of his generation. Allen Curnow has described their "common line of development" in these terms: "A mostly personal lyric impulse in the first place changed early to more or less direct lyric argument in which assertions about New Zealand itself ... became a dominant theme." Later these poets returned to "more personal and universal themes, lest their discovery of New Zealand should end in isolation." After a ritual pilgrimage "Home" to England exposed him to the reality of English life in 1930, Fairburn repudiated his limply derivative early verse. His first book, *He Shall Not Rise,* ended with a poem (from which the title was taken) that, in effect, disowned its own contents. Georgianism, he wrote after returning to New Zealand, was "another string which tripped up the feet of New Zealand poets." Instead they must embrace "the anarchy of life in a new country." Fairburn attempted this in *Dominion,* an ambitious portrait of New Zealand in the depression years, a poem which, in the words of one contemporary, decided "the struggle for poetry in New Zealand – rata blossoms v. reality, spooju v. style." Ranging from intemperate Poundian tirades to Wordsworthian celebrations of Nature, *Dominion* is an uneven but vigorous survey of the history and institutions, the land and the people of New Zealand. Fairburn is most effective and original when the lyrical and satirical modes merge, as in "Conversation in the Bush":

> "Observe the young and tender frond
> Of this punga: shaped and curved
> like the scroll of a fiddle: fit instrument
> to play archaic tunes."
>
> > > > "I see
> the shape of a coiled spring."

Here accurate natural description is made to serve wider purposes; from the speakers' difference of opinion over the shape of a fern leaf can be inferred contrasting aesthetic and political attitudes to the national crisis of the time.

After the thirties Fairburn turned away from national issues. His longer poems became more personal in emphasis (*Three Poems*), his satire more occasional, more amusing, but unfortunately, much slighter. *The Rakehelly Man* contains the best of his comic verse, immensely enjoyable if seldom of permanent interest. Much more of his creative energy went into lyric poetry, the best of which was collected in *Strange Rendezvous*. In his first book Fairburn had written of "the peace/and the forgetting/of the instant of love;/and the flat calm of death," and these traditional themes remain his central preoccupations; but his style matured into a flexible and distinctive idiom, combining a lovely relaxed movement with vividly particular sensations, as in "The Cave":

> We climbed down, and crossed over the sand,
> and there were islands floating in the wind-whipped blue,
> and clouds and islands trembling in your eyes.

Out of the conflict between sexual love on the one hand and time and death on the other Fairburn wrote several lyrics of great intensity ("The Cave," "Tapu," "A Farewell"), but perhaps his most distinctive poem, one of the few in which he achieved total integration of his complex nature, was "Full Fathom Five," both an Arnoldian exploration of the conflict of imagination and reality and an oblique self portrait:

> And eventually and tragically finding he could not drown
> he submitted himself to the judgment of the desert
> and was devoured by man-eating ants
> with a rainbow of silence branching from his lips.

> > > > > > —Peter Simpson

FEARING, Kenneth (Flexner). American. Born in Oak Park, Illinois, 28 July 1902. Educated at public schools in Oak Park; University of Wisconsin, Madison, B.A. 1924. Married 1) Rachel Meltzer in 1933, one son; 2) Nan Lurie in 1945 (divorced, 1958). Free-lance writer in New York City from 1924: contributor to various poetry magazines. Recipient: Guggenheim Fellowship, 1936, 1939; National Institute of Arts and Letters award, 1945. *Died 26 June 1961.*

PUBLICATIONS

Verse

Angel Arms.   1929.
Poems.   1935.
Dead Reckoning.   1938.
Collected Poems.   1940.
Afternoon of a Pawnbroker and Other Poems.   1943.
Stranger at Coney Island and Other Poems.   1948.
New and Selected Poems.   1956.

Fiction

The Hospital.   1939.
Dagger of the Mind.   1941.
Clark Gifford's Body.   1942.
The Big Clock.   1946.
Loneliest Girl in the World.   1951.
The Generous Heart.   1954.
The Crozart Story.   1960.

Reading List: "The Meaning of Fearing's Poetry" by M. L. Rosenthal, in *Poetry*, July 1944.

*   *   *

Poet, novelist, and editor, Kenneth Fearing is associated with the literature of disillusionment which was written in America during the 1930's and 1940's when technological achievements and social institutions appeared incapable of remedying the profound evils of economic depression. Severely affected by the suffering which he encountered in his environment, Fearing became disillusioned with capitalistic systems of government and industry, espousing instead a Marxist belief in the inherent goodness of the common man, whom he hoped would unite with one another and lead the world into a new era of utopian humanism.

Into this crusade for social justice, Fearing enlisted his talents as a writer. His poetry earned him the admiration of his contemporaries and a lasting position of respect in modern literature. The deft ironic tone which characterizes much of Fearing's poetry and which undercuts the optimism of the Whitmanesque lines in which he wrote is admirably suited to capturing his anger and bitterness at the disregard of institutions for the liberties of the individual, and his sympathy and pity for those people who were trapped by social circumstance in sterile urban environments where they were forced by industrial and political taskmasters to lead mechanical lives of quiet desperation.

But if the economic and social conditions of the 1930's provided Fearing with the subject matter for his poetry, they also limited the scope of his poetic growth. In many respects, Fearing's hatreds and fears shackle his imagination to themes and obsessions which do not sustain repeated or extended treatment. As a result, the reader who indulges in more than one volume of Fearing's poems receives the impression that while the setting and characters of his poems may vary from volume to volume the ideas which they embody remain the same. In his best poems, however, Fearing captures the anxieties, hopes, and frustrations of his generation in a manner which reflects both sensitivity and talent, and *Dead Reckoning* and *Afternoon of a Pawnbroker and Other Poems* are deserving of serious critical analysis.

As a novelist, Fearing specialized in pulp thrillers into which he interjected social commentary. His first novel, *The Hospital*, is replete with scandals and intrigues which expose the machinations behind the workings of the medical profession. Equally shocking and equally involved are *Clark Gifford's Body*, a murder mystery which explores the possibility of revolution in America, and *The Generous Heart*, a novel which depicts the graft and greed involved in the misappropriation of funds by a charitable organization. Another novel, *The Big Clock*, proved so popular that it became the subject of a film. Ostensibly about a murder, *The Big Clock* also analyzes the ruthlessness of journalistic rivalry and muckraking.

—James A. Levernier

FitzGERALD, Robert D(avid).   Australian.   Born in Hunters Hill, New South Wales, 22 February 1902. Educated at Sydney Grammar School; Sydney University, 1920–21; Fellow, Institute of Surveyors. Married Marjorie-Claire Harris in 1931; four children. Surveyor, FitzGerald and Blair, 1926–30; Native Lands Commission Surveyor, Fiji, 1931–36; Municipal Surveyor, 1936–39; Surveyor, Australian Department of the Interior, 1939–65, now retired. Visiting Lecturer, University of Texas, Austin, 1963. Recipient: Australian Sesqui-Centenary Poetry Prize, 1938; Australian Literature Society Gold Medal, 1938; Grace Leven Prize, 1952, 1959, 1962; Fulbright grant, 1963; Encyclopedia Britannica Award, 1965. O.B.E. (Officer, Order of the British Empire), 1951. Lives in Hunters Hill, New South Wales.

PUBLICATIONS

Verse

   The Greater Apollo.   1927.
   To Meet the Sun.   1929.
   Moonlight Acre.   1938.
   Heemskerck Shoals.   1949.
   Between Two Tides.   1952.
   This Night's Orbit.   1953.
   The Wind at Your Door.   1959.
   Southmost Twelve.   1962.
   Of Some Country: 27 Poems.   1963.
   (Poems).   1963.
   Forty Years' Poems.   1965.
   Product.   1978.

Other

   The Elements of Poetry.   1963.
   Of Places and Poetry.   1976.

Editor, *Australian Poetry 1942.*   1942.
Editor, (*Poems*), By Mary Gilmore.   1963.
Editor, *The Letters of Hugh McCrae.*   1970.

Reading List: *Six Australian Poets* by T. Inglis Moore, 1942; *FitzGerald* by A. Grove Day, 1973.

*   *   *

Robert D. FitzGerald is the only Australian poet of any real importance whose work can be described as deliberately and consistently philosophical (as distinct from mystical or theosophical), one of the few whose verse generates a continual intellectual excitement, sensuously expressed. In his first two books, *The Greater Apollo* and *To Meet the Sun*, FitzGerald, using metaphor as a scientist uses hypothesis, is already tossing up philosophical ideas: determinism, as in "Meeting"; freewill, as in "Calm"; and concepts of change, endurance, and eternality, as in the sequence "The Greater Apollo." His interest in the last three questions places him in the tradition of Brennan and the 19th-century Romantics of Germany and France, an interest which his family connections may have fostered. A more direct impulse towards exploring these ideas was the reading of A. N. Whitehead's *Science and the Modern World*, with its base of Bergsonian thought, though it would be wrong to assume that FitzGerald is mere versified Whitehead. The analysis of the nature of continuity itself is, indeed, FitzGerald's permanent theme, and the phrase "diamond waterfalls" an early metaphor for it.

Moonlight Acre shows an increasing confidence and craftsmanship, a more idiosyncratic style, probably based on Browning. There is a growing preoccupation with concepts of freedom and a willingness to challenge accepted conventions, as in "Exile," a poem which should be compared with "Law-breakers," written during the Vietnam war thirty years later. The cragginess of the diction and the occasionally tortuous syntax in the longer poems in this book are evidence not of an absence of a lyrical sense, but of the inherent difficulty of the subject matter. FitzGerald can be simple and sensuous if he wants to, as the love-poems and the verses about some of his Fijian encounters indicate.

With "The Hidden Bole," a long elegy on the death of Pavlova, however, FitzGerald reaches his full stature, displaying both intellectual toughness and a lyric sweetness far less characteristic of him. The poem explores the nature of beauty, with its inseparable element of transience; the use of Pavlova's dancing as an image of its perfection parallels Whitehead's statement that "the only endurances are structures of activity." The fusion of the ballet image, with Pavlova as its centre, and the image of the sacred banyan tree with its "hidden bole," the symbol of life, is not accomplished without some strain, but the vigour and excitement of the poem are enough to carry us over the rough place; the last two stanzas, which bring the focus of attention back to Pavlova herself, are an exquisite evocation of the dancer:

> Eyes, were you drunk or blind
> not knowing her steps, although you watched their thief,
> the wind's toe-pointing leaf,
> not seeing her chase the pebbled river?
> She is the prisoned sunshine that became
> delicate contour of escaping fire;
> she is the snowflake blown upon the flame—
> song and the melting wraith of song's desire.

The use of images as hypotheses to be successively eliminated in analysing concepts is employed also in "Essay on Memory." It is an impressive, if not wholly successful poem, and certainly the most interesting of the attempts to provide the country with "a usable past."

"Heemskerck Shoals and "Face of the Waters" and "Fifth Day" (from the volume *This Night's Orbit*) are far more accomplished pieces, the first expressing the paradox that the practical man is often the truest dreamer, the second on the agony of "striving to be" and of "not-being," the third on the impossibility of writing history, using the trial of Warren Hastings as an instance: "history hooks/the observer into the foreground as he looks...."

FitzGerald's most ambitious poem is *Between Two Tides*, though his most disturbing one, morally, is perhaps *The Wind at Your Door*, on a convict theme. *Between Two Tides* has for its subject the struggle for power between two Tongan chiefs, a vehicle for the argument that events present "straws" for man's choosing, that it is his duty to choose, and that by choosing he is able to determine the nature of the "straws" themselves. Human life is the indefinable moment between two tides when man is able to assert his "thusness" through his choosing. The poem is slow-moving but compellingly structured as a series of dissolving views: Finau's tale, filtered through several intermediaries to the poet, who becomes the omniscient narrator interpreting for the reader. In this poem FitzGerald makes use of the early experience of his life in Fiji, which had been working in him for many years below the surface. Unfamiliar setting and exotic characters provide the distancing necessary to an economical working out of the theme, and the result is the first really powerful narrative poem in Australian literature. The interconnections between what men are and the institutions they create are developed perhaps with greater human sympathy and humility in *The Wind at Your Door*. History, the past within us becoming the present and shaping the future, is one of FitzGerald's life-long preoccupations; in it he seems to discern, in spite of relapses into savagery, some secret "force towards order," though he is no facile optimist. His profession, surveying, has been a discernible influence on his work, and so has the Irish component in his ancestry, while his long sojourn in the Fijian Islands gives a mysterious dimension to his work, a perspective that marks him off from his contemporaries, some of whom seem culture-bound in comparison.

Besides his books of verse, FitzGerald has edited a selection of Mary Gilmore's poems, and a selection of the letters of Hugh McCrae. He has also published a book of criticism, *The Elements of Poetry*, robust, sensitive and individual. *Of Places and Poetry* is a collection of family reminiscences, portraits, literary explorations, and essays on the theory and practice of verse. Some of his sketches of literary personalities are illuminating and reasonably objective; his poetic theory is his own and strongly held, if not particularly stimulating, but there is a curious naivety about his prose style which is absent from his verse. Poetry is his native element.

—Dorothy Green

FLECKER, James Elroy. English. Born Herman Elroy Flecker in Lewisham, London, 5 November 1884; grew up in Cheltenham, Gloucestershire. Educated at Cheltenham Ladies College Kindergarten; preparatory school, Cheltenham; Dean Close School, Cheltenham, 1893–1900; Uppingham School, 1901–06; Trinity College, Oxford, 1902–06, B.A. 1906; studied Oriental languages at Caius College, Cambridge, 1908–10. Married Helle Skiadaressi in 1911. Teacher, Hampstead, London, 1907; entered the British diplomatic service, 1910: served in Constantinople, 1910–11; Vice-Consul, Beirut, 1911–13. Tubercular: retired from the diplomatic service and lived in Switzerland, 1913–15. *Died 3 January 1915.*

PUBLICATIONS

Collections

> *Collected Poems,* edited by J. C. Squire.   1916; revised edition, 1946.
> *Collected Prose.*   1920.

Verse

> *The Bridge of Fire.*   1907.
> *Thirty-Six Poems.*   1910; augmented edition, as *Forty-Two Poems,* 1911.
> *The Golden Journey to Samarkand.*   1913.
> *The Burial in England.*   1915.
> *The Old Ships.*   1915.
> *God Save the King.*   1915.
> *Selected Poems.*   1918.
> *Unpublished Poems and Drafts,* edited by Martin Booth.   1971.

Plays

> *Hassan,* revised by Basil Dean (produced 1923).   1922.
> *Don Juan* (produced 1926).   1925.
> *Joseph and Mary,* in *With Pipe and Tabor,* by R. Moorhouse.   1928.

Fiction

> *The Last Generation: A Story of the Future.*   1908.
> *The King of Alsander.*   1914.

Other

> *The Best Man: Eights' Week 1906.*   1906.
> *The Grecians: A Dialogue on Education.*   1910.
> *The Scholar's Italian Book: An Introduction to the Study of the Latin Origins of Italian.*   1911.
> *The Letters to Frank Savery,* edited by Helle Flecker.   1926.
> *Some Letters from Abroad.*   1930.

Reading List: *Flecker: From School to Samarkand* by Thomas S. Mercer, 1952 (includes bibliography); *No Golden Journey* (biography) by John Sherwood, 1973; *Flecker* by John M. Munro, 1976.

*   *   *

Although James Elroy Flecker wrote a number of short prose pieces, fiction, and plays (*Hassan* was magnificently staged by Basil Dean in 1923), he is perhaps best remembered as a poet. Such frequently anthologised poems as "A Ship, An Isle, A Sickle Moon," "The Old Ships," "Tenebris Interlucentem," and "The Golden Journey to Samarkand," later incorporated into *Hassan*, all testify to his skill as a literary craftsman. Therefore, although he is frequently lumped together with the Georgians, Flecker is perhaps best appreciated as a late survival of the European Parnassian tradition, his verses being an expression of the belief that good poetry finds its beauty in perfection of form and clarity of outline. In his more introspective moments, however, Flecker considers the relationship between Art and Life, and speculates whether Art may not be an escape from life rather than an affirmation of it, an idea which he tentatively expresses in "The Old Ships."

Attracted by the exoticism of the East, and finding inspiration in Arabian legend and the local color of the Levant, he nonetheless remained temperamentally attached to his native country, and a number of his poems, for example "Brumana," reflect his nostalgia for the English countryside. While much of his verse owes its origins to literary sources rather than to life, after being struck by tuberculosis in 1910 he wrote poetry of a more somber tone, as for example "In Hospital," which clearly reflects the poet's awareness of the transience of human existence.

While it is easy to dismiss *Hassan* as an oriental extravaganza in the tradition of *Chu Chin Chow*, Flecker's play is far from being a hollow spectacle. Rather, as Priscilla Thouless has noted in *Modern Poetic Drama* (1935), it reflects an artistic dilemma that is central to a proper understanding of Flecker. As she expresses it: "[Flecker] clung to the Parnassian path because he feared self-expression; he feared that if he did not strictly confine himself he would turn to gross egoism, like that of Victor Hugo, or to didacticism like that of Wordsworth. He feared moreover that his 'healthy manliness' might fade away, and that his divided soul might be revealed. In *Hassan* it is revealed, for in *Hassan* we find the hand of the Parnassian and of the Romantic...."

Flecker is admittedly a minor figure, and, although he was writing at a time when poets such as T. S. Eliot and Ezra Pound were shaping the modern aesthetic, his work shows no trace of the forces which were to exert such a profound influence on the development of modern poetry. Essentially he must be regarded as a late practicioner of the doctrine of Art for Art's sake, writing poetry which was devoid of "dullness, weakness, bad workmanship, vulgar thought and shoddy sentiment," as he expressed it in his essay "The Public as Art Critic." For these artistic vices, he believed, were ultimately "slanders on mankind."

—John M. Munro

FLETCHER, John Gould. American. Born in Little Rock, Arkansas, 3 January 1886. Educated at high school in Little Rock, 1899–1902; Phillips Academy, Andover, Massachusetts, 1902–03; Harvard University, Cambridge, Massachusetts, 1903–07. Married 1) Florence Emily Arbuthnot in 1916; 2) Charlie May Simon in 1936. Lived in England, 1908–14, 1916–33: one of the founders of the Imagist group of poets; returned to the United States and settled in Arkansas, 1933: associated with the Agrarian group of writers. Recipient: Pulitzer Prize, 1939. LL.D.: University of Arkansas, Fayetteville, 1933. Member, National Institute of Arts and Letters. *Died 10 May 1950.*

PUBLICATIONS

Verse

The Book of Nature 1910–1912.   1913.
The Dominant City.   1913.

Fire and Wine. 1913.
Fool's Gold. 1913.
Visions of the Evening. 1913.
Irradiations: Sand and Spray. 1915.
Goblins and Pagodas. 1916.
Japanese Prints. 1918.
The Tree of Life. 1918.
Breakers and Granite. 1921.
Preludes and Symphonies. 1922.
Parables. 1925.
Branches of Adam. 1926.
The Black Rock. 1928.
XXIV Elegies. 1935.
The Epic of Arkansas. 1936.
Selected Poems. 1938.
South Star. 1941.
The Burning Mountain. 1946.

Other

La Poésie d'André Fontainas. 1919.
Some Contemporary American Poets. 1920.
Paul Gauguin: His Life and Art. 1921.
John Smith — Also Pocahontas. 1928.
The Crisis of the Film. 1929.
The Two Frontiers: A Study in Historical Psychology (on Russia and America). 1930;
   as *Europe's Two Frontiers,* 1930.
Life Is My Song (autobiography). 1937.
Arkansas. 1947.

Editor, *Edgar Allan Poe.* 1926.

Translator, *The Dance over Fire and Water,* by Elie Favre. 1926.
Translator, *The Reveries of a Solitary,* by Rousseau. 1927.

Reading List: *Fletcher* by Edna B. Stephens, 1967 (includes bibliography); *Fletcher and Imagism* by Edmund S. de Chasca, 1978.

* * *

Although most often linked with the Imagist movement because of his early association with Amy Lowell, John Gould Fletcher belongs to no one "school" of poetry; his work covers a wide range of styles and themes. But in all of his work an emphasis upon the visual is a reflection not only of his interest in art but of his early experience with Imagist philosophy. In 1908, at the age of twenty-two, Fletcher left America for Europe, and spent the next twenty-five years moving between the two continents. In 1913, having published, at his own expense, five volumes of poetry, he went to Paris where he came under the influence of Impressionist art, new music, and Ezra Pound. But it was with Amy Lowell that he aligned himself, joining her Imagist circle in 1914; Lowell included some of Fletcher's poems in her anthologies, he dedicated some of his work to her, and together they formulated a poetic style of "polyphonic prose."

Of Fletcher's many works, the most famous are his "symphonies"; these are expressions of mood symbolized by a distinct color, one for each symphony. They are all divided into movements (the poems of *Sand and Spray* are even given tempo markings), each reflecting another aspect of the color stressed in the imagery of the poem. The result is an effective synaesthetic blend of verbal, visual, and musical elements. In "White Symphony," for instance, mood is reflected in white peonies "like rockets in the twilight," the "white snow-water of my dreams," and a "white-laden" snowy landscape. Fletcher retains the idea of symphonic form in later poems as well. Orientalism, so influential upon the Imagists, also had a profound effect upon Fletcher; Chinese philosophy and Japanese poetry (especially *haiku*) were important to the writing of the symphonies, and Fletcher's viewing of Oriental art exhibited in America in 1914 and 1915 is reflected in *Goblins and Pagodas* and *Japanese Prints*. The subjects of the latter volume are not necessarily Japanese, as Fletcher notes in his preface, "but all illustrate something of the charm I have found in Japanese poetry and art." Here he seeks "to universalize our emotions," to show "that the universe is just as much in the shape of a hand as it is in armies, politicians, astronomy, or the exhortations of gospel-mongers; that style and technique rest on the thing conveyed and not the means of conveyance." This emphasis upon the concrete remains constant throughout all of Fletcher's poetry, which, in general, is fairly traditional in form.

In the 1920's, traveling through the American South, Fletcher met the writers of the agrarian "Fugitive" movement, in whom he had been interested for several years. Although he did not embrace the Fugitives' belief in purely intellectual poetry, he did share their concept of Southern agrarian culture as a bastion against modern industrialism. His contribution to the 1929 Fugitive symposium was a discussion of "Education, Past and Present" (published in 1930 in *I'll Take My Stand*), in which he stressed the importance of encouraging folk education to help the South maintain its distinct culture. In 1933, Fletcher returned to his native Little Rock, and from that point he can be considered a Southern regional writer.

—Jane S. Gabin

FROST, Robert (Lee). American. Born in San Francisco, California, 26 March 1874. Educated at Lawrence, Massachusetts, High School, graduated 1892; Dartmouth College, Hanover, New Hampshire, 1892; Harvard University, Cambridge, Massachusetts, 1897–99. Married Elinor Miriam White in 1895; one son, three daughters. Mill worker and teacher, Lawrence, 1892–97; farmer, Derry, New Hampshire, 1900–12; English Teacher, Pinkerton Academy, Derry, 1905–11; conducted course in psychology, State Normal School, Plymouth, New Hampshire, 1911–12; sold the farm, and lived in England, 1912–15; returned to America and settled on a farm near Franconia, New Hampshire, 1915; Poet-in-Residence, Amherst College, Massachusetts, 1916–20; subsequently Visiting Lecturer at Wesleyan University, Middletown, Connecticut; University of Michigan, Ann Arbor, 1921–23, 1925–26; Dartmouth College; Yale University, New Haven, Connecticut; and Harvard University. A Founder, Bread Loaf School, Middlebury College, Vermont, 1920. Poetry Consultant to the Library of Congress, Washington, D.C., 1958. Recipient: Pulitzer Prize, 1924, 1931, 1937, 1943; New England Poetry Club Golden Rose, 1928; Loines Award, 1931; American Academy of Arts and Letters Gold Medal, 1939; Academy of American Poets Fellowship, 1953; Sarah Josepha Hale Award, 1956; Emerson-Thoreau Medal, 1959; U.S. Senate Citation of Honor, 1960; Poetry Society of America Gold Medal, 1962; MacDowell Medal, 1962; Bollingen Prize, 1963. Litt.D.: Cambridge University, 1957; D.Litt.: Oxford University, 1957. Member, American Academy of Arts and Letters. *Died 29 January 1963.*

PUBLICATIONS

Collections

The Poetry, edited by Edward Connery Lathem.   1969.
Selected Letters, edited by Lawrance Thompson.   1964.
Selected Prose, edited by Hyde Cox and Edward Connery Lathem.   1966.

Verse

Twilight.   1894.
A Boy's Will.   1913.
North of Boston.   1914.
Mountain Interval.   1916.
Selected Poems.   1923.
New Hampshire: A Poem with Notes and Grace Notes.   1923.
West-Running Brook.   1928.
The Lovely Shall Be Choosers.   1929.
Collected Poems.   1930; revised edition, 1939.
The Lone Striker.   1933.
Three Poems.   1935.
The Gold Hesperides.   1935.
From Snow to Snow.   1936.
A Further Range.   1936.
Selected Poems.   1936.
A Considerable Speck.   1939.
A Witness Tree.   1942.
Come In and Other Poems, edited by Louis Untermeyer.   1943; revised edition, as *The Road Not Taken*, 1951.
A Masque of Reason.   1945.
The Courage to Be New.   1946.
Poems.   1946.
Steeple Bush.   1947.
A Masque of Mercy.   1947.
Complete Poems.   1949.
Hard Not to Be King.   1951.
Aforesaid.   1954.
Selected Poems.   1955.
Dedication: The Gift Outright.   1961.
In the Clearing.   1962.
One Favored Acorn.   1969.

Plays

A Way Out (produced 1919?).   1929.
The Cow's in the Corn.   1929.

Other

Two Letters.   1931.
Frost and John Bartlett: The Record of a Friendship, edited by Margaret Bartlett Anderson.   1963.

Letters to Louis Untermeyer. 1963.

Frost: Farm-Poultryman, edited by Edward Connery Lathem and Lawrance Thompson. 1963.

Frost: Life and Talks-Walking, edited by Louis Mertins. 1965.

Frost and the Lawrence, Massachusetts "High School Bulletin": The Beginning of a Literary Career, edited by Edward Connery Lathem and Lawrance Thompson. 1966.

Interviews with Frost, edited by Edward Connery Lathem. 1967.

Family Letters of Robert and Elinor Frost, edited by Arnold Grade. 1972.

Frost on Writing, edited by Elaine Barry. 1973.

A Time to Talk, edited by Robert Francis. 1973.

Bibliography: *A Descriptive Catalogue of Books and Manuscripts in the Clifton Waller Barrett Library, University of Virginia* by Joan St. C. Crane, 1974; *The Critical Reception of Frost: An Annotated Bibliography of Secondary Comment* by Peter VanEgmond, 1974.

Reading List: *Frost: A Collection of Critical Essays* edited by James M. Cox, 1962; *An Introduction to Frost* by Elizabeth Isaacs, 1962; *The Major Themes of Frost* by Radcliffe Squires, 1963; *The Poetry of Frost: Constellations of Intention* by Reuben Brower, 1963; *Frost* by Elizabeth Jennings, 1964; *Frost* by James Doyle, 1965; *Frost* by Philip L. Gerber, 1966; *Frost: The Early Years,* 1966, *The Years of Triumph,* 1970, and *The Later Years,* 1977, by Lawrance Thompson and R. H. Winnick; *Frost* by Elaine Barry, 1973; *Frost: The Work of Knowing* by Richard Poirier, 1977.

*   *   *

In 1959, at a dinner celebrating Robert Frost's eighty-fifth birthday, Lionel Trilling gave an after-dinner address that was later incorporated in "A Speech on Robert Frost: A Cultural Episode." Trilling announced his antipathy for those poems by Frost which expressed a "distaste for the life of the city" and for "the demand that is made upon intellect to deal with whatever are the causes of complexity, uncertainty, anxiety." Then Trilling specified poems he did admire, poems that led him to define Frost as a "terrifying poet" who depicted a "terrifying universe." The speech confused Frost (who was not sure whether he had been attacked or praised), outraged many of his friends, and caused quite a furor.

It would seem ludicrous that as late as at the time of Frost's eighty-fifth birthday there could be so much confusion concerning what constituted Frost's basic point of view. Yet several factors make this situation plausible. For one thing, although such critics as John Crowe Ransom and Randall Jarrell praised Frost's poetry, his work gained comparatively little critical attention in the decades when the practitioners of the New Criticism reigned supreme. Further complications were caused by many of the critics who did laud his work. These admirers touted precisely the glib, sentimental, shallow poems by Frost that Trilling disliked. The main source of the confusion, however, was Robert Frost himself. Because Frost hungered so insatiably for popularity and esteem, he meticulously created a "folksy" public image of himself that his audiences would be entranced by. He never read any of his somber poems in public. He saw to it that his unattractive traits – his obsessive need to win at everything, his violent temper, his delight in back-biting, his race prejudices – remained totally unknown to the public. With equal skill, he hid his family misfortunes – his sister's insanity, his severe marital problems, his son's suicide, a daughter's insanity.

It is no wonder, then, that although Frost began writing in the late 1800's, we are still only beginning to formulate an intelligent evaluation of his poetry. Yet, despite all the obfuscations, such an evaluation is well worth pursuing, for Frost's best poems – and there are many of them – are of a very high quality. Frost was a consummate craftsman. He mastered a variety of forms; he wrote excellent sonnets, heroic couplets, and blank verse poems. His rime patterns are deftly wrought. He was even more adroit in matters of meter and rhythm. He proved repeatedly that there is no reason to believe that traditional rhythmical patterns inevitably lead to monotony.

What ultimately makes Frost's best poems valuable, however, is their dynamic view of our daily life. Frost believed that we live in a God-directed universe, but despite all his religious meditations Frost found God's ways absolutely inscrutable. At his most grim, as represented in "Design," Frost not only acknowledges the presence of the appalling in physical reality, but wonders if there is any cosmic design at all. It is certain in any case, as "Nothing Gold Can Stay" states, that no purity can abide in physical reality. What is pure is almost immediately contaminated. Nature is lovely at times, yet its very loveliness can prove fatally alluring, as the speaker in "Stopping by Woods on a Snowy Evening" testifies. Nor can we imitate the animal world and rely on our instincts; "The White-Tailed Hornet" reports that nature's creatures, acting on pure instinct, often blunder ridiculously.

Man experiences no clarifying visions. "The Fear" insists that we live surrounded by a literal and metaphorical darkness which harbors the hostile and the terrifyingly ambiguous. Weariness and loneliness define the archetypal human being who narrates "Acquainted with the Night." Isolation and poverty can crush a person physically, mentally, and spiritually, as they do characters in "A Servant to Servants" and "The Hill Wife." Moreover, man is badgered by his suppressed desires – the point of "The Sound of the Trees." Yet "The Flood" states that man cannot always control his destructive urges.

Frost also makes it clear that people cannot easily offer each other solace. The difficulty of understanding another human being is sometimes insurmountable. In "Home Burial," a husband and wife attempt to cope with the death of their child in two different ways. Neither can understand the other's attitude or behavior; neither can in any way help the other.

In his recent essay " 'The Death of the Hired Man': Modernism and Transcendence," Warren French pinpoints why Frost's poetry is especially valuable today. French remarks that, aware of modern man's grim situation, Frost – unlike the pre-Modernists – did not proclaim the need for every individual to retreat at all costs to the safety of society; nor did Frost adopt or advocate the lifestyle lauded by Modernist writers – the deliberate withdrawal on the part of the individual from society. Instead, Frost concentrated on what marks him – in French's term – as a "post-Modernist." He struggled to discover what positive course is possible for a man who wants to maintain his individuality without exiling himself from society.

The affirmative albeit starkly limited goal Frost strove for and suggested to others is best indicated by his statement that his poems offer "a momentary stay against confusion." A series of momentary stays, created by the individual, is all man can hope for. As Lawrance Thompson wrote in his introduction to Frost's Selected Letters, Frost "bluntly rejected all the conventional stays which dogmatists call permanent"; they are too inflexible to contend successfully with physical reality's ever-shifting conditions. Frost was equally uninterested in trying to transcend the physical – material – world. He thought that the label "materialist" was used too quickly as a pejorative term. He said that it was "wrong to call anybody a materialist simply because he tried to say spirit in terms of matter, as if that were a sin." Nor did Frost fall back on the Romantic belief that man is basically good. He spurned the view that because man and nature are God's creations, they can do no wrong.

According to Frost, in order to achieve a momentary stay against confusion the first thing man needs is courage. A character in A Masque of Mercy says, "The saddest thing in life/Is that the best thing in it should be courage." Man must also try to maintain his equilibrium. Again and again, as in "The Vantage Point," "Goodbye and Keep Cold," and "To Earthward," Frost underscores the need to have the right perspective on all things, including oneself. Men should focus on the facts – and not daydream. In "Mowing," he declares that "The fact is the sweetest dream that labor knows." "Labor" is another key word. In "Two Tramps in Mud Time," he states that we should work and that our work should be motivated simultaneously by "love" and "need."

In some ways, nature can be supportive. "The Onset" and "The Need of Being Versed in

Country Things" remind us that many things on earth are cyclical; this means that although evil comes to us, it will not last. So, too, nature is a revitalizing force, and sometimes awesomely beautiful, as described in "Iris by Night." It can also startle us out of a black mood created by too much self-centeredness – the development recorded in "Dust of Snow." It should also be remembered, as "Our Hold on the Planet" points out, that nature is at least "one fraction of one per cent" in "favor of man" – otherwise we would never have been able to thrive on earth.

Finally, Frost specifically advises us to preserve our individual integrity, but to link ourselves to society. Frost's emphasis on the value of society (often symbolized by the home) is coupled with his emphasis on the value of love. Love can be tenderly lyrical, as described in "Meeting and Passing." "Putting In the Seed" proclaims that love can be dynamically fertile. Love can alter reality – the point in "Never Again Would Birds' Song Be the Same." Love, breeding forgiveness and acceptance, provides a home against adversity. This is what Mary, in "The Death of the Hired Man," knows to be so, and what her husband Warren comes to realize. They decide to nurse Silas, their old hired man, but also to allow him his self-respect. Perhaps the finest example of Frost's stress on the importance of a viable balance between the individual and society is "The Silken Tent." Here, the woman described is a vibrant individual, yet held – willingly – by "countless ties of love and thought/To everything on earth."

—Robert K. Johnson

FULLER, Roy (Broadbent).   English.   Born in Failsworth, Lancashire, 11 February 1912. Educated at Blackpool High School; qualified as a solicitor, 1933. Served in the Royal Navy as a radar mechanic in East Africa, 1941–43, and as a Lieutenant with the Royal Naval Volunteer Reserve at the Admiralty, London, 1944–46. Married Kathleen Smith in 1936; one son, the poet John Fuller. Assistant Solicitor, 1938–58, Solicitor, 1958–69, and since 1969 Director, Woolwich Equitable Building Society, London. Chairman of the Legal Advisory Panel, 1958–69, and since 1969 Vice-President, Building Societies Association. Chairman, Poetry Book Society, 1960–68; Professor of Poetry, Oxford University, 1968–73; Chairman, Arts Council, 1976–77. Since 1972, Governor of the BBC. Recipient: Arts Council Poetry Award, 1959; Duff Cooper Memorial Prize, 1968; Queen's Gold Medal for Poetry, 1970. Fellow, Royal Society of Literature, 1958. C.B.E. (Commander, Order of the British Empire), 1970. Lives in London.

PUBLICATIONS

Verse

Poems.   1939.
The Middle of a War.   1942.
A Lost Season.   1944.
Epitaphs and Occasions.   1949.
Counterparts.   1954.
Brutus's Orchard.   1957.

Collected Poems, 1936–1961.   1962.
Buff.   1965.
New Poems.   1968.
Off Course.   1969.
Tiny Tears.   1973.
An Old War.   1974.
Waiting for the Barbarians.   1974.
From the Joke Shop.   1975.
The Joke Shop Annexe.   1975.
An Ill-Governed Coast.   1976.

Fiction

The Second Curtain.   1953.
Fantasy and Fugue.   1954.
Image of a Society.   1956.
The Ruined Boys.   1959; as *That Distant Afternoon,* 1959.
The Father's Comedy.   1961.
The Perfect Fool.   1963.
My Child, My Sister.   1965.
The Carnal Island.   1970.

Other

Savage Gold (juvenile).   1946.
With My Little Eye (juvenile).   1948.
Catspaw (juvenile).   1966
Owls and Artificers: Oxford Lectures on Poetry.   1971.
Seen Grandpa Lately? (juvenile).   1972.
Professors and Gods: Last Oxford Lectures on Poetry.   1973.
Poor Roy (juvenile).   1977.

Editor, *Byron for Today.*   1948.
Editor, with Clifford Dyment and Montagu Slater, *New Poems 1952.*   1952.
Editor, *Supplement of New Poetry.*   1964.

Reading List: "The Novels of Fuller" by F. McGuinness, in *London Magazine 3,* 1963; "Private Images of Public Ills: The Poetry of Fuller" by George Woodcock, in *Wascana Review 4,* 1969.

*   *   *

Roy Fuller has consistently striven in his poetry to be intelligent, skilful, and disciplined, which, he persistently maintains in his criticism, many popularly acclaimed artists in contemporary culture are not. He has often been categorised, in consequence, as an opponent of innovation and a supporter of the literary "status quo." His political sympathies, however, have always been with the need for social change. The desire to re-order society is to be seen most clearly in his earliest verse, though even in these poems he does not deal with specific political events or issues. His concern in all his poetry is with the pains and anxieties of the human condition. The war poems, for instance, concentrate not on the global disasters or on individual death and pain, but on the fears, loneliness, and boredom of the ordinary man, isolated by war from loved ones. As the end of the war approaches these individual anxieties re-assert their importance in life – "the permanent and real/Furies are settling in upstairs" ("During a Bombardment by V-Weapons"). Nevertheless, a constant theme in his poetry has been forebodings of the imminent collapse of civilisation, frequently seen as analogous to the fall of the Roman Empire and the ensuing "dark ages," and closely linked with autumnal images and references to the frailty of the human body. Another major preoccupation is the purpose of art and its relation to reality. The poet must continually endeavour to speak relevantly of the times he lives in and to represent reality faithfully, so that "the crude/World and my words marry like a joint" ("Dialogue of the Poet and His Talent"). He is constantly aware, however, of how words fail "to make/a world parallel to blind creation/and replace that with its order" ("Homage to Balthus"). Art, particularly by seductive and sensuous images, distorts and falsifies reality.

The sensuous phrase is not frequent in Fuller's poetry; as he himself says, his verse is "a muted, sparse accompaniment" ("Dedicatory Epistle") to our times. The tone of the poems is meditative and serious, sometimes ironical and self-deprecating ("Chinoiserie"). They often begin with a carefully detailed observation of an object, which provides the starting-point for the poet's thoughts, and in recent years he has frequently interwoven several strands of thought, allowing the separate ideas to resonate and sometimes coalesce, as in "Reading *The Bostonians*." This poem is also the earliest example of his use of syllabic verse, which, he feels, has allowed him to write with greater freedom. The poems since the mid-1950's have become more direct and forceful in style, and have shed much of the early influence of Auden, but his characteristic manner has remained essentially restrained and thoughtful.

This is equally true of Fuller's novels. After two "novels of pursuit" he explored, in *Image of a Society*, the inter-relationship of the social and the personal. While not abandoning this theme entirely, later novels, notably his finest achievement, *My Child, My Sister*, have focussed more directly on the individual consciousness.

—David Astle

GASCOYNE, David (Emery). English. Born in Harrow, Middlesex, 10 October 1916. Educated at Salisbury Cathedral Choir School; Regent Street Polytechnic, London. Lived in France, 1937–39, 1954–65. Recipient: Rockefeller-Atlantic Award, 1949. Fellow, Royal Society of Literature, 1951. Lives on the Isle of Wight.

PUBLICATIONS

Verse

Roman Balcony and Other Poems. 1932.
Man's Life Is This Meat. 1936.
Hölderlin's Madness. 1938.
Poems 1937–1942. 1943.
A Vagrant and Other Poems. 1950.
Night Thoughts. 1956.
Collected Poems, edited by Robin Skelton. 1965.

The Sun at Midnight: Notes on the Story of Civilisation Seen as the History of the Great
Experimental Work of the Supreme Scientist. 1970.
Collected Verse Translations, edited by Robin Skelton and Alan Clodd. 1970.
Three Poems. 1976.

Play

The Hole in the Fourth Wall; or, Talk, Talk, Talk (produced 1950).

Fiction

Opening Day. 1933.

Other

A Short Survey of Surrealism. 1935.
Thomas Carlyle. 1952.

Editor, Outlaw of the Lowest Planet, by Kenneth Patchen. 1946.

Translator, Conquest of the Irrational, by Salvador Dali. 1935.
Translator, with Humphrey Jennings, A Bunch of Carrots: Twenty Poems, by Benjamin
Péret. 1936; revised edition, as Remove Your Hat, 1936.
Translator, What Is Surrealism?, by André Breton. 1936.

Bibliography: "Gascoyne: A Checklist" by A. Atkinson, in Twentieth-Century Literature
6, 1961.

Reading List: "A Voice in the Darkness" by Gavin Ewart, in London Magazine, November
1965; "Gascoyne and the Prophetic Role" by Kathleen Raine, in Defending Ancient Springs,
1967.

*   *   *

While still in his teens, David Gascoyne published two books of poems, a novel, and a
critical work, A Short Survey of Surrealism. His own surrealist poems are, with some of
Dylan Thomas's early verse, almost the only good examples of their kind, but it was not until
the publication in 1943 of Poems 1937–1942 that Gascoyne's remarkable talents came to
fruition. That volume, with illustrations designed by Graham Sutherland, explores themes of
guilt, anguish, and longing for spiritual certainty with unashamed eloquence. He moves
continually in a world filled with mysterious presences and mythical figures, nowhere more
effectively than in "Eve," whom he evokes in the closing lines of the poem:

> Insurgent, wounded and avenging one,
> In whose black sex
> Our ancient culpability like a pearl is set.

In that poem and in poems such as "Winter Garden," "The Fault," and the sequence
"Miserere," Gascoyne achieves an intensity and purity of utterance that he has never
surpassed and seldom equalled. In his next collection, A Vagrant, the eloquence trembles on

the verge of grandiloquence, the images are too often reminiscent of 19th-century romanticism at its least happy; *Night Thoughts*, commissioned for radio, lapses into crude rhetoric and over-emphasis.

Gascoyne has always insisted on the sacred, prophetic nature of poetry, and has admired those who strive to create what Carlyle called "an inspired Poesy and Faith for Man," a quotation that Gascoyne makes use of in his essay on Carlyle. His *Collected Poems* contains enough good poems to ensure that he will continue to be read with admiration by all who respond to the visionary element in poetry, and one can only regret that he has remained relatively silent since then.

—John Press

GILMORE, Mary (Jean). Australian. Born in Cotta Walla, near Goulburn, New South Wales, 16 August 1865. Pupil-teacher in Cootamundra, Albury, and Wagga. Married William Alexander Gilmore in 1897 (separated, 1911); one son. Taught in Silverton, 1888–89, and in Sydney, 1890; relief worker during maritime strike, 1890; emigrated to utopian colony "New Australia," Cosme, Paraguay, 1896: teacher, and Editor of *Cosme Evening Notes*; returned to Australia, 1902: farmer in Casterton, Victoria, 1902–11; settled in Sydney, 1911; Founding Editor of the women's page, *The Worker*, Sydney, 1908–30; Columnist, *Tribune* (communist newspaper), 1952–62. Founding Executive Member, Australian Workers Union (first woman member). D.B.E. (Dame Commander, Order of the British Empire), 1937. *Died 3 December 1962.*

PUBLICATIONS

Collections

(Poems), edited by Robert D. FitzGerald.   1963.
Gilmore: A Tribute, edited by D. Cusack and others.   1965.

Verse

Marri'd and Other Verses.   1910.
The Tale of Tiddley Winks.   1917.
The Passionate Heart.   1918.
The Tilted Cart: A Book of Recitations.   1925.
The Wild Swan.   1930.
The Rue Tree.   1931.
Under the Wilgas.   1932.
Battlefields.   1939.
The Disinherited.   1941.
Pro Patria Australia and Other Poems.   1945.
Selected Verse.   1948; revised edition, 1969.
All Souls.   1954.
Fourteen Men.   1954.

Other

Hound of the Road. 1922.
Old Days, Old Ways: A Book of Recollections.   1934.
More Recollections.   1935.

Bibliography: in *Gilmore: A Tribute,* 1965.

Reading List: *Gilmore* by Sylvia Lawson, 1966; *Three Radicals* by W. H. Wilde, 1969.

*   *   *

Mary Gilmore's long life spanned more than half of Australia's whole history and encompassed the most dramatic and significant events in its struggle for recognition as a nation: gold-rushes, the great strikes of the 1890's leading to the formation of the Labour Party and the consolidation of industrial unionism, Federation, the first World War and Gallipoli, the Depression, the second World War and the Pacific War, and the economic expansion of the cheap oil decades. Mary Gilmore's prose and poetry, her sixty years as a working journalist, reflect all these changes, as well as her personal response to them. This response never wavered from the religious and idealistic principles on which her moral attitudes rested: the principles of the brotherhood of man and of the Christian ethic as revealed towards the end of *Matthew* 25. In accordance with these principles, she extended the meaning of brotherhood to cover the long-forgotten convicts who helped found the country and the dispossessed Aboriginals, at a time when there were few people to see good in either. "Old Botany Bay" and "The Myall in Prison" express the tragedy of both.

Mary Gilmore was of Scottish descent, and her hearing was early attuned to the great ballads, the Bible, and the timeless hymns and psalms of her ancestors. In addition, there was in her a genuine streak of Celtic mysticism, or at least of the "feyness" common to so many Scotchwomen, added to an element of gnomic wisdom, and her work in consequence conveys a curious impression of being spoken by a tribal Wise Woman. All of it is distinguished by a warm, simple, and sincere humanity. In common with the balladists, she has a strength and vitality unusual in women poets. Like most of the balladists, she is a poet of the people and knows their struggles from the inside, not as a spectator. Her verse comes as naturally as song to a bird; she writes with the same unselfconsciousness as would attend the making of bread, and both activities are part of the unity of her personality. Like her contemporary Hugh McCrae, she thinks naturally in images, which are not, unlike McCrae's, merely the result of observation, but are bound up indissolubly with some mental state, mood, or idea:

> Nurse no long grief,
> Lest the heart flower no more;
> Grief builds no barns; its plough
> Rusts at the door.

But a simple, natural style does not always achieve such timeless perfection and Mary Gilmore's art has the defects of its qualities. A reluctance to realise the need for self-criticism, for whatever reason, sometimes results in vagueness, in the commonplace, in facile emotional self-indulgence. Nevertheless the wide range of her subjects and her sympathies, her intelligence and sensitivity, her vigour and individuality, the sense that in reading her we are listening to the voice of a race give her a place of first importance in Australian literature. She speaks in addition for women, not for Australian women alone, though she does that, but for womankind, though she was no feminist: one of the best of her poems is the early "Eve-song." Yet some of the best and the strongest come from her last book, *Fourteen Men,* published in her 90th year, in which all her gifts and her preoccupations are as vital as ever: her awareness of the natural world, her sympathy with humble people, her religious faith, her empathy with Aboriginals, her interest in world affairs, especially in peace movements, her wisdom and her passion and her sense of mystery. The risk is that she may be under-rated: it is rarely pointed out, for instance, how much is owed to her example by Judith Wright.

Mary Gilmore wrote three books of essays and recollections, besides her books of verse: *Hound of the Road*, *Old Days, Old Ways*, and *More Recollections*. These have the same qualities as her verse and bring the era in which she grew up vividly to life. Some of her best work, however, may still lie buried in *The Worker*, the women's page of which she edited for more than twenty years. Other journalistic articles wait for discovery in Argentina newspapers, to which she contributed after the New Australia experiment in Paraguay came to an end.

—Dorothy Green

GINSBERG, Allen.   American. Born in Newark, New Jersey, 3 June 1926. Educated at Paterson High School, New Jersey; Columbia University, New York, B.A. 1948. Served in the Military Sea Transport Service. Associated with the Beat movement and the San Francisco Renaissance in the 1950's. Widely travelled: has participated in many poetry readings and demonstrations. Lived in the Far East, 1962–63. Since 1971, Director, Committee on Poetry Foundation, New York; Director, Kerouac School of Poetics, Naropa Institute, Boulder, Colorado. Recipient: Guggenheim Fellowship, 1965; National Endowment for the Arts grant, 1966; National Institute of Arts and Letters grant, 1969; National Book Award, 1974. Member, National Insitute of Arts and Letters, 1973. Lives in New York City.

PUBLICATIONS

Verse

> *Howl and Other Poems.*   1956; revised edition of *Howl*, as *Howl for Carl Solomon*, 1971.
> *Empty Mirror: Early Poems.*   1961.
> *Kaddish and Other Poems, 1958–1960.*   1961.
> *Reality Sandwiches, 1953–60.*   1963.
> *T.V. Baby Poems.*   1967.
> *Wales – A Visitation, July 29, 1967.*   1968.
> *Scrap Leaves, Tasty Scribbles.*   1968.
> *Planet News, 1961–1967.*   1968.
> *Airplane Dreams: Compositions from Journals.*   1968.
> *Ankor-Wat.*   1969.
> *Iron Horse.*   1972.
> *The Fall of America: Poems of These States 1965–1971.*   1972.
> *The Gates of Wrath: Rhymed Poems 1948–1952.*   1972.

Bixby Canyon Ocean Path Word Breeze.   1972.
New Year Blues.   1972.
Sad Dust Glories.   1975.
First Blues: Rags, Ballads, and Harmonium Songs, 1971–1974.   1975.
Mind Breaths: Poems 1972–1977.   1977.

Plays

Don't Go Away Mad, in *Pardon Me, Sir, But Is My Eye Hurting Your Elbow?,* edited by
Bob Booker and George Foster.   1968.
Kaddish (produced 1972).   1973.

Other

The Yage Letters, with William S. Burroughs.   1963.
Indian Journals: March 1962–May 1963: Notebooks, Diary, Blank Pages,
Writings.   1970.
Improvised Poetics.   1972.
Allen Verbatim: Lectures on Poetry, Politics, Consciousness, edited by Gordon
Ball.   1974.
The Visions of the Great Remembrancer (on Jack Kerouac).   1974.
Chicago Trial Testimony.   1975.
As Ever: The Collected Correspondence of Ginsberg and Neal Cassady.   1977.
Journals: Early Fifties–Early Sixties, edited by Gordon Ball.   1977.

Bibliography: *A Bibliography of the Works of Ginsberg* by George Dowden, 1970.

Reading List: *Howl of the Censor* by J. W. Ehrlich, 1961; *Ginsberg* by Thomas F. Merrill,
1969; *Ginsberg in America* by Jane Kramer, 1969, as *Paterfamilias,* 1970; *Scenes along the
Road* edited by Ann Charters, 1971; *Ginsberg in the '60's* by Eric Mottram, 1972.

*   *   *

Like Whitman, his forebear, Allen Ginsberg is a prolific poet who writes too much: some
of his work is, like Whitman's, unfocused, emotionally scattered, and prone to large
abstractions unrelated to any concrete particularity. And, like Whitman, Ginsberg insists that
any subject is a fit one for poetry. And so, like Whitman, he has been attacked for his
vulgarity, for his failure to be "proper" or dignified; yet at the same time, like both Whitman
and Blake (from whom he has learned much), he appeals to the young, to those who do not
think that poetry and the business of daily life are essentially grave matters whose languages
have to be separated from one another. Ginsberg is a World-Poet, like Neruda and
Yevtushenko, and like Gibran, Tagore, Whitman, and Blake in previous times. And, like each
of these, he has written a quantity of slight but interesting occasional verse, of which
"Portland Coloseum" (in *Planet News*), about a Beatles concert, is representative.

In *Improvised Poetics* Ginsberg talks about writing this poem. "I changed things," he said,
"like *Hands waving* LIKE *myriad snakes of thought* to *Hands waving myriad/snakes of*
thought. Ah ... *The million children* OF *the thousand worlds,* so I just changed *The million*
children,/the thousand worlds." These apparently minor revisions are significant: Ginsberg
talks about his "paragraphal" mode of composition and explains, "when I'd get three or four
[phrases] that made an apposition I'd start a new paragraph." In taking out "a lot of
syntactical fat" and thus "putting two short lines together that had just images in them,"

Ginsberg prunes the lines of prepositions which express relationship and embraces the technique of juxtaposition, learned from Pound. The danger of such technique is that the poem can degenerate into a mere list (although, as Emerson remarked in *The Poet*, "bare lists of words are found suggestive to an imaginative and excited mind"). The value of such appositional language is that it can *imply* cause-and-effect relationships, but it does not state them: cause and effect are not to be assumed in or about the world of event; it is a world of immediacy. That is to say, the reader is moved into a world of event, a place *where things happen*, for (to quote Emerson again) "the quality of the imagination is to flow, and not to freeze." Ginsberg's reader can, therefore, often be overwhelmed by a rush of sensory, social, political and/or intellectual data to very good effect, as in poems like *Howl* or *Kaddish*.

The concern of the poet is for registering the precise nature of the occurrence (his thought, his feeling, the particularities from which they arise) in the here and now. So Ginsberg, like other modernists, finds crucial the accuracy of the poem as notation of the spoken voice or as notation of the processes of thought. The notation is exact: in *Airplane Dreams* the lines of the long poem "New York to San Fran" are, in Ginsberg's words, "hung out on the page a little to the right.... A little bit like diagramming a sentence, you know, the old syntactical diagrammatic method of making a little platform and you put the subject and object on it and hang adjectives and adverbial clauses down" (*Improvised Poetics*). Here is a short sequence from "Portland Coloseum":

> The million children
> the thousand worlds
> bounce in their seats, bash
> each other's sides, press
> legs together nervous
> Scream again & claphand

Like Olson's, Ginsberg's line-breaks serve an emphatic, syntactic purpose, in which the slight hesitancy at the end of the line provides for unexpected semantic conjunctions and emphases, while at the same time they direct the reader's voice into the (in this case slightly nervous) rhythm and rhetorical inflection of the verse.

Such a line, the unit of thought or the unit of speech, reinforces the air of spontaneous improvisation characteristic of much of Ginsberg's work. The publication of *Howl* in 1956, brought Ginsberg to prominence and gave wide currency to the notion that poetry might be a spontaneous art, requiring little or no skill or revision. Deceptively simple in appearance, *Howl* rests on an extensive apprenticeship in rhymed verse (some of which has been published in *The Gates of Wrath*) and in conscious craftsmanship. As Ginsberg wrote to Richard Eberhart, the "general ground plan" of the poem, "quite symmetrical, surprisingly," structures the three sections of the poem round three main devices: the fixed base of "who" and a long line; the repetition and variation of the fixed base "Moloch"; and the "fixed base/reply/fixed base/longer reply" of the final section. Such writing is not always done, of course, in a single extended burst of composition (the result of a fairly extended gestation): Ginsberg's compositions are often leisurely and deliberative, and very often, in revising a poem, Ginsberg in effect composes a completely new one. "Sunflower Sutra," for example, is a revised version of "In Back of the Real." It is fundamentally a different poem that came about as the result of "re-seeing" the same event. With its long lines, its introduction of a second person into the poem, and its focus on the *perceiver* of the flower, "Sunflower Sutra" is both less general and more immediate in its effect. At the same time it is, as is much of Ginsberg's work, more a celebration and affirmation of the individual, of the personal, and of nature than a denunciation of the world of man. Ginsberg's great strengths as poet are to be found in such visionary poems as this, with its long and carefully controlled lines juxtaposed against shorter lines, leading the poem to a crescendo which is not rhetorical only but quite literally *physical*: Ginsberg's long interest in yoga and in the breath as a measure in verse has led him to speculate on the correlations in Sanskrit poetry between prosody and human physiology, and has led him to attempt similar correlations in his own work. At the same time, the unabashed frankness of his words and the declarative nature of much of his writing have made the work accessible to the casual reader, and have thus given Ginsberg a wide following.

—Peter Quartermain

GLOVER, Denis (James Matthews). New Zealander. Born in Dunedin, 10 December 1912. Educated at Auckland Grammar School; Christ's College; Canterbury University College, A.B. Served as an officer in the Royal Navy during World War II: Distinguished Service Cross. Married 1) Mary Granville in 1936, one son; 2) Lyn Cameron in 1972. Taught English at Canterbury University, 1936–38, and typography at the Technical Correspondence Institute, Christchurch. Founder, Caxton Press, Christchurch, 1936; joined Pegasus Press, 1953, and Wingfield Press, 1955. Formerly, Journalist, *The Press*, Christchurch. Former President, New Zealand P.E.N. and Friends of the Turnbull Library, Wellington; Member of the Canterbury University Council, and of the New Zealand State Literary Fund Committee. Recipient: Jessie Mackay Award, 1960. Lives in Wellington.

PUBLICATIONS

Verse

> *Short Reflection on the Present State of Literature in This Country.* 1935.
> *Another Argo*, with Allen Curnow and A. R. D. Fairburn. 1935.
> *Thistledown.* 1935.
> *Six Easy Ways of Dodging Debt Collectors.* 1936.
> *A Caxton Miscellany*, with others. 1937.
> *The Arraignment of Paris.* 1937.
> *Thirteen Poems.* 1939.
> *Cold Tongue.* 1940.
> *Recent Poems*, with others. 1941.
> *The Wind and the Sand: Poems 1933–44.* 1945.
> *Summer Flowers.* 1945.
> *Sings Harry and Other Poems.* 1951.
> *Arawata Bill: A Sequence of Poems.* 1953.
> *Since Then.* 1957.
> *Poetry Harbinger*, with A. R. D. Fairburn. 1958.
> *Enter Without Knocking: Selected Poems.* 1964; revised edition, 1972.
> *Sharp Edge Up: Verses and Satires.* 1968.
> *Myself When Young.* 1970.
> *To a Particular Woman.* 1970.
> *Diary to a Woman.* 1971.
> *Dancing to My Tune.* 1974.
> *Wellington Harbour.* 1974.

Plays

Screenplays: *The Coaster,* 1951; *Mick Stimson,* with John Lang, 1972.

Radio Play: *They Sometimes Float at Sea,* 1970.

Fiction

3 Short Stories.   1936.

Other

Till the Star Speaks.   1939.
D Day.   1944.
A Clutch of Authors and a Clot.   1960.
Hot Water Sailor.   1962.
Glover's Bedside Book.   1963.

Editor, with Ian Milner, *New Poems.*   1934.
Editor, *The Disadvantages of Being Dead and Other Sharp Verses.* by A. R. D. Fairburn.   1958.
Editor, *Cross Currents,* by Merrill Moore.   1961.
Editor, *Collected Poems,* by A. R. D. Fairburn.   1966.
Editor, with Geoffrey Fairburn, *The Woman Problem and Other Prose,* by A. R. D. Fairburn.   1967.

*   *   *

Denis Glover, naval Commander, boxing blue, poet, publisher, printer, "looking rather like Mr. Punch in naval uniform" (John Lehmann, 1941) has been a minor kind of colonial/ Renaissance man. All which helps establish his very distinctive poetic tone, although in parenthesis one might note his admirable wartime prose in *Penguin New Writing* (notably "It Was D-Day"), and his eminently readable autobiography *Hot Water Sailor.* His poetry begins, part Georgian, part Audenesque, in the middle 1930's when that "shock of recognition" of the Depression ignited so much local creativity. He also, with developing elegance, printed and published (under the imprint Caxton Press) his own verse, along with much other significant poetry, fiction, and critical prose, through the next crucial and formative decade.

Early verse presents the dignity of labour ("The Road Builders") and lyric response to landscape ("Holiday Piece"); his very first Caxton Press book, incidentally, with that sharp, irreverent and dangerous wit he still displays, is titled *Six Easy Ways of Dodging Debt Collectors,* with the explanation "Called on the outside, because of the difficulty of selling verse, *Six Easy Ways....*" In *Recent Poems* he moves into his stride with, perhaps most notably, the memorable ballad "The Magpies" with its lyric opening, "When Tom and Elizabeth took the farm/The bracken made their bed," but lamentable conclusion:

> The farm's still there, Mortgage corporations
> Couldn't give it away.
> And *Quardle oodle ardle wardle doodle*
> The magpies say.

The same volume sustains his impudent wit ("Thoughts on Cremation"); *The Wind and the Sand* not only promotes his St. Exupéry-like romanticism but adds themes of nostalgia and mortality and that marine sensibility he alone brings to New Zealand verse.

In my view, *Sings Harry* is his best single volume. This contains "A Note to Lili Kraus" where he articulates a representative local fear of feeling: "Lili, emotion leaves me quite dismayed:/If I'm on fire I call the fire-brigade." Alastair Campbell ("Glover and Georgianism," *Comment 21*) has shown it is through "Harry" (possibly copying Yeats) that Glover finds an emotionally liberating persona. Harry, like his subsequent fellows, 'Wata Bill and Mick Stimson, is that true colonial archetype, a rural male loner. From "Sings Harry to an Old Guitar":

> These songs will not stand −
> The wind and the sand will smother.
>
> Not I but another
> Will make songs worth the bother:
> The rimu or kauri be,
> I'm but the cabbage tree

and from "Sings Harry in the Wind-Break":

> From the cliff-top a boy
> Felt that great motion
> And pupil to the horizon's eye
> Grew wide with vision,

and from "Themes":

> What shall we sing? sings Harry.
>
> Sing all things sweet or harsh upon
> These islands in the Pacific sun,
> The mountains whitened endlessly
> And the white horses of the winter sea.

His subsequent *Arawata Bill*, though ingenious and admired, seems too contrived and rhythmically stiff to create quite the same niche for a wandering prospector. Only perhaps in "Towards Banks Peninsula: Mick Stimson" (*Since Then*) does a similar warmth, more tranquil, infuse his lines: this poem should possibly be linked with "Towards Banks Peninsula: Peraki" (*Poetry Harbinger*) as part of that poetry of the sea prominent in his later work.

—Peter Alcock

GOGARTY, Oliver (Joseph) St. John.   American.   Born in Dublin, Ireland. 17 August 1878; emigrated to the U.S. in 1939: naturalized citizen. Educated at Stonyhurst, Dublin; Clongowes Wood, Kildare; Trinity College, Dublin; Worcester College, Oxford; studied medicine in Vienna; qualified as a surgeon: Fellow of the Royal College of Surgeons of Ireland. Practiced as a nose, throat, and ear surgeon. Senator of the Irish Free State, 1922–36. *Died 22 September 1957.*

PUBLICATIONS

Collections

   The Plays.   1971.

Verse

   Cervantes: Tercentenary of Don Quixote.   1905(?).
   Hyperthuleana.   1916.
   The Ship and Other Poems.   1923.
   Wild Apples.   1928; revised edition, 1930.
   Selected Poems.   1933.
   Others to Adorn.   1938.
   Elbow Room.   1939.
   Perennial.   1944.
   The Collected Poems.   1951.
   Unselected Poems.   1954.

Plays

   Blight: The Tragedy of Dublin, with Joseph O'Connor (produced 1917).   1917.
   The Enchanted Trousers (produced 1919).   1919.
   A Serious Thing (produced 1919).   1919.

Fiction

   Mad Grandeur.   1941.
   Mr. Petunia.   1945.

Other

   As I Was Going down Sackville Street: A Phantasy in Fact.   1937.
   I Follow St. Patrick.   1938.
   Tumbling in the Hay.   1939.
   Going Native.   1940.
   Mourning Becomes Mrs. Spendlove and Other Portraits, Grave and Gay.   1948.
   Intimations.   1950.
   Rolling Down the Lea.   1950.
   It Isn't This Time of Year at All! An Unpremeditated Autobiography.   1954.
   Start from Somewhere Else: An Exposition of Wit and Humor, Polite and Perilous.   1955.
   A Week End in the Middle of the Week and Other Essays on the Bias.   1958.
   William Butler Yeats: A Memoir.   1963.
   Many Lives to Thee: Letters to G. K. A. Bell 1904–1907, edited by James F. Carens.   1971.

Reading List: *Gogarty* by A. Norman Jeffares, 1961; *Gogarty: A Poet and His Times* by Ulick O'Connor, 1964, as *The Times I've Seen*, 1964.

*   *   *

Oliver St. John Gogarty was a friend of James Joyce, a politician (in sympathy with the aims of Sinn Fein and a friend of its founder, Arthur Griffith; a Senator after Home Rule was achieved and the victim of an assassination attempt), and a public figure. But of his two volumes of memoirs, *As I Was Going down Sackville Street* and *Tumbling in the Hay*, it has been well said that Gogarty "eschews perspective like the Chinese" and "allowed his imagination to body forth ideas, without regard to chronology." These brisk and witty evocations of a lost Dublin, its personalities and brilliant conversations, have a vivid informality, and parts of both were transcribed directly from Gogarty's talk. The later autobiography, *It Isn't This Time of Year at All*, is more formalized and rather dull. As a critic, he is negligible, though the brief essays in *Intimations* and *A Week End in the Middle of the Week* can be read with mild pleasure.

As a poet, there was always something amateur about him. He was one of the "gentlemen who wrote with ease," and he was casual about collecting his poems. His happiest vein lay in the occasional and satirical. Attempting a severe neo-classical surface, he is lapidary or nothing (and often nothing): his lyrics tend to suffer from the expected epithet and the routine inversion, but he can offer an occasional Landorian elegance and conciseness and a sharp evocation of the natural scene.

Gogarty's three plays are vigorous and read well, but the characters are too one-dimensional to survive on the stage. The novel *Mr. Petunia*, with its American eighteenth-century background, is a virtuoso piece. Gogarty will probably be remembered first as the original of Joyce's Buck Mulligan in *Ulysses*, and second as a wit. The competing nature of his many talents prevented the full realisation of any.

—Ian Fletcher

GRAVES, Robert (Ranke). English. Born in London, 24 July 1895. Educated at Charterhouse School, Surrey; St. John's College, Oxford, B.Litt. 1926. Served in France with the Royal Welch Fusiliers in World War I; was refused admittance into the armed forces in World War II. Married 1) Nancy Nicholson, one son, two daughters; 2) Beryl Pritchard, three sons, one daughter. Professor of English, Egyptian University, Cairo, 1926. Settled in Deya, Majorca; with the poet Laura Riding established the Seizen Press and *Epilogue* magazine. Left Majorca during the Spanish Civil War: settled in Glampton-Brixton, Devon during World War II; returned to Majorca after the war. Clark Lecturer, Trinity College, Cambridge, 1954; Professor of Poetry, Oxford University, 1961–66; Arthur Dehon Little Memorial Lecturer, Massachusetts Institute of Technology, Cambridge, 1963. Recipient: Bronze Medal for Poetry, Olympic Games, Paris, 1924; Hawthornden Prize, for fiction, 1935; Black Memorial Prize, for fiction, 1935; Femina Vie Heureuse-Stock Prize, 1939; Russell Loines Award, 1958; National Poetry Society of America Gold Medal, 1960; Foyle Poetry Prize, 1960; Arts Council Poetry Award, 1962; Italia Prize, for radio play, 1965; Queen's Gold Medal for Poetry, 1968; Gold Medal for Poetry, Cultural Olympics, Mexico City, 1968. M.A.: Oxford University, 1961. Honorary Fellow, St. John's College, Oxford, 1971. Honorary Member, American Academy of Arts and Sciences, 1970. Lives in Majorca.

PUBLICATIONS

Verse

Over the Brazier. 1916.
Goliath and David. 1916.
Fairies and Fusiliers. 1917.
Treasure Box. 1919.
Country Sentiment. 1920.
The Pier-Glass. 1921.
Whipperginny. 1923.
The Feather Bed. 1923.
Mock Beggar Hall. 1924.
Welchman's Hose. 1925.
(Poems). 1925.
The Marmosite's Miscellany. 1925.
Poems (1914–1926). 1927.
Poems (1914–1927). 1927.
Poems 1929. 1929.
Ten Poems More. 1930.
Poems 1926–1930. 1931.
To Whom Else? 1931.
Poems 1930–1933. 1933.
Collected Poems. 1938.
No More Ghosts: Selected Poems. 1940.
Work in Hand, with Alan Hodge and Norman Cameron. 1942.
(Poems). 1943.
Poems 1938–1945. 1946.
Collected Poems (1914–1947). 1948.
Poems and Satires 1951. 1951.
Poems 1953. 1953.
Collected Poems 1955. 1955.
Poems Selected by Himself. 1957; revised edition, 1961, 1966.
The Poems. 1958.
Collected Poems 1959. 1959.
More Poems 1961. 1961.
Collected Poems. 1961.
New Poems 1962. 1962.
The More Deserving Cases: Eighteen Old Poems for Reconsideration. 1962.
Man Does, Woman Is 1964. 1964.
Love Respelt. 1965.
Collected Poems 1965. 1965.
Seventeen Poems Missing from "Love Respelt". 1966.
Colophon to "Love Respelt". 1967.
(Poems), with D. H. Lawrence, edited by Leonard Clark. 1967.
Poems 1965–1968. 1968.
Poems about Love. 1969.
Love Respelt Again. 1969.
Beyond Giving: Poems. 1969.
Poems 1968–1970. 1970.
The Green-Sailed Vessel. 1971.
Poems 1970–1972. 1972.
Deyá. 1973.

Timeless Meeting: Poems.   1973.
At the Gate.   1974.
Collected Poems 1975.   1975.
New Collected Poems.   1977.

Plays

John Kemp's Wager: A Ballad Opera.   1925.
Much Ado about Nothing, from the play by Shakespeare, textual revisions by Graves
   (produced 1965).

Radio Play: *The Anger of Achilles,* 1964.

Fiction

The Shout.   1929.
No Decency Left, with Laura Riding.   1932.
The Real David Copperfield.   1933; as *David Copperfield by Charles Dickens,
   Condensed by Robert Graves,* edited by Merrill P. Paine, 1934.
*I, Claudius: From the Autobiography of Tiberius Claudius, Emperor of the Romans, Born
   B.C. 10, Murdered and Deified A.D. 54.*   1934.
*Claudius the God and His Wife Messalina: The Troublesome Reign of Tiberius Claudius
   Caesar, Emperor of the Romans (Born B.C. 10, Died A.D. 54), As Described by
   Himself; Also His Murder at the Hands of the Notorious Agrippina (Mother of the
   Emperor Nero) and His Subsequent Deification. As Described by Others.*   1934.
"Antigua, Penny, Puce."   1936; as *The Antigua Stamp,* 1937.
Count Belisarius.   1938.
Sergeant Lamb of the Ninth.   1940; as *Sergeant Lamb's America,* 1940.
Proceed, Sergeant Lamb.   1941.
The Story of Marie Powell: Wife to Mr. Milton.   1943; as *Wife to Mr. Milton: The Story
   of Marie Powell,* 1944.
The Golden Fleece.   1944; as *Hercules, My Shipmate,* 1945.
King Jesus.   1946.
Watch the North Wind Rise.   1949; as *Seven Days in New Crete,* 1949.
The Islands of Unwisdom.   1949; as *The Isles of Unwisdom,* 1950.
Homer's Daughter.   1955.
¡Catacrok! Mostly Stories, Mostly Funny.   1956.
Collected Short Stories.   1964.

Other

*On English Poetry, Being an Irregular Approach to the Psychology of This Art, from
   Evidence Mainly Subjective.*   1922.
The Meaning of Dreams.   1924.
Poetic Unreason and Other Studies.   1925.
*My Head! My Head! Being the History of Elisha and the Shunamite Woman; With the
   History of Moses as Elisha Related It, and Her Questions to Him.*   1925.
Contemporary Techniques of Poetry: A Political Analogy.   1925.
Another Future of Poetry.   1926.
Impenetrability; or, The Proper Habit of English.   1927.
The English Ballad: A Short Critical Survey.   1927.

Lars Porsena; or, The Future of Swearing and Improper Language.   1927; revised edition, as *The Future of Swearing and Improper Language,* 1936.

A Survey of Modernist Poetry, with Laura Riding.   1927.

Lawrence and the Arabs.   1927; as *Lawrence and the Arabian Adventure,* 1928.

A Pamphlet Against Anthologies, with Laura Riding.   1928; as *Against Anthologies,* 1928.

Mrs. Fisher; or, The Future of Humour.   1928.

Goodbye to All That: An Autobiography.   1929; revised edition, 1957, 1960.

But It Still Goes On: An Accumulation.   1930.

Epilogue: A Critical Summary, vols. 1, 2, and 3, with Laura Riding and others.   1935–37.

T. E. Lawrence to His Biographer Robert Graves.   1938.

The Long Week-end: A Social History of Great Britain 1918–1939, with Alan Hodge.   1940.

The Reader over Your Shoulder: A Handbook for Writers of English Prose, with Alan Hodge.   1943.

The White Goddess: A Historical Grammar of Poetic Myth.   1948; revised edition, 1958.

The Common Asphodel: Collected Essays on Poetry 1922–1949.   1949.

Occupation: Writer.   1950.

The Nazarene Gospel Restored, with Joshua Podro.   1953.

The Crowing Privilege: The Clark Lectures 1954–1955; Also Various Essays on Poetry and Sixteen New Poems.   1955; as *The Crowning Privilege: Collected Essays on Poetry,* 1956.

Adam's Rib and Other Anomalous Elements in the Hebrew Creation Myth: A New View.   1955.

The Greek Myths.   2 vols., 1955.

Jesus in Rome: A Historical Conjecture, with Joshua Podro.   1957.

They Hanged My Saintly Billy.   1957; as *They Hanged My Saintly Billy: The Life and Death of Dr. William Palmer,* 1957.

Steps: Stories, Talks, Essays, Poems, Studies in History.   1958.

Five Pens in Hand.   1958.

Food for Centaurs: Stories, Talks, Critical Studies, Poems.   1960.

The Penny Fiddle: Poems for Children.   1960.

Greek Gods and Heroes.   1960; as *Myths of Ancient Greece,* 1961.

Selected Poetry and Prose, edited by James Reeves.   1961.

The Siege and Fall of Troy (juvenile).   1962.

The Big Green Book.   1962.

Oxford Addresses on Poetry.   1962.

The Hebrew Myths: The Book of Genesis, with Raphael Patai.   1964.

Ann at Highwood Hall: Poems for Children.   1964.

Majorca Observed.   1965.

Mammon and the Black Goddess.   1965.

Two Wise Children (juvenile).   1966.

Poetic Craft and Principle: Lectures and Talks.   1967.

Spiritual Quixote.   1967.

The Poor Boy Who Followed His Star (juvenile).   1968.

The Crane Bag and Other Disputed Subjects.   1969.

On Poetry: Collected Talks and Essays.   1969.

Poems: Abridged for Dolls and Princes (juvenile).   1971.

Difficult Questions, Easy Answers.   1972.

Editor, with Alan Porter and Richard Hughes, *Oxford Poetry, 1921.*   1921.

Editor, *John Skelton (Laureate), 1460(?)–1529.*   1927.

Editor, *The Less Familiar Nursery Rhymes*. 1927.

Editor, *Old Soldiers Never Die*, by Frank Richards. 1933.

Editor, *Old Soldier Sahib*, by Frank Richards. 1936.

Editor, *The Comedies of Terence*, translated by Echard. 1962.

Translator, with Laura Riding, *Almost Forgotten Germany*, by George Schwarz.   1936.

Translator, *The Transformations of Lucius, Otherwise Known as The Golden Ass*, by Apuleius. 1950.

Translator, *The Cross and the Sword*, by Manuel de Jesus Galvan. 1954.

Translator, *The Infant with the Globe*, by Pedro Antonio de Alarcon. 1955.

Translator, *Winter in Majorca*, by George Sand. 1956.

Translator, *Pharsalia: Dramatic Episodes of the Civil Wars*, by Lucan. 1956.

Translator, *The Twelve Caesars*, by Suetonius. 1957.

Translator, *The Anger of Achilles: Homer's Iliad*. 1959.

Translator, with Omar Ali-Shah, *Rubaiyyat of Omar Khayaam*. 1967.

Translator, *The Song of Songs*. 1973.

Bibliography: *A Bibliography of the Works of Graves* by Fred H. Higginson, 1966.

Reading List: *Graves* by Martin Seymour-Smith, 1956, revised edition, 1965, 1970; *Graves* by J. M. Cohen, 1960; *Swifter than Reason: The Poetry and Criticism of Graves* by Douglas Day, 1963; *Graves* by George Stade, 1967; *Barbarous Knowledge: Myth in the Poetry of Yeats, Graves, and Muir* by Daniel Hoffman, 1967; *The Poetry of Graves* by Michael Kirkham, 1969; *The Third Book of Criticism* by Randall Jarrell, 1969.

*   *   *

Robert Graves's prolific writings in prose and verse express his own conflicting characteristics. He is at once a Romantic primitive and a classicist; a seeker of ecstasy and of formal perfection. Committed to the life of feeling and the rule of intuition, he is a compulsive systematizer and puzzle-solver. Indeed, Graves is a confirming example of what T. S. Eliot diagnosed as the characteristic modern condition: dissociation of sensibility from thought. Graves's entire career expresses his inspired, inventive, and ingenious efforts to express either side of his essential self; in his best work, both are intertwined.

Graves's childhood and adolescence were typical of his class and time. Son of A. P. Graves, a facile verse-writer and translator from the Irish who was inspector of schools in Dublin, Robert had a proper Edwardian childhood and was schooled at Charterhouse. At the outbreak of the first World War he volunteered and was commissioned in the Royal Welch Fusiliers. His choice of regiment reflects his desire to find his own Celtic roots elsewhere than in the Ireland pre-empted by his father's literary activity. The immediate result of service was his exposure to the horror of trench warfare, severe wounds, being reported dead, return to duty, subsequent hospitalization in England where he was treated for shell-shock by Dr. W. H. R. Rivers, whose patients included Siegfried Sassoon and Wilfred Owen and whose psychiatric theories influenced Graves's aesthetic in the 1920's. The war experience and its aftermath are memorably stated in his autobiography, *Goodbye to All That*, his aesthetic in *Poetic Unreason*.

By 1916 Graves had published his first book of poems, *Over the Brazier*, rather vapid stuff compared to what he would write within a decade. As a war poet Graves did not deal, as did Owen, Sassoon, and Isaac Rosenberg, with reality; his desperately self-protective imagination held fast to nursery and nature images, the pieties of Georgianism. Not until the war was over could Graves grapple with its nightmarish revelation of the madness of reality, as he does in such poems as "In Procession," "Warning to Children," "Alice," "The Cool Web," "In Broken Images," and many others. These are among the most powerful reflections of the disintegration of certainty, the blasting apart of pre-war norms, the guilt of survivors, the desperation of man deprived of the traditional and institutional props of his culture.

With tenacity Graves refused, however, to surrender certain of those institutions and traditions. As a poet he resisted the modernist break-up of meter, form, and linguistic decorum. In its conventional craft his work is thus nearer to that of Hardy and Yeats than to Eliot or Pound. In theme, however, he has not essayed the range of any of these. Besides his poems of psychomachia mentioned above, his principal theme has been the recording of romantic love. In this his work shows affinities to Donne and the Cavalier poets, but Graves's view of love is unique. From the beginning he viewed love as a transcendent ecstasy immutably linked with doom, as in "Love Without Hope" (1925):

> Love without hope, as when the young bird-catcher
> Swept off his tall hat to the Squire's own daughter,
> So let the imprisoned larks escape and fly
> Singing about her head, as she rode by.

This quatrain encapsulates the convictions Graves would raise into myth in *The White Goddess*, that stupendous "historic grammar of poetic myth" which explicates what in his poem "To Juan at the Winter Solstice" he called the "one story and one story only/That will prove worth your telling." The Squire's daughter will become a queen, a goddess, while remaining the mortal woman whom the poet is fated to love; the young bird-catcher is of course the poet whose singing larks were imprisoned in his head (under his tall hat) until he gave them freedom to declare his hopeless adoration. The beloved is in fact the poet's Muse who appears to him as Mother, Lover, and Layer-out, a tripartite pattern of significance Graves traces to the once-universal matriarchal religious states that preceded the patriarchy, repressive of the life of feeling, which the Judeo-Christian tradition has foisted upon the world.

Accept this historiography (with its roots in Celtic and Classical paganism) or not; what is incontestable is that Graves has written a body of love poetry without rival in our time for its intensity, elegance, and occasional lubricity.

As novelist and essayist Graves demonstrates the erudition and intellectual ingenuity that characterize *The White Goddess*. Many of his fictions offer "answers" to conundrums historians not gifted with a poet's intuition have been unable to solve, just as Graves's discursive books often "restore" defective literary or sacred texts (e.g., the ballads, the Bible). His most admired novels, *I, Claudius* and *Claudius the God*, provide the hitherto secret memoirs of Claudius himself and give an even more intimate view than did Suetonius of the depravities of Rome's first family between the reigns of Caesar Augustus and Claudius himself. The latter, shy, stammering, introspective, and wise, has a poet's understanding of the social and personal catastrophes enacted around him. To the alert reader Graves is writing about the decline and fall of the British as well as the Roman empire, as he does overtly in *The Long Week-end*. Other novels present historical cruces from similarly unexpected points of view. *Wife to Mr. Milton* exonerates its heroine against the received calumnies of a poet Graves dislikes intensely. *Sergeant Lamb's America* treats the American Revolution as seen by a predecessor in Graves's own regiment.

Graves's measure for other poets, as for himself, is their participation in "The poetic trance derive[d] from ecstatic worship of the age-old matriarchal Greek Muse, who ruled Sky, Earth, Underworld in triad." In his Oxford lectures, *Mammon and the Black Goddess*, Graves discovers a further stage in his anatomy of love, the stations of the poet's progress. "The Black Goddess... promises a new pacific bond between men and women, corresponding to a final reality of love, in which the patriarchal marriage bond will fade away.... Faithful as Vesta, gay and adventurous as the White Goddess, she will lead man back to that sure instinct of love which he long ago forfeited by intellectual pride." Robert Graves has continued to pour forth poems on his "one story only" past his eightieth year.

—Daniel Hoffman

GREGORY, Horace (Victor).   American.   Born in Milwaukee, Wisconsin, 10 April 1898. Educated at the Milwaukee School of Fine Arts, Summers 1913–16; German-English Academy, Milwaukee, 1914–19; University of Wisconsin, Madison, 1919–23, B.A. 1923. Married the poet Marya Zaturenska in 1925; two children. Free-lance writer, New York and London, 1923–34; Member of the English Department, 1934–60, and since 1960, Professor Emeritus, Sarah Lawrence College, Bronxville, New York. Lecturer, New School for Social Research, New York, 1955–56. Associate Editor, *Tiger's Eye* magazine, New York. Recipient: Levinson Award, 1936; Russell Loines Award, 1942; Guggenheim Fellowship, 1951; Academy of American Poets Fellowship, 1961; Bollingen Prize, 1965; Horace Gregory Foundation Award, 1969. Member, National Institute of Arts and Letters, 1964. Lives in Rockland County, New York.

PUBLICATIONS

Verse

    Chelsea Rooming House.   1930; as *Rooming House,* 1932.
    No Retreat.   1933.
    A Wreath for Margery.   1933.
    Chorus for Survival.   1935.
    Poems 1930–1940.   1941.
    Selected Poems.   1951.
    Medusa in Gramercy Park.   1961.
    Alphabet for Joanna (juvenile).   1963.
    Collected Poems.   1964.
    Another Look.   1976.

Other

    Pilgrim of the Apocalypse: A Critical Study of D. H. Lawrence.   1933; revised edition,
       1957.
    The Shield of Achilles: Essays on Beliefs in Poetry.   1944.
    A History of American Poetry 1900–1940, with Marya Zaturenska.   1946.
    Amy Lowell: Portrait of the Poet in Her Time.   1958.
    The World of James McNeill Whistler.   1959.
    The Dying Gladiators and Other Essays.   1961.
    Dorothy Richardson: An Adventure in Self-Discovery.   1967.
    The House on Jefferson Street: A Cycle of Memories.   1971.
    Spirit of Time and Place: The Collected Essays.   1973.

    Editor, with Eleanor Clark, *New Letters in America.*   1937.
    Editor, *Critical Remarks on the Metaphysical Poets,* by Samuel Johnson.   1943.
    Editor, *The Triumph of Life: Poems of Consolation for the English-Speaking*
       World.   1945.
    Editor, *The Portable Sherwood Anderson.*   1949.
    Editor, *Selected Poetry,* by Robert Browning.   1956.
    Editor, with Marya Zaturenska, *The Mentor Book of Religious Verse.*   1957.
    Editor, with Marya Zaturenska, *The Crystal Cabinet: An Invitation to Poetry.*   1962.
    Editor, with others, *Riverside Poetry 4: An Anthology of Student Verse.*   1962.
    Editor, *Evangeline and Selected Tales and Poems of Longfellow.*   1964.

Editor, *Selected Poems*, by E. E. Cummings.   1965.
Editor, with Marya Zaturenska, *The Silver Swan: Poems of Romance and Mystery*.   1966.
Editor, *Selected Poems of Lord Byron*.   1969.

Translator, *The Poems of Catullus*.   1931.
Translator, *Poems*, by Catullus.   1956.
Translator, *The Metamorphoses*, by Ovid.   1958.
Translator, *Love Poems of Ovid*.   1964.

Reading List: "Gregory Issue" of *Modern Poetry Studies*, May 1973.

*   *   *

Horace Gregory is perhaps best known as the translator of Catullus and Ovid. But he has also published critical studies on Amy Lowell, D. H. Lawrence, James McNeill Whistler and others, as well as collaborating with his wife, the poet Marya Zaturenska, on *A History of American Poetry 1900–1940*.

Elizabeth Drew has written that his "emotional range is perhaps the most comprehensive among modern poets," and Louis Untermeyer wrote that Gregory "does not share Eliot's disillusions or Crane's disorganization," a statement that is unfair to all three poets. However, poems like "Valediction to My Contemporaries" compare interestingly with Hart Crane's "The Bridge" in their language, their idealism, their purposes; and many of Gregory's efforts to recapture in monologues the pathos and cacophony of life in the modern city remind one of Eliot. In the final analysis, however, authenticity and integrity may not be enough; subtleties of syntax, powers of condensation, originality of imagery, distinguish Eliot and Crane from those who wrote with comparable verve.

Gregory is academic, ordered, descriptive, even-paced; he might be quite properly compared with MacLeish for his intellectual ambition, rhetorical power, and sense of American history. Most of his poems are based on classical subjects in one way or another, though he often juxtaposes classical imagery with modernistic impressions; he also has many poems about paintings, European scenes, and – like MacLeish – his country's cultural history. His well-known poem on Emerson recapitulates Emerson's life in an investigation of the intellectual's role ("To know too well, to think too long") in a land where action and immortality are even more akin than rhetoric and relevance. Gregory, like MacLeish, bears a heavy weight of idealism at all times, perhaps more than his country's history can support. Because the idealism is more muted in his Chelsea rooming house poems, they are perhaps more appealing than his poems with more epic ambitions. In poems like "McAlpin Garfinkel, Poet" and "Time and Isidore Lefkowitz", Gregory seems to have absorbed the influence of Edwin Arlington Robinson and to have looked forward to the work of poets like Kenneth Fearing:

> Look at Isidore Lefkowitz,
> biting his nails, telling how
> he seduces Beautiful French Canadian
> Five and Ten Cent Store Girls,
> beautiful, by God, and how they cry
> and moan, wrapping their arms
> and legs around him
> when he leaves them....

In an age when we have come to think of poems as the swiftly captured sound of madness, Gregory's work stands as a celebration of order, with the glimpsed backstreet life crying out to have a part of that order and the consideration due to it.

How can I unlearn
the arts of love within a single hour:
How can I close my eyes before a mirror,
believe I am not wanted, that hands, lips, breast
are merely deeper shadows behind the door
where all is dark?

—David Ray

GUNN, Thom(son William). English. Born in Gravesend, Kent, 29 August 1929. Educated at University College School, London; Trinity College, Cambridge, B.A. 1953, M.A. 1958; Stanford University, California, 1954–55, 1956–58. Served in the British Army, 1948–50. Moved to the United States in 1954. Member of the English Department, University of California, Berkeley, 1958–66. Poetry Reviewer, *Yale Review*, New Haven, Connecticut, 1958–64. Recipient: Maugham Award, 1959; Arts Council of Great Britain award, 1959; National Institute of Arts and Letters grant, 1964; Rockefeller award, 1966; Guggenheim Fellowship, 1971. Lives in San Francisco.

PUBLICATIONS

Verse

(Poems). 1953.
Fighting Terms. 1954; revised edition, 1958.
The Sense of Movement. 1957.
My Sad Captains and Other Poems. 1961.
Selected Poems, with Ted Hughes. 1962.
A Geography. 1966.
Positives, photographs by Ander Gunn. 1966.
Touch. 1967.
The Garden of the Gods. 1968.
The Explorers: Poems. 1969.
The Fair in the Woods. 1969.
Poems 1950–1966: A Selection. 1969.
Sunlight. 1969.
Moly. 1971.
Mandrakes. 1974.
Song Book. 1974.
To the Air. 1974.
Jack Straw's Castle. 1976.
The Missed Boat: Seven Poems. 1976.

Other

Editor, *Poetry from Cambridge 1951–52: A Selection of Verse by Members of the University.* 1952.

Editor, with Ted Hughes, *Five American Poets*.   1963.
Editor, *Selected Poems of Fulke Greville*.   1968.
Editor, *Ben Jonson*.   1974.

Reading List: *Ted Hughes and Gunn* by Alan Bold, 1976.

*   *   *

Thom Gunn's early poetry, written in the 1950's was formally fastidious, intellectually tough, and uncompromisingly rhetorical. The rhetoric led to his name being linked with that of Ted Hughes, for both poets were fascinated with violence as a welcome disruption in the quotidian malaise of social life. Yet the association was deceptive, for the preoccupations of Gunn's poetry have always been radically different from those of Hughes's. Where the latter sought and found a glorious poise and self-sufficiency in predatory animals, Gunn was obsessed from the beginning by the traditional themes of modern western thought. In fact the whole of his career so far could be looked at as a struggle with the categories of Cartesian philosophy. To escape these categories he immersed himself first in existentialism, and then in the mysticism associated with hallucinatory drugs.

In *Fighting Terms* and *The Sense of Movement*, there are a technical expertise and an Elizabethan elegance of argument for which he became justly famous. His major theme was that of rationalist man seeking an identity in which he is not crippled by his intellectualism. The image of head-wounds recurs frequently as a metaphoric representation of a mental anguish which can only be overcome by action, and action in this early poetry often represents an undifferentiated possibility of escape from thought: "I acted, and my action made me wise" ("Incident on a Journey"). Love finds its place in this schema as a strategy or form of covert warfare, a brutalised routine of stimulus and response, as in "Carnal Knowledge":

> I prod, you react. Thus to and fro
> We turn, to see ourselves perform the same
> Comical act inside the tragic game.

In fact, the claims of humanity and companionship are viewed largely as a threat which the isolated ego must negotiate its way past. Gunn's obsessions with military uniform, motorcyclists, and petty criminals suggest a studious avoidance of communication.

"In Santa Maria Del Populo" (*My Sad Captains*) registered a shift of concern towards more sympathetic preoccupations. Life is no longer a vicious game, a mere war of identities. *Positives* in 1966 marks the transition. This volume, combining Gunn's poetry and Ander Gunn's photographs, is his opportunity to shed his previous rhetoric completely, and concern himself at length with the apparently unheroic. Daily, ordinary life from the cradle to the grave is the subject, and it is explored in a binary composition of poetic and photographic images, both concretizing images that might have remained abstract in themselves.

By the time of *Touch* in 1967, Gunn was ready to attempt his most ambitious poem. "Misanthropos" uses the poetic trope of last man/first man on earth to explore his old fixation – the relations of mind to body, and individual to society and environment. By pushing to its furthest extremity his notion of solitary, meditative, but surviving man, this poem releases Gunn into a statement of the need for generosity, for the acceptance of common failings. The poem ends:

> Turn out toward others, meeting their look at full,
> Until you have completely stared
> On all there is to see. Immeasurable,
> The dust yet to be shared.

"Misanthropos" is a poem of sustained energy and courage. His new theme was now, forcibly, the attempt to reconcile individual identity with the unperfected identities which surround it.

Later still, Gunn says of his book *Moly*: "I think of it as being about Odysseus' meeting with Hermes, his eating of that herb, and his reflections on metamorphosis in the remaining walk he has before he reaches the thick stone-built house." Just as Gunn once took the crude mythic postures of the Hell's Angels and turned them to remarkable poetic effect, so in *Moly* he approaches the chaotic dissolution through L.S.D. of San Francisco in the 1960's and uses that to equally remarkable effect. The final poem in the volume, "Sunlight," shows Gunn using his old formalistic inventiveness for the promotion of a libertarian philosophy which would have been unthinkable for him in the 1950's. A hymn to the sun, as the patron saint of all warmth, ends with this invocation:

> Enable us, altering like you, to enter
> Your passionless love, impartial but intense,
> And kindle in acceptance round your centre,
> Petals of light lost in your innocence.

Jack Straw's Castle shows Gunn at his freest, in terms of what he will allow himself to say. But this freedom has nothing to do with formal or metrical sloppiness. It has been earned by the apprenticeship of formal constraint, the meticulous study of his craft. It reinforces the notion that the poet's quest has been essentially coherent. Gunn began with an exploration of the resistance of individual identity to encroachment or possession. If his early verse was at times a celebration of this theme, it soon came to be a questioning of it. In the nature of the American contexts Gunn placed himself in, there was the possibility not only of a further questioning, but of a reversal. There is a sharp distinction, of course, between reversal and regression. In seeking to overcome the Cartesian oppositions he started out with, Gunn has not abandoned his earlier intellectual acerbity. He has sought to overcome a flaw at the centre of western philosophical thought. When the poem "The Geysers" ends:

> I am
> I am raw meat
> I am a god

it is reaching back to a source of unified energy found in Blake. The development of Gunn's poetry can be seen as an attempt to reach back to that fruitful beginning of a tradition still in its infancy.

—Alan Wall

GUSTAFSON, Ralph (Barker). Canadian. Born in Lime Ridge, Quebec, 16 August 1909. Educated at Bishop's University, Lennoxville, Quebec, B.A. 1929, M.A. 1930; Oxford University, B.A. 1933. Married Elisabeth Renninger in 1958. Music Master, Bishop's College School, 1930; Master, St. Alban's School, Brockville, Ontario, 1934; worked for the British Information Services, 1942–46. Since 1960, Music Critic, Canadian Broadcasting Corporation; since 1963, Professor of English and Poet-in-Residence, Bishop's University. Recipient: Prix David, 1935; Canada Council Senior Fellowship, 1959, Award, 1968, 1971; Governor-General's Award, 1974; A. J. M. Smith Award, 1975. M.A.: Oxford University, 1963; D.Litt.: Mount Allison University, Sackville, New Brunswick, 1973. Lives in Quebec.

PUBLICATIONS

Verse

> *The Golden Chalice.* 1935.
> *Alfred the Great* (verse play). 1937.
> *Epithalamium in Time of War.* 1941.
> *Lyrics Unromantic.* 1942.
> *Flight into Darkness: Poems.* 1944.
> *Rivers among Rocks.* 1960.
> *Rocky Mountain Poems.* 1960.
> *Sift in an Hourglass.* 1966.
> *Ixion's Wheel: Poems.* 1969.
> *Theme and Variations for Sounding Brass.* 1972.
> *Selected Poems.* 1972.
> *Fire on Stone.* 1974.

Fiction

> *The Brazen Tower.* 1974.

Other

> *Poetry and Canada.* 1945.
>
> Editor, *Anthology of Canadian Poetry (English).* 1942.
> Editor, *A Little Anthology of Canadian Poets.* 1943.
> Editor, *Canadian Accent: A Collection of Stories and Poems by Contemporary Writers from Canada.* 1944.
> Editor, *The Penguin Book of Canadian Verse.* 1958; revised edition, 1967, 1975.

Bibliography: "Ralph Gustafson: A Bibliography in Progress" by L. M. Allison and W. Keitner, in *West Coast Review,* June 1974.

Reading List: "Ralph Gustafson: A Review and Retrospect" by Robin Skelton, in *Mosaic,* 1974.

*   *   *

Ralph Gustafson is one of the most prolific, various and technically accomplished of contemporary Canadian poets. After a somewhat unpromising start with a volume of romantic lyrics and sonnets and a poetic play on the subject of King Alfred in the mid-thirties, Ralph Gustafson found an original style and an individual voice in the sardonic and tender poetry produced during and after World War II. *Flight into Darkness* assimilated, rather than shook off, influences of Hopkins and Donne and demonstrated the relevance of the metaphysical dialectic to the problem of preserving an individual integrity in the kaleidoscopic new world of the post-war breakdown.

The poet's elliptical and intensely allusive style has taken on a new subtlety and his work a wider field of interest since 1960. Travel across Canada, especially to the Rockies and the mountains of the north-west coast, and to Italy, Greece and the Scandinavian countries, has provided the stimulus for a prolific outburst of poetry in which the themes of nature, art, history, love and sex are given a highly individual treatment. As Earle Birney has written: "Ralph Gustafson has a way all his own of fusing music and passion with sophisticated feeling and graceful craft.... A stylist given to paradox and poetic wit, he is nonetheless serious, and his sensitive judgments rise from a warm heart."

—A. J. M. Smith

GUTHRIE, Ramon. American. Born in New York City, 14 January 1896. Educated at Mt. Hermon, 1912–14; University of Toulouse, Docteur en Droit, 1922; the Sorbonne, Paris, 1919, 1922–23. Served in the American Field Service, 1916–17; United States Army Air Corps, 1917–19; Office of Strategic Services, 1943–45: Silver Star. Married Marguerite Maurey in 1922. Assistant Professor of Romance Languages, University of Arizona, Tucson, 1924–26; Professor of French, 1930–63, and Professor Emeritus, 1963–73, Dartmouth College, Hanover, New Hampshire. Recipient: National Endowment for the Arts grant, 1969, 1971; Marjorie Peabody Waite Award, 1970. M.A., 1939, and D.Litt., 1971, Dartmouth College. *Died 22 November 1973.*

PUBLICATIONS

Verse

Trobar Clus. 1923.
A World Too Old. 1927.
The Legend of Ermengarde. 1929.
Scherzo, From a Poem to be Entitled "The Proud City." 1933.
Graffiti. 1959.
Asbestos Phoenix. 1968.
Maximum Security Ward, 1964–1970. 1970.

Novels

Marcabrun: The Chronicle of a Foundling Who Spoke Evil of Women and of Love and Who Followed Unawed the Paths of Arrogance Until They Led to Madness, and of His Dealings with Women and of Ribald Words, the Which Brought Him Repute as a Great Rascal and as a Great Singer. 1926.
Parachute. 1928.

Other

Editor, with George E. Diller, *French Literature and Thought since the Revolution.* 1942.
Editor, with George E. Diller, *Prose and Poetry of Modern France.* 1964.

Translator, *The Revolutionary Spirit in France and America*, by Bernard Faÿ.   1927.
Translator, *The Other Kingdom*, by David Rousset.   1947.
Translator, *The Republic of Silence*, edited by A. J. Liebling.   1947.

Reading List: *Guthrie Kaleidoscope,* 1963 (includes bibliography by Alan Cooke); "La Poésie de Guthrie" by L. Véza, in *Etudes Anglaises,* January–March 1967.

*   *   *

Ramon Guthrie's last and most important work, *Maximum Security Ward*, appeared when he was seventy-four. Indeed, although he was a contemporary of Cummings and Crane, most of his significant work belongs to the late 1950's and 1960's and is collected in *Graffiti, Asbestos Phoenix*, and *Maximum Security Ward*. All three books contain striking poems, but the cumulative force of the last, which derives from its dramatic center, is by far Guthrie's most sustained success. The speaker, a critically ill and suffering old man, uses all the resources of his imagination, memory, intellect, and humor to overcome his bewildering isolation and disappointment in himself and his fellow human beings. The book is a particularly valuable addition to the genre of the modern lyric sequence.

The best introduction to the poet and his style comes in the first of the forty-nine poems of *Maximum Security Ward*:

> So name her Vivian. I, scarecrow Merlin –
> our Broceliande this frantic bramble of
> glass and plastic tubes and stainless steel –
> could count off such illusions as I have
> on a quarter of my thumbs.

Here are all the hallmarks of Guthrie's mature verse: the passionate immediacy of the speaking voice; the subtle internal rhymes and skilful assonance, alliteration, and colliteration (the use of related consonants); the unpretentious, humorous, colloquial tone combined with a scholarly range of reference and romantic wistfulness; and the recurrent reference to French art and literature, particularly medieval romance, as a psychological touchstone.

Guthrie was bilingual and a Francophile, and his intimate knowledge of France is reflected in his poetry. He lived, studied, and wrote in France during most of the 1920's and sporadically thereafter and knew the expatriate community of artists well. He served in France in two wars, married a Frenchwoman, and taught French literature throughout his academic career. His earliest important literary influences were French, and Proust was his philosophical mentor. But he was an eminently American poet, writing out of the traditions of American verse and at times satirizing his country's hypocrisies and cruelties – particularly her role in Vietnam – for the good of the body politic. Of course, his great subject in *Maximum Security Ward* is supranational: the meaning of the whole human enterprise – what it is to be fully human psychologically, socially, politically – and the role of any artist, whether writer, painter, musician, or sculptor, in uncovering what is essentially a sacred meaning.

A good amateur painter, Guthrie had a visual imagination that matched and reinforced his great love for the texture of language and that enhanced the exquisitely tactile sensuousness of some of his most evocative passages:

> this smooth knoll of your shoulder,
> this cwm of flank, this moss-delineated quite
> un-Platonic cave....

Everywhere about is landscape as far as foot can feel
lamps exude their light on flagstones
there are quaint quiet trains in
corridors of pure perspective

Guthrie's poems are filled with concrete, memorable phrases and imagery; he moves skilfully from tone to tone, from the most jarring to the most lyrical; wit, intelligence, and a deep sympathy and humanity inform his work. It is a pity it is not better known.

—Sally M. Gall

HARDY, Thomas. English. Born in Upper Bockhampton, Dorset, 2 June 1840. Educated in local schools, 1848–54, and privately, 1854–56; articled to the ecclesiastical architect, John Hicks, in Dorchester, 1856–61; studied in evening classes at King's College, London, 1861–67. Married 1) Emma Lavinia Gifford in 1874 (died, 1912); 2) Florence Emily Dugdale in 1914. Settled in London, 1861, to practice architecture, and worked as Assistant to Sir Arthur Blomfield, 1862–67; gave up architecture to become full-time writer; lived in Max Gate, Dorchester, after 1886. Justice of the Peace for Dorset; Member of the Council of Justice to Animals. Recipient: Royal Institute of British Architects medal, for essay, 1863; Architecture Association prize, for design, 1863; Royal Society of Literature Gold Medal, 1912. LL.D.: University of Aberdeen; University of St. Andrews; University of Bristol; Litt.D.: Cambridge University; D.Litt.: Oxford University. Honorary Fellow: Magdalene College, Cambridge; Queen's College, Oxford. Honorary Fellow of the Royal Institute of British Architects, 1920. Order of Merit, 1910. *Died 11 January 1928.*

PUBLICATIONS

Collections

New Wessex Edition of the Works. 1974–
Complete Poems, edited by James Gibson. 1976; revised *Variorum Edition,* 1978.
The Portable Hardy, edited by Julian Moynahan. 1977.
Collected Letters. edited by Richard Little Purdy and Michael Millgate. vol. 1 (of 7), 1978.

Verse

Wessex Poems and Other Verses. 1898.
Poems of the Past and the Present. 1902; revised edition, 1902.
Time's Laughingstocks and Other Verses. 1909.
Satires of Circumstance: Lyrics and Reveries, with Miscellaneous Pieces. 1914.

Selected Poems.   1916; revised edition, as *Chosen Poems.* 1929.
Moments of Vision and Miscellaneous Poems.   1917.
Collected Poems.   1919.
Late Lyrics and Earlier, with Many Other Verses.   1922.
Human Shows, Far Phantasies, Songs, and Trifles.   1925.
Winter Words in Various Moods and Metres.   1928.

Plays

Far from the Madding Crowd, with J. Comyns Carr, from the novel by Hardy (produced 1882).
The Three Wayfarers, from his own story "The Three Strangers" (produced 1893).   1893.
The Dynasts: A Drama of the Napoleonic Wars.   3 vols., 1903–08; vol. 1 revised, 1904; edited by John Wain, 1965.
The Play of Saint George.   1921.
The Famous Tragedy of the Queen of Cornwall (produced 1923).   1923; revised edition, 1924.
Tess of the d'Urbervilles, from his own novel (produced 1924).   In *Tess in the Theatre,* edited by Marguerite Roberts, 1950.

Fiction

Desperate Remedies.   1871; revised edition, 1896, 1912.
Under the Greenwood Tree: A Rural Painting of the Dutch School.   1872; revised edition, 1896, 1912; edited by Anna Winchcombe, 1975.
A Pair of Blue Eyes.   1873; revised edition, 1895, 1912, 1920.
Far from the Madding Crowd.   1874; revised edition, 1875, 1902; edited by James Gibson, 1975.
The Hand of Ethelberta: A Comedy in Chapters.   1876; revised edition, 1895, 1912.
The Return of the Native.   1878; revised edition, 1895, 1912; edited by Colin Tremblett-Wood, 1975.
Fellow Townsmen.   1880.
The Trumpet-Major: A Tale.   1880; revised edition, 1895; edited by Ray Evans, 1975.
A Laodicean; or, The Castle of the De Stancys.   1881; revised edition, 1881, 1896, 1912.
Two on a Tower.   1882; revised edition, 1883, 1883, 1895, 1912.
The Romantic Adventures of a Milkmaid.   1883; revised edition, 1913.
The Mayor of Casterbridge: The Life and Death of a Man of Character.   1886; revised edition, 1895, 1920; edited by F. B. Pinion, 1975; edited by James K. Robinson, 1977.
The Woodlanders.   1887; revised edition, 1895, 1912; edited by F. B. Pinion, 1975.
Wessex Tales, Strange, Lively and Commonplace.   1888; revised edition, 1896.
A Group of Noble Dames.   1891.
Tess of the d'Urbervilles: A Pure Woman Faithfully Presented.   1891; revised edition, 1892, 1895, 1912; edited by Scott Elledge, 1965, revised 1977.
Life's Little Ironies: A Set of Tales.   1894; revised edition, 1912.
Wessex Novels.   16 vols, 1895–96.
Jude the Obscure.   1896; revised edition, 1912; edited by Norman Page, 1978.
The Well-Beloved: A Sketch of Temperament.   1897; revised edition, 1912.
A Changed Man, The Waiting Supper, and Other Tales.   1913.
An Indiscretion in the Life of an Heiress.   1934; edited by Carl J. Weber, 1935.
Our Exploits at West Poley, edited by R. L. Purdy.   1952.

Other

The Dorset Farm Labourer, Past and Present.   1884.
Works (Wessex Edition).   24 vols., 1912–31.
Works (Mellstock Edition).   37 vols., 1919–20.
Life and Art: Essays, Notes, and Letters, edited by Ernest Brennecke.   1925.
The Early Life of Hardy 1840–91, by Florence Hardy.   1928; The Later Years of
   Hardy, 1892–1928, 1930 (dictated to his wife Florence).
Letters of Hardy, edited by Carl J. Weber.   1954.
Notebooks and Some Letters from Julia Augusta Martin, edited by Evelyn
   Hardy.   1955.
Dearest Emmie: Letters to His First Wife, edited by Carl J. Weber.   1963.
The Architectural Notebook, edited by C. J. P. Beatty.   1966.
Personal Writings: Prefaces, Literary Opinions, Reminiscences, edited by Harold
   Orel.   1966.
One Rare Fair Woman (letters to Frances Henniker), edited by Evelyn Hardy and F. B.
   Pinion.   1972.
The Personal Notebooks, edited by Richard H. Taylor.   1978.

Editor, Select Poems of William Barnes.   1908.

Bibliography: Hardy: A Bibliographical Study by R. L. Purdy, 1954, revised edition, 1968;
"Criticism of Hardy: A Selected Checklist" by M. Beebe, B. Culotta, and E. Marcus, in
Modern Fiction Studies, 1960.

Reading List: Hardy of Wessex by Carl J. Weber, 1940, revised edition, 1965; Hardy the
Novelist by David Cecil, 1943; Hardy: The Novels and Stories by Albert Guerard, 1949,
revised edition, 1964; The Pattern of Hardy's Poetry by Samuel Hynes, 1961; Hardy: A
Collection of Critical Essays edited by Albert Guerard, 1963; Hardy by Irving Howe, 1967; A
Hardy Companion, 1968, revised edition, 1976, and Hardy: Art and Thought, 1977, both by
F. B. Pinion; Hardy: His Career as a Novelist by Michael Millgate, 1971; Hardy and British
Poetry by Donald Davie, 1972; Hardy and History by R. J. White, 1974; Young Hardy, 1975,
and The Older Hardy, 1978, both by Robert Gittings; An Essay on Hardy by John Bayley,
1978.

*   *   *

   In his early twenties Thomas Hardy aspired to be a country curate and poet, like William
Barnes. Yet, after a period of intense reading in London, he rejected belief in Providence for
scientific philosophy, based largely on the writings of J. S. Mill, Darwin's The Origin of
Species, and readings in geology and astronomy. Like Mill, Hardy was impressed with
Auguste Comte's emphasis on the need for altruism and a programme of reform based on
education and science. Hardy never forfeited his belief in the Christian ethic; he was
convinced that there was little hope for humanity without enlightened co-operation and
charity. His preface to The Woodlanders suggests that his conscious aim in his last major
novels was to further amelioration through enlisting the sympathetic awareness of his
readers. Humanitarianism combines with his scientific outlook in imaginatively visualized
presentations to maintain his appeal today.
   Hardy's basic ideas did not change greatly and, as his London poems of 1865–67 show,
they were formed early. Events are the result primarily of circumstance or chance, which is
all that is immediately apparent in an evolving network of cause-effect relationships
extending through space and time. In The Woodlanders the "web" which is for ever weaving
shows, for example, a link between the death of Mrs. Charmond and the American Civil

War. Chance includes heredity and character; only when reason prevails is man free to influence the course of events. Such philosophical ideas are inherent, and sometimes explicit, in Hardy's first published novel, *Desperate Remedies*. His previous novel, *The Poor Man and the Lady* (which survives only in scenes adapted to other novels and in "An Indiscretion in the Life of an Heiress"), had been loosely constructed, and too satirical, of London society and contemporary Christianity in particular, to gain acceptance.

In *Desperate Remedies* Hardy merged, for the sake of publication, a tragic situation with a thriller story and a complicated plot (in the manner of Wilkie Collins). Until the sensational dénouement takes over, the writing is enriched with poetical quotations and effects, Shelley's wintry image of adversity determining crisis settings, as in later Hardy novels. A reviewer's commendation of his rustic scenes led to *Under the Greenwood Tree*, which Hardy wrote rapidly, with notable economy, in a happy mood kindled by love of Emma Gifford, a church organist whose blue dress and vanity are the subject of light satire in a novel remarkable for its rustic humour. Though the story of *A Pair of Blue Eyes* was planned before Hardy's first Cornish visit, and its characters are almost wholly fictional, this tragic romance is based on Cornish memories. Often poetic in conception, it suffered from the pressures of serial demands. The heroine's crisis anticipates *Tess*. Writing anonymously for *The Cornhill Magazine*, Hardy was more ambitious in *Far from the Madding Crowd*, showing marked development in Wessex humour and the dramatization of passion. A suggestion that this pastoral work was written by George Eliot made Hardy put aside the story which became *The Woodlanders* for *The Hand of Ethelberta*, a comedy directed by Darwinian ideas and social satire. After a respite, during which he read a great deal, Hardy began *The Return of the Native*, but difficulties with magazine editors made him rewrite much in the first two books. Partly inspired by Arnold, more by Pater's essay on Winckelmann, his theme is hedonism (with a Greek slant) versus altruistic idealism. Life as something to be endured (and avoided by the hedonist) is represented by Egdon Heath. The insignificance of the individual in time (with reference to Egdon) is stressed in a number of scenes, the most important being Darwinian and closely associated with Mrs. Yeobright's death.

Hardy's next novels suggest that he was still searching for the direction his genius should take. After *The Trumpet-Major*, a story dependent for relief on traditional comic types and situations, against a background of threatened Napoleonic invasion, he experimented with a second novel of ideas in *A Laodicean*. Handicapped by prolonged illness, he failed to give artistic cohesion to the theme of Arnold's "imaginative reason," in resolving the conflict between modern technology and a *prédilection d'artiste* for the romantic splendours of the past. Mephistophelian villainy contributes to the counterplot, and continues on a minor scale in *Two on a Tower*, where the story, set against the immensities of stellar space, reveals Hardy's maturing emphasis on altruism. In *The Mayor of Casterbridge* he solved the problem of catering for weekly serialization without detriment to tragic grandeur, his standards being set by the great masterpieces of the past, from classical times onwards. Some of the most moving scenes are in prose of Biblical simplicity or in the vernacular of the unlettered poor. After Henchard's death, Whittle emerges more noble of heart than the shrewd Farfrae or the philosophical Elizabeth-Jane. Hardy had found where his deepest sympathies lay.

Thenceforward his tragedy is centred in the deprivation or ill-chance of the underprivileged: Marty South and Tess, Giles Winterborne and Jude. The tragedy of *The Woodlanders* hinges on false social values which induce Grace Melbury to marry a philanderer whose hypocrisy is veiled in Shelleyan idealism. Tess, as a victim of chance and the embodiment of Christian charity (which suffereth long), is a pure (but not perfect) woman. "Once victim, always victim" echoes Richardson's *Clarissa*, the most important creative influence on *Tess*. *Jude*, the most ambitious and complex of Hardy's tragedies, was not finished to his satisfaction. The Christminster-Crucifixion parallel seems forced at the critical juncture, and hereditary traits of Jude and Sue, with reference to marriage, are too exceptional and peripheral to create convincing tragedy, though the novel contains the most moving dramatic scenes Hardy ever wrote, possibly with his own domestic situation in mind.

He had reason at this time to realize more than ever his readiness to fall imaginatively in love with beautiful women, and he had made it the subject of his satirical fantasy *The Well-Beloved*. One result of this tendency is that his heroines are generally more attractive than his men, Henchard excepted.

Hardy's most characteristic natural settings are psychological rather than scenic, expressing the feelings or situations of his principal characters. His visualizing techniques serve to make his critical scenes more impressive and memorable.

Such was Hardy's sense of the relativity of things that he rarely lost his sense of humour, as may be seen in "A Few Crusted Characters," written as a relief from *Tess*. Among his short stories, there are several, ranging from anecdote to novelette, from humour to satire and tragedy, which rank high in Hardy's fiction.

Violent criticism of *Jude* made Hardy relinquish prose fiction, and return to poetry, sooner than he intended. He had time to prepare for *The Dynasts*, a work he had contemplated in various forms for many years. In this epic drama of the Napoleonic wars, with nations swayed by forces beyond the control of reason, Hardy regards the conflict philosophically through the Spirit of the Years, and tragically through the Spirit of the Pities. It is a work of immense scholarship and artistic proportion, containing some of Hardy finest prose pictures and some moving lyrics. It's main weaknesses are in the verse, however, as well as in the visual and over-mechanical presentation of the Will.

Much of Hardy's early poetry (before and after his novel-writing period) suggests that he did not write it with ease. Rigorously rejecting poetical lushness, he achieved an independence of style reflecting his own observation, thought, vision, and feeling. Integrity shines through his verse even when it is oddly laboured. Impressed by the best of Wordsworth and Browning. he disciplined himself to write lyrical poetry as little removed as possible from the idiom of spoken English; and it is this quality, combined with his personal appeal, which explains the hold he has on modern readers. Most of his poems (and most of his greatest) were composed after he had reached the age of seventy. The autobiographical element is considerable.

Fortified by Arnold's declaration that "what distinguishes the greatest poets is their powerful and profound application of ideas to life," Hardy used verse to promulgate beliefs which he hoped would help to prepare a way for the Positivist religion of humanity. He remained an "evolutionary meliorist" until, in his last years, the prospect of another European war made him place the blame for the Unfulfilled Intention in human affairs, not on abstract Immanent Will, but on the folly of mankind.

His personal poetry has deeper resonances, as may be found particularly in "Poems of 1912–13," written after the death of his first wife. Hardy wrote many narrative poems in dramatic or ballad form. Unusual events and ironies of chance attracted him as much as in his prose; but more important is the poetry which he found in everyday life. "There is enough poetry in what is left, after all the false romance has been extracted, to make a sweet pattern," he affirmed. Many of his poems were composed with song-music in mind, and in stanzas demanding high manipulative skill. So imaginatively sensitive is Hardy to experience that even readers familiar with his poetry continually find something new to admire in movement, expression, or image. His finer poems are surprisingly varied and numerous; in them and elsewhere he modulates language with exquisite art to convey a living voice. The rare distinction of being both a major poet and a major novelist belongs to Thomas Hardy.

—F. B. Pinion

HAYDEN, Robert (Earl). American. Born in Detroit, Michigan, 4 August 1913. Educated at Wayne State University, Detroit, A.B.: University of Michigan. Ann Arbor (Hopwood Award, 1938, 1942), M.A. 1944. Married; one daughter. Teaching Fellow,

University of Michigan, 1944–46; Member of the English Department, Fisk University, Nashville, Tennessee, 1946–68. Visiting Professor, 1968, and since 1969, Professor of English, University of Michigan. Bingham Professor, University of Louisville, Kentucky, Spring 1969; Visiting Poet, University of Washington, Seattle, Summer 1969, University of Connecticut, Storrs, 1971, and Denison University, Granville, Ohio, 1971; Staff Member, Breadloaf Writers Conference, Middlebury, Vermont, 1972. Member, and Poetry Editor, *World Order*, Baha'i Faith. Recipient: Rosenwald Fellowship, 1947; Ford Foundation grant, 1954; World Festival of Negro Arts Poetry Prize, Dakar, Senegal, 1966; Russell Loines Award, 1970; American Academy of Poets Fellowship, 1971. Lives in Ann Arbor, Michigan.

PUBLICATIONS

Verse

Heart-Shape in the Dust.   1940.
The Lion and the Archer, with Myron O'Higgins.   1948.
Figures of Time.   1955.
A Ballad of Remembrance.   1962.
Selected Poems.   1966.
Words in the Mourning Time.   1970.
The Night-Blooming Cereus.   1972.
Angle of Ascent: New and Selected Poems.   1975.

Other

How I Write 1, with Judson Philips and Lawson Carter.   1972.
Nine Black American Doctors (juvenile), with Jacqueline Harris.   1976.

Editor, *Kaleidoscope: Poems by American Negro Poets.*   1967.
Editor, with David J. Burrows and Frederick R. Lapides, *Afro-American Literature: An Introduction.*   1971.

*   *   *

Much in the manner of Countée Cullen, the Harlem Renaissance poet, though more comfortable experimenting with free forms of verse, Robert Hayden has steadfastly claimed refusal to write racial poetry but quite consistently been at his poetic best precisely when he has used the material of the black American experience in his work. He warned in *Kaleidoscope* against placing the black writer in "a kind of literary ghetto," where he would be "not considered a writer but a species of race-relations man, the leader of a cause, the voice of protest." It must be said that even when Hayden employs racial material and themes, he usually molds them into interesting and often exquisite universal shapes that make him far more than a mere "race-relations man." If there is a criticism to be levelled at him, it would be that he is occasionally too academic (indeed, he has spent much of his life in academe), occasionally lapsing into preciousness (e.g., in "Veracruz": "Thus reality/bedizened in the warring colors/of a dream ...").

Mostly, however, Hayden composes with notable power and beauty. For example, his evocation, in "The Ballad of Nat Turner," of the nineteenth-century leader of a slave uprising is perhaps the most succinct and spiritually true in all of imaginative literature. Such poems as

"The Diver" capture the essence of the moment or act (in this case the descent of a sea diver from the sinking "through easeful azure" to the time when "somehow began the measured rise") with the felicitous marriage of sound and sense that is quintessential poetry.

—Alan R. Shucard

HEANEY, Seamus (Justin).   Irish.   Born in Castledawson, County Derry, 13 April 1939. Educated at Anahorish School; St. Columb's College, Derry; Queen's University, Belfast, B.A. (honours) in English 1961. Married Marie Devlin in 1965; two sons. Teacher, St. Thomas's Secondary School, Belfast, 1962–63; Lecturer, St. Joseph's College of Education, Belfast, 1963–66; Lecturer in English, Queen's University, 1966–72; Guest Lecturer, University of California, Berkeley, 1970; moved to County Wicklow, 1972, did regular radio work and teaching at various American universities. Since 1975, Teacher at Carysfort Training College, Dublin. Recipient: Eric Gregory Award, 1966; Cholmondeley Award, 1967; Faber Memorial Prize, 1968; Maugham Award, 1968; Irish Academy of Letters Award, 1971; Denis Devlin Memorial Award, 1973; American-Irish Foundation Award, 1975; National Institute of Arts and Letters E. M. Forster Award, 1975; Duff Cooper Memorial Award, 1976; Smith Literary Award, 1976. Lives in Dublin.

PUBLICATIONS

Verse

Eleven Poems.   1965.
Death of a Naturalist.   1966.
Room to Rhyme, with Dairo Hammond and Michael Longley.   1968.
A Lough Neagh Sequence.   1969.
Door into the Dark.   1969.
Night Drive.   1970.
Boy Driving His Father to Confession.   1970.
Wintering Out.   1972.
North.   1975.
Bog Poems.   1975.
Stations.   1975.
The Watchman's Flute: New Poems.   1978.

Other

Editor, with Alan Brownjohn and Jon Stallworthy, *New Poems 1970–1971.*   1971.
Editor, *Soundings 2.*   1974.

Reading List: *Heaney* by Robert Buttel, 1975.

*   *   *

Seamus Heaney's poetry has been rooted in his rural background, in the activities of farm life, its crafts and skills, its relationship with the land. Many of his early poems celebrate this life and respond sensuously, in image and rhythm, commemorating the crafts of the countryside in their own respect for technical accomplishment. This response to the rural background subsequently involved the auditory imagination. In the accents of the area, in its place-names and historical antecedents, he could hear the divisions of the culture; in the vocables of place he could give intimations of history. He could also detect the divisions in his own experience between the Irish heritage and the English heritage which he had acquired through education and reading.

The dark centres of the past, of the unknown, of the self, of the mysterious region from which poems emerge, found an eloquent metaphor in the bogs of Ireland which preserve objects from the past and at times yield them up. Heaney's discovery of P. V. Glob's *The Bog People* confirmed his faith in this metaphor, and extended his understanding of the violence in Northern Ireland by showing that in the early Iron Age there had been similar blood-lettings. The book enriched his imaginative response to the metaphor of the bog in its moving account, together with its pictures of the Tollund Man, the Grauballe Man, and others, of how ritual sacrifices to the goddess of the earth led, through time and through the preserving and transmuting properties of the bog, to these resurrected objects of beauty. This extension has broadened the scope of his poetry even as it has deepened and confirmed the validity of his trust in his own region. Exploring the implications of the resemblances and associations between Ireland and Scandinavia (for example, in the Viking deposits recently found in Dublin), he writes now with confidence and nonchalance, making bold imaginative leaps across the landscape of northern Europe and backward through literary, linguistic, and geological periods.

—Maurice Harmon

HILL, Geoffrey. British. Born in Bromsgrove, Worcestershire, 18 June 1932. Educated at Fairfield Junior School; County High School, Bromsgrove; Keble College, Oxford. Senior Lecturer in English, University of Leeds. Recipient: Gregory Award, 1961; Hawthornden Prize, 1969; Faber Memorial Prize, 1970; Whitbread Award, 1971; Alice Hunt Bartlett Award, 1971; Heinemann Award, 1972. Fellow, Royal Society of Literature, 1972. Lives in Leeds, Yorkshire.

PUBLICATIONS

Verse

(Poems). 1952.
For the Unfallen: Poems 1952–1958. 1959.
Preghiere. 1964.
King Log. 1968.
Mercian Hymns. 1971.
Somewhere Is Such a Kingdom: Poems 1952–1971. 1975.

Play

   Brand, from the play by Ibsen (produced 1978).   1978.

Reading List: essay by Christopher Ricks, in *London Magazine*, November 1964; "The Poetry of Hill" by Jon Silkin, in *British Poetry since 1960* edited by Michael Schmidt and Grevel Lindop, 1972.

*   *   *

An awareness of history is central to the modernist sensibility, though few poets writing today have made such concerted use of the spirit of the past as Geoffrey Hill. Not surprisingly, his first major collection takes the creation as a starting point, where we are confronted by the violent, menacing nature of this nascent universe:

> The second day I stood and saw
> The osprey plunge with triggered claw,
> Feathering blood along the shore,
> To lay the living sinew bare.

Death figures prominently in a world predatory from its conception, its significance magnified by his retrospective approach; the dead amass in, rather than fade away from, his vision:

> But the dead maintain their ground –
> That there's no getting round –
>
> Who in places vitally rest,
> Named, anonymous.

The manipulation of familiar phrases and the twisting paradoxical progression of thought are symptomatic of a struggle to come to terms with the suffering that surrounds him.
   Hill's ventures to specific moments in history are attempts to give meaning to these perceptions – or at least a context in which they can be analysed. In what is perhaps his best work, "Funeral Music" (*King Log*), Hill effects a subtle interplay between the emblematic ceremonial beheading of three men and a bloody episode from the Wars of the Roses. The poem's contrapuntal movement is firmly structured within a sequence of sonnets – a form of which Hill is particularly fond, its disciplined cohesion an amenable vehicle for his complex syntax, weighted cadences, and dense verbal texture. Fifteenth-century heroic sacrifice, resolute faith, and elaborate ritual are the values to which Hill turns for explanation. His virulent scepticism towards our meaningless religious ceremonies, merely designed to alleviate anxiety, falters under the weight of the past, when the consequences of his negation become clear:

> Though I would scorn the mere instinct of faith,
> Expediency of assent, if I dared,
> What I dare not is a waste history
> Or void rule.

Mercian Hymns marks a new departure. The simultaneity often implied by the interaction of event and sensibility is made overt by Hill's mythopoeic process, where the terrain of Offa's Mercia, resonant of its medieval roots, is furnished with motorways and the shifting reflections of the poet's childhood. The pitfalls of the prose poem format chosen for the hymns are avoided; narrative and catalogue are tightly harnessed to produce a characteristic blend of objectivity and immediacy. And curiously, it is among these strange juxtapositions, when history is most abused, that a sense of chronology, of archetypal pattern, is most apparent.

There is a discernible softening of tone in his recent work, in particular the lyrical tranquillity of "The Pentecost Çastle" (*Agenda*, Autumn–Winter 1972–73, and Autumn 1975), but little sign of abatement in mental anguish if we are to judge from the outstanding sonnet sequence "Lachrimae" (*Agenda*, Winter–Spring 1974–75), written with the martyrdom of Robert Southwell in mind. Endowed with the ultimate justification, suffering is embraced as a necessary, desirable prelude to salvation.

—Garth Clucas

HODGSON, Ralph. English. Born in Yorkshire, 9 September 1871. Journalist in London: Editor, *Fry's Magazine*; Founder, with Lovat Fraser, The Sign of the Flying Fame, 1913; Lecturer in English Studies, Imperial University, Sendai, Japan, 1924–38; settled in Minerva, Ohio. Recipient: Royal Society of Literature Polignac Prize, 1914; National Institute of Arts and Letters award, 1946; Queen's Gold Medal for Poetry, 1954. Member, Order of the Rising Sun, Japan, 1938. *Died 3 November 1962.*

PUBLICATIONS

Verse

    The Last Blackbird and Other Lines. 1907.
    Eye and Other Poems. 1913.
    The Bull. 1913.
    The Song of Honour. 1913.
    The Mystery and Other Poems. 1913.
    Poems. 1917.
    Hymn to Moloch. 1921.
    Silver Wedding and Other Poems. 1941.
    The Muse and the Mastiff. 1942.
    The Skylark and Other Poems, edited by Colin Fenton. 1958.
    Songs to Our Surnames, edited by Colin Fenton. 1960.
    Collected Poems, edited by Colin Fenton. 1961.

Bibliography: *Hodgson: A Bibliography* by Wesley D. Sweetser, 1974.

Reading List: *Withdrawn in Gold: Three Commentaries on Genius* (on Hodgson, James Stephens, and Isak Dinesen) by George B. Saul, 1970.

*   *   *

Immortalized by his life-long friend T. S. Eliot in "Lines to Ralph Hodgson, Esqr.," Hodgson is chiefly remembered as a poet of the Georgian period. After World War I, the Muse seldom visited. His main productions were a collaboration on an English version of *The Manyōshū* while in residency at Imperial University and, finally, broadsheets, titled Flying Scrolls, sent to friends from Minerva, Ohio. The Scrolls, aside from the long poem *The Muse and the Mastiff*, are mostly charming, sagacious, and humorous epigrams in single lines, couplets, triplets, or quatrains ("Oaths in anguish rank with prayers"); but they contribute only slightly to his poetic canon.

The poems frequently anthologized – "Time, You Old Gipsy Man," "Eve," "The Song of Honour," "The Mystery," "Stupidity Street," and "The Bull" – are all from the 1917 *Poems*. Often marked by the pathetic fallacy and tending toward conventional metrical schemes and rapid, regular meter, they are nevertheless unique both in versatility and theme. "Eve," for example, is a remarkably compassionate view of woman's role in the Fall of Man, where Eve is tempted by an unusually seductive Satan in the form of a cobra:

> Soft as a bubble sung
> Out of a linnet's lung
> Soft and most silvery
> "Eva!" he said.

In the pubs, as "the toast goes round," her name is still accompanied by a leer, maligning all women in the name of the first, simply for having been, herself, initially betrayed. "Stupidity Street" reflects both Hodgson's ecological concern and love of birds. Here, as in many of his poems, he deplores their wanton destruction to gratify the gourmet or women's vanity and warns of danger to the balance of nature:

> I saw in vision
> The worm in the wheat
> And in the shops nothing
> For people to eat....

Nature, however, in "The Bull" is both cruel and glorious. The bloody and vanquished leader of "a thousand head," dreaming of the time when "Not a cow that said him nay," now bravely faces the last battle of all and

> Turns to meet the loathly birds
> Flocking round him in the skies
> Waiting for the flesh that dies.

Hodgson's tour de force is the mystical "The Song of Honour," his "Harmonious hymn of being" and "testament of Beautysprite/Upon a flying scroll." Entranced in wonderment at the flooding firmament and triggered by the song of a bird, the poet achieves rapport with "the universal choir." Through repeated use of synecdoche in this relatively short poem, Hodgson successfully suggests both the infinitude of the universe and, at the same time, its organic unity.

Hodgson, like Housman and FitzGerald, though limited in creative scope, produced some minor masterworks. In 1943 (in *Poets Remembered*), viewing himself in the perspective of the Georgian age, he was piercingly realistic: "New Rhythms and a New Age. A New Age that is now actually at this very moment, more than twenty-five years after, dying, discredited, and done with – no more than dead bones and a matter for the sexton."

—Wesley D. Sweetser

HOPE, A(lec) D(erwent). Australian. Born in Cooma, New South Wales, 21 July 1907. Educated at the University of Sydney, B.A. 1928; Oxford University, B.A. 1931. Married Penelope Robinson in 1938; three children. English Teacher, New South Wales Department of Education, 1933–36; Lecturer in English and Education, Sydney Teachers College, 1937–45; Senior Lecturer in English, University of Melbourne, 1945–50. Professor of English, 1951–68, Library Fellow, 1969–72, and since 1968 Professor Emeritus, School of General Studies, Australian National University, Canberra. President, Australian Society of Authors, 1965–66, and Australian Association of Teachers of English, 1966–67. Recipient: Britannica-Australia Award, 1965; Ingram Merrill Foundation Award, 1969. Litt.D.: Australian National University, 1972; University of New England, Armidale, New South Wales. Fellow, Australian Academy of the Humanities. O.B.E. (Officer, Order of the British Empire), 1972. Lives in Canberra.

PUBLICATIONS

Verse

The Wandering Islands. 1955.
Poems. 1960.
(Poems), edited by Douglas Stewart. 1963.
Collected Poems 1930–1965. 1966.
New Poems 1965–1969. 1969.
Dunciad Minor: An Heroick Poem. 1970.
Collected Poems 1930–1970. 1972.
Selected Poems. 1973.
A Late Picking: Poems 1965–1974. 1978.

Other

Australian Literature 1950–1962. 1963.
The Cave and the Spring: Essays on Poetry. 1965.
A Midsummer Eve's Dream: Variations on a Theme by William Dunbar. 1970.
Judith Wright. 1975.

Editor, Australian Poetry 1960. 1960.

Bibliography: Hope: A Bibliography, 1968.

*   *   *

A. D. Hope is learned, passionate, sceptical – and in his work there is an insistent, almost fierce sense of a Western Latin tradition. Perhaps one is misled by the analogy of the Latin line. It may be that the creative impulse is a sense of discrepancy, an aching consciousness of the dissimilarity between the decorative density of Europe and the emptiness of the arid continent. More probably both impulses work together in the Australian sensibility, sharpening into positive existence the Latin elements – not just the linguistic ones – latent in the English language. Certainly, Hope is concerned, in a way most unusual for those currently writing in English, with order and coherence of feeling and with decorum and regularity in presentation. This preoccupation is a constant presence in the poetry, even if not always successfully realised.

Sexual love is a recurrent theme in Hope's work. Occasionally he celebrates it as the beneficent completion of life and personality. More frequently he is concerned with its turbidity and cruelty. He sees it as incestuous, murderous, carnivorous, or absurd. The sense of unalloyed delight in love, spiritual and physical, in, for example, "The Gateway," is comparatively rare in Hope's poetry. It is true that whenever he writes of love he conveys in a masterly way the pleasure of the senses and the richness and beauty of the body. But there is always something else breaking in, something sinister or ugly or mean. Monstrous and cogent memories from the Old Testament and the classics, which supply many of the fictions used in Hope's verse, intrude on the enclosed world of lovers: reminiscences of Circe surrounded by snouted beasts, of Lot and his daughters "crafty from fear, reckless with joy and greed," of Susannah and the seedy hatred of the Elders, of Pasiphae, filled with the bull's monstrous life, of Odysseus and passion punctured by the ridiculous commonplace.

"The End of a Journey" is an example of Hope's supple virtuosity in modulation, from the stately and measured to the casual and throwaway. It calls up the name of Yeats, and Hope has made no secret of his admiration for Yeats and "that noble, candid speech/In which all things worth saying may be said ...," as well as his strong preference for Yeats over Eliot. But while Yeats is clearly a vital (and absorbed) influence on Hope, his idiom is his own, being at once less gorgeous and Byzantine when full out and more flatly contemporary in the lower register.

There is something on occasion nasty, an occasional gratuitous revelling in the garbage-bin (and perhaps also the puritan self-hatred to which this is often a clue), in a few of Hope's poems, as for example in "Rawhead and Bloody Bones":

> This Belly too commits
> By a strange and self abuse,
> Chin-chopper's titbits,
> Meat of his own mint, chews.

But more often some quality in the tone, a quaver of amusement, a glint of wit, a touch of self-mockery, even a cry of innocent astonishment, shows that the macabre is being put to a more complicated and controlled use. It becomes an instrument instead of a dead end, another gateway through which the poet's imagination can enter an odd, disturbed, but somehow valid world.

The grotesque depends on discrepancy, on a measured friction between manner and material or on discordant experiences crushed together. Both types of contrast contribute to the effect of "The Coasts of Cerigo" and "The Kings," as they do in another startling poem in this genre, "The Dinner." "The Dinner" is of unusual interest; we see in the poem how the imagination of a poet of the grotesque hurls itself from the given situation to one at the extreme point of difference. In this violent dialectical swing the shock of the poem comes from our realising that the second stage, in spite of its immense dissimilarity, is really a development of the first, that it was there all the time grinning under the original elegant surface. We notice, too, how Hope arrives like a poetic zoologist at the second fiercely contrasting situation by a kind of compressed evolutionary method which appears in several poems. The reductive habit of the scientist, his concern with origins and causes, becomes in Hope's hands an instrument of poetic exploration.

One of Hope's favoured metres, the rhymed couplet, is handled with remarkable naturalness, and is used as the instrument of strength rather than delicacy. Indeed the heroic couplet, employed in an easy, open way, is splendidly adapted to communicate the peculiar quality of Hope's poetry which one is aware of even in his earliest, lightest pieces. This is its powerfully – almost physically – energetic character. It is muscular, quick, and solid – with the relaxed poise of the gifted athlete who brings all his force to bear rhythmically and without strain.

Hope is the least neurotic of poets and even when he is scrutinising the stages of his own childhood, as in one of his best poems, "Ascent into Hell," his regard is gravely objective without the least touch of narcissistic droop or any suspicion of anxious self-interest. Right from the start of Hope's poetic career, the reader is aware of the formed personality beneath the finished literary character. It is positive, independent, and radical in the Australian manner – in the manner of the Australian *people*, that is; the accepted Australian literary convention lacked precisely this very virtue. It is free of the fog of middle-class pretension and gentility: sharp where that was bland, and harsh where that was cosy. At the same time Hope's poetry asserts a profound commitment to the great constitutive works of the Western – not just the British – tradition, and, not only in poetry but also in thought and morality, accepts and asserts, namely, the principles of an intellectual aristocracy, and in doing so avoids, or ignores, the clogging dangers of Australian democracy. The result is a powerful and unfashionable maturity which joins a naked freshness of original response to a richly realised conception of an ideal order.

—William Walsh

HUGHES, (James) Langston. American. Born in Joplin, Missouri, 1 February 1902. Educated at Central High School, Cleveland, 1916–20; Columbia University, New York, 1921–22; Lincoln University, Pennsylvania (Witter Bynner Award, 1926), B.A. 1929. During World War II, Member of the Music and Writers war boards. Seaman, 1923–25; busboy, Wardman Park Hotel, Washington, D.C., 1925; Madrid Correspondent, Baltimore *Afro-American*, 1937; Columnist, Chicago *Defender*, 1943–67, and New York *Post*, 1962–67. Founder of the Harlem Suitcase Theatre, New York, 1938, New Negro Theatre, Los Angeles, 1939, and Skyloft Players, Chicago, 1941. Visiting Professor in Creative Writing, Atlanta University, Gerogia, 1947; Poet-in-Residence, University of Chicago Laboratory School, 1949. Recipient: Harmon Gold Medal for Literature, 1931; Rosenwald Fellowship, 1931, 1940; Guggenheim Fellowship, 1935; National Institute of Arts and Letters grant, 1946; Anisfield-Wolfe Award, 1953; Spingarn Medal, 1960. D.Litt.: Lincoln University, 1943; Howard University, Washington, D.C., 1963; Western Reserve University, Cleveland, 1964. Member, National Institute of Arts and Letters, 1961, and American Academy of Arts and Sciences. *Died 22 May 1967.*

PUBLICATIONS

Verse

The Weary Blues.   1926.
Fine Clothes to the Jew.   1927.
Dear Lovely Death.   1931.
The Negro Mother and Other Dramatic Recitations.   1931.
The Dream-Keeper and Other Poems.   1932.
Scottsboro Limited: Four Poems and a Play in Verse.   1932.
A New Song.   1938.
Shakespeare in Harlem.   1942.

Jim Crow's Last Stand. 1943.
Lament for Dark Peoples and Other Poems, edited by H. Driessen.   1944.
Fields of Wonder. 1947.
One-Way Ticket. 1949.
Montage of a Dream Deferred. 1951.
Selected Poems. 1959.
Ask Your Mama: 12 Moods for Jazz. 1961.
The Panther and the Lash: Poems of Our Times. 1967.
Don't You Turn Back: Poems (juvenile), edited by Lee Bennett Hopkins.   1969.

Plays

The Gold Piece, in *The Brownies' Book,* July 1921.
Mulatto (produced 1935; original version produced 1939). In *Five Plays,* 1963.
Little Ham (produced 1935).   In *Five Plays,* 1963.
Troubled Island (produced 1935; revised version, music by William Grant Still, produced 1949).   1949.
When the Jack Hollers, with Arna Bontemps (produced 1936).
Joy to My Soul (produced 1937).
Soul Gone Home (produced 1937?).   In *Five Plays,* 1963.
Don't You Want to Be Free?, music by Carroll Tate (produced 1937).   In *One Act Play Magazine,* October 1938.
Front Porch (produced 1938).
The Sun Do Move (produced 1942).
Freedom's Plow (broadcast, 1943).   1943.
Pvt. Jim Crow (radio script), in *Negro Story,* May-June 1945.
Booker T. Washington at Atlanta (broadcast, 1945).   In *Radio Drama in Action,* edited by Eric Barnouw, 1945.
Street Scene (lyrics only), book by Elmer Rice, music by Kurt Weill (produced 1947).   1947.
The Barrier, music by Jan Meyerowitz (produced 1950).
Just Around the Corner (lyrics only), book by Abby Mann and Bernard Drew, music by Joe Sherman (produced 1951).
Simply Heavenly, music by David Martin (produced 1957).   1959.
Esther, music by Jan Meyerowitz (produced 1957).
Shakespeare in Harlem, with James Weldon Johnson (produced 1959).
Port Town, music by Jan Meyerowitz (produced 1960).
The Ballad of the Brown King, music by Margaret Bonds (produced 1960).
Black Nativity (produced 1961).
Gospel Glow (produced 1962).
Tambourines to Glory, music by Jobe Huntley, from the novel by Hughes (produced 1963).   In *Five Plays,* 1963.
Five Plays (includes *Mulatto, Soul Gone Home, Little Ham, Simply Heavenly, Tambourines to Glory*), edited by Webster Smalley.   1963.
Jericho-Jim Crow (produced 1963).
The Prodigal Son (produced 1965).

Screenplay: *Way Down South,* with Clarence Muse, 1939.

Radio scripts: *Jubilee,* with Arna Bontemps, 1941; *Brothers,* 1942; *Freedom's Plow,* 1943; *John Henry Hammers It Out,* with Peter Lyons, 1943; *In the Service of My Country,* 1944; *The Man Who Went to War,* 1944 (UK); *Booker T. Washington at Atlanta,* 1945; *Swing Time at the Savoy,* with Noble Sissle, 1949.

Television scripts: *The Big Sea,* 1965; *It's a Mighty World,* 1965; *Strollin' Twenties,* 1966.

Fiction

Not Without Laughter. 1930.
The Ways of White Folks (stories). 1934.
Simple Speaks His Mind. 1950.
Laughing to Keep from Crying (stories). 1952.
Simple Takes a Wife. 1953.
Simple Stakes a Claim. 1957.
Tambourines to Glory. 1958.
The Best of Simple. 1961.
Something in Common and Other Stories. 1963.
Simple's Uncle Sam. 1965.

Other

Popo and Fifina: Children of Haiti (juvenile), with Arna Bontemps. 1932.
The Big Sea: An Autobiography. 1940.
The First Book of Negroes (juvenile). 1952.
The First Book of Rhythms (juvenile). 1954.
Famous American Negroes (juvenile). 1954.
The Sweet Flypaper of Life, with Roy De Carava (on Harlem). 1955.
Famous Negro Music-Makers (juvenile). 1955.
The First Book of Jazz (juvenile). 1955; revised edition, 1962.
A Pictorial History of the Negro in America, with Milton Meltzer. 1956; revised edition, 1963.
I Wonder As I Wander: An Autobiographical Journey. 1956.
The First Book of the West Indies (juvenile). 1956; as *The First Book of the Caribbean,* 1965.
The Langston Hughes Reader. 1958.
Famous Negro Heroes of America (juvenile). 1958.
The First Book of Africa (juvenile). 1960; revised edition, 1964.
Fight for Freedom: The Story of the NAACP. 1962.
Black Magic: A Pictorial History of the Negro in American Entertainment, with Milton Meltzer. 1967.
Black Misery. 1969.
Good Morning, Revolution: Uncollected Social Protest Writings, edited by Faith Berry. 1973.

Editor, *Four Lincoln University Poets.* 1930.
Editor, with Arna Bontemps, *The Poetry of the Negro 1746–1949: An Anthology.* 1949; revised edition, 1970.
Editor, with Waring Guney and Bruce M. Wright, *Lincoln University Poets.* 1954.
Editor, with Arna Bontemps, *The Book of Negro Folklore.* 1958.
Editor, *An African Treasury: Articles, Essays, Stories, Poems by Black Africans.* 1960.
Editor, *Poems from Black Africa.* 1963.
Editor, *New Negro Poets: USA.* 1964.
Editor, *The Book of Negro Humor.* 1966.
Editor, *La Poésie Negro-Américaine* (bilingual edition). 1966.
Editor, *Anthologie Africaine et Malgache.* 1966.

Editor, *The Best Short Stories by Negro Writers: An Anthology from 1899 to the Present.* 1967.

Translator, with Mercer Cook, *Masters of the Dew,* by Jacques Roumain. 1947.
Translator, with Ben Frederic Carruthers, *Cuba Libre,* by Nicolás Guillén. 1948.
Translator, *Gypsy Ballads,* by Federico García Lorca. 1951.
Translator, *Selected Poems of Gabriela Mistral.* 1957.

Bibliography: *A Bio-Bibliography of Hughes, 1920–1967* by Donald C. Dickinson, 1967, revised edition, 1972.

Reading List: *Hughes* by James A. Emanuel, 1967; *Hughes: A Biography* by Milton Meltzer, 1968; *Hughes, Black Genius: A Critical Evaluation* edited by Therman B. O'Daniel, 1971 (includes bibliography); *Hughes: An Introduction to the Poetry* by Onwuchekwa Jemie, 1977; *Hughes: The Poet and His Critics* by Richard K. Barksdale, 1977.

*   *   *

As impressive as Langston Hughes is for his versatility and productivity, his claim to enduring literary importance rests chiefly on his poetry and his Simple sketches. In his poetry his sure lyric touch, his poignant insight into the urban black folk soul rendered with remarkable fidelity to a variety of black idioms, his negative capability of subordinating his own personality so as to convey a vivid impression of scene or incident or mood or character, and his willingness to experiment are his richest endowments, though one also often finds in his verse the comic sense (often ironic or bittersweet), the broad democratic faith, and the total understanding of character which so irradiate the Simple tales.

Although Hughes wrote some verse without specific racial reference, the three major categories of his poetry comprise poems related to black music, poems of racial protest, and poems of racial affirmation. These categories naturally overlap, but it is convenient to discuss them separately. For the entire course of his literary career, Hughes was fascinated by black music: blues, jazz in its several varieties, and gospel. The classic blues stanzaic form, consisting of a statement of a problem or situation in the first line repeated in the second (often with a slight variation) followed by a third line resolving, interpreting, or commenting on the first two, appears frequently in Hughes, as in the following from "Red Sun Blues":

> Gray skies, gray skies, won't you let the sun shine through?
> Gray skies, gray skies, won't you let that sun shine through?
> My baby's left me, I don't know what to do.

Elsewhere, as in the title poem of *The Weary Blues*, Hughes uses the blues and bluesmen as subject in a poem which may incorporate blues stanzas but has its own larger structure. His poems deriving from jazz are more complicated in their experimentation. Taken together, they provide a kind of poetic graph of developments in jazz from the Harlem cabaret life of the exuberant 1920's, through the boogie-woogie of the 1930's and the bebop of the 1940's, to the progressive jazz of the 1950's. From such early examples as "Jazzonia" and "The Cat and the Saxophone" to the ambitious later works *Montage of a Dream Deferred* and *Ask Your Mama*, Hughes used the varieties of jazz as both subject and style, designing the last-named work for musical accompaniment and often reading his poetry on tour to a jazz background. Though less prominently than blues and jazz, spirituals and gospel music figure also in Hughes's poetry (for example, the "Feet of Jesus" section in *Selected Poems*), as well as in his numerous song-plays.

As a poet of racial protest Hughes was less strident than some other well-known black writers, but not necessarily less trenchant or effective. Such poems as "I, Too" and "Let America Be America Again" express a wistful longing for racial equality. Others, such as "Brass Spittoons" and "Ballad of the Landlord" develop miniature dramas of the hardships and injustices of black life in a racist society. Some of the later poems included in the "Words on Fire" section of *The Panther and the Lash* sound notes of rising militancy. Surely among Hughes's best poems in this category are "American Heartbreak," whose laconic understatement achieves a sense of bitter finality, and "Song for a Dark Girl," a starkly tragic and strangely beautiful lyric about a girl's response to the lynching of her lover. Whether wistful, dramatic, angry, or tragic in mood, Hughes was always alive throughout his career to the oppression of his people.

He was equally sensitive to the dignity with which they endured or resisted that oppression. "Mother to Son" and "The Negro Mother" are among his many poems celebrating the black quest for freedom and social justice. Hughes was one of the first writers to use "soul" in a special racial sense, as in his very early poem "The Negro Speaks of Rivers." Color itself delights the poet in the carefully crafted "Dream Variation" and the delicious "Harlem Sweeties." And his comic vision to be developed in such loving detail in the Simple sketches is prefigured in "Sylvester's Dying Bed" and the Madam Alberta K. Johnson poems. Lowlife and working class blacks, shunned by bourgeois spokesmen of the Harlem Renaissance, often receive special tribute in Hughes's poems of racial affirmation.

Hughes's interest in fiction developed later than his instinct for poetry. The novels *Not Without Laughter* and *Tambourines to Glory* are highly readable if somewhat weak in structure. The best of his sixty-six published short stories are proficient in technique and perceptive in their treatment of a variety of human situations. The most striking achievement in fiction is the creation of Jesse B. Semple. As Richard K. Barksdale has noted, Simple "had just the right blend of qualities to be Black America's new spokesman — just enough urban humor, cynicism, and sardonic levity and just enough down-home simplicity, mother-wit, innocence, and naiveté" (*Black Writers of America*, edited by Richard Barksdale and Keneth Kinnamon). The marvelous talk elicited from this fully realized black working man by the middle-class, intellectual narrator of the sketches constitutes one of the most valuable treasures of American literary humor.

In drama Hughes is perhaps more important for the extent of his activity and the stimulus he gave to black theater than for the intrinsic artistic merit of his own plays. As translator, anthologist, historian, and biographer he played a major role in popularizing Afro-American, Afro-Caribbean, and African subjects. As devoted friend and sponsor of generations of aspiring writers he was at the center of black literary activity for more than four decades. Together with his own accomplishments as poet and humorist, these efforts constitute a total contribution to literature matched by that of few writers in this century.

—Keneth Kinnamon

HUGHES, Ted. English. Born in Mytholmroyd, Yorkshire, in 1930. Educated at Mexborough Grammar School, Yorkshire; Pembroke College, Cambridge, B.A. 1954, M.A. 1959. Served in the Royal Air Force for two years. Married 1) Sylvia Plath, *q.v.*, in 1956 (died, 1963), one son, one daughter; 2) Carol Orchard in 1970. Worked as a rose gardener and night watchman; reader for the Rank Organisation. Since 1965, Editor, with Daniel Weissbort, *Modern Poetry in Translation* magazine, London. Recipient: New York Poetry Center First Publication Award, 1957; Guinness Award, 1958; Guggenheim Fellowship, 1959; Maugham Award, 1960; Hawthornden Prize, 1961; City of Florence International

Poetry Prize, 1969; Queen's Gold Medal for Poetry, 1974. O.B.E. (Officer, Order of the British Empire), 1977. Lives in England.

PUBLICATIONS

Verse

The Hawk in the Rain.   1957.
Lupercal.   1960.
Selected Poems, with Thom Gunn.   1962.
The Burning of the Brothel.   1966.
Recklings.   1966.
Scapegoats and Rabies: A Poem in Five Parts.   1967.
Animal Poems.   1967.
Five Autumn Songs for Children's Voices.   1968.
The Martyrdom of Bishop Farrer.   1970.
A Crow Hymn.   1970.
A Few Crows.   1970.
Crow: From the Life and Songs of the Crow.   1970; revised edition, 1972.
Crow Wakes: Poems.   1971.
Poems, with Ruth Fainlight and Alan Sillitoe.   1971.
Eat Crow.   1972.
Selected Poems 1957–1967.   1972.
In the Little Girl's Angel Gaze.   1972.
Cave Birds.   1975.
Earth-Moon.   1976.
Eclipse.   1976.
Gaudete.   1977.
Chiasmadon.   1977.

Plays

The Calm (produced 1961).
The Wound (broadcast, 1962).   In Wodwo, 1967.
Seneca's Oedipus (produced 1968).   1969.
Beauty and the Beast (televised, 1968; produced 1971).   In The Coming of the King and Other Plays, 1970.
The Coming of the King and Other Plays (juvenile) (includes The Tiger's Bones; Beauty and the Beast; Sean, The Fool, The Devil and the Cats).   1970; augmented edition, as The Tiger's Bones and Other Plays for Children (includes Orpheus), 1973.
Sean, The Fool, The Devil and the Cats (produced 1971).   In The Coming of the King and Other Plays, 1970.
The Coming of the King (televised, 1972).   In The Coming of the King and Other Plays, 1970.
Orghast (produced 1971).
The Iron Man (juvenile), from his own story (televised, 1972).   1973.
The Story of Vasco, music by Gordon Crosse, from a play by Georges Schehadé (produced 1974).   1974.

Radio Plays: The House of Aries, 1960; A Houseful of Women, 1961; The Wound, 1962; Difficulties of a Bridegroom, 1963; Dogs, 1964.

Televison Plays (juvenile): *Beauty and the Beast,* 1968; *The Coming of the King,* 1972; *The Iron Man,* 1972.

Other

Meet My Folks! (juvenile).   1961.
The Earth-Owl and Other Moon-People (juvenile).   1963.
How the Whale Became and Other Stories (juvenile).   1963.
Nessie the Mannerless Monster (juvenile).   1964; as *Nessie the Monster,* 1974.
Wodwo (miscellany).   1967.
The Iron Man: A Story in Five Nights (juvenile).   1968; as *The Iron Giant,* 1968.
Poetry Is (juvenile).   1970.
Season Songs (juvenile).   1975.
Moon-Whales and Other Poems (juvenile).   1976.
Moon-Bells (juvenile).   1978.

Editor, with Patricia Beer and Vernon Scannell, *New Poems 1962.*   1962.
Editor, with Thom Gunn, *Five American Poets.*   1963.
Editor, *Here Today.*   1963.
Editor, *Selected Poems,* by Keith Douglas.   1964.
Editor, *Poetry in the Making: An Anthology of Poems and Programmes from "Listening and Writing."*   1967.
Editor, *A Choice of Emily Dickinson's Verse.*   1971.
Editor, *A Choice of Shakespeare's Verse.*   1971; as *Poems: With Fairest Flowers While Summer Lasts: Poems from Shakespeare,* 1971.
Editor, *Selected Poems,* by Yehuda Amichai.   1971.
Editor, *Crossing the Water,* by Sylvia Plath.   1971; as *Crossing the Water: Transitional Poems,* 1971.

Translator, with János Csokits, *Selected Poems,* by János Pilinszky.   1976.

Reading List: *The Art of Hughes* by Keith Sagar, 1975; *Hughes and Thom Gunn* by Alan Bold, 1976.

*   *   *

Few young poets can have won the instant and universal critical acclaim for a first volume which Ted Hughes received in 1957 for *The Hawk in the Rain.* The reasons, in retrospect, are plain to see. Hughes's poetry broke upon a dead decade in English literature; into the social-democratic sheepishness of "The Movement" and the *New Lines* anthology, it brought "a sudden sharp hot stink of fox" ("The Thought-Fox"), reiterating the perennial Romantic notion of poetic inspiration as something atavistic and instinctual, a thing of the blood and gut. This was a poetry harsh, jagged, and abrasive, which, though it often rhymed, apparently did so as a kind of disdainful concession to order – where downbeat, unstressed, half- or near-rhymes suggested the recalcitrance of a turbulent, energetic world reluctant to be constrained by considerations of urbanity or the kind of formal nicety dear to "The Movement." This was clearly a poetry that had been shaped by the Cambridge English School's predilection for the muscularity, the wrenched syntax and scansion, and the extraordinary yokings of vocabulary and image in John Donne's verse. In "Wind," Hughes doesn't simply break the "rule" about not splitting adjective from noun by enjambment: he goes further and hyphenates the adjective across the line-ending, in outrageous mimesis of the action: "The wind flung a magpie away and a black-/Back gull bent like an iron bar slowly." But an equally powerful influence must have been Hughes's transfer from the English Tripos to Archaeology and Anthropology, which confirmed that taste for the primitive and the exotic, the alien, and the mythic, that finds its fullest expression in *Crow*. Finally, and a crucial component of Hughes's appeal, he brought a breath of provincial fresh air into an increasingly drab metropolitan culture. The Macmillan era needed its prophets, its avatars of an order beyond the bland superficialities of affluence and consumerism. Hughes was a grammar-school boy and shopkeeper's son from the West Riding; the burliness of his North Country physique was reproduced in the abrupt angularity of his verse; for the literary fashion-mongers of the capital, Hughes, therefore, despite his Cambridge degree, became another of those recurring discoveries of the Romantic era, the noble poetic savage, warbling his native woodnotes wild to an appreciative audience.

This is most obvious in his constant flirtation with the apocalyptic mode. In "The Horses," for example, he emerges from a world locked in "Evil air, a frost-making stillness," where "my breath left tortuous statues in the iron light" and the horses stand "megalith-still," to a vision of the sudden, cataclysmic dawn which is the objective correlative of his own anarchic feelings:

> Slowly detail leafed from the darkness. Then the sun
> Orange, red, red, erupted
>
> Silently, and splitting to its core tore and flung cloud,
> Shook the gulf open, showed blue,
>
> And the big planets hanging. ...

Though the poem then draws us back ("in the fever of a dream") to a restored stasis ("Hearing the horizons endure"), this experience is repeated throughout the early poetry. In "Famous Poet" poetry itself, "set/To blink behind bars at the zoo," still offers a glimpse of "a time when half the world still burned," and, in "Macaw and Little Miss," "The Jaguar," "Esther's Tomcat," and all those other caged or semi-domesticated carnivores in Hughes's bestiary, we are offered images of a lost world of the instincts repeatedly associated with a feudal or primordial ethos of cruelty, superstition, and a barbarous grandeur of speech and gesture. In "Pike," "An Otter," and "February" the self is drawn in fascination to this world, yet at the same time struggles to preserve the poise exemplified in "To Paint a Water Lily" ("still/As a painting, trembling hardly at all,.../Whatever horror nudge her root") or "The Retired Colonel," "Honouring his own caricature" amidst "a pimply age." One way of maintaining balance in *Lupercal*, staving off the return of the repressed, is the distancing irony which allows the poet to dissociate himself from the pretensions, for example, of "Hawk Roosting," a meritocrat whose solipsistic smugness is acutely caught in the boast with which the poem ends:

> Nothing has changed since I began.
> My eye has permitted no change.
> I am going to keep things like this.

(This humorous streak, underestimated in Hughes's work, is very apparent in his rather whimsical stories for children, and reaches the proportions of black farce in *Crow*.)

If, in his earlier books, nature was a viscous, glutinous realm seeking to engulf the mutinous spirit, by the time of *Wodwo* it has dried out. This is the poetry of an increasingly barren struggle for survival, in a landscape as bleak and relentless as that depicted in "Pibroch." In "Gog" the self wakes to its own desolation ("I ran and an absence bounded beside me"), to an unexplained guilt and self-questioning in a world where "Everywhere the dust is in power" and "The rider of iron, on the horse shod with vaginas of iron,/Gallops over the womb that makes no claim, that is of stone." That north country poem of a delusive quest through arid lands, *Sir Gawain and the Green Knight*, supplies both title and epigraph to this volume, as well as the theme of an endless warring – whether the Viking Raids of "The Warriors of the North," the Great War translated into a Beckettian charade in the radio-play "The Wound," or the twentieth-century massacres of Dresden, Buchenwald, and the Gulags, culmination of "a hundred and fifty million years of hunger" in which "Killing gratefully as breathing/Moulded the heart and mouth" ("Karma").

Crow offers a grim, sardonic vision of a world in which the worst has already happened; in the raucous, acerbic tones of Donne's satires it submits all human pretensions to Crow's cold nihilistic scrutiny. Man is "a walking/Abattoir/Of innocents," hypocritically justifying his lust for survival with a flood of words (language and its duplicity, as lie, jest, vow, curse, and prayer is a recurring motif). Crow, for whom even birth is "A Kill," who struggles into existence over the body of his mother ("Crow and Mama") cannot afford such luxuries: charity, love, compunction, remorse, forgiveness are all denied him by life itself; to come into existence is to give pain, to survive is to survive at the expense of others. Crow triumphs over Death in the "Examination at the Womb Door" in which he answers all the questions successfully, but it is only a provisional victory. *Crow* is a bitter parody of all creation myths, in which sexuality is a mutual devouring from which one emerges into the dark cycles of renewal and destruction. In "Crow's First Lesson" God tries to teach him to say "Love." But Crow's gape gives birth successively to shark, bluefly, tsetse, and mosquito, homing on "their sundry fleshpots." Another attempt retches up "Man's bodiless prodigious head" and then "woman's vulva" which "dropped over man's neck and tightened." As "God struggled to part them, cursed, wept – /Crow flew guiltily off." In such brutal parables, Hughes's considerable talent approaches "the bottom of all things" of which he writes in "How Water Began to Play"; whether it ends up, like water, "Utterly worn out," or "utterly clear," the future has yet to show.

—Stan Smith

JARRELL, Randall. American. Born in Nashville, Tennessee, 6 May 1914. Educated at Vanderbilt University, Nashville, B.S. in psychology 1936 (Phi Beta Kappa), M.A. in English 1939. Served as a celestial navigation tower operator in the United States Army Air Corps, 1942–46. Married Mary Eloise von Schrader in 1952. Instructor in English, Kenyon College, Gambier, Ohio, 1937–39, University of Texas, Austin, 1939–42, and Sarah Lawrence College, Bronxville, New York, 1946–47; Associate Professor, 1947–58, and Professor of English, 1958–65, Women's College of the University of North Carolina (later, University of North Carolina at Greensboro). Lecturer, Salzburg Seminar in American Civilization, 1948; Visiting Fellow in Creative Writing, Princeton University, New Jersey, 1951–52; Fellow, Indiana School of Letters, Bloomington, Summer 1952; Visiting Professor of English, University of Illinois, Urbana, 1953; Elliston Lecturer, University of Cincinnati, Ohio, 1958; Phi Beta Kappa Visiting Scholar, 1964–65. Acting Literary Editor, *The Nation*, New York, 1946–47; Poetry Critic, *Partisan Review*, New Brunswick, New Jersey, 1949–53, and *Yale Review*, New Haven, Connecticut, 1955–57; Member of the Editorial Board, *American Scholar*, Washington, D.C., 1957–65. Consultant in Poetry, Library of Congress, Washington, D.C., 1956–58. Recipient: Guggenheim Fellowship, 1946; National Institute of

Arts and Letters grant, 1951; National Book Award, 1961; Oliver Max Gardner Award, University of North Carolina, 1962; American Association of University Women Juvenile Award, 1964; Ingram Merrill Award, 1965. D.H.L.: Bard College, Annandale-on-Hudson, New York, 1962. Member, National Institute of Arts and Letters; Chancellor, Academy of American Poets, 1956. *Died 14 October 1965.*

PUBLICATIONS

Collections

> *The Complete Poems.* 1969.
> *The Achievement of Jarrell: A Comprehensive Selection of His Poems,* edited by Frederick J. Hoffman. 1970.

Verse

> *Five Young American Poets,* with others. 1940.
> *Blood for a Stranger.* 1942.
> *Little Friend, Little Friend.* 1945.
> *Losses.* 1948.
> *The Seven-League Crutches.* 1951.
> *Selected Poems.* 1955.
> *Uncollected Poems.* 1958.
> *The Woman at the Washington Zoo: Poems and Translations.* 1960.
> *Selected Poems.* 1964.
> *The Lost World: New Poems.* 1965.
> *Jerome: The Biography of a Poem.* 1971.

Play

> *The Three Sisters,* from a play by Chekhov (produced 1964). 1969.

Fiction

> *Pictures from an Institution: A Comedy.* 1954.

Other

> *Poetry and the Age* (essays). 1953.
> *A Sad Heart at the Supermarket: Essays and Fables.* 1962.
> *The Gingerbread Rabbit* (juvenile). 1964.
> *The Bat-Poet* (juvenile). 1964.
> *The Animal Family* (juvenile). 1965.
> *The Third Book of Criticism* (essays). 1969.
> *Fly by Night* (juvenile). 1976.
> *A Bat Is Born* (juvenile). 1977.
> *Kipling, Auden & Co.* 1979.

Editor, *The Anchor Book of Stories.* 1958.
Editor, *The Best Short Stories of Kipling.* 1961; as *In the Vernacular: The English in India* and *The English in England,* 2 vols., 1963.
Editor, *Six Russian Short Novels.* 1963.

Translator, with Moses Hadas, *The Ghetto and the Jews of Rome,* by Ferdinand Gregorovius. 1948.
Translator, *The Rabbit Catcher and Other Fairy Tales of Ludwig Bechstein.* 1962.
Translator, *The Golden Bird and Other Fairy Tales,* by the Brothers Grimm. 1962.
Translator, *Snow White and the Seven Dwarfs: A Tale from the Brothers Grimm.* 1972.
Translator, *The Juniper Tree and Other Tales,* by the Brothers Grimm. 1973.
Translator, *Goethe's Faust: Part One.* 1974; *Part Two,* 1978.

Bibliography: *Jarrell: A Bibliography* by Charles M. Adams, 1958, supplement in *Analects 1,* Spring 1961; "A Checklist of Criticism on Jarrell 1941–70" by D. J. Gilliken, in *Bulletin of the New York Public Library,* April 1971.

Reading List: *Jarrell 1914–1965* edited by Robert Lowell, Peter Taylor, and Robert Penn Warren, 1967; *The Poetry of Jarrell* by Suzanne Ferguson, 1971; *Jarrell* by M. L. Rosenthal, 1972.

*   *   *

Shortly after his death, the elegant, brilliant, and quixotic Randall Jarrell was eulogized by Karl Shapiro as the greatest poet-critic since T. S. Eliot. At a memorial service at Yale, such men as Robert Lowell, Robert Penn Warren, and Richard Eberhart came to honor their dead friend as a master among men of their craft. Robert Lowell called him "the most heartbreaking English poet of his generation." Celebrated as well was Jarrell's literary criticism, for in work like *Poetry and the Age,* he had altered dominant critical trends and tastes. He had brought Walt Whitman into prominence, and had imparted new light on Frost, Stevens, Williams, and Marianne Moore, among others; he had attacked the New Critics, and he had affirmed the relevance of art to life. Not unlike Ezra Pound, Jarrell was one of those truly committed critics who, although a poet himself, had helped the writers around him to define twentieth century art.

As Walter Rideout in his essay in *Poets in Progress* (edited by Edward Hungerford, 1962) has noted, when Jarrell published his *Selected Poems* in 1955, he grouped them in such a way as to obscure the rather marked delineations in central subject matter that had distinguished volume from volume. The style of his first book, however, *Blood for a Stranger,* is noticeably derivative, and shows the influence of Allen Tate, John Crowe Ransom, and particularly W. H. Auden in its experiments with villanelles, sestinas, and unusual rhyming patterns, as well as in its intellectual brilliance and metaphysical questionings. The volume cries out against a world politically heaving itself toward catastrophe. Jarrell's tone is one of existential loneliness and despair.

Little Friend, Little Friend and *Losses* are less formal; Jarrell establishes a more direct and characteristic tone; the poet seems, in fact, personally more attracted to death. Jarrell's ambiguous view of humanity, man as murderer and victim, innocent and guilty, ultimately like the child facing the "capricious infinite" parental power, found its perfect expression in these war poems. But Jarrell's war poems treat the human condition, their central image, man as soldier/prisoner. Jarrell dramatizes man's guilt and suffering upon a stage of world-wide struggle. *Losses* treats all sorts of prisoners – children, black Americans, DP's at Haifa, Jews in concentration camps – and focuses upon how each is a victim within "the necessities that governed every act." Even the enemy contains the child, who, called upon to commit a

terrible violence, is himself an innocent. Utilizing the perspective of the child, Jarrell makes
the outcome of war the product of innocence:

> The other murderers troop in yawning;
> Three of them play Pitch, one sleeps, and one
> Lies counting missions, lies there sweating
> Till even his heart beats: One; One; One.
> O *murderers*! ... Still, this is how it's done.

Reality is defined as nightmare, "experience" before and after life, the dream. In "The Death
of the Ball Turret Gunner," he writes: "From my mother's sleep I fell into the State/... I
woke to black flak and the nightmare fighters." Jarrell supports no conventional political
position, no "program for chance." Instead, the man-child is "a ticket/Someone bought and
lost on, a stray animal/... Bewildered .../What have you understood, to die?" His
compassion extends even to the enemy; the powerful also suffer: "Who will teach the
Makers how to die?" he writes.

Jarrell's great and fertile period concluded with *The Seven-League Crutches*. The early
works focused upon lost childhood and innocence, the terrible shock of awareness of adult
hypocrisy and social disintegration. Jarrell now moves away from more public concerns to
private life; his poems are more relaxed. Although the theme of illness remains in the poems
about children, his work is more psychological, more dream-filled. One senses now, in
addition, "a way out," in the face of "Necessity": "Man you must learn to live/though you
want nothing but to die." Stoical, compassionate, and even at times capable of a bittersweet
humor, some of Jarrell's most mature work now appears. Man may perhaps even transcend
Necessity through the imaginative life, the creation and perception of art.

After this Jarrell turned to fairy tale and became preoccupied with children's stories, with
German Romanticism. The fairy tale offered him the innocent's victory over the potent and
evil forces of the universe. In "The Märchen" (Grimm's Tales), he wrote, for example:

> We felled our islands there, at last, with iron.
> The sunlight fell to them, according to our wish,
> And we believed, till nightfall, in that wish;
> And we believed, till nightfall, in our lives.

The title poem of *The Woman at the Washington Zoo*, a return to Jarrell's more formal
style of the 1940's, crystallizes the poet's concern with aging and loneliness. The woman cries
out for relief, for transformation again, from her empty life: "the world goes by my cage and
never sees me." She cries: "You know what I was,/You see what I am: change me, change
me!"

In *The Lost World*, published after a nervous breakdown, many of his recurrent themes
appear: loneliness, lovelessness, age, lost youth, the world's hypocrisy, and, as Robert Lowell
put it, childhood, "above all childhood!" *The Lost World* fails to exhibit the brilliance, power,
elegance, and diversity that characterize his earlier work. More importantly, there is about it
too much of a confessional quality; the poems are awkward and read like revelations on the
analyst's couch. The speaker appears filled with a sense of guilt and helplessness. He tries to
forgive, especially, his parents, but he is unsuccessful. In "The Piano Player," for example, he
confesses: "I go over, hold my hands out, play I play − /If only, somehow, I had learned to
live!" His childhood football hero, Daddy Lipscomb, admits: "I've been scared/Most of my
life. You wouldn't think so to look at me./It gets so bad I cry myself to sleep." Many of these
poems contain a female persona, a woman sometimes unfaithful to her lover, often cruel to
people and animals to the point of murder, but, most frequently, unmitigatingly unkind to
her child. Although one senses Jarrell's attempt to understand and forgive these people, the
poet remains in despair: "I identify myself, as always/With something that there's something
wrong with."

One feels a debt toward Jarrell for his enormous encouragement and advice to the poets of his time. But one must regard him as well as an important poet with a brilliant intelligence, elegance, and humor. Jarrell's uniqueness remains in his special combination of sophistication with undiminished yearnings for childhood, that bittersweet faith that through art, or dreams, or fairy tales, one could regain childhood innocence and joy and negate the inevitable processes of aging, isolation, and death.

—Lois Gordon

JEFFERS, (John) Robinson. American. Born in Pittsburgh, Pennsylvania, 10 January 1887. Tutored by his father; attended schools in Switzerland and Germany; University of Western Pennsylvania, Pittsburgh, 1902; Occidental College, Los Angeles, California, 1903–05, graduated 1905; University of Zurich; University of Southern California, Los Angeles, M.A.; School of Medicine, University of Southern California; studied forestry at the University of Washington, Seattle. Married Una Call Kuster in 1913. Turned to writing after inheriting a modest income, 1912; after 1924 lived in seclusion in a house he built on the California coast near Carmel. Recipient: Academy of American Poets Fellowship, 1958; Shelley Memorial Award, 1961. D.Litt.: Occidental College, 1937. Member, National Institute of Arts and Letters. *Died in January 1962.*

PUBLICATIONS

Collections

Selected Poems. 1965.
Selected Letters 1897–1962, edited by Ann N. Ridgeway. 1968.

Verse

Flagons and Apples. 1912.
Californians. 1916.
Tamar and Other Poems. 1924.
Roan Stallion, Tamar, and Other Poems. 1925.
The Women at Point Sur. 1927.
Poems. 1928.
An Artist. 1928.
Cawdor and Other Poems. 1928.
Dear Judas and Other Poems. 1929.
Stars. 1930.
Apology for Bad Dreams. 1930.
Descent to the Dead: Poems Written in Ireland and Great Britain. 1931.
Thurso's Landing and Other Poems. 1932.
Give Your Heart to the Hawks and Other Poems. 1933.
Solstice and Other Poems. 1935.

The Beaks of Eagles. 1936.
Such Counsels You Gave to Me and Other Poems. 1937.
The Selected Poetry. 1938.
Be Angry at the Sun. 1941.
The Double Axe and Other Poems. 1948.
Hungerfield and Other Poems. 1954.
The Beginning and the End and Other Poems. 1963.

Plays

Medea, from a play by Euripides (produced 1947). 1946.
The Cretan Women, from a play by Euripides (produced 1954?). In *From the Modern Repertory 3,* edited by Eric Bentley, 1956.

Other

Poetry, Gongorism, and a Thousand Years. 1949.
Themes in My Poems. 1956.

Bibliography: *The Critical Reception of Jeffers: A Bibliographical Study* by Alex Vardamis, 1972.

Reading List: *The Loyalties of Jeffers* by Radcliffe Squires, 1956; *Jeffers* by Frederic I. Carpenter, 1962; *The Stone Mason of Tor House: The Life and Work of Jeffers* by Melba B. Bennett, 1966; *Jeffers: Fragments of an Older Fury* by Brother Antoninus (William Everson), 1968; *Jeffers, Poet of Inhumanism* by Arthur B. Coffin, 1971; *Jeffers* by Robert Brophy, 1973.

*   *   *

In 1925 *Roan Stallion, Tamar, and Other Poems* established Robinson Jeffers as one of the major poets of his generation. But beginning in 1927 with *The Women at Point Sur* his repeated use of forbidden themes alienated many readers, and in 1941 his opposition to American participation in World War II all but destroyed his reputation. Since his death in 1962 a better perspective has been achieved, and now he is recognized as one of the most powerful – if also most controversial – of modern poets.

Most of his volumes include one or more long narrative poems, together with many shorter lyrics. And these longer poems all deal, either implicitly or explicitly, with the materials of myth. His *Medea,* for instance, is a free adaptation of the play of Euripides, but *Solstice* attempts to domesticate the violent Greek myth in a realistic California setting. His most successful narrative poems, such as "Roan Stallion" which describes a woman's passionate adoration of a horse, use mythical materials most unobtrusively. But the aura of myth and the forbidden passions which the old myths described, such as incest, parricide, and the love of man for beast, all trouble the narrative poetry of Jeffers.

Besides these myths, his poetry gives vivid expression to an extraordinary sense of place. The wild coast of the country south of Carmel, where he lived all his creative life, provides both actual setting and the conviction of immediate reality for all his poems, both narrative and lyric. But most significant of all is the symbolic nature of this actual country. Here is "Continent's End," both in fact and in idea, "the long migrations' end," where human civilization now faces "the final Pacific" and looks Westward toward its first beginnings in "mother Asia."

In his poetry this realistic sense of place combines with a consciousness of the symbolic significance of this place and a remembrance of the prehistoric origins of civilization suggested by the ancient myths. At its best this poetry realizes a vision of human history unique in its temporal scope and its imaginative power. It is small wonder if it sometimes fails to unify these disparate elements and to realize this all-inclusive vision.

The volume which first established Jeffers's reputation probably remains his best, and the three narrative poems which it includes illustrate the various combinations of narrative realism with mythical symbolism which his later poetry developed. "Roan Stallion" is most completely realistic, and perhaps for this reason has remained the favorite of traditional minded readers. "Tamar" is most extreme, both in plot and in technique, although the strange story of incest plays itself out in a California setting. "The Tower Beyond Tragedy" retells the story of the Oresteia in its original Greek setting, but with modern characterization.

The heroine of "Roan Stallion" is named "California," and both name and plot recall the Greek myth of Europa. But the god-like stallion remains simply an animal, and the woman's adoration for him remains psychological. Meanwhile the mythical dimensions of the naturalistic story are emphasized by poetic suggestion:

> The fire threw up figures
> And symbols meanwhile, racial myths formed and
> dissolved in it, the phantom rulers of humanity
> That without being are yet more real than what
> they are born of, and without shape, shape that
> which makes them.

"Tamar" is a very different poem, perhaps unique in literature. Its incestuous heroine rejects all the inhibitions of civilization, but her seemingly realistic actions are motivated by passages of dream, vision, and racial memory until the modern story seems to reenact the earliest creation myths of the incestuous union of Coelus and Terra, of gods and men. The heroine's absolute rejection of morality is paralleled only by that of the later *Women at Point Sur*. But here the repeated use of dream and vision transforms the realistic story into the realm of timeless myth.

"The Tower Beyond Tragedy" narrates the plot of the Oresteia in realistic terms, but focuses on the character of Cassandra and her predictions of doom. Midway through the poem these enlarge into an all-embracing prophecy of the ultimate destruction of future empires, ending with "a mightier to be cursed and a higher for malediction," America. The poem concludes with the refusal of Orestes to inherit Mycenae, or imperial power, and an eloquent poetic statement of his philosophy of total detachment in a "tower beyond tragedy."

This denunciation of imperial power and this celebration of human detachment is also the theme of many of Jeffers' best shorter poems, such as "Shine, Perishing Republic" and "Continent's End." Other lyrics celebrate simply the beauty of nature, such as "Night" and "Boats in a Fog." Perhaps the best of his short poems is "To the Stone Cutters," which treats the ancient theme of mutability.

After the *Roan Stallion* volume, *The Women at Point Sur* narrated a story of the total rejection of traditional morality by a renegade Christian minister. But this longest of Jeffers' poems was also most realistic, so that the mythical and instinctual incest of "Tamar" became calculated and explicit. Actually the poem recalls the story of Euripides' *Bacchae*, which Jeffers also used in his short poem "The Humanist's Tragedy," but the longer poem abandoned all reference to myth and symbol. Although most contemporary readers rejected it, Jeffers' chief modern disciple, William Everson (Brother Antoninus), has praised it highly in *Fragments of an Older Fury*.

In *Dear Judas* Jeffers retold the gospel story with new characterization, as he had retold the Oresteia in "The Tower Beyond Tragedy." The striking originality of his conception and the soaring poetry with which he clothed it make the poem memorable. But his rejection of Christian orthodoxy seemed blasphemous to many readers. "The Loving Shepherdess," a companion narrative poem, created a character of such beauty that her story seems unique among Jeffers' dark tragedies.

In the 1930's Jeffers turned to a series of more realistic long poems with contemporary California settings, without mythical overtones. "Cawdor," "Thurso's Landing," and "Give Your Heart to the Hawks" all take place in "Jeffers Country" south of Carmel, and all develop their tragic stories effectively. Only some names and passages of poetic commentary suggest larger themes. Near the end of "Thurso's Landing" the poet comments:

> The platform is like a rough plank theatre-stage
> Built on the brow of the promontory: as if our blood had labored all around the earth from Asia
> To play its mystery before strict judges at last, the final ocean and sky, to prove our nature
> More shining than that of the other animals. It is rather ignoble in its quiet times, mean in its pleasures,
> Slavish in the mass; but at stricken moments it can shine terribly against the dark magnificence of things.

After 1935 Jeffers published new volumes every few years, but only a few of the narrative poems achieved excellence. "At the Birth of an Age" develops incidents from the Niblung Saga, but the poetry overshadows the story, and the mythical and philosophic elements which it illustrates find powerful expression. The second narrative poem in *The Double Axe*, entitled "The Inhumanist," creates a hermit-hero who gives expression to Jeffers' philosophy both in speech and in action. Finally, "Hungerfield" creates a brief modern myth recalling that of Herakles.

Many readers prefer Jeffers' shorter poems to his long narratives. His "Apology for Bad Dreams" offers both illustration and explanation of the violent imagery and pessimistic philosophy which characterize all his poetry. A later poem, "The Bloody Sire," gives perfect expression to this philosophy of violence, ending: "Who would remember Helen's face/ Lacking the terrible halo of spears?"

Much of the difficulty of his poetry stems from his insistence upon the philosophy of "Inhumanism," which he attempted to define in his later writing. His opposition both to human self-importance and to the classical tradition of humanism emphasized instead the modern search for objective truth. In contrast to T. S. Eliot's traditional classicism, Jeffers celebrated the values of science and discovery.

—Frederic I. Carpenter

JOHNSON, James Weldon. American. Born in Jacksonville, Florida, 17 June 1871. Educated at Atlanta University, A.B. 1894, A.M. 1904; also studied at Columbia University, New York, for three years. Married Grace Nail in 1910. Principal, Stanton Central Grammar School for Negroes, Jacksonville; helped found *Daily American*, Jacksonville; admitted to the Florida Bar, and practised in Jacksonville, 1897–1901; moved to New York, to collaborate with his brother, the composer J. Rosamond Johnson, in writing popular songs and light opera, 1901–06; United States Consul in Puerto Cabello, Venezuela, 1906–09, and Corinto, Nicaragua, 1909–12; Executive Secretary, National Association for the Advancement of Colored People, 1916–30; Spence Professor of Creative Literature, Fisk University, Nashville, Tennessee, 1930–38; Visiting Professor of Creative Literature, New York

University, 1934. Columnist, New York *Age*. Director, American Fund for Public Service; Trustee, Atlanta University. Recipient: Spingarn Medal, 1925; Du Bois Prize for Negro Literature, 1933. Litt.D.: Talladega College, Alabama, 1917; Howard University, Washington, D.C., 1923. Member, Academy of Political Science. *Died 26 June 1938*.

PUBLICATIONS

Verse

> *Fifty Years and Other Poems.*   1917.
> *God's Trombones: Seven Negro Sermons in Verse.*   1927.
> *Saint Peter Relates an Incident of the Resurrection Day.*   1930.
> *Saint Peter Relates an Incident: Selected Poems.*   1935.

Plays

> *Goyescas; or, The Rival Lovers*, from a play by Fernando Periquet, music by Enrique Granados (produced 1915).   1915.
> *Shakespeare in Harlem*, with Langston Hughes (produced 1959).

Fiction

> *The Autobiography of an Ex-Colored Man.*   1912.

Other

> *The Changing Status of Negro Labor.*   1918.
> *Africa in the World Democracy*, with Horace M. Kallen.   1919.
> *Self-Determining Hayti.*   N.d.
> *Lynching: America's National Disgrace.*   1924.
> *The Race Problem and Peace.*   1924.
> *Fundamentalism Versus Spiritualism: A Layman's Viewpoint.*   1925.
> *Native African Races and Culture.*   1927.
> *Legal Aspects of the Negro Problem.*   N.d.
> *Black Manhattan.*   1930.
> *The Shining Life.*   1932.
> *Along This Way* (autobiography).   1933.
> *Negro Americans, What Now?*   1934.

> Editor, *The Book of American Negro Poetry*.   1922; revised edition, 1931.
> Editor, *The Book of American Negro Spirituals*.   1925; *Second Book*, 1926.

Reading List: *Roots of Negro Racial Consciousness: Three Harlem Renaissance Authors* (on Countée Cullen, Claude McKay, and Johnson) by Stephen H. Bronz, 1964; *Johnson, Black Leader, Black Voice* by Eugene D. Levy, 1973 (includes bibliography).

*   *   *

James Weldon Johnson's literary output is slight but it is a solid achievement and one that proves crucial when viewed in the perspective of an Afro-American aspiring to authorship in the United States in the early twentieth century. In *God's Trombones: Seven Negro Sermons in Verse* Johnson achieves a considerable success in melding Afro-American folk and Euro-American sophisticated modes of expression to gain the kind of artistic synthesis he hoped would assist in confirming the right to full citizenship for peoples of African descent in the United States, by virtue of a demonstrated capacity (which their detractors would argue they did not possess) to contribute significantly to the formation of a national culture. This task of recuperation becomes a theme in Johnson's influential picaresque novel now regarded as a classic, *The Autobiography of an Ex-Colored Man*, first published anonymously in 1912. The novel's "tragic mulatto" protagonist is a trained musician who earns his way as an inspired ragtime pianist. He professes, however ironically (and it is to Johnson's skillful manipulation of irony that the novel owes the greater part of its success), to bring "glory and honour to the Negro race." This he intends to achieve through compositions in the European classical tradition incorporating elements of Afro-American folk music, the projected field research for which, however, never gets done. Further insight into Johnson's recuperative aims is available in the important Prefaces to the two editions of his equally influential and classic anthology, *The Book of American Negro Poetry*. In these he compares the Afro-American poet's need to achieve a distinct mode of expression rooted in and supportive of Afro-American life ("a form that will express the racial spirit by symbols from within" rather than from without), to that recognized by the Irish poet-playwright J. M. Synge which led to the assimilation of indigenous folk material into his works.

Johnson's accidental death cut short his efforts but his poems in *God's Trombones* record a significant step in the direction he envisioned. This work has continued to serve as an inspiration and a model for Afro-American writers. Stylistically inspired by the folk preaching Johnson observed in Afro-American churches, the poems assume the form and essential rhythm of the sermons and prayers he heard. As such they score a marked stylistic departure from the prevailing Anglo-American poetic tradition of the day. Also, they constitute a corrective to the artificial and, as Johnson saw it, denigrating folk speech of the stereotype-fostering dialect mode that had been grafted onto that tradition, including its use in Johnson's own early dialect poetry. On the Euro-American side, the poems in *God's Trombones* are biblical-Whitmanesque, gaining an appeal at once sophisticated and folk oriented. Similarly, *The Autobiography of an Ex-Colored Man* delineates the artistic defusing of the various stereotypes Afro-American writers were coming to recognize as an obligatory function of their works. Toward that end, Johnson imbues his protagonist with the superficialities of the "tragic mulatto" stereotype but protrays him with psychological verisimilitude and with irony, thus enabling the stereotypical aspect to achieve a virtual self-destruction. He thus carries forward a tradition of corrective aesthetics pioneered by his predecessors, the Afro-American writers Charles W. Chesnutt and, to a lesser degree, Paul Laurence Dunbar.

—Alvin Aubert

JONES, David (Michael).   English.   Born in Brockley, Kent, 1 November 1895. Educated at Camberwell School of Art, London, 1910–14; Westminster School of Art, London, 1919–21. Served with the Royal Welch Fusiliers, 1915–18. Worked with Eric Gill in Wales, 1924–27. Engraver, book illustrator, painter and water colourist: exhibitions – National Gallery, London, 1940, 1941, 1942; Paris, 1945; Brooklyn, New York, 1952–53; one-man shows – Edinburgh and the Tate Gallery, London 1954–55; National Book League, London, 1972. Works in the collections of the Tate Gallery; Victoria and Albert Museum, London; National Museum of Wales, Cardiff; Sydney Art Gallery; Toronto Art Gallery; Arts Council of Great Britain, London; British Council, London. Recipient: Hawthornden Prize, 1938; Russell Loines Award, 1954; Welsh Arts Council Award, 1960, 1969; Royal National Eisteddfod of Wales Gold Medal for Fine Arts, 1964; Corporation of London Midsummer Prize, 1968. D.Litt.: University of Wales, 1960. Honorary Member, Royal Society of Painters in Water Colours; Fellow, Royal Society of Literature. C.B.E. (Commander, Order of the British Empire), 1955; Companion of Honour, 1974. *Died 28 October 1974.*

PUBLICATIONS

Verse

>   *The Anathemata: Fragments of an Attempted Writing.*   1952.
>   *The Fatigue.*   1965.
>   *The Tribune's Visitation.*   1969.
>   *The Sleeping Lord and Other Fragments.*   1974.
>   *The Kensington Mass,* edited by René Hague.   1975.

Other

>   *In Parenthesis: Seinnyessit e Gledyf ym Penn Mameu.*   1937.
>   *David Jones* (paintings).   1949.
>   *Epoch and Artist: Selected Writings,* edited by Harman Grisewood.   1959.
>   *An Introduction to The Rime of the Ancient Mariner.*   1972.
>   *Use and Sign.*   1975.
>   *Letters to Vernon Watkins,* edited by Ruth Pryor.   1976.
>   *The Dying Gaul and Other Writings,* edited by Harman Grisewood.   1978.

Bibliography: *Jones: An Annotated Bibliography and Guide to Research* by Samuel Rees, 1977.

Reading List; *Jones: Artist and Writer* by David Blamires, 1971; *Jones: An Exploratory Study of the Writings* by Jeremy Hooker, 1975; *Jones,* 1975, and *A Commentary on The Anathemata of Jones,* 1977, both by René Hague.

*   *   *

Before David Jones achieved any literary recognition he was already well-known as a watercolourist and engraver. Indeed, throughout his life he continued to draw and paint, making some of his finest and most complex pictures in the latter part of his life. He also fused poetry and painting in highly idiosyncratic calligraphic inscriptions, reproductions of which adorn some of his books.

David Jones was not a typical man of letters. His reading of contemporary English literature included Hopkins and Eliot, but little beyond that. His knowledge of the past centred on such figures as Chaucer, Langland, Malory, Shakespeare, Milton, Coleridge, Browning, and Quiller-Couch's *Oxford Book of English Verse,* together with whatever he could find translated of the ancient literature of Wales. Legend, tradition, myth, and romance were of more consequence to him than realism or romanticism. His range of non-literary interests was formidable and fed directly, but with a proper metamorphosis, into his own writing. He was passionately concerned to expound the fundamental nature of man as an artist or maker (to use a favourite word of his), whether in the earliest shapes of palaeolithic art or in the abstract art of his own time, and this was inextricably linked with his understanding of man as a religious animal. He had been brought up in the Church of England by an evangelically minded Welsh father and an English mother from London, but his way of looking at the world led him in 1921 to become a Roman Catholic. Belonging to the Catholic circles in which Eric Gill moved, he met many of the radical Catholics of the day. He was deeply influenced by Thomism and the philosophy of Maritain, and his acquaintance with the theology of Maurice de la Taille, regarded with great suspicion in the 1920's, proved to be seminal in the writing of *The Anathemata*.

David Jones's first book, *In Parenthesis*, is certainly one of the most enduring works to have emerged from the First World War. Begun as late as 1927 or 1928 and not published until 1937, it is an extraordinary distillation, part prose, part poetry, of Jones's indelible experiences as a private soldier in the trenches. It is not autobiography, but rather a transmutation of typical and individual experiences centred on a man, John Ball, who belongs to a mixed company of Londoners and Welshmen. From the initial parade-ground muddles and embarkation for France the narrative moves gradually into episodes of trench life realized in acute sensory detail and with variation of mood from wry humour to stark pathos, culminating in the summer battle of the Somme. While obviously a "war book" in terms of its primary subject-matter, *In Parenthesis* relates this searing action to the continuities of Welsh and English tradition, so that telling phrases from, for example, the old Welsh elegiac poem *The Gododdin* and Malory illuminate the present day. Despite its daunting range of literary and Biblical allusion *In Parenthesis* never loses touch with concrete actuality.

The Anathemata is like no other work, though it shares the modernist, allusive poetic techniques of Joyce, Eliot, and Pound, deepened and extended from *In Parenthesis*. It was considered by David Jones as his most important work. Based on the narrative structure of the Tridentine mass, it is also a celebration of the history and essence of Britain from the earliest geological times to the pre-industrial period. The first four sections constitute an exploration, through the recurring metaphor of the voyage, of man in pre-history and history from the roots of Western culture in the ancient Near East, through Greece, Troy, and Rome to early Celtic Britain and the Anglo-Saxon settlement. The last four sections focus respectively on London as the image of the city, presided over by woman in all her guises; the tree as the keel of a ship, as mast and military engine, and as the Christian Cross; birth and incarnation; death, sacrifice and salvation. Such a bald summary does no justice to the rich mosaic of the poem, its constant references back and forwards, its emotional and spiritual reverberations. Everywhere the poet strives to bring together and interpret

> The adaptations, the fusions
> the transmogrifications
> > but always
> the inward continuities
> > of the site
> > of place.

The Anathemata was sub-titled "fragments of an attempted writing," and *The Sleeping Lord* presents further fragments of this writing. They are more sharply focussed on the military levelling situation of the Roman Empire at the time of Christ, depicted with telling irony, with accompanying and contrasting pictures of Celtic culture from that period and somewhat later. The separate pieces have a strong political dimension which is the more universal in application as the empires of today are never explicitly brought on to the scene. The splits in allegiance between "everything presuming difference/and all the sweet remembered demarcations" on the one hand and "the fact of empire" on the other are nowhere mere movingly expressed than in *The Tribune's Visitation*.

Although David Jones did not publish much in his lifetime, he was a prolific writer and wrote acutely and feelingly on the relationship of art and religion, the meaning of tradition, and the importance of Welsh culture for Britain. *Epoch and Artist*, a collection of broadcast talks, book reviews, essays, and letters, and a fascinating *Introduction to The Rime of the Ancient Mariner* were published in his later years. *The Dying Gaul*, a similar collection to *Epoch and Artist*, was published posthumously. So also was a brief poetic fragment, *The Kensington Mass*. It is now becoming clear that David Jones was a prolific letter-writer, and individual letters and complete sets of correspondence, shedding light on his working methods, his tireless mind, and his lovable, humble personality, have already appeared.

—David Blamires

KAVANAGH, Patrick. Irish. Born in Inniskeen, 21 October 1904. Educated at Kednaminsha National School, 1910–16. Married Katherine Moloney in 1967. Farmer and shoemaker, Inniskeen, 1920–36; lived in London and Dublin, 1936–42; Columnist ("City Commentary"), *Irish Press*, Dublin, 1942–44; Film Critic and Feature Writer, *The Standard*, Dublin, 1943–49; Editor, *Kavanagh's Weekly*, Dublin, 1952; Contributor, *Nimbus* magazine, London, 1954, *The Farmer's Journal*, Dublin, 1958–63, and *RTV-Guide*, Dublin, 1963–67; Extra-Mural Lecturer, University College, Dublin, 1956–59. Recipient: A E Memorial Award, 1940; Arts Council of Great Britain Award, 1967. *Died 30 November 1967.*

PUBLICATIONS

Collections

Complete Poems, edited by Peter Kavanagh. 1972.

Verse

Ploughman and Other Poems. 1936.
The Great Hunger. 1942.
A Soul for Sale. 1947.
Recent Poems. 1958.
Come Dance with Kitty Stobling and Other Poems. 1960.
Collected Poems. 1964.

Plays

Self Portrait (televised, 1962). 1964.
Tarry Flynn (produced 1966).

Television Feature: *Self Portrait,* 1962.

Fiction

Tarry Flynn.   1948.
By Night Unstarred, edited by Peter Kavanagh.   1977.

Other

The Green Fool (autobiography).   1938.
Collected Pruse.   1967.
Lapped Furrows: Correspondence, 1933–1967, Between Patrick and Peter Kavanagh, With Other Documents, edited by Peter Kavanagh.   1969.
November Haggard: Uncollected Prose and Verse, edited by Peter Kavanagh.   1971.
A Kavanagh Anthology, edited by Eugene Platt.   1973.

Bibliography: *Garden of the Golden Apples: A Bibliography of Kavanagh* by Peter Kavanagh, 1972.

Reading List: *Clay Is the Word: Kavanagh 1904–1967* by Alan Warner, 1973.

*   *   *

The early poems of Patrick Kavanagh arise like prayers from the ragged fields of his native Monaghan. As he claimed in the first poem of his *Collected Poems,* he wished to find "a star-lovely art/In a dark sod," and on occasions he succeeded.

The best of the verse in *Ploughman and Other Poems* has fibre in its unashamed paganism: he addresses the blackbird, "O pagan poet you/And I are one/In this – we lose our God/At set of sun." The Irish countryman's adherence to the elder faiths underlies his Catholicism just as vestiges of Gaelic lyricism echo behind the influence of English rural singers. Kavanagh never decisively made, however, the choice he offered himself between Venus and the Virgin: the weak verse in his first volume exhibits a cloying devotionalism and piety. Yet even in an otherwise discountable poem, tiny miracles of wings open out of clay that surprise the poet, one feels, as much as the reader. The poet never lost this gift: "My hills hoard the bright shillings of March/While the sun searches in every pocket" ("Shancoduff"); "The axle-roll of a rut-locked cart/Broke the burnt stick of noon in two" ("Spraying the Potatoes").

The "thrill/Of common things raised up to angelhood" is Kavanagh's enduring theme and pursuit, and it is not surprising that the mystical innocence he sought and that relates him to poets like Vaughan and Clare should often collapse into wilful naivety or bathos. The poet's stated distinction between the virtues of parochialism and the vices of provincialism is, though, a valid one. It permitted a sense of freedom and authority ("A road, a mile of kingdom, I am king/Of banks and stones and every blooming thing"), and even of immortality ("I cannot die/Unless I walk outside these whitethorn hedges").

Walk outside them he did, which Kavanagh lyrically describes in his autobiographical works *The Green Fool* and *Tarry Flynn.* In his long and justly famous poem, *The Great Hunger,* Kavanagh turned upon the Irish rural life he had left: not its physical beauty, but its sexual frustration and the priestly interference with the minds and bodies as well as souls of the country people. The poet later repudiated his most ambitious and varied poem, considering it to have "some kinetic vulgarity." He was in error: his portrait of a small unmarried farmer, Patrick Maguire, "whose spirit/Is a wet sack flapping about the knees of time" is an unforgettable and powerful indictment.

One half of Kavanagh's poetic character desired lyrical repose, and he believed that the poet's authority "Is bogus if the sonorous beat is broken/By disturbances in human hearts": his goal was to be "Passive, observing with a steady eye." The other, maverick half grew increasingly combative – even litigious – and prosaic, and in later poems, such as "The Paddiad" (*Come Dance with Kitty Stobling*), he abandoned poetry like that of *The Great Hunger* which required passionate engagement, and instead tried to write satire that too often sank into invective and doggerel. The satire fails because it springs from self-pity rather than social indignation, and, if on occasions self-pity is transformed into genuine poetry, it is not satire but the lyrical balladry of "If Ever You Go to Dublin Town."

Repose was hard won. In the mid-1950's he had an operation for lung cancer, in the wake of which he lost his messianic compulsion: "My purpose in life was to have no purpose." "Canal Bank Walk," "Lines Written on a Seat on the Grand Canal" and "The Hospital" are fine sonnets, in the last of which Kavanagh described as the poet's purpose what he had in fact been attempting all along in his best lyrical poems – snatching out of time "the passionate transitory." Posterity will rescue from time at least a score of Kavanagh's poems, passionate and enduring.

—John Wilson Foster

KEYES, Sidney (Arthur Kilworth). English. Born in Dartford, Kent, 27 May 1922. Educated at Dartford Grammar School; Queen's College, Oxford (Editor, *Cherwell*). Commissioned in the West Kent Regiment, and killed in action in Tunisia, 1943. Recipient: Hawthornden Prize, 1944. *Died 29(?) April 1943.*

PUBLICATIONS

Collections

    Collected Poems, edited by Michael Meyer. 1945.
    Minos of Crete: Plays and Stories, edited by Michael Meyer. 1948.

Verse

    The Iron Laurel. 1942.
    The Cruel Solstice. 1943.

Plays

    Hosea: A Modern Morality (produced 1941). In *Minos of Crete: Plays and Stories,* 1948.
    Minos of Crete, in *Minos of Crete: Plays and Stories.* 1948.

Other

    Editor, with Michael Meyer, *Eight Oxford Poets.* 1941.

Reading List: *Keyes: A Biographical Inquiry* by John Guenther, 1967; *Not Without Glory: Poets of the Second World War* by Vernon Scannell, 1976.

*   *   *

Keyes's writing life consisted of his last two years at school, eighteen months at Oxford, and a year of army training. That from so little of life he completed two accomplished collections of poems (within a year gathered into a posthumous *Collected Poems* along with a useful memoir and notes), and the plays and stories of *Minos of Crete*, indicates the precocious nature of his achievement. His misfortune was to be instantly lauded as his war's successor to Owen: a claim doomed to emphasise his limitations in view of the fact that he died at the age of twenty within two weeks of reaching the Tunisian Front and not one of his poems was written from experience of battle. In consequence, today his false reputation is remembered and his work largely unread. In fact he was a promising poet with a niche in literary history as one of the Oxford poets of 1940–1942 who tried to move through romanticism away from what they regarded as "the Audenian school of poets": he was a friend of John Heath-Stubbs and contemporary of the more brilliant Drummond Allison (1921–43).

Keyes's first collection shows a surprisingly adept apprentice poet, already at eighteen able to take something of Yeats's resonance, to draw from his reading his own themes of pain and death, and to find in the seer-poets he admired echoes of his own generation's fate, as in "Poem for May the First":

> I praise this unheroic generation
> Anchored to earth and confident and hopeless
> Of bloom this May as any wry-limbed cypress.

His is a poetry of the eloquent gesture, succeeding through its assimilation of elegiac cadence. Clare, Wordsworth, Yeats, and Schiller are given tribute through monologue or elegy, and in the important sequence "The Foreign Gate" Keyes echoes Dante to extend his lament to the dead of war:

> "Remember the torn lace, the fine coats slashed
> With steel instead of velvet, Künersdorf
> Fought in the shallow sand was my relief."
> "I rode to Naseby" ...
>   "At Dunkirk I
> Rolled in the shallows, and the living trod
> Across me for a bridge ..."

Keyes more often brings specific images of this kind to bear on the poems of his second collection. Still he aspires to the grand symbolic presentation of experience, seeking, as he wrote in a letter of January 1943 (quoted in *Collected Poems*), to synthesise the discoveries of Rilke and Yeats. But it is the short poems which grow from his experience of love – "The True Heart," "Seascape," "The Kestrels" – which show his talent developing:

> When I would think of you, my mind holds only
> The small defiant kestrels – how they cut
> The raincloud with sharp wings, continually circling
> Above the storm rocked elm, with passionate cries.

—Desmond Graham

KINSELLA, Thomas. Irish. Born in Dublin, 4 May 1928. Educated at University College, Dublin. Married Eleanor Walsh in 1955; two daughters, one son. Worked in the Irish Civil Service, 1948 until his retirement from the Department of Finance, 1965; Writer-in-Residence, 1965–67, and Professor of English, 1967–70, Southern Illinois University, Carbondale. Since 1970, Professor of English, Temple University, Philadelphia. Director, Dolmen Press, Dublin, and Cuala Press, Dublin; Founder, Peppercanister publishers, Dublin, 1972. Artistic Director, Lyric Players Theatre, Belfast. Recipient: Guinness Award, 1958; Irish Arts Council Triennial Book Award, 1961; Denis Devlin Memorial Award, 1967, 1970; Guggenheim Fellowship, 1968, 1971. Member, Irish Academy of Letters, 1965. Lives in Dublin.

PUBLICATIONS

Verse

The Starlit Eye. 1952.
Three Legendary Sonnets. 1952.
The Death of a Queen. 1956.
Poems. 1956.
Another September. 1958; revised edition, 1962.
Moralities. 1960.
Poems and Translations. 1961.
Downstream. 1962.
Six Irish Poets, with others, edited by Robin Skelton. 1962.
Wormwood. 1966.
Nightwalker. 1967.
Nightwalker and Other Poems. 1968.
Poems, with Douglas Livingstone and Anne Sexton. 1968.
Tear. 1969.
Butcher's Dozen. 1972.
A Selected Life. 1972.
Finistere. 1972.
Notes from the Land of the Dead and Other Poems. 1972.
New Poems, 1973. 1973.
Selected Poems 1956–1968. 1973.
Vertical Man: A Sequel to A Selected Life. 1973.
The Good Fight: A Poem for the Tenth Anniversary of the Death of John F. Kennedy. 1973.
One. 1974.
A Technical Supplement. 1976.

Other

Davis, Mangan, Ferguson? Tradition and the Irish Writer, with W. B. Yeats. 1970.

Editor, Selected Poems of Austin Clarke. 1976.

Translator, The Breastplate of St. Patrick, 1954; as Faeth Fiadha: The Breastplate of St. Patrick, 1957.
Translator, The Exile and Death of the Sons of Usnech, by Longes Mac n-Usnig. 1954.

Translator, *Thirty Three Triads, Translated from the XII Century Irish.*   1955.
Translator, *The Tain.*   1969.

Bibliography: by Hensley Woodbridge, in *Eire-Ireland,* 1966.

Reading List: "Kinsella Issue" of *Hollins Critic 4,* 1968; *Eight Contemporary Poets* by Calvin Bedient, 1974; *The Poetry of Kinsella* by Maurice Harmon, 1974.

*   *   *

In *Nightwalker,* a long poem near mid-career, Thomas Kinsella aptly called himself "a vagabond/tethered." His work is distinguished by an effort to test and extend the limits of his own imaginative process, pitting his restless energies against a "will that gropes for/ structure." During the 1970's, Kinsella's work moved deeply and specifically into the weird environs of the imagination, making them a primary subject of his broodings, as in "Hen Woman" (*Notes from the Land of the Dead*):

> There is no end to that which,
> not understood, may yet be noted
> and hoarded in the imagination,
> in the yolk of one's being, so to speak,
> there to undergo its (quite animal) growth.

The act of writing became, with *Notes from the Land of the Dead,* a "fall," a journey down into "the heart of the pit" from which to emerge "carrying my prize." In *A Technical Supplement,* Kinsella explicitly assumes "the beginning/must be inward. Turn inward. Divide." Turning inward, he places under scrutiny the matter of cognition and perception, knowing he can only achieve a temporary order with it. The work is located where anticipated connections are not always possible and therefore not always insisted upon. The stress is internal – the impulse shaping itself – rather than external and imposed. The terms of his inward turnings – tearings, "vital spatterings," self-surgeries, the "great private blade" – are harsh, unlike the pleasing grace of such early poems as "Fifth Sunday after Easter" (*Poems and Translations*):

> April's sweet hand in the margins betrayed
> Her character in late cursive daffodils;
> A gauche mark, but beautiful: a maid.

That early poetry, from *Another September* through *Wormwood,* was characterized by traditional, formal logic and structure, narrative drive, and rich description. It was poetry of married love, ordeal, erosion. Its language, approaching maturity in such poems as "A Country Walk" or "Mirror in February," was packed and lush, serviceable for material which dealt with "the swallowing and absorption of bitterness." The final effort in this manner, "Phoenix Park," articulated certain "laws of order" such as the principle

> That life is hunger, hunger is for order,
> And hunger satisfied brings on new hunger
> Till there's nothing to come

After a pause during which Kinsella escalated his effort to finish translating the early Irish epic, *The Tain,* his poems occupy a mythic territory of dark caves and the sea, of snakes and "animal action." They have been characterized by an apparent formlessness, a charged language at once compressed and wildly associative – a language of trance – and a "difficult" density. For poems of the sources and processes of self and imagination, this form is direct and appropriate; the material is allowed to define its own "random/persistent coherences."

Having evolved the agitated Nightwalker and subsequent versions of him — William Skullbullet in *A Technical Supplement* or the possessed man with "the brainworm" that "will not sleep" in "The Clearing" — Kinsella discovered that only by turning finally inward, under enormous pressure and with less reliance on the old supports of persona or technique, could he find the satisfaction of capturing "in absolute hunger" the things of the mind that dominate him, as in "The Oldest Place" (*One*):

> We would need to dislodge
> the flesh itself, to dislodge that
> — shrivel back to the first drop
> and be spat back shivering into
> the dark beyond our first father

—Floyd Skloot

KLEIN, A(braham) M(oses).   Canadian.   Born in Montreal, Quebec, 14 February 1909. Educated at McGill University, Montreal, B.A. 1930; University of Montreal, B.C.L. 1933; called to the Bar of Quebec, 1933. Married Bessie Koslov in 1935; two sons, one daughter. Practised law in Montreal from 1933; subsequently also worked in public relations. Director of Education, Zionist Organization of Canada, 1936–37; Editor, *Canadian Zionist* and *Canadian Jewish Chronicle*. Special Lecturer in Poetry, McGill University, 1946–47; a Founder, *Preview*, *First Statement*, and *Northern Review* magazines, Montreal, in the 1940's. Recipient: Edward Bland Fellowship Prize, 1947; Governor-General's Award, 1949; Province of Quebec Literary Prize, 1952; Kovner Memorial Award, 1952; Lorne Pierce Gold Medal, 1957. *Died 21 August 1972.*

PUBLICATIONS

Collections

   Collected Poems, edited by Miriam Waddington.   1974.

Verse

   Hath Not a Jew....   1940.
   Poems.   1944.
   The Hitleriad.   1944.
   Seven Poems.   1947.
   Huit Poèmes Canadiens (En Anglais).   1948.
   The Rocking Chair and Other Poems.   1948.

Play

Hershel of Ostropol, in *Canadian Jewish Chronicle 26* and *27,* 1939.

Fiction

The Second Scroll.   1951.

Other

Translator, *From Palestine to Israel,* by Moishe Dickstein.   1951.
Translator, *Of Jewish Music, Ancient and Modern,* by Israel Rabinovitch.   1952.

Reading List: *Klein* edited by Tom Marshall, 1970; *Klein* by Miriam Waddington, 1970.

*   *   *

The condition of being Jewish, or more positively the fierce sense of Jewish identity, is
the generating feeling and the constitutive, substantial experience of all A. M. Klein's best
poetry up to *The Rocking Chair,* where indeed it is still present if in a calmer, more implied
manner. And the condition of being Jewish, as Klein felt it, is more perplexing a question
than whether or not Klein lost his faith, or regained it, or didn't, as though this were a matter
that could be defined in a chart or scheduled on a timetable once for all. The pattern of being
Jewish revealed in *Hath Not a Jew* and *Poems* includes, it seems to me, at least three notes:
first, the consciousness of the divine as totally other, as the unnameable, unqualified, and
absolute ground of being; second, the enjoyment of a rich immediacy of life, and custom,
habit, rite, symbol, food, of innumerable significant particulars; and third, stretching between
the consciousness of the first and the living of the second, the vital sense of a continuous
tradition: a tradition, it may be added, in which doubt and the questioning of reason have
their place. To celebrate, to recall, to represent, and in doing so, to defend: these are the aims,
not always separate one from another, which inform many of the poems, aims themselves
subordinate to the larger purpose of sustaining the tradition and defining the human reality of
the Jewish experience.

Klein's evocation of the Jewish sensibility is both broad and fine, joining the accuracy of
the intent observer to the warmth of recovered personal experience. It includes history, the
poet's own life, festivals, characters, fairy-tales, legends, psalms, the memories of a child, as
well as carolling children's songs. It takes in not only sages and saints, children and elves,
spidery logicians and gloomy puritans, but also Chaucerian rogues, clowns and dwarfs,
unabashed hypocrites, the querulous devotee, the furious preacher, the bawling junk man,
the matchmaker − "cupid in a caftan" − and the deprecating self, like the mild Moses who so
spared everybody trouble "that in his tomb/He will turn dust to save some room." The rich
portraiture and the manifold differences of an old complex society derive from the poet's own
life, and especially his childhood, and from a wide erudition fed on Jewish learning and
European tradition. The tone is variously reverential and sarcastic, disillusioned and pious,
indignant and resigned, witty and sad; the diction is biblical and lavish but also homely and
colloquial; and the rhythms, whether solemn or nimble, organic and unforced: the whole is
the product of a rarely civilised mind in possession of a marvellously humane tradition.

The world constituted in these Jewish poems has solidity and bloom and an intensely
living presence, and just occasionally a taste of molasses. It is also torn and stricken by
history, its existence constantly menaced and intermittently ravaged, so that one receives the
paradoxical impression of something both ancient and brimming with life standing

precariously on the edge of dissolution or – since this phrase may suggest the possibility of inward collapse – expecting some oceanic invasion. Working from deep within this tradition Klein's sensibility manifests the opposed attitudes corresponding to the double character of the Jewish universe: the tenderness and reverence for the humanity embodied in the tradition together with the keenest relish for its unique savour, and the hard reaction to external hostility, a stony pride of resistance.

Klein is one of the few serious Canadian writers untroubled by the problem of identity and free of its attendant, modish hysteria about alienation. His work has in it all the richness, the inclusiveness, of the Jewish character and mind, the product of an ancient, sophisticated, oppressed, and still living tradition. At the same time he is alert to the several nuances of contemporary Canadian life, and the marriage of a suffering but essential serenity with a nervous and accurate response make for a poetry which is altogether independent but also splendidly central.

The Rocking Chair, Klein's final appearance as a poet (apart from the verse in *The Second Scroll*), came out in 1948. A case could be made for its being the best single book of verse ever to be published in Canada and one of the best in English anywhere since the war. Not that it is by any means flawless. There is more than a suspicion of North American molasses in "The Sugaring," as well as rather too much unassimilated Hopkins, a degree too feverish a nostalgia in "The Sisters of the Hôtel Dieu," and more than a hint of linguistic intoxication in "Montreal," repeated readings of which leave one irritated at its contrivance and artificiality. In the achieved poems an imagination charged with history and a consciousness clarified by an ancient coherence are brought to bear on persons, places, things, processes, and conditions – saltily, stingingly, fresh, and Canadian. The past in the poet is locked with the present in the object. The effect is to produce a reality which has both roundness and depth. Each clean surface is backed by a thick supporting texture of allusion and reference from history, literature, traditional assumption, and racial memory and luminous Jewish reverence for the life of the word and the book, an unbroken order or human experience. The interior of the refrigerator deepens into a Laurentian village, "tiered and bright"; the commercial bank opens into a flowering jungle concealing silent beasts pawing the ground; bakers at their ovens appear as Levites at their altars; the dress manufacturer as he fishes becomes "at the end of his filament,/a correspondent of water and of fish"; the Quebec liquor commission store turns magically into Ali Baba's cave, offering the pleasures of "the sycophancy of glass, the palm's cool courtier,/and the feel of straw, all rough and rustical"; the break-up of the ice raises from the tomb "the pyramid fish, the unlockered ships,/and last year's blue and bloated suicides"; the social guilt implied in the pawnshop makes it "Our own gomorrah house,/the sodom that merely to look at makes one salt."

Klein's creative generosity, that is, works first to establish the being of the object, event, place, or experience at the centre of the poem, and then to enlarge its significance. The essential quality and inward shape sustain the meaning. So that, for example, in "The Rocking Chair," "Grain Elevator," "The Spinning Wheel," the thing becomes an image, the image a symbol, the symbol a style of life and feeling. Each of the major poems in *The Rocking Chair* testifies to the ease and authority with which Klein treats his Canadian theme. In this work we see detachment telescoped into identity. In none of the poems is the Jew in Klein ousted by the Canadian. Rather a sensibility fed by one of the most ancient sources of human quality shows itself superbly qualified to cope with a new hospitality to experience, and to see in the Canadian example the universal human thing. So that these poems work by combining distance and intimacy, perspective and grain, and find "the thing that makes them one" in what is common and human.

> Or find it, find it, find it commonplace
> but effective, valid, real, the unity
> In the family feature, the not unsimilar face....

The ironic truth of our strange age, enunciated by Klein in "Portrait of the Poet as

Landscape," a poem notable for its wit, strength, and undespairing acceptance of a despairing part, is that the making of these creative connections, the articulation of our human experience, is the business of someone who has been dismissed from real society, the poet. He is missing but not missed, "a Mr. Smith in a hotel register − /incognito, lost...."

—William Walsh

KUNITZ, Stanley (Jasspon).   American.   Born in Worcester, Massachusetts, 29 July 1905. Educated at Harvard University, Cambridge, Massachusetts (Garrison Medal, 1926), A.B. (summa cum laude) 1926 (Phi Beta Kappa), A.M. 1927. Served in the United States Army, 1943–45: Staff Sergeant. Married 1) Helen Pearce in 1930 (divorced, 1937), one daughter; 2) Eleanor Evans in 1939 (divorced, 1958); 3) Elise Asher in 1958. Editor, *Wilson Library Bulletin*, New York, 1928–43; Member of the Faculty, Bennington College, Vermont, 1946–59; Professor of English, State University of New York at Potsdam, 1949–50, and Summers 1949–53; Lecturer, and Director of the Poetry Workshop, New School for Social Research, New York, 1950–57; Visiting Professor of Poetry, University of Washington, Seattle, 1955–56; Visiting Professor of English, Queens College, Flushing, New York, 1956–57, and Brandeis University, Waltham, Massachusetts, 1958–59; Director, YM-YWHA Poetry Workshop, New York, 1958–62; Danforth Visiting Lecturer, various American colleges, 1961–63; Fellow, 1969, and Visiting Professor of Poetry, 1970, Yale University, New Haven, Connecticut. Lecturer, 1963–67, and since 1967 Adjunct Professor of Writing, Graduate School of the Arts, Columbia University, New York. Since 1968, Chairman, Writing Department, Fine Arts Work Center, Provincetown, Massachusetts; since 1969, Editor, Yale Series of Younger Poets, Yale University Press. Formerly, Cultural Exchange Lecturer, U.S.S.R. and Poland. Consultant in Poetry, Library of Congress, Washington, D.C., 1974–76. Recipient: Guggenheim Fellowship, 1945; Amy Lowell Traveling Fellowship, 1953; Harriet Monroe Award, 1958; Pulitzer Prize, 1959; Ford Foundation grant, 1959; National Institute of Arts and Letters grant, 1959; Brandeis University Creative Arts Award, 1964; Academy of American Poets Fellowship, 1968; American Academy of Arts and Letters Award of Merit, 1975; Translation Center grant, 1975. Litt.D.: Clark University, Worcester, Massachusetts, 1961. Member, American Academy of Arts and Letters; Chancellor, Academy of American Poets, 1970. Lives in New York City.

PUBLICATIONS

Verse

Intellectual Things.   1930.
Passport to the War: A Selection of Poems.   1944.
Selected Poems 1928–1958.   1958.
The Testing-Tree.   1971.
The Terrible Threshold: Selected Poems, 1940–1970.   1974.

Other

A Kind of Order, A Kind of Folly: Essays and Conversations.   1975.

Editor, *Living Authors: A .Book of Biographies.*   1931.
Editor, with Howard Haycraft and Wilbur C. Hadden, *Authors Today and Yesterday: A Companion Volume to "Living Authors".*   1933.
Editor, with others, *The Junior Book of Authors.*   1934; revised edition, 1961.
Editor, with Howard Haycraft, *British Authors of the Nineteenth Century.*   1936.
Editor, with Howard Haycraft, *American Authors, 1600–1900: A Biographical Dictionary of American Literature.*   1938.
Editor, with Howard Haycraft, *Twentieth Century Authors: A Biographical Dictionary of Modern Literature.*   1942; *First Supplement,* with Vineta Colby, 1955.
Editor, with Howard Haycraft, *British Authors Before 1800: A Biographical Dictionary.*   1952.
Editor, *Poems,* by John Keats.   1964.
Editor, with Vineta Colby, *European Authors, 1000–1900: A Biographical Dictionary of European Literature.*   1967.
Editor and Translator, with Max Hayward, *Poems of Akhmatova.*   1973.

Translator, with others, *Antiworlds and the Fifth Ace,* by Andrei Voznesensky.   1967.
Translator, with others, *Stolen Apples,* by Yevgeny Yevtushenko.   1972.
Translator, with others, *Story under Full Sail,* by Andrei Voznesensky.   1974.

Reading List: "The Poetry of Kunitz" by James Hagstrum, in *Poets in Progress,* edited by Edward Hungerford, 1962; *The Comtemporary Poet as Artist and Critic* edited by Anthony Ostroff, 1964; "Man with a Leaf in His Head" by Stanley Moss, in *The Nation,* 20 September 1971.

*   *   *

Stanley Kunitz's *Selected Poems 1928–1958* offers us a good standard of the classic forms and modes of American poetry that largely governed poets of these three decades. Kunitz has more often fought the form imposed on his sometimes extravagant lyrical language than given in to it, and where this creative conflict between a restless content and a rigid, enveloping form is sustained the result has unusual vigor and freshness. The effect is of loosely woven statements held under intense pressure of symmetry and repeated rhythm, as in this nervous, jaggedly expressed love lyric, "Green Ways":

> Let me not say it, let me not reveal
> How like a god my heart begins to climb
> The trellis of the crystal
> In the rose-green moon;
> Let me not say it, let me leave untold
> This legend, while the nights snow emerald.
>
> Let me not say it, let me not confess
> How in the leaflight of my green-celled world
> In self's pre-history
> The blind moulds kiss;
> Let me not say it, let me but endure
> This ritual like feather and like star.

Let me proclaim it – human be my lot! –
How from my pit of green horse-bones
I turn, in a wilderness of sweat,
To the moon-breasted sibylline,
And lift this garland, Danger, from her throat
To blaze it in the foundries of the night.

But "Green Ways" is the balance that Kunitz has not always been able to strike in his poetry; here passion and form give way to each other, but in some of his work the feeling has been too thoroughly subdued by order and conscious craft, creating a lyric that is too dry and rehearsed in its utterance. But even in the severest of his poems, the reader is aware of the intensity of the poet's mind, the irrepressible energy of his imagination.

Often called the poet's poet, a term he has tended to dismiss more vigorously in later years, Kunitz has himself defended the unruly side of the poetic medium. As editor of the Yale Younger Poets Series, Kunitz has been enthusiastic in his advocacy of a poetry of process and impulsive strategies. In his occasional and critical prose, he has also tended to favor the ungoverned muse: in his essay "A Kind of Order" he says: "With young writers I make a nuisance of myself talking about order, for the good reason that order is teachable; but in my bones I know that only the troubled spirits among them, those who recognize the disorder without and within, have a chance to become poets."

In the strictest balance, however, Kunitz's *Selected Poems* conveys, even it its most rigid formulations of lyric, a stubbornly individual mind that has known all the extremes of feeling and mood. "Night-Piece," "The Man Upstairs" with its Eliotic strain of irony and wit, the poems gathered under the section "The Terrible Threshold" and much else in this collection are provocative and vital.

—Paul Christensen

LARKIN, Philip (Arthur).   English.   Born in Coventry, Warwickshire, 9 August 1922. Educated at King Henry VIII School, Coventry; St. John's College, Oxford, B.A. 1943, M.A. 1947. Held posts in various U.K. libraries, 1943–55. Since 1955, Librarian, Brynmor Jones Library, University of Hull, Yorkshire. Jazz Feature Writer, *Daily Telegraph*, London, 1961–71; Visiting Fellow, All Souls College, Oxford, 1970–71. Recipient: Arts Council Prize, 1965; Queen's Gold Medal for Poetry, 1965; Cholmondeley Award, 1973; Russell Loines Award, 1974; Yorkshire Art Association Award, 1975; FVS Foundation of Hamburg Shakespeare Prize, 1976. D.Litt.: Queen's University of Belfast, 1969; University of Leicester, 1970; University of Warwick, 1973; University of St Andrews, 1974; University of Sussex, Brighton, 1974. Honorary Fellow, St. John's College, Oxford, 1973. Fellow, and Benson Medallist, 1975, Royal Society of Literature; Honorary Member, American Academy of Arts and Sciences, 1975. C.B.E. (Commander, Order of the British Empire), 1975. Lives in Hull, Yorkshire.

PUBLICATIONS

Verse

The North Ship.   1945; revised edition, 1966.
XX Poems.   1951.

(Poems).   1954.
The Less Deceived.   1955.
The Whitsun Weddings.   1964.
High Windows.   1974.

Fiction

Jill.   1946; revised edition, 1964.
A Girl in Winter.   1947.

Other

All What Jazz: A Record Diary 1961–68.   1970.

Editor, with Bonamy Dobrée and Louis MacNeice, *New Poems 1958.*   1958.
Editor, *The Oxford Book of Twentieth Century Verse.*   1973.

Reading List: *Larkin* by David Timms, 1973; *An Uncommon Poet for the Common Man: A Study of Larkin's Poetry* by Lolette Kuby, 1974; *Larkin* by Alan Brownjohn, 1975.

*   *   *

For more than twenty years Philip Larkin has been the most admired poet of his generation in England, though his reputation has not extended to other parts of the English-speaking world. American readers, for instance, seem to have difficulty in tuning into Larkin's accents or appreciating his themes. His first collection, *The North Ship*, attracted little attention; indeed it was scarcely known until a new edition appeared in 1966. Larkin's earliest poetry was rhetorical and Yeatsian. He soon decided that Yeats was not the right model for him, and that his true poetic master was Thomas Hardy, whom he still admires enormously. But something permanent remained from the Yeatsian phase: the capacity to produce a rich, emphatic, memorable line, and great skill in handling complex stanza forms. *The North Ship* was followed in the late forties by two accomplished novels, *Jill* and *A Girl in Winter*, both studies of sensitive, lonely young people, drawing in part on autobiographical material. But Larkin seems to have made a deliberate decision not to continue with fiction and has since restricted himself to poetry. His first mature collection, *The Less Deceived*, made a considerable impact, but Larkin writes poems slowly and infrequently, and only two collections have been published since then.

Yet though Larkin's rate of production is not high his poetic craftsmanship is exemplary, and is admired even by readers who find his emotional range too narrow. He is a formally traditional poet, in the line of Hardy, Graves, Edward Thomas, and the best of the Georgians, and on the face of it he has little time for the modernism of Eliot and Pound. Nevertheless, his diction and metrics show that he has not been unaffected by poetic modernism. Even though he no longer writes fiction, Larkin brings a novelist's power of observation to the writing of poetry: he notes carefully, if without enthusiasm, the changing appearance of things in post-war English society. He writes coolly, sometimes affectionately, about provincial or suburban landscape and the frequent defeats and occasional triumphs of everyday human existence. Critics who deplore his seeming narrowness have referred to Larkin's "suburban mental ratio." He has indeed caught in his poetry something of the urbanized or suburbanized way of life of most contemporary English people, even the very tones of voice, as well as a certain familiar atmosphere of resentment and small aims and ideals. This sense of recognition certainly accounts for part of his appeal.

But he is far more than a social observer or commentator in verse, however acute and sensitive. Compared with the great poets of the recent past – the heroic generation of modernism – he is undeniably narrow; but he is also deep, in his own characteristic way. Each of his mature volumes contains one or two longish, finely wrought poems which touch on the major and perennial themes of existence: death in "Church Going" (*The Less Deceived*); love and marriage in the title poem of *The Whitsun Weddings*, and love and death in "An Arundel Tomb" in the same collection; old age in "The Old Fools" and death in "The Building" (*High Windows*). Each of his collections, too, contains a number of short lyrics, sometimes difficult, but all of marked aesthetic intensity and at times hauntingly beautiful: "Coming," "Going," "Age," "Absences," "Water," "Days," "Afternoons." Larkin's mood is, admittedly, often bleak or sad or autumnal, occasionally even despairing. But certain poems attain a note of celebration, like "The Trees" or "Show Saturday" (*High Windows*). Profoundly agnostic, Larkin still finds value and consolation in the recurring rituals that bring human beings together, like a funeral, a wedding, an annual horse-show. Reading Larkin one misses large gestures of affirmation or defiance – the kind of thing he found he could not accept in Yeats – and their absence can be a little lowering. But Larkin's poetry offers many satisfactions: like other good poets he has made positive poems out of negative feelings.

—Bernard Bergonzi

LAWRENCE, D(avid) H(erbert). English. Born in Eastwood, Nottinghamshire, 11 September 1885. Educated at Nottingham High School, 1898–1901; University College, Nottingham, now University of Nottingham, 1906–08: teacher's certificate, 1908. Eloped with Frieda Weekley in 1912, married in 1914. Worked for a firm of surgical appliance makers, Nottingham, 1901; teacher in Eastwood and Ilkeston, Nottinghamshire, 1902–06; teacher at the Davidson Road School, Croydon, Surrey, 1908–12; full-time writer from 1912; lived in Germany, 1912–14; in England, 1914–19; Editor, with Katherine Mansfield and John Middleton Murry, *The Signature* magazine, 1915; prosecuted for obscenity (*The Rainbow*), 1915; left England, 1919, and travelled in Australia, Mexico, Sicily, and Sardinia; lived in the southwestern United States, Mexico, and Italy. Also a painter: one-man show, London, 1929 (closed by the police). Recipient; Black Memorial Prize, 1921. *Died 2 March 1930.*

PUBLICATIONS

Collections

    Collected Letters, edited by Harry T. Moore.   2 vols., 1962.
    Complete Poems, edited by Vivian de Sola Pinto and F. Warren Roberts.   2 vols., 1964.
    Complete Plays.   1965.
    A Selection, edited by R. H. Poole and P. J. Shepherd.   1970.

Verse

    Love Poems and Others.   1913.
    Amores.   1916.

Look! We Have Come Through! 1917.
New Poems. 1918.
Bay. 1919.
Tortoises. 1921.
Birds, Beasts, and Flowers. 1923.
Collected Poems. 2 vols., 1928.
Pansies. 1929.
Nettles. 1930.
Last Poems, edited by Richard Aldington and Giuseppe Orioli. 1932.
Fire and Other Poems. 1940.

Plays

The Widowing of Mrs. Holroyd (produced 1920). 1914.
Touch and Go. 1920.
David (produced 1927). 1926.
A Collier's Friday Night (produced 1965). 1934.
The Daughter-in-Law (produced 1967). In *Complete Plays*, 1965.
The Fight for Barbara (produced 1967). In *Complete Plays*, 1965.
The Married Man, and *The Merry-Go-Round*, in *Complete Plays*. 1965.

Fiction

The White Peacock. 1911; edited by Harry T. Moore, 1966.
The Trespasser. 1912.
Sons and Lovers. 1913; edited by Julian Moynahan, 1968; *A Facsimile of a Manuscript*, edited by Mark Schorer, 1978.
The Prussian Officer and Other Stories. 1914.
The Rainbow. 1915.
Women in Love. 1920.
The Lost Girl. 1920.
Aaron's Rod. 1922.
England My England and Other Stories. 1922.
The Ladybird, The Fox, The Captain's Doll. 1923; as *The Captain's Doll: Three Novelettes*, 1923.
Kangaroo. 1923.
The Boy in the Bush, with M. L. Skinner. 1924.
St. Mawr, Together with The Princess. 1925.
The Plumed Serpent (Quetzalcoatl). 1926.
Sun (story). 1926; unexpurgated edition, 1928.
Glad Ghosts (story). 1926.
Rawdon's Roof (story). 1928.
The Woman Who Rode Away and Other Stories. 1928.
Lady Chatterley's Lover. 1928; *The First Lady Chatterley* (first version), 1944; *La Tre Lady Chatterley* (three versions), in Italian, 1954; *John Thomas and Lady Jane* (second version), 1972.
The Escaped Cock. 1929; as *The Man Who Died*, 1931.
The Virgin and the Gipsy. 1930.
Love among the Haystacks and Other Pieces. 1930.
The Lovely Lady (stories). 1933.
A Modern Lover (stories). 1934.
A Prelude (story). 1949.

The Princess and Other Stories, and *The Mortal Coil and Other Stories*, edited by Keith Sagar.   2 vols., 1971.

Other

Twilight in Italy.   1916.
Movements in European History.   1921; revised edition, 1926.
Psychoanalysis and the Unconscious.   1921.
Sea and Sardinia.   1921.
Fantasia of the Unconscious.   1922.
Studies in Classic American Literature.   1923; edited by Armin Arnold, as *The Symbolic Meaning: The Uncollected Versions*, 1962.
Reflections on the Death of a Porcupine and Other Essays.   1925.
Mornings in Mexico.   1927.
The Paintings of Lawrence.   1929.
My Skirmish with Jolly Roger (introduction to *Lady Chatterley's Lover*).   1929; as *A Propos of Lady Chatterley's Lover*, 1930.
Pornography and Obscenity.   1929.
Assorted Articles.   1930.
Apocalypse.   1931.
Letters, edited by Aldous Huxley.   1932.
Etruscan Places.   1932.
We Need One Another.   1933.
Phoenix: The Posthumous Papers, edited by Edward D. McDonald.   1936.
The Paintings, edited by Mervyn Levy.   1964.
Phoenix II: Uncollected, Unpublished, and Other Prose Works, edited by F. Warren Roberts and Harry T. Moore.   1968.
Lawrence in Love: Letters to Louie Burrows, edited by James T. Boulton.   1968.
Centaur Letters, edited by Edward D. McDonald.   1970.
Letters to Martin Secker, 1911–30, edited by Martin Secker.   1970.
The Quest for Ranamim: Letters to S. S. Koteliansky, 1914–30, edited by G. J. Zytaruk.   1970.
Letters to Thomas and Adele Seltzer: Letters to His American Publishers, edited by Gerald M. Lacy.   1976.

Translator, with S. S. Koteliansky, *All Things Are Possible*, by Leo Shestov.   1920.
Translator, *Mastro-Don Gesualdo*, by Giovanni Verga.   1923.
Translator, *Little Novels of Sicily*, by Giovanni Verga.   1925.
Translator, *Cavalleria Rusticana and Other Stories*, by Giovanni Verga.   1928.
Translator, *The Story of Doctor Manente*, by A. F. Grazzini.   1929.
Translator, with S. S. Koteliansky, *The Grand Inquisitor*, by Dostoevsky.   1930.

Bibliography: *A Bibliography of Lawrence* by F. Warren Roberts, 1963.

Reading List: *The Intelligent Heart*, 1954, revised edition, as *The Priest of Love*, 1974, and *The Life and Works of Lawrence*, revised edition, 1964, both by Harry T. Moore; *Lawrence, Novelist* by F. R. Leavis, 1955; *The Love Ethic of Lawrence* by Mark Spilka, 1955, and *Lawrence: A Collection of Critical Essays* edited by Spilka, 1963; *The Dark Sun: A Study of Lawrence* by Graham Hough, 1956; *Lawrence: A Composite Biography* edited by Edward Nehls, 3 vols., 1957–59; *The Deed of Life: The Novels and Tales of Lawrence* by Julian Moynahan, 1963; *Lawrence* by R. P. Draper, 1964, and *Lawrence: The Critical Heritage* edited by Draper, 1970; *Double Measure: A Study of the Novels and Stories of Lawrence* by

George H. Ford, 1965; *The Art of Lawrence* by Keith Sagar, 1966; *Acts of Attention: The Poems of Lawrence* by Sandra M. Gilbert, 1972; *Lawrence* by Frank Kermode, 1973.

* * *

D. H. Lawrence's background, which was an important influence on his work, is best described in his own essay "Nottingham and the Mining Countryside." Life in late nineteenth-century Eastwood, he says, "was a curious cross between industrialism and the old agricultural England of Shakespeare and Milton and Fielding and George Eliot." His father, a semi-literate miner who spoke the Nottinghamshire and Derbyshire dialect, was essentially working-class in habits and outlook, but his mother, who had been a schoolteacher, spoke "King's English" and prided herself on her superiority to the world into which she had married. Their son owed much to both. It was his mother who encouraged him to develop his intelligence and took pride in his educational achievements, but it was from his father's sensuousness and the "intimate community" of the miners that he derived his later belief in the overriding importance of non-intellectual contact between men and women and of intuitive awareness rather than scientific knowledge.

Lawrence's first important novel, *Sons and Lovers*, is a study of working-class life seen from within. In it he draws extensively on his own background and personal experience. Mr. and Mrs. Morel are fictional portraits of his mother and father, and their son Paul has much in common with Lawrence himself. Similarly, his youthful sweetheart, Jessie Chambers, is reflected in the character of Miriam Leivers, and the farm where she lives is based on the Haggs', near Eastwood, which helped to give Lawrence his deep understanding of, and passion for, English country life. The theme of the novel is mother-love as a dominating and destructive force. Lawrence himself comments that Mrs. Morel's sons, William and Paul, are "urged into life by their reciprocal love of their mother.... But when they come to manhood, they can't love, because their mother is the strongest power in their lives, and holds them" (letter of 14 November 1912). But the mother is also a vital, energetic force in Paul's life. Although her opposition to Miriam as a sweetheart for her son is in part the result of jealousy (they compete for the same intellectual interest), it is also based on a shrewd recognition that Miriam's soulful possessiveness is inimical to her son's fulfilment.

The sensuousness which Paul Morel inherits from his father finds expression in his purely physical relationship with Clara. In this part of the novel, as in certain passages of natural description which have a powerful, but indefinable, symbolic quality, Lawrence anticipates the exploration of unconscious influences on human relationships which becomes the primary theme of his two greatest novels, *The Rainbow* and *Women in Love*. Here Lawrence makes important innovations in characterization. The emphasis on analysis of motives and moral choice typical of nineteenth-century realism gives way to a sense that a subterranean life force takes over and directs the main characters at critical moments in their relations with each other. As Lawrence puts it, "You mustn't look in my novel [*The Rainbow*] for the old stable *ego* – of the character ... don't look for the development of the novel to follow the lines of certain characters: the characters fall into the form of some other rhythmic form, as when one draws a fiddle bow across a fine tray delicately sanded, the sand takes lines unknown" (letter of 5 June 1914).

In *The Rainbow* three generations of the Brangwen family struggle successively to find a balanced relationship in which their strong, instinctive sense of oneness with the natural world is harmonised with the conscious intelligence and mechanical sophistication which are increasingly the marks of modern industrialised society. A tentative resolution is achieved in the first generation when Tom and Lydia meet, like a rainbow, "to the span of the heavens" with their child Anna "free to play in the space beneath, between"; but in the succeeding generations the struggle is both intensified and less satisfactory in outcome, culminating in the complete collapse of the relationship between Ursula and Skrebensky in the third generation.

The method Lawrence employs in *The Rainbow* is highly original, and yet the result is not an obviously "experimental" novel such as Joyce's *Ulysses* or Virginia Woolf's *The Waves*. It is still, like *Sons and Lovers,* in many respects a vivid record of life in the English midlands of the late nineteenth and early twentieth century, and it has many scenes of compelling emotional realism; but it transcends these to become a symbolist exploration of human relations seen in the context of the natural rhythm of life itself, and expressed in a language which has strong biblical overtones. The result is a work which is often repetitive, sometimes obscure, and occasionally pretentious, but always bristling with a compelling immediacy of experience which demands an intensely personal response from the reader.

Women in Love (originally conceived as an integral part of *The Rainbow*) continues the experiences of Ursula into a new relationship with Rupert Birkin, which is presented as the creative counterpart to the destructive relationship between her sister, Gudrun, and Birkin's friend, Gerald Crich. Marriage and personal fulfilment through the sexual relationship remains the theme of this novel, but a further dimension is added to it by Birkin's role as prophet of a new conception of "polarity" between man and woman, which involves both mutual commitment and a balanced independence. Birkin also believes in the need for a relationship of "blood brotherhood" between man and man to complement the marital relationship between man and woman. Altogether *Women in Love* is the most ambitious of Lawrence's novels. Criticism of social and economic conditions, a major preoccupation with Lawrence during and after the war years, mounts here to a sweeping denunciation of the devitalised materialism of contemporary England, and is skilfully interlocked with symbolic scenes which, like those of *Sons and Lovers* and *The Rainbow*, remain mysteriously evocative while being more purposefully organised in accordance with an almost epic, or mythic, design. Some of the faults of *The Rainbow* remain, and Lawrence's didacticism is at times excessive (though this is qualified by the self-criticism which is incorporated into the character of Birkin), but despite these flaws *Women in Love* is Lawrence's masterpiece and one of the undoubted classics of modern literature.

The novels which follow *Women in Love* are disappointingly inferior. The best of these is *Lady Chatterley's Lover* which has a tautness of structure and clarity of theme lacking in *Aaron's Rod* and *Kangaroo*, while its return to the treatment of the sexual relationship in warm, personal terms is a welcome contrast to the doctrinaire abstractions and the pseudo-religious revivalism of *The Plumed Serpent*. But even *Lady Chatterley* has an unsatisfactorily simplified schematic quality compared with *Sons and Lovers*, *The Rainbow*, and *Women in Love*.

There is, however, no reason to suspect a flagging of creative effort if one takes into account the tales, poems, travel books, and critical essays, and the marvellous spontaneity of the stream of letters, written without any thought of publication, which continued to flow from Lawrence's pen in the years after 1916. His special flair for the short story genre is apparent in his earliest work, in tales of the Nottingham environment such as "Odour of Chrysanthemums" and "Daughters of the Vicar," which show remarkable skill in combining atmosphere, psychological truth, and moral discrimination in terms of what makes for and against living fulfilment. These qualities are continued in the "long short stories" of his middle period, but joined with a more highly developed capacity for conveying levels of meaning which are subversive of conventionally accepted standards. In "The Ladybird" this is suggested through the dark, hypnotic influence of Count Psanek on Lady Daphne, a forerunner of the relationship between Mellors and Connie in *Lady Chatterley*, though the story is marred by the self-consciously "poetic" prose in which it is written. (A more successful attempt at the same theme is made in *The Virgin and the Gipsy*.) The colloquial freedom and syntactic naturalness of "The Fox" and "The Captain's Doll" are more characteristic of Lawrence's short story style, though in themselves they have quite separate and distinct virtues. "The Fox" is a powerful fusion of realism and symbolism, while "The Captain's Doll" is a triumph of tone and humour, looking forward to the more specifically satirical short stories such as "Things" and "The Man Who Loved Islands."

The best of Lawrence's prose work in his last years is to be found in *The Man Who Died* (first printed as *The Escaped Cock*), a re-interpretation of Christianity through the story of

Jesus risen in the flesh to a new appreciation of the sensuous world and physical love. Like the travel book *Etruscan Places*, it is essentially a visionary work, offering a criticism of the modern world, but indirectly through an imaginative re-creation of a way of life enhanced by the vitality and sense of wonder which have all but disappeared from the present. In this respect it is akin to the poetry of Lawrence's *Last Poems*, which meditate on death, but in so doing heighten his keen sense of the lambent, instantaneous quality of life.

The rare achievement of Lawrence's poetry has still not been given the recognition which it deserves. When writing in traditional forms, i.e., mostly in his early verse, he often seems ill-at-ease, struggling to say something for which his medium is unsuited, but in the more fluent mode of free verse, which he used with an instinctive sense of rhythm and appropriate line length that exerted its own flexible control, he found the perfect means for communicating "direct utterance from the instant whole man" (Preface to the American edition of *New Poems*). The themes are often those of the novels and stories, but the implicit disclaimer of finality enables him to give those themes a freshness and tentativeness of expression which is a welcome relief from the assertiveness of the prose. "End of Another Home Holiday," for example, achieves a delicacy of poise between disapproval of, and sympathy for, maternal love which is perhaps finer than that of *Sons and Lovers*; and the poems of *Birds, Beasts, and Flowers*, especially "Snake" and the first part of "Fish," communicate (better than, for example, the short novel *St. Mawr* does) that sense of the inviolable otherness of the living, non-human world which acts by its very presence as a criticism of man's abuse of his own instinctual being.

His early dialect verse, like the best of his plays (*The Widowing of Mrs. Holroyd* and especially *The Daughter-in-Law*), faithfully reflects the mocking, un-stuffy, working-class voice of his Nottinghamshire background; and it is this tone of voice which gives the verse of *Pansies* and *Nettles* (labelled "satirical doggerel" by W. H. Auden) its mocking, deflationary humour. Here Lawrence, the prophet, brings himself down to earth and saves himself from his own messianic over-assertiveness. As he puts it in the poem "St. Matthew":

> So I will be lifted up, Saviour,
> But put me down again in time Master,
> Before my heart stops beating, and I become what I am not.

—R. P. Draper

LAYTON, Irving (Peter). Canadian. Born in Neamtz, Rumania, 12 March 1912; emigrated to Canada in 1913. Educated at Alexandra Public School, Montreal; Byron Bing High School, Montreal; MacDonald College, Sainte Anne de Bellevue, Quebec, B.Sc. in agriculture 1939; McGill University, Montreal, M.A. 1946. Served in the Canadian Army, 1942–43: Lieutenant. Married 1) Betty Frances Sutherland in 1946; one son, one daughter; 2) the writer Aviva Cantor in 1961, one son. Lecturer, Jewish Public Library, Montreal, 1943–58; high school teacher in Montreal, 1954–60; Part-time Lecturer, 1949–65, and Poet-in-Residence, 1965–66, Sir George Williams University, Montreal; Writer-in-Residence, University of Guelph, Ontario, 1968–69. Since 1969, Professor of English Literature, York University, Toronto. Co-Founding Editor, *First Statement*, later *Northern Review*, Montreal, 1941–43; former Associate Editor, *Contact* magazine, Toronto, and *Black Mountain Review*, North Carolina. Recipient: Canada Foundation Fellowship, 1957; Canada Council Award, 1959, 1967, and senior arts grant and travel grant, 1973; Governor-General's Award, 1960; President's Medal, University of Western Ontario, 1961. D.C.L.: Bishop's University, Lennoxville, Quebec, 1970. Lives in Toronto.

PUBLICATIONS

Verse

Here and Now.   1945.
Now Is the Place: Stories and Poems.   1948.
The Black Huntsman.   1951.
Cerberus, with Raymond Souster and Louis Dudek.   1952.
Love the Conqueror Worm.   1953.
In the Midst of My Fever.   1954.
The Cold Green Element.   1955.
The Blue Propeller.   1955.
The Blue Calf and Other Poems.   1956.
Music on a Kazoo.   1956.
Improved Binoculars: Selected Poems.   1956.
A Laughter in the Mind.   1958; augmented edition, 1959.
A Red Carpet for the Sun: Collected Poems.   1959.
The Swinging Flesh (poems and stories).   1961.
Balls for a One-Armed Juggler.   1963.
The Laughing Rooster.   1964.
Collected Poems.   1965.
Periods of the Moon.   1967.
The Shattered Plinths.   1968.
The Whole Bloody Bird (obs, aphs, and pomes).   1969.
Selected Poems, edited by Wynne Francis.   1969.
Five Modern Canadian Poets, with others, edited by Eli Mandel.   1970.
Collected Poems.   1971.
Nail Polish.   1971.
Lovers and Lesser Men.   1973.
Selected Poems.   1974.
The Pole Vaulter.   1974.
Seventy-Five Grub Poems.   1974.
The Unwavering Eye: Selected Poems, 1969–1975.   1975.
Selected Poems.   1977.

Other

Engagements: The Prose of Layton, edited by Seymour Mayne.   1972.
Taking Sides: The Collected Social and Political Writings, edited by Howard Aster.   1977.

Editor, with Louis Dudek, *Canadian Poems 1850–1952.*   1952
Editor, *Pan-ic: A Selection of Contemporary Canadian Poems.*   1958.
Editor, *Poems for 27 Cents.*   1961.
Editor, *Love Where the Nights Are Long: Canadian Love Poems.*   1962.
Editor, *Anvil: A Selection of Workshop Poems.*   1966.
Editor, *Poems to Colour: A Selection of Workshop Poems.*   1970.
Editor, *Anvil Blood: A Selection of Workshop Poems.*   1973.

Bibliography: "Layton: A Bibliography in Progress 1931–1971" by Seymour Mayne, in *West Coast Review*, January 1973.

Reading List: "That Heaven-Sent Lively Ropewalker, Layton" by Hayden Carruth, in *Tamarack Review,* Spring 1966; *Layton* by Eli Mandel, 1969.

*   *   *

Irving Layton is undoubtedly the most prolific of Canadian poets; since his first book, *Here and Now,* appeared in 1945, hardly a year has passed without another volume or at least a brochure of his verse appearing. He has also written some short stories and a few polemical essays, the best of which were collected by his fellow poet, Seymour Mayne, in a volume entitled *Engagements.* As an editor he has been involved in a number of North American verse magazines, including *First Statement* and *Contact* in Canada, and *Black Mountain Review* in the United States. But is is essentially as a poet that Layton sees himself and makes sure that the world sees him.

Layton is a poet of various styles and equally various levels of quality; he belongs to no school and has borrowed effects from all of them. Readers are often puzzled that so much energy and so much genuine talent should be accompanied by such an evident lack of self-criticism – a lack which means that more than half of any volume Layton publishes is likely to consist of poems that should never have passed beyond the writer's desk. At the same time they are often stirred to admiration by his best poems which, as Northrop Frye has pointed out, reveal Layton as "an erudite elegiac poet, whose technique turns on an aligning of the romantic and the ironic."

Layton's work can really be considered in three phases. He first published, largely at his own expense, a series of thin volumes of verbose and flamboyant verses strong in self-advertisement and in cheap shocks for respectable minds. By the early 1950's, however, Layton was beginning to find himself; in volumes like *The Cold Green Element* his real power as a poet of compassion, in love with the splendour and sad with the transience of life, begins to emerge. It is admirably exemplified in the poem – obliquely celebrating Layton's hero Nietzsche – "The Birth of Tragedy":

> A quiet madman, never far from tears,
> > I lie like a slain thing
> > under the green air the trees
> inhabit, or rest upon a chair
> > towards which the inflammable air
> tumbles on many robins' wings;
> > noting how seasonably
> > leaf and blossom uncurl
> and living things arrange their death,
> while someone from afar off
> blows birthday candles for the world.

The period from about 1953 to 1965 can perhaps be regarded as the climax of Layton's career, when he wrote the series of vivid and moving lyrics and elegies that make his *Collected Poems* of 1965 the true core of his work, its best items rarely equalled by any of the many volumes he has published during the years since then.

It was during the 1960's that Layton moved out of small-press printing into commercial publication, while writing as prolifically as he had always done; in this decade also he became the most popular among the Canadian poets who during this period turned public entertainer, his combination of inspired rhetoric and sexual clowning making him popular with the young audience of the period's counter-culture. What has been really surprising, in view of the volume of work that Layton has continued to produce, is the lack of real change or development in his work since the middle 1960's. His poetry remains essentially didactic and constantly agitated; one encounters repeatedly – and to the degree of boredom – the familiar obsessions with sex, with the poet's ego, with the poet's detractors, with those the poet despises, the glorifications of creativity and life as against order and art, of Dionysus as against Apollo, the hatred of critics, the love for the trival and juvenile epigram, the deliberate Nietzschean waywardness. What has declined is the immediacy of the lyric urge. In recent years Layton has written no poems that really compare with the earlier series of splendidly passionate and compassionate elegies on the human and animal condition which place Layton among the best Canadian poets.

—George Woodcock

LEE, Laurie.   British.   Born in Stroud, Gloucestershire, 26 June 1914. Educated at Slad Village School, Gloucestershire, and Stroud Central School. During World War II made documentary films for the General Post Office film unit, 1939–40, and the Crown Film Unit, 1941–43, and travelled as a scriptwriter to Cyprus and India; Publications Editor, Ministry of Information, 1944–46; member of the Green Park Film Unit, 1946–47. Married Catherine Francesca Polge in 1950; one daughter. Caption Writer-in-Chief, Festival of Britain, 1950–51. Recipient: Atlantic Award, 1944; Society of Authors Traveling Award, 1951; Foyle Award, 1956; Smith Literary Award, 1960. Fellow, Royal Society of Literature. M.B.E. (Member, Order of the British Empire), 1952. Lives in Stroud, Gloucestershire.

PUBLICATIONS

Verse

The Sun My Monument.   1944.
The Bloom of Candles: Verse from a Poet's Year.   1947.
My Many-Coated Man   1955.
(Poems).   1960.

Plays

The Voyage of Magellan: A Dramatic Chronicle for Radio (broadcast, 1946).   1948.
Peasants' Priest (produced 1947).   1952.

Screenplays: *Cyprus Is an Island,* 1946; *A Tale in a Teacup,* 1947.

Radio Play: *The Voyage of Magellan*   1946.

Other

Land at War.   1945.
We Made a Film in Cyprus, with Ralph Keene.   1947.
An Obstinate Exile.   1951.
A Rose for Winter: Travels in Andalusia.   1955.

Cider with Rosie (autobiography).   1959; as *The Edge of Day: A Boyhood in the West of England,* 1960.

Man Must Move: The Story of Transport (juvenile), with David Lambert.   1960; as *The Wonderful World of Transport,* 1960.

The Firstborn (essay).   1964.

As I Walked Out One Midsummer Morning (autobiography).   1969.

I Can't Stay Long.   1975.

Editor, with Rex Warner and Christopher Hassall, *New Poems 1954.*   1954.

Translator, *The Dead Village,* by Avigdor Dagan.   1943.

*   *   *

To the general public Laurie Lee is known more for his magazine articles and his evocatively nostalgic prose works (high on the paperback best-seller lists) than as a poet. However, it is as a poet that he merits attention, since his lyrical, sensuous prose style, exploring the sources and stimulus of his imaginative and physical creativity, might be seen as a part of his poetic life. The biographical works like *Cider with Rosie* crystallize in a personal perspective landscapes and characters representative of an historical moment or ethnic atmosphere. The poems, by contrast, lacking the self-dramatization which characterizes the prose reminiscences, are self-contained miniatures confronting personal experience with the control and economy necessary to avoid over-sentimentality and luxuriant romanticism.

Some have seen echoes of Lorca in his verse, others recognize the English tradition of lyrical enthusiasm for love, the power of nature, and acute sense experience. Lee has the ability to contain feeling within the apposite word and passing analogy that transfer a mood, emotion and physical presence to the reader without effort, as in "Day of These Days":

> As bread and beanflowers
> the touch of their lips
> and their white teeth sweeter than cucumbers.

Always, his imagery is drawn from the earth, juxtaposing the body and nature, the senses with the other three elements. Even in his poems of pain and despair, "Black Edge," for instance, we are sustained by the positive keenness of response and the richness of his verbal dexterity.

—B. C. Oliver-Morden

LEVERTOV, Denise. American.   Born in Ilford, Essex, England, 24 October 1923; emigrated to the United States, 1948; naturalized, 1955. Educated privately. Married the writer Mitchell Goodman in 1947; one son. Poetry Editor, *The Nation,* New York, 1961; taught at the YM-YWHA Poetry Center, New York, 1964; Honorary Scholar, Radcliffe Institute for Independent Study, Cambridge, Massachusetts, 1964–66; Visiting Lecturer, City College of New York, 1965, Drew University, Madison, New Jersey, 1965, Vassar College, Poughkeepsie, New York, 1966–67, and University of California, Berkeley, 1969; Visiting Professor, Massachusetts Institute of Technology, Cambridge, 1969–70; Artist-in-Residence,

Kirkland College, 1970–71; Elliston Lecturer, University of Cincinnati, Spring 1973. Visiting Professor, 1973–74, 1974–75, and since 1975 Professor, Tufts University, Medford, Massachusetts. Recipient: Longview Award, 1961; Guggenheim Fellowship, 1962; National Institute of Arts and Letters grant, 1966, 1968; Lenore Marshall Prize, 1976. D.Litt.: Colby College, Waterville, Maine, 1970; University of Cincinnati, 1973. Lives in New York City.

PUBLICATIONS

Verse

The Double Image.   1946.
Here and Now.   1957.
Overland to the Islands.   1958.
5 Poems.   1958.
With Eyes at the Back of Our Heads.   1959.
The Jacob's Ladder.   1961.
O Taste and See: New Poems.   1964.
City Psalm.   1964.
Psalm Concerning the Castle.   1966.
The Sorrow Dance.   1967.
Three Poems.   1968.
A Tree Telling of Orpheus.   1968.
The Cold Spring and Other Poems.   1968.
A Marigold from North Vietnam.   1968.
Embroideries.   1969.
Relearning the Alphabet.   1970.
Summer Poems 1969.   1970.
A New Year's Garland for My Students, MIT 1969–70.   1970.
To Stay Alive.   1971.
Footprints.   1972.
The Freeing of the Dust.   1975.

Fiction

In the Night: A Story.   1968.

Other

The Poet in the World (essays).   1973.
Conversation in Moscow.   1973.

Editor, *Out of the War Shadow: An Anthology of Current Poetry.*   1967.
Editor and Translator, with Edward C. Dimock, Jr., *In Praise of Krishna: Songs from the Bengali.*   1967.

Translator, *Selected Poems of Guillevic.*   1969.

Bibliography: *A Bibliography of Levertov* by Robert A. Wilson, 1972.

Reading List: *Levertov* by Linda Wagner, 1967.

*   *   *

By her own admission, Denise Levertov began writing as a "British Romantic with almost Victorian background" and has since become one of the powerful probing voices of contemporary American poetry. Her outspoken advocacy of women's liberation, her opposition to the Vietnam War, her adherence generally to the values of the political left came about through the gradual transformations of awareness since publishing *Here and Now* in 1957.

Raised and educated in a literary household in England, she published a first book of poems, *The Double Image*, in 1946. In 1948 she emigrated to the United States with her American husband, the novelist Mitchell Goodman, whose friendship with Robert Creeley led to her association with the Black Mountain movement and the journal *Origin*, which began publishing her work. Her early poems show the influence of Williams and Olson in their diction and form, but by the middle of the 1950's, Robert Duncan encouraged her to experiment more boldly with mythic perception of her identity and circumstances. She has since explained her own poetic in the essay "Organic Form," which distinguishes between a free verse of disjointed statements and organic poetry, where "form," all facets of technique, is "a revelation of content." But her poems retain traditional verse conventions, and she has occasionally attacked the improvisatory mode of other poets.

In her first substantial work, *With Eyes at the Back of Our Heads*, her poems moved to frank self-disclosures, in an effort to grasp a personal identity underlying sexual stereotype. In "The Goddess," one of the finest poems of the volume, she dramatizes her awakening to an inner nature after her expulsion from "Lie Castle," where she has been flung

> across the room, and
> room after room (hitting the walls, re-
> bounding – to the last
> sticky wall – wrenching away from it
> pulling hair out!)
> til it lay
> outside the outer walls!
>
> There in the cold air
> lying still where her hand had thrown me,
> I tasted the mud that splattered my lips
> the seeds of a forest were in it,
> asleep and growing! I tasted
> her power!

O Taste and See pursues the implications of "The Goddess" by boldly reaching into the feminine psyche to discover its raw vitality, as in this startling image of appetite:

> In the black of desire
> we rock and grunt, grunt and
> shine

Beginning with *Relearning the Alphabet*, she has moved beyond purely personal issues to larger political concerns, war resistance, women's liberation, poverty and oppression in the Third World. The poems of *To Stay Alive* and *Footprints*, many taking a longer, serial form, follow her increasingly activist participation in various resistance movements of the last two decades.

—Paul Christensen

LEWIS, Alun.   Welsh.   Born in Aberdare, South Wales, in 1915. Educated at University College of Wales, Aberystwyth, B.A. in history; University of Manchester, M.A. Teacher at Pengam. Served in the British Army: died in the Arakan on active service, 1944. *Died in 1944.*

PUBLICATIONS

Collections

Selected Poetry and Prose, edited by Ian Hamilton.   1966.

Verse

Raiders' Dawn and Other Poems.   1942.
Ha! Ha! among the Trumpets: Poems in Transit.   1945.

Fiction

The Last Inspection (stories).   1942.

Other

Letters from India.   1946.
In the Green Tree (letters; includes stories).   1948.

Reading List: "Lewis" by Gwyn Jones in *Welsh Review 3,* 1944; in *The Open Night* by John Lehmann, 1952; articles by John Stuart Williams in *Anglo-Welsh Review 14,* 1964–65; *Lewis* by Alun John, 1970.

*   *   *

Alun Lewis, Anglo-Welsh poet and short story writer, was born in a small valley near Aberdare in 1915. He grew up in a bi-lingual mining community, attended the local secondary school, and read history at the University College of Wales, Aberystwyth. After taking his Master's at Manchester, he became a teacher at Pengam. This seems to have been a temporary expedient while he waited for the war that seemed inevitable. In the meantime he wrote poems and short stories which were published in periodicals as different as *Lilliput* and *The Welsh Review.*

His reputation as an Anglo-Welsh writer remains uncertain, perhaps because the term has begun to impose its own stereotypes. While the quality of his short stories is acknowledged – he has been compared at his best with Chekhov – he has not, as a poet, received the kind of acclaim that has been given Dylan Thomas. This may be because he is in the end a different kind of poet, a poet of the relationship between man and the "complexity of the universe." He disturbs more often than he comforts. It may be worth noting that Robert Graves considered him a truer poet than Dylan Thomas. The integrity of his concern with the conflict between "self-pity and pity for the world" supports this claim.

He was already a writer of some achievement before he became a soldier – more than a third of the poems in his first collection, *Raiders' Dawn*, were written before September 1939 – but there is little doubt that his service experience in England and in India compelled an extension of sensibility upon a mind "honest with itself and humble, clear-sighted and receptive." Having rejected what he called "Virgil's imperial gaze" he achieved an economy and authority in stories like "The Orange Grove" and in poems like "The Peasants" in which "the material and the spiritual" are never separate. His death on active service in the Arakan in 1944 deprived us of a writer of unusual talent who had already achieved much and promised a great deal more.

—John Stuart Williams

LINDSAY, (Nicholas) Vachel.   American.   Born in Springfield, Illinois, 10 November 1879. Educated at Hiram College, Ohio, 1897–1900; studied for the ministry; studied art at the Chicago Art Institute, 1901, and New York Art School, 1905. Married Elizabeth Conner in 1925; one son, one daughter. Pen and ink designer, 1900–10; lecturer on the history of art, 1905–10; also travelled through the U.S. living by reciting his poems, 1906–12; after 1912 became known for his verses and was thereafter in demand as lecturer and reader. Taught at Gulf Park College, Mississippi, 1923–24. Litt.D.: Hiram College, 1930. Member, National Institute of Arts and Letters. *Died* (by suicide) *5 December 1931.*

PUBLICATIONS

Collections

   Selected Poems, edited by Mark Harris.   1963.

Verse

   The Tramp's Excuse and Other Poems.   1909.
   Rhymes to Be Traded for Bread.   1912.
   General William Booth Enters into Heaven and Other Poems.   1913.
   The Congo and Other Poems.   1914.
   The Chinese Nightingale and Other Poems.   1917.
   The Golden Whales of California and Other Rhymes in the American Language.   1920.
   The Daniel Jazz and Other Poems.   1920.
   Going-to-the-Sun.   1923.
   Collected Poems.   1923; revised edition, 1925.
   Going-to-the-Stars.   1926.
   The Candle in the Cabin: A Weaving Together of Script and Singing.   1926.
   Johnny Appleseed and Other Poems (juvenile).   1928.
   Every Soul Is a Circus.   1929.
   Selected Poems, edited by Hazelton Spencer.   1931.

Other

   The Village Magazine.   1910.

Adventures While Preaching the Gospel of Beauty.   1914.
The Art of the Moving Picture.   1915; revised edition, 1922.
A Handy Guide for Beggars, Especially Those of the Poetic Fraternity.   1916.
The Golden Book of Springfield, Being a Review of a Book That Will Appear in 2018.   1920.
The Litany of Washington Street (miscellany).   1929.
Letters to A. Joseph Armstrong, edited by Armstrong.   1940.

Reading List: *Lindsay: A Poet in America* by Edgar Lee Masters, 1935; *The West-Going Heart: A Life of Lindsay* by Eleanor Ruggles, 1959; *Lindsay* by Raymond Purkey, 1968; *Lindsay: Fieldworker for the American Dream* by Ann Massa, 1970.

*   *   *

Vachel Lindsay was a man out of phase with his time. He was also a writer who had the misfortune to be judged solely on the basis of his poetry, even though he produced a sizeable corpus of prose, work which he felt to be ultimately more important than his poetry. While it is true that he has recently begun to receive the critical appreciation and intepretation he deserves, it is equally true that he is still considered by many to be a writer (and reciter) of verse – a 20th-century troubadour who toured the country reciting his poems to hugely enthusiastic audiences, a propagandist for America whose exhortations were clothed in bombast, naivety, sentimentality, and theatrics, a phenomenon whose time had already come and gone. His role as social critic was unrecognized and such prose works as *Adventures While Preaching the Gospel of Beauty*, *The Art of the Moving Picture*, *A Handy Guide for Beggars*, and *The Golden Book of Springfield* were virtually ignored.

Lindsay's early books of verse, *General William Booth Enters into Heaven and Other Poems* and *The Congo and Other Poems*, established his reputation as a herald of the New Poetry. They mark a dramatic break with the genteel, derivative verse that then dominated the American literary scene, while marking a continuity with the Whitmanesque mode. His best poems ring with genuine music and vibrate with energy, and Lindsay's theatrical recitation of them established his reputation as an entertainer. But the latter reputation eclipsed the former and clung to him throughout the remainder of his life. His problem was two-fold: his superb qualities as an entertainer and the public's refusal to accept his definition of the role of the poet.

Lindsay felt poetry should serve the masses; that art for art's sake had no place on the American scene; that elitism in poetry was a negative and destructive force; and that Americans had to be awakened to the fact that they were allowing their country's true destiny to slip away. Lindsay considered his poetry to be the best means by which he could jolt the people into an awareness of what was happening; when they were made aware of it they would then fall in line behind him and join his efforts to recapture and restore to America its original promise.

But Lindsay's vision of America was not the vision of the American majority. Moreover, his pessimism and fundamentalist viewpoint (both of America's problems and of the solutions to them) were anathema to political, social, and literary arbiters of the day. And finally, since Lindsay believed poetry to be a social as opposed to artistic instrument (content should take precedence over style), he was not part of the imagist movement which influenced the course of 20th-century American poetry from his day to the present.

Lindsay never recovered from the realization that the people wanted only entertainment from him and that his crusade for "religion, equality and beauty," his "gospel," was doomed. He died by his own hand, a bitter and psychotic man, "Staking his last strength and his final fight/That cost him all, to set the old world right" ("Litany of the Heroes").

—Catherine Seelye

LIVESAY, Dorothy. Canadian. Born in Winnipeg, Manitoba, 12 October 1909. Educated at Trinity College, University of Toronto, 1927–31, B.A. 1931; the Sorbonne, Paris, diploma, 1932; London Institute of Education, 1959; University of British Columbia, Vancouver, M.Ed. 1966. Married Duncan Macnair in 1937 (died); one son and one daughter. Social worker, Englewood, New Jersey, 1935–36, and Vancouver, 1936–39, 1953–55; Correspondent, Toronto *Daily Star*, 1946–49; Documentary Scriptwriter, Canadian Broadcasting Corporation, 1950–55; Lecturer in Creative Writing, University of British Columbia, 1955–56, 1965–66; High School Teacher, Vancouver, 1956–58; UNESCO English Specialist, Paris, 1958–60, and Zambia, 1960–63; Writer-in-Residence, University of New Brunswick, Fredericton, 1966–68; Associate Professor of English, University of Alberta, Edmonton, 1968–71; Visiting Lecturer, University of Victoria, British Columbia, 1974–75; Writer-in-Residence, University of Manitoba, Winnipeg, 1975–77, and University of Ottawa, 1977. Editor, *CV/II* magazine. Recipient: Governor-General's Award, 1945, 1948; Lorne Pierce Medal, 1947; President's Medal, University of Western Ontario, 1954; Canada Council grant, 1958, 1964, 1971, 1977. D.Litt.: University of Waterloo, Ontario, 1973.

PUBLICATIONS

Verse

> *Green Pitcher.* 1928.
> *Signpost.* 1932.
> *Day and Night.* 1944.
> *Poems for People.* 1947.
> *Call My People Home.* 1950.
> *New Poems.* 1955.
> *Selected Poems 1926–1956.* 1957.
> *The Colour of God's Face.* 1965.
> *The Unquiet Bed.* 1967.
> *The Documentaries: Selected Longer Poems.* 1968.
> *Plainsongs.* 1969; revised edition, 1971.
> *Disasters of the Sun.* 1971.
> *Collected Poems: The Two Seasons.* 1972.
> *Nine Poems of Farewell 1972–1973.* 1973.
> *Ice Age.* 1975.

Fiction

> *A Winnipeg Childhood* (stories). 1973.

Other

> *Right Hand, Left Hand* (memoirs). 1977.

> Editor, *The Collected Poems of Raymond Knister.* 1949.
> Editor, with Seymour Mayne, *Forty Women Poets of Canada.* 1971.

Reading List: "Livesay: The Love Poetry" by P. Stevens, in *Canadian Literature,* Winter 1971; "Livesay's Two Seasons" by Robin Skelton, in *Canadian Literature,* Autumn 1973.

*   *   *

Dorothy Livesay's efflorescence in her later years is remarkable in Canadian poetry. Her two early collections demonstrated a controlled, precise lyric verse, often praised at the time for its "feminine images" and "intense feeling." Reviewers of her overtly political work from the 1930's were reluctant to acknowledge her leftist views, although her reputation as a craftsman was well established by the time her *Selected Poems* appeared; after E. J. Pratt and Earle Birney, and with F. R. Scott, A. M. Klein, and A. J. M. Smith she was considered to be one of the country's half-dozen best poets. With seven new volumes published during the last two decades, together with her *Collected Poems* and a selection, she is now widely regarded as the most mature voice in Canadian feminist poetry. Livesay has long insisted on a "way of looking" that is distinctively from a "womans's eye," and she has edited an anthology of women poets from Canada. *Collected Poems* and *Ice Age* include all her substantial poetry.

Livesay's semi-autobiographical prose reminiscences of her youth, *A Winnipeg Childhood,* suggest the constrained literary environment reflected in her first precocious volume of verse and its sequel. Her personal preoccupations through the 1930's and later can be summed up as "love, politics, the Depression and feminism." A communist for much of that time, she was only occasionally heard in public as a revolutionary; the appearance of *Day and Night* during the Second World War revealed the strength of her commitment to the struggle against fascism and industrial capitalism. Despite the obtrusive rhetoric, her sympathies with the victims of economic and military oppression are strongly realised in the longer poetry of the 1930's and 1940's: the title poems of *Day and Night* and *Call My People Home* (a radio documentary on Japanese-Canadians interned in 1941), and "Prophet of the New World," about the nineteenth-century mystic and revolutionary Riel.

New Poems marked a substantial development. Her usual tight control, frequently emphasized by rhyme, was sharpened by a more objective tone. Later collections continue to demonstrate the dialectic structure of her work, while increasingly they embody "that pull between community and private identity that is characteristic of being a woman." In *The Unquiet Bed* Livesay had found an appropriately intimate voice, one patterned by natural speech rhythms yet preserving the sharp irony which characterizes her most acute work. The "great game" of love can involve both "an itch for the seven-inch/reach" and confidence that "aloneness is the only bliss." In her latest poetry she is secure in her stance as both observer and participant, poet and woman, listening with her "third ear" and knowing that "in the small womb/lies all the lightning."

—Bruce Nesbitt

LOWELL, Amy (Lawrence).   American.   Born in Brookline, Massachusetts, 9 February 1874. Educated privately. Travelled a good deal abroad; associated with the Imagists in London, 1913, and thereafter promoted their work in America. Lecturer, Brooklyn Institute of Arts and Sciences, 1917–18. Recipient: Pulitzer Prize, 1926. Litt.D.: Baylor University, Waco, Texas, 1920. *Died 12 May 1925.*

PUBLICATIONS

Collections

> The Complete Poetical Works.   1955.
> A Shard of Silence: Selected Poems, edited by Glenn Richard Ruihley, 1957.

Verse

> A Dome of Many-Coloured Glass.   1912.
> Sword Blades and Poppy Seed.   1914.
> Men, Women, and Ghosts.   1916.
> Can Grande's Castle.   1918.
> Pictures of the Floating World.   1919.
> Legends.   1921.
> Fir-Flower Tablets: Poems Translated from the Chinese by Florence Ayscough, English Versions by Lowell.   1921.
> A Critical Fable.   1922.
> What's O'Clock, edited by Ada Dwyer Russell.   1925.
> East Wind, edited by Ada Dwyer Russell.   1926.
> The Madonna of Carthagena.   1927.
> Ballads for Sale, edited by Ada Dwyer Russell.   1927.

Play

> Weeping Pierrot and Laughing Pierrot, music by Jean Hubert, from a work by Edmond Rostand.   1914.

Fiction

> Dream Drops; or, Stories from Fairy Land, with Elizabeth Lowell and Katherine Bigelow Lowell.   1887.

Other

> Six French Poets: Studies in Contemporary Literature.   1915.
> Tendencies in Modern American Poetry.   1917.
> John Keats.   2 vols., 1925.
> Poetry and Poets: Essays, edited by Ferris Greenslet.   1930.
> Florence Ayscough and Lowell: Correspondence of a Friendship, edited by Harley Farnsworth MacNair.   1946.

Reading List: Lowell: A Critical Appreciation by Bryher, 1918; Lowell: A Chronicle, with Extracts from Her Correspondence by S. Foster Damon, 1935; Lowell: Portrait of the Poet in Her Time by Horace Gregory, 1958; Lowell by Frank C. Flint, 1969; The Thorn of a Rose: Lowell Reconsidered by Glenn Richard Ruihley, 1975.

*   *   *

Even more than is commonly the case with rebel poets and personalities, Amy Lowell was subjected to heavy-handed abuse as well as uncritical admiration in her own life-time, there was little or no understanding of the nature of her work, and, following her untimely death in 1925, a shift in poetic fashions all but obliterated the memory of her unusual achievements. The reasons for that eclipse lie both in the poet and in her audience. Lowell was one of the most prolific and most uneven poets ever to appear in America. Because so much of her poetry was bad, it was easy to judge her harshly. Moreover, her best and most characteristic poetry was very puzzling to conventional readers and remains so to this day. The language of these poems is chiefly pictorial, with the result that she was dismissed as a writer who touched only the physical surfaces of the world and so failed to illuminate any of its deeper meanings. As for the defects in her audience, the misreading of the poet was due to the ignorance and superficiality of the literary journalists of her day. After her death, the misunderstanding was perpetuated by the "new critics" who scorned writers who fell outside the pale of the poetry of wit and cultural memory promoted by T. S. Eliot and Ezra Pound. Though Lowell, at her best, is a writer of extraordinary verve, freshness, and beauty of expression, she was little better understood fifty years after her death than she was in 1912 when she published her first book of poems, *A Dome of Many-Coloured Glass*.

This book was rightly criticized for its feebleness and conventionality of expression; but it has one merit unnoticed by the interpreters of her poetry. The poems are written in a late Romantic style of direct statement and they chart with unusual thoroughness all of the facets of her idealistic and mystical thought. After 1912, as suggested above, Miss Lowell expressed herself imagistically. To a poet concerned with extrarational areas of experience, the new style was a great advance over the confines of logical statement, but it also led to the failures of communication which have persisted to the present day. Fortunately, we can study the poems published in *A Dome* and so know precisely the content of her thought and the beliefs she had adopted, as a substitute for Christianity, to explain her own insights into reality.

The most important of these concerns the existence of a transcendent power that permeates the world and accounts for the divinity that the poet sensed in all created things. In her poem "Before the Altar," a lonely and penniless worshipper offers his life and being as sacrifice to this Power, which she also celebrates in "The Poet," another early poem. Moved by the awesome splendors of creation, the poet is urged, she says, to forsake the ordinary pleasures of life to pursue the ideality symbolized by the "airy cloudland palaces" of sunset. Such a man, she says, "spurns life's human friendships to profess/Life's loneliness of dreaming ecstasy." In much of Lowell's most admirable imagistic poetry, this mystical conception of reality is rendered by means of her "numinous landscape" or scene, as in the poems "Ombre Chinoise" or "Reflections" where the physical objects concerned are presented with a kind of divine nimbus.

The realm of ideality envisioned in these four poems is sometimes perceived as a solution to the painful incompletions of life. This is the second major theme in Lowell's poetry, and the incompletion is most tragic in the case of the denial of love. Such denial is a spiritual *malaise*, in her view, because she identifies love not with sex but with inner emotional development. "Patterns," which is this author's most famous poem, dramatizes the withering of spirit resultant on the death of the heroine's lover. The poem is highly voluptuous and insists strongly on the physical beauties of lover and lady and the formal, spring-time garden where the poem is set, but the heroine's decision to live a loveless, celibate life calls attention to the deeper meaning of the relationship.

The spirituality that is implicit in romantic attachments includes recognition of an element of divinity in the beloved. The achievement of love as sacred rite is a third principal theme in Lowell's writings and it occurs in many of her most striking poems, beginning with a loose effusion in *A Dome* but ending with the sublimity of "In Excelsis" and her six sonnets written to Eleonora Duse. The loved one as sacred presence or, at the least, a part of an all-encompassing Divinity is consistent with the poet's preoccupation with a transcendent reality and completes the circle of her themes by returning her thought to its starting place. In terms of individual poems, Lowell's treatment of these themes is so varied and intermixed with nearly all the other issues of life that only a long survey can do them justice. But it is important to note that Lowell approached life *as a mystic* at a profound, intuitive level, and the imagistic mode in which she cast her poems was the one best suited to her gifts and the visionary character of her poetry. As poet her contribution is a revivification of the human sense of the beauties and mysteries of existence.

In addition to the solitary, contemplative role of poet that she adopted for herself, Lowell fulfilled another dynamic "political" role in the far-reaching effort she made to obtain public acceptance of the "new poetry" that appeared in America in 1912. The role she played was political in that the new poetry, seemingly odd and irregular in its form, challenged nearly all established social norms and ideals. Through her critical writings as well as her countless public appearances as lecturer and reader, Lowell assumed leadership of this movement and was responsible for a large measure of its success in creating a new poetic taste and awareness in America.

—Glenn Richard Ruihley

LOWELL, Robert (Traill Spence, Jr.). American. Born in Boston, Massachusetts, 1 March 1917. Educated at St. Mark's School, Southboro, Massachusetts; Harvard University, Cambridge, Massachusetts, 1935–37; Kenyon College, Gambier, Ohio, 1938–40, A.B. (summa cum laude) 1940 (Phi Beta Kappa). Conscientious objector during World War II: served prison sentence, 1943–44. Married 1) the writer Jean Stafford in 1940 (divorced, 1948); 2) the writer Elizabeth Hardwick in 1949 (divorced, 1972), one son; 3) the writer Caroline Blackwood in 1972, one son. Editorial Assistant, Sheed and Ward, publishers, New York, 1941–42; taught at the University of Iowa, Iowa City, 1949–50, 1952–53; Salzburg Seminar on American Studies, 1952; Boston University; New School for Social Research, New York; Harvard University; Professor of Literature, University of Essex, Wivenhoe, Colchester, 1970–72. Consultant in Poetry, Library of Congress, Washington, D.C., 1947–48; Visiting Fellow, All Souls College, Oxford, 1970. Recipient: Pulitzer Prize, 1947; National Institute of Arts and Letters grant, 1947; Guggenheim Fellowship, 1947, 1974; Harriet Monroe Poetry Award, 1952; Guinness Prize, 1959; National Book Award, 1960; Bollingen Poetry Translation Award, 1962; New England Poetry Club Golden Rose, 1964; Ford Foundation grant, for drama, 1964; Obie Award, for drama, 1965; Sarah Josepha Hale Award, 1966; Copernicus Award, 1974; National Medal for Literature, 1977. Member, American Academy of Arts and Letters. *Died 12 September 1977.*

PUBLICATIONS

Verse

Land of Unlikeness. 1944.
Lord Weary's Castle. 1946.
Poems 1938–1949. 1950.
The Mills of the Kavanaughs. 1951.
Life Studies. 1959; augmented edition, 1959, 1968.
Imitations. 1961.

For the Union Dead.   1964.

Selected Poems.   1965.

The Achievement of Lowell: A Comprehensive Selection of His Poems, edited by William
    J. Martz.   1966.

Near the Ocean.   1967.

The Voyage and Other Versions of Poems by Baudelaire.   1968.

Notebook 1967–1968.   1969; augmented edition, as *Notebook,* 1970.

For Lizzie and Harriet.   1973.

History.   1973.

The Dolphin.   1973.

Poems: A Selection, edited by Jonathan Raban.   1974.

Selected Poems.   1976.

Day by Day.   1977.

Plays

Phaedra, from the play by Racine (produced 1961).   In *Phaedra and Figaro,* 1961.

The Old Glory (Benito Cereno and *My Kinsman, Major Molineux)* (produced
    1964).   1964;   expanded version, including *Endecott and the Red Cross* (produced
    1968),   1966.

Prometheus Bound, from a play by Aeschylus (produced 1967).   1969.

Other

Editor, with Peter Taylor and Robert Penn Warren, *Randall Jarrell 1914–1965.*   1967.

Reading List: *Lowell: The First Twenty Years* by Hugh B. Staples, 1962; *The Poetic Themes
of Lowell* by Jerome Mazzaro, 1965; *Lowell: A Collection of Critical Essays* edited by Thomas
Parkinson, 1968; *The Public Poetry of Lowell* by Patrick Cosgrave, 1970; *Lowell: A Portrait
of the Artist in His Time* edited by Michael London and Robert Boyars, 1970 (includes
bibliography by Jerome Mazzaro); *Lowell* by Richard J. Fein, 1970; *Critics on Lowell:
Readings in Literary Criticism* edited by Jonathan Price, 1972; *The Poetic Art of Lowell* by
Marjorie G. Perloff, 1973; *Pity the Monsters: The Political Vision of Lowell* by Alan
Williamson, 1974; *Lowell* by John Crick, 1974.

*   *   *

Robert Lowell has been described as "a poet of restlessness without repose" (John Crick).
His career is the history of violent changes in subject matter, and in manner, which often
annoyed and confused his critics. Even now, after his death, there is little general agreement
about his stature. But perhaps, even in this, Lowell is a *representative* figure: the last thirty
years (Lowell's publishing history runs from 1944 to 1977) have witnessed a fragmentation
of culture that denies us the sorts of certainty about the status that it was once possible to
accord to Eliot, or to Yeats. This period will never, one suspects, be accepted as "The Age of
Lowell." Individual poets seem no longer capable of this sort of centrality of significance.

But if any poet in this period has – perhaps sometimes with too earnest a deliberateness –
lived through, proved upon his pulses, the central concerns, preoccupations, and pains of his
time, it is Lowell. The career may, conveniently, be seen in three parts: the early poetry of
Lowell's Catholicism that embraces *Land of Unlikeness, Lord Weary's Castle,* and *The Mills
of the Kavanaughs;* the mid-period poetry of personal breakdown and political concern that
includes *Life Studies, For the Union Dead,* and *Near the Ocean;* and the final period that saw

the various attempts to create a larger, freer form through the subsequent stages of *Notebook*, *History*, *For Lizzie and Harriet*, and *The Dolphin*, a period concluding with the sustained elegiac note of *Day by Day*.

On the face of it, the three phases of the career seem to have little in common, apart from certain stylistic tics — most notably, and often irritatingly, Lowell's penchant for the triple adjective and the attention-seeking oxymoron. Some insight into an underlying continuity in Lowell's "one life, one writing" may be provided by remarking on his exceptional insistence on revising himself in public. One of the most upsetting aspects of *Notebook*, for many of its reviewers, was the shock of coming across familiar Lowell lines either in very different contexts, or procrusteanly racked into the uniform regularity of the book's "sonnets." Lowell's apparently cavalier freedom with his own published work suggests not so much a desire to do a little better what he has done brilliantly before, but rather a deep-seated impatience with his own enormous talent and with poetry itself. In the poem "Tired Iron" in *The Dolphin*, there is an almost Beckettian dismissal of the work, even as he is engaged on it — "I can't go on with this, the measure is gone." It is possible to see in Lowell, as in some of the greatest artists of the second half of the twentieth century, a radical dissatisfaction with art itself, with its consolations, its sense of order, its morality. What gives Lowell's dissatisfaction its unique savour is his refusal of the obvious alternative of a bleak nihilism in favour of a worried, guilty commitment to a traditional New England liberalism. The oddity of Robert Lowell's sensibility is perhaps suggested in a shorthand way by pointing to the poems in *Notebook* and *History* dedicated to Eugene McCarthy and Robert Kennedy: an existential absurdist clinging precariously to sanity celebrates the pragmatic politics of liberal capitalism.

Dissatisfaction, restlessness, unease: these are the signatures of Lowell's work. The early formalist poetry nominally takes its cue from Allen Tate and the Southern Fugitives. In fact, the formal majesty of the poems is everywhere disturbed by a raucous alliterative bellowing; the Catholicism is everywhere collapsed into savage heresy and blasphemy:

> O Mother, I implore
> Your scorched, blue thunderbreasts of love to pour
> Buckets of blessings on my burning head.

If this is rhetoric, it is a rhetoric of desperation. Even in the more tender poems — "The Quaker Graveyard in Nantucket" and "Mother Marie Therese" — Lowell's sonic boom threatens his formal perfection. His dissatisfaction compels him almost to wring the neck of his magnificent rhetoric. Such dissatisfactions led to a long silence during "the tranquillized Fifties," a silence during which the dissatisfactions of his personal life involved periods in mental hospitals. The silence was broken only at the end of the decade by the publication of *Life Studies*, a book in an entirely different mode and manner; Lowell was now so dissatisfied with his earlier work that he attempted almost its polar opposite, a poetry close to Chekhovian prose. This is the one work of Lowell's about which almost all critics agree: it was *the* book of its time, following, with total assurance, a direction more hesitantly beginning to be taken by some of his contemporaries, profoundly influential in its discovery of a new sort of personal voice. It signals, in "Beyond the Alps," Lowell's break with Catholicism, and it proceeds to worry out, "confessionally," the psychic disturbances and extremities of his harrowing personal experience. This is a poetry resolutely committed to walking naked; but the voice is moving and desperate and rises to a unique and instantly recognisable "Lowellian" pathos:

> A car radio bleats,
> 'Love, O careless Love ...' I hear
> my ill-spirit sob in each blood cell,
> as if my hand were at its throat ...
> I myself am hell,
> nobody's here —.

But, unlike that of some poets who crawled in under the mantle of "confessional" poetry, Lowell's writing refuses the temptations of an easy solipsism. Christopher Ricks, in a *New Statesman* review of *For the Union Dead* (26 March 1965), maintained that "The singular strength of Robert Lowell's poetry has always been a matter of his power to enforce a sense of context." The work after *Life Studies* evidences a desire to speak, out of personal pain and catastrophe, about society and politics, and about literature, religion, and history, the sustaining "outer contexts" of our lives. Restlessly moving away from the "prose" style of *Life Studies*, Lowell wrote, in the central poems of *Near the Ocean* – especially, perhaps, in "Waking Early Sunday Morning" – the greatest elegies for a generation that suffered the Vietnam war and the threat of nuclear extinction, and he wrote them, with his casually characteristic refusal of the obvious, in a finely judged, perfectly achieved neo-classical form that recalls that other poet of the barbarities of which a "civilised" society is capable, Andrew Marvell:

> Pity the planet, all joy gone
> from this sweet volcanic cone;
> peace to our children when they fall
> in small war on the heels of small
> war – until the end of time
> to police the earth, a ghost
> orbiting forever lost
> in our monotonous sublime.

In *For the Union Dead*, the forms are again free, though the relatively uncluttered simplicity of these poems belies a carefully crafted subtlety of association, allusion, and symbolism. These haunted, nostalgic poems begin in a consideration of the joys and pains of personal relationship but extend themselves into the troubles of political life. The volume's title-poem relates private and public breakdown in a muted poetry of understatement, working by implication and suggestion. The poem's final stanza is as devastating as anything in Lowell, but the devastation comes across quietly, hesitantly, thrown off almost parenthetically compared to the aggressive climaxes of the poems in *Lord Weary's Castle*:

> The Aquarium is gone. Everywhere,
> giant finned cars nose forward like fish;
> a savage servility
> slides by on grease.

The ability to relate his own trouble to the trouble of his times is the impulse behind *Notebook*. This, and the works that grew out of it, are the most ambitious of Lowell's writing: he is attempting a large, inclusive form, a form for all occasions, in the manner of Pound's *Cantos*, of Berryman's *Dream Songs*. In the poems in the sequence – all irregular fourteen-liners – that deal with "history," there is too often the feeling of formal monotony, rhythmic inertia, a tired, mechanical repetitiveness. The lack of a real voice, and the absence of anything but the most straightforward chronology to serve as "plot," render *History* a generally wearying experience. The failure derives, perhaps, from Lowell's refusal to admit that a sonnet sequence, or its equivalent, is really capable of handling only limited types of material. The larger successes of *For Lizzie and Harriet* and *The Dolphin* are perhaps the result of their being more traditionally plotted around the themes and occasions of personal love and marriage. The idea of writing "history" as a sequence of sonnets has an almost wilful perversity about it, as though Shakespeare had decided to put the material of the history plays, as well as the story of his "two loves," into a sonnet sequence.

But such perversity, and the overall failure of a single book, are perhaps the inevitable price of an heroic refusal to repeat himself, a nervous, restless desire to define and re-define the protean self. "We are words," Lowell insists in a poem in *History* addressed to Berryman,

"John, we used the language as if we made it." The claim is large; it is characteristic of Lowell's proud ambition that he should make it for himself; but in the formal variety, the technical ingenuity, and the inventiveness of his poems – and of his translations and plays – he comes, at the very least, close to justifying it.

—Neil Corcoran

MacDIARMID, Hugh. Pseudonym for Christopher Murray Grieve. Scottish. Born in Langholm, Dumfriesshire, 11 August 1892. Educated at Langholm Academy; Broughton Student Centre, Edinburgh; University of Edinburgh. Married 1) Margaret Skinner in 1918 (divorced, 1932), one son and one daughter; 2) Valda Trevlyn in 1934, one son. Journalist, 1912–15, 1920–30: Editor, *The Scottish Chapbook,* Montrose, Angus, 1922–23, *The Scottish Nation*, Montrose, Angus, 1923, *The Northern Review*, Edinburgh, 1924, and *The Voice of Scotland*, Dunfermline, Fife, 1938–39, Glasgow, 1945–49, and Edinburgh, 1955–58. A Founder, Scottish Nationalist Party; Founder, Scottish Centre of P.E.N. Recipient: Foyle Prize, 1963; Scottish Arts Council Award, 1969. LL.D.: University of Edinburgh, 1957. Professor of Literature, Royal Scottish Academy, 1974; Honorary Fellow, Modern Language Association of America. Granted Civil List pension, 1951. *Died 9 September 1978.*

PUBLICATIONS

Verse

> *Annals of the Five Senses.* 1923.
> *Sangschaw.* 1925.
> *Penny Wheep.* 1926; edited by John C. Weston, 1971.
> *A Drunk Man Looks at the Thistle.* 1926; revised edition, 1956.
> *The Lucky Bag.* 1927.
> *To Circumjack Cencrastus; or, The Curly Snake.* 1930.
> *First Hymn to Lenin and Other Poems.* 1931.
> *Second Hymn to Lenin.* 1932.
> *Tarras.* 1932.
> *Scots Unbound and Other Poems.* 1932.
> *Stony Limits and Other Poems.* 1934.
> *Selected Poems.* 1934.
> *Second Hymn to Lenin and Other Poems.* 1935.
> *Direadh.* 1938.
> *Speaking for Scotland.* 1939.
> *Cornish Heroic Song for Valda Trevlyn.* 1943.
> *Selected Poems,* edited by R. Crombie Saunders. 1944.
> *Speaking for Scotland: Selected Poems.* 1946.
> *Poems of the East-West Synthesis.* 1946.

A Kist of Whistles: New Poems.   1947.

Selected Poems, edited by Oliver Brown.   1954; as *Poems*, 1955.

In Memoriam James Joyce: from A Vision of World Language.   1955.

Stony Limits and Scots Unbound and Other Poems.   1956.

Three Hymns to Lenin.   1957.

The Battle Continues.   1957.

The Kind of Poetry I Want.   1961.

Collected Poems.   1962; revised edition, edited by John C. Weston, 1967.

Bracken Hills in Autumn.   1962.

The Blaward and the Skelly.   1962.

Poems to Paintings by William Johnstone 1933.   1963.

Two Poems: The Terrible Crystal, A Vision of Scotland.   1964.

The Ministry of Water: Two Poems.   1964.

Six Vituperative Verses.   1964.

Poet at Play and Other Poems, Being a Selection of Mainly Vituperative Verses.   1965.

The Fire of the Spirit: Two Poems.   1965.

Whuculls.   1966.

On a Raised Beach.   1967.

A Lap of Honour.   1967.

Early Lyrics, Recently Discovered among Letters to His Schoolmaster and Friend, George Ogilvie, edited by J. K. Annand.   1968.

A Clyack-Sheaf.   1969.

More Collected Poems.   1970.

Selected Poems, edited by David Craig and John Manson.   1970.

The MacDiarmid Anthology: Poems in Scots and English, edited by Michael Grieve and Alexander Scott.   1972.

Song of the Seraphim.   1973.

Direadh I, II, and III.   1974.

The Complete Poems, edited by Michael Grieve and W. R. Aitken.   2 vols., 1978.

The Socialist Poems, edited by T. S. Law and Thurso Berwick.   1978.

Other

Contemporary Scottish Studies: First Series.   1926.

The Present Position of Scottish Music.   1927.

Albyn; or, Scotland and the Future.   1927.

The Present Position of Scottish Arts and Affairs.   1928.

The Scottish National Association of April Fools.   1928.

Scotland in 1980.   1929.

Warning Democracy.   1931.

Five Bits of Miller.   1934.

At the Sign of the Thistle: A Collection of Essays.   1934.

Scottish Scene; or, The Intelligent Man's Guide to Albyn, with Lewis Grassic Gibbon.   1934.

Charles Doughty and the Need for Heroic Poetry.   1936.

Scottish Eccentrics.   1936.

Scotland and the Question of a Popular Front Against Fascism and War.   1938.

The Islands of Scotland: Hebrides, Orkneys and Shetlands.   1939.

Lucky Poet: A Self-Study in Literary and Political Ideas, Being the Autobiography of MacDiarmid.   1943.

Cunninghame Graham: A Centenary Study.   1952.

The Politics and Poetry of MacDiarmid.   1952.

Francis George Scott: An Essay on the Occasion of His Seventy-Fifth Birthday, 25th January 1955. 1955.

Burns Today and Tomorrow. 1959.

The Man of (Almost) Independent Mind (on Hume). 1962.

When the Rat Race Is Over: An Essay in Honour of the Fiftieth Birthday of John Gawsworth. 1962.

MacDiarmid on Hume. 1962.

The Ugly Birds Without Wings. 1962.

The Company I've Kept (autobiography). 1966.

The Uncanny Scot: A Selection of Prose, edited by Kenneth Buthlay. 1968.

Selected Essays, edited by Duncan Glen. 1969.

An Afternoon with MacDiarmid: Interview at Brownsbank on 25th October 1968, with Duncan Glen. 1969.

On Metaphysics and Poetry, edited by Walter Perrie. 1974.

John Knox, with Campbell Maclean and Anthony Ross. 1976.

Editor, *Northern Numbers, Being Representative Selections from Certain Living Scottish Poets.* 2 vols., 1920–21.

Editor, *Robert Burns, 1759–1796.* 1926.

Editor, *Living Scottish Poets.* 1931.

Editor, *The Golden Treasury of Scottish Poetry.* 1940.

Editor, *Auntran Blads: An Outwale o Verses,* by Douglas Young. 1943.

Editor, *William Soutar: Collected Poems.* 1948.

Editor, *Poems,* by Robert Burns. 1949.

Editor, with Maurice Lindsay, *Poetry Scotland Four.* 1949.

Editor, *Scottish Arts and Letters: Fifth Miscellany.* 1950.

Editor, *Selections from the Poems of William Dunbar.* 1952.

Editor, *Selected Poems of William Dunbar.* 1955.

Editor, *Love Songs,* by Burns. 1962.

Editor, *Henryson.* 1970.

Translator, *The Handmaid of the Lord,* by Ramon Maria de Tenreiro. 1930.

Translator, *The Birlinn of Clanranald,* by Alexander MacDonald. 1935.

Translator, with Elspeth Harley Schubert, *Harry Martinson: Aniara: A Review of Man in Time and Space.* 1963.

Translator, *The Threepenny Opera,* by Brecht. 1973.

Reading List: *The Politics and Poetry of MacDiarmid* by Arthur Leslie, 1952; *MacDiarmid: A Festschrift* edited by K.D. Duval and others, 1962; *MacDiarmid and the Scottish Renaissance* by Duncan Glen, 1964; *"MacDiarmid" (C. M. Grieve)* by Kenneth Buthlay, 1964; *The Golden Lyric: An Essay on the Poetry of MacDiarmid* by Iain Crichton Smith, 1967; *MacDiarmid: A Critical Survey* edited by Duncan Glen, 1972 (includes bibliography by W. R. Aitken); *MacDiarmid: An Illustrated Biography of Christopher Murray Grieve* by Gordon Wright, 1977.

*   *   *

Hugh MacDiarmid established himself as a poet of importance when he turned from writing verse in English to writing short lyrics in his native Scots. These are the poems collected in *Sangschaw* and *Penny Wheep.* The best of the lyrics in these volumes equal anything in the whole tradition of the lyric poem in Scots – "The Watergaw," "The Eemis Stane," "Empty Vessel," "Crowdieknowe," and the four-part sequence "Au Clair de la

Lune." These poems were almost immediately recognised as something quite unique in Scots poetry after the long period of imitation Burnsian verse. They not only demonstrate the usual seemingly effortless lyric cry and an equally effortless "leap into the symbol," but also show, which is more unusual at least in the Scots tradition, a seeming impersonality of stance which is yet also universally human.

If the short lyrics of *Sangschaw* and *Penny Wheep* jolted the Scottish literary scene out of its set ways, then the publication in 1926 of the 2685-line poem *A Drunk Man Looks at the Thistle* came like "the shock of a childbirth in church," as David Daiches has memorably written. *A Drunk Man* takes up the lyricism of the short poems and extends it into a long work concerned with heaven and hell and all else besides. It leaps into metaphysical speculation in verse where the real and the imaginary are as one; it contains satirical writing equal to anything in Scottish verse, including Burns's "Holy Willie's Prayer." It achieves its unquestioned unity by what may seem at first to be a disorganised flow of magnificent and varied verse. Here MacDiarmid is in full control of many verse forms, each suited to the content of the section where it is employed; the lyricism is fully at one with a speculative mind of huge imagination. This work is now being increasingly recognized as the greatest long poem in the Scots tradition.

MacDiarmid tried to repeat the success and something of the techniques of *A Drunk Man* in his next work, *To Circumjack Cencrastus*, but, despite some very fine successes including a masterly translation into English of Rilke's "Requiem – Für eine Freundin," this work lacks the unity of its predecessor, and, more important, too many passages lack poetry. But *Cencrastus* was followed by many more important poems in Scots, including some very fine short lyrics, especially "At My Father's Grave" (*First Hymn to Lenin*) and "Milk-Wort and Bog Cotton" and "The Back o' Beyond" (*Scots Unbound*). But to this period also belong poems which show a continued or even further-devoloped ability to combine lyricism with speculative thought in longer works – *Tarras*, "Water of Life," "Excelsior," "Harry Semen," and the two magnificent poems "By Wauchopeside" and "Whuchulls." Also belonging to this most creative period in the early 1930's is the beautiful long work "Water Music" in which the sounds of the Scots language are exploited as never before or since. The wonderfully conversational yet technically exact "The Seamless Garment" also belongs to this period, as do the first two Hymns to Lenin. Soon, however, MacDiarmid was turning from Scots to English and soon to an English of extended vocabulary.

To some critics MacDiarmid's finest achievement in English is to be found among the group of short poems published in *Second Hymn to Lenin*. The number of fully realised poems in this work are not numerous but the few that are make an imposing group. They certainly include: "Lo! A Child Is Born," "On the Ocean Floor," "O Ease My Spirit," and "The Two Parents." Others might see the long poem "On a Raised Beach," with its use of specialised English language, as MacDiarmid's finest poetry in English; other major long poems in English included in *Stony Limits* are the title poem, "A Point of Honour," "Lament for the Great Music," and at least parts of "Ode to All Rebels." Also in this volume are the magnificent four lines of "The Skeleton of the Future," which is perhaps the greatest, if also the shortest, expression of MacDiarmid's commitment to communism. The eight lines of "Skald's Death" are also very fine and "With the Herring Fishers" shows him still to be a master of the short lyric in Scots. *Stony Limits* also printed his most famous, or most popular, Scottish nationalist poem "The Little White Rose," but it is not one of his better poems.

By 1939 MacDiarmid had turned to the very long "poems of fact" or "world-view," the poems of his last creative period. These "world-view" poems are really one very long and unfinished, or unfinishable, work; separately published parts include *In Memoriam James Joyce* and *The Kind of Poetry I Want*, although both were perhaps largely written in the late 1930's or early 1940's and revised later. These long poems have not received the critical recognition given to other aspects of MacDiarmid's work. The temptation with these works is to pick out the passages which rise almost to lyric heights, passages such as "In the Fall" in *In Memoriam James Joyce*, but to do this is to work against their true poetry and energy. One poem of this period stands as a separate work, "The Glass of Pure Water" (*Poetry Scotland*,

1943); *Direadh I, II, and III*, first printed in MacDiarmid's autobiography *Lucky Poet*, are also excellent for leading a hesitant reader into the longer works.

This later work requires reading in mass, and the publication of *The Complete Poems* may lead to a reconsideration of it. But even without critical acclaim for this later work Hugh MacDiarmid has a body of achieved poetry which establishes him as not only the widest ranging but also as one of the greatest of Scottish poets.

—Duncan Glen

MACKENZIE, Kenneth (Ivo). Pseudonym: Seaforth Mackenzie.   Australian.   Born in Perth, Western Australia, in 1913. Educated at Muresk Agricultural College; studied arts and law at the University of Western Australia, Perth. Married Kate Loveday in 1934; one daughter and one son. Lived in Kurrajong from 1948. Recipient: Commonwealth Literary Fund grant, 1948, 1951, 1955. *Died in January 1955.*

PUBLICATIONS

Collections

   The Poems, edited by Evan Jones and Geoffrey Little.   1972.

Verse

   Our Earth.   1937.
   The Moonlit Doorway.   1944.

Fiction

   The Young Desire It.   1937.
   Chosen People.   1938.
   Dead Men Rising.   1951.
   The Refuge: A Confession.   1954.

Other

   Editor, *Australian Poetry, 1951–52.*   1952.

Reading List: "A Dead Man Rising: The Poetry of Mackenzie" in *Australian Quarterly 36,* 1964, and *Mackenzie,* 1969, both by Evan Jones; "Mackenzie's Novels" by Peter Cowan, in *Meanjin 24,* 1965; "Mackenzie's Fiction" by R. G. Geering, in *Southerly 26,* 1966.

*   *   *

Many of Kenneth Mackenzie's poems were not published until 1972, seventeen years after his death. On the basis of his two early books *Our Earth* and *The Moonlit Doorway*, it was possible to regard him mainly as a love-poet, sensual and egoistic. The new volume, almost but not quite complete, revealed that the love-poems were far less dominant than poems about death and nothingness, and that fear of death gave way to a quiet longing for death, or "his brother sleep," submerged beneath the fear in the early verse. Mackenzie's decision to be a writer, and above all, a poet, in a country in which, in his day, it was almost impossible to exist by the pen, kept him all his short life in stark poverty, not mitigated by his alcoholism. One of the editors of his *Poems* has pointed out the remarkable parallels between his life and Dylan Thomas's, though Thomas seems to have died of too much success while Mackenzie succumbed to failure. Yet the disorders of his life were not reflected in the tone of his verse, which became more measured, serene, and controlled as outward circumstances deteriorated. His essential solitariness, with his retreat to the bush, became in the end a source of strength, and the last poems, especially those about the natural world, have a freshness, a joy, and a confidence which have no other source except in this sense of freedom from all earthly ties.

Existential guilt and anxiety are constant notes in the verse from the beginning, as the first poem in *The Moonlit Doorway*, "Heat," indicates. It is the first of many "river" poems, which gains an ironic significance from hindsight: Mackenzie was to drown in a river at the age of forty-two. Of the thirty-five poems on the subject of death, some are associated with love, but many more with fear or anxiety. Mackenzie's adult world is on the whole a painful, candle-lit world, full of dark presences and the need for expiation which is never quite remorse. Many of the poems lament the lost innocence of childhood, and parenthood was not for him a source of joy, as it was for Judith Wright, but an occasion for apology or a plea for forgiveness:

> What shall I say to you in my defence?
> What can I say to mate you with your stars?
> I shall say this: I got you unawares.

The sense of guilt, the anxiety, are conveyed quite often in images of murder, as in "Going Upstairs," for example, a striking if melodramatic poem, which nevertheless displays a gift for the theatrical in the proper sense of the word. It is a remarkable example of Mackenzie's gift for finding a situation to contain emotional mysteries without lapsing into frigid allegory, and the swift transition from the heroic to the sordid and the ridiculous is beautifully accomplished. A similar piece of reductionism occurs in "A Conqueror," one of the best and most neglected of Australian war-poems. The private murders and betrayals of lovers have their counterpart on the world's stage, where the lust for power, which lovers too often mistake for love, becomes destructive on a grand scale.

The poems of the final ten years are much preoccupied with physical pain, his own and other men's, in hospital. Some are pleas for oblivion, but one at least calls in question the genuineness of the death-wish, and prays for time to amend and praise. Mackenzie's poems have the faults associated with these themes. The great deliberation and the unrelenting control give an impression of slowness and monotony. It is best to read them a few at a time. He also has one of the defects of the solitary: frequent outbursts of garrulity. Lacking companionship, he conducts an eternal argument with himself, always "fighting a battle on the brink of time." He also has the narrow range of the solitary, though within that range he saw very deeply, as the references to his wife in "Two Trinities" reveal. His work is self-regarding, ego-centric, but not self-deluding − he does not romanticize his weaknesses, and with all his faults remains on the right side of the thin line between sensitivity and self-indulgence.

He wrote four novels, largely as pot-boilers. But *The Refuge*, about an extraordinary relationship between a journalist, his refugee second wife, and his son by his first wife, is as sensitive, perceptive, and compelling as the best of his verse.

—Dorothy Green

MacLEISH, Archibald. American. Born in Glencoe, Illinois, 7 May 1892. Educated at the Hotchkiss School, Lakeville, Connecticut; Yale University, New Haven, Connecticut, A.B. 1915; Harvard University, Cambridge, Massachusetts, LL.B. 1919. Served in the United States Army, 1917–19: Captain. Married Ada Hitchcock in 1916; three children. Lecturer in Government, Harvard University, 1919–21; Attorney, Choate Hall and Stewart, Boston, 1920–23; Editor, *Fortune* magazine, New York, 1929–38; Curator of the Niemann Foundation, Harvard University, 1938; Librarian of Congress, Washington, D.C., 1939–44; Director, United States Office of Facts and Figures, 1941–42, Assistant Director of the Office of War Information, 1942–43, and Assistant Secretary of State, 1944–45, Washington, D.C. Chairman of the United States Delegation to the UNESCO drafting conference, London, 1945, and Member of the Executive Board, UNESCO, 1946. Rede Lecturer, Cambridge University, 1942; Boylston Professor of Rhetoric and Oratory, Harvard University, 1949–62; Simpson Lecturer, Amherst College, Massachusetts, 1964–67. Recipient: Shelley Memorial Award, 1932; Pulitzer Prize, 1933, 1953, for drama, 1959; New England Poetry Club Golden Rose, 1934; Bollingen Prize, 1952; National Book Award, 1953; Sarah Josepha Hale Award, 1958; Antoinette Perry Award, 1959; National Association of Independent Schools Award, 1959; Academy of American Poets Fellowship, 1965; Academy Award, 1966; National Medal for Literature, 1978. M.A.: Tufts University, Medford, Massachusetts, 1932; Litt.D.: Wesleyan University, Middletown, Connecticut, 1938; Colby College, Waterville, Maine, 1938; Yale University, 1939; University of Pennsylvania, Philadelphia, 1941; University of Illinois, Urbana, 1947; Rockford College, Illinois, 1952; Columbia University, New York, 1954; Harvard University, 1955; Carleton College, Northfield, Minnesota, 1956; Princeton University, New Jersey, 1965; University of Massachusetts, Amherst, 1969; York University, Toronto, 1971; LL.D.: Dartmouth College, Hanover, New Hampshire, 1940; Johns Hopkins University, Baltimore, 1941; University of California, Berkeley, 1943; Queen's University, Kingston, Ontario, 1948; University of Puerto Rico, Rio Piedras, 1953; Amherst College, Massachusetts, 1963; D.C.L.: Union College, Schenectady, New York, 1941; L.H.D.: Williams College, Williamstown, Massachusetts, 1942; University of Washington, Seattle, 1948. Commander, Legion of Honor; Commander, El Sol del Peru. President, American Academy of Arts and Letters, 1953–56. Lives in Massachusetts.

PUBLICATIONS

Verse

    Songs for a Summer's Day (A Sonnet-Cycle). 1915.
    Tower of Ivory. 1917.
    The Happy Marriage and Other Poems. 1924.
    The Pot of Earth. 1925.
    Streets in the Moon. 1926.

The Hamlet of A. MacLeish. 1928.
Einstein. 1929.
New Found Land: Fourteen Poems. 1930.
Before March. 1932.
Conquistador. 1932.
Frescoes for Mr. Rockefeller's City. 1933.
Poems 1924–1933. 1933; as *Poems,* 1935.
Public Speech: Poems. 1936.
Land of the Free – U.S.A. 1938.
America Was Promises. 1939.
Actfive and Other Poems. 1948.
Collected Poems 1917–1952. 1952.
Songs for Eve. 1954.
Collected Poems. 1963.
"The Wild Old Wicked Man" and Other Poems. 1968.
The Human Season: Selected Poems 1926–1972. 1972.
New and Collected Poems 1917–1976. 1976.

Plays

Nobodaddy. 1926.
Union Pacific (ballet scenario; produced 1934). In *The Book of Ballets,* 1939.
Panic: A Play in Verse (produced 1935). 1935.
The Fall of the City: A Verse Play for Radio (broadcast, 1937). 1937.
Air Raid: A Verse Play for Radio (broadcast, 1938). 1938.
The States Talking (broadcast, 1941). In *The Free Company Presents,* edited by James Boyd, 1941.
The American Story: Ten Radio Scripts (includes *The Admiral; The American Gods; The American Name; Not Bacon's Bones; Between the Silence and the Surf; Discovered; The Many Dead; The Names for the Rivers; Ripe Strawberries and Gooseberries and Sweet Single Roses; Socorro, When Your Sons Forget)* (broadcast, 1944). 1944.
The Trojan Horse (broadcast, 1952). 1952.
This Music Crept by Me upon the Waters (broadcast, 1953). 1953.
J.B.: A Play in Verse (produced 1958). 1958.
The Secret of Freedom (televised, 1959). In *Three Short Plays,* 1961.
Three Short Plays: The Secret of Freedom, Air Raid, The Fall of the City. 1961.
Our Lives, Our Fortunes, and Our Sacred Honor (as *The American Bell,* music by David Amram, produced 1962). In *Think,* July–August 1961.
Herakles: A Play in Verse (produced 1965). 1967.
An Evening's Journey to Conway, Massachusetts: An Outdoor Play (produced 1967). 1967.
Scratch, suggested by *The Devil and Daniel Webster* by Stephen Vincent Benét (produced 1971). 1971.
The Great American Fourth of July Parade (produced 1975). 1975.

Screenplays: *Grandma Moses,* 1950; *The Eleanor Roosevelt Story,* 1965.

Radio Plays: *The Fall of the City,* 1937; *King Lear,* from the play by Shakespeare, 1937; *Air Raid,* 1938; *The States Talking,* 1941; *The American Story* series, 1944; *The Son of Man,* 1947; *The Trojan Horse,* 1952; *This Music Crept by Me upon the Waters,* 1953.

Television Play: *The Secret of Freedom,* 1959.

Other

Housing America, by the Editors of Fortune.   1932.
Jews in America, by the Editors of Fortune.   1936.
Background of War, by the Editors of Fortune.   1937.
The Irresponsibles: A Declaration.   1940.
The Next Harvard, As Seen by MacLeish   1941.
A Time to Speak: The Selected Prose.   1941.
The American Cause.   1941.
A Time to Act: Selected Addresses.   1943.
Poetry and Opinion: The Pisan Cantos of Ezra Pound: A Dialogue on the Role of
   Poetry.   1950.
Freedom Is the Right to Choose: An Inquiry into the Battle for the American
   Future.   1951.
Poetry and Journalism.   1958.
Poetry and Experience.   1961.
The Dialogues of MacLeish and Mark Van Doren, edited by Warren V. Busch.   1964.
The Eleanor Roosevelt Story.   1965.
A Continuing Journey.   1968.
The Great American Frustration.   1968.
Riders of the Earth: Essays and Reminiscences.   1978.

Editor, Law and Politics, by Felix Frankfurter.   1962.

Bibliography: A Catalogue of the First Editions of MacLeish by Arthur Mizener, 1938;
MacLeish: A Checklist by Edward J. Mullahy, 1973.

Reading List: MacLeish by Signi Lenea Falk, 1965; MacLeish by Grover C. Smith, 1971.

*   *   *

By 1940, Archibald MacLeish had written numerous books of poems, and was a well-known writer. He was also the target of adverse criticism. MacLeish's early work is too derivative. It abounds with the distracting influence of Eliot and Pound, among others. MacLeish writes on the same subjects as Eliot and Pound and from exactly their point of view. MacLeish's early long poems proved very weak. His most famous one is Conquistador, which won him the first of three Pulitzer Prizes. It is a verbose, unqualified glorification of Spain's slaughter and enslavement of Mexican Natives, and is, at best, unthinkingly adolescent. Other works in this period are marred by the confusing about-face MacLeish executes concerning the role of the poet. In his "Invocation to the Social Muse," MacLeish criticizes those who would urge the poet to concentrate on social issues. These issues, however, soon become central to his own work. MacLeish proceeds to sermonize, harangue – and produce much poor poetry, especially in Public Speech and his plays for radio.

Yet, despite the inferior work written in these decades, MacLeish was beginning to compile an outstanding body of lyric poetry. Some of the short poems in Streets in the Moon and New Found Land hold up very well. "L'an trentiesme de mon eage" is a superior presentation on the subject of the lost generation. Other fine peoms include "Eleven," "Immortal Autumn," and "Memorial Rain." "Ars poetic" develops the stimulating idea that "A poem should not mean/But be." Perhaps the best of all is "The End of the World," a dramatization of the belief that the universe is basically meaningless. Poems 1924–1933 brought together such superior lyrics as "Pony Rock," "Unfinished History," and "Lines for an Interment."

What became increasingly apparent in the 1940's and thereafter is that MacLeish's primary strength as a writer resides in the lyric form. In fact, MacLeish has done most of his best work after the age of fifty.

Even some of MacLeish's later plays and long poems, two genres he never really excels at, rise above the mediocre. The full-length play *J.B.*, despite its bland poetry and tepid main character, effectively dramatizes the tragedies that engulf J.B. and offers a frequently rousing debate between Mr. Zuss (representing orthodox religion) and Nickles (representing a pragmatic outlook). MacLeish's one-act play *This Music Crept by Me upon the Waters* is also successful. The main characters, Peter and Elizabeth, are interesting; the plot builds in suspense; and the poetry and the theme (a preference for the present over the past) are powerful. *Actfive* is MacLeish's best long poem. The first section, which delineates modern man's basic predicament, is quite absorbing.

Still, it is MacLeish's lyric poetry that will be remembered the longest. Starting with the poems collected in 1948, the number of excellent lyrics mounts steadily. For this reason, the critical neglect MacLeish has suffered in recent years is unjust. These later lyrics center on three sometimes overlapping subjects. One presents MacLeish's increasing awareness of the mystery that permeates human experience. Earlier in his life, he wrote several poems that spoke confidently, if not cockily about setting out on explorations; now he writes "Voyage West," a sensitive expression of the uncertainty involved in a journey. Significantly, "Poet's Laughter" and "Crossing" are full of questions, while "The Old Man to the Lizard" and "Hotel Breakfast" end with questions, not answers. MacLeish sums up his sense of the mysterious in "Autobiography" when he says, "What do I know of the mystery of the universe?/Only the mystery."

MacLeish has also written several tender eulogies and epitaphs. Two such poems about his mother are "The Burial" and "For the Anniversary of My Mother's Death." A pair of even finer poems, "Poet" and "Hemingway," have Ernest Hemingway for their subject. Other outstanding poems in this vein include "Edwin Muir," "Cummings," and "The Danger in the Air."

Finally, MacLeish has written a host of fine poems about old age. The difficulty of creativity when one is no longer young is described in "They Come No More, Those Words, Those Finches." Tiredness is poignantly depicted in "Walking" and "Dozing on the Lawn." "Ship's Log" records the narrowing awareness of the old. Here, MacLeish states: "Mostly I have relinquished and forgotten/Or grown accustomed, which is a way of forgetting." Yet " 'The Wild Old Wicked Man' " presents an old person's wisdom and passion. In the two poems concerning "The Old Gray Couple," he offers the reader a moving portrait of the final, deepest stage of human love. Lastly, using Odysseus as narrator, MacLeish chooses human love (symbolized by his aging wife) and mortal life over love for the abstract (symbolized by the goddess Calypso) and the metaphysical in his lovely poem "Calypso's Island." This poem declares, "I long for the cold, salt,/Restless, contending sea and for the island/Where the grass dies and the seasons alter."

—Robert K. Johnson

MacNEICE, (Frederick) Louis. English. Born in Belfast, Northern Ireland, 12 September 1907. Educated at Sherborne School; Marlborough; Merton College, Oxford, 1926–30, B.A. (honours) in classics and philosophy 1930. Married 1) Mary Ezra in 1930 (divorced, 1937), one son; 2) the singer Hedli Anderson in 1942, one daughter. Lecturer in Classics, University of Birmingham, 1930–36; Lecturer in Greek, Bedford College, University of London, 1936–40; Visiting Lecturer in English, Cornell University, Ithaca,

New York, 1940; Feature Writer and Producer, BBC, London, 1941–49; Director, British Council Institute, Athens, 1950–51; Visiting Lecturer in Poetry and Drama, Sarah Lawrence College, Bronxville, New York, 1954–55. Clark Lecturer, Cambridge University, 1963. Recipient: Premio d'Italia, for radio play, 1959. D.Litt.: Queen's University of Belfast, 1957. C.B.E. (Commander, Order of the British Empire), 1958. *Died 3 September 1963.*

PUBLICATIONS

Collections

> *The Collected Poems*, edited by E. R. Dodds.   1966.

Verse

> *Blind Fireworks.*   1929.
> *Poems.*   1935.
> *Letters from Iceland*, with W. H. Auden.   1937.
> *The Earth Compels.*   1938.
> *Autumn Journal: A Poem.*   1939.
> *The Last Ditch.*   1940.
> *Selected Poems.*   1940.
> *Poems 1925–1940.*   1940.
> *Plant and Phantom.*   1941.
> *Springboard: Poems 1941–1944.*   1944.
> *Holes in the Sky: Poems 1944–1947.*   1948.
> *Collected Poems 1925–1948.*   1949.
> *Ten Burnt Offerings.*   1952.
> *Autumn Sequel: A Rhetorical Poem in XXVI Cantos.*   1954.
> *Visitations.*   1957.
> *Eighty-Five Poems, Selected by the Author.*   1959.
> *Solstices.*   1961.
> *The Burning Perch.*   1963.
> *The Revenant: A Song-Cycle for Hedli Anderson.*   1975.

Plays

> *The Station Bell* (produced 1935).
> *The Agamemnon,* from the play by Aeschylus (produced 1936).   1936.
> *Out of the Picture* (produced 1937).   1937.
> *Christopher Columbus* (broadcast 1942).   1944.
> *The Dark Tower and Other Radio Scripts* (includes *Sunbeams in His Hat* and *The March Hare Saga).*   1947.
> *Faust,* parts 1 and 2 (abridged version), from the play by Goethe (broadcast 1949).   1951.
> *Traitors in Our Way* (produced 1957).
> *The Mad Island and The Administrator: Two Radio Plays.*   1964.
> *One for the Grave: A Modern Morality Play* (produced 1966).   1968.
> *Persons from Porlock and Other Plays for Radio* (includes *Enter Caesar, East of the Sun and West of the Moon, They Met on Good Friday).*   1969.

Screenplay: *The Conquest of Everest*, 1953.

Radio Plays and Features: *Word from America*, 1941; *Cook's Tour of the London Subways*, 1941; *The March of the 10,000*, 1941; *The Stones Cry Out* (series), 1941; *Freedom's Ferry*, 1941; *Dr. Chekhov*, 1941; *The Glory That Is Greece*, 1941; *Rogue's Gallery*, 1941; *Salute to the New Year*, 1941; *Vienna*, 1942; *Salutation to Greece*, 1942; *Calling All Fools*, 1942; *Salute to the U.S.S.R.*, 1942; *Alexander Nevsky*, 1942; *The Debate Continues*, 1942; *Black Gallery* (series), 1942; *The Undefeated of Yugoslavia*, 1942; *Britain to America*, 1942; *The United Nations: A Tribute*, 1942; *Halfway House*, 1942; *Salute to the U.S. Army*, 1942; *Christopher Columbus*, 1942; *Salute to Greece*, 1942; *Salute to the United Nations*, 1943; *Two Men and America*, 1943; *The Four Freedoms* (series), 1943; *Long Live Greece*, 1943; *Zero Hour*, 1943; *The Death of Byron*, 1943; *Sicily and Freedom*, 1943; *The Death of Marlowe*, 1943; *Independence Day*, 1943; *Four Years at War*, 1943; *Lauro de Bosis: The Story of My Death*, 1943; *The Spirit of Russia*, 1943; *The Fifth Freedom*, 1943; *Ring in the New*, 1943; *The Sacred Band*, 1944; *Sunbeams in His Hat*, 1944; *The Nosebag*, 1944; *This Breed of Men*, 1944; *D Day*, 1944; *He Had a Date*, 1944; *Why Be a Poet?*, 1944; *The Golden Ass*, 1944; *Cupid and Psyche*, 1944; *The Year in Review*, 1944; *A Roman Holiday*, 1945; *The March Hare Resigns*, 1945; *London Victorious*, 1945; *A Voice from Norway*, 1945; *The Dark Tower*, 1946; *Salute to All Fools'*, 1946; *Poetry Promenade* (series), 1946; *Enter Caesar*, 1946; *The Careerist*, 1946; *Agamemnon*, 1946; *Book of Verse* (series), 1946; *Aristophanes: Enemy of Cant*, 1946; *The Heartless Giant*, 1946; *The Death of Gunnar*, 1947; *The Burning of Njal*, 1947; *Portrait of Rome*, 1947; *"Autumn Journal": A Selection*, 1947; *India at First Sight*, 1948; *Portrait of Delhi*, 1948; *The Road to Independence*, 1948; *Pakistan*, 1948; *The Two Wicked Sisters*, 1948; *No Other Road*, 1948; *Trimalchio's Feast*, 1948; *The Queen of Air and Darkness*, 1949; *Louis MacNeice Reads His Poetry*, 1949; *Faust* (six parts), 1949; *Portrait of Athens*, 1951; *Burnt Offerings*, 1951; *In Search of Anoyia*, 1951; *Delphi: The Centre of the World*, 1952; *One Eye Wild*, 1952; *The Twelve Days of Christmas*, 1953; *Time Hath Brought Me Hither*, 1953; *Return to Atlantis*, 1953; *Where No Wounds Were*, 1954; *Prisoner's Progress*, 1954; *Autumn Sequel* (series), 1954; *Return to a School*, 1954; *The Waves*, from the novel by Virginia Woolf, 1955; *The Fullness of the Nile*, 1955; *The Star We Follow*, with Ritchie Calder, 1955; *Also among the Prophets*, 1956; *Bow Bells*, 1956; *Spires and Gantries*, 1956; *Carpe Diem*, 1956; *From Bard to Busker*, 1956; *Nuts in May*, 1957; *An Oxford Anthology*, 1957; *The Stones of Oxford*, 1957; *Border Ballads*, 1958; *All Fools' at Home*, 1958; *Health in Their Hands*, 1958; *New Poetry*, 1959; *Scrums and Dreams*, 1959; *Poems by Tennyson*, 1959; *They Met on Good Friday*, 1959; *Mosaic of Youth*, 1959; *East of the Sun and West of the Moon*, 1959; *The Odyssey* (series), with others, 1960; *The Administrator*, 1961; *Poems of Salvatore Quasimodo*, 1961; *Let's Go Yellow*, 1961; *The Mad Islands*, 1962; *Latin Poetry*, 1963; *New Poetry*, 1963; *Mediaeval Latin Poetry*, 1963; *Persons from Porlock*, 1963; *Ireland, My Ireland*, 1976.

Fiction

Roundabout Way.   1932.

Other

I Crossed the Minch (travel and verse).   1938.
Modern Poetry: A Personal Essay.   1938.
Zoo.   1938.
The Poetry of W. B. Yeats.   1941.

Meet the U.S. Army. 1943.
The Penny That Rolled Away (juvenile). 1954; as *The Sixpence That Rolled Away,*
   1956.
Astrology, edited by Douglas Hill. 1964.
Varieties of Parable (lectures). 1965.
The Strings Are False: An Unfinished Autobiography, edited by Elton R. Dodds. 1965.

Editor, with Stephen Spender, *Oxford Poetry 1929.* 1929.
Editor, with Bonamy Dobrée and Philip Larkin, *New Poems 1958: A P.E.N.*
   Anthology. 1958.

Bibliography: *A Bibliography of the Works of MacNeice* by C. M. Armitage and Neil Clark,
1973.

Reading List: *MacNeice* by John Press, 1965; *Spender, Day Lewis, MacNeice* by Derek
Stanford, 1969; *MacNeice* by Elton E. Smith, 1970; *Apollo's Blended Dream: A Study of the
Poetry of MacNeice* by William T. McKinnon, 1971; *The Poetry of MacNeice* by D. B. Moore,
1972; *Time Was Away: The World of MacNeice* edited by Terence Brown and Alec Reid,
1974; *MacNeice: Sceptical Vision* by Terence Brown, 1975.

*   *   *

Even if Louis MacNeice had never written a line of original poetry he would still be
remembered as a versatile and prolific man of letters. Despite the technical skill and the
arduous labour that MacNeice lavished on it, his translation of Goethe's *Faust* was only a
partial success, but his version of the *Agamemnon* of Aeschylus has been justly praised as a
remarkable achievement by classical scholars and by readers of poetry who have no Greek.
His essay *Modern Poetry* remains the best guide to what the most intelligent young poets of
the 1930's were trying to achieve; *The Poetry of W. B. Yeats,* written before the flood of
Yeatsian exegesis had gathered strength, conveys MacNeice's admiration for a major poet,
but makes some pertinent criticisms of Yeats's metaphysical and political attitudes; *Varieties
of Parable,* published two years after MacNeice's death and unrevised by him, contains
illuminating reflections on writers as dissimilar as Spenser, George Herbert, and Beckett, for
whom he felt an intuitive sympathy. He was also what he called a "radio practitioner," the
author of over 150 radio scripts, only a few of which have been published. And his
unfinished autobiography, *The Strings Are False,* is unusually perceptive and honest.

Yet it is as a poet the MacNeice will be deservedly remembered. Although he was, at the
time, classified as "a poet of the thirties," part of the pantomime monster that Roy Campbell
dubbed MacSpaunday, he was a highly individual poet whose temperament, convictions, and
poetic achievement differentiated him sharply from Auden, Spender, and Day Lewis, with
whom he was so often ranked.

MacNeice loved the brilliance of the visible world, the surfaces of things, the life-
quickening moments that suddenly awaken the lucky man who is blessed by those visitants.
He rejected the Platonic belief in "a transcendental radiance" that, as MacNeice put it,
imposed "a white-out on everything." An early poem, "Snow," makes explicit those implicit
assumptions that colour his lyrics of the 1930's:

> World is crazier and more of it than we think,
> Incorrigibly plural. I peel and portion
> A tangerine and spit the pips and feel
> The drunkenness of things being various.

One of his best known poems of the period, "The Sunlight on the Garden," still retains its vividness, partly because it moves to a tune that continues to delight us with its ingenious elegance:

> The sunlight on the garden
> Hardens and grows cold,
> We cannot cage the minute
> Within its nets of gold,
> When all is told
> We cannot beg for pardon

There is in his early verse an underlying sadness that springs from the recognition of transience. The dazzle on the sea, the momentary sunlight, even that brief awareness of timelessness in the presence of the beloved – "Time was away and somewhere else" – would, he knew, be obliterated by the turbulence of the universal flux.

His longer poems of the 1930's that wrestle with this problem are less satisfying than the short lyrics. *Autumn Journal* is, however, a highly successful poem because, as the title implies, it is not an attempt to express a systematic philosophy but a series of observations on a variety of themes, of reactions to the events of the day in the private and public worlds. The metres of the poem are irregular, the rhyme-schemes are flexible, and the poem's themes are as diverse in range as those in Byron's *Don Juan*: civil war, political satire, autobiographical digressions, memories of a broken marriage, philosophical argument, and an evocation of ancient Greece that displays MacNeice's gifts at their most brilliant.

During the war years and the late 1940's, MacNeice's poetry becomes darker and more reflective, less given to recording the surfaces of things, less gay in its music:

> Because the velvet image,
> Because the lilting measure
> No more convey my meaning.

The ravages of war, the burning of London by enemy planes, the apparent triumph of a principle that is radically hostile to life – those are the themes that run through his poems of the decade, poems whose titles and imagery remind us that MacNeice, the son of a Bishop, was haunted always by the symbols and the morality of a Christianity that he had reluctantly but firmly rejected. No poem of his is more impressive or more universal than "Prayer Before Birth":

> I am not yet born; O hear me,
> Let not the man who is beast or who thinks he is God come near me.

Between 1948 and 1957 MacNeice published three long poems: his translation of *Faust* which, although only two-thirds of the length of the original, still ran to 8000 lines; *Ten Burnt Offerings*, ten medium-length poems described by the author as "experiments in dialectical structure"; and *Autumn Sequel*, "a rhetorical poem" in twenty-six cantos. All three of the poems were broadcast by the BBC before publication, and all have been generally considered among the least satisfactory of his works. *Autumn Journal* had been successful because of its formal variety and flexibility; *Autumn Sequel*, which MacNeice described as an attempt to marry myth to "actuality," is written in *terza rima*, a medium that has proved as dangerous to English writers of long poems as Shakespearean blank verse to aspiring poetic dramatists.

Happily MacNeice was revisited by the lyrical impulse – his first collection of short poems since *Holes in the Sky* was appropriately entitled *Visitations*. In the spring and early summer of 1960, says MacNeice, "I underwent one of those rare bursts of creativity when the poet is first astonished and then rather alarmed by the way the mill goes on grinding." The resulting volume, *Solstices*, was followed by a posthumous collection, *The Burning Perch*. The variety of moods and the mastery of tone are impressive in these poems. One section of "Notes for a Biography" is a bitter virtuso parody of "Bonny Dundee"; "Beni Hasan" contemplates with serene gravity the prospect of death that came to the poet on the Nile; in "The Habits" MacNeice faces the truth about his own nature. Not surprisingly, he was "taken aback" when assembling the poems for *The Burning Perch* "by the high proportion of sombre pieces, ranging from bleak observation to thumbnail nightmares." One poem in particular, "The Taxis," is a kind of ghost story suffused with sardonic mirth:

> In the third taxi he was alone tra-la
> But the tip-up seats were down and there was an extra
> Charge of one-and-sixpence and an odd
> Scent that reminded him of a trip to Cannes.

Auden and MacNeice were the finest poets of their generation: it is by no means certain that Auden was the more distinguished of the two.

—John Press

MASEFIELD, John (Edward). English. Born in Ledbury, Herefordshire, 1 June 1878. Educated at King's School, Warwick. Served in the Red Cross in France and Gallipoli during World War I. Married Constance de la Cherois-Crommelin in 1903 (died, 1960); one son and one daughter. Indentured on the merchant training ship *Conway*, 1891–93; apprenticed on a windjammer, 1894; Sixth Officer, White Star liner *Adriatic*; worked at various odd jobs in New York City, and Yonkers, New York, 1896–97; Literary Editor, *Speaker* magazine, after 1900; Feature Writer for the *Manchester Guardian*. President, Incorporated Society of Authors, Playwrights, and Composers, 1937–67; Member, Book and Periodicals Committee, British Council, London, and lectured for the British Council in various European countries. Recipient: Polignac Prize, 1912; Shakespeare Prize, University of Hamburg, 1938; Foyle Prize, 1962; National Book League Award, 1964. D.Litt.: Oxford University, 1922; LL.D.: University of Aberdeen, 1922. Poet Laureate, 1930 until his death. Order of Merit, 1935; Companion of Literature, Royal Society of Literature, 1961. *Died 12 May 1967.*

PUBLICATIONS

Collections

   A Selection of Poems, edited by John Betjeman.   1978.

Verse

   Salt-Water Ballads.   1902.
   Ballads.   1903; revised edition, as *Ballads and Poems*, 1910.
   The Everlasting Mercy.   1911.

The Story of a Round-House and Other Poems.   1912; revised edition, 1913.
The Widow in the Bye Street.   1912.
The Daffodil Fields.   1913.
Dauber.   1913.
Philip the King and Other Poems.   1914.
Good Friday and Other Poems.   1916.
Sonnets.   1916.
Poems.   1916; revised edition, 1923, 1929; as *Collected Poems,* 1935.
Sonnets and Poems.   1916.
Lollingdon Downs and Other Poems.   1917.
Cold Cotswolds.   1917.
Rosas.   1918.
Reynard the Fox; or, The Ghost Heath Run.   1919.
Animula.   1920.
Enslaved.   1920.
Enslaved and Other Poems.   1920.
Right Royal.   1920.
King Cole.   1921.
The Dream.   1922.
Selected Poems.   1922; revised edition, 1938.
King Cole and Other Poems.   1923.
The Dream and Other Poems.   1923.
The Collected Poems.   1923; revised edition, 1932, 1935, 1938, 2 vols., 1948.
Sonnets of Good Cheer to the Lena Ashwell Players.   1926.
Midsummer Night and Other Tales in Verse.   1928.
South and East.   1929.
The Wanderer of Liverpool (verse and prose).   1930.
Poems of the Wanderer: The Ending.   1930.
Minnie Maylow's Story and Other Tales and Scenes.   1931.
A Tale of Troy.   1932.
A Letter from Pontus and Other Verse.   1936.
The Country Scene in Poems and Pictures.   1937.
Tribute to Ballet in Poems and Pictures.   1938.
Some Verses to Some Germans.   1939.
Shopping in Oxford.   1941.
Gautama the Enlightened and Other Verse.   1941.
Natalie Maisie and Pavilastukay: Two Tales in Verse.   1942.
A Generation Risen.   1942.
Land Workers.   1942.
Wonderings: Between One and Six Years.   1943.
On the Hill.   1949.
In Praise of Nurses.   1950.
The Bluebells and Other Verse.   1961.
Old Raiger and Other Verse.   1964.
In Glad Thanksgiving.   1967.

Plays

The Campden Wonder (produced 1907).   In *The Tragedy of Nan and Other Plays,* 1909.
The Tragedy of Nan (produced 1908).   In *The Tragedy of Nan and Other Plays,* 1909.
The Tragedy of Nan and Other Plays (includes *The Campden Wonder* and *Mrs. Harrison*).   1909.

The Tragedy of Pompey the Great (produced 1910).   1910; revised version (produced 1914), 1914.

Anne Pedersdotter, from a play by Hans Wiers-Jenssen (as *The Witch*, produced 1910).   1917.

Philip the King (produced 1914).   In *Philip the King and Other Poems*, 1914.

The Faithful (produced 1915).   1915.

Good Friday: A Play in Verse (produced 1917).   1916.

The Sweeps of Ninety-Eight (produced 1916).   With *The Locked Chest*, 1916.

The Locked Chest (produced 1920).   With *The Sweeps of Ninety-Eight*, 1916.

Melloney Holtspur (produced 1923).   1922.

Esther and *Berenice*, from plays by Racine.   2 vols., 1922.

A King's Daughter: A Tragedy in Verse (produced 1923).   1923.

Tristan and Isolt: A Play in Verse (produced 1923).   1927.

The Trial of Jesus (produced 1926).   1925.

Verse and *Prose Plays*.   2 vols., 1925.

The Coming of Christ (produced 1928).   1928.

Easter: A Play for Singers.   1929.

End and Beginning.   1933.

A Play of Saint George.   1948.

Fiction

A Mainsail Haul (stories).   1905; revised edition, 1913.

A Tarpaulin Master (stories).   1907.

Captain Margaret: A Romance.   1908.

Multitude and Solitude.   1909.

The Street of To-Day.   1911.

Sard Harker.   1924.

Odtaa.   1926.

The Hawbucks.   1929.

The Bird of Dawning: or, The Fortune of the Sea.   1933.

The Taking of the Gry.   1934.

Victorious Troy; or, "The Hurrying Angel."   1935.

Eggs and Baker; or, The Days of Trial.   1936.

The Square Peg; or, The Gun Fella.   1937.

Dead Ned: The Autobiography of a Corpse.   1938.

Live and Kicking Ned: A Continuation of the Tale of Dead Ned.   1939.

Basilissa: A Tale of the Empress Theodora.   1940.

Conquer: A Tale of the Nika Rebellion in Byzantium.   1941.

Badon Parchments.   1947.

Other

Sea Life in Nelson's Time.   1905.

On the Spanish Main; or, Some English Forays on the Isthmus of Darien.   1906.

Chronicles of the Pilgrim Fathers.   1910.

A Book of Discoveries (juvenile).   1910.

Lost Endeavour (juvenile).   1910.

Martin Hyde, The Duke's Messenger (juvenile).   1910.

Jim Davis; or, The Captive of the Smugglers (juvenile).   1911.

William Shakespeare.   1911; revised edition, 1954.

John M. Synge: A Few Personal Recollections.   1915.

Gallipoli. 1916.

The Old Front Line; or, The Beginning of the Battle of the Somme. 1917.

The War and the Future. 1918; as *St. George and the Dragon*, 1919.

The Poems and Plays. 2 vols., 1918.

The Battle of the Somme. 1919.

John Ruskin. 1920.

The Taking of Helen. 1923.

The Taking of Helen and Other Prose Selections. 1924; as *Recent Prose,* 1924; revised edition, 1932.

The Midnight Folk (juvenile). 1927.

The Conway: From Her Foundation to the Present Day. 1933; revised edition, 1953.

The Box of Delights; or, When the Wolves Were Running (juvenile). 1935.

Collected Works. 10 vols., 1935–38.

Some Memories of W. B. Yeats. 1940.

In the Mill (autobiography). 1941.

The Nine Days' Wonder: The Operation Dynamo. 1941.

The Twenty Five Days. 1941.

I Want! I Want! 1944.

New Chum (autobiography). 1944.

A Macbeth Production. 1945.

Thanks Before Going. 1946; revised edition, 1947.

A Book of Both Sorts: Selections from the Verse and Prose. 1947.

A Book of Prose Selections. 1950.

St. Katherine of Ledbury and Other Ledbury Papers. 1951.

So Long to Learn: Chapters of an Autobiography. 1952.

An Elizabethan Theatre in London. 1954.

The Story of Ossian. 1959.

Grace Before Ploughing: Fragments of Autobiography. 1966.

Editor, with Constance Masefield, *Lyrists of the Restoration.* 1905.

Editor, *The Poems of Robert Herrick.* 1906.

Editor, *Dampier's Voyages.* 2 vols., 1906.

Editor, *A Sailor's Garland.* 1906.

Editor, *The Lyrics of Ben Jonson, Beaumont, and Fletcher.* 1906.

Editor, with Constance Masefield, *Essays, Moral and Polite, 1660–1714.* 1906.

Editor, *An English Prose Miscellany.* 1907.

Editor, *Defoe* (selections). 1909.

Editor, *The Loyal Subject,* in *The Works of Beaumont and Fletcher,* edited by A. H. Bullen. 1910.

Editor, *My Favourite English Poems.* 1950.

Translator, *Polyxena's Speech from the Hecuba of Euripides.* 1928.

Bibliography: *Bibliography of Masefield* by C. H. Simmons, 1930.

Reading List: *Masefield* by L. A. G. Strong, 1952; *Masefield* by Muriel Spark, 1953; *Masefield* by Margery Fisher, 1963; *Remembering Masefield* by Corliss Lamont, 1971; *Masefield* by Sanford Sternlicht, 1977.

*   *   *

At one time an author with a very large and devoted following, John Masefield lost much of his readership and his reputation declined during the last quarter century of his life. Some explanations may be adduced for this. In the first place, much of his writing is concerned with seafaring or with country life. But the seafaring he had himself experienced was in the age of sail, and other forms of transportation have rendered that era obsolete; the heroisms of the merchant seaman confronting wind and water, isolated from all contact with land, are no longer popular. As for the stories of country life, the rural west midlands of England he wrote about have decisively changed. If it is an exaggeration to say his England is scarcely rural any longer, yet technology, political evolution, and a social revolution have almost entirely subsumed a pattern of living which had prevailed for generations. The once familiar settings of his work are now remote. And if Masefield did not keep pace in his writings with the vast and rapid changes in transport, applied politics, and urbanization, still less did he heed the changes in poetic techniques that were expressive of those changes. He was, it might seem, a conservative in all ways. Nevertheless, Masefield had some exceptional powers, and it is not improbable that, when he is no longer regarded as "old fashioned," but as a poet of his own time, and eminently of the 1920's, he will be cherished as a poet for whom the term Georgian is quite inadequate to define his breadth, vigour, and abundance, or his innovatory tendencies, once startling, almost outrageous, though now softened and blurred through subsequent, and far more radical, tendencies.

He celebrated his favourite subjects of the sea and the countryside copiously, and in almost every form of verse and prose – lyric, dramatic, narrative, autobiographical. Yet though he achieved successes in every mode of writing, it is above all as a narrative writer that he should be valued. He is a superb straightforward story-teller. But, excellent as many of the prose stories are, it is as a story-teller in verse that he must be accounted a great master, one of the few great masters in that genre since Chaucer. The prose stories can be considered as sailors yarns: *Captain Margaret* and *The Bird of Dawning* are models of a good, clear, honest style. Of the sinuosities of a Conrad, or the psychological subtleties of a Kipling, Masefield is utterly innocent. Instead, there is a candid and unclouded focus on character and event, on people and things and deeds. Nouns or pronouns and verbs, the staple of any writing, are functional therefore to an abnormal degree in Masefield's prose stories. Sentiment, if not passion, is genuine and moving.

The objectivity and solidity of his prose, and its other virtues, are present in his narrative poems, but, under the exciting condensation of metre, rhyme, or stanza, they there attain a striking intensity – an intensity only rarely found in his chief exemplar, Chaucer. Three stories in verse, set in the countryside, are to be especially commended: *The Everlasting Mercy*, *The Widow in the Bye Street*, and *Reynard the Fox*. The first of these tells of a young reprobate, converted from drunken debauchery and crime, by a non-conforming preacher. The second, truly tragic, related in the rime-royal stanza of Chaucer's *Prioress's Tale*, follows the career of a poor widow's son to his death on the scaffold for committing a murder. The third tells of a fox hunt and imaginatively appreciates both the skill and enjoyment of the hunters, and the terror of their victim. In all three the pacing of the narrative, the economy in matching episode to space, the gradations towards climax are magnificently controlled.

Traditional as are Masefield's forms, he was pioneering in his diction. *The Everlasting Mercy* surprised readers with the rude oaths of the rough peasants. Max Beerbohm wrote "A simple swearword in a rustic slum,/A simple swearword is to some,/To Masefield something more." That "something more" was the poetic shock to be gained by admitting the violent and brutal slang and monosyllabic oaths into a context illustrating divine mercy.

In all his story-poems cited, bold and accurate observation and suspense play their part in a series of situations leading to powerful climax. In most of them, Masefield's imaginative compassion shows him in advance of his time. There is no doubt that the execution of the young murderer in *The Widow in the Bye Street* rouses in the reader, because it did in Masefield, pity and terror.

Many of his shorter poems, as those in the collection *Salt-Water Ballads*, are likewise narrative in structure. His best known poem, "Cargoes," is a history of freight shipping in miniature, but its popularity should not be allowed to obscure the splendour of his longer works.

—Francis Berry

MASON, R(onald) A(lison) K(ells).   New Zealander.   Born in Auckland, 10 January 1905.
Educated at Panmore School; Auckland Grammar School, 1917–22; Auckland University
College, 1926–29, 1938–39, B.A. in classics 1939. Married Dorothea Mary Mould in 1964.
Part-time tutor, University Coaching College, Auckland, 1923–29; company secretary,
1933–35; Editor, *Phoenix*, 1933; public works foreman, 1936–39; Editor, *In Print*, 1941–43;
Assistant Secretary, Auckland General Labourers Union, and Editor, *Challenge*, 1943–54;
landscape gardener from 1956, and part-time school teacher from 1965. Founder Member
and Officer, People's Theatre and New Theatre Group, Auckland, 1940–43; first President,
New Zealand-China Society. Recipient: New Zealand State Literary Fund award, 1961;
Robert Burns Fellowship, University of Otago, 1962. *Died in 1971.*

PUBLICATIONS

Verse

In the Manner of Men.   1923.
The Beggar.   1924.
Penny Broadsheet.   1925.
No New Thing: Poems 1924–1929.   1934.
End of Day.   1936.
This Dark Will Lighten: Selected Poems 1923–1941.   1941.
Recent Poems, with others.   1941.
Collected Poems.   1962.

Plays

To Save Democracy, in *Tomorrow*, 27 April 1938.
Squire Speaks: A Radio Play.   1938.
China (produced 1943).   In *China Dances*, 1962.
Refugee (produced 1945).
Daddy, Paddy, and Marty, in *The People's Voice*, April 1950.
Strait Is the Gate (produced 1964).

Other

Frontier Forsaken.   1947.
Rex Fairburn.   1962.
China Dances (miscellany).   1962.

Reading List: *Mason* by Charles Doyle, 1970.

*   *   *

If any New Zealand poet before James K. Baxter has a claim to continuing international
recognition, R. A. K. Mason is the prime candidate. An independent New Zealand poetry
begins in 1923 with the publication of Mason's *In the Manner of Men*.

A poet by nature rather than conscious intellectual development, Mason had done most of
his best work by the time he was thirty. The poems in his first important small collection *The*

Beggar were almost all written before he was eighteen. Although a handful of pieces were added to his last major collection, *This Dark Will Lighten*, the bulk of his slender collected poems were written by 1929 and published, after a series of printing delays, in *No New Thing*.

During the 1930's Mason became more consciously literary and this reduced the tension of his poems. He also turned towards Marxism and developed an interest in a kind of didactic drama. Possibly for these reasons, and because of the thinness of the cultural context in which he had to work, he wrote few poems in the latter half of his life, with the scathing "Sonnet to MacArthur's Eyes" (1950) a notable exception. From 1931 to 1956 he wrote chiefly leftist political journalism, first mainly for the *People's Voice* and then *Challenge*. One small book, *Frontier Forsaken*, deals with the disastrous effects of European colonisation on the Cook Islands. Still of some interest are several of Mason's plays, such as *Squire Speaks* and *China*, the latter a manifestation of his longtime interest in revolutionary China.

Strongly influenced by the Latin classics (especially Horace and Catullus), many of Mason's best poems are rooted also in the New Testament, particularly Christ's Passion. His central theme was grief at the body's death, an unappeasable hunger for personal immortality. From these concerns came his finest poems, such as "Footnote to John, II iv," "On the Swag," "Flow at Full Moon," "Judas Iscariot" (of which Dylan Thomas asked, "Didn't that poem shock people in New Zealand?"), and other compelling pieces, such as "After Death," "The Lesser Stars," and "The Spark's Farewell to its Clay."

Although a major figure in his own country, Mason has had no followers. In style and personality he is idiosyncratic, and the religious element is important to what is best in him; he is thus an odd poet to have sprung from a secular welfare-state society. The meeting-ground is a curious species of puritanism common to the poet and the national psyche.

—Charles Doyle

MASTERS, Edgar Lee. American. Born in Garnett, Kansas, 23 August 1868; brought up in Lewistown, Illinois. Educated at schools in Lewistown; Knox College, Galesburg, Illinois, 1889; studied law in his father's law office; admitted to the Illinois Bar, 1891. Married 1) Helen M. Jenkins in 1898 (divorced, 1925), three children; 2) Ellen Coyne in 1926. Practised law in Chicago, 1891–1921, when he retired and moved to New York, to devote himself to writing, Recipient: Twain Medal, 1927; Academy of American Poets Fellowship, 1946. *Died 5 March 1950.*

PUBLICATIONS

Collections

  Selected Poems, edited by Denys Thompson. 1972.

Verse

  A Book of Verses. 1898.
  The Blood of the Prophets. 1905.
  Songs and Sonnets. 2 vols., 1910–12.
  Spoon River Anthology. 1915; revised edition, 1916.

The Great Valley.   1916.
Songs and Satires.   1916.
Toward the Gulf.   1918.
Starved Rock.   1919.
Domesday Book   1920.
The Open Sea.   1921.
The New Spoon River.   1924.
Selected Poems.   1925.
The Fate of the Jury: An Epilogue to Domesday Book.   1929.
Lichee Nuts.   1930.
The Serpent in the Wilderness.   1933.
Invisible Landscapes.   1935.
The Golden Fleece of California.   1936.
Poems of People.   1936.
The New World.   1937.
More People.   1939.
Illinois Poems.   1941.
Along the Illinois.   1942.
Harmony of Deeper Music: Posthumous Poems, edited by Frank K. Robinson.   1976.

Plays

Maximilian.   1902.
Althea.   1907.
The Trifler.   1908.
The Leaves of the Tree.   1909.
Eileen.   1910.
The Locket.   1910.
The Bread of Idleness.   1911.
Lee: A Dramatic Poem.   1926.
Jack Kelso: A Dramatic Poem.   1928.
Gettysburg, Manila, Acoma.   1930.
Godbey: A Dramatic Poem.   1931.
Dramatic Duologues (includes Henry VIII and Ann Boleyn, Andrew Jackson and Peggy
    Eaton, Aaron Burr and Madam Jumel, Rabelais and the Queen of Whims).   1934.
Richmond: A Dramatic Poem.   1934.

Fiction

Mitch Miller.   1920.
Children of the Market Place.   1922.
Skeeters Kirby.   1923.
The Nuptial Flight.   1923.
Mirage.   1924.
Kit O'Brien.   1927.
The Tide of Time.   1937.

Other

The New Star Chamber and Other Essays.   1904.
Levy Mayer and the New Industrial Era: A Biography.   1927.

Lincoln, The Man.   1931.
The Tale of Chicago.   1933.
Vachel Lindsay: A Poet in America.   1935.
Across Spoon River: An Autobiography.   1936.
Whitman.   1937.
Mark Twain: A Portrait.   1938.
The Sangamon (on the Sangamon River).   1942.

Editor, *The Living Thoughts of Emerson.*   1940.

Bibliography: *Masters: Catalogue and Checklist* by Frank K. Robinson, 1970.

Reading List: *The Chicago Renaissance in American Letters* by Bernard Duffey, 1954; *The Vermont Background of Masters* by Kimball Flaccus, 1955; in *America's Literary Revolt* by Michael Yatron, 1959; *Spoon River Revisited* by Lois Hartley, 1963; *Masters: The Spoon River Poet and His Critics* by John T. Flanagan, 1974.

*   *   *

One of the ancient Greek poets has written: "No man knows happiness; all men/Learn misery who live beneath the sun," thereby anticipating the spirit of Edgar Lee Masters's *Spoon River Anthology.* Though the book was brilliantly successful, the road to it was a long and arduous one. Seventeen years earlier Masters's first book of poems was an ignominious failure. The next few books were also unsuccessful. By this date the poet was a well-known lawyer, a robust man about town in Chicago who had made an unsuitable marriage but never allowed matrimony to interfere with his libertine instincts. The contrast between the poems, classic in form and hackneyed in thought, and their lusty author led one literary friend of Masters, the editor of *Reedy's Mirror*, to nudge him in the direction of a more original subject-matter. In any case, at the age of forty-five, Masters had failed at poetry, the one great passion of his life, and in his personal life. His one transcendent gift, fascination with human nature and insight into its workings, had found expression only in his legal career where he had espoused the cause of lower-class victims of capitalist greed.

This was the situation in May 1914, when the poet's mother arrived to visit him. According to Masters, this lady was witty, acutely observant, and "full of divinations" into the lives of the townspeople they had known in Petersburg and Lewistown, Illinois. Mother and son reviewed these lives, reviving emotions and interests that had long been dormant in the poet's mind. The result was the sudden eruption of his latent gifts as chronicler of a whole community of inter-related lives. Between May and December, though under heavy pressure from his legal duties, Masters composed the 214 epitaphs that were published that year in *Reedy's Mirror*. Other than the memory of his neighbors, the chief sources of inspiration were the polished epigrams of the *Greek Anthology* and the stimulus of the American free verse revolt that had just burst on a startled, genteel reading public. These three sources, along with the sobering reflections on human mortality induced by his mother's visit, produced "the most read and talked of volume of poetry that has ever been written in America."

Five years after the publication of *Spoon River*, Masters retired from the law and devoted himself to the writing of thirty or more books of poetry, novels, biographies, and Illinois history and geography. Though he showed a dogged determination to succeed, he never caught fire again. His first great achievement was his last and the remaining thirty-five years of his life were an embarrassing anticlimax as his first forty-five were a despairing preparation. Masters's own life, which he includes in his book under the name Webster Ford, was one of the most curious and ironical of the tales he tells there.

The anthology, as expanded and republished in 1916, contains a short prologue, "The

Hill," and 243 individual epitaphs. The verses, of a marvelous concision and vitality, relate only the most essential features of the speakers' lives. Each soul, speaking for himself from the grave, bares his innermost nature and the secrets of his life, his own self-portrait being qualified by the words of those with whom his fate was interlocked, so that nineteen separate story lines are developed. Each epitaph has its own tone and style; each speaker treats the climactic experiences or insights of his life. Depending on the character of the speaker, the language varies from mystical utterance downwards to sonorous rhetoric and racy colloquialism. The criticism that the style is prosy and flat, made by Floyd Dell and others when the book first appeared, is traceable to the lack of conventional prettiness in meter and rhyme. Though rarely "pretty," many of the poems are written in a highly imaginative metaphoric style, all are freshly conceived on the basis of a unifying rhetorical design with ample use of every form of verbal patterning, many are haunting, and some contain images of real beauty.

Without the power of its language, *Spoon River* would never have aroused its readers as it did. But its essence is in its portraiture. As few other authors have done, and no other author, perhaps, in the compass of a single book, Masters produced a "summation" and "universal depiction of life." Every variety of human nature is represented: celebrants at life's feast and neurasthenics, rowdies and lovers, pious Christians and atheists, rapists and whores, society women and laundresses, scientists and factory hands, clairvoyants, preachers, and a stable boy who sees the face of God. One of the largest groups is the philosophers. Masters was a zealous scholar and had read widely in several languages. Along with the anti-Christian and libertarian elements in his make-up, there was also the social idealist, the cosmic optimist, and the mystic that he counted as his essential self. The epitaphs of the philosophers are usually limited to one strand of thought from which one may infer their life and character, and their reflections are framed in such a way that they are as dramatic as the life histories.

Two criticisms of Masters should be considered here. The first is that the poet is preoccupied with sex, and much of the anthology is sordid and obscene. This charge, originating with Amy Lowell and others, is curious because there are only a dozen poems that are chiefly concerned with sex, none of these is salacious, and they tend to show that the wages of sin are death. The basis of the complaint lies in the candor with which Masters treats sex wherever it appears in life. Readers had been conditioned to literature in which the subject-matter was not actual life but a given writer's conception of it so that much of the earth and roots had been removed — as well as the uppermost reaches of branches that were beyond the interests of a workaday world. One of the novelties of Masters's treatment was to eliminate authorial censorship and to allow his characters, based as they were on real-life persons, to speak honestly of their lives. Though this was not his intention, the result was the first exposé of village life, which set a new pattern for literature, while the poet's views are said to have influenced subsequent writing between the two world wars.

According to the second objection, the poet falsified the American mid-western town by presenting an overly sensationalistic and pessimistic account of its life. It is true that the incidence of crime and sudden death is greater than one would normally find, but Masters was not writing a sociological report. The epitaphs taken together form a highly patterned comical tragedy that represents life as it works on the human imagination. At some moment all of these disasters actually happen to someone, but the book, as Alice Henderson remarked, is also steeped in a "flaming idealism." There are many heroes and noble souls, and the final impression that it makes is of the dignity, stoic courage, and resilience of humanity in its hapless "fool's errand" to the grave. In writing these portraits, Masters creates the bond of understanding and sympathy with a many-faced humanity that motivated his own legal work for luckless victims of circumstances.

—Glenn Richard Ruihley

McAULEY, James (Phillip). Australian. Born in Lakemba, New South Wales, 12 October 1917. Educated at Fort Street High School, Sydney; University of Sydney, M.A., Dip. Ed. Married Norma Abernethy in 1942; four sons, one daughter. Lecturer in Government, Australian School of Pacific Administration, 1946–60; Professor of English, University of Tasmania, Hobart, 1961–76. Founding Editor, *Quadrant*, Sydney, 1956–76. Recipient: Carnegie grant, 1967. Fellow, Australian Academy of the Humanities. *Died 15 October 1976.*

PUBLICATIONS

Verse

The Darkening Ecliptic, with Harold Stewart. 1944; as *Poems,* 1961.
Under Aldebaran. 1946.
A Vision of Ceremony. 1956.
The Six Days of Creation. 1963.
(Poems). 1963.
Caption Quiros: A Poem. 1964.
Surprises of the Sun. 1969.
Collected Poems 1936–1970. 1971.

Other

Poetry and Australian Culture, with *Felons and Folksongs* by Russell B. Ward. 1955.
The End of Modernity: Essays on Literature, Art, and Culture. 1959.
C. J. Brennan. 1963.
Edmund Spenser and George Eliot: A Critical Excursion. 1963.
A Primer of English Versification. 1966; as *Versification: A Short Introduction,* 1966.
The Personal Element in Australian Poetry. 1970.
Christopher Brennan. 1973.
The Grammar of the Real: Selected Prose 1959–1974. 1976.
A Map of Australian Verse. 1976.

Editor, *Generations: Poetry from Chaucer to the Present Day.* 1969.

Reading List: *McAuley: Tradition in Australian Poetry* by Leonie Kramer, 1957; *McAuley* by Vivian Smith, 1965, revised edition, 1970.

* * *

James McAuley's work is zestful and, after his conversion to Roman Catholicism in 1952, certain. His was a full life and a firm faith.

Even before 1952, in his first collection *Under Aldebaran* there is much that speaks his dissatisfaction with a materialist society of narrow views and short perspectives. "The True Discovery of Australia," ironic and Gulliverian, has the local reference that the later "Letter to John Dryden" extends in scope. The alignment with Swift and Dryden reminds us not only of McAuley's classicism but also of his focus upon the European inheritance. His editing of *Quadrant* and his work for the Australian Association for Cultural Freedom should be seen as part of the same context as his regard for traditional values, which has received its most closely argued expression in his two prose works, *The End of Modernity* and *The Grammar of the Real*. His most ambitious poem, *Captain Quiros*, records its hero's voyage to establish New Jerusalem in the southern seas. The voyage can easily be applied to McAuley's own spiritual experience in a world from which he felt increasingly isolated but for which he never despaired.

As a poet he applied the strictest standards to sustain the pure dialect of the tribe, working persistently in traditional measures and wanting no other. As early as 1944 with Harold Stewart he perpetrated the Ern Malley hoax, by which several ridiculous pieces were taken seriously by the *avant-garde* as the work of a newly discovered poet. Like Spenser, McAuley "celebrates" secular and divine love, and his second collection was called *A Vision of Ceremony*. For him, in his own phrases, "Beauty is order" ("Envoi") and "Only the simplest forms can hold/A vast complexity" ("An Art of Poetry").

—Arthur Pollard

McKAY, Claude. Jamaican. Born Festus Claudius McKay in Sunny Ville, Clarendon Parish, Jamaica, 15 September 1889. Educated at grammar school in Jamaica; Tuskegee Institute, Alabama, 1912; Kansas State College, Manhattan, 1912–14. Married Eulalie Imelda Edwards in 1914 (separated, 1914), one daughter. Policeman in Jamaica; migrated to New York City, did various jobs and opened a restaurant, 1914; Staff Member, *Workers' Dreadnought* communist newspaper, London, 1920; Staff Member, 1921–22, and Co-Editor, with Michael Gold, 1922, *The Liberator*, New York; visited Russia, 1922–23, and lived in Europe and Tangier, 1923–34, then returned to the United States: writer for the WPA (Works Progress Administration) in the late 1930's. Recipient: Harmon Prize, 1929. *Died 22 May 1948.*

PUBLICATIONS

Collections

Selected Poems. 1953.
The Passion of McKay: Selected Prose and Poetry 1912–1948, edited by Wayne Cooper. 1973.

Verse

Constab Ballads. 1912.
Songs from Jamaica. 1912; with *Constab Ballads,* as *The Dialect Poetry,* 1972.
Songs of Jamaica. 1912.
Spring in New Hampshire and Other Poems. 1920.
Harlem Shadows. 1922.

Fiction

Home to Harlem. 1928.
Banjo: A Story Without a Plot. 1929.

Gingertown (stories).   1932.
Banana Bottom.   1933.

Other

Negry v Amerike (Negroes in America).   1923.
A Long Way from Home (autobiography).   1937.
Harlem: Negro Metropolis.   1940.

Bibliography: "McKay" by Manuel D. Lopez, in *Bulletin of Bibliography,* October–December 1972.

Reading List: *Roots of Negro Racial Consciousness: Three Harlem Renaissance Authors* by Stephen H. Bronz, 1964; *The West Indian Novel and Its Background* by Kenneth Ramchand, 1970; *McKay: The Black Poet at War* by Addison Gayle, Jr., 1972.

*   *   *

Claude McKay attempted throughout his career to resolve the complexities surrounding the black man's paradoxical situation in the West. A widely travelled man, he lived for twelve years (1922–1934) in Great Britain, Russia, Germany, France, Spain and Morocco. It is during these years that a new wave of Afro-American writing, now widely known as the Harlem Renaissance, spread across the American continent. McKay is generally credited with having inspired the Renaissance with his militant poem "If We Must Die" (1919) when the nation was gripped with the Great Red Scare and racial riots in the Northern cities. Later, however, the self-exiled McKay developed an ambivalent relationship with the New Negroes of the 1920's; he did not share the "social uplift" philosophy of Alian Locke and W. E. B. DuBois although he had affinities as writer with Jean Toomer, Langston Hughes and Zora Neale Hurston. McKay is also considered a pioneer in the development of West Indian fiction, though he never returned to the land of his birth, Jamaica, having left it at age 23. Today, many regard his fiction as his most valuable contribution, but McKay also published four collections of poems, an autobiography, many essays, and a sociological study of Harlem.

It is as a poet that McKay first won attention in both the West Indies and the United States. In 1912, before he went to Kansas as an agriculture student (hoping to become the prophet of scientific farming on his return home!), he had published two volumes of dialect verse, *Songs of Jamaica* and *Constab Ballads*, and won himself a reputation as "the Jamaican Bobby Burns." Soon, he was drawn towards the intricacies of the American colour caste and he decided to cast his lot with working-class Afro-Americans. McKay was both stimulated and angered by the American environment – "Although she feeds me bread of bitterness/... I love this cultured hell that tests my youth!" ("America"). His background in the Jamaican society where the blacks formed a majority often gave him an edge as poet-observer over black American artists whose careers were sometimes wrecked by a debilitating bitterness. In his poems of personal love and racial protest, McKay gave strong expression to joy and anger, pride and stoicism. "If We Must Die," although not his best poem, won him great popularity because it powerfully evoked, in lines charged with emotion, the militant mood of Afro-American communities over the treatment meted out to black soldiers returning from World War I. The poem achieved a kind of universality in spite of its trite diction, as was well-demonstrated when Winston Churchill related it to the Allied cause by reading it to the House of Commons during World War II.

McKay's influence on later black poetry is measured better by the power of his sentiment than by any innovations in form, style or diction. McKay empathises with the sufferings of working-class blacks in the many poems of *Harlem Shadows*, but he succeeds best when he focusses on an individual's tragedy to protest against the forces of oppression. This is evident in poems such as "The Harlem Dancer," where a young female dancer is surrounded by a crowd of "wine-flushed, bold-eyed boys" which has no inkling of her soulful pride. In "Baptism," he expresses a Victorian stoicism that asserts the individual's victory through the harshest of tests. McKay often tried his hand at the sonnet form, using irregular rhyme and metre to achieve his own poetic ends. "One Year After," dealing with inter-racial love in a two-sonnet sequence, anticipates contemporary black attitudes in attributing the failure of a black-white relationship not to society's pressures but to the lover's black pride: "Not once in all our days of poignant love/Did I a single instant give to thee/My undivided being wholly free." McKay also wrote many poems about love and sex that had little to do with racial conflict and in some of these (e.g., "Flower of Love" and "A Red Flower") – as often in his fiction, especially in *Home to Harlem* – he creates erotic effects through suggestive portrayals of sexual pleasure. And yet, McKay's link to the more recent black literature is based primarily on his protest poems and his three novels.

McKay wrote both short stories and novels. *Gingertown*, his only collection of short stories, is important mainly as a source of clues and parallels to his development as novelist-thinker. The three novels – *Home to Harlem*, *Banjo*, and *Banana Bottom* – together form a thematic trilogy exploring the Western black man's special situation against the Manichean opposition between "instinct" and "intellect." *Home to Harlem* and *Banjo*, both essentially plotless novels, raise issues relating to the black's alleged primitivism, and its possible uses in an age when the fear of standardization was obsessive. The two protagonists – Jake and Banjo respectively – are rollicking roustabouts, taking life and women as they come. Their life of instinctive simplicity is, however, not without a Hemingway-like code. If they would not scab against a fellow worker, they would not be gullible enough to join a union either. As lovers, they do not permit themselves to become pimps or demean themselves to satisfy their women's masochistic desires. In the sexual metaphor that is McKay's lens in all the three novels, sexual deviations and perversions symbolize the pernicious influence of white values on black lives. In *Banana Bottom*, there is a tentative resolution of these conflicts in the character of Bita Plant who (like McKay himself) cannot allow self-hatred to reject native traditions completely even as she continues to find uses in her life for Western thought. Bita is, in some ways, a dramatization of the tangled thought on the significance of race and heritage in modern life that McKay had filtered through the character of Ray, who appears in both *Home to Harlem* and *Banjo*.

There is no hint in either his autobiography, *A Long Way from Home*, or his sociological study, *Harlem: Negro Metropolis*, of McKay's conversion in 1944 to Roman Catholicism, an astonishing turnabout by any standards. McKay's autobiography is unusual in not giving any details of his personal life, although useful as a mirror to his independence in the midst of stimulating encounters with issues, places, and people (including Frank Harris, H. G. Wells, Isadora Duncan, Sinclair Lewis). The section on his Russian visit is particularly valuable in determining a phase of his uneasy relationship with the leftist movement, from the days of his association with Max Eastman and *The Liberator* to the anti-Communist sentiments of his final years. *Harlem: Negro Metropolis* offers a scathing view of Harlem's community life and the obsessive fight of its leaders against segregation. The reviewers criticized the book justifiably for its frequent failures in objectivity. Although McKay never became an apologist for capitalist imperialism, he did try in his last years to vindicate his conversion to Catholicism in his essay "On Becoming a Roman Catholic" and in many letters to his life-long friend, Max Eastman. One cannot, however, help feeling that a tired McKay surrendered his difficult search for the positive meanings of black life by giving in to the traditional discipline of the Roman Church. As he himself put it in a letter (16 October 1944) to Eastman: "It seems to me that to have a religion is very much like falling in love with a woman. You love her for her ... Beauty, which cannot be defined."

—Amritjit Singh

MERRILL, James (Ingram). American. Born in New York City, 3 March 1926. Educated at Lawrenceville School; Amherst College, Massachusetts, B.A. 1947. Served in the United States Army, 1944–45. Recipient: National Book Award, 1967; Bollingen Prize, 1973. Member, National Institute of Arts and Letters, 1971. Lives in Connecticut.

PUBLICATIONS

Verse

Jim's Book: A Collection of Poems and Short Stories.   1942.
The Black Swan.   1946.
First Poems.   1951.
Short Stories.   1954.
The Country of a Thousand Years of Peace and Other Poems.   1959; revised edition, 1970.
Selected Poems.   1961.
Water Street.   1962.
The Thousand and Second Night.   1963.
Violent Pastoral.   1965.
Nights and Days.   1966.
The Fire Screen.   1969.
Two Poems.   1972.
Braving the Elements.   1972.
The Yellow Pages: 59 Poems.   1974.
Yannina.   1973.
Divine Comedies.   1976.

Plays

The Bait (produced 1953). In Artists' Theatre: Four Plays, edited by Herbert Machiz,   1960.
The Immortal Husband (produced 1955). In Playbook: Plays for a New Theatre,   1956.

Fiction

The Seraglio.   1957.
The (Diblos) Notebook.   1965.

Reading List: Alone with America by Richard Howard, 1969; "Feux d'Artifice" by Stephen Yenser, in Poetry, June 1973.

*   *   *

James Merrill's books of poems are like the rings of a tree: each extends beyond the content, expression, outlook, and craft of the previous work. Merrill has patiently, even doggedly, pursued his craft, giving each poem, however short or terse or ephemeral, a certain lapidary sheen and hardness. Merrill's complete output of verse, fiction, and plays is characterized by an absorption with technique and difficulty.

But his earliest poems are overworked with rhyme scheme, metric pattern, enamelled diction. Merrill came onto the literary scene during the vogue of revived metaphysical poetry, verse wrought in a traditional manner with high polish and much verbal flourishing under formal restraint. Such is the poetry of his first major book, *The Country of a Thousand Years of Peace*, with its elegant experiences, its widely cultivated tastes, its voice of leisured travel and gracious living – the poetry, in other words, of an American aristocrat. *Water Street* continues this elegant discourse on the vicissitudes of life, love, travel, the perennially chilly rooms and beds of his daily life.

But with *The Fire Screen* a new dimension to the persona comes into view: his life in Greece, where the warm sun, the old culture, the intimacy of life release a deeper self-awareness into his poems. Instead of the isolated, inward existence of New England, here the speaker is thrust into a more primal and assertive culture where his passions and convictions are awakened. There are also poems of return to the northeastern United States, lyrics of resignation and quiet regrets. In the American edition is the too-long verse narrative "The Summer People," with its heavy-handed irony; Robert Lowell said more about the vacation culture in his one page poem "Skunk Hour." *Braving the Elements* is both freer in its verse forms and more open and intimate in its content. Instead of the choppy quality of his earlier, too tightly wrought lines, there is now a smooth, conversational rhythm in his three or four line stanza structures. "Days of 1935," "18 West 11th Street" (which laments the death of young anti-war radicals), and "Days of 1971" are open, intimate revelations of the poet's mind.

Merrill's progress is toward a compromise between rigid formalism and the open poem, where craft would continue to discipline the choice and assembly of language but where the content would be free to take its own course. That balance is reached in the long sequence "The Book of Ephraim" in *Divine Comedies*. The twenty-six alphabetically ordered parts are interwoven through a leisurely plot where the poet and his lover communicate with the spirit of Ephraim through the Ouija board, whose insight and wit make life seem a mere changing room in a vast spiritual universe. In discovering this broader realm, Merrill is dazzling as a conversational poet. Ephraim's reckless honesty about the other side enables the speaker to unravel a complex plot of lives and after-lives, including his own father's, in a humorous, novel-like progression of poems. The verse never impedes the narrative; it enhances it with its exuberance of puns, amazing condensations of ideas and observations, feats of beautiful lyric sound.

The success of this sequence makes clear Merrill's earlier difficulties with orthodox convention: his verve and spontaneity of imagination, his life as a contemporary, were too straitened by the demands of closed forms of verse. Merrill has seized upon the cut-and-paste, leaping perceptual technique of today's poets without relinquishing his skill to craft the diction of his now fluid poems.

—Paul Christensen

MERWIN, W(illiam) S(tanley). American. Born in New York City, 30 September 1927. Educated at Princeton University, New Jersey, A.B. in English 1947. Married Diana Whalley in 1954. Tutor to Robert Graves's son, Majorca, 1950; Playwright-in-Residence, Poet's Theatre, Cambridge, Massachusetts, 1956–57; Poetry Editor, *The Nation*, New York, 1962; Associate, Theatre de la Cité, Lyons, France, 1964–65. Recipient: National Institute of Arts and Letters grant, 1957; Arts Council of Great Britain bursary, 1957; Rabinowitz Research Fellowship, 1961; Ford Foundation grant, 1964; Chapelbrook Award, 1966; National Endowment for the Arts grant, 1968; P.E.N. Translation Prize, 1969; Rockefeller Foundation grant, 1969; Pulitzer Prize, 1971; Academy of American Poets Fellowship, 1973; Shelley Memorial Award, 1974.

PUBLICATIONS

Verse

A Mask for Janus. 1952.
The Dancing Bears. 1954.
Green with Beasts. 1956.
The Drunk in the Furnace. 1960.
The Moving Target. 1963.
The Lice. 1967.
Three Poems. 1968.
Animae. 1969.
The Carrier of Ladders. 1970.
Signs, with A. D. Moore. 1971.
Chinese Figures: Second Series. 1971.
Japanese Figures. 1971.
Asian Figures. 1972.
Writings to an Unfinished Accompaniment. 1973.
The Compass Flower. 1977.

Plays

Darkling Child, with Dido Milroy (produced 1956).
Favor Island (produced 1957).
Eufemia, from the play by Lope de Rueda, in Tulane Drama Review, December 1958.
The Cid, from a play by Corneille (produced 1960). In The Classic Theatre, edited by Eric Bentley, 1961.
The Gilded West (produced 1961).
Turcaret, from the play by Alain Lesage, in The Classic Theatre, edited by Eric Bentley, 1961.
The False Confession, from a play by Marivaux (produced, 1963). In The Classic Theatre, edited by Eric Bentley, 1961.
Yerma, from the play by Garcia Lorca (produced 1966).
Iphigenia at Aulis, with George E. Dimock, Jr., from a play by Euripides. 1978.

Other

A New Right Arm (essay). N.d.
Selected Translations, 1948–1968. 1968.
The Miner's Pale Children. 1970.
Houses and Travellers: A Book of Prose. 1977.

Editor, West Wind: Supplement of American Poetry. 1961.

Editor, with J. Moussaieff Masson, *Classical Sanskrit Love Poetry*.   1977

Translator, *The Poem of the Cid*.   1959.
Translator, *The Satires of Perseus*.   1961.
Translator, *Some Spanish Ballads*.   1961; as *Spanish Ballads*,   1961.
Translator, *The Life of Lazarillo de Tormes: His Fortunes and Adversities*.   1962.
Translator, *The Song of Roland*, in *Medieval Epics*.   1963.
Translator, *Transparence of the World: Poems of Jean Follain*.   1969.
Translator, *Products of the Perfected Civilization: Selected Writings*, by Sebastian
    Chamfort.   1969.
Translator, *Voices: Selected Writings of Antonio Porchia*.   1969.
Translator, *Twenty Love Poems and a Song of Despair*, by Pablo Neruda.   1969.
Translator, with others, *Selected Poems: A Bilingual Edition*, by Pablo Neruda, edited by
    Nathaniel Tarn.   1969.
Translator, with Clarence Brown, *Selected Poems of Osip Mandelstam*.   1973.
Translator, *Vertical Poetry*, by Robert Juarrox.   1977.

Bibliography: in "Seven Princeton Poets," in *Princeton Library Chronicle*, Autumn 1963.

Reading List: "Merwin Issue" of *Hollins Critic*, June 1968.

*   *   *

W. S. Merwin's writing career erupted suddenly in 1952 with the publication of *A Mask for Janus*. Both it and *The Dancing Bears* are books of traditional poetry, stressing short, consciously crafted lines that move with densely worded statement. *Dancing Bears*, slightly freer in form and showing more confidence in composition, is dry and bookish, but Merwin has exercised his skill in these earliest volumes, and his intelligence and promise are evident throughout.

In *Green with Beasts* and *The Drunk in the Furnace* Merwin is in greater control of his imagination, and the experience in his lyrics is suddenly intense and compelling. The mythic content of *Green with Beasts* anticipates the bold explorations of subjectivity of later volumes. But sheer variety of tone and diction, clarity of image, leaps of thought and perception give *Green with Beasts* surges of power. *The Drunk in the Furnace* retreats slightly from the daring pursuit of the earlier volume, but the ordinary world is rediscovered here, especially in the title poem, in which the poet discovers a man living contentedly in an abandoned furnace. The landscape of these mature works is charged with magic and the fabulous, and the drunk rattling his bottle of liquor against the iron walls of his home is typical of the uncanny world in which Merwin has rooted his lyric.

By 1960, Merwin appears to have exhausted his interest in traditional English poetry, for in translating certain Spanish poets he discovered surrealist techniques that continue to affect his unique, wistfully lyrical style. The problem with *The Moving Target*, however, is the emphasis given to a disembodied voice whose lyric statements arise from unstated situations and have little or no core of argument. There is a sameness to this poetry as each poem passes into the other with its silky array of words touching briefly on the particulars of life.

In his most recent volumes, Merwin has written what appears to be the stages of a spiritual progress. Each volume is intent to mine a deeper layer of the subjective mind, to test the limits of perception where it borders on fantasy and archetypal thought, to let merge the states of dream and waking. *The Lice* is composed in the soft, remote language of surrealist lyrics and offers a distant reflection of the turbulence of the 1960's, without indictment or direct reference to actual events. A sense of political terror and unrest pervades these sombre poems. *The Carrier of Ladders* broods on absence of meaning, on death, on spiritual transcendence of the objective and alien landscape. In *Writings to an Unfinished Accompaniment*. Merwin comes to an end of the disjunctive, loosely imagistic poem. A noticeable change of attention takes over in *The Compass Flower* where the quotidian is suddenly fresh and vital, and his poems come to crisp focus on objects of immediate experience.

—Paul Christensen

MEW, Charlotte (Mary). English. Born in London, 15 November 1869. Educated privately. Death of her father, 1897, left family in greatly reduced circumstances; brother and sister confined to mental institutions; following death of remaining sister, became mentally ill and died by suicide. Granted Civil List pension, 1922. *Died 24 March 1928.*

PUBLICATIONS

Collections

Collected Poems. 1953.

Verse

The Farmer's Bride. 1916; revised edition, 1921; as *Saturday Market,* 1921.
The Rambling Sailor. 1929.

Reading List: "Mew" by Harold Monro, in *Some Contemporary Poets,* 1920.

* * *

Charlotte Mew began writing short stories, poems, and occasional articles of criticism (e.g., a defense of Emily Brontë in *Temple Bar*, 1904) in the 1890's. Although her stories found a ready market in the *English Woman, Temple Bar*, the *Egoist*, and other journals, she was a severe self-critic and chose to publish very little of what she wrote. One of her best stories, "Passed" (*Yellow Book*, 1894), is based on her voluntary social work; it is a highly introspective account of the speaker's new insights after being led to a sordid room where a prostitute lies dead by suicide. Because of fear of hereditary insanity, Charlotte and her sister Anne had renounced marriage, and many of her stories and poems have the theme of renunciation. The mysterious "A White Night" (*Temple Bar*, 1903) involves the living burial of a woman, who accepts this fate, by a company of monks in a Spanish church.

As a poet, Charlotte Mew was "discovered" by Alida Klemantaski; her husband, Harold Monro, published a book of 17 of her poems in 1916. In "The Farmer's Bride," the title poem, the awkward farmer longs for his frightened, deranged young wife: "She sleeps up in the attic there/Alone, poor maid. 'Tis but a stair/Betwixt us. Oh! my God! the down,/The soft young down of her, the brown,/The brown of her – her eyes, her hair, her hair!" The powerful monologue "Madeleine in Church" gives a wry stoical interpretation, typical of Charlotte's attitude toward herself: "It seems too funny all we other rips/Should have immortal souls ..." and "I do not envy Him His victories, His arms are full of broken things,/ But I shall not be in them." Charlotte Mew insisted that her occasional long lines not be run-over in the printing. She usually used rhyme. Most of her poems are short, and in inventive irregular stanzas, expressive of their strong, controlled emotion.

The painful death of Anne left Charlotte deranged. Her poems "Ken" and "On the Asylum Road" had told of insane persons being taken to dreary hospitals. The room given her in a hospital had no view but a neighboring brick wall. She had once written: "Lord, when I look at lovely things which pass,/... Can I believe there is a heavenlier world than this?" She poisoned herself in 1928.

—Alice R. Bensen

MILLAY, Edna St. Vincent.   American.   Born in Rockland, Maine, 22 February 1892. Educated at schools in Rockland and Camden, Maine; Barnard College, New York; Vassar College, Poughkeepsie, New York, graduated 1917. Married Eugen Jan Boissevain in 1923. Worked as a free-lance writer in New York City; also associated with the Provincetown Players. Recipient: Pulitzer Prize, 1923. Litt.D.: Tufts University, Medford, Massachusetts; Colby College, Waterville, Maine; University of Wisconsin, Madison; L.H.D.: New York University. Member, American Academy of Arts and Letters. *Died 19 October 1950.*

PUBLICATIONS

Collections

> *Letters,* edited by Allan Ross Macdougall.   1952.
> *Collected Poems,* edited by Norma Millay.   1956.

Verse

> *Renascence and Other Poems.*   1917.
> *A Few Figs from Thistles.*   1920.
> *Second April.*   1921.
> *The Ballad of the Harp-Weaver.*   1922.
> *The Harp-Weaver and Other Poems.*   1923; as *Poems,* 1923.
> *(Poems),* edited by Hughes Mearns.   1927.
> *The Buck in the Snow and Other Poems.*   1928.
> *Poems Selected for Young People.*   1929.
> *Fatal Interview: Sonnets.*   1931.
> *Wine from These Grapes.*   1934.
> *Conversation at Midnight.*   1937.
> *Huntsman, What Quarry?*   1939.
> *Make Bright the Arrows: 1940 Notebook.*   1940.

Collected Sonnets. 1941.
The Murder of Lidice. 1942.
Collected Lyrics. 1943.
Mine the Harvest: A Collection of New Poems, edited by Norma Millay. 1954.

Plays

Aria da Capo (produced 1921). 1921.
The Lamp and the Bell (produced 1921).   1921.
Two Slatterns and a King: A Moral Interlude (produced 1921).   1921.
The King's Henchman, music by Deems Taylor (produced 1927).   1927.
The Princess Marries the Page. 1932.

Other

Distressing Dialogues. 1924.
Fear. 1927(?).

Translator, with George Dillon, *Flowers of Evil,* by Baudelaire. 1936.

Bibliography: *A Bibliography of the Works of Millay* by Karl Yost, 1937.

Reading List: *The Indigo Bunting: A Memoir of Millay* by Vincent Sheean, 1957; *Restless Spirit: The Life of Millay* by Miriam Gurko, 1962; *Millay* by Norman A. Brittin, 1967; *Millay* by James Gray, 1967; *The Poet and Her Book: A Biography of Millay* by Jean Gould, 1969.

*   *   *

If it is true that "You cannot touch a flower without disturbing a star," then the whole firmament must have been tremulous at the birth of Edna St. Vincent Millay. A woman of pronounced and strongly held convictions, she was catapulted to fame in 1920 by her book *A Few Figs from Thistles,* and became the prototype of the "new, emancipated women." The unheard of freedom which this lady demanded – freedom in love, freedom of thought in matters of morality and religion, equal rank with the male, and, above all, the freedom to act out her own individuality unhampered by outworn social codes – was one that was needed to counteract the deadening effects of Victorian proprieties. The rebellion that Millay promoted opened many new paths for the adventuresome human spirit and she is not to be blamed if the new freedoms are often abused. As she noted in one of her finest sonnets, "What rider spurs him," civilization is a contest fought in the dark against tremendous obstacles and requiring a continuous forward motion to counteract the destructive and stultifying tendencies in human nature. It is curious that Millay, the proponent of new, creative designs for life, clothed her verse in traditional forms and language, while T. S. Eliot, who harked to the past and worshipped authority as the solution to the world's ills, developed a new language and style for poetry. His contribution was also a forward motion for poetry, but the great admiration for this poet among academicians served for many years to minimize the recognition of the achievements of lyrical poets such as Millay.

More, perhaps, than any other poet in English, Millay's stance vis-à-vis the universe was one of a human being almost totally absorbed in her own human situation, whose reactions to that situation, including, of course, the condition of the whole human race, are nearly always of an immediate, personal character. She does not stand outside herself but reports all the tumults of existence as they reverberate in her own being. Since she was a personality more than life-size and was gifted with "a high sense of drama," her personalist approach created poetry of great vitality and conviction. On the other hand, being caught in the cage of personal, individual existence becomes suffocating, and, in her case, largely excluded awareness of the strange Otherness of things, the transcendent order of reality that we call the Divine.

Such as it was, however, Millay's outlook produced a large body of lyrical works of the highest distinction and expressiveness. It is easy to understand Louis Untermeyer's hyperbolic statement in 1923 that "Renascence," written when Millay was nineteen years old, was "possibly the most astonishing performance of this generation." Sentiments of great verve and freshness are given classic expression in a style that is always concise and musical. As James Gray says, the content of her poetry is equally attractive since it consists of her own version of the ageless contest between life and death, in both the physical and spiritual senses, the raptures and failures of love, and the ever-present struggle between the processes of decay and rebirth. There are times, as suggested above, when the reader may feel oppressed by the weight of her tortured self-absorption, but this is the price that must be paid for the sharply etched and poignant account of her soul's turnings.

—Glenn Richard Ruihley

* * *

MONRO, Harold (Edward). English.   Born in Brussels, Belgium, 14 March 1879. Educated at Radley; Caius College, Cambridge. Served in an anti-aircraft battery during World War I. Married Alida Klemantaski in 1920; one son. Founder, *Poetry Review*, London, 1912, and Poetry Bookshop, Bloomsbury, London, 1912; Editor, *Poetry and Drama*, 1913–14; Founder Editor, *The Monthly Chapbook*, London, 1919–21. *Died 16 March 1932.*

PUBLICATIONS

Collections

   Collected Poems, edited by Alida Monro.   1933.

Verse

   Poems.   1906.
   Judas.   1907.
   Before Dawn: Poems and Impressions.   1911.
   Children of Love.   1914.
   Trees.   1916.
   Strange Meetings.   1917.
   Real Property.   1922.
   The Earth for Sale.   1928.

Play

One Day Awake: A Morality. 1922.

Other

Proposals for a Voluntary Nobility, with Maurice Browne. 1907.
The Evolution of the Soul. 1907.
The Chronicle of a Pilgrimage: Paris to Milan on Foot. 1909.
Some Contemporary Poets (1920). 1920.
The War Memorial in Battersea Park. 1924.

Editor, *Twentieth Century Poetry: An Anthology.* 1929.

Reading List: in *Polite Essays* by Ezra Pound, 1937; in *The Georgian Revolt* by R. H. Ross, 1965; *Monro and the Poetry Bookshop* by Joy Grant, 1967 (includes bibliography).

*   *   *

Of all the Georgian poets, Harold Monro came nearest to dealing with the concerns of life around him. His central position as organiser of the Poetry Bookshop, and of readings and discussions held there as part of his attempt to popularise poetry, made him seem to relegate his own work to a secondary role. Those who like to imagine that the making of poetry is a full-time occupation sometimes sneer at Monro and his fellow Georgians as "weekending with their talents" (overlooking the fact that one of the mightiest of symphonists, Gustav Mahler, was also a week-end and summer-holiday composer). Strength is seemingly lent to this absurd argument by the fact that Monro's sonnet-sequence "Week-end" was for many years his most frequently anthologised piece.

> The train! The twelve o'clock for paradise.
>   Hurry, or it will try to creep away.
> Out in the country everyone is wise:
>   We can be wise only on Saturday.
> There you are waiting, little friendly house:
>   Those are your chimney-stacks with you between,
> Surrounded by old trees and startled cows,
>   Staring through all your windows at the green....

Week-ending has become a popular pastime throughout much of Europe, and Monro catches its sense of quasi-romantic release better than anyone.

Like Coventry Patmore, whose rhymed *vers libres* Munro emulated in his later work, he was much concerned with the small things of domestic life, but seen in their relation to practical use as well as for what they are themselves. In a strange way, quite early he left behind the mood for Georgian poetry (though not always the tone), and looked forward to the urban poetry of Eliot and his followers. Thus, eight years before the publication of *The Waste Land*, Monro, in "London Interior," was writing:

> The evening will turn grey.
> It is sad in London after two.
> All, all the afternoon,
> What can old men, old women do?

It is sad in London when the gloom
Thickens, like wool,
In the corners of the room;
The sky is shot with steel,
Shot with blue.

The bells ring the slow time;
The chairs creak, the hours climb;
The sunlight lays a streak upon the floor.

He himself, in a late poem which both he and his wife (but not this critic) regarded as his best, "Midnight Lamentation," observed: "I think too much of death;/There is a gloom/when I can't hear your breath/calm in some room." A sense of alienation, of unhappiness, pervades most of what he wrote, as alcohol eventually pervaded his later life. The tendency to both melancholy and alcoholism was perhaps an inheritance of his Lowland Scots ancestry. His achievement, though a minor one, is distinctive, and his best work should be better known than it is.

—Maurice Lindsay

* * *

MONTAGUE, John (Patrick).   Irish.   Born in Brooklyn, New York, 28 February 1929. Educated at St. Patrick's College, Armagh; University College, Dublin, B.A. in English and history 1949, M.A. 1951; Yale University, New Haven, Connecticut (Fulbright Scholar), 1953–54; University of Iowa, Iowa City, M.F.A. 1955. Married 1) Madeleine de Brauer in 1956; 2) Evelyn Robson in 1971. Worked for the State Tourist Board, Dublin, 1956–61; taught at the Poetry Workshop, University of California, Berkeley, Spring 1964 and 1965, University College, Dublin, Spring/Summer 1967 and Spring 1968, and at the Experimental University of Vincennes, France. Currently, Lecturer in Poetry, University College, Cork. Member, Irish Academy of Letters.

PUBLICATIONS

Verse

  Forms of Exile.   1958.
  The Old People.   1960.
  Poisoned Lands and Other Poems.   1961.
  All Legendary Obstacles.   1966.
  Patriotic Suite.   1966; *Home Again*, 1967; *Hymn to the New Omagh Road*, 1968; *The Bread God: A Lecture, with Illustrations in Verse*, 1968; *A New Siege*, 1969; complete version, as *The Rough Field*, 1972.
  A Chosen Light.   1967.

The Planter and the Gael, with John Hewitt. 1970.
Tides. 1970.
A Fair House (translations from Irish). 1973.
The Cave of Night. 1974.
O'Riada's Farewell. 1974.
A Slow Dance. 1975.
The Great Cloak. 1978.

Fiction

Death of a Chieftain and Other Stories. 1964.

Other

Editor, *The Dolmen Miscellany of Irish Writing*. 1962.
Editor, with Liam Miller, *A Tribute to Austin Clarke on His Seventieth Birthday*. 1966.
Editor, *The Faber Book of Irish Verse*. 1974; as *The Book of Irish Verse*, 1977.

Reading List: *Montague* by Frank Kersnowski, 1975.

* * *

Only gradually has John Montague's precise mastery of the lyric sequence been so closely attended as the discovery of Thomas Kinsella and Seamus Heaney at the start and close of the 1960's. Dating from 1958, Montague's collections span more than Heaney's pagan pastorals and Kinsella's nightmare-torn memoirs, for brighter, fresher influences on Montague have been the Americans William Carlos Williams and Robert Duncan. Although *Poisoned Lands* displays forms grounded in a classical Irish schooling, it draws innovation and humor from Lawrence and Auden. Only later in sequences like *All Legendary Obstacles* and in triptychs like the title poem of *A Chosen Light* do Montague's adult and perplexing, for some, traits appear: a personal reticence alluding to, not confessing, private crises; and a delight in the open forms of extensive sequences. One can feel in these both Yeats and the new American poets – Snyder, Bly, Creeley – standing near:

> (next to the milk-white telephone)
>
> A minute wind –
> Mill casting its pale light
> Over unhappiness, ceaselessly
> Elaborating its signals
>
> Not of help, but of neutral energy.

The Rough Field, begun in 1958, is an epic sequence of ten sequences, or cantos; it charts by turns a vision of the moral geography of Montague's Ulster heritage and of his spiralling progress through its torn world back to its *garbh acaidh. The Rough Field* may best be read, keeping in mind its titular metaphor, as a social allegory whose moral impulse springs from illuminations of a newly ordered self, and these require a myth able to span his cantos' local subjects and ambitious themes. Montague found such a myth in those love poems of *A Chosen Light*, resolved later in the darker lyrics of *Tides*. These employ an ancient Irish genre, the *aisling*, to spin autobiography into a romance of the self renewed. *The Rough Field* ends with the romantic parable of "The Wild Dog Rose":

> Briefly
> the air is strong with the smell
> of that weak flower, offering
> its crumbling yellow cup
> and pale bleeding lips
> fading to white
> at the rim
> of each bruised and heart-
> shaped petal.

That emblem of grace renewed enables Montague's persona to become a culture hero – scapegoat or celebrant – on a pilgrimage back to spiritual yet visible origins.

—Thomas Dillon Redshaw

MOORE, Marianne (Craig). American. Born in Kirkwood, Missouri, 15 November 1887. Educated at the Metzger Institute, Carlisle, Pennsylvania; Bryn Mawr College, Pennsylvania, B.A. 1909; Carlisle Commercial College, Pennsylvania, 1910. Head of the Commercial Studies Department, United States Indian School, Carlisle, 1911–15; worked as a private tutor and secretary in New York City, 1919–21, and as a Branch Librarian for the New York Public Library system, 1921–25; Acting Editor, *The Dial*, 1926 until it ceased publication, 1929. Visiting Lecturer, Bryn Mawr College, 1953; Ewing Lecturer, University of California, Berkeley, 1956. Recipient: Hartsock Memorial Prize, 1935; Shelley Memorial Award, 1941; Harriet Monroe Poetry Award, 1944; Guggenheim Fellowship, 1945; National Institute of Arts and Letters grant, 1946, and Gold Medal, 1953; Pulitzer Prize, 1952; National Book Award, 1952; Bollingen Prize, 1953; Poetry Society of America Gold Medal, 1960, 1967; Brandeis University Creative Arts Award, 1963; Academy of American Poets Fellowship, 1965; MacDowell Medal, 1967; National Medal for Literature, 1968. Litt.D.: Wilson College, Chambersburg, Pennsylvania, 1949; Mount Holyoke College, South Hadley, Massachusetts, 1950; University of Rochester, New York, 1951; L.H.D.: Rutgers University, New Brunswick, New Jersey, 1955; Smith College, Northampton, Massachusetts, 1955; Pratt Institute, Brooklyn, New York, 1959; D.Litt.: New York University, 1967; Washington University, St. Louis, Missouri, 1967; Harvard University, Cambridge, Massachusetts, 1969. Member, American Academy of Arts and Letters, 1955. *Died 5 February 1972.*

PUBLICATIONS

Verse

Poems. 1921.
Observations. 1924.

Selected Poems.   1935.
The Pangolin and Other Verse.   1936.
What Are Years?   1941.
Nevertheless.   1944.
Collected Poems.   1951.
Like a Bulwark.   1956.
O to Be a Dragon.   1959.
Eight Poems.   1962.
The Arctic Ox.   1964.
Tell Me, Tell Me: Granite, Steel, and Other Topics.   1966.
The Complete Poems.   1967.
Unfinished Poems.   1972.

Play

The Absentee, from a story by Maria Edgeworth.   1962.

Other

Predilections.   1955.
Idiosyncracy and Technique: Two Lectures.   1958.
Letters from and to the Ford Motor Company, with David Wallace.   1958.
A Moore Reader.   1961.
Dress and Kindred Subjects.   1965.
Poetry and Criticism.   1965.

Editor, with W. H. Auden and Karl Shapiro, *Riverside Poetry 1953: Poems by Students in Colleges and Universities in New York City.*   1953.

Translator, with Elizabeth Mayer, *Rock Crystal: A Christmas Tale,* by Adalbert Stifter.   1945.
Translator, *The Fables of La Fontaine.*   1954; *Selected Fables,* 1955.
Translator, *Puss in Boots, The Sleeping Beauty, and Cinderella: A Retelling of Three Classic Fairy Tales,* by Charles Perrault.   1963.

Bibliography: *Moore: A Descriptive Bibliography* by Craig S. Abbott, 1977.

Reading List: *The Achievement of Moore: A Biography, 1907–1957* by Eugene P. Sheehy and Kenneth A. Lohf, 1958; *Moore* by Bernard F. Engel, 1964; *Moore* by Jean Garrigue, 1965; *Moore: An Introduction to the Poetry* by George W. Nitchie, 1969; *Moore* by Sister M. Thérèse, 1969; *Moore: A Collection of Critical Essays* edited by Charles Tomlinson, 1970; *Moore: The Cage and the Animal* by Donald Hall, 1970; *Moore: Poet of Affection* by Pamela White Hadas, 1977.

*   *   *

Marianne Moore seems the best poet of her sex to have written in the United States during this century. Her poetry is richer and more inclusive than that of H. D. or of Elizabeth

College; and in the 1920's she was associated with the New York magazine *The Dial*, becoming its editor from 1926 to 1929. Like Williams, she was a naturalist in her subject-matter, and would not have disagreed with Pound's programme for Imagism. Many of the American modernist poets learned to purge their beams at her empirical eye. Yet Eliot, who could not have accepted William's *dictum* "No ideas but in things," also admired Marianne Moore's poetry for the distinction of its language. In his preface to her *Selected Poems*, he judged that she was "one of those few who have done the language some service in my lifetime."

Marianne Moore appears at first an idiosyncratic writer. She chooses odd subjects and sees them from odd angles; she is miscellaneous in her subject-matter and unpredictable in her reflections; she writes in a chopped prose in lines of spectacular irregularity, but with metrical distinctness and, surprisingly often, rhyme. Yet her style, for all its asymmetry, is rapid, clear, unself-concerned, flexible, and accurate, and her work gradually discloses her exceptional sanity, intelligence, and imaginative depth. Unmistakably modern, she has no modernist formlessness; curious and precise, she is too brave in her vision to be an old maid. Some of these paradoxical qualities appear in her openings, which demand attention by their directness, as in "The Steeple-Jack":

> Dürer would have seen a reason for living
>   in a town like this, with eight stranded whales
> to look at; with the sweet sea air coming into your house
> on a fine day, from water etched
>   with waves as formal as the scales
> on a fish.

or "Silence":

> My father used to say,
> "Superior people never make long visits,
> have to be shown Longfellow's grave
> or the glass flowers at Harvard.
> Self-reliant like the cat —
> that takes its prey to privacy,
> the mouse's limp tail hanging like a shoelace from its mouth —
> they sometimes enjoy solitude..."

or "To a Snail":

> If "compression is the first grace of style,"
> you have it. Contractility is a virtue
> as modesty is a virtue.

or "Poetry":

> I, too, dislike it.
>   Reading it, however, with a perfect contempt for it, one discovers in
> it, after all, a place for the genuine.

This last is a complete poem, and unusually brief, although most of her poems are meditations of this characteristic briskness. "The Steeple-Jack" is a classic among her longer poems, as is "A Grave," which begins:

Bishop, to name two who resemble her in their fastidious interest in natural history – Miss Moore's predilection and habitual material. Herself of the modernist generation of Stevens, Williams, Pound, and Eliot, she knew Williams, Pound, and H. D. in her days at Bryn Mawr

> Man looking into the sea,
> taking the view from those who have as much right to it as you have to it yourself,
> it is human nature to stand in the middle of a thing,
> but you cannot stand in the middle of this;
> the sea has nothing to give but a well excavated grave.

The resonance of that last line states openly, with "an elegance of which the source is not bravado," the essential seriousness which Marianne Moore often took pains to bury deep in her bright-eyed concern with the external world, of which she was such a connoisseur. Like La Fontaine, whose *Fables* she translated, she was fundamentally a humane moralist, however passionate and fine her observation of animals, baseball-players, and nature's remoter aspects; and she was fundamentally serious despite her turn for the smacking epigram.

Her career illuminated the American scene for an exceptionally long time, and to increasing recognition. Her powers did not diminish, but her idiosyncrasy and allusiveness intensified. Thoroughly American and modern, she demonstrated the possibility of a highly civilised and eclectic mind operating with discrimination and unsentimental enjoyment on the premise basic to so much modern American poetry, that everything that is human is material for poetry: "Whatever it is, let it be without/affectation" ("Love in America").

—M. J. Alexander

MOORE, T(homas) Sturge. English.   Born in Hastings, Sussex, 4 March 1870; brother of the philosopher G. E. Moore. Educated at Dulwich College to age 14; Croydon and Lambeth art schools. Married Marie Appia in 1903; one son and one daughter. Author, art historian, and wood engraver. Member, Academic Committee, Royal Society of Literature. Granted Civil List pension, 1920. *Died 18 July 1944.*

PUBLICATIONS

Verse

Two Poems.   1893.
The Vinedresser and Other Poems.   1899.
Danaë.   1903.
The Centaur's Booty.   1903.
The Rout of the Amazons.   1903.
The Gazelles and Other Poems.   1904.
Pan's Prophecy.   1904.
To Leda and Other Odes.   1904.

Theseus, Medea, and Lyrics.   1904.
The Little School: A Posy of Rhymes.   1905; revised edition, 1917.
The Sea Is Kind.   1914.
Danaë, Aforetime, Blind Thamyris.   1920.
Judas.   1923.
Mystery and Tragedy: Two Dramatic Poems.   1930.
Nine Poems.   1930.
The Poems.   4 vols., 1931–33.
Selected Poems, edited by Marie Sturge Moore.   1934.
The Unknown and Known, and a Dozen Odd Poems.   1939.

Plays

Aphrodite Against Artemis (produced 1906).   1901.
Absalom: A Chronicle Play.   1903.
Mariamne.   1911.
A Sicilian Idyll, and Judith: A Conflict.   1911.
Judith: A Conflict (produced 1916).   In *A Sicilian Idyll, and Judith*, 1911.
The Wilderness, with Gustave Ferrari (produced 1915).
Tragic Mothers: Medea, Niobe, Tyrfing.   1920.
Medea (produced 1924).   In *Tragic Mothers*, 1920.
The Powers of the Air.   1920.
Roderigo of Bivar.   1925.
Bee-Bee-Bei, music by Edmund Rubbra (produced 1933).

Other

Altdorfer.   1900.
A Brief Account of the Origin of the Eragny Press, and a Note on the Relation of the Printed Book as a Work of Art to Life.   1903.
Albert Dürer.   1905.
Correggio.   1906.
Art and Life (essays).   1910.
Hark to These Three Talk about Style.   1915.
Some Soldier Poets.   1919.
(Woodcuts).   1921.
Armour for Aphrodite (aesthetics).   1929.
Yeats and Moore: Their Correspondence 1901–1937, edited by Ursula Bridge.   1953.
Contributions to the Art of the Book and Collaboration with Yeats, edited by Malcolm Easton.   1970.

Editor, *The Passionate Pilgrim and the Songs in Shakespeare's Plays*.   1896.
Editor, *The Vale Shakespeare*.   39 vols., 1900–03.
Editor, *Little Engravings*.   1902.
Editor, *Poems from Wordsworth*.   1902.
Editor, *A Selection from the Poems of Michael Field*.   1923.
Editor, with D. C. Sturge Moore, *Works and Days, from the Journal of Michael Field*.   1933.
Editor, with Cecil Lewis, *Self-Portrait, Taken from the Journals and Letters of Charles Ricketts, R.A.*   1939.

Translator, *The Centaur, The Bacchante*, by Maurice de Guérin.   1899.

Reading List: *Moore and the Life of Art* by F. L. Gwynn, 1951 (includes bibliography).

* * *

T. Sturge Moore was educated at Croydon Art School where he met Charles Shannon, and by Shannon was persuaded to proceed to Lambeth Art School where Shannon's associate Charles Ricketts was teaching. By 1888 Moore was part of Rickett's "Vale" circle and contributed poems, woodcuts, and wood engravings to such periodicals as Rickett's *Dial* and Shannon and Gleeson White's *Pageant*. His first and best volume of verse, *The Vinedresser and Other Poems*, appeared in 1899. Though he published prolifically both poetry and poetic drama, he never won popular acclaim, though respected by fellow practitioners. Laurence Binyon early on pointed out the limitations of Moore's style, which were never overcome: a deficiency in clean phrasing, a choke of consonants, and obscurity of syntax. His subject matter was invariably remote, ideal, literary. He was, however, skilled in the evocation of colourful and densely realised Arcadian scenes which reflect the enthusiasm of the autodidact for classical story. He was also a great reviser of earlier poets' work, an interesting mode of composition, and one which has been recently practiced by such poets as George MacBeth.

Moore, as befitted the brother of the distinguished Cambridge philosopher G. E. Moore, was something of aesthetician. His *Art and Life* elaborates a comparison between Flaubert and Blake, somewhat in Flaubert's favour; *Armour for Aphrodite* develops his theory of beauty as creative tension – like Yeats he adds the element of struggle to the Paterian aesthetic. Moore was a skilled designer of books and bookplates. His design for *Axel* is brilliantly complex in the Ricketts manner, while his series of covers for Yeats's later poems were composed in accordance with programmes suggested by the poet. The letters he exchanged with Yeats in the later 1920's and the 1930's are fascinating examples of Moore's gifts for philosophical argument besides radiating flashes of critical insight.

—Ian Fletcher

MORAES, Dom(inic Frank). Indian. Born in Bombay, 19 July 1938; son of Frank Moraes, editor of the *Indian Express*. Educated at Jesus College, Oxford, 1956–59, B.A. in English 1959. Married 1) Judith St. John in 1963 (divorced), one son; 2) Leela Naidu in 1970. Formerly, scriptwriter, Granada Television; Documentary Filmmaker. Since 1971, Editor, *The Asian Magazine*, Hong Kong. Since 1973, Consultant, United Nations Fund for Population Activities. Recipient: Hawthornden Prize, 1958.

PUBLICATIONS

Verse

A Beginning. 1957.
Poems. 1960.
John Nobody. 1965.
Poems 1955–1965. 1966.
Bedlam Etcetera. 1966.

Other

   Green Is the Grass (on cricket).   1951.
   Gone Away: An Indian Journal.   1960.
   My Son's Father: An Autobiography.   1968; as *My Son's Father: A Poet's
      Autobiography,* 1969.
   The Tempest Within: An Account of East Pakistan.   1971.
   From East and West: A Collection of Essays.   1971.
   A Matter of People.   1974; as *This Burdened Planet,* 1974.

   Editor, *Voices for Life: Reflections on the Human Condition.*   1975.

   Translator, *The Brass Serpent,* by T. Carmi.   1964.

*   *   *

Dom Moraes, the son of the distinguished journalist and writer Frank Moraes, is in several ways an interesting literary figure. One of the best known Indian poets writing in English, there is in his poetry, paradoxically, very little of specific "Indianness." In fact, as he himself put it once: "English is the language I think in and write in; I even dream in it ... I don't speak any Indian language – neither Hindi nor my native Konkani." And he spent the most formative years of his life – from 15 to 30 – in England.

Moraes's poetic talent has been an extremely precocious one: at eighteen, he won the Hawthornden Prize for his first collection of poems, *A Beginning*; his second, *Poems* was a Poetry Book Society choice. The most remarkable quality of his poetry is an unusual combination of romantic näiveté with a deep, underlying ironic thrust. This stems from a recurring feeling of loneliness threatening, in the initial stages, to become obsessive self-indulgence: "I have grown up, I think, to live alone,/To keep my old illusions, sometimes dream/Glumly that I am unloved and forlorn ..." ("Autobiography"). This apparently "fluent sentimentality" in fact tempts one, as Harry Fainlight has put it (*Encounter*, November 1961) "to write the whole thing off as a luxury product, the lispings of an elite-poet." The näiveté, however, is only apparent, for there is "deceptive strength in this kind of verse; having the courage of one's own naivety is a difficult and promising thing and certainly a much sounder basis for growth than the clever apeing of maturity ...."

This growth registers itself in his gradual awareness of contemporary reality: the loss of identity rendered acute by his dichotomous background as an Indian writing in English, the increasing eruption of violence and disorder. If the Indian landscape is dotted with "hawks," "doe-like girls, the sun, endless delay/Bullocks and Buicks, statesmen like great auks," ("John Nobody") and "the consumptive beggars" with "the thin voice of a shell" ("Gone Away"), he realizes that this is an extension of disorder all over, symbolized by such events as the trial of Milovan Djilas and the atrocities of the Nazis.

From this awareness of a searing landscape arises the insistent longing for love ("Except in you I have no rest/For always with you I am safe"), for the tranquil, almost mystical, vision. This is expressed with great subtlety in, for instance, "Bells for William Wordsworth," in which the Wordsworthian vision does not remain a mere academic exercise ("His work is carefully studied in colleges still") but becomes a significant mode for his own regaining of tranquillity: "I have seen him risen again with the crocus in Spring./I have turned my ear to the wind, I have heard him speaking." The longing for the tranquil vision, for Moraes, is innate to the poet's vocation itself, his preoccupation with words: "I have spent several years fighting with words/And they fight back with words that perplex" ("A Small Whimper"). And eventually it is art that encapsules reality in a deathless way; for, like the stranger catching a "glimpse" of "the miles-off sea" even in the midst of ruins ("kanheri caves"), art ensures resurrection.

Poetry seems to Moraes, however, aesthetically to insulate one from the rough and tumble of life. Probably this accounts for his constant roving and, like V. S. Naipaul, interspersing his creative with non-fictional writing: travelogue, reportage, film-making. *Gone Away* (a record of his travel in India) and *My Son's Father* (autobiography) are written with great subtlety and insight and seem inalienable parts of his creative writing itself.

Moraes's weakness as a poet, however, seems to be the lack of a controlling, focussing centre. In spite of his work's wide-ranging implications, arising out of the incorporation of myth, anthropology, and medieval references, there is an absence of firm roots. Hence the irritating sense of non-belonging perceptible in his poetry.

—M. Sivaramkrishna

MUIR, Edwin.   Scottish.   Born in Deerness, Orkney, 15 May 1887. Educated at Kirkwall Burgh School, Orkney. Married Willa Anderson in 1919; one child. Worked in various commercial and ship building offices in Glasgow, and as a journalist and translator: Staff Member, *New Age*, London, 1919–21; lived in Prague after 1920; fiction reviewer, *The Listener*, 1933–45; Co-Editor, *The European Quarterly*, 1934; worked for the British Council in Edinburgh during World War II, in Prague, 1945–48, and Rome, 1948–50; Warden of Newbattle Abbey College, Dalkeith, 1950–55; Charles Eliot Norton Professor of Poetry, Harvard University, Cambridge, Massachusetts, 1955–56; retired to Swaffham Prior, near Cambridge, 1957; Visiting Winston Churchill Professor, University of Bristol, 1958. Recipient: Foyle Prize, 1950; Heinemann Award, 1953; Frederick Niven Literary Award, 1953; Russell Loines Award, 1957; Saltire Society Prize, 1957. Ph.D.: Charles University, Prague, 1947; LL.D.: University of Edinburgh, 1947; Docteur-ès-Lettres: University of Rennes, 1949; Litt.D.: University of Leeds, 1955; Cambridge University, 1958. Fellow, Royal Society of Literature, 1953. C.B.E. (Commander, Order of the British Empire), 1953. *Died 3 January 1959.*

PUBLICATIONS

Collections

Selected Poems.   1965.
Selected Letters, edited by P. H. Butter.   1974.

Verse

First Poems.   1925.
Chorus of the Newly Dead.   1926.
Six Poems.   1932.
Variations on a Time Theme.   1934.
Journeys and Places.   1937.
The Narrow Place.   1943.
The Voyage and Other Poems.   1946.

The Labyrinth.   1949.
Collected Poems 1921–1951, edited by J. C. Hall.   1952.
Collected Poems 1921–1958, edited by Willa Muir and J. C. Hall.   1960; revised
    edition, 1963.
One Foot in Eden.   1956.

Fiction

The Marionette.   1927.
The Three Brothers.   1931.
Poor Tom.   1932.

Other

We Moderns: Enigmas and Guesses.   1918.
Latitudes.   1924.
Transition: Essays on Contemporary Literature.   1926.
The Structure of the Novel.   1928.
John Knox: Portrait of a Calvinist.   1929.
Scottish Journey.   1935.
Social Credit and the Labour Party: An Appeal.   1935.
Scott and Scotland: The Predicament of the Scottish Writer.   1936.
The Present Age, from 1914.   1939.
The Story and the Fable: An Autobiography.   1940; revised edition, as *An
    Autobiography,* 1954.
The Scots and Their Country.   1946.
Essays on Literature and Society.   1949; augmented edition, 1965.
The Estate of Poetry (lectures).   1962.

Editor, with others, *Orion: A Miscellany 1–2.*   2 vols., 1945.
Editor, *New Poets.*   1959.

Translator, with Willa Muir, of more than 40 books by Kafka, Hermann Broch, Gerhart
Hauptmann, Lion Feuchtwanger, Shalom Asch, Heinrich Mann, and other authors,
1925–48.

Bibliography: *Bibliography of the Writings of Muir* by Elgin W. Mellown, 1964, revised
edition, 1966; *A Checklist of the Writings of Muir* by Elgin W. Mellown and Peter C. Hoy,
1971.

Reading List: *Muir* by J. C. Hall, 1956; *Muir,* 1962, and *Muir: Man and Poet,*1966, both by
P. H. Butter; *Barbarous Knowledge: Myth in the Poetry of Yeats, Graves, and Muir* by Daniel
Hoffman, 1967; *Belonging: A Memoir* by Willa Muir, 1969; *The Poetry of Muir: The Field of
Good and Ill* by Elizabeth L. Haberman, 1971; *Verging on Another World: Notes Towards an
Understanding of Muir's Poetry* by Martin Booth, 1978.

*   *   *

Not until he was over thirty did Edwin Muir recover from the need to protect himself from
a hostile environment and regain something of his childhood's vividness of seeing. Then he
was able to look back over the intervening period of sleep-walking, and in so doing to see not

his "own life merely, but all human life," beneath the story of one man the fable of Man. His early poems are already expressions of this imaginative vision, but are limited in range and in skill. The language is sometimes stiff, the rhythms lacking in flexibility. Gradually he extended his range, finding value in the journey through the labyrinth of time as well as in the goal of a re-entered Eden, combining myth and dream with a profound understanding of what was happening immediately around him. Gradually his language and his rhythms became more flexible and varied. He remained open to experience until the end, and wrote a large proportion of his best poems when over sixty.

Stories are innumerable, the fable one. So to some Muir's poems, tending towards a common centre, appear monotonous. But they approach that centre from many points – from common things such as a dying wasp, a departing swallow, from ordinary human love ("The Confirmation") as well as from stranger experiences of neurosis ("The Strange Return") and dream vision ("The Combat," "The Transfiguration," "The Brothers"). At his best we have "the ordinary day" as well as "the deepening trance" in which Angel and girl, time and the timeless, meet ("The Annunciation"). Some would like more of the ordinary day, particular girls as well as "the girl." But in days when we are so often offered nothing but raw fragments of experience, that is a minor complaint. Everything in his work is distilled, seen imaginatively, meaningful.

Neither his language nor his rhythms draw attention to themselves, and anyone looking for great linguistic inventiveness or rhythmical excitement will be disappointed; but if one looks at subtle and slight changes of rhythm and the exact placing of ordinary words so as to control their meaning, one comes to see, with T. S. Eliot, that "possessed by his vision, he found, almost unconsciously, the right, the inevitable way of saying what he wanted to say."

Next in value to his poetry is his *Autobiography*, especially the early part of it originally published as *The Story and the Fable*. Written in beautifully lucid, quietly rhythmical prose, it does not tell of sensational events, but is nevertheless exciting, being felt as both strange and familiar. However different our particular experiences we yet feel his journey as our own. At the same time the book has, more than the poetry, the grittiness of actual life. Incidents, places, people are evoked with vivid particularity, as well as being felt as strangely representative.

Muir wrote over a thousand reviews as well as several volumes of literary and social criticism; and he and his wife translated over forty books, mostly from German. His criticism is given life by the same passionate search for values as is his creative work. In the 1920's, in a series of essays on contemporary writers, he wanted to examine "the assumptions on which people live, as well as those on which they could conceivably live"; and at the end of his life he was stressing above all the value of the imagination, not only as the main thing we look for in literature, but also as that which we most need in life in order to "apprehend ... living creatures in their individuality," and to see life whole and in proper proportion. Most of the best of his criticism is in *The Structure of the Novel* and in *Essays on Literature and Society*; but even his ephemera, such as the fortnightly reviews of new novels in *The Listener*, has an extraordinarily high level of fairness, wit, quick perception of new merit, and sharp questioning of the merely fashionable.

Willa Muir, the better linguist, bore by far the larger share of the burden of translating. (Working separately from her he could make mistakes, as in his translations from Hölderlin's *Patmos*.) But they worked together on the translations from Kafka and Broch. Reading Kafka, he felt greatness in every sentence, and he despaired of being able to translate him without injury. "The word order of Kafka is naked and infallible," not only expressing meanings but "involved as part of it." In English the word order has to be changed, and an attempt made to write prose "as natural in the English way as his was in his own way." With Broch the problem is different. The style is self-consciously difficult – and different in each book of *The Sleepwalkers* – "the writer battling with his own style" to express the almost inexpressible and to mirror the disintegration of values which is his central subject. I cannot judge of their fidelity, but these translations are works of art in their own right, the making of them part of Muir's search for meaning.

None of Muir's three novels is satisfying as a whole, though all contain fine imaginative passages – for instance, the strange dreams and visions of Hans in *The Marionette*, David's dreams in *The Three Brothers*, Mansie's experience of a May Day parade in Glasgow and his encounter with a horse in *Poor Tom*. In them Muir's own past presses too strongly on a fictional structure too slight to contain and transform it. The right forms for this material were to be found in autobiography and in poetry.

—P. H. Butter

NASH, (Frederick) Ogden. American. Born in Rye, New York, 19 August 1902. Educated at St. George's School, Newport, Rhode Island, 1917–20; Harvard University, Cambridge, Massachusetts, 1920–21. Married Frances Rider Leonard in 1931; two daughters. Taught for one year at St. George's School, Newport; worked briefly as a bond salesman on Wall Street, 1924; worked in the editorial and publicity departments of Doubleday Doran, publishers, New York, 1925, and joined John Farrar and Stanley Rinehart when they left the firm to set up their own publishing house; Member, Editorial Staff, *The New Yorker* magazine; later retired from publishing to devote himself to his own writing. Recipient: Sarah Josepha Hale Award, 1964. Member, National Institute of Arts and Letters. *Died 19 May 1971.*

PUBLICATIONS

Collections

I Wouldn't Have Missed It: Selected Poems, edited by Linell Smith and Isabel Eberstadt.   1975.

Verse

Free Wheeling.   1931.
Hard Lines.   1931.
Hard Lines and Others.   1932.
Happy Days.   1933.
Four Prominent So and So's, music by Robert Armbruster.   1934; as *Four Prominent Bastards Are We,* 1934.
The Primrose Path.   1935.
The Bad Parents' Garden of Verse.   1936.
Bon Voyage.   1936.
I'm a Stranger Here Myself.   1938.
The Face Is Familiar: Selected Verse.   1940; revised edition, 1954.
Good Intentions.   1942.
The Nash Pocket Book.   1944.
Many Long Years Ago.   1945.

Selected Verse.   1946.
Nash's Musical Zoo.   1947.
Versus.   1949.
Family Reunion.   1950.
The Private Dining Room and Other New Verses.   1953.
You Can't Get There from Here.   1957.
Verses from 1929 On.   1959; as *Collected Verse from 1929 On,* 1961.
Scrooge Rides Again.   1960.
Everyone But Thee and Me.   1962.
Marriage Lines: Notes of a Student Husband.   1964.
The Mysterious Ouphe.   1965.
A Nash Omnibook.   1967.
Santa Go Home: A Case History for Parents.   1967.
There's Always Another Windmill.   1968.
Funniest Verses, edited by Dorothy Price.   1968.
Bed Riddance: A Posy for the Indisposed.   1970.
The Old Dog Barks Backwards.   1972.

Plays

One Touch of Venus, with S. J. Perelman, music by Kurt Weill, from *The Tinted Venus*
    by F. Anstey (produced 1943).   1944.
Sweet Bye and Bye (lyrics only), book by S. J. Perelman and Al Hirschfield, music by
    Vernon Duke (produced 1946).
Two's Company (lyrics only; revue) (produced 1952).
The Littlest Revue, with others (produced 1956).
The Beauty Part, with S. J. Perelman (produced 1961).   1963.

Screenplays: *The Firefly,* with Frances Goodrich and Albert Hackett, 1937; *The Shining
Hour,* with Jane Murfin, 1938; *The Feminine Touch,* with George Oppenheimer and
Edmund L. Hartmann, 1941.

Other

The Cricket of Carador (juvenile), with Joseph Alger.   1925.
Born in a Beer Garden; or, She Troupes to Conquer, with Christopher Morley and Cleon
    Throckmorton.   1930.
Parents Keep Out: Elderly Poems for Youngerly Readers (juvenile).   1951.
The Christmas That Almost Wasn't (juvenile).   1957.
The Boy Who Laughed at Santa Claus (juvenile).   1957.
Custard the Dragon (juvenile).   1959.
A Boy Is a Boy: The Fun of Being a Boy (juvenile).   1960.
Custard the Dragon and the Wicked Knight (juvenile).   1961.
The New Nutcracker Suite and Other Innocent Verses (juvenile).   1962.
Girls Are Silly (juvenile).   1962.
The Adventures of Isabel (juvenile).   1963.
A Boy and His Room (juvenile).   1963.
The Untold Adventures of Santa Claus (juvenile).   1964.
The Animal Garden (juvenile).   1965.
The Cruise of the Aardvark (juvenile).   1967.
The Scroobious Pip (juvenile), by Edward Lear (completed by Nash).   1968.

Editor, *Nothing But Wodehouse*.   1932.

Editor, *The Moon Is Shining Bright as Day: An Anthology of Good Humored Verse*.   1953.

Editor, *I Couldn't Help Laughing: Stories* (juvenile).   1957.

Editor, *Everybody Ought to Know: Verses Selected and Introduced*.   1961.

*   *   *

Ogden Nash's career as a writer of light verse began in the 1930's when he accepted defeat as a poet. Realizing that his serious verses were tongue-tied and sentimental, he began constructing a peculiar form of doggerel which broke all rules of symmetry and harmony in poetry. Lines grew as long as subway trains, capped by rhymes as outrageous as cocktail party chatter; philosophical questions were mocked by horse-sensical conclusions: "What is life? Life is stepping down a step or sitting on a chair,/And it isn't there." Though it wasn't great poetry, it made Nash America's most popular comic poet.

With these techniques, Nash was able to express poetically the plain-spoken American's frustration with poetic complication, as well as the conviction that, really, poetry is just prose that rhymes. (Or should be, Nash hints: "One thing that literature would be greatly the better for/Would be a more restricted use of simile and metaphor.") In the Introduction to the 1975 Nash collection *I Wouldn't Have Missed It*, Archibald MacLeish gave away the secret: "Nothing ... suggests the structure of verse but the rhymes" which are used baldly to shoehorn sentences into what looked like verse. Basing his poems not on the poetic line, but on the sentence, Nash became (in his work) a "wersifier" painting men, women, and society from their poetic backsides.

Like his wersification, Nash's subjects come straight out of everyday life: summer colds and Monday mornings, leaky faucets and crashing bores. He is assailed by the mundane torments of living, perplexed by the oddities and failings of human nature, and mystified by women, just as they are by men. Yet no matter how disastrous life may be, Nash reassures us that perhaps it isn't so bad after all: "When I consider how my life is spent,/I hardly ever repent."

—Walter Bode

NEILSON, (John) Shaw.   Australian.   Born in Peoria, South Australia. 22 February 1872. Educated at State School, Peoria; State School, Minimay, Victoria, 1885–86. Farmer in the bush country, 1902–22; also wrote for the *Bulletin*, Sydney, 1900, *The Book Fellow*, 1907 and from 1911, and *Clarion*, 1908; Messenger, Country Roads Board, Melbourne, 1928–41. Granted Commonwealth Literary Fund pension, 1922. *Died 12 May 1942.*

PUBLICATIONS

Collections

The Poems, edited by A. R. Chisholm.   1965.

Verse

> *Heart of Spring.*   1919.
> *Ballad and Lyrical Poems.*   1923.
> *New Poems.*   1927.
> *Collected Poems,* edited by R. H. Croll.   1934.
> *Beauty Imposes: Some Recent Verse.*   1938.
> *Unpublished Poems,* edited by James Devaney.   1947.
> *Witnesses of Spring: Unpublished Poems,* edited by Judith Wright.   1970.

Bibliography: *Neilson: An Annotated Bibliography and Checklist 1893–1964* by Hugh Anderson, 1964.

Reading List: *Neilson* by James Devaney, 1944; *Neilson* by Judith Wright, 1963 (biography and selected verse); *Neilson* by H. J. Oliver, 1968; *Neilson* by Hugh Anderson and L.J. Blake, 1972.

* * * * *

Shaw Neilson's work is hard to characterize. He is purely a lyrical poet, and his subjects are those of traditional lyric: the cycle of natural renewal, love, the spring, the beauty and pathos of young girls, children, the way of the animals as superior to the ways of men. Although he knew and loved the Australian back country, his poetry is not particularly tinged with local colour; his tone is not assertively tough nor is he in search of the Australian identity. In a sense, his poems could have emerged from several cultures: delicately mystical, occasionally reminiscent of Blake, or Walter de la Mare, or, in a poem like "The Long Week End" with the colloquially bitter-sweet irony of its refrain, calling to mind John Crowe Ransom:

> Sweet is the white, they say, she will ascend
> To an unstinted country where the days
> Gone without malice there she stays and stays
> Upon the long weekend.

His central poem, "The Orange Tree," is pure poetry, language at its most literary and innocent, the Tree representing the eternal life cycle. The poem is a dialogue between a young girl who hears the deep words of the tree and a sophisticated interlocutor who tries futilely to match his questions with the "mystery" of life, and who is imperatively silenced by the girl at the end of the poem, where questioning is stilled in affirmation:

> Listen! the young girl said. For all
>   Your hapless talk you fail to see
> There is a light, a step, a call
>   This evening in the Orange Tree.
>
> Is it, I said, a waste of love
>   Imperishably old in pain,
> Moving as an affrighted dove
>   Under the sunlight or the rain? ...

Silence! The young girl said. Oh, why
   Why will you talk to weary me?
Plague me no longer now for I
   Am listening like the Orange Tree.

—Ian Fletcher

NEMEROV, Howard. American. Born in New York City, 1 March 1920. Educated at
Fieldston School, New York; Harvard University, Cambridge, Massachusetts, A.B. 1941.
Served in the Royal Canadian Air Force, and the United States Air Force, 1941–45: First
Lieutenant. Married Margaret Russell in 1944; three children. Instructor in English,
Hamilton College, Clinton, New York, 1946–48; Member of the Literature Faculty,
Bennington College, Vermont, 1948–66; Professor of English, Brandeis University,
Waltham, Massachusetts, 1966–69. Since 1969, Professor of English, Washington
University, St. Louis. Visiting Lecturer, University of Minnesota, Minneapolis, 1958–59;
Writer-in-Residence, Hollins College, Virginia, 1962–64; Consultant in Poetry, Library of
Congress, Washington, D.C., 1963–64. Associate Editor, *Furioso*, Madison, Connecticut,
later Northfield, Minnesota, 1946–51. Recipient: National Institute of Arts and Letters grant,
1961; New England Poetry Club Golden Rose, 1962; Brandeis University Creative Arts
Award, 1962; National Endowment for the Arts grant, 1966; Theodore Roethke Award,
1968; Guggenheim Fellowship, 1968; St. Botolph's Club Prize, 1968; Academy of American
Poets Fellowship, 1970. D.L.: Lawrence University, Appleton, Wisconsin, 1964; Tufts
University, Medford, Massachusetts, 1969. Fellow, American Academy of Arts and Sciences,
1966. Member, American Academy of Arts and Letters, 1976. Lives in St. Louis.

PUBLICATIONS

Verse

   The Image and the Law. 1947.
   Guide to the Ruins. 1950.
   The Salt Garden. 1955.
   Mirrors and Windows. 1958.
   New and Selected Poems. 1960.
   The Next Room of the Dream: Poems and Two Plays. 1962.
   Five American Poets, with others, edited by Ted Hughes and Thom Gunn. 1963.
   The Blue Swallows. 1967.
   The Winter Lightning: Selected Poems. 1968.
   The Painter Dreaming in the Scholar's House. 1968.
   Gnomes and Occasions: Poems. 1972.
   The Western Approaches: Poems 1973–1975. 1975.
   Collected Poems. 1977.

Fiction

The Melodramatists. 1949.
Federigo; or, The Power of Love. 1954.
The Homecoming Game. 1957.
A Commodity of Dreams and Other Stories. 1959.
Stories, Fables, and Other Diversions. 1971.

Other

Poetry and Fiction: Essays. 1963.
Journal of the Fictive Life. 1965.
Reflexions on Poetry and Poetics. 1972.
Figures of Thought: Speculations on the Meaning of Poetry and Other Essays. 1978.

Editor, *Poets on Poetry.* 1965.

Reading List: *Nemerov* by Peter Meinke, 1968; *The Critical Reception of Nemerov: A Selection of Essays and a Bibliography* edited by Bowie Duncan, 1971; *The Shield of Perseus* by Julia Bartholomay, 1972.

* * *

Although Howard Nemerov has written a journal, two collections of short stories, three novels, and much fine criticism (including exceptionally perceptive essays on Wallace Stevens, Dylan Thomas, and Vladimir Nabokov), his primary importance is as a poet. He is a superior craftsman, particularly skilled at blank verse. Moreover, the content of his poetry is penetrating. Perhaps the foremost reason for this richness in content is that Nemerov believes that a major function of the poet is to scrutinize and describe reality precisely as it is. "The Private Eye" makes it clear that the artist should strip himself of preconceptions. In "Vermeer," Nemerov praises this painter for taking "what is, and seeing it as it is."

Despite the fact that reality contains patterns, Nemerov finds that, fundamentally, reality is primitive and chaotic. "The Town Dump" and "The Quarry" stress the relentless chaotic decay occurring in our world, while raw primitiveness is emphasized in "Lobsters." "Nightmare" shows that the primitive also exists within the human being. Nor is any Dionysian oneness fusing man and nature possible. Instead, nature is apt to paralyze man's will, as it does the speaker's in "Death and the Maiden."

Man, then, is a very limited creature, a main point in both of his verse plays, *Endor* and *Cain*, as well as in "Runes." For Nemerov the other major function of the artist is to create some kind of comforting order, even though this order is only temporary. Nemerov stresses this point again and again in such poems as "Elegy for a Nature Poet" and "Lines and Circularities." The artist can also remind us that nature can be lovely and exhilarating. However, we must not think that human creations can "replace" reality – the warning given in "Projection."

Because nature is ceaselessly changing, Nemerov suggests that man, too, should be flexible. "Lot Later" dramatizes this point. Inflexibility will trap man, for even sanctified history can later be proven false, the theme in "To Clio, Muse of History." Nevertheless, man should not let himself be crippled by cynicism, as is the Minister in *Endor.*

Nemerov's poetry is valuable because it incisively presents us with a no-nonsense view of the world, a view that is stark, but not entirely negative. In "The View from an Attic Window," he declares that we live amid chaos, that our individual lives are short, and that, as a result, "life is hopeless," yet "beautiful" – and we should try to endure and to grow. "Small Moment" states that if we do fully accept reality, we will also embody vibrant love.

—Robert K. Johnson

NICHOLSON, Norman (Cornthwaite). English. Born in Millom, Cumberland, 8 January 1914. Educated at local schools. Married Yvonne Gardner in 1956. Frequent public lecturer. Recipient: Heinemann Award, 1945; Cholmondeley Award, 1967; Northern Arts Association grant, 1969; Society of Authors bursary, 1973; Queen's Gold Medal for Poetry, 1977. M.A.: University of Manchester, 1959; Open University, 1975. Fellow, Royal Society of Literature, 1945. Lives in Cumbria.

PUBLICATIONS

Verse

> *Selected Poems,* with J. C. Hall and Keith Douglas.   1943.
> *Five Rivers.*   1944.
> *Rock Face.*   1948.
> *The Pot Geranium.*   1954.
> *Selected Poems.*   1966.
> *No Star on the Way Back: Ballads and Carols.*   1967.
> *A Local Habitation.*   1972.
> *Cloud on the Black Combe.*   1975.
> *Stitch and Stone: A Cumbrian Landscape.*   1975.

Plays

> *The Old Man of the Mountains* (produced 1945).   1946.
> *Prophesy to the Wind* (produced 1949).   1950.
> *A Match for the Devil* (produced 1953).   1955.
> *Birth by Drowning* (produced 1959).   1960.

> Television Play: *No Star on the Way Back,* 1963.

Fiction

> *The Fire of the Lord.*   1944.
> *The Green Shore.*   1947.

Other

> *Man and Literature.*   1943.
> *Cumberland and Westmorland.*   1949.

H. G. Wells. 1950.
William Cowper. 1951.
The Lakers: The Adventures of the First Tourists. 1955.
Provincial Pleasures. 1959.
William Cowper (not the same as the 1951 book). 1960.
Portrait of the Lakes. 1963.
Enjoying It All (radio talks). 1964.
Greater Lakeland. 1969.
Wednesday Early Closing (autobiography). 1975.

Editor, *An Anthology of Religious Verse Designed for the Times.* 1942.
Editor, *Wordsworth: An Introduction and Selection.* 1949.
Editor, *Poems,* by William Cowper. 1951.
Editor, *A Choice of Cowper's Verse.* 1975.

Reading List: *Nicholson* by Philip Gardner, 1973.

*　　*　　*

Norman Nicholson is a regional poet who, living and writing in the shadow of Wordsworth on the western edge of Cumbria, has yet asserted his own distinctive and authentic voice. The Cumbria he celebrates is partly the industrialized region of mines, blast furnaces, and slag-banks surrounding his home town, Millom, but it stretches beyond these to include the neighbouring coast and the dales and fells of Lakeland. From *Five Rivers* onwards Nicholson's strength has always been his response to this landscape, a response in which imaginative perception, an acuity of vision akin to that of the painter, blends with historical awareness to give a satisfying sense that here is a poet who "deals largely with substantial things." Botany and geology, a feeling for soil and stone, and a love of local history authenticate his landscapes. He combines reflection with description, directness with reticence. In his concern for order, clarity, and control he is in the classical tradition. His mind is, however, fertile in the production of images, and he has a strong sense of colour.

He is also a religious poet. Some of the poems in *Five Rivers*, retelling biblical stories in a modern, somewhat surrealist manner, now seen over-ambitious. The shorter ones (e.g., "Shepherd's Carol") succeed better. *The Old Man of the Mountains*, Nicholson's best known verse-play, is a retelling of the story of Elijah and the raven, given a modern setting on the Cumberland fells, and quite effectively pillories modern man's materialism and greed.

Despite many appealing poems in *Five Rivers* and *Rock Face*, Nicholson's work is probably seen at its best in *The Pot Geranium* and *A Local Habitation*. In the former, depth of feeling combined with technical mastery gives a new assurance of tone. Poems like "On Duddon Marsh" recreate their subject in precise and evocative detail. Others, like "Fossils," penetrate imaginatively into the life of inanimate rocks. (The animism of his portrayal of Nature has always been a notable feature.) There also appear here poems in the personal, anecdotal style – concerned with people as well as places – that he was to develop in *A Local Habitation*: the splendid "Rising Five"; "The Buzzer," an almost Proustian realisation; and the sharply observed "Five Minutes."

"My ways are circumscribed," the poet confesses in the title-poem "The Pot Geranium." In *A Local Habitation* this has ceased to matter; his confidence in the value of that life now leads him to write of it in an engagingly relaxed, intimate, and sometimes humorous way. (The subject-matter of some of the poems is expanded in his highly readable autobiography, *Wednesday Early Closing*.) In earlier volumes Nicholson's concern to moralise his song is sometimes rather too obvious and the application forced. Here, especially in the serenely beautiful "September on the Mosses," the physical and moral visions are fused. The local habitation convincingly mirrors the universal.

—Joan Grundy

NOYES, Alfred.   English.   Born in Wolverhampton, 16 September 1880. Educated at Exeter College, Oxford, 1898–1901. Married 1) Garnet Daniels in 1907 (died, 1926); 2) Mary Wild-Blundell in 1927; one son and two daughters. Delivered the Lowell Lectures in the U.S., 1913; Professor of Modern English Literature, Princeton University, New Jersey, 1914–23; returned to England and lived by his writing; became a Roman Catholic, 1927. Litt.D.: Yale University, New Haven, Connecticut, 1913; LL.D: University of Glasgow, 1927; University of California, Berkeley, 1944; L.H.D.: Syracuse University, New York, 1942. C.B.E. (Commander, Order of the British Empire), 1918. *Died 28 June 1958.*

PUBLICATIONS

Collections

   Collected Poems.   1947; revised edition, edited by Hugh Noyes, 1963, 1966.

Verse

   The Loom of Years.   1902.
   The Flower of Old Japan: A Dim Strange Tale for All Ages.   1903.
   Poems.   1904.
   The Forest of Wild Thyme: A Tale for Children under Ninety.   1905.
   Drake: An English Epic.   2 vols., 1906–08.
   Poems.   1906.
   Forty Singing Seamen and Other Poems.   1907.
   The Golden Hynde and Other Poems.   1908.
   The Enchanted Island and Other Poems.   1909.
   In Memory of Swinburne.   1909.
   Collected Poems.   4 vols., 1910–27; vols. 1 and 2 revised, 1928.
   The Prayer for Peace.   1911.
   The Carol of the Fir Tree.   1912.
   Tales of the Mermaid Tavern.   1913.
   Two Christmas Poems.   1913.
   The Wine-Press: A Tale of War.   1913.
   A Tale of Old Japan.   1914.
   The Searchlights.   1914.
   The Lord of Misrule and Other Poems.   1915.
   A Salute from the Fleet and Other Poems.   1915.
   Songs of the Trawlers.   1916.
   The Avenue of the Allies, and Victory.   1918.

The New Morning.   1918.
The Elfin Artist and Other Poems.   1920.
Selected Verse.   1921.
The Torch-Bearers.   3 vols., 1922–30.
Songs of Shadow-of-a-Leaf and Other Poems.   1924.
Princeton, May 1917; The Call of the Spring.   1925.
Dick Turpin's Ride and Other Poems.   1927.
Ballads and Poems.   1928.
The Strong City.   1928.
Poems: The Author's Own Selection for Schools.   1935.
The Cormorant.   1936.
Youth and Memory.   1937.
Wizards.   1938.
If Judgment Comes.   1941.
Poems of the New World.   1942.
Shadows on the Down and Other Poems.   1945.
The Assumption: An Answer.   1950.
A Roehampton School Song.   1950.
Daddy Fell into the Pond and Other Poems for Children.   1952.
A Letter to Lucian and Other Poems.   1956.

Plays

Orpheus in the Underworld, with Frederic Norton and Herbert Beerbohm Tree
(produced 1911).
Sherwood; or, Robin Hood and the Three Kings.   1911; revised version, as *Robin Hood*
(produced 1926), 1926.
Rada: A Drama of War.   1914; revised version, as *A Belgian Christmas Eve,* 1915.

Fiction

Walking Shadows (stories).   1918.
Beyond the Desert: A Tale of Death Valley.   1920.
The Hidden Player.   1924.
The Return of the Scare-Crow.   1929; as *The Sun Cure,* 1929.
The Last Man.   1940; as *No Other Man,* 1940.
The Devil Takes a Holiday.   1955.

Other

William Morris.   1908.
Mystery Ships: Trapping the "U"-Boat.   1916.
What Is England Doing?   1916.
Open Boats.   1917.
Some Aspects of Modern Poetry.   1924.
New Essays and American Impressions.   1927.
The Opalescent Parrot: Essays.   1929.
Tennyson.   1932.
The Unknown God.   1934.
Happiness and Success, with S. Baldwin.   1936.
Voltaire.   1936.

Orchard's Bay (essays; includes verse).   1939; as *The Incompleat Gardener,* 1955.
Pageant of Letters (essays).   1940.
The Edge of the Abyss (lectures).   1942.
The Secret of Pooduck Island (juvenile).   1943.
Portrait of Horace.   1947.
Two Worlds for Memory (autobiography).   1953.
The Accusing Ghost; or, Justice for Casement.   1957.

Editor, *The Magic Casement: An Anthology of Fairy Poetry.*   1908.
Editor, *The Minstrelsy of the Scottish Border,* edited by Sir Walter Scott.   1908.
Editor, *The Temple of Beauty: An Anthology.*   1910.
Editor, *A Book of Princeton Verse.*   1916.
Editor, *Helicon Poetry Series.*   4 vols., 1925.
Editor, *The Golden Book of Catholic Poetry.*   1946.

Reading List: *Noyes* by Walter Jerrold, 1930; *Noyes* by D. G. Larg, 1936; "The Poetic Achievement of Noyes" by Derek Stanford, in *English 12,* 1958.

*   *   *

Alfred Noyes's verse chimed well with the increasingly strident jingoism of the Edwardian era, earning him a place in innumerable school anthologies. His two-volume epic on Drake, serialized in *Blackwood's Magazine,* set the pattern for writing which repeatedly turned for inspiration to the sea and its heroes. Yet the hortatory, hectoring rhetoric of poems such as "In Time of War" or "Nelson's Year" (which, beginning " 'Hasten the Kingdom, England,' " casts the British Empire in a divine crusade to unify the "striving nations," "England's Rose of all the roses/Dawning wide and ever wider o'er the kingdom of mankind") conceals a deeper unease and anxiety. "The Phantom Fleet" reveals this as a doubt about England's capacity to resist the challenge of the newer maritime powers, summoning the ghosts of Nelson and the Elizabethan privateers to defend a nation "resting on her past" which has neglected her "first, last line," the Fleet.

The same insecurity pervades the personal verse, where jaunty self-confidence jostles a stale world-weariness ("The heart in its muffled anguish, the sea in its mournful voice"). Frustrated, cramped, disenchanted in an age of positivism and commerce, this grocer's son from Wolverhampton sought in fantasy an escape from "the solemn sin of truth." *The Forest of Wild Thyme* leads us as children off "to hunt the fairy gleam/That flutters through the unfettered dream." But the long-sought Flower of Old Japan turns out to be no exotic growth, but "a white/English daisy," and we are brought back, in a sentimentalism of the hearth, to see that "All the fairy tales were true,/And home the heart of fairy-land." The same domestication of the exotic underlies the Imperial dream: "A Song of England" sees her dutiful sons shipped overseas, only to find in her "silent purple harmonies" the truly magical landscape, towards which they "grope in dreams." Noyes thus manages to reconcile Little Englandism with the imperial theme. The true "Empire Builders" are similarly found, in a characteristic movement, on native soil, in the lowly round of "many a country cottage-home" or the City's "roaring streets." The heavy rhythms, emphatic rhymes and rollicking fourteeners of his Kiplingesque ballads likewise suggest the robustness of the spiritual invalid, compensating for the sado-masochistic weakness of, e.g., "The Mystic" ("My soul lay stabbed by all the swords of sense") or the fin-de-siècle cadences of "In the Heart of the Woods"; and indeed, Noyes ultimately found his refuge from desolation in Catholicism.

There is much in his verse of the sensuous languors of the early Keats; much of the alliterative opulence of Poe, Swinburne and the Decadents ("dim as a dream, rich as a reverie," "perfumed with old regret and dead desire"). Even at his best, as in the unexpected imitation of Gautier, "Art," the terseness of his model –

> Yes! Beauty still rebels!
> Our Dreams like clouds disperse:
>   She dwells
> In agate, marble, verse

– is marred by a prolixity that overextends a simple idea into stanza after stanza of amplification. In form and sentiment vatic, maudlin, sententious, Noyes displays the self-indulgence of his age. His work would have benefitted from the discipline recommended in the closing stanza of this poem: "Take up the sculptor's tool!"

—Stan Smith

O'HARA, Frank (Francis Russell O'Hara).   American.   Born in Baltimore, Maryland, 27 June 1926. Educated privately in piano and musical composition, 1933–43; at New England Conservatory of Music, Boston, 1946–50; Harvard University, Cambridge, Massachusetts, 1946–50, B.A. in English 1950; University of Michigan, Ann Arbor (Hopwood Award, 1951), M.A. in English 1951. Served in the United States Navy 1944–46. Staff Member, 1951–54, Fellowship Curator, 1955–64, Associate Curator, 1965, and Curator of the International Program, 1966, Museum of Modern Art, New York. Editorial Associate, *Art News* magazine, New York, 1954–56; Art Editor, *Kulchur Magazine*, New York, 1962–64. Collaborated in several poem-painting and poem-lithograph projects. Recipient: Ford Foundation Fellowship, for drama, 1956. *Died 25 July 1966.*

PUBLICATIONS

Collections

>   *Collected Poems,* edited by Donald Allen.   1971.
>   *Selected Poems,* edited by Donald Allen.   1974.

Verse

>   *A City Winter and Other Poems.*   1952.
>   *Oranges.*   1953.
>   *Meditations in an Emergency.*   1956.
>   *Hartigan and Rivers with O'Hara: An Exhibition of Pictures, with Poems.*   1959.
>   *Second Avenue.*   1960.
>   *Odes.*   1960.
>   *Featuring O'Hara.*   1964.
>   *Lunch Poems.*   1964.
>   *Love Poems: Tentative Title.*   1965.

Five Poems.   1967.
Two Pieces.   1969.
Odes.   1969.
Hymns of St. Bridget, with Bill Berkson.   1974.
Poems Retrieved, 1951–1966, edited by Donald Allen.   1975.
Early Poems, 1946–1951, edited by Donald Allen.   1976.

Plays

Try! Try! (produced 1951; revised version, produced 1952).   In *Artists' Theatre,* edited
   by Herbert Machiz, 1960.
Change Your Bedding (produced 1952).
Love's Labor: An Eclogue (produced 1959).   1964.
Awake in Spain (produced 1960).   1960.
The General Returns from One Place to Another (produced 1964).

Screenplay: *The Last Clean Shirt.*

Other

Jackson Pollock.   1959.
A Frank O'Hara Miscellany.   1974.
Art Chronicles 1954–1966.   1974.
Standing Still and Walking in New York, edited by Donald Allen.   1975.
Early Writings, edited by Donald Allen.   1977.

Editor,   *Robert   Motherwell: A   Catalogue   with   Selections   from   the   Artist's
   Writings.*   1966.

Reading List: *O'Hara, Poet among Painters* by Marjorie Perloff, 1977.

*   *   *

Frank O'Hara's status as an important poet of the post-World War II era has only recently
been established. During his lifetime he was known only to a circle of friends, many of them
painters in New York whom he knew from his work as an Associate Curator of the Museum
of Modern Art. But his canon is large and runs to more than five hundred pages of text in
Donald Allen's edition of *The Collected Poems.*

O'Hara was cavalier about his reputation as a poet and reluctant to have his poetry in print.
As a result, his work largely went unnoticed in the review columns; when his name did
surface, he was taken lightly. Only very recently has his work received serious critical
attention; Marjorie Perloff's book vigorously argues his major status as an innovator of
lyrical poetry. Perloff and others consider O'Hara to have had an influence on younger poets
comparable to Charles Olson, Robert Creeley, and Allen Ginsberg.

O'Hara's poetry from 1951 to 1954 shows the influence of Pound, William Carlos
Williams, and Auden. His early poems, collected in *A City Winter and Other Poems,* are
lyrical and strive very deliberately for surprising effects. His friend, the poet John Ashbery,
once commented that this was O'Hara's "French Zen period," which is an astute observation
of the lushly surrealistic language of these poems. As he commented in an early poem,
"Poetry":

> The only way to be quiet
> is to be quick, so I scare
> you clumsily, or surprise
> you with a stab. A praying
> mantis knows time more
> intimately than I and is
> more casual.

Auden once wrote to caution O'Hara against tiring the reader with an excess of surreal statements, and he appears to have heeded his counsel, for in the poetry of the later 1950's, gathered in *Meditations in an Emergency* and *Lunch Poems*, he exerted greater control over the structure of his poems and gave himself more intense freedom in brief, dazzling displays of lyrical exuberance.

In *Second Avenue* and other longer poems – "Easter," "In Memory of My Feelings," "Ode to Michael Goldberg('s Birth and Other Births)" and the late "Biotherm (for Bill Berkson)" – O'Hara, like Pushkin and Byron before him, created perhaps the essential hero of urban cultural life, a sophisticated romantic who thrives on the city's alien and exotic elements. His many shorter poems are briefer expressions of this same captivating persona.

O'Hara also succeeds in rendering consciousness and its fringe states with intense accuracy and daring in a style partly influenced by the methods and experiments of the Abstract Expressionist painters. O'Hara wrote several plays, and essays on contemporary painting collected in *Standing Still and Walking in New York* and *Art Chronicles 1954–1966*. Although not a theorist or trained critic of painting, his eye was sensitive to technique and his instinct sharp in discerning the great works of his time.

—Paul Christensen

OKARA, Gabriel (Imomotimi Gbaingbain). Nigerian. Born in Bumodi, Ijaw District, Rivers State, Western Nigeria, 21 April 1921. Educated at the Government College, Umuahia; trained as a bookbinder; studied journalism at Northwestern University, Evanston, Illinois, 1956. Principal Information Officer, Eastern Regional Government, Enugu, until 1967; Biafran Information Officer, Nigerian Civil War, 1967–69; travelled to the United States, with Chinua Achebe and Cyprian Ekwensi, to seek help for Biafra, 1969. Since 1972, Director of the Rivers State Publishing House, Port Harcourt. Recipient: Nigerian Festival of the Arts award, 1953.

PUBLICATIONS

Verse

The Fisherman's Invocation.   1978.

Fiction

The Voice.   1964.

Reading List: *Mother Is Gold* by Adrian A. Roscoe, 1971; *Culture, Tradition, and Society in the West African Novel* by Emmanuel Obiechina, 1975.

* * *

Gabriel Okara has written plays, translated folk material from Ijaw into English, and prepared documentary material for broadcasting. He is known almost exclusively, however, as a poet and as the author of an experimental novel, *The Voice*.

In 1953 Okara's poem "The Call of the River Nun" won the best all-round award in the Nigerian Festival of Arts. Like much of his poetry it has undercurrents of melancholy. The poet writes, with a slightly adolescent plangency, of how the River Nun beckons him into the mainstream of life. Later poems have been more symbolic including "The Snow Flakes Sail Gently Down," invoking impressions of exile while wintering in America:

> Then I dreamed a dream
> in my dead sleep. But I dreamed
> not of earth dying and elms a vigil
> keeping. I dreamed of birds, black
> birds flying in my inside, nesting
> and hatching on oil palms, bearing suns
> for fruits and with roots denting the
> uprooters' spades.

Okara's poems are deeply felt and usually introspective, though he is as concerned for the loss of traditional life in Nigeria as he is for his own state of mind brought about by the transition.

The Voice enjoys a reputation as a *succès d'estime*, for Okara attempted a semi-poetic novel which would render into an English equivalent some of the rhythms and sense of imagery found in his own vernacular, Ijaw. The novel is referred to whenever the possibilities of an African English are discussed. It is a short, partly allegorical novel presenting a struggle between the individual and his community; it is so lucid and distilled that it is likely to survive as a classic of African writing. In many ways *The Voice* is the archetypal rural novel in West Africa, confronting old and new values in a modern setting and demonstrating the rooted idealism which many African writers in the early 1960's believed to be the salvation of Africa. Okolo, whose name means "voice," embodies the author's faith in the liberty of personal conscience.

—Alastair Niven

OKIGBO, Christopher (Ifenayichukwu). Nigerian. Born in Ojoto, Onitsha Province, East Central State, 16 August 1932. Educated at the Government College, Umuahia; University College, Ibadan, 1951–56, B.A. in classics 1956. Served as a Major in the Biafran Army: killed in action, 1967. Married Sefi, daughter of the Attah of Igberra, in 1963; one daughter. Worked for the Nigerian Tobacco Company and the United African Company; Private Secretary to the Federal Minister of Research and Information, 1956–58; Latin Teacher, Fiditi Grammar School, near Ibadan, 1959–60; Librarian, University of Nigeria, Nsukka, then Enugu, 1960–62; West Africa Representative, Cambridge University Press, 1962–66. West African Editor, *Transition* magazine, Kampala, Uganda; Editor, Mbari Press,

Ibadan. Founder, with Chinua Achebe, of Citadel Books Ltd., Enugu, 1967. Recipient: Dakar Festival of Negro Arts Poetry Prize, 1966. *Died in August 1967.*

PUBLICATIONS

Verse

Heavensgate.   1962.
Limits.   1964.
Labyrinths, with Path of Thunder.   1971.

Reading List: *The Trial of Okigbo* by Ali A. Mazrui, 1971; *Okigbo: Creative Rhetoric* by Sunday O Anozie, 1972.

*   *   *

In the Introduction to *Labyrinths*, Christopher Okigbo wrote:

Although these poems were written and published separately, they are, in fact, organically related.

Heavensgate was originally conceived as an Easter sequence. It later grew into ... an offering to Idoto, the village stream of which I drank, in which I washed, as a child....

Limits and *Distances* are man's outer and inner worlds projected.... Both parts of *Silences* were inspired by the Western Nigeria crisis of 1962, and the death of Patrice Lamumba....

Labyrinths is thus a fable of man's perennial quest for fulfilment ... a poet-protagonist is assumed throughout ... larger than Orpheus: one with a load of destiny on his head, rather like Gilgamesh, like Aeneas ... like the Fisher King of Eliot's *Waste Land....*

The comment makes very clear the kind of poet Okigbo was. He had an urgent sense of the poetic future of a country only recently released from pre-literacy. His education in Classical and British literature combined with his life's knowledge of Ibo ethic, myth, and verbal folk poetry allowed him to see man's past as much more interwoven than has been supposed and African culture no less rich than that of the West. Okigbo's poetry does not try to merge Ibo, Nigerian, African backgrounds or poetry with British or Classical, but to show them as if from one, perhaps the same, antecedent. In *Silences* he writes, "One dips one's tongue in ocean, and begins / To cry to the mushroom of the sky."

Okigbo made no effort to solve problems which such attitudes as that of the Negritude of the 1950's posed. English was for him his own tongue, and he did not think of using any other for his poetry. In fact, there are strong echoes from other English writers – in *Limits*, for instance, of Eliot, John Wain, even de la Mare – mingled with references to Ibo myth and ritual:

Hurry on down–
Thro' the cinder market –
Hurry on down
in the wake of the dream;

> Hurry on down –
>   To rockpoint of Cable,
>
> To pull by the rope
>   the big white elephant ...
>
> *& the mortar is not yet dry*
> *& the mortar is not yet dry....*

Okigbo's double background makes for richness of substance and metaphor. Intensity of feeling carries this intellectual poet still further. He acknowledges his debt to Gerard Manley Hopkins in his " Lament of the Silent Sisters," a poem prophetic of his own death:

> Chorus: We carry in our worlds that flourish
>   Our worlds that have failed ...
>
> Crier: This is our swan song
>   This is the sigh of our spirits.

Okibo was a religious, philosophic poet of great promise.

—Anne Tibble

OLSON, Charles (John).   American.   Born in Worcester, Massachusetts, 27 December 1910. Educated at Wesleyan University, Middletown, Connecticut, B.A. 1932, M.A. 1933; Yale University, New Haven, Connecticut; Harvard University, Cambridge, Massachusetts. Taught at Clark University, Worcester, and Harvard University, 1936–39; Instructor and Rector, Black Mountain College, North Carolina, 1951–56; taught at the State University of New York at Buffalo, 1963–65, and the University of Connecticut, Storrs, 1969. Recipient: Guggenheim grant (twice); Wenner-Gren Foundation grant, to study Mayan hieroglyphics, 1952; National Endowment for the Arts grant, 1966, 1968. *Died 10 January 1970.*

PUBLICATIONS

Verse

Corrado Cagli March 31 Through April 19 1947.   1947.
Y & X.   1948.
Letter for Melville 1951.   1951.
This.   1952.
In Cold Hell, in Thicket.   1953.
The Maximus Poems 1–10.   1953.
Ferrini and Others, with others.   1955.
Anecdotes of the Late War.   1955.
The Maximus Poems 11–22.   1956.

O'Ryan 2 4 6 8 10.   1958; expanded edition, as *O'Ryan 12345678910,* 1965.
Projective Verse.   1959.
The Maximus Poems.   1960.
The Distances: Poems.   1960.
Maximus, From Dogtown I.   1961.
Signature to Petition on Ten Pound Island Asked of Me by Mr. Vincent Ferrini.   1964.
West.   1966.
Charles Olson Reading at Berkeley, edited by Zoe Brown.   1966.
Before Your Very Eyes!, with others.   1967.
The Maximus Poems, IV, V, VI.   1968.
Reading about My World.   1968.
Added to Making a Republic.   1968.
Clear Shifting Water.   1968.
That There Was a Woman in Gloucester, Massachusetts.   1968.
Wholly Absorbed into My Own Conduits.   1968.
Causal Mythology.   1969.
Archaeologist of Morning: The Collected Poems Outside the Maximus Series.   1970.
The Maximus Poems, Volume Three, edited by Charles Boer and George F. Butterick.   1975.

Plays

The Fiery Hunt and Other Plays.   1977.

Fiction

Stocking Cap: A Story.   1966.

Other

Call Me Ishmael: A Study of Melville.   1947.
Apollonius of Tyana: A Dance, with Some Words, for Two Actors.   1951.
Mayan Letters, edited by Robert Creeley.   1953.
A Bibliography on America for Ed Dorn.   1964.
Pleistocene Man: Letters from Olson to John Clarke during October, 1965.   1968.
Human Universe and Others Essays, edited by Donald Allen.   1965.
Proprioception.   1965.
Selected Writings, edited by Robert Creeley.   1966.
Letters for "Origin," 1950–1956, edited by Albert Glover.   1969.
The Special View of History, edited by Ann Charters.   1970.
Poetry and Truth: The Beloit Lectures and Poems, edited by George F. Butterick.   1971.
Additional Prose: A Bibliography on America, Proprioception, and Other Notes and Essays, edited by George F. Butterick.   1974.
The Post Office: A Memoir of His Father.   1975.
Olson and Ezra Pound: An Encounter at St. Elizabeth's, edited by Catherine Seelye.   1975.
Muthologos: The Collected Lectures and Interviews, edited by George F. Butterick.   1976.

Bibliography: *A Bibliography of the Works of Olson* by George F. Butterick and Albert Glover, 1967.

Reading List: *Olson/Melville: A Study in Affinity* by Ann Charters, 1968; *A Guide to the Maximus Poems of Olson* by George F. Butterick, 1978; *Olson: Call Him Ishmael* by Paul Christensen, 1978.

*   *   *

Although any final judgment regarding the work and influence of the poet Charles Olson remains controversial, he must nevertheless be regarded as a seminal force in the reshaping of American poetry written since World War II. Olson showed little inclination to be a poet until his mid-thirties. Shortly after the death of Roosevelt, however, Olson left government and committed himself to a literary career. By then he had written only the draft of a short book on Melville, *Call Me Ishmael*, and several conventional poems published in popular magazines. From these unpromising beginnings, Olson began writing in earnest in the late 1940's. With the help of Edward Dahlberg, a completely revised *Call Me Ishmael* was published in 1947; two years later, Olson composed "The Kingfishers," among the most innovative poems to have emerged since World War II. And in 1950, largely from the example of the techniques employed in "The Kingfishers," and ideas taken from a variety of sources, including William Carlos Williams, Pound, Dahlberg and his close friend Robert Creeley, Olson synthesized the provocative and highly influential manifesto, "Projective Verse."

This essay established a new set of conventions for the short poem. In place of the old rules of repetitive measure, rhyme, and fixed stanza, Olson introduced the principle that "form is an extension of content," or that form is the result of allowing content to assume its own partly accidental shape during composition. Around this main principle are certain technical corollaries: for example, the poet, rather than treating his theme in an orderly progression of ideas, should instead rush from "perception to perception" until his argument is exhausted. The poet should allow the rhythm of his breath during composition to determine the length of each line, so that he has scored it for the reading voice. And in fitting words together in the line itself, the poet should let sound, rather than sense, determine syntax. A logic of the ear should take precedence over intellect in the fashioning of language.

Olson suggested that all of these new conventions were dependent on a new stance to experience, which he called Objectism. The poet should no longer consider his mind a clearing house of data, from which to select bits of information for his poems. Rather, the poet should include the rest of his organism in the act of perception and awareness, and should feel himself rush out of his private emotion into the realms of phenomena free of self-consciousness and inhibition. Objectism called for the poet to accept himself as merely another object inhabiting the phenomenal welter making up the world. The techniques advised in the first half of the essay, then, are all the means of making experience direct and unmediated for the poet who plunges fully into the phenomena around him.

"The Kingfishers" satisfies most of the conditions of composition set forth in the "Projective Verse" essay. Its form is the result of a rush of discourse on a series of loosely related topics, of experiments in combinations of sounds, and of the arrangement of words in clusters to show the changing shape of his thinking moment by moment. This striking poem creates the feeling of having kept pace with the random and shifting content of the poet's awareness.

Olson's projective methodology and the example of "The Kingfishers" are clearly efforts to explore and even to track the behavior of the imagination. More significant is the fact that Olson's poetic brings poetry into the general current of free-forming methods then being applied to the other arts: atonal, free-form jazz composition, abstract expressionism, improvisational theater, and kinetic sculpture.

Olson went on to refine the doctrine now known as Objectism in subsequent essays and lectures, but his several collections of short poems and the long, sequential work *The Maximus Poems* are the basis of his reputation and influence as a poet. In 1953, Robert Creeley published Olson's first full-length volume of poems, *In Cold Hell, in Thicket*, which contains not only "The Kingfishers" but many of Olson's boldest shorter poems. Many, but by no means all, of these shorter poems are composed in the projective mode; others are written in a more leisurely-paced free verse style. The whole work is concerned with the burdens of tradition and influence the poet must cast off to pursue his own direction. The poet argues, often petulantly, against Ezra Pound, whom Olson identifies as his spiritual father and arch rival.

Creeley later edited Olson's *Selected Writings*, further establishing Olson's reputation as a key figure of the new poetry. A more finished and elaborate poetry emerges in *The Distances*, but there is less bold experiment in these maturer lyrical poems. Olson had moved to less defined areas of awareness; many of the poems are startling reenactments of dreams, in which the supralogical narratives are skillfully and persuasively dramatized, and there is a greater interest in myth and the content and forms of consciousness.

But the primary text for judging Olson as poet rests with his central work, the long, epical *Maximus* sequence, begun in the late 1940's and sustained to the last months of his life. The work remains unfinished, although the final volume, found among the poet's papers, has been edited and published. The work in one way is a celebration of the seacoast town of Gloucester, Massachusetts, where communal spirit among the fishermen thrived before industry was established; in another, it is close scrutiny of life in America and a search for an alternative ideology rooted in new spiritual awareness.

In the first volume, *The Maximus Poems*, Olson's persona, Maximus, named after an itinerant Phoenician mystic of the fourth century A.D., surveys contemporary Gloucester and finds its citizenry in disarray and the local culture ugly and alien. This judgment prompts a systematic inquiry into the origins of Gloucester and of America, which takes up the remainder of the volume. In the second volume, *Maximus IV,V VI*, the speaker widens his interests to include mythological lore, the history of human migration, religious literature, and the finer details of Gloucester's past, which seem to Maximus to re-enact certain of the myths and fables of the ancient world. The final volume, more somber in mood and subject, continues Maximus's intense survey of Gloucester and himself. A vision of a new cosmos is summoned in these poems, in the hope of redeeming and possibly reconstituting the communal ethos of Gloucester's past. But that hope gives way to remorse and disparagement of the reckless present and its deadening commercial enterprises.

The poem is among the more ambitious experiments in sustained narrative in the post-war period; it ranks in conception and execution with other verse epics of the modern period, including Pound's *Cantos*, Williams's *Paterson*, and Hart Crane's *The Bridge*. Although Olson is less musical in his language, and at times a dry poet given to long quotation from historic documents, the sweep of his thought and the scope of his imaginative arguments distinguish him as a major American poet of the Whitman tradition.

—Paul Christensen

OWEN, Wilfred (Edward Salter). English. Born in Oswestry, Shropshire, 18 March 1893. Educated at Birkenhead Institute, Cheshire, 1899–1907; Shrewsbury Technical School, Shropshire, 1907–11. Served in the Artists' Rifles and the Manchester Regiment, 1915–18: military cross; killed in action. Pupil and lay assistant to Herbert Wigan, Vicar of Dunsden, Oxfordshire, 1911–13; Tutor in English, Berlitz School, Bordeaux, 1913–14; private tutor in Bordeaux, 1914–15. *Died 4 November 1918.*

PUBLICATIONS

Collections

Poems, edited by Siegfried Sassoon.   1920.
Poems, edited by Edmund Blunden.   1931.
Collected Poems, edited by C. Day Lewis.   1963; revised edition, 1964.
Collected Letters, edited by Harold Owen and John Bell.   1967.
War Poems and Others, edited by Dominic Hibberd.   1973.

Bibliography: Owen: A Bibliography by William White, 1967.

Reading List: Owen: A Critical Study by D. S. R. Welland, 1960, revised edition, 1978; Journey from Obscurity: Owen, 1893–1918 by Harold Owen, 3 vols., 1963–65; Heroes' Twilight by Bernard Bergonzi, 1965; Owen by G. M. White, 1969; Out of Battle: Poetry of the Great War by Jon Silkin, 1972; Owen by Jon Stallworthy, 1974; Owen by Dominic Hibberd, 1975.

*   *   *

In the unfinished draft Preface for the volume of poems that he never lived to see in print, Wilfred Owen wrote, "My subject is War, and the pity of War," and it has since been too often assumed that the War which he made his subject made him a poet. In fact, he had discovered his vocation at the age of ten or eleven and at once bound himself apprentice to the great Romantics, Coleridge, Keats, and Shelley, steeping himself in their writings, studying their lives, in a single-minded endeavour to make himself a poet.

He came, therefore, to the Great War with a developed technique and an imagination in large measure prepared to receive and record the experience of the trenches. His religious upbringing and subsequent doubts, a compassionate humanism derived from his literary masters, boyhood interests in botany and archaeology, all shaped him for his subject as for no other. He had, however, written none of the poems by which he is now known when, after four harrowing months at the Front, he was found in May 1917 to be suffering from shell-shock and invalided back to Craiglockhart War Hospital on the outskirts of Edinburgh. There he had the good fortune to meet Siegfried Sassoon, whose first fiercely realistic "war poems" had just appeared in The Old Huntsman and Other Poems. Under their influence and with the encouragement and expert guidance of the older man, Owen was soon producing poems purged of an adolescent, sub-Keatsian luxuriance and far superior to any he had written before. Initially, some like "The Dead-Beat" and "Dulce et Decorum Est" relied too heavily on the colloquial shock-tactics that Sassoon had perfected. Although Owen shared his friend's indignation at the war-mongering of clerics, journalists, and politicians, the incompetence of the General Staff, and the activities of war-profiteers, elegy was a mode more suited to his temperament than satire or simple exposure of the horrors of war.

Helping him with the final revisions to "Anthem for Doomed Youth," Sassoon "realized that his verse, with its sumptuous epithets and large-scale imagery, its noble naturalness and the depth of meaning, had impressive affinities with Keats, whom he took as his supreme exemplar. This new sonnet was a revelation.... It confronted me with classic and imaginative serenity." That poem was a reply to a Prefatory Note in an anthology, Poems of Today (1916), whose anonymous author had written that one of the youngest of the poets represented had "gone singing to lay down his life for his country's cause," and that in the arrangement of the book "there is no arbitrary isolation of one theme from another; they mingle and interpenetrate throughout, to the music of Pan's flute, and of Love's viol, and the bugle-call of Endeavour, and the passing-bell of Death." Similar responses to the pronouncements of other authors were to produce many of Owen's most powerful poems: "Apologia pro Poemate Meo" prompted by a remark of Robert Graves's, "For God's sake cheer up and write more optimistically – the war's not ended yet but a poet should have a spirit above wars"; the fragment "Cramped in that funnelled hole" prompted, perhaps unconsciously, by Tennyson's "The Charge of the Light Brigade"; and "S.I.W." subverting its epigraph from Yeats's play *The King's Threshold*.

Throughout his months at Craiglockhart Owen suffered from the horrendous nightmares that are the principal symptom of shell-shock. His experience of battle, banished from his waking mind, erupted into his dreams and thence into his poems. In "The Sentry" he remembers

> Those other wretches, how they bled and spewed,
> And one who would have drowned himself for good, –
> I try not to remember these things now.

But when he tries to forget them, there returns the memory of the blinded sentry vainly trying to see the struck match held before his eyes: " 'I can't,' he sobbed. Eyeballs, huge-bulged like squids',/Watch my dreams still.... " Those tormented eyes stare also from such other poems as "Dulce et Decorum Est," "Greater Love," and "Mental Cases." Another obsessive image is of a subterranean Hell. Derived from the lurid descriptions of the wages of sin heard as a child, this appears in pre-war poems about the excavations at Uriconium and the double grave of a mother and daughter. Experience of the trenches expanded that metaphor into the symbol of mythic significance that dominates so many of the mature poems, among them "Cramped in that funnelled hole," "Miners," and "Strange Meeting."

The distinctive music of such later poems owes much of its power to Owen's mastery of alliteration, onomatopoeia, assonance, half-rhyme, and the pararhyme that he pioneered. This last, the rhyming of two words with identical or similar consonants but differing, stressed vowels (as *Flashes/Fleshes* and *hall/Hell*), of which the second is usually the lower in pitch, produces effects of dissonance, failure, and unfulfilment that subtly reinforce his themes.

In the year of life left to him after leaving Craiglockhart in November 1917, he matured rapidly both as man and poet. Success as a soldier, marked by the award of the Military Cross, and as a poet, which had won him "the recognition of his peers," gave him a new confidence. He wrote more eloquently than other poets of the tragedy of boys killed in battle because, as a latent homosexual, he felt that tragedy more acutely, and in his later elegies a disciplined sensuality, a passionate intelligence find their fullest, most moving, and memorable expression.

—Jon Stallworthy

PAGE, P(atricia) K(athleen). Canadian. Born in Swanage, Dorset, England, 23 November 1916; emigrated to Canada, 1919. Educated at St. Hilda's School for Girls, Calgary, Alberta; Art Students' League, and Pratt Institute, New York; studied art privately in Brazil and New York. Married William Arthur Irwin in 1950; three step-children. Formerly, sales clerk and radio actress, St. John, New Brunswick; filing clerk and historical researcher, Montreal, and a Founding Editor, *Preview*, Montreal; Script Writer, National Film Board, Ottawa, 1946–50. Painter, as P. K. Irwin: one-man shows at Picture Loan Society, Toronto, 1960; Galeria de Arte Moderna, Mexico City, 1962, and Art Gallery of

Greater Victoria, 1965; works included in the collections of the National Gallery of Canada, Ottawa; Art Gallery of Toronto; Vancouver Art Gallery. Recipient: Governor-General's Award, 1955. Member, Academia Brazileira de Letras, Rio de Janeiro. Lives in Victoria, British Columbia.

PUBLICATIONS

Verse

   Unit of Five, with others. 1944.
   As Ten as Twenty. 1946.
   The Metal and the Flower. 1954.
   Cry Ararat! Poems New and Selected. 1967.
   Leviathan in a Pool. 1973.

Fiction

   The Sun and the Moon. 1944.
   The Sun and the Moon and Other Fictions. 1973.

Reading List: *The Bush Garden: Essays on the Canadian Imagination* by Northrop Frye, 1971; "The Poetry of Page" by A. J. M. Smith, in *Canadian Literature,* Autumn 1971.

*   *   *

P. K. Page is a poet with two careers. She played a considerable role among the Montreal poets of the early 1940's, being one of the founding editors of the historic Canadian poetry magazine *Preview*, and she continued writing verse until the early 1950's. There followed a period of travel in Latin America, Australia, and the United States, during which she wrote comparatively little, and developed a parallel talent as a painter under the name of P. K. Irwin. Returning to Canada in 1964, she began to write poetry again, and in recent years has reoccupied her leading position among active Canadian writers.

P. K. Page's early poetry tended to take on some of the flavour of English 1930's verse, concerning itself with themes of social protest and showing the formal influence of Auden and Spender. By the end of the 1940's she was moving into a more individual kind of expression, terse and ironic, and was concerning herself less with socio-political situations than with individual predicaments – the plights of solitary people or of those whom circumstances subjected to contempt; satire and compassion are unusually mingled in these middle poems.

In her later work, P. K. Page has moved towards a stark, purified poetry of great tonal attractiveness, and at the same time towards metaphysical intents, and an almost mystical concern for the view out from the mind towards images that promise integration. Her poem, "Cry Ararat!," in the volume with the same name, is typical of this trend, as the final lines eloquently demonstrate:

   The leaves that make the tree by day,
   the green twig the dove saw fit
   to lift across a world of water
   break in a wave about our feet.

The bird in the thicket with his whistle
the crystal lizard in the grass
the star and shell
tassel and bell
of wild flowers blowing where we pass,
this flora-fauna flotsam, pick and touch,
requires the focus of the total I.

A single leaf can block a mountainside;
all Ararat be conjured by a leaf.

As well as her poetry and painting, P. K. Page has produced a small amount of fiction. The novel she published in 1944 under the pseudonym of Judith Cape, *The Sun and the Moon*, was a work of romantic symbolism, and the same is true of her haunting and highly ambivalent short stories.

—George Woodcock

PATCHEN, Kenneth. American. Born in Niles, Ohio, 13 December 1911. Educated at Warren High School, Ohio; the Experimental College, University of Wisconsin, Madison, 1928–29. Married Miriam Oikemus in 1934. Also an artist: one-man show of books, graphics, and paintings, Corcoran Gallery, Washington, D.C., 1969. Recipient: Guggenheim Fellowship, 1936; Shelley Memorial Award, 1954; National Endowment for the Arts Distinguished Service Grant, 1967. *Died 8 January 1972.*

PUBLICATIONS

Verse

Before the Brave. 1936.
First Will and Testament. 1939.
The Teeth of the Lion. 1942.
The Dark Kingdom. 1942.
Cloth of the Tempest. 1943.
An Astonished Eye Looks Out of the Air, Being Some Poems Old and New Against War and in Behalf of Life. 1945.
Outlaw of the Lowest Planet, edited by David Gascoyne. 1946.
Selected Poems. 1946; revised edition, 1958, 1964.
Pictures of Life and of Death. 1947.
They Keep Riding Down All the Time. 1947.
Panels for the Walls of Heaven. 1947.
Patchen: Man of Anger and Light, with A Letter to God by Kenneth Patchen, with Henry Miller. 1947.
CCCLXXIV Poems. 1948.

To Say If You Love Someone and Other Selected Love Poems.   1948.
Red Wine and Yellow Hair.   1949.
Fables and Other Little Tales.   1953.
The Famous Boating Party and Other Poems in Prose.   1954.
Orchards, Thrones and Caravans.   1955.
Glory Never Guesses: Being a Collection of 18 Poems with Decorations and Drawings.   1956.
A Surprise for the Bagpipe Player: A Collection of 18 Poems with Decorations and Drawings.   1956.
When We Were Here Together.   1957.
Hurrah for Anything: Poems and Drawings.   1957.
Two Poems for Christmas.   1958.
Poem-scapes.   1958.
Pomes Penyeach.   1959.
Poems of Humor and Protest.   1960.
Because It Is: Poems and Drawings.   1960.
A Poem for Christmas.   1960.
The Love Poems.   1960.
Patchen Drawing-Poem.   1962.
Picture Poems.   1962.
Doubleheader.   1966.
Hallelujah Anyway.   1966.
Where Are the Other Rowboats?   1966.
But Even So (includes drawings).   1968.
Love and War Poems, edited by Dennis Gould.   1968.
Selected Poems.   1968.
The Collected Poems.   1968.
Aflame and Afun of Walking Faces: Fables and Drawings.   1970.
There's Love All Day, edited by Dee Danner Barwick.   1970.
Wonderings.   1971.
In Quest of Candlelighters.   1972.

Plays

Now You See It (Don't Look Now) (produced 1966).
Lost Plays, edited by Richard Morgan.   1977.

Radio Play: *City Wears a Slouch Hat,* 1942.

Fiction

The Journal of Albion Moonlight.   1941.
The Memoirs of a Shy Pornographer: An Amusement.   1945.
Sleepers Awake.   1946.
See You in the Morning.   1948.

Other

Patchen: Painter of Poems (exhibition catalogue).   1969.
The Argument of Innocence: A Selection from the Pictureworks, edited by Peter Veres.   1975.

Bibliography: *Patchen: A First Bibliography* by Gail Eaton, 1948.

Reading List: *Patchen: A Collection of Essays* edited by Richard Morgan, 1977.

*   *   *

Kenneth Patchen is in the tradition of American poets that descends from Walt Whitman through William Carlos Williams to the Black Mountain poets, and beyond them to such younger writers as Galway Kinnell and Michael Waters. That is to say, Patchen is a "redskin" poet as opposed to a "paleface." His poems do not make use of European-inspired formal devices; his language is deliberately a "barbaric yawp" (Whitman's famous phrase from *Song of Myself*); and his subject-matter is drawn from his own very American experiences. He is a poet of the open air and the open road, a hunter after experience, claiming a kind of mystical connection with the animals he kills (in this he is very like Hemingway, James Dickey, and, perhaps, Robinson Jeffers); his style is free-ranging, colloquial, wise-cracking, but also unembarrassedly ready with the big word, the huge emotion. In short, he sounds very like Carl Sandburg.

Yet Patchen is a self-conscious poet. He may *play* the cracker-barrel philosopher, but as Thomas Hardy said of William Barnes, "He sings his native woodnotes wild with a great deal of art." Look, for example, at so small a poem as "In Memory of Kathleen":

> How pitiful is her sleep.
> Now her clear breath is still.
>
> There is nothing falling tonight,
> Bird or man,
> As dear as she.
>
> Nowhere that she should go
> Without me. None but my calling.
>
> O nothing but the cold cry of the snow.

It is a very finely written poem of grief, and a subtle one. The play on "pitiful" is perhaps obvious; but the way in which "falling" anticipates the cry of the snow is not so obvious, yet entirely just; as is the extraordinarily compacted "None but my calling." "None" comes from the earlier "nowhere," and it means that Patchen finds himself utterly alone: she has gone where he can't follow, there is only *his* calling, *his* voice to be heard. That, and the cry of the snow: whiteness, death, its falling reminding him that she, too, has fallen in death. Glanced casually over, this little poem may seem hopelessly slight; looked at more carefully, it emerges as the work of a considerable poet.

Patchen doesn't always write with this degree of tense urgency. It is, I think, characteristic of his kind of poetry that there should be a great deal of sprawl about it; and while one may salute the energy that has led him to produce so many volumes of verse – he must be one of the most unflaggingly fertile of twentieth-century American poets – it is also possible to wish that some of his work had been more intensively worked over. There is, for instance, a wonderful idea, partly spoiled, in *First Will and Testament* which has at its core a play for voices, featuring a Mr. Kek and his brothel, to which come, in turn, a group of famous poets, Donne, Marvell, Jonson, etc.; and then jazzmen Beiderbecke, Armstrong, Allen; gangsters, sportsmen – all outsiders, all seeking warmth and love and a good time, and trying to escape "the enemy." Much of this is obviously borrowed from Auden, but it has some fizzing wit and a great deal of hard-hitting panache that are Patchen's own. The trouble is that it degenerates into Cummings-like sentimentality: all picaros are better than all lawmen; to be an artist you have to be on the outside, a society reject, a bum. In other words the play is written out of cliché, so that although it has local life it is finally soggy.

This criticism applies to a good deal of his work. Yet nothing I say here is intended to detract from the vitality of his best writing, which can crop up anywhere, and is just as likely to show itself in a late volume, like *When We Were Here Together*, as in an early one, such as *Before the Brave*.

—John Lucas

p'BITEK, Okot. Ugandan. Born in Gulu, Acoli District, Northern Uganda, in 1931. Educated at Gulu High School; King's College, Budo, Uganda; University of Bristol, Certificate in Education; University of Wales, Aberystwyth, LL.B.; Oxford University, B.Litt. in social anthropology 1963. Lecturer in Sociology at Makerere University College, and Director of the Uganda National Theatre and Uganda National Cultural Center, all Kampala, 1964–68; Founder, Kisumu Arts Festival, Kenya, 1968; Fellow, International Writing Program, University of Iowa, Iowa City, 1969–70; Senior Research Fellow, Institute of African Studies, Nairobi, 1971. Lives in Kisumu, Kenya.

PUBLICATIONS

Verse

> *Lak tar miyo kinyero wi lobo?* (in Acoli: Are your teeth white, then laugh!).   1953.
> *The Song of Lawino* (translated from Acoli by the author).   1966.
> *Song of Ocol.*   1970.
> *The Song of a Prisoner.*   1970.
> *Two Songs: The Song of a Prisoner, The Song of Malaya.*   1971.
> *The Horn of My Love* (Acoli traditional songs, translated by the author).   1974.
> *The Hare and the Hornbill.*   1978.

*   *   *

Okot p'Bitek is a scholar as well as a poet and a novelist. *Song of Lawino* is a traditional story in verse of an Acoli wife, as if told by herself, of her husband's turning, in his desire to be "modern," to Clementine who "aspires/To look like a white woman" ("And she believes/ That this is beautiful"):

> I do not deny
> I am a little jealous.
> It is no good lying,
> We all suffer from a little jealousy....
>
> How many kids
> Has this woman sucked?
> The empty bags on her chest
> Are completely flattened, dried.
> Perhaps she has aborted many!
> Perhaps she has thrown her twins
> In the pit latrine!

The story contains a revealing character-sketch of the husband, Okol, floundering among the problems of *Uhuru* (freedom). It is a useful stroke to have made a woman the mouthpiece while there are still too few women writing in Africa. *Two Songs: Song of a Prisoner, Song of Malaya* are in similar, short-lined, graphic verse, the first song from the mouth of a man, the second from an unmarried woman. They are biting yet compassionate satires on an emergent African society torn between its own rich traditions and a seductive, materialist modernity passed on by British and American "imperialist progress"; *Song of a Prisoner* reveals, behind this "false dawn" of assassinations, corruption great and small, tyrants and blustering power, an enduring reality of life outside the "brash new towns" – the burning optimism of the people of Africa in the face of hardship and humiliation as in the known face of hunger: "Brother/How could I/So poor/Cold/Limping/Weak/Hungry like an empty tomb/A young tree/Burnt out/By the fierce wild fire/Of Uhuru/How could I/Inspire you/To such heights of brutality?"

What p'Bitek is writing is essentially a new kind of verse. Not only is he combining modern verse-form with oral form and content: he is showing how that form *is* the oral form. Yet, beside his stark concern with human essentials, the content of some modern Western verse can sound trivial, precious, oblique, too personal, materialist. Almost the only other poetry like p'Bitek's, since the 1960's, has come from South Africa, Russia, Chile, East Europe. In his own preface to *The Horn of My Love*, he explains: "Missionaries, anthropologists, musicologists and folklorists have plucked songs, stories, proverbs, riddles etc. from their social backgrounds and, after killing them by analysis, have buried them in inaccessible and learned journals, and in expensive technical books. I believe that literature, like all the other creative arts, is there, first and foremost, to be enjoyed." Writing by Africans alone, p'Bitek thinks, can secure the development of African literature.

—Anne Tibble

PLATH, Sylvia. American. Born in Boston, Massachusetts, 27 October 1932. Educated at Smith College, Northampton, Massachusetts, B.A. (summa cum laude) in English 1955; Harvard University, Cambridge, Massachusetts, Summer 1954; Newnham College, Cambridge (Fulbright Scholar), 1955–57, M.A. 1957. Married the poet Ted Hughes, *q.v.*, in 1956; one daughter and one son. Guest Editor, *Mademoiselle* magazine, New York, Summer 1953; Instructor in English, Smith College, 1957–58; moved to England, 1959. Recipient: Yaddo Fellowship, 1959; Cheltenham Festival Award, 1961; Saxon Fellowship, 1961. *Died* (by suicide) *11 February 1963.*

PUBLICATIONS

Verse

A Winter Ship. 1960.
The Colossus and Other Poems. 1960; as The Colossus, 1967.
Ariel. 1965.
Uncollected Poems. 1965.
Fiesta Melons. 1971.

Crossing the Water, edited by Ted Hughes. 1971; as *Crossing the Water: Transitional Poems*, 1971.
Crystal Gazer and Other Poems. 1971.
Lyonesse: Hitherto Uncollected Poems. 1971.
Winter Trees. 1971.
Pursuit. 1973.

Play

Three Women: A Monologue for Voices (broadcast 1962; produced 1973).

Radio Play: *Three Women*, 1962.

Fiction

The Bell Jar. 1961.

Other

Letters Home: Correspondence 1950–1963, edited by Aurelia Schober Plath. 1975.
The Bed Book (juvenile). 1976.
Plath: A Dramatic Portrait (miscellany), edited by Barry Kyle. 1976.
Johnny Panic and the Bible of Dreams, and Other Prose Writings. 1977.

Editor, *American Poetry Now: A Selection of the Best Poems by Modern American Writers*. 1961.

Bibliography: *A Chronological Checklist of the Periodical Publications of Plath* by Eric Homberger, 1970; *Plath and Anne Sexton: A Reference Guide* by Cameron Northouse and Thomas P. Walsh, 1975.

Reading List: *The Art of Plath: A Symposium* edited by Charles Newman, 1970 (includes bibliography); *Plath* by Eileen M. Aird, 1973; *Plath: Method and Madness* by Edward Butscher, 1976, and *Plath: The Woman and Her Work* edited by Butscher, 1977; *Plath: Poetry and Existence* by David Holbrook, 1976.

*   *   *

The adolescent heroine of Sylvia Plath's only novel, *The Bell Jar*, has looked into her grave and seen a sobering and a maddening truth. Her suicidal hysteria, like that which finally took her author, is the anguish of a being who has realized her own gratuitousness, "Factitious, artificial, sham." What she has called her "self," that unique and coddled ego, is no more than a nexus of donated being, a field of battle where the conflicting forces of her environment, her familial and social experience, clash, divide, and coalesce. Plath herself wrote of the poem "Daddy" as "spoken by a girl with an Electra complex. Her father died while she thought he was God. Her case is complicated by the fact that her father was also a Nazi and her mother very possibly Jewish. In the daughter the two strains marry and paralyze each other – she has to act out the awful little allegory before she is free of it." While the details hardly correspond accurately to Plath's own biography, their symbolic function in the emotional ecology of her work is clear. The title poem of *The Colossus* acknowledges such a condition: addressed to her dead father ("I shall never get you put together entirely") it is self-consciously post-Freudian and pre-Christian: "A blue sky out of the Oresteia/Arches above us"; if her father is now no more than a "Mouthpiece of the dead," this is equally true of all selves, whose "hours are married to shadow," the marionettes of an unconscious in whose formation they had no hand. "Poem for a Birthday" is a complex dramatic monologue in which a psyche struggles towards birth, in "the city of spare parts" which is the world. Its voice is a Cinderella or Snow-White princess in nightmare exile among incomprehensible and uncomprehending powers, feeling herself "Duchess of Nothing," "housekeep[ing] in Time's gut end" and "married [to] a cupboard of rubbish." It is a representative text.

The imagery of Plath's poems undergoes endless transformations, in which the links are often suppressed or arbitrary: sudden shifts of tack and emotion lead off in unexpected directions. Her poetic narratives fork and proliferate in this way because, in unfolding the implications of a sequence of images, she uncovers the complex and contradictory possibilities condensed within them, the infantile traumas lying treacherously beneath the surface of adult experience. The same image can be charged with quite contradictory emotional valencies. The bee, for example, a recurring motif (her father was an apiculturalist), stirs rich, ambiguous feelings. It is a female, a source of honey and creativity, but it has a male sting; the hive includes drudges and drones, but also that dark leonine queen at the core; in "The Swarm" and "The Arrival of the Bee-Box", bees are the collective "black, intractable mind" of a genocidal Europe and the "swarmy," "angrily clambering" impulsions of the individual unconscious. Such transitions express her own sense of the self, not as a hierarchically ordered pyramid, but as an ensemble of possibilities, in which none usurps precedence for long, and to which only a provisional coherence can be given, in the specifying of a name and image ("The Arrival of the Bee-Box," after toying with the starvation or release of the bees which threaten and fascinate, concludes, "The box is only temporary"). Self for Plath is either a rigid, false *persona* or an amorphous, uncongealed, and fluid congeries, like the bee-swarm itself, undergoing constant metamorphosis, continually dying and being reborn in the mutations of the imagery. In "Elm," the social self speaks as a tree, rooted in its context, wrenched violently by a wind that "will tolerate no bystanding." But such fixity is an illusion, for its roots reach down to the dissolute sea, its branches "break up in pieces that fly about like clubs," it is dragged by the moon (usually the image of a sterile maternal force), and it contains subversive lives which are part of itself yet frighteningly independent:

> I am inhabited by a cry.
> Nightly it flaps out
> Looking, with its hooks, for something to love.
>
> I am terrified by this dark thing
> That sleeps in me;
> All day I feel its soft, feathery turnings, its malignity.

Plath repeatedly sees relationships as predatory, exploitative, and destructive, yet desired and necessary, as in "The Rabbit-Catcher" ("And we too had a relationship,/Tight wires between us,/Pegs too deep to uproot, and a mind like a ring/Sliding shut on some quick thing,/The constriction killing me also"). In "Tulips," even the smiles of husband and children, in a photograph, "catch onto my skin, little smiling hooks," while identity itself, in "The Applicant," is seen as a collection of functions, answers to others' questions, a poultice for their wounds, apple for their eyes, "A living doll" which is the accretion of artificial limbs and artificial commitments.

This aspect of her verse has made her co-option by the women's movement inevitable. But it is also just. Plath is, in fact, a profoundly political poet, who has seen the generic nature of these private catastrophes of the self, their public origin in a civilization founded on mass-manipulation and collective trickery. Esther Greenwood, in *The Bell Jar*, links her electric shock treatment with the electrocution which is the Rosenbergs' punishment for rebellion against the American way of life: she fears most of all being consigned to the charity wards, "with hundreds of people like me, in a big cage in the basement. The more hopeless you were, the further away they hid you." In a century which has shut away millions, in hospitals, concentration camps, and graveyards, where the self can be "wiped out ... like chalk on a blackboard" by administrative *diktat*, Plath sees a deep correspondence between the paternal concern of the psychiatrist and the authority of the modern state, even in its most extreme variants: both presuppose the self as victim, passive and compliant, as *sine qua non* of any "final solution." For Plath, concerned that "personal experience shouldn't be a kind of shut box and mirror-looking narcissistic experience," but "should be generally relevant, to such things as Hiroshima and Dachau and so on," the refusal to collaborate was a profoundly positive act, the assertion not of the nihilism of which she has been accused but of a more exacting and scrupulous conscience. If, in poems such as "Daddy" and "Lady Lazarus," she veers close to disintegration, she also promises a breakthrough into a resurrection which sheds the constricting husks of the past, a vengeful return which is only justice:

> So, so. Herr Doktor.
> So, Herr Enemy.
> I am your opus,
> I am your valuable,
> The pure gold baby
>
> That melts to a shriek.
> I turn and burn,
> Do not think I underestimate your great concern....
>
> Herr God, Herr Lucifer
> Beware
> Beware.
>
> Out of the ash
> I rise with my red hair
> And I eat men like air.

—Stan Smith

POUND, Ezra (Weston Loomis).   American.   Born in Hailey, Idaho, 30 October 1885. Educated at Hamilton College, Clinton, New York, Ph.B. 1905; University of Pennsylvania, Philadelphia, M.A. 1906. Married Dorothy Shakespear in 1914. Taught at Wabash College, Crawfordsville, Indiana, 1906; travelled in Spain, Italy, and France, 1906–07; lived in London, 1908–20, in Paris, 1920–24, and in Rapallo, Italy, 1924–45: one of the creators of the Imagist movement; English Editor of *Poetry*, Chicago, 1912–19; Founder, with Wyndham Lewis, of *Blast*, 1914; English Editor of *The Little Review*, Chicago, 1917–19; Paris Correspondent of *The Dial*, 1922; Founder and Editor of *The Exile*, 1927–28. Broadcast over Italian Radio to the United States after 1941, in support of fascism, and was arrested and jailed for these broadcasts by the United States Army in 1945; imprisoned near Pisa, found unfit to stand trial for treason, and committed to St. Elizabeth's Hospital, Washington, D.C.; released in 1958; returned to Italy. Recipient: Academy of American Poets Fellowship, 1963; National Endowment for the Arts grant, 1967. *Died 1 November 1972.*

PUBLICATIONS

Collections

Selected Prose 1909–1965, edited by William Cookson.   1973.
Selected Poems 1908–1959.   1975.

Verse

A Lume Spento.   1908.
A Quinzaine for This Yule.   1908.
Personae.   1909.
Exultations.   1909.
Provença: Poems Selected from Personae, Exultations, and Canzoniere.   1910.
Canzoni.   1911.
Riposte.s.   1912.
Lustra.   1916.
Lustra, with Earlier Poems.   1917.
Quia Pauper Amavi.   1919.
The Fourth Canto.   1919.
Umbra: The Early Poems.   1920.
Hugh Selwyn Mauberley.   1920.
Poems, 1918–21, Including Three Portraits and Four Cantos.   1921.
A Draft of XVI Cantos.   1925.
Personae: The Collected Poems.   1926; revised edition, 1949; as *Personae: Collected Shorter Poems,* 1952; as *Collected Shorter Poems,* 1968.
Selected Poems, edited by T. S. Eliot.   1928; revised edition, 1949.
A Draft of Cantos 17–27.   1928.
A Draft of XXX Cantos.   1930.
Homage to Sextus Propertius.   1934.
Eleven New Cantos: XXXI–XLI.   1934; as *A Draft of Cantos XXXI–XLI,* 1935.
Alfred Venison's Poems, Social Credit Themes.   1935.
The Fifth Decad of Cantos.   1937.
A Selection of Poems.   1940.
Cantos LII–LXXI.   1940.
The Pisan Cantos.   1948.
The Cantos.   1948; revised edition, 1965; revised edition, as *Cantos No. 1–117, 120,* 1970.
Selected Poems.   1949; revised edition, 1957.
Section: Rock-Drill: 86–95 de los Cantares.   1955.
Thrones: 96–109 de las Cantares.   1959.
A Lume Spento and Other Early Poems.   1965.
Canto CX.   1965.
Selected Cantos.   1967.
Cantos 110–116.   1967.
Drafts and Fragments, Cantos CX–CXVII.   1968.
Collected Early Poems, edited by Michael John King.   1976.

Other

The Spirit of Romance.   1910; revised edition, 1953.

"Noh" or Accomplishment: A Study of the Classical Stage of Japan, with Ernest
    Fenollosa.   1916; as *The Classical Noh Theatre of Japan*, 1959.
Gaudier-Brzeska: A Memoir.   1916; revised edition, 1959.
Pavannes and Divisions.   1918.
Instigations.   1920.
Indiscretions; or Une Revue de Deux Mondes.   1923.
Antheil and The Treatise on Harmony.   1924.
Imaginary Letters.   1930.
How to Read.   1931.
ABC of Economics.   1933.
ABC of Reading.   1934.
Make It New: Essays.   1934.
Social Credit: An Impact.   1935.
Jefferson and/or Mussolini.   1935; revised edition, as *Jefferson e Mussolini*, 1944.
Polite Essays.   1937.
Guide to Kulchur.   1938; as *Culture*, 1938.
What Is Money For?   1939.
Carta da Visita.   1942; translated by John Drummond, as *A Visiting Card*, 1952.
L'America, Roosevelt, e le Cause della Guerra Presente.   1944; translated by John
    Drummond, as *America, Roosevelt, and the Causes of the Present War*, 1951.
Oro e Lavoro.   1944; translated by John Drummond, as *Gold and Labour*, 1952.
Introduzione alla Natura Economica degli S.U.A.   1944; translated by Carmine Amore,
    as *An Introduction to the Economic Nature of the United States*, 1950.
Orientamenti.   1944.
If This Be Treason.   1948.
The Letters of Pound, 1907–1941, edited by D. D. Paige.   1950.
Patria Mia.   1950; as *Patria Mia and The Treatise on Harmony*, 1962.
The Translations of Ezra Pound, edited by Hugh Kenner.   1953; revised edition, 1970.
Secondo Biglietto da Visita.   1953.
Literary Essays, edited by T. S. Eliot.   1954.
Pavannes and Divagations.   1958.
Impact: Essays on Ignorance and the Decline of American Civilization, edited by Noel
    Stock.   1960.
EP to LU: Nine Letters Written to Louis Untermeyer by Ezra Pound, edited by J. Albert
    Robbins.   1963.
Pound/Joyce: The Letters of Ezra Pound to James Joyce, edited by Forrest Read.   1967.
Redondillas: or, Something of That Sort.   1967.
The Caged Panther: Ezra Pound at St. Elizabeth's (includes 53 letters), by Harry M.
    Meachum.   1967.
DK: Some Letters of Pound, edited by Louis Dudek.   1974.
Pound and Music: The Complete Criticism, edited by R. Murray Schafer.   1977.

Editor, *Des Imagistes: An Anthology*.   1914.
Editor, *Catholic Anthology, 1914–1915*.   1915.
Editor, *Poetical Works of Lionel Johnson*.   1915.
Editor, *Passages from the Letters of John Butler Yeats*.   1917.
Editor, *Profile: An Anthology*.   1932.
Editor, *Rime*, by Guido Cavalcanti.   1932.
Editor, *Active Anthology*.   1933.
Editor, *The Chinese Written Character as a Medium for Poetry: An Ars Poetica*. by
    Ernest Fenollosa.   1936.
Editor, *De Moribus Brachmanorum, Liber Sancto Ambrosio Falso Adscriptus*.   1956.
Editor, with Marcella Spann, *Confucius to Cummings: An Anthology of Poetry*.   1964.

Translator, *The Sonnets and Ballate of Guido Cavalcanti.* 1912; as *Pound's Cavalcanti Poems,* 1966.
Translator, *Cathay: Translations.* 1915.
Translator, with Ernest Fenollosa, *Certain Noble Plays of Japan.* 1916.
Translator, *Dialogues of Fontenelle.* 1917.
Translator, *The Natural Philosophy of Love,* by Rémy de Gourmont. 1922.
Translator, *The Call of the Road,* by Edouard Estaunié. 1923.
Translator, *Ta Hio: The Great Learning,* by Confucius. 1928.
Translator, *Digest of the Analects,* by Confucius. 1937.
Translator, *Italy's Policy of Social Economics 1939–1940,* by Odon Por. 1941.
Translator, with Alberto Luchini, *Ta S'en Dai Gaku, Studio Integrale,* by Confucius. 1942.
Translator, *Ciung Iung, l'Asse che non Vacilla,* by Confucius. 1945.
Translator, *The Unwobbling Pivot and The Great Digest,* by Confucius. 1947.
Translator, *Confucian Analects.* 1951.
Translator, *The Classic Anthology Defined by Confucius.* 1954.
Translator, *Women of Trachis,* by Sophocles. 1956.
Translator, *Moscardino,* by Enrico Pea. 1956.
Translator, *Rimbaud* (5 poems). 1957.
Translator, with Noel Stock, *Love Poems of Ancient Egypt.* 1962.

Bibliography: *A Bibliography of Pound* by Donald Gallup, 1963, revised edition, 1969.

Reading List: *Pound: His Metric and Poetry* by T. S. Eliot, 1917; *The Poetry of Pound,* 1951, and *The Pound Era,* 1971, both by Hugh Kenner; *A Primer of Pound* by M. L. Rosenthal, 1960; *Pound* by G. S. Fraser, 1960; *Pound, Poet as Sculptor,* 1964, and *Pound,* 1976, both by Donald Davie; *The Life of Pound* by Noel Stock, 1970: *Pound: The Critical Heritage* edited by Eric Homberger, 1972; *Pound, The Last Rower: A Political Profile* by C. David Heymann, 1976; *Time in Pound's Work* by William Harmon, 1977.

* * *

In his preface to his little book on popular music, *All What Jazz,* the poet Philip Larkin names the jazz musician Charlie Parker, Picasso, and Ezra Pound as standing for all that he most detests in "modernism" in the arts. Larkin is probably, without being among the startlingly great, the most distinguished poet we have in England at this moment. I am not competent to speak about Parker. But Cubism, invented by Picasso and Braque, is, in spite of its comparatively short life in its pure form, the greatest revolution in painting since the first adequate exploitation of perspective, anatomy, and the golden section at the Renaissance. Similarly, for good or evil, modern poetry would not be what it is (or have been what it was) without Pound. It may be true that what Pound had personally to say through the medium of verse was either not very interesting or, as in his praise of Fascism, positively dangerous. He remains the greatest technical inventor in poetry in his century, and the history of twentieth-century poetry would be quite different without him. As an observer of life, Larkin is in many ways a more complex and subtle man than Pound. Still, if Larkin had never existed, we should lack four slim volumes of carefully undertoned verse, but the history of poetry in our century would be much what it is already.

Yet the comparison of Picasso and Pound is critically apt. Both, the one in Spain, the other in the American mid-west, started out of the main stream. When Picasso came to Paris from Spain, he left a country that had not even caught up with Impressionism. When Pound came to England in 1908, with his first volume *A Lume Spento* privately printed in Venice, he was imitating the poets of the 1890's, including Yeats in his very early phase, Swinburne, and the Pre-Raphaelites: he was about thirty years behind the times. T. E. Hulme and other members of the Poets' Club, now forgotten, were already experimenting with what was to be called Imagism, and an Englishman, F. S. Flint, was to work out its theory; it was left to Pound, when he got round to it in 1912, only to give it a name. His own Imagist poems are among the best, but not perhaps so good as the very best of his American acquaintance, Hilda Doolittle. Of his poems before *The Cantos*, the best are two translations, "The Seafarer" (his Anglo-Saxon was self-taught, and some of the lines are sonorous but meaningless) and "Cathay" (adapted from the American scholar Ernest Fenollosa's attempts to translate classical Chinese poetry through a knowledge of the Chinese ideograms), and the two-part *Hugh Selwyn Mauberley*.

A study of cultural decay in England since the Pre-Raphaelites, *Mauberley* begins with a mock-epitaph for Pound and an ironic but affectionate picture of the tradition of the Pre-Raphaelites and Decadents from which he derives; its second half deals with an imaginary character, Hugh Selwyn Mauberley, who chooses to drift hedonistically to his death. Yet the final poem created by Pound at the end of his section is a seventeenth-century pastiche, the final poem created by Mauberley; transforming hair into metal and flesh into porcelain under the electric light is very startlingly "modern." There is a sense also that the Mauberley figure, for all his drifting, feels more deeply than the satirically observant Pound figure. Like *The Waste Land*, of which it is in some sense a forerunner, *Hugh Selwyn Mauberley* has still to be satisfactorily construed. (There is likewise no agreed judgment about whether the startling mistranslations in *Homage to Sextus Propertius* are blunders or are satirical, though some intention to satirise the British Empire is obvious.)

Pound then embarked on a poem of enormous length, *The Cantos*. This is, in a certain sense, a modern epic, except that the heroic role is played now by Odysseus and now by a Renaissance adventurer like Sigismundo de Malatesta, and the sage figure now by Confucius and now by one of the American founding fathers like Jefferson or John Adams. The poem throughout assumes a knowledge in the reader of Pound's raw material and a knowledge of the economics of Major Douglas ("Can't move them with a cold thing like economics") and of exactly what Pound means by usury. There are very dull patches in the middle, but the account of Pound's imprisonment by American troops in Pisa (*The Pisan Cantos*) at the time of the Allied invasion of Italy is vivid. The later cantos are more fragmentary and harder to understand. The poem is a failure as a whole, but an amazing manual of poetic techniques.

—G. S. Fraser

PRATT, E(dwin) J(ohn).   Canadian.   Born in Western Bay, Newfoundland, 4 February 1883. Draper's apprentice, St. John's, Newfoundland, 1898–1901; educated at Methodist College, St. John's, 1901–03; school teacher and student preacher, Newfoundland, 1903–07; Victoria College, University of Toronto, 1907–17, B.A. 1911, B.D. 1913, M.A. 1915, Ph.D. 1917; ordained in the Methodist Church. Demonstrator and Lecturer in Psychology, University College, 1911–17, and Associate Professor of English, 1919–33, Professor of English, 1933–53, and Emeritus Professor, 1953–64, Victoria College, University of Toronto. Editor, *Canadian Poetry* magazine, Toronto, 1936–42; Member, Editorial Board, *Saturday Night*, Toronto, 1952. Recipient: Governor-General's Award, 1937, 1949, 1952; Lorne Pierce Gold Medal, 1940; University of Alberta Gold Medal for Literature, 1951; Canada Council grant, 1958, and medal, 1961. D.Litt.: University of Manitoba, Winnipeg, 1945; McGill University, Montreal, 1949; University of Toronto, 1953; Assumption University, Windsor, Ontario, 1955; University of New Brunswick, Fredericton, 1957; University of Western Ontario, London, 1957; Memorial University of Newfoundland, St.

John's, 1961; LL.D.: Queen's University, Kingston, Ontario, 1949; D.C.L.: Bishop's University, Lennoxville, Quebec, 1949. Fellow, Royal Society of Canada, 1930. C.M.G. (Companion, Order of St. Michael and St. George), 1946. *Died 26 April 1964.*

PUBLICATIONS

Collections

  Selected Poems, edited by Peter Buitenhuis.   1968.

Verse

  Rachel: A Story of the Sea.   1917.
  Newfoundland Verse.   1923.
  The Witches' Brew.   1925.
  Titans.   1926.
  The Iron Door: An Ode.   1927.
  The Roosevelt and the Antinoe.   1930.
  Verses of the Sea.   1930.
  Many Moods.   1932.
  The Titanic.   1935.
  The Fable of the Goats and Other Poems.   1937.
  Brébeuf and His Brethren.   1940.
  Dunkirk.   1941.
  Still Life and Other Verse.   1943.
  Collected Poems.   1944; revised edition, edited by Northrop Frye, 1958.
  They Are Returning.   1945.
  Behind the Log.   1947.
  Ten Selected Poems.   1947.
  Towards the Last Spike: A Verse Panorama of the Struggle to Build the First Canadian Transcontinental.   1952.
  Here the Tides Flow.   1962.

Other

  Studies in Pauline Eschatology and Its Background.   1917.

  Editor, *Under the Greenwood Tree,* by Thomas Hardy.   1937.
  Editor, *Heroic Tales in Verse.*   1941.

Reading List: *Pratt: The Man and His Poetry* by H. W. Wells and C. F. Klinck, 1947; *The Poetry of Pratt* by John Sutherland, 1956; *Pratt* by Milton T. Wilson, 1969; *Pratt* by David G. Pitt, 1969; *Pratt: The Evolutionary Vision* by Sandra Djwa, 1974.

*   *   *

Widely regarded as Canada's pre-eminent narrative poet, E. J. Pratt embodied in his work a nineteenth-century concern for social Darwinism and an evolving "instinct for what is imaginatively central in Canadian sensibility" (Northrop Frye). An ordained Methodist minister who wrote his M.A. and Ph.D. theses on demonology and Pauline eschatology, he experienced a crisis of faith which has caused him to be viewed variously an an atheist, Christian humanist, and agnostic. Similar ambiguity has hedged judgements about his shorter lyric poems and longer comic extravaganzas. His narrative fables and epics, particularly *Brébeuf and His Brethren*, best demonstrate his pre-occupation with themes of primaeval conflict, his fascination with technical language, and his dexterity in establishing the dramatic coherency of his stories in verse.

Four collections of Pratt's shorter poems were published between 1923 and 1943 (*Newfoundland Verse, Many Moods, The Fable of the Goats*, and *Still Life*); with some of his later poems, most are included in the second edition of the *Collected Poems*. Their tone is remarkably consistent: calm and flat, covering a moment of violence and usually concluding with a rhetorical comment. Pratt was not attracted by post-Edwardian experiments in form, and very few of these poems are in free verse. He almost never wrote about love. His most frequently anthologized short works, such as "The Shark" and "Sea-Gulls," centre on Newfoundland and the sea, or on the simultaneity of the evolutionary process, as in "The Prize Cat" and "From Stone to Steel."

Pratt's early personal and stylistic difficulties in reconciling orthodox Christianity with the aftermath of the First World War, a natural world indifferent to man, are evident in his first narratives: "Clay" (1917, published in part in *Newfoundland Verse*) and *Rachel. The Witches' Brew*, a farce about the effects of alcohol on fish, pointed more clearly to the elastic line, hyperbolic language, and juxtaposition of sober detail with vaulting commentary, all of which would mark his mature long poems. The formulation of *The Iron Door* as a dream-vision did not bear out his attempt to rationalize belief in the face of his mother's death. Thereafter he would continue to construct epic battles as metaphors for the persistence and frailty of human will, the kind of battles he dramatized in "The Cachalot" and "The Great Feud." Published together as *Titans*, his first major work, both poems set out struggles between evolutionary Titans and Olympians: in the first, a giant squid against a sperm whale, and in the second (sub-titled "A Dream of a Pleiocene Armageddon") the animals of the land led by an ape against those of the sea, with admixtures of grotesque comedy. Man kills one victor and is himself drowned in "The Cachalot"; man's solitary ancestor remains alive in "The Great Feud."

Pratt's poetic response to the political and economic dialectic of the 1930's was curiously muted. "The Fable of the Goats," omitted from the *Collected Poems*, offers peace in our time as a solution to the Spanish Civil War. His choice of the metaphor of a gigantic dinner for "The Depression Ends" appears perversely blinkered as a political statement. More characteristic of his larger attitudes are two of the three epics set at sea: *The Roosevelt and the Antinoe* and *The Titanic*, with their themes of human rescue partially thwarted and of the limits of technology in saving man. The American ship *Roosevelt* aids the sinking British *Antinoe*, but the sea can master both. The iceberg of *The Titanic* assumes a related role, a morally neutral force which seems – but only seems – to strike man down for his pride and arrogance. The Second World War provided Pratt with a properly grand stage for his complicated concept of heroism: rhetorically in the propagandistic *Dunkirk*; intimately in the North Atlantic convoy duty described in *Behind the Log*; and mythically in "The Truant," a debate between representative man and the Panjandrum who personifies the mechanistic principle of the universe, the perfect dictator. That Pratt should later describe Canada's far western mountain ranges as "seas" is appropriate, as is his concern with individual rather than collective human effort in his last narrative, *Towards the Last Spike*. Here the construction of the transcontinental railway in the 1870's and 1880's is transmuted into an ironic commentary on the triumph of will over environment, the need to establish an empire of communication over what man sees to be moral chaos, and the belief that technological progress is a metaphor for human evolution.

Brébeuf and His Brethren, Pratt's finest (and longest) narrative, is patterned on the way of the cross in its exploration of faith in seventeenth-century New France. (It is partly based on events chronicled in the Jesuit *Relations*.) The conflict of Indian and priest moves to the inevitable martyrdom of Brébeuf and Lalement. Pratt's objectivity, careful pacing, and smooth manipulation of a quarter-century's dialogue and description conclude with a contemporary Mass at the shrine of the martyrs. The final ironies of the poem characterize Pratt's own views on man's fate in a world always new to him. The value of human life lies in the persistence of individual struggle against our collective self-willed suicide.

—Bruce Nesbitt

PURDY, Al(fred Wellington).   Canadian.   Born in Wooller, Ontario, 30 December 1918. Educated at Dufferin Public School, Trenton, Ontario; Albert College, Belleville, Ontario; Trenton Collegiate Institute, Ontario. Served with the Royal Canadian Air Force during World War II. Married Eurithe Parkhurst in 1941; one son. Has held numerous jobs; taught at Simon Fraser University, Burnaby, British Columbia, Spring 1970; Poet-in-Residence, Loyola College, Montreal, 1973; Artist-in-Residence, University of Manitoba, Winnipeg, 1975–76. Recipient: Canada Council Fellowship, 1960, 1965, Senior Literary Fellowship, 1968, 1971, award, 1973, and grant, 1974; President's Medal, University of Western Ontario, 1964; Governor-General's Award, 1966. Lives in Ontario.

PUBLICATIONS

Verse

>   *The Enchanted Echo.*   1944.
>   *Pressed on Sand.*   1955.
>   *Emu, Remember!*   1956.
>   *The Crafte So Longe to Lerne.*   1959.
>   *Poems for All the Annettes.*   1962.
>   *The Blur in Between: Poems 1960–61.*   1962.
>   *The Cariboo Horses.*   1965.
>   *North of Summer: Poems from Baffin Island.*   1967.
>   *Poems for All the Annettes* (selected poems).   1968.
>   *Wild Grape Wine.*   1968.
>   *Spring Song.*   1968.
>   *Love in a Burning Building.*   1970.
>   *The Quest for Ouzo.*   1970.
>   *Selected Poems.*   1972.
>   *Hiroshima Poems.*   1972.
>   *On the Bearpaw Sea.*   1973.
>   *Sex and Death.*   1973.
>   *In Search of Owen Roblin.*   1974.
>   *Sundance at Dusk.*   1976.

Other

Editor, *The New Romans: Candid Canadian Opinions of the United States.*   1968.
Editor, *Fifteen Winds: A Selection of Modern Canadian Poems.*   1969.
Editor, *I've Tasted My Blood: Poems 1956–1968,* by Milton Acorn.   1969.
Editor, *Storm Warning: The New Canadian Poets.*   1971.

Reading List: *Purdy* by George Bowering, 1970.

*   *   *

From an unpromising beginning in the early 1940's, Al Purdy has made himself one of the liveliest, most prolific, and most respected Canadian poets. He is also one of the four or five most accomplished. From a purveyor of banalities, both in theme and technique, he has developed into a subtle and wide-ranging craftsman, ear and eye sensitively attuned to the human scene. A self-taught poet, he took a long time to work through certain habits and attitudes gathered in from the British tradition, but by the late 1950's his distinctive gifts had begun to show through. Eclectic in means, Protean in personality, his work seems to have cohered through the discovered sense of *locus* first apparent in such poems as "At Roblin Lake" (*The Crafte So Longe to Lerne*).

His work advanced greatly in the early 1960's, as is evident in *Poems for All the Annettes*, a collection full of a new energy, in which an earlier introversion has given way, importantly, to a telling exploration of individual relationships, as in "House Guest" and "Archaeology of Snow." Beyond this, Purdy shows in poems such as "The Old Woman and the Mayflowers" how a landscape may discover its myths in the character of its people.

The Cariboo Horses is in many ways Purdy's best book. In a book in which time and space, spartan time and empty − or snow-filled − space, predominate, he makes effective technical use of the continuous-present verb form. If *Poems for All the Annettes* marks the moment when Purdy's creative energies gathered decisively, *The Cariboo Horses* follows up by confirming that he is a *Canadian* poet. The book includes "The Madwoman in the Train," remarkable both as a subtle handling of the traditional sestina and as a deployment of psychological perspective.

It was Purdy who started the trend in Canada towards books of poems with a single, usually historical, thematic focus − in *North of Summer*. But his real métier is a kind of discursive lyric which he has, with mastery, made peculiarly his own. From *Wild Grape Wine* to *Sundance at Dusk* his repeated tactic has been to infuse information (geographical, historical, cultural, scientific) with emotion, as in "The Runners," "The Horses of the Agawa," and "Sundance." He handles the contemporary device of minimal punctuation well, and his best work evinces an easy and energetic handling of line and a peculiarly personal tone which is compounded of nostalgia and irony. The strong personality which gives his work its particular quality is held in balance by a high degree of professionalism.

—Charles Doyle

RAINE, Kathleen (Jessie).   English.   Born in London, 14 June 1908. Educated at County High School, Ilford; Girton College, Cambridge, M.A. in natural sciences 1929. Married the poet Charles Madge (divorced); one daughter and one son. Research Fellow, Girton College,

Cambridge, 1955–61; Andrew Mellon Lecturer, National Gallery of Art, Washington, D.C., 1962. Recipient: Arts Council award, 1953; Chapelbrook Award; Cholmondeley Award, 1970; Smith Literary Award, 1972. D.Litt.: University of Leicester, 1974. Lives in London.

PUBLICATIONS

Verse

> *Stone and Flower: Poems 1935–43.*   1943.
> *Living in Time.*   1946.
> *The Pythoness and Other Poems.*   1949.
> *Selected Poems.*   1952.
> *The Year One.*   1952.
> *The Collected Poems.*   1956.
> *The Hollow Hill and Other Poems, 1960–1964.*   1965.
> *Six Dreams and Other Poems.*   1968.
> *Ninfa Revisited.*   1968.
> *The Lost Country.*   1971.
> *On a Deserted Shore.*   1973.
> *The Oval Portrait and Other Poems.*   1977.

Other

> *William Blake.*   1951; revised edition, 1965, 1969.
> *Coleridge.*   1953.
> *Poetry in Relation to Traditional Wisdom.*   1958.
> *Defending Ancient Springs* (essays).   1967.
> *Blake and Tradition.*   1968.
> *William Blake.*   1971.
> *Faces of Day and Night* (autobiography).   1972.
> *Yeats, The Tarot and the Golden Dawn.*   1972.
> *Farewell Happy Fields: Memories of Childhood.*   1973.
> *Blake and Antiquity.*   1974.
> *David Jones: Solitary Perfectionist.*   1974; revised edition, 1975.
> *A Place, A State: A Suite of Drawings,* drawings by Julian Trevelyan.   1974.
> *The Land Unknown* (autobiography).   1975.
> *The Inner Journey of the Poet.*   1976.
> *The Lion's Mouth* (autobiography).   1977.

> Editor, with Max-Pol Fouchet, *Aspects de Littérature Anglaise, 1918–1945.*   1947.
> Editor, *Letters of Samuel Taylor Coleridge.*   1950.
> Editor, *Selected Poems and Prose of Coleridge.*   1957.
> Editor, with George Mills Harper, *Thomas Taylor the Platonist: Selected Writings.*   1969.
> Editor, *A Choice of Blake's Verse.*   1974.
> Editor, *Shelley.*   1974.

> Translator, *Talk of the Devil,* by Dénis de Rougemont.   1945.
> Translator, *Existentialism,* by Paul Foulquié.   1948.
> Translator, *Cousin Bette,* by Balzac.   1948.

Translator, *Lost Illusions,* by Balzac.   1951.
Translator, with R. M. Nadal, *Life's a Dream,* by Calderón.   1968.

Reading List: *Raine* by Ralph J. Mills, Jr., 1967.

*   *   *

Kathleen Raine is very much a poet on her own in the modern world, and her contribution to literature is difficult to classify. She belongs, perhaps, to the same poetic group as T. S. Eliot, David Gascoyne, St. John Perse, and Hugo Manning. A biologist by training, influenced by the writings of Jung and Blake, she has drawn greatly on nature and philosophy for her writings. She has made a lifelong study of the sources of tradition and makes great use of symbolism. Poetry for her is only authentic if it makes use of perennial philosophy and ancient wisdom expressed in traditional language. Her early poems had a spareness and directness about them which, coupled with a natural lyrical movement and a clear eye for significant detail, soon established her as a poet of consequence. Her later work, though often couched in simple language, is not so easy to comprehend at a first reading, since much of it conceals deep private experiences. She is essentially a poet in the Platonic tradition, who has always defended the ancient springs of civilisation, especially when these are of Christian origin. She has an individual and high-minded vision, both of life and literature, and in later years has displayed a deep sense of anger and passion against contemporary ignorance, and what she believes to be false Communistic ideas.

As a scholar she has made a name for herself in the English-speaking world by her writings about William Blake and Thomas Taylor, and is accepted as one of the leading authorities on both of them. Blake, for her, is an archetype which all poets should follow, in that he laid such great emphasis upon the powers of imagination and the need for mankind to retain his primeval innocence. Her autobiographies are very personal and often harrowing, especially *The Lion's Mouth*, revealing her complete dedication to poetry, even at the expense of everything else in her life. Her protestations, and her courage to speak out against the dilution of life and literature in the contemporary world, have brought her much criticism and misunderstanding, but they have not affected her honesty or swayed her opinions. Her poetry can be tender and straightforward on the one hand, and difficult and obscure on the other, but both styles reveal a unique gift of unusual brilliance.

—Leonard Clark

RANSOM, John Crowe. American. Born in Pulaski, Tennessee, 30 April 1888. Educated at Vanderbilt University, Nashville, Tennessee, B.A. 1909 (Phi Beta Kappa); Christ Church, Oxford (Rhodes Scholar), 1910–13, B.A. 1913. Served in the United States Army, 1917–19. Married Robb Reavill in 1920; three children. Assistant in English, Harvard University, Cambridge, Massachusetts, 1914; Member of the Faculty, 1914–27, and Professor of English, 1927–37, Vanderbilt University; Carnegie Professor of Poetry, 1937–58, and Professor Emeritus, 1959–74, Kenyon College, Gambier, Ohio. Visiting Lecturer in English, Chattanooga University, Tennessee, 1938; Visiting Lecturer in Language and Criticism, University of Texas, Austin, 1956. Member of the Fugitive Group of Poets: Founding Editor, with Allen Tate, *The Fugitive*, Nashville, 1922–25; Editor, *Kenyon Review*, Gambier, Ohio, 1937–59. Formerly, Honorary Consultant in American

Letters, Library of Congress, Washington, D.C. Recipient: Guggenheim Fellowship, 1931; Bollingen Prize, 1951; Russell Loines Award, 1951; Brandeis University Creative Arts Award, 1958; Academy of American Poets Fellowship, 1962; National Book Award, 1964; National Endowment for the Arts award, 1966; Emerson-Thoreau Medal, 1968; National Institute of Arts and Letters Gold Medal, 1973. Member, American Academy of Arts and Letters, and American Academy of Arts and Sciences. *Died 3 July 1974.*

PUBLICATIONS

Verse

Poems about God. 1919.
Armageddon, with *A Fragment* by William Alexander Percy and *Avalon* by Donald Davidson. 1923.
Chills and Fever. 1924.
Grace after Meat. 1924.
Two Gentlemen in Bonds. 1927.
Selected Poems. 1945; revised edition, 1963, 1969.

Other

God Without Thunder: An Unorthodox Defense of Orthodoxy. 1930.
Shall We Complete the Trade? A Proposal for the Settlement of Foreign Debts to the United States. 1933.
The World's Body. 1938; revised edition, 1968.
The New Criticism. 1941.
A College Primer of Writing. 1943.
Poems and Essays. 1955.
Beating the Bushes: Selected Essays 1941–1970. 1972.

Editor, *Topics for Freshman Writing: Twenty Topics for Writing, with Appropriate Material for Study.* 1935.
Editor, *The Kenyon Critics: Studies in Modern Literature from the "Kenyon Review."* 1951.
Editor, *Selected Poems,* by Thomas Hardy. 1961.

Bibliography: "Ransom: A Checklist, 1967–76" by T. D. Young, in *Mississippi Quarterly 30,* 1976–77.

Reading List: *Ransom* by John L. Stewart, 1962; *The Poetry of Ransom: A Study of Diction, Metaphor, and Symbol* by Karl F. Knight, 1964; *The Equilibrist: A Study of Ransom's Poems 1916–1963* by Robert Buffington, 1967; *Ransom: Critical Essays and a Bibliography* edited by T. D. Young, 1968, and *Gentleman in a Dustcoat: A Biography of Ransom* by Young, 1976; *Ransom* by Thornton H. Parsons, 1969; *Ransom: Critical Principles and Preoccupations* by James E. Morgan, 1971; *The Poetry of Ransom* by Miller Williams, 1972.

*   *   *

As poet, teacher, critic, and editor, John Crowe Ransom was one of the most influential men of his generation. Although scholars and critics have agreed that Ransom commands an eminent position, they have disagreed on the precise nature of his contribution. The priorities Ransom established for his literary career displeased some of his friends. He was, as Allen Tate once said, "one of the great elegiac poets of the English language," who produced ten or twelve almost perfect lyrics which will be read as long as poetry is regarded as a serious art. Yet the major portion of his creative energies were devoted to the writing of poetry only for a very brief period. During the remainder of a long and active literary career, much of his thought and most of his effort were expended on speculations on the nature and function of poetic discourse; on the significance of religious myth, the need for an inscrutable God; and on discussions of the proper relations that should exist between man, God, and nature.

Most of the poetry for which Ransom will be remembered was written between 1922 and 1925 and published in *Chills and Fever* and *Two Gentlemen in Bonds*. During the winter of 1922 Ransom read at one of the Fugitive meetings his poem "Necrological," which convinced Allen Tate that almost "overnight he had left behind him the style of his first book [*Poems about God*] and, without confusion, had mastered a new style." All of his best poems are written in this "new style," what critics have come to refer to as his "mature manner": the subtle irony, the nuanced ambiguities, the wit, and the cool detached tone. In these poems Ransom uses a simple little narrative as a means of presenting the "common actuals"; an innocent character is involved in a common situation and through this involvement he comes to have a fuller understanding of his own nature. Few poets of his generation have been able to represent with greater accuracy and precision the inexhaustible ambiguities, the paradoxes and tensions, the dichotomies and ironies that make up the life of modern man. His poetry reiterates a few themes: man's dual nature and the inevitable misery and disaster that accompany the failure to recognize and accept this basic truth; mortality and the fleetingness of youthful vigor and grace, the inevitable decay of feminine beauty; the disparity between the world as man would have it and as it actually is, between what people want and need emotionally and what is available for them, between what man desires and what he can get; the necessity of man's simultaneous apprehension of nature's indifference and mystery and his appreciation of her sensory beauties; the inability of modern man, in his incomplete and fragmentary state, to experience love.

Throughout his career Ransom maintained that human experience can be fully realized only through art. In many of his critical essays – some of which are collected in *The World's Body*, *The New Criticism*, and *Beating the Bushes* – Ransom tries to define the unique nature of poetic discourse, which functions to "induce the mode of thought that is imaginative rather than logical," to recover "the denser and more refractory original world which we know loosely through our perceptions and memories." That which we may learn from poetry is "ontologically distinct" because it is the "kind of knowledge by which we must know what we have arranged that we cannot know otherwise." Only through poetry, which is composed of a "loose logical structure with a good deal of local texture," can man recover the "body and solid substance of the world." The basic kind of data which science can collect reduces the "world to a scheme of abstract conveniences." Whereas science is interesting only in *knowing*, art has a double function; it wants both to *know* and to *make*.

In many of his later essays Ransom attempts to demonstrate how the critic should react in his efforts to define the nature of poetic discourse and to justify its existence in a society becoming more and more enamored of the quasi-knowledge and the false promises of science. In essay after essay he insists that the truths that poetry contains can be obtained only through a detailed analytical study of the poems themselves, and he repeats one theme: without poetry man's knowledge of himself and his world is fragmentary and incomplete.

—T. D. Young

READ, Sir Herbert (Edward). English. Born at Muscoates Grange, Kirbymoorside, Yorkshire, 4 December 1893. Educated at Crossley's School, Halifax, Yorkshire; University of Leeds. Commissioned in The Green Howards, 1915, and fought in France and Belgium, 1915–18: Captain, 1917; Military Cross, Distinguished Service Order, 1918; mentioned in despatches. Married 1) Evelyn Roff; 2) Margaret Ludwig; four sons and one daughter. Assistant Principal, The Treasury, London, 1919–22; Assistant Keeper, Victoria and Albert Museum, London, 1922–31; Watson Gordon Professor of Fine Arts, University of Edinburgh, 1931–33; Editor, *Burlington Magazine*, London, 1933–39; Sydney Jones Lecturer in Art, University of Liverpool, 1935–36; Editor, English Master Painters series, from 1940. Leon Fellow, University of London, 1940–42; Charles Eliot Norton Professor of Poetry, Harvard University, Cambridge, Massachusetts, 1953–54; A. W. Mellon Lecturer in Fine Arts, Washington, 1954; Senior Fellow, Royal College of Art, London, 1962; Fellow, Center for Advanced Studies, Wesleyan University, Middletown, Connecticut, 1964–65. Trustee, Tate Gallery, London, 1965–68. President, Society for Education Through Art, Yorkshire Philosophical Society, Institute of Contemporary Arts, and British Society of Aesthetics. Recipient: Erasmus Prize, 1966. Prof. Honorario: University of Cordoba, Argentina, 1962; Doctor of Fine Arts: State University of New York at Buffalo, 1962; Litt.D.: University of Boston, 1965; University of York, 1966. Honorary Fellow, Society of Industrial Artists; Foreign Corresponding Member, Académie Flamande des Beaux Arts, 1953; Foreign Member, Royal Academy of Fine Arts, Stockholm, 1960; Honorary Member, American Academy of Arts and Letters, 1966. Knighted, 1953. *Died 12 June 1968.*

PUBLICATIONS

Verse

Songs of Chaos. 1915.
Auguries of Life and Death. 1919.
Eclogues: A Book of Poems. 1919.
Naked Warriors. 1919.
Mutations of the Phoenix. 1923.
Collected Poems, 1913–1925. 1926; revised edition, 1946, 1966.
The End of a War. 1933.
Poems 1914–34. 1935.
Thirty-Five Poems. 1940.
A World Within a War. 1944.
Moon's Farm, and Poems Mostly Elegiac. 1955.

Plays

Aristotle's Mother: An Argument in Athens (broadcast 1946). In *Imaginary Conversations: Eight Radio Scripts,* edited by Rayner Heppenstall, 1948.
Thieves of Mercy (broadcast 1947). In *Imaginary Conversations: Eight Radio Scripts,* edited by Rayner Heppenstall, 1948.
Lord Byron at the Opera (broadcast 1953). 1963.
The Parliament of Women. 1961.

Radio Plays: *Artistotle's Mother,* 1946; *Thieves of Mercy,* 1947; *Lord Byron at the Opera,* 1953.

Fiction

The Green Child: A Romance.   1935.

Other

English Pottery: Its Development from Early Times to the End of the Eighteenth Century,
    with B. Rackham.   1924.
In Retreat.   1925.
English Stained Glass.   1926.
Reason and Romanticism: Essays in Literary Criticism.   1926.
English Prose Style.   1928; revised edition, 1952.
Phases of English Poetry.   1928; revised edition, 1950.
The Sense of Glory: Essays in Criticism.   1929.
Staffordshire Pottery Figures.   1929.
Wordsworth.   1930; revised edition, 1949.
Ambush.   1930.
Julien Benda and the New Humanism.   1930.
The Meaning of Art.   1931; as *The Anatomy of Art,* 1932; revised edition, 1936, 1949,
    1951, 1968.
Form in Modern Poetry.   1932.
Art Now: An Introduction to the Theory of Modern Painting and Sculpture.   1933;
    revised edition, 1936, 1948, 1961.
The Innocent Eye.   1933.
Art and Industry: The Principles of Industrial Design.   1934; revised edition, 1944,
    1953, 1957.
Essential Communism.   1935.
In Defence of Shelley and Other Essays.   1936.
Art and Society.   1937; revised edition, 1945.
Collected Essays in Literary Criticism.   1938; as *The Nature of Literature,* 1956.
Poetry and Anarchism.   1938.
Annals of Innocence and Experience.   1940; revised edition, 1946; as *The Innocent Eye,*
    1947.
The Philosophy of Anarchism.   1940.
To Hell with Culture: Democratic Values Are New Values.   1941.
Education Through Art.   1943.
The Politics of the Unpolitical.   1943.
The Education of Free Men.   1944.
Flicker, with Toni del Renzio and R. S. O. Poole.   1944.
A Coat of Many Colours: Occasional Essays.   1945; revised edition, 1956.
The Grass Roots of Art: Four Lectures.   1946; revised edition, 1955.
Coleridge as Critic.   1949.
Education for Peace.   1949.
Existentialism, Marxism, and Anarchism: Chains of Freedom.   1949.
Byron.   1951.
Contemporary British Art.   1951; revised edition, 1965.
The Philosophy of Modern Art: Collected Essays.   1952.
The True Voice of Feeling: Studies in English Romantic Poetry.   1953.
Anarchy and Order: Essays in Politics.   1954.
Icon and Idea: The Function of Art in the Development of Human Consciousness.   1955.
The Art of Sculpture (lectures).   1956.
The Significance of Children's Art: Art as a Symbolic Language.   1957.
The Tenth Muse: Essays in Criticism.   1957.

A Concise History of Modern Painting.   1959; revised edition, 1968.
The Forms of Things Unknown: Essays Towards an Aesthetic Philosophy.   1960.
Truth Is More Sacred: A Critical Exchange on Modern Literature, with Edward
   Dahlberg.   1961.
A Letter to a Young Painter (essays).   1962.
The Contrary Experience: Autobiographies.   1963.
Selected Writings.   1963.
To Hell with Culture and Other Essays on Art and Society.   1963.
Art and Education.   1964.
A Concise History of Modern Sculpture.   1964.
Henry Moore: A Study of His Life and Work.   1965.
The Origins of Form in Art.   1965.
The Redemption of the Robot: My Encounter with Education Through Art.   1966.
T.S.E.: A Memoir (on Eliot).   1966.
Art and Alienation: The Role of the Artist in Society.   1967.
Poetry and Experience.   1967.
The Cult of Sincerity.   1968.
Essays in Literary Criticism: Particular Studies.   1969.

Editor, *Speculations: Essays on Humanism and the Philosophy of Art,* by T. E. Hulme,
   1923.
Editor, *Form in Gothic,* by W. R. Worringer.   1927.
Editor, *Notes on Language and Style,* by T. E. Hulme.   1929.
Editor, with Bonamy Dobrée, *The London Book of English Prose.*   1931; as *The Book of
   English Prose,* 1931; revised edition, 1949.
Editor, *The English Vision.*   1933.
Editor, *Unit 1: The Modern Movement in English Architecture, Painting, and
   Sculpture.*   1934.
Editor, with Denis Saurat, *Selected Essays and Critical Writings,* by A. R.
   Orage.   1935.
Editor, *Surrealism.*   1936.
Editor, *The Knapsack: A Pocket-Book of Prose and Verse.*   1939.
Editor, *Kropotkin: Selections from His Writings.*   1942.
Editor, *The Practice of Design.*   1946.
Editor, with Bonamy Dobrée, *The London Book of English Verse.*   1949; revised
   edition, 1952.
Editor, *Outline: An Autobiography, and Other Writings,* by Paul Nash.   1949.
Editor, with Michael Fordham and Gerhard Adler, *The Collected Works of C. J.
   Jung.*   17 vols., 1953–73.
Editor, *This Way Delight: A Book of Poetry for the Young.*   1956.
Editor, *Origins of Western Art.*   1965.

Translator, with M. Ludwig, *Radio,* by M. Arnheim, 1936.

Reading List: *Read: An Introduction* edited by Henry Treece, 1944; *Read* by Francis Berry,
1953, revised edition, 1961; *Read: A Memorial Symposium* edited by Robin Skelton, 1970; *A
Certain Order: The Development of Read's Theory of Poetry* by Worth T. Harder, 1971;
Read: The Stream and the Source by George Woodcock, 1972.

*   *   *

Sir Herbert Read was of the same generation as Rosenberg and Owen. But Read survived
the War, the crude fact of which permitted him to write what some may think of as not only

his finest "war poem," but perhaps his best poem of all, *The End of a War* (written between 1931–2, and published 1933). Like Blunden and Sassoon, as a survivor he continued to be haunted by his experience of trench combat. Unlike Sassoon, his poetry continued to express his apprehension of war's social destructiveness, and the few lessons that might be obtained from it.

In a sense, "The Happy Warrior" can serve as a model for the former. It looks backwards with adverse judgment on Wordsworth's apparently theoretical appraisal of the "Character of the Happy Warrior," and projects on to it an experienced and thus realistic understanding of how war erodes all that best restraining consciousness which is the hallmark of civilization:

> I saw him stab
> And stab again
> A well-killed Boche.

The poem is also notable for its successful handling of the theme in imagistic form, and in this it is somewhat exceptional, for the hard edge and the controlling image are not, of themselves, attributes that can best explore the discursive nature and evaluation of such experiences as the war forced upon each person. Read noted in his autobiographies *The Contrary Experience* that Imagism could not cope with war's experiences properly; yet in all his war poems, even *The End of a War*, the kind of relation between image, rhythm, syntax, and lineation is one that developed from Imagism's original tenets. What Read cannot make Imagism do, however, is to unfold narrative, and he is therefore forced, in *The End of a War*, to have a prefacing prose note which situates the narrative facts which may then be used as the basis for philosophic and/or sensuous projection. This solution is not an integral one, for the formal means of verse are themselves supported by the external prose activity.

Of all the war poets Yeats chose only Read's long poem for his *The Oxford Book of Modern Verse* (1936), and something of Yeats's preference for the distancing of suffering reflected in such a choice may help us to arrive at evaluating a complex poem that finally asserts a tentative optimism.

—Jon Silkin

REXROTH, Kenneth. American. Born in South Bend, Indiana, 22 December 1905; moved to Chicago, 1917. Educated at the Art Institute, Chicago; New School for Social Research, New York; Art Students' League, New York. Conscientious objector during World War II. Married 1) Andree Dutcher in 1927 (died, 1940); 2) Marie Kass in 1940 (divorced, 1948); 3) Marthe Larsen in 1949 (divorced, 1961), two children; 4) Carol Tinker in 1974. Past occupations include farm worker, factory hand, and insane asylum attendant. Painter: one-man shows in Los Angeles, New York, Chicago, San Francisco, and Paris. Columnist, *San Francisco Examiner*, 1958–68. Since 1953, San Francisco Correspondent for *The Nation*, New York; since 1968, Columnist for *San Francisco Magazine* and the *San Francisco Bay Guardian*, and Lecturer, University of California at Santa Barbara. Co-Founder, San Francisco Poetry Center. Recipient: Guggenheim Fellowship, 1948; Shelley Memorial Award, 1958; Amy Lowell Fellowship, 1958; National Institute of Arts and Letters grant, 1964; Fulbright Senior Fellowship, 1974; Academy of American Poets Copernicus Award, 1975. Member, National Institute of Arts and Letters. Lives in Santa Barbara, California.

PUBLICATIONS

Verse

In What Hour. 1941.
The Phoenix and the Tortoise. 1944.
The Art of Wordly Wisdom. 1949.
The Signature of All Things: Poems, Songs, Elegies, Translations, and Epigrams. 1950.
The Dragon and the Unicorn. 1952.
In Defence of the Earth. 1956.
The Homestead Called Damascus. 1963.
Natural Numbers: New and Selected Poems. 1963.
The Complete Collected Shorter Poems. 1967.
The Collected Longer Poems. 1968.
The Heart's Garden, The Garden's Heart. 1967.
The Spark in the Tinder of Knowing. 1968.
Sky Sea Birds Trees Earth House Beasts Flowers. 1970.
New Poems. 1974.

Plays

Beyond the Mountains (includes *Phaedra, Iphigenia, Hermaios, Berenike*) (produced 1951). 1951.

Other

Bird in the Bush: Obvious Essays. 1959.
Assays (essays). 1961.
An Autobiographical Novel. 1966.
Classics Revisited. 1968.
The Alternative Society: Essays from the Other World. 1970.
With Eye and Ear (literary criticism). 1970.
American Poetry in the Twentieth Century. 1971.
The Rexroth Reader, edited by Eric Mottram. 1972.
The Elastic Retort: Essays in Literature and Ideas. 1973.
Communalism: From Its Origins to the 20th Century. 1975.

Editor, *Selected Poems,* by D. H. Lawrence. 1948.
Editor, *The New British Poets: An Anthology.* 1949.
Editor, *Four Young Women: Poems.* 1973.
Editor, *Tens: Selected Poems 1961–1971,* by David Meltzer. 1973.
Editor, *The Selected Poems of Czeslav Milosz.* 1973.
Editor, *Seasons of Sacred Lust,* by Kazuko Shiraishi. 1978.

Translator, *Fourteen Poems,* by O. V. de L.-Milosz. 1952.
Translator, *100 Poems from the Japanese.* 1955.
Translator, *100 Poems from the Chinese.* 1956.
Translator, *30 Spanish Poems of Love and Exile.* 1956.
Translator, *100 Poems from the Greek and Latin.* 1962.
Translator, *Poems from the Greek Anthology.* 1962.
Translator, *Selected Poems,* by Pierre Reverdy. 1969.

Translator, *Love and the Turning Earth: 100 More Classical Poems.*   1970.
Translator, *Love and the Turning Year: 100 More Chinese Poems.*   1970.
Translator, *100 Poems from the French.*   1970.
Translator, with Ling O. Chung, *The Orchid Boat: Women Poets of China.*   1972.
Translator, *100 More Poems from the Japanese.*   1976.

Readling List: *Rexroth* by Morgan Gibson, 1972.

*   *   *

Kenneth Rexroth is a man of letters in the tradition of Robert Graves, W. H. Auden, and Edmund Wilson, although he has chiefly been a consolidator and synthesizer of others' ideas; this is true of his verse as well as of his many polemical essays on American culture. Rexroth came to literature with an amazing intelligence, so wide and retentive of the bewildering cross currents of thought in the twentieth century that his writings capture the essence of each decade in the broad span of his works, which cover the play *Beyond the Mountains*; *An Autobiographical Novel*; translations, encompassing poems in Japanese, Chinese, French, Greek, and Spanish; criticism; and his own vast collections of poetry. Without pedantry or empty imitation, Rexroth has tapped the spirit of each of the major figures that emerged in his lifetime and illuminated it in his own boldly assertive style. An early interest in Asian poetry followed from Pound, whom Rexroth praised and criticized in his critical study, *American Poetry in the Twentieth Century*.

Rexroth's longer poems resemble the casual, narrative style of Auden, although comparisons should not be taken too far. In his polemic essays, his style and approach to the basic issues of American culture, industrial economy, depersonality in the mass population, and commerciality, are reminiscent of the early essays of Edmund Wilson, Paul Goodman, and Edward Dahlberg. Rexroth's poems on nature anticipated by many years the accurate, sensitive naturalist poems of Gary Snyder, who has in turn influenced Rexroth in his most recent work.

It is therefore difficult to isolate Rexroth from the stream of literature and ideas in which he has fashioned his work. But an essential Rexroth is perceptible in his elegant love poems and landscape meditations, gathered in *The Collected Shorter Poems*. These reveries and amorous lyrics present an unguarded, visionary persona unlike any in American poetry, as in "Camargue":

> Green moon blaze
> Over violet dancers
> Shadow heads catch fire
> Forget forget
> Forget awake aware dropping in the well
> Where the nightingale sings
> In the blooming pomegranate
> You beside me
> Like a colt swimming slowly in kelp
> In the nude sea
> Where ten thousand birds
> Move like a waved scarf
> On the long surge of sleep

The shorter poetry is brief, lyrical, touching on love, travels, occasionally social comment. The strain of the didactic is strong in Rexroth's work, especially in the long travelogue poem, *The Dragon and the Unicorn*.

Rexroth's polemical criticism of American literature and idealogy is contained in a number of volumes, *With Eye and Ear*, *The Alternative Society*, *Communalism*, and *American Poetry in the Twentieth Century*, where he is intensely perceptive and iconoclastic. In the last, he argues persuasively that American poetry should be traced not from Europe but from Native Indian cultures. As a figure central to most of the major phases of American writing throughout the century, Rexroth is a watershed of literary ideas and principles, and a writer who has communicated a stubborn, wilful intellect in a century of increasing squeamishness and doubt.

—Paul Christensen

RICH, Adrienne (Cecile). American. Born in Baltimore, Maryland, 16 May 1929. Educated at Roland Park Country School, Baltimore, 1938–47; Radcliffe College, Cambridge, Massachusetts, 1947–51, A.B. (cum laude) 1951 (Phi Beta Kappa). Married Alfred Conrad in 1953 (died, 1970); three sons. Lived in the Netherlands, 1961–62; taught at the YM-YWHA Poetry Center Workshop, New York, 1966–67; Visiting Poet, Swarthmore College, Pennsylvania, 1966–68; Adjunct Professor, Graduate Writing Division, Columbia University, New York, 1967–69; Lecturer, 1968–70, Instructor, 1970–71, and Assistant Professor of English, 1971–72, City College of New York; Fannie Hurst Visiting Professor of Creative Writing, Brandeis University, Waltham, Massachusetts, 1972–73; Lucy Martin Donnelly Fellow, Bryn Mawr College, Pennsylvania, 1975. Since 1976, Professor of English, Douglass College, Rutgers University, New Brunswick, New Jersey. Member, Advisory Board, Feminist Press, Westbury, New Jersey. Recipient: Guggenheim Fellowship, 1952, 1961; Ridgely Torrence Memorial Award, 1955; Friends of Literature Grace Thayer Bradley Award, 1956; National Institute of Arts and Letters award, 1960; Amy Lowell Traveling Scholarship, 1962; National Translation Center grant, 1968; National Endowment for the Arts grant, 1969; Shelley Memorial Award, 1971; Ingram Merrill Foundation grant, 1973; National Book Award, 1974. D.Litt.: Wheaton College, Norton, Massachusetts, 1967. Lives in New York City.

PUBLICATIONS

Verse

A Change of World.   1951.
(*Poems*).   1952.
The Diamond Cutters and Other Poems.   1955.
Snapshots of a Daughter-in-Law: Poems 1954–1962.   1963.
Necessities of Life: Poems 1962–1965.   1966.
Selected Poems.   1967.
Leaflets: Poems 1965–1968.   1969.
The Will to Change: Poems 1968–1970.   1971.
Diving into the Wreck: Poems 1971–1972.   1973.
Poems Selected and New 1950–1974.   1975.
The Dream of a Common Language: Poems 1974–1977.   1978.

Other

Of Woman Born: Motherhood as Experience and Institution.   1976.

Reading List: "Voice of the Survivor: The Poetry of Rich" by Willard Spiegelman, in *Southwest Review,* Autumn 1975; *Rich's Poetry* edited by Barbara Charlesworth Gelpi and Albert Gelpi, 1975.

*   *   *

Adrienne Rich's comments on her early poems offer the best insight into the shape of her career. In "When We Dead Awaken: Writing as Re-Vision" (1971) she notices that "Beneath the conscious craft are glimpses of the split I even then experienced between the girl who wrote poems, who defined herself in writing poems, and the girl who defined herself by her relationships with men." In other contexts Rich extends her use of the term "splits" to explain the structure of all contemporary problems – artistic, psychological, and social. Insofar as she defines her poetry in terms of a response to splits within and without, Rich accepts the modernist premise that the poet begins his or her work in a fragmented world.

Her early poems in *A Change of World* and *The Diamond Cutters* use their mastery of formal elements to control and order the splits. The poems in *Snapshots of a Daughter-in-Law* continue the intense examination of experience, but they no longer insist on bringing all tensions under control by the end of the poem and risk very dearly bought defenses in order to get closer to the actual dynamics of experience. With this change of stance, her poems begin to confront the tensions she finds in the world with an eye towards changing the world, or changing that part of herself which formerly had been intimidated by the tensions. Rather than protecting the self or the poet's voice from the tensions in the world, these poems begin the process of integrating the self in order to encounter the world in a full and direct attempt to overcome the limitations of experience, or of that intimidating experience of the early poems. So, while speakers in the early poems took comfort and defined success in closing shutters and other protective habits developed by experience, the speaker in "The Phenomenology of Anger" (1972) finds the simmering frustrations and tensions a source of energy, and enjoys speculating on the shape of future experiences when the force of the anger breaks out from its containment.

Having begun this intense exploration of self and world, she finds a sense of wholeness in poems such as "Planetarium" (1971) and "Diving into the Wreck" (1973) which develop images that respect the integrity of conflicts within and without and still enable a holistic view of self and world. In one of Rich's latest and longest poems, "From an Old House in America," she extends the possibilities of her sense of an integrated identity to social and political contexts. She finds not only a positive definition of self, as she had in "Diving into the Wreck," but she also finds a place in which the self can work and interact in a positive and effective fashion. The speaker in "From an Old House in America" begins with a positive and comfortable sense of self and then extends her social and political connections with other inhabitants of the house, with other American women, contemporaries and ancestors, and finally, with all women in all places. In this re-integration of poet and world Rich gets beyond the self-conscious impasse of modernist aesthetics and begins the process of changing the world with a public voice whose authority and promise grow out of its successful resolution of "splits" in the world.

—Richard C. Turner

RICKWORD, (John) Edgell. English. Born in Colchester, Essex, 22 October 1898. Educated at Colchester Grammar School; Pembroke College, Oxford. Served in the Artists' Rifles, 1916–18; invalided out of the army. Editor, *Calendar of Modern Letters,* 1925–27; Associate Editor, *Left Review,* 1934–38; Editor, *Our Time,* 1944–47; also contributed to various other London journals. Recipient: Arts Council Prize, 1966.

PUBLICATIONS

Verse

>   *Behind the Eyes.* 1921.
>   *Invocations to Angels, and The Happy New Year.* 1928.
>   *Twittingpan and Some Others.* 1931.
>   *Collected Poems.* 1947.
>   *Fifty Poems.* 1970.
>   *Behind the Eyes: Selected Poems and Translations.* 1976.

Fiction

>   *Love One Another: Seven Tales.* 1929.

Other

>   *Rimbaud: The Boy and the Poet.* 1924; revised edition, 1963.
>   *William Wordsworth 1770–1850.* 1950.
>   *Gillray and Cruikshank: An Illustrated Life of James Gillray (1756–1815) and of George Cruikshank (1792–1878),* with Michael Katanka. 1973.
>   *Essays and Opinions 1921–1931,* edited by Alan Young. 1974.
>
>   Editor, *Scrutinies of Various Writers.* 1928; vol. 2, 1931.
>   Editor, with Jack Lindsay, *A Handbook of Freedom: A Record of English Democracy Through Twelve Centuries.* 1939.
>   Editor, *Soviet Writers Reply to English Writers' Questions.* 1948.
>   Editor, *Further Studies in a Dying Culture,* by Christopher Caudwell. 1949.
>   Editor, *Radical Squibs and Loyal Ripostes: Satirical Pamphlets of the Regency Period, 1819–1821.* 1971.
>
>   Translator, with Douglas Mavin Garman, *Charles Baudelaire: A Biography,* by François Porché. 1928.
>   Translator, *La Princesse aux Soleils, and Harmonie,* by Ronald Firbank. 1973 (translation into English).

Reading List: "The Poetic Mind of Rickword" by David Holbrook, in *Essays in Criticism,* July 1962.

*   *   *

Edgell Rickword's experience of the war was profound and unforgettable. He was almost sixteen when it began, joined the Artists' Rifles in 1916, and was invalided out of the army after the Armistice. His first book of poetry, *Behind the Eyes*, appeared in 1921 and revealed a preoccupation with images of a nightmarish intensity, images of battle, physical suffering, bodily decay, and the transience of beauty. There is an elegant strength in Rickword's handling of these subjects, the poems never collapsing into hysteria or incoherence. The fixed, rational gaze straight into the face of modern horrors is unswerving in its honesty and resolution, as in "Trench Poets":

> I knew a man, he was my chum,
> but he grew darker day by day,
> and would not brush the flies away,
> nor blanch however fierce the hum
> of passing shells....

Invocations to Angels saw, alongside this lyrical evocation of disaster, Rickword writing in a satirical mode. Pieces like "Poet to Punk" showed him producing the kind of verse that was to become predominant by the time of *Twittingpan and Some Others*. It is a public poetry pressed into being by political needs. It found its most famous expression in a poem published in *Left Review* in 1938. "To the Wife of a Non-Interventionist Statesman" is a powerful and accurate satire, enlisted on behalf of the Spanish republican cause, but widening its polemic to include a vision of the future at home:

> Euzkadi's mines supply the ore
> to feed the Nazi dogs of war:
> Guernika's thermite rain transpires
> in doom on Oxford's dreaming spires:
> in Hitler's frantic mental haze
> already Hull and Cardiff blaze....

Rickword also made some excellent translations of Rimbaud and produced a critical study of the French poet which still stands as a formidable achievement. *Rimbaud: The Boy and the Poet* was described by Enid Starkie in 1954 as the finest work on Rimbaud to have appeared in any country up to that date. Rickword's critical work has, in fact, been at least as important as his poetry. In editing *The Calendar of Modern Letters* from 1925 to 1927, he not only helped to raise the standards of critical debate at the time, but made possible the founding five years later of *Scrutiny*. Whether writing for the *New Statesman*, *The Times Literary Supplement*, *The Calendar* itself, or the *Daily Herald*, Rickword maintained the same unfaltering level of critical shrewdness and intellectual acuity. When his political commitments led him in the 1930's to the Communist Party, and the editorship for a time of *Left Review*, this did not represent the collapse of his critical standards, as some of his more condescending later admirers have said. His influence on *Left Review* was a highly beneficial one, widening the scope of the journal and increasing its sensitivity to contemporary literature.

Edgell Rickword was one of the first critics in England to understand the nature of modernism, and to grasp the revolutionary nature of the achievements of Eliot and Pound. His unquestionable integrity frequently led him into difficulties, and left him, in the cold-war atmosphere after 1945, in a kind of wilderness. The re-discovery and re-examination of his work in the 1970's has been long overdue.

—Alan Wall

RIDING, Laura. American. Born Laura Reichenthal in New York City, 16 January 1901; adopted the surname Riding in 1926. Educated at Cornell University, Ithaca, New York. Married 1) Louis Gottschalk; 2) the poet and critic Schuyler B. Jackson in 1941 (died, 1968). Associated with the Fugitive group of poets; lived in Europe, 1926–39; associated with Robert Graves, in establishing the Seizen Press and *Epilogue* magazine; returned to America, 1939, renounced poetry, 1940, and has since devoted herself to the study of linguistics. Recipient: Guggenheim Fellowship, 1973. Lives in Florida.

PUBLICATIONS

Verse

The Close Chaplet. 1926.
Voltaire: A Biographical Fantasy. 1927.
Love as Love, Death as Death. 1928.
Poems: A Joking Word. 1930.
Twenty Poems Less. 1930.
Though Gently. 1930.
Laura and Francisca. 1931.
The Life of the Dead. 1933.
The First Leaf. 1933.
Poet: A Lying Word. 1933.
Americans. 1934.
The Second Leaf. 1935.
Collected Poems 1938.
Selected Poems: In Five Sets. 1970.

Fiction

Experts Are Puzzled (stories). 1930.
No Decency Left, with Robert Graves. 1932.
14A, with George Ellidge. 1934.
Progress of Stories. 1935.
Convalescent Conversations. 1936.
A Trojan Ending. 1937.
Lives of Wives (stories). 1939.

Other

A Survey of Modernist Poetry, with Robert Graves. 1927.
A Pamphlet Against Anthologies, with Robert Graves. 1928; as *Against Anthologies,* 1928.
Contemporaries and Snobs. 1928.
Anarchism Is Not Enough. 1928.
Four Unposted Letters to Catherine. 1930.
The Telling. 1972.
It Has Taken Long (selected writings), in "Riding Issue" of *Chelsea 35.* 1976

Editor, *Everybody's Letters.* 1933.

Editor, *Epilogue 1–3*.   3 vols., 1935–37.
Editor, *The World and Ourselves: Letters about the World Situation from 65 People of Different Professions and Pursuits*.   1938.

Translator, *Anatole France at Home,* by Marcel Le Goff.   1926.
Translator, with Robert Graves, *Almost Forgotten Germany,* by Georg Schwarz.   1936.

Bibliography: by Alan Clark, in *Chelsea 35,* 1976.

Reading List: *Riding's Pursuit of Truth* by Joyce Piell Wexler, 1977.

*   *   *

Laura Riding is, according to Kenneth Rexroth in *American Poetry in the Twentieth Century*, "the greatest lost poet in American literature." The inaccessibility of her poetry, both in the literal and figurative sense, partially accounts for this lack of attention. Since the publication of her substantial *Collected Poems* in 1938, she has published no new poetry and has allowed the re-issue of only one slender volume selected from the earlier edition. Hence her poetry is hard to find, and, once found, hard to follow. Her brief poem, "Grace," illustrates her obscurity:

> This posture and this manner suit
> Not that I have an ease in them
> But that I have a horror
> And so stand well upright –
> Lest, should I sit and, flesh-conversing, eat,
> I choke upon a piece of my own tongue-meat.

Characteristic of other poems by Riding, this one is virtually unadorned, with the single concrete image withheld until the last two lines. The subject matter is, typically and paradoxically, an examination of an interior feeling, a topic that one does not expect to find treated with this austerity.

Riding's definition of a poem in the preface to the *Collected Poems* is "an uncovering of truth of so fundamental and general a kind that no other name besides poetry is adequate except truth." This definition, if tautological, is indicative of Riding's strong commitment to purity in the language. This strong belief impelled her eventually to abandon the writing of poetry, for she found that she could not reconcile the necessity to keep the language pure with the desirability of making the poems sensuously appealing to the readers.

Riding's undeservedly neglected fiction has received even less attention than her poetry. Her *Progress of Stories*, a collection marked by impressive variety and a somewhat flamboyant wit, is unlike her poetry in tone although it treats similar themes. The comic sketch, "Eve's Side of It," for instance, complements such feminist poems as "Divestment of Beauty" and "Auspice of Jewels." She has deliberately adopted a lighter vein for these stories, she explains in the preface, because she is tired of the accusation of obscurity and being made "a scape goat for the incapacity of people to understand what they only pretend to want to know."

Of her numerous theoretical studies, the two she wrote in collaboration with Robert Graves are best known. Compared to her other works, *A Survey of Modernist Poetry* is a model of lucidity. It suggests a method of textual scrutiny that possibly influenced William Empson's *Seven Types of Ambiguity*. While the work of E. E. Cummings most often provides examples for the book, Riding's poem "The Rugged Back of Anger" is examined. To apply

Riding's critical method to her poetry is helpful in understanding this austere and significant poet.

—Nancy C. Joyner

ROBINSON, Edwin Arlington. American. Born in Head Tide, Maine, 22 December 1869; grew up in Gardiner, Maine. Educated at Gardiner High School, graduated 1888; Harvard University, Cambridge, Massachusetts, 1891–93. Free-lance writer in Gardiner, 1893–96; settled in New York City, 1896; worked as Secretary to the President of Harvard University, 1897; returned to New York, settled in Greenwich Village, and held various jobs, including subway-construction inspector, 1903–04; through patronage of Theodore Roosevelt, who admired his poetry, became Clerk in the United States Customs House, New York, 1904–10; spent summers at the MacDowell Colony, Peterborough, New Hampshire, 1911–34. Recipient: Pulitzer Prize, 1922, 1925, 1928; National Institute of Arts and Letters Gold Medal, 1929. Honorary degrees: Yale University, New Haven, Connecticut, 1922, and Bowdoin College, Brunswick, Maine. Member, American Academy of Arts and Letters. *Died 6 April 1935.*

PUBLICATIONS

Collections

>   *Collected Poems.* 1937.
>   *Selected Letters,* edited by Ridgely Torrence and others. 1940.
>   *Tilbury Town: Selected Poems,* edited by Lawrance Thompson. 1953.
>   *Selected Early Poems and Letters,* edited by Charles T. Davis. 1960.
>   *Selected Poems,* edited by Morton Dauwen Zabel. 1965.

Verse

>   *The Torrent and the Night Before.* 1896; revised edition, as *The Children of the Night,*
>   1897.
>   *Captain Craig.* 1902; revised edition, 1915.
>   *The Town Down the River.* 1910.
>   *The Man Against the Sky.* 1916.
>   *Merlin.* 1917.
>   *Lancelot.* 1920.
>   *The Three Taverns.* 1920.
>   *Avon's Harvest.* 1921.
>   *Collected Poems.* 1921.
>   *Roman Bartholow.* 1923.
>   *The Man Who Died Twice.* 1924.
>   *Dionysus in Doubt.* 1925.
>   *Tristram.* 1927.

Collected Poems.   5 vols., 1927.
Sonnets 1889–1927.   1928.
Fortunatus.   1928.
Three Poems.   1928.
Modred: A Fragment.   1929.
The Prodigal Son.   1929.
Cavender's House.   1929.
The Glory of the Nightingales.   1930.
Matthias at the Door.   1931.
Poems, edited by Bliss Perry.   1931.
Nicodemus.   1932.
Talifer.   1933.
Amaranth.   1934.
King Jasper.   1935.
Hannibal Brown: Posthumous Poem.   1936.

Plays

Van Zorn.   1914.
The Porcupine.   1915.

Other

Letters to Howard George Schmitt, edited by Carl J. Weber.   1940.
Untriangulated Stars: Letters to Harry de Forest Smith 1890–1905, edited by Denham
    Sutcliffe.   1947.
Letters to Edith Brower, edited by Richard Cary.   1968.

Editor, *Selections from the Letters of Thomas Sergeant Perry.*   1929.

Bibliography: *A Bibliography of the Writings and Criticisms of Robinson* by Lillian Lippincott, 1937; supplements by William White, in *Colby Library Quarterly,* 1965, 1969.

Reading List: *Robinson: A Biography* by Hermann Hagedorn, 1938; *Robinson* by Yvor Winters, 1946, revised edition, 1971; *Robinson: The Literary Background of a Traditional Poet* by Edwin S. Fussell, 1954; *Where the Light Falls: A Portrait of Robinson* by Chard Powers Smith, 1965; *Robinson: A Poetry of the Act* by W. R. Robinson, 1967; *Robinson: A Critical Introduction* by Wallace L. Anderson, 1967; *Robinson: The Life of Poetry* by Louis O. Coxe, 1968; *Robinson* by Hoyt C. Franchere, 1968; *Appreciation of Robinson* (essays) edited by Richard Cary, 1969; *Robinson: Centenary Essays* edited by Ellsworth Barnard, 1969.

*   *   *

More than any other poet of his time, Edwin Arlington Robinson made poetry his career. He neither travelled nor taught, married nor made public appearances. Aside from a handful of prose pieces and two unsuccessful plays, he devoted himself exclusively to the writing of poetry, publishing many volumes of verse in a forty-year period. He suffered during the first half of his career from neglect and near impoverishment; he suffered during his last years from an excess of adulation. After his signal success of *Tristram,* for which he won his third Pulitzer Prize, he was hailed as America's foremost poet. Although his reputation has diminished since his death, he is nevertheless established as the most important poet writing in America at the turn of the century and has a firm place as one of the major modern poets.

He was, as Robert Frost noted in his preface to *King Jasper*, "content with the old way to be new." The old way was his unwavering insistence on traditional forms. His poems demonstrate his facility in an impressive variety of verse forms, from blank verse in most of the long narratives to Petracharan sonnets and villanelles in his shorter work, but he was positively reactionary in his dismissal of the then current *vers libre* movement. In a letter, he once placed free verse along with prohibition and moving pictures as "a triumvirate from hell, armed with the devil's instructions to abolish civilization."

Robinson was new in his attitudes in and toward his poetry. He may be called an impersonal romantic, breaking with the nineteenth-century tradition by objectifying and dramatizing emotional reactions while at the same time emphasizing sentiment and mystical awareness. His combination of compassion and irony has become a familiar stance in modern poetry, and his celebrated advocacy of triumphant forbearance in the face of adversity anticipates the existential movement. In a letter to *The Bookman* in 1897, responding to the charge that he was pessimistic, he wrote, "This world is not a 'prison house,' but a kind of spiritual kindergarten where millions of bewildered infants are trying to spell God with the wrong blocks." While he was reluctant to be classified as an exponent of any formal philosophical or theological stance, he was entirely willing, in and out of his poetry, to condemn materialistic attitudes. Robinson's use of humor within his serious poetry, such as in *Amaranth*, placed a new importance on the comic.

While Robinson frequently wrote poems on conventional topics, his subject matter was new in his heavy emphasis on people. Unlike other romantic poets, he generally avoided the celebration of natural phenomena, bragging to a friend about his first volume that one would not find "a single red-breasted robin in the whole collection." Many of his short poems are character sketches of individuals, anticipating Edgar Lee Masters's *Spoon River Anthology*. All of the long narratives deal with complicated human relationships. Frequently they explore psychological reactions to a prior event, such as *Avon's Harvest*, Robinson's "ghost story" about a man destroyed by his own hatred, and *Cavender's House*, a dialogue between a man and his dead wife which deals with questions of jealousy and guilt. The people inhabiting Robinson's books include imaginary individuals; characters modeled on actual acquaintances, such as Alfred H. Louis in *Captain Craig*; figures from history, such as "Ben Jonson Entertains a Gentleman from Stratford," "Rembrandt to Rembrandt," and "Ponce de Leon"; and mythic figures, notably characters from the Bible and Arthurian legend.

Edwin S. Fussell, in his book on Robinson, devotes separate chapters to the English Bible and the Greek and Roman classics as significant influences on Robinson's work. English poets of particular importance to him are Shakespeare, Wordsworth, Kipling, Tennyson, and Robert Browning, although Robinson objected to the inevitable comparison between his character analyses and those of Browning. Among American poets Robinson found Emerson to be his most significant precursor. Because of his narrative impulse, his work is also compared to the fiction of Hawthorne and Henry James.

Robinson is best known today for his earliest work, the short sketches of characters, chiefly failures, who reside in Tilbury Town, the name he uses for Gardiner, Maine. Partially because of the frequency of their being anthologized, "Richard Cory," "Miniver Cheevy," and "Mr. Flood's Party" are his most famous poems. "Eros Turannos" has been singled out by Louis O. Coxe as the most impressive Tilbury poem. Also highly regarded are a few of the poems of medium length, notably "Isaac and Archibald" and "Aunt Imogen."

Not all of Robinson's poems are narratives, and some of the symbolic lyrics have been highly praised, particularly "For a Dead Lady" and the poem about which Theodore Roosevelt wrote, "I am not sure I understand 'Luke Havergal,' but I am sure that I like it." "The Man Against the Sky," the title poem of the first volume that received pronounced critical approval, is an ironic meditation on possibilities of philosophical attitudes. It has received a great deal of critical attention from both admirers and detractors. Robinson said that the poem "comes as near as anything to representing my poetic vision."

Critics have tended to neglect Robinson's long narratives, those thirteen book-length poems that occupied most of his attention during the second half of his career. According to his earliest biographer, Hermann Hagedorn, the difficulty Robinson had with *Captain Craig*, first in getting a publisher and then in the adverse critical reaction, was a devastating experience for the young poet. Until he issued his first *Collected Poems* in 1921, Robinson alternated his long poems with volumes of shorter, more readily acceptable pieces. After he was thoroughly established, however, he concentrated on the long narratives. Though these poems sometimes lend themselves to verbosity and repetition, they nevertheless provided Robinson with his most congenial form, allowing him to combine his talents of narration, characterization, and symbolic discursiveness.

—Nancy C. Joyner

RODGERS, W(illiam) R(obert).   Irish.   Born in Belfast, 1 August 1909. Educated at the Queen's University of Belfast, B.A. 1931. Married 1) Mary Harden Waddell in 1936 (died, 1953), two daughters; 2) Marianne Helweg in 1953, one daughter. Ordained in the Presbyterian Church, 1935: Minister, Loughgall Presbyterian Church, County Armagh, 1935 until he resigned, 1946; BBC Producer and Scriptwriter, associated with Third Programme productions on Ireland and Irish literary characters, 1946–66; Writer-in-Residence, Pitzer College, Claremont, California, 1966–68; Lecturer at California State Polytechnic College, San Luis Obispo, 1968. Recipient: Dublin Arts Council grant, 1968; Chapelbrook Foundation grant, 1968. Member, Irish Academy of Letters, 1951. *Died 1 February 1969.*

PUBLICATIONS

Collections

Collected Poems.   1971.

Verse

Awake! and Other Poems.   1941.
Europa and the Bull and Other Poems.   1952.

Play

Radio Play: *The Return Room,* 1955.

Other

The Ulstermen and Their Country.   1947.
Ireland in Colour: A Collection of Forty Colour Photographs.   1957.

Irish Literary Portraits (radio interviews). 1972.
Essex Roundabout. 1973.

Reading List: "The Poetry of Rodgers" by Robert Greacen, in *Poetry Quarterly 12*, 1950–51; *Rodgers* by Darcy O'Brien, 1970; in *Northern Voices: Poets from Ulster* by Terence Brown, 1975.

*   *   *

W. R Rodgers published two volumes of poetry which were notable for their extraordinary, baroque verbal textures. Rodgers managed his effects as a poet through exuberant use of such techniques as assonance, internal rhyming, punning, and alliteration. Critics often compared his verse to the work of Gerard Manley Hopkins but it is important to note that Rodgers began his verbal experiments and achieved his own recognisable manner before he read that poet.

Rodgers employs verbal peculiarities to express his awareness of clash, strife, creative confusion in the natural and the psychological orders. His sense of the landscape is of a proliferation of vigorously alive phenomena engaged in a vital struggle, while his sense of human psychology is compact of sexual and religious conflicts, releasing the self into moments of ebullient celebration. Linguistic, sensuous, and moral intensity are features of his work, though an impression of excess and almost irresponsible loquacity is an aspect that some readers may find oppressive. His finest achievements were a number of brief, brilliantly energetic lyric poems of which "The Lovers" in his first volume, *Awake and Other Poems*, and "Lent" in his second, *Europa and the Bull and Other Poems*, can be cited as particularly successful examples.

Rodgers published a number of short prose travel pieces and a quantity of literary journalism, but apart from his poetry his most significant work was as a radio broadcaster. He wrote a number of radio portraits of Irish writers for the BBC and his radio feature *The Return Room* is one of the most successful evocations of life in the poet's native city of Belfast.

—Terence Brown

ROETHKE, Theodore (Huebner).   American.   Born in Saginaw, Michigan, 25 May 1908. Educated at John Moore School, Saginaw, 1913–21; Arthur Hill High School, Saginaw, 1921–25; University of Michigan, Ann Arbor, 1925–29, B.A. 1929 (Phi Beta Kappa), M.A. 1936; Harvard University, Cambridge, Massachusetts, 1930–31. Married Beatrice O'Connell in 1953. Instructor in English, 1931–35, Director of Public Relations, 1934, and Varsity Tennis Coach, 1934–35, Lafayette College, Easton, Pennsylvania; Instructor in English, Michigan State College, East Lansing, Fall 1935; Instructor, 1936–40, Assistant Professor, 1940–43, and Associate Professor of English Composition, 1947, Pennsylvania State University, College Park; Instructor, Bennington College, Vermont, 1943–46; Associate Professor, 1947–48, Professor of English, 1948–62, and Honorary Poet-in-Residence, 1962–63, University of Washington, Seattle. Recipient: Yaddo fellowship, 1945; Guggenheim grant, 1945, 1950; National Institute of Arts and Letters grant, 1952; Fund for the Advancement of Education Fellowship, 1952; Ford Foundation grant, 1952, 1959; Pulitzer Prize, 1954; Fulbright Fellowship, 1955; Borestone Mountain Award, 1958;

National Book Award, 1959, 1965; Bollingen Prize, 1959; Poetry Society of America Prize, 1962; Shelley Memorial Award, 1962. D.H.L.: University of Michigan, 1962. *Died 1 August 1963.*

PUBLICATIONS

Collections

On the Poet and His Craft: Selected Prose, edited by Ralph J. Mills, Jr.   1965.
Collected Poems.   1966.
Selected Letters, edited by Ralph J. Mills., Jr.   1968.
Selected Poems, edited by Beatrice Roethke.   1969.

Verse

Open House.   1941.
The Lost Son and Other Poems.   1948.
Praise to the End!   1951.
The Waking: Poems 1933–1953.   1953.
Words for the Wind: The Collected Verse.   1957.
The Exorcism.   1957.
Sequence, Sometimes Metaphysical, Poems.   1963.
The Far Field.   1964.
Two Poems.   1965.

Other

I Am! Says the Lamb (juvenile).   1961.
Party at the Zoo (juvenile).   1963.
Straw for the Fire: From the Notebooks of Theodore Roethke, 1943–1963, edited by David Wagoner.   1972.
Dirty Dinky and Other Creatures: Poems for Children, edited by Beatrice Roethke and Stephen Lushington.   1973.

Bibliography: *Roethke: A Bibliography* by James R. McLeod, 1973.

Reading List: *Roethke* by Ralph J. Mills, Jr., 1963; *Roethke: Essays on His Poetry* by Arnold S. Stein, 1965; *Roethke: An Introduction to His Poetry* by Karl Malkoff, 1966; *The Glass House: The Life of Roethke* by Allan Seager, 1968; *Profile of Roethke* by William Heyen, 1971; *Roethke's Dynamic Vision* by Richard Allen Blessing, 1974; *Roethke: The Garden Master* by Rosemary Sullivan, 1975; *The Echoing Wood of Roethke* by Jenijoy La Belle, 1976.

*   *   *

Theodore Roethke's posthumous collection, *The Far Field,* is a résumé and retrospect of a lifetime's preoccupations, acknowledging its debt to those poets who have confronted the mystery of personal extinction – the later Eliot and Yeats and that "Whitman, maker of catalogues" whose "terrible hunger for objects" is repeated in these writings of a man who has "moved closer to death, lived with death." Roethke always felt "the separateness of all things," the fragility of being. In "The Dream" he had written "Love is not love until love's vulnerable"; "The Abyss" adds a new, desperate urgency to the theme, poised on a dark stair that "goes nowhere," knowing the abyss is "right where you are − /A step down the stair." Yet if this last volume broods over childhood initiations into mortality, it also celebrates the spontaneous impulse towards life, light, growth in which he shares:

> Many arrivals make us live: the tree becoming
> Green, a bird tipping the topmost bough,
> A seed pushing itself beyond itself....
>
> What does what it should do needs nothing more.
> The body moves, though slowly, towards desire.
> We come to something without knowing why.

Summoned once more to the field's end, in old age Roethke returned to "the first heaven of knowing," that second-childhood of radical innocence which has always been the American visionary's home. If "Old men should be explorers," he replies to the Eliot of *Four Quartets*, "I'll ben an Indian./Iroquois," thus unashamedly assuming the role of the noble savage in retreat, whose "journey into the interior," into the heart of the continent, is also a "long journey out of the self," into the unconscious and preconscious, the elemental life of the planet.

There is a paradoxical resolution of stasis and motion throughout Roethke's work. "The Sententious Man" claims to "know the motion of the deepest stone"; in "The Far Field," imagery of dwindling, darkening, and decline shifts into sudden surges and spurts of life, as not only air, fire, and water but even earth takes on the fluidity which leaves no ground secure: "the shale slides dangerously," dust blows, rubble falls, the arroyo cracks, the swamp is "alive with quicksand." Amid this movement the self floats unperturbed: "I rise and fall in the slow sea of a grassy plain" (the theological punning here recurs throughout his verse); "And all flows past.... I am not moving but they are," for the soul, preparing itself for death, has finally found that longed-for "imperishable quiet at the heart of form." Throughout his verse, the *field* is a complex metaphor: it is the green field of nature, the field of perception, and, at their intersection, a heraldic field in which matter blazons forth spirit, where "All finite things reveal infinitude," disclosing, in the words of one of his earliest poems, "skies of azure/The pageantry of wings the eyes' right treasure."

Movement from closure to openness, finitude to immensity, has been the characteristic rhythm of all his poetry. The title poem of *Open House* proclaims this:

> My secrets cry aloud....
> My heart keeps open house,
> My doors are widely swung....
> I'm naked to the bone
> With nakedness my shield.
> Myself is what I wear.

The Lost Son pokes around in origins, under stones, in drains and subsoil, to find the answer to his most basic question: "Where do the roots go?" Roethke felt himself at home amidst the abundant verminous life of a vegetable nature which (as in "Cuttings, *later*") strains like a saint to rise anew in "This urge, wrestle, resurrection of dry sticks" − a world to which he was introduced in his florist father's greenhouses, where he learnt to "study the lives on a leaf: the little/Sleepers, numb nudgers"; and not only to study, but to find in them, as in the "Shoots [which] dangled and drooped,/Lolling obscenely" in "Root Cellar," an imagery of his own instinctual life. He was impressed by the stubborn persistence of this residual realm: "Nothing would give up life:/Even the dirt kept breathing a small breath."

His poems are rites of passage, exits and entrances where "the body, delighting in thresholds,/Rocks in and out of itself." *Praise to the End* employs the bouncy rhythms and inconsequential surrealism of nursery rhyme and baby talk, used to such effect in his poems for children, to enact the birth or rebirth of the scattered psyche (Roethke suffered from periodic mental illness) out of a tangle of instinctual impulses – eating, touching, snuffling, sucking, licking – in all of which identity is constituted as *lack* ("I Need, I Need"), a fall from innocence into disenchantment which brings us to our proper selfhood, aware of time and consequence, and able to announce "I'm somebody else now." In "Give Way, Ye Gates," one line of six verbs charts the whole pilgrimage through need, mutuality, and loss into separated being: "Touch and arouse. Suck and sob. Curse and mourn." The technique of this volume is a riddling, exclamatory questioning, like that of an insistent child who neither expects nor receives an answer, wanting only confirmation of its own puzzling existence. Yet this catechism of the "happy asker" reveals a world of correspondences where everything *is* an answer to everything else, and the creatures sing their own richness and diversity: "A house for wisdom. A field for revelation./Speak to the stones and the stars answer."

In his love poems this most physical of poets assumes a metaphysical lightness and delicacy, a clarity of syntax and almost allegoric translucence of imagery which recall Renaissance neo-platonism and the courtly love of the troubadours. His women (even the "woman lovely in her bones") are the Beatrices of a rarefied sensuality, "know[ing] the speech of light" and "cry[ing] out loud the soul's own secret joy"; but even here Roethke's playfulness is preserved in sudden unexpected carnalities of language ("pure as a bride.../ And breathing hard, as that man rode/Between those lovely tits"). "The Renewal" shows love to be the force that moves the stars, reducing to a oneness knowing and motion, the dualities of his universe, just as "Words for the Wind," which provided the title for his *Collected Verse*, sees it as both the journey and the destination of the soul:

> I cherish what I have
> Had of the temporal:
>
> I am no longer young
> But the wind and waters are;
> What falls away will fall;
> All things bring me to love.

—Stan Smith

ROSENBERG, Isaac. English. Born in Bristol, 25 November 1890; family lived in Whitechapel, London, after 1897. Educated at Baker Street School, Stepney, London, 1899–1904; apprentice engraver, Carl Hentschel Company, London, 1904–07; attended evening classes at the London College of Printing, 1907–10; studied at the Slade School of Art, London, 1911–14 (Jewish Educational Aid Society grant, 1912). Visited South Africa, 1914–15; served in the British Army in World War I, 1915–18; killed in action. *Died 1 April 1918.*

PUBLICATIONS

Collections

> *Collected Works: Poetry, Prose, Letters, and Some Drawings*, edited by Gordon
> Bottomley and Denys Harding.   1937; revised edition of poetry section, as *Collected
> Poems*, 1949.
> *Collected Works*, edited by Ian Parsons.   1976.

Verse

> *Night and Day*.   1912.
> *Youth*.   1915.
> *Poems*, edited by Gordon Bottomley.   1922.

Play

> *Moses*.   1916.

Reading List: in *Heroes' Twilight* by Bernard Bergonzi, 1965; *Out of Battle: The Poetry of the First World War* by Jon Silkin, 1972; *Rosenberg: The Half Used Life* by Jean Liddiard, 1975; *Journey to the Trenches* by Joseph Cohen, 1975.

*   *   *

Isaac Rosenberg was killed on the western front on 1 April 1918. His parents were immigrants from Czarist Russia who left to avoid anti-semitism and forced conscription. The family moved to the ghetto of East London in 1897 where there was already a sizable Jewish community – a community that at one time supported a Yiddish theatre and newspaper. But although Rosenberg rejected Hebrew and the concomitant way of orthodox Judaism, Jewish culture, in the widest sense, was an essential part of his upbringing. Kenneth Allott noted in *The Penguin Book of Contemporary Verse* that for him Rosenberg's poems "are spoilt ... by his appetite for the extravagant and his rebarbative diction." Allott's taste was formed round the cool clinching wit of Auden, and the fact is that Rosenberg's poetry is imaginatively vigorous, an attribute that never had much in it for Auden, or, one supposes, Allott. Rosenberg's imagination is robust whether he is structuring a re-shaping of consciousness, as he is in his playlet *Moses* or the dramatic "Amulet/Unicorn" fragments; or in the metaphor of Absalom's hair ("Chagrin"), or the re-informed lovers of the "Grecian Urn" as we find them in "Daughters of War" and the third stanza of "Dead Man's Dump." Rosenberg was afraid of his poetry being thin, especially in ideas. He need not have worried, for, as in "Dead Man's Dump," the ideas are not only substantial but often subtle:

> What fierce imaginings their dark souls lit?
> Earth! have they gone into you!
> Somewhere they must have gone,
> And flung on your hard back
> Is their soul's sack
> Emptied of God-ancestralled essences.
> Who hurled them out? Who hurled?

Rosenberg mourns not only the body and *its* death, but, surprisingly perhaps for a Jewish writer with his concern for the total being, also the death of the soul. The "soul's sack" may be the body, but it is, more subtly and crucially, as likely to be the soul's amnion, whose contents are evacuated with the death of the flesh. Thus with the soul's death also die the essences originated by God, and this religious apprehension of what is destroyed by the human activity of war achieves the status of tragic assertion.

The language in this stanza is robust and dense, and ultimately registers tenderness and pain, responses that are more intimate and singular than the compassion Wilfred Owen articulates. Even in the work that is not ostensibly about the War (like the playlet *Moses* and the "Amulet/Unicorn" fragments), there is a greater immediacy concerning the nature of destruction in Rosenberg's work than in Owen's. As Walter Benjamin said of Brecht in "The Author as Producer": "He goes back, in a new way, to the theatre's greatest and most ancient opportunity: the opportunity to expose the present." Just so; and it is also true of Rosenberg. "Dead Man's Dump," like Owen's "Strange Meeting," is indeed a poem concerned with the imminent destruction of an at least partly humane civilisation; and as the destruction occurs the value shows up. But where Owen recollects in pity, narratively, Rosenberg's apprehensions are evolved dramatically in the present, as that is *made* by man. And this exposing of the present happens elsewhere in Rosenberg. It occurs in the trick played on God in the ingenious, Donne-like "God made Blind." In *Moses*, the protagonist has just murdered the sadistic Egyptian overseer Abinoah (whose daughter Moses is in love with) only to find that he must face the Egyptian Prince Imra and his glimmering cohorts that have come to arrest him. In "The Unicorn," the women are abducted in a kind of Sabine rape. In Owen's "Strange Meeting," the resulting admonition may be as dire as it is in Rosenberg's "Dead Man's Dump." Possibly more so. But it is not as sensuously disturbing. Samuel Johnson observed that the business of the poet was to strike through to the reader's *senses*. Rosenberg's sensuous apprehensions delay the workings of valuation until the experience is complete, and there is nowhere else that the mind can go but to full judgment.

—Jon Silkin

RUKEYSER, Muriel. American. Born in New York City, 15 December 1913. Educated at Fieldston School, New York, 1919–30; Vassar College, Poughkeepsie, New York; Columbia University, New York, 1930–32. Has one son. Vice-President, House of Photography, New York, 1946–60; taught at Sarah Lawrence College, Bronxville, New York, 1946, 1956–57. Since 1967, Member, Board of Directors, Teachers–Writers Collaborative, New York. President, P.E.N. American Center, 1975–76. Recipient: Harriet Monroe Award, 1941; National Institute of Arts and Letters Award, 1942; Guggenheim Fellowship, 1943; American Council of Learned Societies Fellowship, 1963; Swedish Academy translation award, 1967. D.Litt.: Rutgers University, New Brunswick, New Jersey, 1961. Member, National Institute of Arts and Letters. Lives in New York City.

PUBLICATIONS

Verse

Theory of Flight. 1935.
U.S. 1. 1938.

Mediterranean. 1938.
A Turning Wind. 1939.
The Soul and Body of John Brown. 1940.
Wake Island. 1942.
Beast in View. 1944.
The Children's Orchard. 1947.
The Green Wave. 1948.
Orpheus. 1949.
Elegies. 1949.
Selected Poems. 1951.
Body of Waking. 1958.
Waterlily Fire: Poems 1932–1962. 1962.
The Outer Banks. 1967.
The Speed of Darkness. 1968.
29 Poems. 1970.
Breaking Open. 1973.
The Gates. 1976.

Play

The Color of the Day (produced 1961).

Fiction

The Orgy. 1965.

Other

Willard Gibbs (biography). 1942.
The Life of Poetry. 1949.
Come Back Paul (juvenile). 1955.
One Life (biography of Wendell Willkie). 1957.
I Go Out (juvenile). 1961.
Bubbles (juvenile). 1967.
Poetry and Unverifiable Fact: The Clark Lectures. 1968.
The Traces of Thomas Hariot. 1971.

Translator, with others, *Selected Poems of Octavio Paz.* 1963; revised edition, 1973.
Translator, *Sun Stone,* by Octavio Paz. 1963.
Translator, with Leif Sjöberg, *Selected Poems of Gunnar Ekelöf.* 1967.
Translator, *Three Poems by Gunnar Ekelöf.* 1967.
Translator, with others, *Early Poems 1935–1955,* by Octavio Paz. 1973.

* * *

Much has been said about the feminine voice in poetry, usually by critics. No one seems to know exactly what the "true" feminine voice is, except that somewhere between the despair and the joy of woman's second-class existence, a kind of experience is finally being written. Sylvia Plath wrote from this sensibility and a number of new lady poets have missed the joy expressed between the lines, where Plath had made words that work together. The assumption that despair should somehow outweigh joy in serious feminine poetry results from the Dickinson (and now, Plath) tradition.

Reading the work of Muriel Rukeyser, one quickly learns that feminism is not so easily defined. Once again, the near-answer is revealed for what it is, and we are thrown back to the poem itself. Rukeyser's work can be despairing, but her responses have larger potential. Even in moments of sad recollection, as in "Effort at Speech Between Two People," Rukeyser's voice is not entirely despondent:

> When I was three, a little child read a story about a rabbit
> who died, in the story, and I crawled under a chair   :
> a pink rabbit   :   it was my birthday, and a candle
> burnt a sore spot on my finger, and I was told to be happy.

Here, Rukeyser has successfully combined the elements of mature narrative with a verbal sense of what it was like to live through that third birthday. The poem is not cute, in any of its aspects, and in spite of succeeding lines ("I am unhappy. I am lonely. Speak to me.") never indulges in outright despondency. It is the hope for communication that has initially caused the poem which survives, echoed by lively images, and imbuing the poem ultimately with a sense of optimism.

Rukeyser's work is always tough, however, and never assumes the false authority that is so often mistaken for wisdom. She investigates nearly every aspect of life, from the desperate haircutting of a boy who needs work to "The Power of Suicide," one of her tight, excellent four-line poems:

> The potflower on the windowsill says to me
> In words that are green-edged red leaves:
> Flower   flower   flower   flower
> Today for the sake of all the dead   Burst into flower.

The simplicity of such a poem makes explication impossible: what gimmicks of "style" has the poet employed? One knows only that the poem is bound by a natural rhythm, and seems to relate a part of the poet's experience.

Some of Rukeyser's long poems, in particular "The Speed of Darkness," are among the finest we'll have to carry with us into the next century. Her vocabulary is truly of our generation, but she's writing poems of a longer endurance:

> Whoever despises the clitoris despises the penis
> Whoever despises the penis despises the cunt
> Whoever despises the cunt despises the life of the child.
>
> Resurrection music,   silence,   and surf.

In "Waterlily Fire," she curiously mixes hard consonant sounds with a softer, feminine voice:

> We pray : we dive into each other's eyes
> Whatever can come to a woman can come to me.
> This the long body : into life from the beginning....

The toughness of these poems suggests that "feminine," with all its present connotations, is not the correct adjective for Miss Rukeyser's work. The frankness of her love poems (read "What I See") combined with her muted optimism also makes for memorable poetry.

For the moment, such "optimism" seems the only valid voice that any poet, regardless of sex, can bring to his work. Anything else is a lie, or why would the poet trouble to write at all?

Muriel Rukeyser's poetry *is* feminine, but only because the poet is a lady. It is enduring because the poet has retained all of her "seventeen senses," and utilizes every one of them in her work.

—Geof Hewitt

SANDBURG, Carl.   American.   Born in Galesburg, Illinois, 6 January 1878. Educated at Lombard College, Galesburg, 1898–1902. Served as a Private in the 6th Illinois Volunteers during the Spanish American War, 1899. Married Lillian Steichen in 1908; three daughters, including the poet Helga Sandburg. Associate Editor, *The Lyceumite*, Chicago, 1907–08; District Organizer, Social-Democratic Party, Appleton, Wisconsin, 1908; City Hall Reporter for the *Milwaukee Journal*, 1909–10; Secretary to the Mayor of Milwaukee, 1910–12; worked for the *Milwaukee Leader* and *Chicago World*, 1912; worked for *Day Book*, Chicago, 1912–17, also Associate Editor, *System: The Magazine of Business*, Chicago, 1913; Stockholm Correspondent, 1918, and Manager of the Chicago Office, 1919, Newspaper Enterprise Association; Reporter, Editorial Writer, and Motion Picture Editor, 1917–30, and Syndicated Columnist, 1930–32, *Chicago Daily News*; Lecturer, University of Hawaii, Honolulu, 1934; Walgreen Foundation Lecturer, University of Chicago, 1940; weekly columnist, syndicated by the *Chicago Daily Times*, from 1941. Recipient: Poetry Society of America Award, 1919, 1921; Friends of Literature Award, 1934; Roosevelt Memorial Association prize, for biography, 1939; Pulitzer Prize, for history, 1940, and for poetry, 1951; American Academy of Arts and Letters Gold Medal, 1952; National Association for the Advancement of Colored People Award, 1965. Litt.D.: Lombard College, 1928; Knox College, Galesburg, Illinois, 1929; Northwestern University, Evanston, Illinois, 1931; Harvard University, 1940; Yale University, New Haven, Connecticut, 1940; New York University, 1940; Wesleyan University, Middletown, Connecticut, 1940; Lafayette College, Easton, Pennsylvania, 1940; Syracuse University, New York, 1941; Dartmouth College, Hanover, New Hampshire, 1941; University of North Carolina, Chapel Hill, 1955; Uppsala College, New Jersey, 1959; LL.D.: Hollins College, Virginia, 1941; Augustana College, Rock Island, Illinois, 1948; University of Illinois, Urbana, 1953. Commander, Order of the North Star, Sweden, 1953. Member, American Academy of Arts and Letters, 1940. *Died 22 July 1967.*

PUBLICATIONS

Collections

  The Letters, edited by Herbert Mitgang.   1968.

Verse

  In Reckless Ecstasy.   1904.
  The Plaint of the Rose.   1904(?).

Incidentals.   1904.
Joseffy.   1910.
Chicago Poems.   1916.
Cornhuskers.   1918.
Smoke and Steel.   1920.
Slabs of the Sunburnt West.   1922.
(*Poems*), edited by Hughes Mearns.   1926.
Selected Poems, edited by Rebecca West.   1926.
Good Morning, America.   1928.
The People, Yes.   1936.
Bronze Wood.   1941.
Complete Poems.   1950; revised edition, 1970.
Harvest Poems 1910–1960, edited by Mark Van Doren.   1960.
Six New Poems and a Parable.   1961.
Honey and Salt.   1963.
Breathing Tokens, edited by Margaret Sandburg.   1978.

Fiction

Remembrance Rock.   1948.

Other

You and Your Job.   1908.
The Chicago Race Riots, July 1919.   1919.
Rootabaga Stories (juvenile).   1922.
Rootabaga Pigeons (juvenile).   1923.
Abraham Lincoln: The Prairie Years.   2 vols., 1926 (selection, for children, as *Abe
     Lincoln Grows Up,* 1928); *Abraham Lincoln: The War Years,* 4 vols., 1939; revised
     abridgement, as *Storm over the Land,* 1942; one volume selection *The Prairie Years
     and War Years,* 1954.
Rootabaga Country (juvenile).   1929.
Steichen, The Photographer.   1929.
Early Moon (juvenile).   1930.
Potato Face (juvenile).   1930.
Mary Lincoln, Wife and Widow, with Paul M. Angle.   1932.
Home Front Memo.   1943.
The Photographs of Abraham Lincoln, with Frederick Hill Meserve.   1944.
Lincoln Collector: The Story of Oliver R. Barrett's Great Private Collection.   1949.
Always the Young Strangers (autobiography).   1953; selection, for children, as *Prairie-
     Town Boy,* 1955.
The Sandburg Range (miscellany).   1957.
Wind Song (juvenile).   1960.

Editor, *American Songbag.*   1927; *New American Songbag,* 1950.
Editor, *A Lincoln and Whitman Miscellany.*   1938.

Screen documentary: *Bomber* 1945.

Bibliography: *Sandburg: A Bibliography* by Thomas S. Shaw, 1948.

Reading List: *Sandburg: A Study in Personality and Background* by Karl W. Detzer, 1941; *Sandburg* by Harry Golden, 1961; *Sandburg* by Richard H. Crowder, 1964; *Sandburg* by Mark Van Doren, 1969 (includes bibliography); *Sandburg: Lincoln of Our Literature* by North Callahan, 1970; *Sandburg, Yes* by W. G. Rogers, 1970; *Sandburg* by Gay Wilson Allen, 1972.

*   *   *

Harriet Monroe's magazine *Poetry* in 1914 gave conspicuous position to Carl Sandburg's early poems. Readers were drawn by his Whitman-like quality, now vigorous and rugged, now gentle and compassionate. His books *Chicago Poems* and *Cornhuskers* set the pace and established him as a leading American poet. His free-verse lines were, at their best, musical and varied. His subject matter was generally quarried from the cities and countryside of the Midwest. His themes were built on concern for the common man, concomitant with his interest in Socialism. Out of the Great Depression came his book *The People, Yes*, consisting of folk sayings cemented together by optimistic prophecies to the effect that the ordinary man would eventually receive his due. Sandburg's last book of poems, *Honey and Salt*, continued to substantiate his thesis that the life of "the family of man" is not all sweet, that it is tempered by the sobering experience of everyday existence and even by tragedy. In this book the old poet, through his reliance on a proliferation of color images unusual in a writer at the end of his career, proved to be as vigorous as a tyro one-third his age.

The People, Yes had been a product of Sandburg's interest in folklore. Two collections of the songs of the people established him as something of an authority: *The American Songbag* and the expanded *New American Songbag*. In fact, for the twenty years preceding World War II Sandburg traveled widely singing these songs to large audiences, accompanying himself on the guitar.

In prose biography Sandburg showed a skillful hand. He wrote of his wife's brother in *Steichen, The Photographer* and of the wife of his life-long hero in *Mary Lincoln, Wife and Widow*. His most famous prose work remains his 6-volume biography of Lincoln. If in this monumental work (without footnotes and index) he occasionally rearranged the chronology and indeed embroidered the facts, he nevertheless produced a rich and sensitive portrait, filled with incident, pointed up with insight, and made brilliant with poetic truth. His *Always the Young Strangers* tells the story of his own growing-up with a remarkable analytical objectivity in an enchanting style as engrossing as a novel.

Remembrance Rock was something else again. Commissioned by Metro-Goldwyn-Mayer to write a "great American novel" later to be made into a scenario for a moving picture, Sandburg turned out a wooden, repetitive piece of fiction, not only very long, but very tiresome. Like *The People, Yes* the book is packed with songs, proverbs, anecdotes, folk customs. Effective in a Depression poem, this subject matter was ill suited to the novel form. In spite of the book's ineptness, however, Sandburg was continuing to show his integrity and generosity, his hatred of bigotry, his consuming love for his native country.

He was popular with children. His *Rootabaga Stories*, *Rootabaga Pigeons*, and *Potato Face* enjoyed wide readership. The fantasy, inventiveness, humor, and light-heartedness in these stories were similar to many of the traits in his poems, selections from which, indeed, were collected in anthologies intended for children.

Sandburg no doubt will long be remembered for his Lincoln biography and for many of his poems. The reader can recall the alternating robustiousness and pathos of "Chicago," the delicate imagism of "Fog," the loud anger of "To a Contemporary Bunkshooter," the wholesome aspiration of *The People, Yes*. Even though one cannot place him in the very top rank of American poets, it is possible to say that to have read Sandburg is to have been the companion of a deeply rooted and dedicated citizen of the United States and of a conscious craftsman skilled in communicating the basic emotions, especially as felt by the "ordinary" person. It must be emphasized that Sandburg was moved not just by the masses, what he lovingly called "the mob." True, he was sympathetic with his "people" as they struggled toward the stars (one of his early poems chanted, "I am the people, the mob"), but his many poems about individuals showed him to be actively aware of the inescapable fact that every man and woman experiences troubles and ecstasies (e.g., "The Hangman at Home," "Helga," "Ice Handler," "Mag"). Furthermore, though Sandburg is linked with Lindsay and Masters as an Illinois poet, he is seen to be, on careful study, a poet of universals. If his most frequent subjects are the little people of his home state, his themes are nonetheless the concerns of all people everywhere.

—Richard H. Crowder

SASSOON, Siegfried (Lorraine).   English.   Born in Kent, 8 September 1886. Educated at Marlborough Grammar School; Clare College, Cambridge. Served in the Army during World War I: Captain; Military Cross. Married Hester Getty in 1933; one son. Literary Editor, *Daily Herald*, London, 1919; lectured in the United States, 1920. Recipient: Hawthornden Prize, 1928; Black Memorial Prize, 1928; Queen's Gold Medal for Poetry, 1957. D.Litt.: Oxford University, 1965. Honorary Fellow, Clare College, Cambridge, 1953. C.B.E. (Commander, Order of the British Empire), 1951. *Died 1 September 1967.*

PUBLICATIONS

Verse

Poems.   1906.
Sonnets and Verses.   1909.
Sonnets.   1909.
Twelve Sonnets.   1911.
Poems.   1911.
Melodies.   1912.
An Ode for Music.   1912.
The Daffodil Murderer.   1913.
Discoveries.   1915.
Morning-Glory.   1916.
The Redeemer.   1916.
To Any Dead Officer.   1917.
The Old Huntsman and Other Poems.   1917.
Four Poems.   1918.
Counter-Attack and Other Poems.   1917.
Picture-Show.   1919.
The War Poems.   1919.
Lines Written in the Reform Club.   1921.
Recreations.   1923.
Lingual Exercises for Advanced Vocabularians.   1925.
Selected Poems.   1925.
Satirical Poems.   1926.
The Heart's Journey.   1927.

Poems. 1931.
The Road to Ruin. 1933.
Vigils. 1934.
Rhymed Ruminations. 1939.
Poems Newly Selected, 1916–1935. 1940.
(Poems). 1943.
Collected Poems. 1947.
Common Chords. 1950.
Emblems of Experience. 1951.
The Tasking. 1954.
An Adjustment. 1955.
Sequences. 1956.
Poems, edited by D. Silk. 1958.
Lenten Illuminations, Sight Sufficient. 1958.
The Path to Peace: Selected Poems. 1960.
Collected Poems, 1908–1956. 1961.
An Octave: 8 September 1966. 1966.

Plays

Orpheus in Diloeryum. 1908.
Hyacinth: An Idyll. 1912.
Amyntas: A Mystery. 1912.

Fiction

Something about Myself (story). 1966.

Other

Memoirs of a Fox-Hunting Man. 1928; *Memoirs of an Infantry Officer,* 1930; *Sherston's Progress,* 1936; complete version as *The Complete Memoirs of George Sherston,* 1937; selection, as *The Flower Show Match and Other Pieces,* 1941.
The Old Century and Seven More Years (autobiography). 1938.
The Weald of Youth (autobiography). 1942.
Siegfried's Journey, 1916–1920 (autobiography). 1945.
Meredith. 1948.
Letters to a Critic, edited by Michael Thorpe. 1976.

Editor, *Poems,* by Wilfred Owen. 1920.

Bibliography: *A Bibliography of Sassoon* by Geoffrey Keynes, 1962, addenda by D. Farmer, in *Publications of the Bibliographical Society of America 63,* 1969.

Reading List: *Sassoon: A Critical Study* by Michael Thorpe, 1966; *Out of Battle: Poetry of the Great War* by Jon Silkin, 1972; *Sassoon: A Poet's Pilgimage* by Felicitas Corrigan, 1973.

*   *   *

Memorably courageous both as soldier and as pacifist, Siegfried Sassoon is usually associated with the First World War. He began to write before it and continued after it for almost half a century, but the war provoked his fiercest writing: verse of an adrenalin-intensity next to which his other work seems desultory and tame.

Sassoon's early poetry evokes a pastoral dream-world, stocked rather conventionally with Georgian fauna and flora – "vagrom-hearted" boys, the "daffodilly," and the "windy lea." *Memoirs of a Fox-Hunting Man* lovingly documents in prose the actual world he knew: at first, a leisured country-life existence of spacious assurances, seasonal pleasures, and decorous ritual that now seems almost equally in the realm of idyll. Then, after 1914, the narrative draws Sassoon out from the tranquillities of "Rooks ... cawing in the vicarage elms" to the "continuous rumble and grumble of bombardment." The eye that pleasurably dawdled over rural vistas becomes focussed on mechanised slaughter.

In response, his poetry completely alters. "My trench-sketches," he said, "were like rockets, sent up to illuminate the darkness." The image is appropriate: like the rockets, these war-verses are fuelled with acrid energy; like them, in a burst of heat, they shed light on the appalling. These "harsh, peremptory, and colloquial stanzas with a knock-out blow in the last line" are anti-war propaganda. They were, Sassoon explained, "deliberately written to disturb complacency," and they attempt to do this in two ways: by reporting the atrocities of the Western Front, and by indicting those responsible for them. With unflinching realism, Sassoon depicts the hideous charnel mess into which the men are trapped, the "Golgotha" where they display courage and *camaraderie* but also fear and hysteria, unglamorous symptoms of the healthy urge to keep alive. Pity predominates in this graphic reportage: bitterness, in the contemptuous vignettes of those held to blame – "scarlet Majors," "fierce-browed prelates," "Yellow-Pressmen," and the "smug-faced crowds" with their jingoistic stridency. Two civilian categories arouse particular resentment: an older generation of fathers and "arm-chair" generals, safely bellicose, and women, dupes and feeders of the martial-glory myth. Hurriedly and rather roughly shaped, these verses are not made for detailed contemplation but convey with efficient rapidity a scalding-hot indignation at the war.

Sassoon's later poetry never regained this power. Urbane, sometimes felicitously phrased occasional verse, it progresses rather unexcitingly in traditional directions. There are love-poems blurred over with a faintly melancholy reticence; some gentle satires; ambulating meditations upon past and present; versified responses to art-galleries, concerts, monuments. In the main, an elegiac note prevails. Ghosts and memories drift wanly in and out of stanzas. Wistful for past splendours and stabilities, the verses pause fondly to contemplate painted Victorian skies where "Large clouds, like safe investments, loitered by," or an old lady's "black-lace-mittened hands" crumbling rusks to feed the peacocks. These poems are the product and a record of that genteel cultural tradition into which the First World War so shatteringly broke: obliterating, Sassoon felt, many old decencies, and inspiring, he displayed, some impressive new ones.

—Peter Kemp

SCHWARTZ, Delmore.   American.   Born in Brooklyn, New York, 8 December 1913. Educated at the University of Wisconsin, Madison, 1931; New York University (Editor, *Mosaic* magazine), 1933–35, B.A. in philosophy 1935; Harvard University, Cambridge, Massachusetts, 1935–37. Married 1) Gertrude Buckman (divorced); 2) Elizabeth Pollet in 1949. Briggs-Copeland Instructor in English Composition, 1940, Instructor in English, 1941–45, and Assistant Professor of English, 1946–47, Harvard University. Fellow, Kenyon School of English, Gambier, Ohio, Summer 1950; Visiting Professor at New York

University, Indiana School of Letters, Bloomington, Princeton University, New Jersey, and University of Chicago. Editor, 1943–47, and Associate Editor, 1947–55, *Partisan Review*, New Brunswick, New Jersey; associated with *Perspectives* magazine, New York, 1952–53; Literary Consultant, New Directions, publishers, New York, 1952–53; Poetry Editor and Film Critic, *New Republic* magazine, Washington, D.C., 1955–57. Recipient: Guggenheim Fellowship, 1940; National Institute of Arts and Letters grant, 1953; Bollingen Prize, 1960; Shelley Memorial Award, 1960. *Died 11 July 1966.*

PUBLICATIONS

Collections

    Selected Essays, edited by Donald A. Dike and David H. Zucker.   1970.
    What Is to Be Given: Selected Poems, edited by Douglas Dunn.   1976.

Verse

    In Dreams Begin Responsibilities (includes short story and play).   1938.
    Genesis: Book One (includes prose).   1943.
    Vaudeville for a Princess and Other Poems (includes prose).   1950.
    Summer Knowledge: New and Selected Poems 1938–1958.   1959.

Play

    Shenandoah; or, The Naming of the Child.   1941.

Fiction

    The World Is a Wedding and Other Stories.   1949.
    Successful Love and Other Stories.   1961.

Other

    Editor, *Syracuse Poems 1964.*   1965.

    Translator, *A Season in Hell* (bilingual edition), by Arthur Rimbaud.   1939.

Bibliography: in *Selected Essays,* 1970.

Reading List: *Schwartz* by Richard McDougall, 1974; *Schwartz: The Life of an American Poet* by James Atlas, 1977.

*   *   *

It is difficult, reading Delmore Schwartz, to disentangle the poetry from the legend. The darling of the group of American intellectuals associated with the *Partisan Review* in the

1930's and 1940's — to which he contributed as poet, critic, and short story writer, and eventually became co-editor — Schwartz had a career worthy of the last *poète maudit*. A precociously brilliant first book, *In Dreams Begin Responsibilities*, was followed by a tragic decline into alcohol, insanity, and an early death, alone, in a seedy Manhattan hotel. Posthumously, Schwartz has undergone a literary "canonisation" in one of the most heartbreaking sequences of John Berryman's *Dream Songs* and as the eponymous "hero" of Saul Bellow's *Humboldt's Gift*. The life is forbiddingly close to stereotyped, "romantic" conceptions of "the Poet."

And Schwartz almost certainly saw himself in something like this role. The titles alone of some of his best known poems — "Do Others Speak of Me Mockingly, Maliciously?," "All of Us Always Turning Away for Solace" — suggest his fundamental view of the poet as one isolated from his tribe, cut off, as in the marvellous "The Heavy Bear Who Goes with Me," from contact even with his own body. The characteristic Schwartzian stance is apparent in his "Sonnet: O City, City": we live

> Where the sliding auto's catastrophe
> Is a gust past the curb, where numb and high
> The office building rises to its tyranny,
> Is our anguished diminution until we die.

In the same poem, however, he longs for an alternative human sympathy, "the self articulate, affectionate and flowing." Between these terms the course of his poetry runs.

It is a poetry that rarely loses touch with political and historical realities: "The Ballad of the Children of the Czar" and the verse play *Shenandoah* poignantly express Schwartz's understanding of his family's experience as Jewish immigrants to the States. There is the larger feeling, in many poems, of human beings *imprisoned* in time, bearing the guilt of generations, and Schwartz probes at his guilts and anxieties in a way that occasionally, as in "Prothalamion," points forward to the "confessional" poetry to be written by his more famous contemporaries Berryman and Lowell. The guardian angels of these poems, figures which haunt Schwartz's imagination and are returned to with obsessive insistence, are the heroic solitaries — Faust, Socrates, "Tiger Christ," "Manic-depressive Lincoln," and, above all, Hamlet.

But there is also in Schwartz, if less insistently, an energetically vibrant language and feeling, a kind of robust dandyism, as in "Far Rockaway":

> The radiant soda of the seashore fashions
> Fun, foam, and freedom. The sea laves
> The shaven sand. And the light sways forward
> On the self-destroying waves.

Douglas Dunn, in his introduction to *What Is to Be Given*, has referred to Schwartz's "sometimes dispiriting ebullience," and it is this that many critics have objected to in the later work. A poem like "Seurat's Sunday Afternoon along the Seine" certainly needs to be read without the expectation of those judicious ironies on which most modern poetry thrives. But, *relaxed into*, the stretch and sweep, the sheer verbal intoxication of the poem, carry persuasive power.

Schwartz is a poet, and a critic, too little read and too little understood. Recent re-publications, however, suggest that his work will survive, along with the best of his generation.

—Neil Corcoran

SCOTT, Duncan Campbell. Canadian. Born in Ottawa, Ontario, 2 August 1862. Educated at Smiths Falls High School, Ontario, 1874–75; Wesleyan College, Stanstead, Quebec, 1877–79. Married 1) Belle Warner Botsford in 1894 (died, 1929), one daughter; 2) Desiree Elise Aylen in 1931. Joined Department of Indian Affairs, Ottawa, 1879: Clerk Third Class, 1879–93; Chief Clerk, 1893–96; Secretary of the Department, 1896–1909; Superintendent of Indian Education, 1909–23; Deputy Superintendent General, 1923 until his retirement, 1932. Columnist, *Toronto Globe*, 1892–93; President, Ottawa Drama League; President, Canadian Authors Association, 1931–33. Recipient: Lorne Pierce Medal, 1927. D.Litt.: University of Toronto, 1922; LL.D.: Queen's University, Kingston, Ontario, 1939. Fellow, 1899, Honorary Secretary, 1911–21, and President, 1921–22, Royal Society of Canada; Fellow, Royal Society of Literature (England). C.M.G. (Companion, Order of St. Michael and St. George), 1934. *Died 19 December 1947.*

PUBLICATIONS

Collections

Selected Poems. 1951.
Selected Stories, edited by Glenn Clever. 1972.

Verse

The Magic House and Other Poems. 1893.
Labor and the Angel. 1898.
New World Lyrics and Ballads. 1905.
Via Borealis. 1906.
Lines in Memory of Edmund Morris. 1915.
Lundy's Lane and Other Poems. 1916.
To the Canadian Mothers, and Three Other Poems. 1917.
Beauty and Life. 1921.
Byron on Wordsworth, Being Undiscovered Stanzas of Don Juan. 1924 (?).
The Poems. 1926.
The Green Cloister: Later Poems. 1935.

Plays

Pierre (produced 1921). In *Canadian Plays from Hart House Theatre 1,* edited by Vincent Massey, 1926.
Prologue (produced 1923). In *The Poems,* 1926.
Joy! Joy! Joy! (produced 1927).

Fiction (stories)

In the Village of Viger. 1896.
The Witching of Elspie. 1923.

Other

John Graves Simcoe (biography). 1905.

Notes on the Meeting Place of the First Parliament of Upper Canada and the Early Buildings at Niagara. 1913.
The Administration of Indian Affairs in Canada. 1931.
Walter J. Phillips, R.C.A. (biography). 1947.
The Circle of Affection and Other Pieces in Prose and Verse. 1947.
Some Letters, edited by Arthur S. Bourinot. 1959; *More Letters,* 1960.

Editor, *The Poems of Archibald Lampman.* 1900; selection, 1947.
Editor, with Pelham Edgar, *The Makers of Canada.* 20 vols., 1903–08.
Editor, *The People of the Plains,* by Amelia Anne Paget. 1909.
Editor, *Lyrics of Earth: Sonnets and Ballads,* by Archibald Lampman. 1925.

Reading List: *Ten Canadian Poets* by Desmond Pacey, 1958; essay by A. J. M. Smith, in *Our Living Tradition* edited by R. McDougall, 1959.

*   *   *

Duncan Campbell Scott had a long poetic career; his first book, *The Magic House,* appeared in 1893, and his last, *The Circle of Affection,* appeared in the year of his death, 1947. He also had experiences unusual among poets in his day, for in 1879 he became a clerk in the Indian Branch in Ottawa, and continued in the service until 1932. In his work Scott had to undertake long, arduous journeys into the northern wilderness where he came into close contact with Indians, Métis, loggers, and trappers; he treasured these experiences, and the tales he heard on his travels, for use in his poetry.

Scott was not only a poet. He published two volumes of short stories, *In the Village of Viger* and *The Witching of Elspie,* both of them set in the pietist and superstition-ridden rural Quebec of the late nineteenth century. Some of these stories are humorous, others are eerie, and others have a grim starkness that reminds one of some of Scott's own poems about Indian life. His play *Pierre* was also set among French Canadians.

It is as a poet, however, that Scott is most interesting. His first volume, *The Magic House,* consisted mainly of descriptive lyrics, conventional in form and sentiment. But in his second book, *Labor and the Angel,* he displayed a real distinctiveness, not only in the romantic narrative poem "The Piper of Arll," but also in the first of his poems about the northland wilderness and the harsh life of the nomad Indian hunters. His experiences in the north continued to haunt him, and almost every later volume down to *The Green Cloister* in 1935 contained Indian poems, of which "The Onondaga Madonna," "At Gull Lake, 1810," and "The Forsaken," a poignant narrative of an old woman left to die by her tribe, are among the best-known of Canadian poems.

Scott in fact wrote two very different kinds of poem. There were the conventional and rather Tennysonian lyrics, concerned often with wild nature, sonorous and mood-provoked but essentially unexperimental, and there were the poems of the northern wilderness and of Indian life in which he strived for a stark and vivid authenticity and achieved it by breaking away from Victorian conventions to use irregular verse forms, hard images, and often harsh words. In these northern poems Scott, more than any of his contemporaries, anticipated the poets of the 1930's who took Canadian poetry out of its colonial past and into modern times.

—George Woodcock

SCOTT, F(rancis) R(eginald).   Canadian.   Born in Quebec City, 1 August 1899. Educated at Quebec High School; Bishop's College, Lennoxville, Quebec, B.A. 1919; Magdalen College, Oxford (Rhodes Scholar), 1920–23, B.A. 1922, B.Litt. 1923; McGill University, Montreal, B.C.L. 1927; called to the Quebec Bar, 1927; Queen's Counsel, Quebec, 1961. Married Marian Mildred Dale in 1928; one son. Teacher, Quebec High School, 1919, Bishop's College School, Lennoxville, 1920, and Lower Canada College, Montreal, 1923; Assistant Professor of Federal and Constitutional Law, 1928–34, Professor of Civil Law, 1934–54, Macdonald Professor of Law, 1955–67, Dean of the Faculty of Law, 1961–64, and Visiting Professor in the French Canada Studies Programme, 1967–69, McGill University. Visiting Professor, University of Toronto Law School, 1953–54, Michigan State University, East Lansing, 1957, and Dalhousie University, Halifax, Nova Scotia, 1969–71. Co-Founding Editor, with A. J. M. Smith, *McGill Fortnightly Review*, Montreal, 1925–27; Editor, *Canada Mercury*, 1928, *Canada Forum*, 1936–39, *Preview*, Montreal, 1942–45, and *Northern Review*, Montreal, 1945–47. President, League for Social Reconstruction, 1935–36; Member, National Council, Penal Association of Canada, 1935–46; Member, National Executive, Canadian Institute of International Affairs, 1935–50; National Chairman, Canadian Cooperative Commonwealth Federation Party, 1942–50; U.N. Technical Assistant, Burma, 1952; Chairman, Legal Research Committee, Canadian Bar Association, 1954–56; Chairman, Canadian Writers Conference, 1955; Civil Liberties Counsel before the Supreme Court of Canada, 1956–64; Member, Royal Commission on Bilingualism and Biculturalism, 1963–71. Recipient: Guggenheim Fellowship, 1940; Royal Society of Canada Lorne Pierce Medal, 1962; Banff Springs Festival Gold Medal, 1958; Quebec Government Prize, 1964; Canada Council Molson Award, 1965, and grant, 1974. LL.D.: Dalhousie University, 1958; University of Manitoba, Winnipeg, 1961; Queen's University, Kingston, Ontario, 1964; University of British Columbia, Vancouver, 1965; University of Montreal, 1966; Osgoode Hall Law School, Downsview, Ontario, 1966; McGill University, 1967; LL.B.: University of Saskatchewan, Saskatoon, 1965. Fellow, Royal Society of Canada, 1947. Honorary Member, American Academy of Arts and Sciences, 1967. C.C. (Companion, Order of Canada), 1967. Lives in Montreal.

PUBLICATIONS

Verse

Overture.   1945.
Events and Signals.   1954.
The Eye of the Needle: Satires, Sorties, Sundries.   1957.
Signature.   1964.
Selected Poems.   1966.
Trouvailles: Poems from Prose.   1967.
The Dance Is One.   1973.

Other

Canada Today: A Study of Her National Interests and National Policy.   1938.
Make This Your Canada: A Review of C. C. F. History and Policy, with David Lewis.   1943.
Canada after the War: Attitudes of Political, Social, and Economic Policies in Post-War Canada, with Alexander Brady.   1944.
Cooperation for What? United States and Britain's Commonwealth.   1944.

The World's Civil Service. 1954.
Evolving Canadian Federalism. 1958.
The Canadian Constitution and Human Rights (radio talks). 1959.
Civil Liberties and Canadian Federalism. 1959.
Dialogue sur la Traduction, with Anne Hébert. 1970.
Essays on the Constitution. 1977.

Editor, with A. J. M. Smith, *New Provinces: Poems of Several Authors.* 1936.
Editor, with A. J. M. Smith, *The Blasted Pine: An Anthology of Satire, Invective and Disrespectful Verse, Chiefly by Canadian Writers.* 1957; revised edition, 1967.
Editor, with Michael Oliver, *Quebec States Her Case: Speeches and Articles from Quebec in the Years of Unrest.* 1964.

Translator, *St. Denys Garneau and Anne Hébert.* 1961.
Translator, *Poems of French Canada.* 1976.

Reading List: *Ten Canadian Poets* by Desmond Pacey, 1958; *The McGill Movement: A. J. M. Smith, Scott, and Leo Kennedy* edited by Peter Stevens, 1969; "The Road Back to Eden: The Poetry of Scott," in *Queen's Quarterly,* Autumn 1972.

*   *   *

The humanistic irony which informs F. R. Scott's finest work has characterized his multiple career since the 1930's: political theorist academic lawyer, satirist, translator, editor, and, above all, socially sensitive poet. His most mature poetry is best seen in his *Selected Poems* and its sequel, *The Dance Is One.* Scott's early verse was influenced by imagism and marked by a strong formal sense, both of which served him well in tracing the harsh environment of northern Quebec and Canada. His precise, occasionally brittle diction matched the dominant imagery of stone, water, snow, and ice. Many of his descriptions of man's place in this "inarticulate, arctic" landscape have come to be regarded as major statements in the transformation of colonial romanticism into modernism in Canadian poetry. Later his rhythms became looser and his verse more free, but his fascination with the relation of language and meaning is still reflected in the concreteness and careful rhetoric of even his most delicate lyrics.

Language as playful dance is central to Scott's aesthetic, just as satire is an essential part of his humanism. Here his political and social vision finds its best expression in verse, and his popular reputation is largely founded on his acerbic humour. His targets are usually institutional and structural dangers, follies, and quirks, rather than individual foibles, for he has been a socialist nearly as long as he has written poetry. *The Eye of the Needle* and *Trouvailles* (a collection of found poems) gather his most familiar observations on Canadian politics, history, literature, class structure, bi-culturalism, and social stupidities – the subjects of his co-edited anthology of "satire, invective and disrespectful verse."

That Scott should have received a Governor-General's Award, not for his poetry but for the retrospective collection *Essays on the Constitution,* is itself ironic, notwithstanding his substantial contributions to Canadian law, legal education, and constitutional theory. The essays incorporate forty years' writing on civil liberties, federalism (both topics of a separate book), human rights, labour relations, public policy, and sovereignty – issues with which he had been actively involved since the beginning of his career as a professor of law. Scott is well-known for his participation in two major civil rights cases in Quebec during the 1950's, and for his role in the founding of the Co-operative Commonwealth Federation (C.C.F., now N.D.P.), the first successful democratic socialist party in Canada. Less known are his pamphlets and books on law and politics, both polemical and academic. As national chairman of the C.C.F., he co-authored a lengthy statement on the history and principles of the party, *Make This Your Canada.*

Scott's strong beliefs about the bilingual nature of Canadian federation are mirrored in his translations of Québécois poetry into English. His *Dialogue sur la Traduction* records progressively his various translations of Anne Hébert's "Tombeau des Rois," and his correspondence with her. His translated *Poems of French Canada* is evidence of his conviction that "translation is not only an art in itself, it is also an essential ingredient in Canada's political entity."

—Bruce Nesbitt

SERVICE, Robert (William). Canadian. Born in Preston, Lancashire, England, 16 January 1874; emigrated to Canada, 1894. Educated at Hill Head High School, Glasgow; University of Glasgow. Served as an ambulance driver, 1914–16, and in Canadian Army Intelligence, 1916–18. Married Germaine Bourgoin in 1913; one daughter. Worked in the Commercial Bank of Scotland; in the Canadian Bank of Commerce, Kamloops, 1904, Whitehorse, 1904–07, Dawson, 1908–10, and Victoria, 1910–12; War Correspondent, *Toronto Star,* 1912. Travelled in Russia, Africa and the South Seas; lived in France from 1912. *Died 11 September 1958.*

PUBLICATIONS

Collections

    Collected Poems.   1961.
    Later Collected Verse.   1965.

Verse

    Songs of a Sourdough.   1907.
    The Spell of the Yukon and Other Verses.   1907.
    Ballads of a Cheechako.   1909.
    Rhymes of a Rolling Stone.   1912.
    The Rhymes of a Red-Cross Man.   1916.
    Selected Poems.   1917.
    The Shooting of Dan McGrew and Other Verses.   1920.
    Ballads of a Bohemian.   1921.
    Complete Poetical Works.   1921; as *Collected Verse,* 1930.
    Complete Poems.   1933.
    Twenty Bath-Tub Ballads.   1939.
    Bar-Room Ballads.   1940.
    Complete Poems.   1940.
    Songs of a Sun-Lover.   1949.

Rhymes of a Roughneck. 1950.
Lyrics of a Lowbrow. 1951.
Rhymes of a Rebel. 1952.
Songs for My Supper. 1953.
Carols of an Old Codger. 1954.
More Collected Verse. 1955.
Rhymes for My Rags. 1956.
Songs of the High North. 1958.

Fiction

The Trail of '98. 1910.
The Pretender. 1914.
The Poisoned Paradise. 1922.
The Roughneck. 1923.
The Master of the Microbe. 1926.
The House of Fear. 1927.

Other

Why Not Grow Young? or, Living for Longevity. 1928.
Ploughman of the Moon: An Adventure in Memory. 1945.
Harper of Heaven: A Further Adventure in Memory. 1948.

Reading List: *Service* by Carl F. Klinck, 1976.

*   *   *

Robert Service arrived in Alaska too late for the Gold Rush of 1898, but his successful career rested almost exclusively on two narrative poems about it: "The Shooting of Dan McGrew" and "The Cremation of Sam McGee." He wrote these and other, similar *Songs of a Sourdough* (as he titled his first collection) largely to amuse companions in the Yukon where he worked in a bank. The popularity of this early work – 1,700 copies were sold from galley sheets alone, by word of mouth among the typesetters and proof-readers, apparently – insured Service's financial security. He further chronicled that final American horizon in *The Trail of '98*, a novel purporting to be "an authentic record ... tragic and moral in its implications" but which sacrificed characterization for melodrama and substituted lyrical flights about the terrain for psychological probing of motives and actions. Service seems to have read little, declaring late in life, "The Classics! Well, most of them bore me/The Moderns I don't understand." He aspired to be "The Bret Harte of the Northland," however, and obviously he knew the work of such oddly matched influences as Rudyard Kipling and Eugene Field.

Service abandoned the Yukon for France shortly after his early success and never returned. His popular verse narratives about Claw-Fingered Kitty, Pious Pete, One-Eyed Mike, The Dago Kid, Gum-Boot Ben, and Muckluck Meg afforded him the leisure to please readers content with romanticized tragedies and comic turns decked out in neat rhymes. (Service later guessed he had written about 30,000 couplets during his career.) Other novels followed as well, all either mysterious, violent, coarse, or lurid: *The Pretender* is about the literary life in the Latin Quarter before the First World War; *The Poisoned Paradise* complicates the same subject with gambling during the 1920's; *The House of Fear*, an overwrought gothic horror story, concluded his half-dozen ventures in this genre.

Some of Service's war poems, in *The Rhymes of a Red-Cross Man*, are of interest because they capture conflicting attitudes toward patriotism and fear through the colloquial speech of enlisted men. Two volumes of autobiography, although of little historical value, offer a readable account of a comfortable man well aware of his modest talents. "For God-sake, don't call me a poet,/For I've never been guilty of that," he wrote in one of the rhymed homilies that filled some 2,000 pages of published work. Well into his eighties, he wrote to his publisher: "Alas, my belly is concave,/My locks no longer wavy;/But though I've one foot in the grave,/The other's in the gravy."

Robert Service was probably too aware of his limitations to be an entirely successful novelist: his own sense of irony too often takes over, alienating his readers from his characters. This is particularly true in *The Trail of '98*, his most valuable work of fiction. His verse narratives, however, are always likely to draw readers who enjoy romance and adventure laced with inexhaustible rhyme and wit.

—Bruce Kellner

SEXTON, Anne (Harvey).   Born in Newton, Massachusetts, 9 November 1928. Educated at Garland Junior College, Boston, 1947–48. Married Alfred M. Sexton in 1948 (divorced, 1974); two daughters. Fashion Model, Boston, 1950–51; Scholar, Radcliffe Institute for Independent Study, Cambridge, Massachusetts, 1961–63; Teacher, Wayland High School, Massachusetts, 1967–68; Lecturer in Creative Writing, 1970–71, and Professor of Creative Writing, 1972–74, Boston University. Crawshaw Professor of Literature, Colgate University, Hamilton, New York, 1972. Recipient: Bread Loaf Writers Conference Robert Frost Fellowship, 1959; American Academy of Arts and Letters Traveling Fellowship, 1963; Ford Foundation grant, 1964; Shelley Memorial Award, 1967; Pulitzer Prize, 1967; Guggenheim Fellowship, 1969. Litt.D.: Tufts University, Medford, Massachusetts, 1970; Regis College, Weston, Massachusetts, 1971; Fairfield University, Connecticut, 1971. Honorary Member, Phi Beta Kappa, 1968. *Died 4 October 1974.*

PUBLICATIONS

Verse

To Bedlam and Part Way Back.   1960.
All My Pretty Ones.   1962.
Selected Poems.   1964.
Live or Die.   1966.
Poems, with Douglas Livingstone and Thomas Kinsella.   1968.
Love Poems.   1969.
Transformations.   1971.
The Book of Folly.   1972.
O Ye Tongues.   1973.

The Death Notebooks. 1974.
The Awful Rowing Towards God. 1975.
45 Mercy Street, edited by Linda Gray Sexton. 1976.

Play

Mercy Street (produced 1969).

Other

Eggs of Things (juvenile), with Maxine Kumin. 1963.
More Eggs of Things (juvenile), with Maxine Kumin. 1964.
Joey and the Birthday Present (juvenile), with Maxine Kumin. 1971.
The Wizard's Tears (juvenile), with Maxine Kumin. 1975.
Sexton: A Self-Portrait in Letters, edited by Linda Gray Sexton and Lois Ames. 1977.

Bibliography: *Sylvia Plath and Sexton: A Reference Guide* by Cameron Northouse and Thomas P. Walsh, 1975.

Reading List: *Sexton: The Artist and Her Critics* edited by J. D. McClatchy, 1978.

* * *

Anne Sexton is known primarily for her remarkable imagery and apparent personal honesty in poems ranging from the formally structured early work (*To Bedlam and Part Way Back*) to the quasi-humorous prose poems of *Transformations* and the evocative free form poetry of *Love Poems*. Sexton had published much of her most mature work in the years immediately preceeding her evident suicide, and her critical reputation has yet to acknowledge that last productive period.

Sexton was a model who married, reared two daughters, and came to poetry through a workshop at Boston University conducted by Robert Lowell. Influenced by Lowell and the writing of W. D. Snodgrass to break the restraint and intellectualism common to American poetry during the 1950's, Sexton wrote such moving personal poems as "The Double Image." Her consideration here of the relationship among a mother, daughter, and grandchild is important not only for the technical prowess with which she handled a possibly sentimental subject, but for the genuine insight into the women's condition. Encouraged by her friendship with Sylvia Plath, who also was a student in the Lowell workshop, Sexton mined areas of theme and image that were virtually unknown to contemporary poetry. "Those Times" re-creates her own childhood as a time of torment; "Little Girl, My String Bean, My Lovely Woman" celebrates her joy in her daughter; "Flee on Your Donkey" plumbs the depths of personal despair; "Menstruation at Forty" questions the mortality image from a feminine view – most of Sexton's poems are adventurous in that she is writing not only about unconventional subjects, but her quick progression from image to image lends an almost surreal effect to the poetry.

Rather than simply describing Sexton's work as "confessional," the over-used label that attached itself to any writing that seemed autobiographical in origin (as what poetry is, finally, not?), readers should be aware that her work manages to distill the apparently autobiographical details into an imagistic whole which convinces any reader of its authenticity. The life in Sexton's poems is the life of the imagination, regardless of whether or not she has used the facts from her own existence in the re-creation of that life. Once the poems from the late collections have been assimilated with the earlier work, her continuous interest in religious themes and images will become as noticeable as her use of feminine psychology and concerns. Sexton's importance to American poetry will not rest simply on her mental stability or instability, her suicide, or her use of personal detail in her work; her importance will rest, finally, on her ability to craft poems that moved the reader to the act of understanding.

—Linda W. Wagner

SHAPIRO, Karl (Jay).   Born in Baltimore, Maryland, 10 November 1913. Educated at the University of Virginia, Charlottesville, 1932–33; Johns Hopkins University, Baltimore, 1937–39; Pratt Library School, Baltimore, 1940. Served in the United States Army, 1941–45. Married 1) Evalyn Katz in 1945 (divorced, 1967); 2) Teri Kovach in 1969; two daughters, and one son. Associate Professor of Writing, Johns Hopkins University, 1947–50; Visiting Professor, University of Wisconsin, Madison, 1948, and Loyola University, Chicago, 1951–52; Lecturer, Salzburg Seminar in American Studies, 1952; State Department Lecturer, India, 1955; Visiting Professor, University of California, Berkeley and Davis, 1955–56, and University of Indiana, Bloomington, 1956–57; Professor of English, University of Nebraska, Lincoln, 1956–66, and University of Illinois, Chicago Circle, 1966–68. Since 1968, Professor of English, University of California at Davis. Editor, *Poetry*, Chicago, 1950–56, *Newberry Library Bulletin*, Chicago, 1953–55, and *Prairie Schooner*, Lincoln, Nebraska, 1956–66. Consultant in Poetry, Library of Congress, Washington, D.C., 1946–47. Recipient: National Institute of Arts and Letters grant, 1944; Guggenheim Fellowship, 1944, 1953; Pulitzer Prize, 1945; Shelley Memorial Award, 1946; Kenyon School of Letters Fellowship, 1956, 1957; Bollingen Prize, 1969. D.H.L.: Wayne State University, Detroit, 1960; D.Litt.: Bucknell University, Lewisburg, Pennsylvania, 1972. Fellow in American Letters, Library of Congress; Member, American Academy of Arts and Sciences, and National Institute of Arts and Letters. Lives in Davis, California.

PUBLICATIONS

Verse

    Poems. 1935.
    Five Young American Poets, with others. 1941.
    Person, Place, and Thing. 1942.
    The Place of Love. 1942.
    V-Letter and Other Poems. 1944.
    Essay on Rime. 1945.
    Trial of a Poet and Other Poems. 1947.
    Poems 1940–1953. 1953.
    The House. 1957.
    Poems of a Jew. 1958.
    The Bourgeois Poet. 1964.
    Selected Poems. 1968.
    White-Haired Lover. 1968.

Adult Bookstore.   1976.
Collected Poems 1940–1977.   1978.

Play

The Tenor, music by Hugo Weisgall.   1956.

Fiction

Edsel.   1970.

Other

Poets at Work: Essays Based on the Modern Poetry Collection at the Lockwood Memorial Library, University of Buffalo, with others, edited by Charles D. Abbot.   1948.
English Prosody and Modern Poetry.   1947.
A Bibliography of Modern Prosody.   1948.
Beyond Criticism.   1953; as *A Primer for Poets,* 1965.
In Defense of Ignorance (essays).   1960.
Start with the Sun: Studies in Cosmic Poetry, with James E. Miller, Jr., and Bernice Slote.   1960.
A Prosody Handbook, with Robert Beum.   1965.
Randall Jarrell.   1967.
To Abolish Children and Other Essays.   1968.
The Poetry Wreck: Selected Essays 1950–1970.   1975.

Editor, with W. H. Auden and Marianne Moore, *Riverside Poetry 1953: Poems by Students in Colleges and Universities in New York City.*   1953.
Editor, *American Poetry.*   1960.
Editor, *Prose Keys to Modern Poetry.*   1962.

Bibliography: *Shapiro: A Bibliography* by William White, 1960.

*   *   *

Karl Shapiro is a poet of great versatility who has a sophisticated command of prosody and a sharp ear for speech rhythms and verbal harmonies. He is a man of considerable erudition, though he never finished college, and a serious though good-humored social critic. Since his first volume of poems in 1935, he has published continuously. As poet and critic, he always has taken an iconoclastic stance. He attacks intellectual poetry, poseurs, stuffed shirts, and the establishment with great vigor, and as a result has been a controversial figure. As editor of *Poetry* and *The Prairie Schooner* for 16 years, he was a significant force in contemporary poetry, and as a professor he has taught two decades of aspiring writers.

When Shapiro published *Selected Poems,* he ignored his first volume, about which he writes in "Recapitulations":

> My first small book was nourished in the dark,
> Secretly written, published, and inscribed.
> Bound in wine-red, it made no brilliant mark.
> Rather impossible relatives subscribed.

His first recognition came in 1941 when he appeared in *Five Young American Poets*. His next volume, *Person, Place, and Thing*, contains excellent poems of social comment in traditional form. "The Dome of Sunday" comments in sharp, clear imagery cast in blank verse on urban "Row houses and row-lives"; "Drug Store" observes youth culture satirically in unrhymed stanzas; "University [of Virginia]" mounts a low-keyed attack: "To hurt the Negro and avoid the Jew/Is the curriculum."

V-Letter and Other Poems contains some of the best poems to come out of World War II, some of which are "V-Letter," "Elegy for a Dead Soldier," "Troop Train," "The Gun," "Sunday: New Guinea," and "Christmas Eve: Australia." The form usually is rhymed stanzas, even *terza rima*, and here Shapiro's social comment finds a wider context. There also begin to be foreshadowings of later preoccupations: religious themes and attacks on intellectualism. "The Jew" anticipates *Poems of a Jew*, and "The Intellectual" ("I'd rather be a barber and cut hair/Than walk with you in gilt museum halls") looks toward attacks on Pound and Eliot in *In Defense of Ignorance*.

Although Shapiro does not write long poems (the exception is *Essay on Rime*, a youthful treatise on the art of poetry in which "Everything was going to be straightened out"), *Poems 1940–1953* contains an evocative, seven-part sequence telling the story of Adam and Eve. (This interest in myth reasserts itself in *Adult Bookstore* in a poignant version in 260 lines of "The Rape of Philomel.") This volume also contains "Israel," occasioned by the founding of that country: "When I see the name of Israel high in print/The fences crumble in my flesh.... " As a boy Shapiro grew up in a Russian-Jewish family not particularly religious, and after his bar mitzvah "I lost all interest in what I had learned." But *Poems of a Jew* explores his Jewishness with pride, wit, and irony, beginning with "The Alphabet" ("letters ... strict as flames," "black and clean" and bristling "like barbed wire").

As early as 1942 Shapiro had published a prose-poem, "The Dirty Word," but in 1964 he turned to this form exclusively in *The Bourgeois Poet*, dropping the kind of verses he previously had thought best, "the poem with a beginning, a middle, and an end ... that used literary allusion and rhythmic structuring and intellectual argument." He wanted a medium in which he could say anything he pleased – ridiculous, nonsensical, obscene, autobiographical, pompous. The individual pieces cover a wide variety of topics and, as earlier, they comment on persons, places, things. The longest (14 pages), "I Am an Atheist Who Says His Prayers," which reminds one of Shapiro's enthusiasm for Whitman, could have been called "Song of Myself." These prose poems (or free verse set as prose paragraphs) had a mixed reception. But Adrienne Rich noted that in his new style Shapiro was going through a "constant revising and purifying of his speech," as all poets must, and she thought parts of this volume were "a stunning success."

In *White-Haired Lover*, a cycle of middle-aged love poems, Shapiro returned to traditional forms, often the sonnet. This also is true of *Adult Bookstore*, a collection that ranges widely in subject. "The Humanities Building," "A Parliament of Poets," and the title poem show that Shapiro has not lost the wit, irony, and technique that have always characterized his work. "The Heiligenstadt Testament" is a splendid dramatic monologue of Beethoven's deathbed delirium, and among the poems occasioned by his move to California are "Garage Sale" ("This situation .../Strikes one as a cultural masterpeice") and a perfect Petrarchan sonnet on freeways and California suburbia.

The Poetry Wreck, which contains Shapiro's most important critical statements, throws light on his poetry, his sources, his beliefs. The derogatory essays on Pound and Eliot are reprinted along with admiring appraisals of W. H. Auden ("Eliot and Pound had rid the poem of emotion completely ... Auden reversed the process"), William Carlos Williams, "whose entire literary career has been dedicated to the struggle to preserve spontaneity and immediacy of experience," Whitman, Dylan Thomas, Henry Miller, and Randall Jarrell. Jarrell, whose "poetry I admired and looked up to most after William Carlos Williams," once said in a passage Shapiro quotes: "Karl Shapiro's poems are fresh and young and rash and live; their hard clear outline, their flat bold colors create a world like that of a knowing and skillful neo-primitive painting, without any of the confusion or profundity of atmosphere, or aerial perspective, but with notable visual and satiric force."

—James Woodress

SIMPSON, Louis (Aston Marantz). American. Born in Jamaica, West Indies, 27 March 1923; became a U.S. citizen. Educated at Munro College, Jamaica, 1933–40, Cambridge Higher Schools Certificate 1940; Columbia University, New York, B.S. 1948, A.M. 1950, Ph.D. 1959. Served in the United States Army, 1943–45: Purple Heart and Bronze Star. Married 1) Jeanne Claire Rogers in 1949 (divorced, 1954), one son; 2) Dorothy Roochvarg in 1955, one son and one daughter. Editor, Bobbs-Merrill Publishing Company, New York, 1950–55; Instructor, Columbia University, 1955–59; Professor of English, University of California, Berkeley, 1959–67. Since 1967, Professor of English, State University of New York at Stony Brook. Recipient: American Academy in Rome Fellowship, 1957; Edna St. Vincent Millay Award, 1960; Guggenheim Fellowship, 1962, 1970; American Council of Learned Societies Grant, 1963; Pulitzer Prize, 1964; Columbia University Medal for Excellence, 1965; American Academy of Arts and Letters award, 1976. Lives in Port Jefferson, New York.

PUBLICATIONS

Verse

The Arrivistes: Poems 1940–1949.   1949.
Good News of Death and Other Poems.   1955.
A Dream of Governors.   1959.
At the End of the Open Road.   1963.
Five American Poets, with others, edited by Thom Gunn and Ted Hughes.   1963.
Selected Poems.   1965.
Adventures of the Letter I.   1971.
Searching for the Ox: New Poems and a Preface.   1976.

Plays

The Father Out of the Machine: A Masque, in Chicago Review, Winter 1951.
Andromeda, in Hudson Review, Winter 1956.

Fiction

Riverside Drive.   1962.

Other

James Hogg: A Critical Study. 1962.
Air with Armed Men (autobiography). 1972; as *North of Jamaica,* 1972.
Three on the Tower: The Lives and Works of Ezra Pound, T. S. Eliot, and William Carlos Williams. 1975.

Editor, with Donald Hall and Robert Pack, *New Poets of England and America.* 1957.
Editor, *An Introduction to Poetry.* 1967.

Reading List: *Simpson* by Ronald Moran, 1972.

*   *   *

Always more of a "paleface" than a "redskin" (to adopt Philip Rahv's famous categorization of American writers), Louis Simpson took some time to find his own poetic voice. His early poetry is heavily dependent on John Crowe Ransom, and much of the work of his first two volumes, *The Arrivistes* and *Good News of Death,* seems to derive from art rather than life. The exception comes with a remarkable group of war poems, especially "Carentan O Carentan" and "The Battle," which, with the exception of Randall Jarrell's, seem to me the best poems to have come from American poets' confrontation with World War II.

A Dream of Governors is a tired, "literary" volume, full of echoes of such poets as Nemerov, Hecht, and Wilbur, all of them more polished performers than Simpson himself. Reading it, you feel that Simpson's talent is all but dead. But *At the End of the Open Road* achieves a remarkable break-through. Gone are the formal posturings, the conventional subjects, the making of poems out of poems, that featured so heavily in the earlier volumes. It is as though Simpson has suddenly found his true subject, and with it an answerable style. Instead of trying to be like other poets, he is now content to be himself: he lets his Jewishness into the poetry, his sense of being something of an outcast, but an outcast who nevertheless knows he belongs to America, and who therefore sets out to celebrate his country, whenever he can find it and whatever it may prove to be. As the title of the volume hints, Simpson turns, as so many American poets have found themselves turning, to Walt Whitman. The Whitman he responds most deeply to is the poet who could embrace multitudes, engage contradictions, responsibly accept irresponsibility: whose gigantic achievement was to perceive the noble folly of American dreams. "All the grave weight of America/Cancelled! Like Greece and Rome./The future in ruins." Those lines come from "Walt Whitman at Bear Mountain," one of Simpson's best poems.

Most of the poems of *At the End of the Open Road* are written in an informal, loose-limbed manner, which more powerfully and convincingly convey the sense of a personal voice than the earlier poems had managed to do. And where Simpson does return to a more formal mode, as in the extraordinarily fine, wittily melancholic "My Father in the Night Commanding No," he does it without leaning on any other poet. Some of the finest poems in this remarkable volume are ones where Simpson broods on the inescapable fact of his Jewishness. He prods at it like an aching tooth, fascinated by it, yet fearing the pain it causes. The best of these is undoubtedly "A Story about Chicken Soup."

In *Adventures of the Letter I,* Simpson attempted to make further use of the style he had discovered for himself: musing, wryly observant, quizzical, contemplative. I think of it as a volume in which Simpson is marking time. There are no poems in it as good as the best of the previous volume; and yet it is an utterly readable, enjoyable piece of work by a poet who, having found his own voice, can be relied on not to bore. Like Whitman, Simpson has become at the very least a good companion.

—John Lucas

SITWELL, Dame Edith.   English.   Born in Scarborough, Yorkshire, 7 September 1887; sister of the poets Sir Osbert Sitwell, *q.v.*, and Sir Sacheverell Sitwell, *q.v.* Educated privately at her father's house, Renishaw Hall, Derbyshire. Visiting Professor, Institute of Contemporary Arts, London, 1957. Recipient: Royal Society of Literature Benson Medal, 1934; Foyle Poetry Prize, 1958; Guinness Poetry Award, 1959. Litt.D.: University of Leeds, 1948; D.Litt.: University of Durham, 1948; Oxford University, 1951; University of Sheffield, 1955; University of Hull, 1963. Honorary Associate, American Institute of Arts and Letters, 1949. Vice-President, 1958, and Companion of Literature, 1963, Royal Society of Literature. D.B.E. (Dame Commander, Order of the British Empire), 1954. *Died 9 December 1964.*

PUBLICATIONS

Collections

   Fire of the Mind (selections), edited by Elizabeth Salter and Allanah Harper, 1976.

Verse

   The Mother and Other Poems.   1915.
   Twentieth-Century Harlequinade and Other Poems, with Osbert Sitwell.   1916.
   Clowns' Houses.   1918.
   The Wooden Pegasus.   1920.
   Façade, music by William Walton.   1922.
   Bucolic Comedies.   1923.
   The Sleeping Beauty.   1924.
   Troy Park.   1925.
   Poor Young People and Other Poems, with Osbert and Sacheverell Sitwell.   1925.
   Elegy on Dead Fashion.   1926.
   Poem for a Christmas Card.   1926.
   Rustic Elegies.   1927.
   Five Poems.   1928.
   Gold Coast Customs.   1929.
   Collected Poems.   1930.
   In Spring.   1931.
   Epithalamium.   1931.
   Five Variations on a Theme.   1933.
   Selected Poems, with an Essay.   1936.
   Poems New and Old.   1940.
   Street Songs.   1942.
   Green Song and Other Poems.   1944.
   The Weeping Babe: Motet for Soprano Solo and Mixed Choir, music by Michael
      Tippett.   1945.
   The Song of the Cold.   1945; revised edition, 1948.
   The Shadow of Cain.   1947.
   The Canticle of the Rose: Selected Poems 1920–1947.   1949.
   Poor Men's Music.   1950.
   Façade and Other Poems.   1950.
   Selected Poems.   1952.
   Gardeners and Astronomers.   1953.

Collected Poems.   1954.
(Poems).   1960.
The Outcasts.   1962; augmented edition, as Music and Ceremonies, 1963.

Plays

The Sleeping Beauty (masque), music by Leighton Lucas (produced 1936).
The Last Party (radio play), in Twelve Modern Plays, edited by J. Hampden.   1938.

Fiction

I Live under a Black Sun.   1937.

Other

Children's Tales from the Russian Ballet.   1920; as The Russian Ballet Gift Book, 1922.
Poetry and Criticism.   1925.
Alexander Pope.   1930.
Bath.   1932.
The English Eccentrics.   1933; revised edition, 1957.
Aspects of Modern Poetry.   1934.
Victoria of England.   1936.
Trio: Dissertations on Some Aspects of National Genius, with Osbert and Sacheverell
    Sitwell.   1938.
English Women.   1942.
A Poet's Notebook.   1943; revised edition, 1950.
Fanfare for Elizabeth.   1946.
A Notebook on William Shakespeare.   1948.
The Queens and the Hive.   1962.
Taken Care Of: An Autobiography.   1965.
Selected Letters, 1919–1964, edited by John Lehmann and Derek Parker.   1970.

Editor and Contributor, Wheels.   6 vols., 1916–21.
Editor, The Pleasures of Poetry: A Critical Anthology.   3 vols., 1930–32.
Editor, Edith Sitwell's Anthology.   1940.
Editor, Look! The Sun (anthology of poetry).   1941.
Editor, Planet and Glow-Worm: A Book for the Sleepless.   1944.
Editor, A Book of Winter.   1950.
Editor, The American Genius: An Anthology of Poetry, with Some Prose.   1951.
Editor, A Book of Flowers.   1952.
Editor, The Atlantic Book of British and American Poetry.   1958.
Editor, Poems of Our Time 1900–1960 (supplement only).   1959.
Editor, Swinburne: A Selection.   1960.

Bibliography: A Bibliography of Edith, Osbert, and Sacheverell Sitwell by Richard Fifoot,
1963; revised edition, 1976.

Reading List: The Three Sitwells by R. L. Mégroz, 1927; A Celebration for Sitwell: Essays
edited by José Garcia Villa, 1948; Triad of Genius by M. Wykes-Jones, 1953; Sitwell: The
Hymn to Life by G. Singleton, 1961; Sitwell: A Critical Essay by Ralph J. Mills, Jr., 1966;

The Last Years of a Rebel: A Memoir of Sitwell by Elizabeth Salter, 1967; *Sitwell: The Symbolist Order* by J. D. Brophy, 1968; *A Nest of Tigers: Edith, Osbert, and Sacheverell Sitwell in Their Times* by John Lehmann, 1968.

*   *   *

During her lifetime, there were vehement differences of opinion about the worth of Edith Sitwell's poetry. Since her death it has attracted little serious criticism. She was her own worst enemy, courting attention by almost mountebank behaviour, deliberately provoking attack and then reacting with insolence or even spite. Yet she was not a charlatan, as her detractors alleged. She was a dedicated poet, passionately interested in revitalising the language of poetry through technical innovations.

She and her two equally remarkable brothers belonged to the artistic avant-garde of the early 1920's, on whom Diaghilev's Russian Ballet made an ineradicable impression. Edith Sitwell's earlier poems are highly stylised, indeed deliberately artificial. Their rhythms reflect those of the dance, their dominant imagery is pastoral or fairy-tale. *Façade*, in which she collaborated with William Walton, has had a more than ephemeral success. The lyrics on the printed page may seem, at best, engaging trivia; spoken or chanted, the verbal patterns offset by the musical, their artistic value is doubled.

Edith Sitwell's poetry was always inventive. Her feeling for individual words was sensuous. For her they possessed texture, colour, and weight as well as sonority. She valued poems as artefacts, and her own for two decades were remarkable for surface brilliance and ingenuity rather than for any depth of feeling, far less intensity of thought. World War II however had a profound effect on her. The volumes published during the 1940's contain poems far more serious and moving than their predecessors. The three Poems for an Atomic Age, particularly "The Shadow of Cain," are remarkable expressions of anguish, as is the rather earlier "Still Falls the Rain."

Edith Sitwell's approach to poetics, as to criticism and biography, was essentially non-academic. Her biographical study of Pope manifested a sympathetic appreciation of his artistry and wit at a time when his poetry was still undervalued. *A Poet's Notebook* affords a good insight into her mind, revealing the eclecticism of her taste and her serious (if highly idiosyncratic) engagement with major as well as minor English and French writers. She was able to recognise creative promise in the living, and launched Dylan Thomas into the literary world of London. A fastidious writer of prose, she developed in *English Eccentrics* biographical themes that suited her admirably. For she was, though too self-consciously, an eccentric, a non-conformist, prepared at all times to assert her own convictions. She deliberately cultivated an aristocratic stance (to which she was entitled by birth), and enhanced her Gothic beauty with spectacular clothes. Many were alienated by her theatricality and offended by her arrogance. Nevertheless, she took her art extremely seriously, and at her best could communicate an original vision with a fine command of rhythm, imagery, and diction.

—Margaret Bottrall

SITWELL, Sir (Francis) Osbert; 5th baronet, 1942. English. Born in London, 6 December 1892; brother of the poets Dame Edith Sitwell, *q.v.*, and Sir Sacheverell Sitwell, *q.v.* Educated at Eton College. Served as a Captain in the Grenadier Guards, 1912–18, and fought in France; invalided home, 1916. With his brother Sacheverell, and others, organized the Exhibition of Modern French Art, London, 1919. Justice of the Peace, Derbyshire, 1939; Chairman, Management Committee, Society of Authors, London, 1944–45, 1946–48, 1951–53; Trustee, Tate Gallery, London, 1951–58. LL.D.: University of St. Andrews, Scotland, 1946; D.Litt.: University of Sheffield, 1951. Fellow, and Companion of Literature, 1967, Royal Society of Literature. Honorary Associate, American Academy of Arts and Letters, 1950; Honorary Fellow, Royal Institute of British Architects, 1957. C.B.E. (Commander, Order of the British Empire), 1956; C.H. (Companion of Honour), 1958. *Died 4 May 1969.*

PUBLICATIONS

Verse

Twentieth-Century Harlequinade and Other Poems, with Edith Sitwell.   1916.
The Winstonburg Line: 3 Satires.   1919.
Argonaut and Juggernaut.   1919.
At the House of Mrs. Kinfoot: Consisting of Four Satires.   1921.
Out of the Flame.   1923.
Poor Young People and Other Poems, with Edith and Sacheverell Sitwell.   1925.
England Reclaimed: A Book of Eclogues.   1927; *Wrack at Tidesend: A Book of Balnearics,* 1952; *On the Continent: A Book of Inquilinics,* 1958; complete version, as *Poems about People; or, England Reclaimed,* 1965.
Miss Mew.   1929.
Collected Satires and Poems.   1931.
Three-Quarter Length Portrait of Michael Arlen.   1931.
A Three-Quarter Length Portrait of Viscountess Wimborne.   1931.
Mrs. Kimber.   1937.
Selected Poems Old and New.   1943.
Four Songs of the Italian Earth.   1948.
England Reclaimed and Other Poems.   1949.

Plays

All at Sea: A Social Tragedy for First-Class Passengers Only, with Sacheverell Sitwell (as *For First Class Passengers Only,* produced 1927).   1927.
Gentle Caesar, with Rubeigh J. Minney.   1942.
Demos the Emperor: A Secular Oratorio.   1948.

Fiction

Triple Fugue (stories).   1924.
Before the Bombardment.   1926.
The Man Who Lost Himself.   1929.
Dumb-Animal and Other Stories.   1930.
Miracle on Sinai: A Satirical Novel.   1933.
Those Were the Days: Panorama with Figures.   1938.
Open the Door! A Volume of Stories.   1941.
A Place of One's Own.   1941.
The True Story of Dick Whittington: A Christmas Story of Cat-Lovers.   1945.

Alive – Alive Oh! and Other Stories.   1947.
Death of a God and Other Stories.   1949.
Collected Stories.   1953.
Fee Fi Fo Fum! A Book of Fairy Stories.   1959.
A Place of One's Own and Other Stories.   1961.

Other

Who Killed Cock Robin? Remarks on Poetry, On Criticism, and, as a Sad Warning, The Story of Eunuch Arden.   1921.
Discursions on Travel, Art, and Life.   1925.
C. R. W. Nevinson.   1925.
The People's Album of London Statues, illustrated by Nina Hamnett.   1928.
Dickens.   1932.
Winters of Content: More Discursions on Travel, Art, and Life.   1932.
Brighton, with Margaret Barton.   1935.
Penny Foolish: A Book of Tirades and Panegyrics.   1935.
Trio: Dissertations on Some Aspects of National Genius, with Edith and Sacheverell Sitwell.   1938.
Escape with Me! An Oriental Sketch-Book.   1939.
Sing High! Sing Low! A Book of Essays.   1944.
A Letter to My Son.   1944.
Left Hand, Right Hand! An Autobiography: Left Hand, Right Hand!   1944 (as *The Cruel Month,* 1945); *The Scarlet Tree,* 1946; *Great Morning!,* 1947; *Laughter in the Next Room,* 1948; *Noble Essences or Courteous Revelations, Being a Book of Characters,* 1950.
Winters of Content and Other Discursions on Mediterranean Art and Travel.   1950.
The Four Continents, Being More Discursions on Travel, Art, and Life.   1954.
Tales My Father Taught Me: An Evocation of Extravagant Episodes (autobiography).   1962.
Pound Wise (essays).   1963.
Queen Mary and Others (essays).   1974.

Editor, with Margaret Barton, *Sober Truth: A Collection of Nineteenth-Century Episodes, Fantastic, Grotesque, and Mysterious.*   1930.
Editor, with Margaret Barton, *Victoriana: A Symposium of Victorian Wisdom.*   1931.
Editor, *Belshazzar's Feast,* music by William Walton.   1931.
Editor, *Two Generations* (writings by Georgiana Caroline Sitwell and Florence Alice Sitwell).   1940.
Editor, *A Free House! or, The Artist as Craftsman, Being the Writings of W. R. Sickert.*   1947.

Bibliography: *A Bibliography of Edith, Osbert, and Sacheverell Sitwell* by Richard Fifoot, 1963; revised edition, 1976.

Reading List: *The Three Sitwells* by R. L. Mégroz, 1927; *Sitwell* by Roger Fulford, 1951; *Triad of Genius* by M. Wykes-Jones, 1953; *A Nest of Tigers: Edith, Osbert, and Sacheverell Sitwell in Their Times* by John Lehmann, 1968.

*   *   *

Sir Osbert Sitwell's early works showed talent but an uncertain sense of direction. As a poet, with a taste for the grotesque and odd but not for direct satire, and lacking a lyrical voice, he came a poor third to his sister Edith and his brother Sacheverell. A novel like *Before the Bombardment* and a set of stories like *Triple Fugue* owed perhaps, as Evelyn Waugh suggested, something to the grotesque fantasies of Ronald Firbank but there was something morose about the humour, and even a certain glum pity.

It was not until the set of five autobiographies, named after the opening volume *Left Hand, Right Hand*, and published after the Second World War, that Sir Osbert's gifts expressed themselves richly and fully. In his father, Sir George Reresby Sitwell, he had to his hand, or from the facts of memory created, one of the great comic characters in English fiction, and in the loyal valet Henry Moat a sort of Sancho Panza to Sir George's Don Quixote. It is interesting how the treatment of Sir George becomes more and more affectionate as the autobiography progresses. Sir George was not at all an evil man, but he was completely self-centred, though with some interests, like that in ornamental gardens, which his children shared. He was incapable of even trying to grasp anybody else's point of view. But Sir Osbert gradually comes to see that the pain he inflicted on his family was not deliberate and that he compensated, in a way, as they grew older, by presenting them with the delight of a living legend. The richness of Sir Osbert's own sense of scene and character and his brilliant gift for digression give him in the end a legendary quality himself.

—G. S. Fraser

SITWELL, Sir Sacheverell; 6th baronet, 1969. Born in Scarborough, Yorkshire, 15 November 1897; younger brother of the poets Dame Edith Sitwell, *q.v.*, and Sir Osbert Sitwell, *q.v.* Educated at Eton College; Balliol College, Oxford. Served in the Grenadier Guards in World War I. Married Georgia Doble in 1925; two sons. With his brother Osbert, and others, organized the Exhibition of Modern French Art, London, 1919. Justice of the Peace, 1943; High Sheriff of Northamptonshire, 1948–49. Freeman, City of Lima, Peru, 1960. Lives in Towcester, Northamptonshire.

PUBLICATIONS

Verse

> *The People's Palace.*   1918.
> *The Parrot.*   1923.
> *Doctor Donne and Gargantua: First Canto.*   1921; *Canto the Second,* 1923; *Canto the Third,* 1926; *The First Six Cantos,* 1930.
> *The Hundred and One Harlequins.*   1922.
> *The Thirteenth Caesar and Other Poems.*   1924.
> *Poor Young People and Other Poems,* with Edith and Osbert Sitwell.   1925.
> *Exalt the Eglantine and Other Poems.*   1926.
> *The Cyder Feast and Other Poems.*   1927.
> *Two Poems, Ten Songs.*   1929.
> *Canons of Giant Art: Twenty Torsos in Heroic Landscapes.*   1933.

Collected Poems.   1936.
Selected Poems.   1948.
Tropicalia.   1972.
To Henry Woodward.   1972.
Agamemnon's Tomb.   1972.
Rosario d'Arabeschi, Basalla ("as the Moors call it") and Dionysia, A Triptych of Poems,
    The Strawberry Feast, Ruralia, To E. S., Variations upon Old Names of Hyacinths,
    Lily Poems, The Archipelago of Daffodils, A Charivari of Parrots, Flowering Cactus, A
    Look at Sowerby's English Mushrooms and Fungi, Auricula Theatre, Lyra Varia, The
    House of the Presbyter, Nigritian, Twelve Summer Poems of 1962, Doctor Donne and
    Gargantua (Cantos Seven and Eight), Badinerie, An Indian Summer, Temple of
    Segesta, L'Amour au Théâtre Italien, A Notebook on My New Poems, Nymphis et
    Fontibus, and Nymphaeum, A Pair of Entr'actes for August Evenings, A Second
    Triptych of Poems, Harlequinade, Brother and Sister: A Ballad of the Paralelo
    Tropicalia, Little Italy in London.   29 vols., 1972–77.
J. S. Bach, Liszt, Domenico Scarlatti, from "Credo; or, An Affirmation."   1976.

Plays

All at Sea: A Social Tragedy for First-Class Passengers Only, with Osbert Sitwell (as *For*
    First Class Passengers Only, produced 1927).   1927.

Ballet: *The Triumph of Neptune,* 1926.

Other

Southern Baroque Art: A Study of Painting, Architecture and Music in Italy and Spain of
    the 17th and 18th Centuries.   1924.
All Summer in a Day: An Autobiographical Fantasia.   1926.
German Baroque Art.   1927.
A Book of Towers and Other Buildings of Southern Europe.   1928.
The Gothick North: A Study of Medieval Life, Art, and Thought (The Visit of the Gypsies,
    These Sad Ruins, The Fair-Haired Victory).   1929.
Beckford and Beckfordism: An Essay.   1930.
Far From My Home: Stories: Long and Short.   1931.
Spanish Baroque Art: With Buildings in Portugal, Mexico, and Other Colonies.   1931.
Mozart.   1932.
Liszt.   1934; revised edition, 1955.
Touching the Orient: Six Sketches.   1934.
A Background for Domenico Scarlatti, 1685–1757; Written for His Two Hundred and
    Fiftieth Anniversary.   1935.
Dance of the Quick and the Dead: An Entertainment of the Imagination.   1936.
Conversation Pieces: A Survey of English Domestic Portraits and Their Painters.   1936.
Narrative Pictures: A Survey of English Genre and Its Painters.   1937.
La Vie Parisienne: A Tribute to Offenbach.   1937.
Roumanian Journey.   1938.
Edinburgh, with Francis Bamford.   1938.
German Baroque Sculpture.   1938.
Trio: Dissertations on Some Aspects of National Genius, with Edith and Osbert
    Sitwell.   1938.
The Romantic Ballet in Lithographs of the Time, with Cyril W. Beaumont.   1938.
Old Fashioned Flowers.   1939.

Mauretania: Warrior, Man, and Woman. 1940.

Poltergeists: An Introduction and Examination Followed by Chosen Instances. 1940.

Sacred and Profane Love. 1940.

Valse des Fleurs: A Day in St. Petersburg and a Ball at the Winter Palace in 1868. 1941.

Primitive Scenes and Festivals. 1942.

The Homing of the Winds and Other Passages in Prose. 1942.

Splendours and Miseries. 1943.

British Architects and Craftsmen: A Survey of Taste, Design, and Style During Three Centuries 1600 to 1830. 1945; revised edition, 1946.

The Hunters and the Hunted. 1947.

The Netherlands: A Study of Some Aspects of Art, Costume and Social Life. 1948; revised edition, 1974.

Morning, Noon and Night in London. 1948.

Theatrical Figures in Porcelain: German 18th Century. 1949.

Spain. 1950; revised edition, 1951.

Cupid and the Jacaranda. 1952.

Truffle Hunt with Sacheverell Sitwell. 1953.

Fine Bird Books 1700–1900, with Hanasyde Buchanan and James Fisher. 1953.

Selected Works. 1953.

Portugal and Madeira. 1954.

Old Garden Roses: Part One, with James Russell. 1955.

Selected Works. 1955.

Denmark. 1956.

Great Flower Books 1700–1900: A Bibliographical Record of Two Centuries of Finely-Illustrated Flower Books, with Wilfrid Blunt and Patrick M. Synge. 1956.

Arabesque and Honeycomb. 1957.

Malta. 1958.

Austria. 1959.

Lost in the Dark Wood (vol. 1 of *Journey to the Ends of Time*). 1959.

Bridge of the Brocade Sash: Travels and Observations in Japan. 1959.

Golden Wall and Mirador: From England to Peru. 1961.

The Red Chapels of Banteai Srei, and Temples in Cambodia, India, Siam, and Nepal. 1962; as *Great Temples of the East,* 1963.

Monks, Nuns, and Monasteries. 1965.

Southern Baroque Revisited. 1967.

Baroque and Rococo. 1967.

Gothic Europe. 1969.

For Want of a Golden City (autobiography). 1973.

The Netherlands. 1974.

Notebook on "Twenty Canons of Giant Art." 1976.

A Note for Bibliophiles. 1976.

A Study of J. S. Bach's Organ Preludes and Fugues. 1977.

Editor, *Gallery of Fashion 1790–1822, from Plates by Heideloff and Ackermann.* 1949.
Editor, *Great Houses of Europe,* photographs by E. Smith. 1961.

Bibliography: *A Bibliography of Edith, Osbert, and Sacheverell Sitwell* by Richard Fifoot, 1963; revised edition, 1976.

Reading List: *The Three Sitwells* by R. L. Mégroz, 1927; *Triad of Genius* by M. Wykes-Jones, 1953; *A Nest of Tigers: Edith, Osbert, and Sacheverell Sitwell in Their Times* by John

Lehmann, 1968; *Sitwell: A Symposium* edited by Derek Parker, 1975; *Hand and Eye* edited by Geoffrey Elborn, 1977.

*   *   *

Sir Sacheverell Sitwell is possibly the most productive but also the least obtrusive of the Sitwell trio, Edith, Osbert, and Sacheverell, of whom he was the youngest. His two earliest prose books, *Southern Baroque Art* and the poetic autobiographical fantasia *All Summer in a Day*, show his great gift, in which he perhaps excelled both his brother and sister, of combining picturesque but precise description with the evocation of a mood. He is a tremendous traveller, from Mauretania to Japan, and from Denmark to Spain, and anybody who has covered the same ground will find that Sir Sacheverell (he inherited the family baronetcy on the death of his brother Osbert) sharpens his own memory, and gives it more exactness. But travel is only one of his interests; he has written books on musicians as various as Offenbach and Mozart, on old garden roses, on British architects and craftsmen, on theatrical figures in porcelain, and a bibliographical study, written with collaborators, of great flower books. If one has a criticism of his enormous output in prose it is that though his eye and ear are magically alert he has never shown much curiosity about human character. The world for him is a raree-show, of which men and women are a very minor part. Yet he uses music, landscape, flowers, and architecture to evoke recurrent though evanescent human moods. Since his *Selected Poems* of 1948, the changes in poetic fashion have reduced publication of his verse. But a small press in Northamptonshire has published over 20 small volumes since 1972. They have probably had few readers, but they show an advance on his earlier work. He is a writer who awaits revaluation and rediscovery.

—G. S. Fraser

SLESSOR, Kenneth.   Australian. Born in Orange, New South Wales, 27 March 1901. Educated at Mowbray House School, Chatswood; North Shore School, Sydney, 1910–19; Sydney Grammar School. Married 1) Noela Senior in 1922 (died 1945); 2) Pauline Wallace in 1951 (marriage dissolved, 1961), one son. Reporter for *The Sun*, Sydney, 1920–24, 1926; a Founding Editor, *Vision*, 1923–24; staff member of *Punch*, Melbourne, and the *Melbourne Herald*, 1925; staff member, 1927, Associate Editor, 1936, and Editor, *Smith's Weekly*, Sydney, and Editor-in-Chief of Smith's Newspapers, 1939; Official War Correspondent for the Australian Forces in the U.K., the Middle East, Greece, and New Guinea, 1940–44; Leader Writer and Literary Editor of *The Sun*, Sydney, 1944–57; Editor of *Southerly*, Sydney, 1956–61; Leader Writer for the *Daily Telegraph*, Sydney, 1957–69. Member of the Advisory Board, Commonwealth Literary Fund, from 1953, and the National Literature Board of Review, from 1968. O.B.E. (Officer, Order of the British Empire), 1959. *Died in 1971.*

PUBLICATIONS

Verse

Thief of the Moon.   1924.
Earth-Visitors.   1926.

Trio, with Harley Matthews and Colin Simpson.   1931.
Darlinghurst Nights.   1931.
Cuckooz Contrey.   1932.
Five Bells: XX Poems.   1939.
One Hundred Poems, 1919–1939.   1944; revised edition, as *Poems*, 1957.

Other

Portrait of Sydney.   1951.
The Grapes Are Growing: The Story of Australian Wine.   1963.
Life at the Cross (on King's Cross, Sydney).   1965.
Canberra.   1966.
Bread and Wine: Selected Prose.   1970.

Editor, with Jack Lindsay, *Poetry in Australia.*   1923.
Editor, *Australian Poetry.*   1945.
Editor, with John Thompson and R. G. Howarth, *The Penguin Book of Australian Verse.*   1958.

Reading List: *Slessor* by Max Harris, 1963; *Slessor* by Graham Burns, 1963; *Slessor* by Clement Semmler, 1966; *Critical Essays on Slessor* edited by A. K. Thomson, 1968; *Slessor* by Herbert C. Jaffa, 1971.

*   *   *

Kenneth Slessor's considerable reputation in Australia as a poet rests on a collection of 104 poems containing what he wished to preserve. After 1947 he ceased to write verse, because, he said, he had nothing more to say. Slessor is given most of the credit for having introduced modernism into Australian poetry, and, along with his contemporary FitzGerald, he certainly announced many of the themes to be developed by younger writers: time, history, voyages, symbolic landscape. Slessor is also pre-eminently the poet of the city of Sydney and its harbour near which he lived most of his adult life. His excursions into the countryside produce little but images of horror and sterility.

Much of his work in the early 1920's was influenced by his association with the artist Norman Lindsay and his son Jack in literary enterprises intended to bring about a cultural renascence in Australia, free from "decadent" European modernism as well as from nationalism. The basis of these ideas was a woolly kind of Nietzscheanism, a rather frenzied vitalism which found curiously static expression in Norman Lindsay's drawings of satyrs and centaurs. Slessor's poems "Thieves' Kitchen," with its romantic abstractions, and "Marco Polo," with its decorative gestures and its undergraduate finale, for all their rhythmic energy are hardly less factitious than the drawings, though pieces like "Heine in Paris" and "Nuremburg" show a genuine individuality and a luxuriant imagination. Slessor's preoccupation with historical subjects was mainly a form of escape from an unsatisfactory present; history was not a process of which he was a living part and which required understanding. All Slessor's dissatisfactions with the modern world, his distress at the eternal flux of life, his sense of the frustration of man's aspirations, issue simply in rage or lamentation. There is no attempt to reason out an explanation why the world has come to be the way it is, no suggestion that poetry might contribute its mite towards the mitigation of human misery. A late poem like "Gulliver," for example, a horrifying indictment of man trapped in the trivialities of modern life, differs from the youthful "Marco Polo" only in its surface realism, its conversational tone, its physical immediacy. The yearning to be "anywhere but here" is the same.

The difference between Slessor and the poet he most resembles, Thomas Hardy, is instructive. Among the poets known to have influenced Slessor, Tennyson, de la Mare, Housman, and T. S. Eliot, Hardy's name is never mentioned. But his debt to Hardy is acknowledged in a short story Slessor wrote for the magazine *Vision* in 1923; it is clear that he took the image of the face trapped behind a pane of glass, which haunts his verse from first to last, from Hardy's "The Face at the Casement" on which he based his story. Hardy took a dim view of man's estate: man seemed to be nothing but the puppet of blind forces, a spectacle to make the gods yawn (as in Slessor's "The Old Play"). One may not like the metaphysic Hardy constructed to deal with the universe he saw, but at least it made possible a way of life not in danger of collapsing into dandyism. Slessor concurs with Hardy's pessimism, his nostalgia, but he has no countervailing argument: it is a concurrence only in mourning. Slessor remained a romantic throughout his career, but what appealed to him in romanticism was its grotesque, flamboyant aspects and a certain mindless sensuality, not its confrontation with a vision of what man might be.

Nevertheless, in spite of reservations about the intellectual content of Slessor's poems, his contribution towards liberating the language of Australian poetry can hardly be over-estimated, and, in spite of the contradictions of the *Vision* program (a national re-birth without nationalism), Slessor developed new lyrical energies in proliferating images and exploring rhythmical possibilities with a zest that denies the elegiac mood characteristic of so much of his verse. He and FitzGerald set new standards in poetry, Slessor in his dedication to technical perfection, FitzGerald in his insistence on solid content and precise thinking.

It is not surprising that an elegy is the peak of Slessor's achievement: the long poem *Five Bells* which re-lives the drowning of an artist friend in Sydney Harbour. All Slessor's preoccupations are gathered up in this poem: his favourite image, the pane of glass, which becomes the port-holes of space through which the dead man is desperately trying to communicate with the living: his other favourite image, the sea, whose eternal movement represents the flux, the destructive aspect of time; the harbour, which represents some sort of permanence within this flux; the sense of human alienation, of fruitful contacts, frustrated by separation or death; of self-alienation, the figure at the window watching a life in which he can never take part. The poem opens with the sound of ship's bells in the harbour marking the watches against a memorable vision of the water at night:

> Deep and dissolving verticals of light
> Ferry the falls of moonshine down. Five bells
> Coldly rung out in a machine's voice. Night and water
> Pour to one rip of darkness, the Harbour floats
> In air, the Cross hangs upside down in water.

The bell recalls the image of the dead Joe and starts off a series of agonised attempts to reconstruct his life and find a meaning in it. All Slessor can remember in the end are little disconnected episodes and the poem comes slowly to an end, not with the conclusion that there is nothing to know but that the poet himself is inadequate to the effort of knowing it. Like all good elegies, *Five Bells* is at once a cry of grief for a particular being and a lament for the general human condition. Protest against death is Slessor's most constant theme, but his anguish does not lead him into nihilism: he does not prefer non-being to the pain of knowing he must die. Slessor's defence against the charge of nihilism can be seen in the last two lines of "South Country," which indicates that death, the norm, is threatened by life, not the other way round: "Something below pushed up a knob of skull,/Feeling its way to air."

The poem "Sleep" reveals Slessor's facility in image-making. Here we find a single idea under the control of one dominating image, and the result is a perfect unity of form and concept. One of the last poems, "Beach Burial," is even more memorable, a triumph of vowel and consonantal music and rhythmical fitness, as well as a most moving and humble tribute to the drowned merchant seamen of the Second World War. *Bread and Wine*, a collection of his best journalistic pieces, includes some fine examples of his work as a war correspondent, as well as his rare literary criticism. The excellence of his prose makes one regret that so much of his talent was expended on ephemeral journalism.

—Dorothy Green

SMITH, A(rthur) J(ames) M(arshall).   American.   Born in Montreal, Quebec, Canada, 8 November 1902; emigrated to the United States, 1930; naturalized, 1941. Educated at McGill University, Montreal (Editor, *McGill Literary Supplement*), B.Sc. in arts 1925, M.A. 1926; University of Edinburgh, 1926–28, Ph.D. 1931. Married Jeannie Dougal Robins in 1927; one son. Assistant Professor, Ball State Teachers College, Muncie, Indiana, 1930–31; Instructor, Doane College, Crete, Nebraska, 1934–35; Assistant Professor, University of South Dakota, Vermillion, 1935–36. Instructor, 1931–33, since 1936 Member of the English Department, and since 1960 Professor of English and Poet-in-Residence, Michigan State University, East Lansing; now retired. Visiting Professor, University of Toronto, 1944–45, University of Washington, Seattle, 1949, Queen's University, Kingston, Ontario, 1952, 1960, University of British Columbia, Vancouver, 1956, Dalhousie University, Halifax, Nova Scota, 1966–67, Sir George Williams University, Montreal, Summers 1967, 1969, State University of New York at Stony Brook, 1969, and McGill University, 1969–70. Recipient: Guggenheim Fellowship, 1941, 1942; Governor-General's Award, 1944; Rockefeller Fellowship, 1944; Lorne Pierce Medal, 1966; Canada Centennial Medal, 1967; Canada Council Medal, 1968. D.Litt.: McGill University, 1958; LL.D.: Queen's University, 1966; Dalhousie University, 1969; D.C.L.: Bishop's University, Lennoxville, Quebec, 1967. Lives in East Lansing, Michigan.

PUBLICATIONS

Verse

> *News of the Phoenix and Other Poems.*   1943.
> *A Sort of Ecstasy: Poems New and Selected.*   1954.
> *Collected Poems.*   1962.
> *Poems: New and Collected.*   1967.

Other

> *Some Poems of E. J. Pratt: Aspects of Imagery and Theme.*   1969.
> *Towards a View of Canadian Letters: Selected Critical Essays 1928–1972.*   1973.

> Editor, with F. R. Scott, *New Provinces: Poems of Several Authors.*   1936.
> Editor, *The Book of Canadian Poetry.*   1943.
> Editor, *Seven Centuries of Verse: English and American, from the Early English Lyrics to the Present Day.*   1947.
> Editor, *The Worldly Muse: An Anthology of Serious Light Verse.*   1951.
> Editor, with M. L. Rosenthal, *Exploring Poetry.*   1955; revised edition, 1973.

Editor, with F. R. Scott, *The Blasted Pine: An Anthology of Satire, Invective and Disrespectful Verse, Chiefly by Canadian Writers*.   1957; revised edition, 1967.
Editor, *The Oxford Book of Canadian Verse: In English and French*.   1960; revised edition, 1965.
Editor, *Masks of Fiction: Canadian Critics on Canadian Prose*.   1961.
Editor, *Masks of Poetry: Canadian Critics on Canadian Verse*.   1962.
Editor, *Essays for College Writing*.   1965.
Editor, *The Book of Canadian Prose*.   2 vols, 1965–73.
Editor, *100 Poems: Chaucer to Dylan Thomas*.   1965.
Editor, *Modern Canadian Verse: In English and French*.   1967.
Editor, *The Collected Poems of Anne Wilkinson and a Prose Memoir*.   1968.
Editor, *The Canadian Century* (anthology).   1975.

Reading List: *Ten Canadian Poets* by Desmond Pacey, 1958; *The McGill Movement: Smith, F. R. Scott, and Leo Kennedy* edited by Peter Stevens, 1969; *Odysseus Ever Returning* by George Woodcock, 1970.

*   *   *

Though almost his whole academic life was lived in the United States, A. J. M. Smith has been one of the most influential figures in the Canadian modernist movement, as an editor and anthologist, as a critic, and as a poet. In the *McGill Literary Supplement* and the *McGill Fortnightly Review* he and F. R. Scott, while still students between 1924 and 1927, virtually launched the evolution that took Canadian poetry out of the colonial into the cosmopolitan stage; and as early as 1928, in a historic article in the *Canadian Forum* entitled "Wanted – Canadian Criticism," Smith put forward the argument that to be mature in a creative sense, a culture needed also a tradition of criticism. Over the years he has done a great deal to create that tradition in the essays on Canadian poets and on their cultural ambiance which in 1973 he collected in *Towards a View of Canadian Letters*.

But Smith's essays are hardly more than an iceberg's tip in considering his importance as a critic, which is much more substantially expressed in the series of notable anthologies in which he revealed the nature of Canadian poetry as an identifiable tradition. These begin with *New Provinces*, in which he and F. R. Scott gathered in 1936 the work of the few modernist poets then working in Canada. A few years later, Smith published *The Book of Canadian Poetry*, which he specifically entitled "a critical and historical anthology"; this was the first work that went through the whole of Canadian poetry from its colonial beginnings and performed an act of critical evaluation which established the important Canadian poets and their dominant manners and themes. Selection itself was, in this pioneer collection, a critical act; few people have disputed the canon of significant Canadian poetry which Smith established in *The Book of Canadian Poetry* and reinforced in successive editions. In 1960 he published *The Oxford Book of Canadian Verse*, the first definitive anthology of poems in Canada's two major languages, and in 1967 *Modern Canadian Verse: In English and French*. In all these volumes the selection was reinforced by perceptive commentary, and, if Smith's anthologies are not unquestioningly accepted as the definitive statements on the development of poetry in Canada, they have greatly influenced trends in literary history and critical evaluation alike.

As a poet Smith (who began to attract international attention during the 1930's when his work was published in journals like *New Verse*) is an artist whose self-criticism has been almost fanatical. His four volumes of highly metaphysical poetry, beginning with *News of the Phoenix* and ending with *Poems: New and Selected*, are rigorously chosen, and in every case except the first book contain old poems carefully revised, as well as new ones; the *Collected Poems* honed down the canon to a hundred pieces, all that Smith wished to keep from more than thirty years writing poetry.

Comparing these poems which appear again and again in different versions, one has the impression that Smith is a poet little bound by time. He began to attract attention in the 1930's, but Yeats and the Sitwells seem his natural siblings rather than the Auden-Spender circle. And if the world Smith creates in his poems is autonomous in time – a kind of poetic Laputa that might dip down as easily in the seventeenth century as in the twentieth – it seems equally free in place.

Admittedly, there are a very few poems which seem to declare a parochial preference. Smith proclaims his intention

> To hold in a verse as austere
> As the spirit of prairie and river,
> Lonely, unbuyable, dear,
> The North, as a need and for ever.

But even in his rather imagistic poems on Canadian landscapes the result has little of guidebook topography; rather, the glimpse one receives is of a detached and personal world, so that the familiar cedar and firs and wild duck calls in a poem like "The Lonely Land" lead us into a country in feeling as mythological as any painted by Poussin for the encounter of Gods and mortals:

> This is a beauty
> of dissonance
> this resonance
> of stony strand
> this smoky cry
> curled over a black pine
> like a broken
> and wind-battered branch
> when the wind
> bends the tops of the pines
> and curdles the sky
> from the north.

Smith's aims are spareness, clarity, balance, the austerity of a latter-day classicism enriched by the discoveries of the Symbolists and the Imagists. Unlike the wildly intuitive versifier he celebrated in "One Sort of Poet," Smith never sings, "*Let it come! Let it come!*" His poems are carefully worked to the last safe moment of polishing. One is aware of the unending search for words that are "crisp and sharp and small," for a form as "skintight" as the stallions of his "Far West." Occasionally the visions clarified through Smith's bright glass are too sharp for comfort, the detachment too remote for feeling to survive. More often, they are saved by the dense impact of the darker shapes that lie within the crystal, the "shadows I have seen, of me deemed deeper/That backed on nothing in the horrid air."

It is this enduring sense of the shapeless beyond shape that gives Smith's best poems their peculiar rightness of tension, and make his austerities so rich in implication.

—George Woodcock

SMITH, Stevie (Florence Margaret Smith). English. Born in Hull, Yorkshire, 20 September 1902. Educated at Palmers Green High School, London, and the North Collegiate

School for Girls. Secretary to Neville Pearson, Newnes Publishing Company, London, 1923–53. Occasional writer and broadcaster for the BBC. Member, Literature Panel, Arts Council of Great Britain. Recipient: Cholmondeley Award, 1966; Queen's Gold Medal for Poetry, 1969. *Died 8 March 1971.*

PUBLICATIONS

Collections

Collected Poems, edited by James MacGibbon.   1975.

Verse

A Good Time Was Had by All.   1937.
Tender Only to One: Poems and Drawings.   1938.
Mother, What Is a Man? Poems and Drawings.   1942.
Harold's Leap.   1950.
Not Waving But Drowning: Poems.   1957.
Selected Poems.   1962.
The Frog Prince and Other Poems.   1966.
The Best Beast: Poems.   1969.
Scorpion and Other Poems.   1972.

Fiction

Novel on Yellow Paper; or, Work It Out for Yourself.   1936.
Over the Frontier.   1938.
The Holiday.   1949.

Other

Some Are More Human than Others: Sketch-Book.   1958.
Cats in Colour.   1959.

Editor, T. S. Eliot: A Symposium for His 70th Birthday.   1958.
Editor, The Batsford Book of Children's Verse.   1970; as The Poet's Garden, 1970.

Reading List: *Ivy and Stevie: Ivy Compton-Burnett and Stevie Smith: Conversations and Reflections* by Kay Dick, 1971.

*   *   *

Stevie Smith was primarily a poet of the odd, the disconcerting, the unexpected. She seems to have formed her characteristic style as early as the 1930's, though it was not until the publication of her *Selected Poems* and a selection in the Penguin Modern Poets series in the early 1960's that she reached a substantial audience. She was adept at playing one emotion off against another within a poem – quirkiness of a wild-eyed eccentricity against plain common sense, levity against loneliness, sharpness against dreaminess. There is much humour, and often zany comedy, in her work, but at the same time a sense of isolation and blankness, and a preoccupation with death.

Her verse forms and her language may strike some readers as naive; they take elements from nursery rhymes, from banal songs, from hymns, and play sly and outrageous tricks with them. In fact she was a sophisticated artist, and her effects are calculated. She can show asperity and a kind of gleeful malice, and the force of these is made the stronger by the child-like stumbling or sing-song with which she displays them.

Religion and the religious life fascinated and repelled her. Apart from hymns, she was soaked in the Authorised Version of the Bible, and was indignant about what she took to be the commonplace flatness of the *New English Bible*. Within the range of her distinctive poetic voice, she was very varied, sustaining a gruesome narrative (as in "Angel Boley"), facing death with poignant cheerfulness (as in "Black March" and "Scorpion"), or simply using words with playful lunacy, as in "Tenuous and Precarious" ("two Romans"). Her best-known poem, "Not Waving, But Drowning," is a small classic of elegiac gaiety and sardonic stoicism. Her three novels (especially *Novel on Yellow Paper*) have their admirers, and they share characteristics with her verse; but it is as a poet that she is remembered, and is likely to go on being so.

—Anthony Thwaite

SMITH, Sydney Goodsir. Scottish. Born in Wellington, New Zealand, 26 October 1915. Educated at the University of Edinburgh; Oriel College, Oxford, M.A. Taught English to the Polish Army in Scotland for the War Office. Married; two children. Joined the British Council, Edinburgh, 1945; worked as a free-lance writer, journalist and broadcaster. Recipient: Atlantic-Rockefeller Award, 1946; Festival of Britain Scots Poetry Prize, 1951; Thomas Urquhart Award, 1962. *Died in January 1975.*

PUBLICATIONS

Collections

Collected Poems. 1976.

Verse

Skail Wind. 1941.
The Wanderer and Other Poems. 1943.
The Deevil's Waltz. 1946.
Selected Poems. 1947.
Under the Eildon Tree: A Poem in xxiv Elegies. 1948.
The Aipple and the Hazel. 1951.
So Late in the Night: Fifty Lyrics 1944–1948. 1952.
Cokkils 1953.

Omens: Nine Poems.   1955.
Orpheus and Euridice: A Dramatic Poem.   1955.
Figs and Thistles.   1959.
The Vision of the Prodigal Son.   1960.
Kynd Kittock's Land.   1965.
Girl with Violin.   1968.
Fifteen Poems and a Play.   1969.
Gowdspink in Reekie.   1974.

Play

The Wallace: A Triumph (produced 1960).   1960.

Fiction

Carotid Cornucopius: Caird o the Cannon Gait and Voyeur o the Outluik Touer: A Drammatick, Backside, Bogbide, Bedride or Badside Buik, by Gude Schir Skidderie Smithereens.   1947.

Other

A Short Introduction to Scottish Literature.   1951.

Editor, *Robert Fergusson 1750–1774: Essays by Various Hands to Commemorate the Bicentenary of His Birth.*   1952.
Editor, *Gavin Douglas: A Selection of His Poetry.*   1959.
Editor, with J. Delancey Ferguson and James Barke, *The Merry Muses of Caledonia,* by Robert Burns.   1959.
Editor, with others, *Hugh MacDiarmid: A Festschrift.*   1962.
Editor, *Bannockburn: The Story of the Battle and Its Place in Scotland's History.*   1965.
Editor, *A Choice of Burns's Poems and Songs.*   1966.

Reading List: "The Poetry of Smith" by Norman MacCaig in *Saltire Review 1*, April 1954; *Smith* by Hugh MacDiarmid, 1963; Essay by Thomas Crawford, in *Studies in Scottish Literature* edited by G. Ross Roy, 1969.

*   *   *

Sydney Goodsir Smith, after MacDiarmid, is in some ways the most powerful poet of the Scottish Renaissance Movement using only the Scots tongue. It was not indigenous to him, and in daily life he spoke what could only be described as Oxford English, though warmed by an aroused concern not usually associated with such a sound.

Like most post-Burns Scots-writing poets, Smith thus fabricated his language, a process not fully developed in his first book, *Skail Wind.* By the time of *The Deevil's Waltz,* however, he was beginning to master his language, ridding himself of the thick sound-play which marred his earlier verses. There were already signs of the strong lyric side to his talent, as in "Largo," in which the feeling of impotence against impersonal forces is symbolised by the last fishing-boat sailing from the Fife harbour:

> And never the clock rins back,
> The free days are owre;
> The warld shrinks, we luik
> Mair t'oor maisters ilka hour....

Smith's mature work is mostly love-poetry. Love and thought, sex and emotion, illumine a single total experience, for Smith as for Burns before him.

> I loe* ma luve in a lamplit bar   *love
> Braw on a wuiden stool,
> Her knees cocked up and her neb* doun   *nose
> Slorpan a pint o yill.*   *ale

His supreme achievement, *Under the Eildon Tree*, ranks with MacDiarmid's *A Drunk Man Looks at the Thistle*. Using the myth of Thomas the Rhymer, the poet laments the loves of some of the world's great lovers as reflected through his own experience of the passion. Allusions to mythology and world literature abound, but are skilfully woven into the texture of the verse in the Poundian manner. Smith's series of elegies, both moving and funny, give the impression of absolute word-rightness that comes only with a masterpiece.

> Ah, she was a bonnie cou!
> Saxteen, maybe sevinteen, nae mair,
> Her mither in attendance, *comme il faut*
> *Pour les jeunes filles bien élevées,*
>   Drinkan like a bluidie whaul tae!
> Wee briests, round and ticht and fou*   *full
> Like sweet Pomona in the orange grove;
> Her shanks were lang, but no ower lang, and plump,
>   A lassie's shanks,
> Wi the meisurance o'Venus –
>   Achteen inch the hoch* frae heuchle-bane* til knap,   *thigh; hip bone
>   Achteen inch the cauf frae knap* til cuit*   *knee-cap; ankle
> As is the true perfection calculate
> By the Auntients efter due regaird
> For this and that....

His difficulty in later years arose from the youthfully orientated nature of his favourite subject, although the plight of a meths-drinker and the peculiarities of his much-loved Edinburgh also moved his muse to memorable heights. Sometimes, when writing in strict forms, he would allow a rhythmic falter. He is also one of the few twentieth-century poets who almost totally eschewed imagery, relying on word-manipulation, description, and the association of ideas to gain his effects.

His play *The Wallace*, written for an Edinburgh International Festival, proved to be a patriotic exercise too dependent on rhetoric for lasting conviction, while his Joycean prose-fantasy in Scots, *Carotid Cornucopias*, though clever and amusing, is prevented by the evident artificiality of the language from touching those depths of associative meaning achieved in its model *Ulysses*.

—Maurice Lindsay

SNODGRASS, W(illiam) D(ewitt). American. Born in Wilkinsburg, Pennsylvania, 5 January 1926. Educated at Geneva College, Beaver Falls, Pennsylvania, 1943–44, 1946;

University of Iowa, Iowa City, 1949–55, B.A. 1949, M.A. 1951, M.F.A. 1953. Served in the United States Navy, 1944–46. Married 1) Lila Jean Hank in 1946 (divorced, 1953), one daughter; 2) Janice Wilson in 1954 (divorced, 1966), one son and one step-daughter; 3) Camille Rykowski in 1967. Instructor in English, Cornell University, Ithaca, New York, 1955–57, University of Rochester, New York, 1957–58, and Wayne State University, Detroit, 1959–67. Since 1968, Professor of English and Speech, Syracuse University, New York. Visiting Teacher, Morehead Writers Conference, Kentucky, Summer 1955, and Antioch Writers Conference, Yellow Springs, Ohio, Summers 1958–59. Recipient: Ingram Merrill Foundation Award, 1958; Longview Award, 1959; Poetry Society of America Special Citation, 1960; Yaddo Resident Award, 1960, 1961, 1965; National Institute of Arts and Letters grant, 1960; Pulitzer Prize, 1960; Guinness Award, 1961; Ford Foundation Fellowship, for drama, 1963; Miles Award, 1966; National Endowment for the Arts grant, 1966; Academy of American Poets Fellowship, 1972; Guggenheim Fellowship, 1972. Member, National Institute of Arts and Letters, 1972; Fellow, Academy of American Poets, 1973. Lives in Erieville, New York.

PUBLICATIONS

Verse

> *Heart's Needle.*   1959.
> *After Experience: Poems and Translations.*   1968.
> *Remains.*   1970.
> *The Führer Bunker: A Cycle of Poems in Progress.*   1977.

Other

> *In Radical Pursuit: Critical Essays and Lectures.*   1975.

> Editor, *Syracuse Poems 1969.*   1969.

> Translator, with Lore Segal, *Gallows Songs,* by Christian Morgenstern.   1967.

Bibliography: *Snodgrass: A Bibliography* by William White, 1960.

*   *   *

In his essay "A Poem's Becoming" (*In Radical Pursuit*), W. D. Snodgrass charts the evolution of his verse from the the densely composed, ambiguous lyrics of his early years at the University of Iowa to a style of "becoming," in which a dramatic action unfolds through the speaker's intimate disclosures and self-revelations. But throughout his transitions to a freer mode of lyric delivery, he has remained a technically conservative poet, writing most work in tightly rhymed patterns and in set metrical rhythms.

Although the craftsmanship of *Heart's Needle* and *After Experience* is at once lustrous and immaculate, Snodgrass is chiefly to be noted for having given voice to the inner life of the average middle-class American who came to maturity during World War II. Like Lowell, whom he studied under, Snodgrass bases the speaker in his poems on his own life, from service in the war to graduate student days in Iowa to teaching posts around the country. His poems, however, are a careful selection of experiences that capture the disappointments, vicissitudes, and angst of a whole generation of Americans. The most emphatic theme of *Heart's Needle* and *After Experience* is a sense of an increasingly depersonalized identity as social life grows more rationalized.

Heart's Needle begins with the disenchantments of returning veterans, who, in "Returned to Frisco, 1946," reenter civilian life

> free to prowl all night
> Down streets giddy with lights, to sleep all day,
>
> Pay our own way and make our own selections;
> Free to choose just what they meant we should....

With this hint at authoritarianism, Snodgrass chronicles the life of the post-war American who carries pent-up, even violent, emotions under a carefully trained surface. Some of these poems have their speaker worry that he has grown too fearful and timid, as in "Home Town," where he has pursued, then eluded a bold, young girl:

> Pale soul, consumed by fear
> of the living world you haunt,
> have you learned what habits lead you
> to hunt what you don't want;
> learned who does not need you;
> learned you are no one here?

The lovely, complex music of the final sequence, "Heart's Needle," captures this likeable, confused new Everyman as he struggles to remain parent to his young daughter. Snodgrass gives these ten poems his richest, most daringly metaphorical speech.

After Experience continues the Everyman chronicle of *Heart's Needle*, but this volume is less carefully structured and often less resonant in its language. Many of the poems take up themes of captivity, terror, potential violence, and disaster. Typical is "Lobsters in the Window," with its moving depiction of the near-frozen lobster seen through a restaurant window:

> He's fallen back with the mass
> Heaped in their common trench
> Who stir, but do not look out
> Through the rainstreaming glass,
> Hear what the newsboys shout,
> Or see the raincoats pass.

The closing section of the volume features skilful translations of a number of poets, particularly Rilke.

—Paul Christensen

SNYDER, Gary (Sherman).   American.   Born in San Francisco, California, 8 May 1930. Educated at Reed College, Portland, Oregon, B.A. in anthropology 1951; Indiana University, Bloomington, 1951–52; University of California, Berkeley, 1953–56; studied Buddhism in

Japan, 1956, 1964, 1965–68. Married 1) Alison Gass in 1950 (divorced, 1951); 2) the poet Joanne Kyger in 1960 (divorced, 1964); 3) Masa Uehara in 1967; two children. Held various jobs, including seaman and forester, 1948–56; Lecturer in English, University of California, Berkeley, 1964–65. Recipient: Bollingen Foundation Research Grant for Buddhist Studies, 1965; National Institute of Arts and Letters prize, 1966; Frank O'Hara Prize, 1967; Guggenheim Fellowship, 1968; Pulitzer Prize, 1975. Lives in California.

PUBLICATIONS

Verse

   Riprap.   1959.
   Myths and Texts.   1960; revised edition, 1978.
   Hop, Skip, and Jump.   1964.
   Nanoa Knows.   1964.
   Riprap and Cold Mountain Poems.   1965.
   Six Sections from Mountains and Rivers Without End.   1965; augmented edition, 1970.
   Three Worlds, Three Realms, Six Roads.   1966.
   A Range of Poems.   1966.
   The Back Country.   1967.
   The Blue Sky.   1969.
   Sours of the Hills.   1969.
   Regarding Wave.   1970.
   Manzanita.   1971.
   Anasazi.   1971.
   The Fudo Trilogy: Spell Against Demons, Smokey the Bear Trilogy, The California Water Plan.   1973.
   Turtle Island.   1974.

Other

   Four Changes.   1969.
   Earth House Hold: Technical Notes and Queries to Fellow Dharma Revolutionaries.   1969.
   On Bread and Poetry: A Panel Discussion, with Lew Welch and Philip Whalen.   1976.
   The Old Ways (essays).   1977.

Bibliography: in *Schist 2,* Summer 1974.

Reading List: "Snyder Issue" of *In Transit,* 1969.

*   *   *

Gary Snyder's writing is the chronicle of an itinerant visionary naturalist. His poetry contains few technical innovations, but consolidates the Imagist ideas of Pound and Williams and the free forms of Olson and the Beat poets. The poetry is wholly absorbed in the chronicle of the poet's wanderings, his religious training in Japan, and his mythic and cultural perception of nature and experience.

Snyder organizes most of his poetry according to experience rather than theme. In *Riprap,* the crisp, taciturn Imagist poems narrate his days as "look out" and "choker" in the remote reaches of the American northwest, and then his first trip to Japan on merchant tankers. The charm of these poems lies in the frank, modest, often tender lyric nature of the young observer, as in "Piute Creek":

> No one loves rock, yet we are here.
> Night chills. A flick
> In the moonlight
> Slips into Juniper shadow:
> Back there unseen
> Cold proud eyes
> Of cougar and Coyote
> Watch me rise and go.

Cold Mountain Poems contains translations of the Chinese poet, Han-Shan, in which Snyder shows skill as an interpreter and cunning in the choice of a poet like himself in vision and inclination. Han-Shan was a mountain recluse, whose regard for the mystery of nature is intense but not ponderous.

Myths and Texts, written before *Riprap* but not published until 1960, is the best orchestrated and developed of his works. By dividing the book into three parts, "Logging," "Hunting," and "Burning," Snyder creates an initiation ritual for his persona, who enters nature as a destroyer (working for logging companies), then as hunter, who must understand his prey to succeed, and who returns from these encounters awed by the power and will of nature. The themes of his early books establish the lines of development of his succeeding works. In *The Back Country*, he narrates experience from early years in Washington and Oregon, his departure for Japan in 1956, his later return to California. The volume has some notational lyrics, but the concision and intensity of most of the poems are deeply effective and dramatic.

Earth House Hold, a collection of prose, powerfully states the depth of his regard for the natural world and shows the maturing intellectual and spiritual subtlety of his mind over the twenty years it records. Snyder, now a cult figure of the ecology movement, carefully traces the evolution of his thought from jottings of natural phenomena to notes for the making of tribal culture in the post-industrial era. An able prose writer, Snyder is both factual and commanding as a theorist of a new pastoral ideology.

Regarding Wave and *Turtle Island* continue the chronicle of the poet through family life and residence in the United States, where environmental abuse has stirred him to a lyricism of greater and greater activism. The final passages of *Turtle Island* are a series of prose tracts on conservation addressed directly to the reader.

—Paul Christensen

SORLEY, Charles Hamilton. Scottish. Born in Aberdeen, 19 May 1895. Educated at King's College Choir School, Cambridge, 1904–08; Marlborough College, 1908–13; studied in Germany, 1914. Commissioned 2nd Lieutenant in the Suffolk Regiment, 1914, and rose to the rank of Captain: trained troops in England, 1914–15; served in France and Belgium, 1915; killed in action at Hulluch. *Died 13 October 1915.*

PUBLICATIONS

Verse

Marlborough and Other Poems.   1916; revised edition, 1916.
(Poems).   1931.

Other

Letters from Germany and from the Army, edited by W. R. Sorley.   1916.
The Letters of Sorley, with a Chapter of Biography, edited by W. R. Sorley.   1919.

Reading List: *The Ungirt Runner: Sorley, Poet of World War I* by Thomas B. Swann, 1965 (includes bibliography); in *Heroes' Twilight* by Bernard Bergonzi, 1965; *Out of Battle: Poetry of the Great War* by Jon Silkin, 1972.

*   *   *

Charles Hamilton Sorley was the only young English poet of the 1914–18 war who had more than a superficial knowledge of pre-war Germany, where he had spent several months after leaving Marlborough College and before taking up his place at Oxford. Right from the start he detested the mendacious vulgarity of anti-German propaganda, and saw the conflict between England and Germany as a fratricidal struggle. In what was probably his last poem, the sonnet that begins "When you see millions of the mouthless dead," Sorley accepts the triumph of death over all who had once been loved: "None wears the face you knew./Great death has made all his for evermore."

Sorley's reputation as a poet depends on a handful of poems inspired by his love of the Marlborough downs and by his reaction to the war. They do not compare in quality with the finest poems of Owen, Rosenberg, and Blunden, but they are remarkable achievements for a man of Sorley's age who had experienced only a few weeks' fighting before his death in action, and before the bloody slaughter in the mud of Flanders that shocked Owen and his fellow poets into maturity.

Sorley's poems, first published in *Marlborough and Other Poems,* are much better known than his letters, which are still in print nearly sixty years after their publication in 1919. Yet his letters display more unmistakably than his poems Sorley's remarkable intellectual power and moral insight. They reveal the complexity and ambiguity of his feelings about the war, as well as an ability to convey the horror and excitement aroused by the spectacle of carnage, and give an inkling of what he might have achieved had he lived.

—John Press

SOUSTER, (Holmes) Raymond.   Canadian.   Born in Toronto, Ontario, 15 January 1921. Educated at University of Toronto schools; Humberside Collegiate Institute, Toronto, 1938–39. Served in the Royal Canadian Air Force, 1941–45. Married Rosalie Lena Geralde in 1947. Since 1939, Staff Member, and currently Securities Custodian, Canadian Imperial

Bank of Commerce, Toronto. Editor, *Direction*, Sydney, Nova Scotia, 1943–46; Co-Editor, *Contact*,Toronto, 1952–54; Editor, *Combustion*,Toronto, 1957–60. Chairman, League of Canadian Poets, 1968–72. Recipient: Governor-General's Award, 1965; President's Medal, University of Western Ontario, 1967; Centennial Medal, 1967. Lives in Toronto.

PUBLICATIONS

Verse

Unit of Five, with others, edited by Ronald Hambleton.   1944.
When We Are Young.   1946.
Go to Sleep, World.   1947.
City Hall Street.   1951.
Cerberus, with Louis Dudek and Irving Layton.   1952.
Shake Hands with the Hangman.   1953.
A Dream That Is Dying.   1954.
For What Time Slays.   1955.
Walking Death.   1955.
Selected Poems, edited by Louis Dudek.   1956.
Crêpe-Hanger's Carnival: Selected Poems 1955–58.   1958.
Place of Meeting: Poems 1958–60.   1962.
A Local Pride.   1962.
12 New Poems.   1964.
The Colour of the Times: The Collected Poems.   1964.
Ten Elephants on Yonge Street.   1965.
As Is.   1967.
Lost and Found: Uncollected Poems.   1968.
So Far So Good: Poems 1938–1968.   1969.
The Years.   1971.
Selected Poems.   1972.
Change-Up: New Poems.   1974.
Rain Check.   1975.
Extra Innings.   1977.

Fiction

The Winter of the Time.   1949.
On Target.   1973.

Other

Editor, *Poets 56: Ten Younger English-Canadians.*   1956.
Editor, *Experiment: Poems 1923–1929,* by W. W. E. Ross.   1958.
Editor, *New Wave Canada: The New Explosion in Canadian Poetry.*   1966.
Editor, with John Robert Colombo, *Shapes and Sounds: Poems of W. W. E. Ross.*   1968.
Editor, with Douglas Lochhead, *Made in Canada: New Poems of the Seventies.*   1970.
Editor, with Richard Woollatt, *Generation Now* (textbook).   1970.
Editor, with Douglas Lochhead, *100 Poems of Nineteenth Century Canada* (textbook).   1973.

Editor, with Richard Woollatt, *Sights and Sounds* (textbook). 1973.
Editor, with Richard Woollatt, *These Loved, These Hated Lands* (textbook). 1974.

Reading List: "Groundhog among the Stars" by Louis Dudek, in *Canadian Literature,* Autumn 1964; "To Souster with Vermont" by Hayden Carruth, in *Tamarack Review,* Winter 1965.

*   *   *

Raymond Souster represents the second generation of modern Canadian poets, the poets who rejected the influence of the English poets of the 1930's who had dominated their predecessors, and looked to American poets like Ezra Pound and William Carlos Williams, less as models than as guides to the acquisition of a way of speaking proper to their experience as North Americans. What distinguishes Souster from the poets with whom he shared that direction in the 1940's, such as Irving Layton and Louis Dudek, is the modesty of presence and the quietness of voice he has adopted. His work is entirely lacking in the histrionics of being a poet.

There are other items of traditional poetic baggage Souster has abandoned in his efforts to write a poetry of direct experience. He avoids not only metrical forms but also recondite allusions, archaisms, even symbolism – everything, in other words, that can impede his search for the pure image, or even the pure imageless voice that can convey truly an experience or an emotion.

Souster's poems tend to be short, colloquial in diction, frequently epigrammatic, aiming at the sharp and often ironic insight into a specific situation that expands in the mind to an insight into existence itself. He has been writing with such consistent regularity over the past thirty years that his books offer many examples of the kind of self-contained yet resonantly allusive poem which, at his best, he creates. A good example, for its combination of brevity and intensity, is the six-line poem "The Six-Quart Basket":

> The six-quart basket
> one side gone
> half the handle torn off
>
> sits in the centre of the lawn
> and slowly fills up
> with the white fruits of the snow.

Other poems are less lucid because their feeling is darker, and, for all Souster's evident enjoyment of the bright surface of the earth and the occasional haunting nostalgia of his poems, the dominant mood that underlies them is perhaps best summed up in his own lines:

> life isn't a matter of luck
> of good fortune, it's whether
> the heart can keep singing
> when there's really no reason
> why it should

—George Woodcock

SPENCER, Bernard. English. Born in Madras, India, 30 November 1909. Educated at Marlborough College; Corpus Christi College, Oxford. Reviewer for the *Morning Post* and *Oxford Mail*; subsequently a schoolteacher: Classics Master at Westminster School, London; helped Geoffrey Grigson to edit *New Verse* in the late 1930's, and, with Lawrence Durrell and Robin Fedden, edited *Personal Landscape*, Middle East, 1942–45; joined the British Council, 1940: Lecturer, Institute of English Studies, Salonika; served five years in Egypt, two years in Italy; Director of Studies, British Institute, Madrid, 1948–49; served at London headquarters, 1950–53, Madrid, 1954, Athens, 1955, London, 1956–58, Spain and Turkey, 1959–62, and in Vienna, 1962–63. *Died 12 September 1963.*

PUBLICATIONS

Verse

> *Aegean Islands and Other Poems.* 1946.
> *The Twist in the Plotting: Twenty Five Poems.* 1960.
> *With Luck Lasting.* 1963.
> *Collected Poems.* 1965.

Other

> Editor, with Stephen Spender, *Oxford Poetry 1930.* 1930.
> Editor, with R. Goodman, *Oxford Poetry 1931.* 1931.
> Editor, with others, *Personal Landscape.* 1945.

> Translator, with Lawrence Durrell and Nanos Valaortis, *The King of Asine and Other Poems,* by George Seferis. 1948.

Reading List: articles by John Betjeman and Lawrence Durrell, in *London Magazine,* 1963–64.

*   *   *

Although Bernard Spencer was a contemporary of Auden, MacNeice, and Spender and, like them, was a frequent contributor to *New Verse*, he brought out no collection of poems before the appearance of *Aegean Islands* in 1946. While sharing the contemptuous hostility displayed by Auden and his friends towards the idiocy and cruelty of capitalism, Spencer was less concerned than they with the social pattern of Britain, perhaps because of his sojourn on the shores of the Mediterranean in the late 1930's and during the war. He was one of the moving spirits in the publication of *Personal Landscape*, a periodical devoted largely to the work of writers whom the chances of war had brought to Egypt as civilians or as members of the armed forces.

Spencer is essentially a lyrical poet, keenly responsive to the landscapes and seascapes in which he found himself. He loved the Mediterranean, the lands of the olive and the grape, where it was still possible to follow a way of life not distorted by the demands of industrialism and the dictates of greed. But he was too acute and honest an observer to pretend that the traditional culture of the Mediterranean could survive, uninfected by war and revolution. Bernard Spencer's two later collections, *The Twist in the Plotting* and *With Luck Lasting*, celebrate the sensuous properties of the world in which he rejoiced, but recognize, with sad irony, the despoiling of landscapes and lives by human wickedness and folly. In "The Rendezvous" he revisits a city made hideous by slogans of hate:

> And true
> to loves love never thought of, here
> with bayonet and with tearing fence,
> with cry of crowds and doors slammed to,
> waits the once known and dear, once chosen
> city of our rendezvous.

He deserves to be more widely read than at present and to be recognized as one of the most gifted poets of his generation.

—John Press

SPENDER, Stephen (Harold).   English.   Born in London, 28 September 1909; son of the writer Harold Spender. Educated at University College School, London; University College, Oxford. Served as a fireman in the National Fire Service, 1941–44. Married 1) Agnes Marie Pearn in 1936; 2) Natasha Litvin in 1941, one son and one daughter. Editor, with Cyril Connolly, *Horizon* magazine, London, 1939–41; Counsellor, UNESCO Section of Letters, 1947; Co-Editor, 1953–66, and Corresponding Editor, 1966–67, *Encounter* magazine, London; Contributor, *Art and Literature*, 1964–66. Elliston Lecturer, University of Cincinnati, 1953; Beckman Professor, University of California, Berkeley, 1959; Visiting Professor, Northwestern University, Evanston, Illinois, 1963; Clark Lecturer, Cambridge University, 1966; Visiting Professor, University of Connecticut, Storrs, 1968–70; Mellon Lecturer, Washington, D.C., 1968; Northcliffe Lecturer, University of London, 1969; Visiting Lecturer, University of Florida, Gainesville, 1976. Since 1970, Professor of English Literature, University College, University of London. Consultant in Poetry, Library of Congress, Washington, D.C., 1965–66. Honorary Member, Phi Beta Kappa, Harvard University, Cambridge, Massachusetts; Fellow, Institute of Advanced Studies, Wesleyan University, Middletown, Connecticut, 1967. Recipient: Queen's Gold Medal for Poetry, 1971. D.Litt.: University of Montpellier; Loyola University, Chicago. Honorary Fellow, University College, Oxford, 1973. Honorary Member, American Academy of Arts and Letters, 1969. C.B.E. (Commander, Order of the British Empire), 1962. Lives in London.

PUBLICATIONS

Verse

Nine Experiments by S. H. S., Being Poems Written at the Age of Eighteen.   1928.
20 Poems.   1930.
Poems.   1933; revised edition, 1934.
Vienna.   1934.
The Still Centre.   1939.
Selected Poems.   1940.

Ruins and Visions. 1942.
Spiritual Exercises (To Cecil Day Lewis). 1943.
Poems of Dedication. 1947.
Returning to Vienna 1947: Nine Sketches. 1947.
The Edge of Being. 1949.
Collected Poems 1928–1953. 1955.
Selected Poems. 1964.
The Generous Days: Ten Poems. 1969; augmented edition as *The Generous Days,* 1971.

Plays

Trial of a Judge (produced 1938). 1938.
Danton's Death, with Goronwy Rees, from a play by Georg Büchner (produced 1939). 1939.
To the Island (produced 1951).
Mary Stuart, from the play by Schiller (produced 1957). 1959.
Lulu, from the play by Frank Wedekind (produced 1958).
Rasputin's End, music by Nicholas Nabokov. 1963.

Fiction

The Burning Cactus (stories). 1936.
The Backward Son. 1940.
Engaged in Writing, and The Fool and the Princess. 1958.

Other

The Destructive Element: A Study of Modern Writers and Beliefs. 1935.
Forward from Liberalism. 1937.
The New Realism: A Discussion. 1939.
Life and the Poet. 1942.
Jim Braidy: The Story of Britain's Firemen, with William Sansom and James Gordon. 1943.
Citizens in War – and After. 1945.
Botticelli. 1945.
European Witness (on Germany). 1946.
Poetry since 1939. 1946.
World Within World: The Autobiography of Spender. 1951.
Europe in Photographs. 1951.
Shelley. 1952.
Learning Laughter (on Israel). 1952.
The Creative Element: A Study of Vision, Despair, and Orthodoxy among Some Modern Writers. 1953.
The Making of a Poem (essays). 1955.
The Imagination in the Modern World: Three Lectures. 1962.
The Struggle of the Modern. 1963.
Ghika: Paintings, Drawings, Sculpture, with Patrick Leigh Fermor. 1964.
The Magic Flute: Retold. 1966.
The Year of the Young Rebels. 1969.
Love-Hate Relations: A Study of Anglo-American Sensibilities. 1974.

Eliot.   1975.
The Thirties and After.   1978.

Editor, with Louis MacNeice, *Oxford Poetry 1929.*   1929.
Editor, with Bernard Spencer, *Oxford Poetry 1930.*   1930.
Editor, with John Lehmann and Christopher Isherwood, *New Writing, New Series I* and
    II. 1938–39.
Editor, with John Lehmann, *Poems for Spain.*   1939.
Editor, *A Choice of English Romantic Poetry.*   1947.
Editor, *Selected Poems,* by Walt Whitman.   1950.
Editor, with Elizabeth Jennings and Dannie Abse, *New Poems 1956.*   1956.
Editor, *Great Writings of Goethe.*   1958.
Editor, *Great German Short Stories.*   1960.
Editor, *The Writer's Dilemma.*   1961.
Editor, with Donald Hall, *The Concise Encyclopedia of English and American Poets and
    Poetry.* 1963; revised edition, 1970.
Editor, with Irving Kristol and Melvin J. Lasky, *Encounters: An Anthology from Its First
    Ten Years.* 1963.
Editor, *Selected Poems,* by Abba Kovner and Nelly Sachs.   1971.
Editor, *A Choice of Shelley's Verse.*   1971.
Editor, *D. H. Lawrence: Novelist, Poet, Prophet.*   1973.
Editor, *The Poems of Percy Bysshe Shelley.*   1974.
Editor, *W. H. Auden: A Tribute.*   1975.

Translator, *Pastor Hall,* by Ernst Toller.   1939.
Translator, with J. L. Gili, *Poems,* by García Lorca.   1939.
Translator, with J. B. Leishman, *Duino Elegies,* by Rainer Maria Rilke.   1939; revised
    edition, 1948.
Translator, with J. L. Gili, *Selected Poems,* by García Lorca.   1943.
Translator, with Frances Cornford, *Le Dur Désir de Durer,* by Paul Eluard.   1950.
Translator, *The Life of the Virgin Mary (Das Marien-Leben)* (bilingual edition), by Rainer
    Maria Rilke.   1951.
Translator, with Frances Fawcett, *Five Tragedies of Sex* (includes *Spring's Awakening,
    Earth-Spirit, Pandora's Box, Death and Devil, Castle Wetterstein*), by Frank
    Wedekind. 1952.
Translator, with Nikos Stangos, *Fourteen Poems,* by C. P. Cavafy.   1977.

Bibliography: *Spender: Works and Criticism: An Annotated Bibliography* by H. B. Kulkarni,
1977.

Reading List: *Spender, MacNeice, Day Lewis: A Critical Essay* by Derek Stanford, 1969;
Spender and the Thirties by Andrew K. Weatherhead, 1974; *"The Angry Young Men"* of the
Thirties: Day Lewis, Spender, MacNeice, Auden by Elton E. Smith, 1975.

*   *   *

Stephen Spender's crucial epoch was the "pink decade," 1930–39, in which intellectuals
began by hoping for revolutionary achievements from Soviet Communism and ended (with
the Berlin-Moscow Non-Aggression Concordat) with the disillusioned admission that Russia
was subject to the same compromises as other sovereign states. A profoundly personal poet,
Spender diagnosed England's loss of personal belief (*The Destructive Element*) as the disease
that produced the observable symptoms of decaying cities, factories abandoned or short-
handed, widespread unemployment (*Trial of a Judge*), corrupt and ineffectual political

leadership (canto 2, *Vienna*), and aristocratic stupidity ("The Cousins," 1936). Indeed, even the most enlightened leaders were fumbling and distracted ("Exiles from Their Land," *The Still Centre*), and individual illness was only a fractured segment of the vast malaise of the age ("The Dead Island," 1936). So sensitive an individualist that boarding school was unmitigated purgatory, Spender urged his liberal friends to surrender to the discipline of communism because it was the only force capable of defeating fascism (*Forward from Liberalism*). Invoking the sanction of Joseph Conrad and Henry James in his criticism, he warned writers that, although reality is dangerous to idealists, it is the final test of relevant, revolutionary art. Later he admitted he could no longer accept the Party's dogmatic dismissal of all non-communist writers as having nothing relevant to say.

In both his personal and political life, Spender has always been obsessed with relationship: person to person, person to group. Thus the autobiographic statement of his development tended to become the record of a coming revolutionary world conflict. But he often seems to have been left with opposing convictions: the 1920's was the last age in which an individual, by himself, could influence history; yet, by the end of the 1930's, he was reluctant to choose between East and West, socialism and capitalism. He simply wanted the freedom to be and to express his uniquely gifted self. Thus his poetry often took the two-sided form of compulsive compassion for the suffering of others, coupled with a masochistic insistence on sharing that suffering.

Without the playful and mordant wit of MacNeice and Auden, his poetry has always risen on Romantic wings and engaged the sympathy of its audience by its touching idealism.

—Elton E. Smith

STAFFORD, William (Edgar). American. Born in Hutchinson, Kansas, 17 January 1914. Educated at the University of Kansas, Lawrence, B.A. 1936, M.A. 1947; University of Iowa, Iowa City, Ph.D. 1954. Conscientious Objector during World War II; active in Pacifist organizations, and since 1959 Member, Oregon Board, Fellowship of Reconciliation. Married Dorothy Hope Frantz in 1944; two daughters and two sons. Member of the English Department, 1948–54, 1957–60, and since 1960, Professor of English, Lewis and Clark College, Portland, Oregon. Assistant Professor of English, Manchester College, Indiana, 1955–56; Professor of English, San Jose State College, California, 1956–57. Consultant in Poetry, Library of Congress, Washington, D.C., 1970–71. United States Information Agency Lecturer in Egypt, Iran, Pakistan, India, Nepal, and Bangladesh, 1972. Recipient: Yaddo Foundation Fellowship, 1955; National Book Award, 1963; Shelley Memorial Award, 1964; National Endowment for the Arts grant, 1966; Guggenheim Fellowship, 1966; Melville Cane Award, 1974. D.Litt.: Ripon College, Wisconsin, 1965; Linfield College, McMinnville, Oregon, 1970. Lives in Portland, Oregon.

PUBLICATIONS

Verse

West of Your City. 1960.
Traveling Through the Dark. 1962.

Five American Poets, with others, edited by Thom Gunn and Ted Hughes.   1963.
Five Poets of the Pacific Northwest, with others, edited by Robin Skelton.   1964.
The Rescued Year.   1966.
Eleven Untitled Poems.   1968.
Weather.   1969.
Allegiances.   1970.
Temporary Facts.   1970.
Poems for Tennessee, with Robert Bly and William Matthews.   1971.
Someday, Maybe.   1973.
That Other Alone.   1973.
In the Clock of Reason.   1973.
Going Places.   1974.
Stories That Could Be True: New and Collected Poems.   1977.

Other

Down in My Heart (experience as a conscientious objector during World War II).   1947.
Friends to This Ground: A Statement for Readers, Teachers, and Writers of Literature.   1967.
Leftovers, A Care Package: Two Lectures.   1973.

Editor, with Frederick Candelaria, *The Voices of Prose*.   1966.
Editor, *The Achievement of Brother Antoninus: A Comprehensive Selection of His Poems*.   1967.
Editor, with Robert H. Ross, *Poems and Perspectives*.   1971.

Reading List: "Stafford Issue" of *Northwest Review*, Spring 1974, and of *Modern Poetry Studies*, Spring 1975.

*   *   *

William Stafford's poetry exemplifies the best of what is left of American transcendentalism. Like Emerson and Thoreau, he regards the human imagination as "salvational," and many of his poems are about the capacity of the imagination to derive meaning and awe from the world. Like the transcendentalists Stafford also regards the natural world as a possible model for human behavior:

> The earth says every summer have a ranch
> that's minimum: one tree, one well, a landscape
> that proclaims a universe – sermon
> of the hills, hallelujah mountain,
> highway guided by the way the world is tilted.

But, although in Stafford's poems Nature ("the landscape of justice") evinces both a glimmer of consciousness and a strict propriety of process, it contains few prescriptions definite enough to be useful guides to human behavior. It provides only distant analogues. Nor is Nature a comforting maternal presence. If there be any one lesson which the human species might draw from natural process, it is humility, to know your place, to have local priorities. Stafford has an organic conception of poetry, which also recalls the transcendentalists. For him, poetry is a manifestation of the "deepest [truest] place we have":

> They call it regional, this relevance –
> the deepest place we have: in this pool forms
> the model of our land, a lonely one,
> responsive to the wind. Everything we own
> has brought us here: from here we speak.

Composition is thus, for Stafford, a means of bringing to light the dark processes of the self:

> I do tricks in order to know:
> Careless I dance,
> then turn to see
> the mark to turn God left for me.

The style of Stafford's poems is quiet and colloquial. Few of them are very long. Throughout his poetry, certain words recur with an intensionally symbolic meaning. The most prominent of these words are "dark," "deep," "cold," "far," "God," and "home." Many of his earlier poems are rhymed, some heavily, some with slant or touch rhyme. His earlier work shows a fondness for sprung rhythm rather than quantitative metric. Since 1960 his work has grown steadily more relaxed in form and more rhetorically inventive. Typical of such inventiveness is the poem "Important Things":

> Like Locate Knob out west
> of town where maybe the world
> began. Like the rusty wire
> sagged in the river for a harp
> when floods go by.
> Like a way of talking, the slur
> in hello to mean you and God
> still think about justice.
> Like being alone, and you are
> alone, like always.
> You always are.

—Jonathan Holden

STEAD, C(hristian) K(arlson). New Zealander. Born in Auckland, 17 October 1932. Educated at Mount Albert Grammar School; University of Auckland, B.A. 1954, M.A. (honours) 1955; University of Bristol (Michael Hiatt Baker Scholar), Ph.D. 1961. Married Kathleen Elizabeth Roberts in 1955; two daughters and one son. Lecturer in English, University of New England, Armidale, New South Wales, 1956–57. Lecturer in English, 1959–61, Senior Lecturer, 1962–63, Associate Professor, 1964–67, and since 1967 Professor of English, University of Auckland. Chairman, New Zealand Literary Fund Advisory Committee. Recipient: Poetry Awards Incorporated prize, 1955; Winn-Manson Katherine Mansfield Award, for fiction and for essay, 1960, and Fellowship, 1972; Nuffield Travelling Fellowship, 1965; Jessie McKay Award, 1972; New Zealand Book Award, 1975. Lives in Auckland.

PUBLICATIONS

Verse

Whether the Will Is Free: Poems 1954–62.   1964.
Crossing the Bar.   1972.
Quesada: Poems 1972–1974.   1975.

Fiction

Smith's Dream.   1971.

Other

The New Poetic: Yeats to Eliot.   1964.

Editor, *New Zealand Short Stories: Second Series.*   1966.
Editor, *Measure for Measure: A Casebook.*   1971.
Editor, *The Letters and Journals of Katherine Mansfield: A Selection.*   1977.

Reading List: essay by Roy Fuller, in *London Magazine,* July 1964; by James Bertram in *Islands 2,* 1972.

*   *   *

   C. K. Stead's *The New Poetic* illustrates his robust, clear-eyed criticism and special skill in the analysis of a text. Many consider Stead's chief distinction as a writer is as a critic. The most substantial of his prose writings is *Smith's Dream,* a kind of political novel set in a New Zealand that has become dominated by a Fascist dictator who is supported by a strong American military presence. The author's interest is in events rather than the springs of action, personal or political, and he shows considerable narrative skill. The tale has been made into the film *Sleeping Dogs.*
   As a poet Stead is not prolific but through his three volumes of verse he has established a solid reputation in his country. *Whether the Will Is Free* is apprentice work strongly influenced by the poets he has chosen for models. The best-known of these early poems is "Pictures from a Gallery Underseas." Stead's poetry has the qualities of good expository prose, clarity, firmness of exposition, and a strong sense of organisation. Its inspiration is often literary but the language has the vitality of common speech and a natural rhythm. The poems in *Crossing the Bar* are poems of statement rather than exploration. He comments on American politics, the nature and importance of poetry, literary events like Auden's sixtieth birthday. There are, too, personal poems like the moving "A Small Registry of Births and Deaths" on his experience of fatherhood. Caesar is a dominant figure in the book. From him the poet has learnt his style, his Rome anticipates modern America: "What Wolf began, Eagle accomplishes." A good deal of Stead's political thinking is summed up in a striking statement of the consequences of political miscalculation: "Minerva had a mouse in mind./It was a weasel, tore her beak." Caesar the victorious soldier is Stead himself fighting that campaign with his "Enemy, brother, Lucifer/My own self" whose outcome is poetry.
   The title sequence of *Quesada* is an extended allusion to the questing Don Quixote. The style of the volume is more relaxed than that of the other books, and more open to experience. Confessedly secular in outlook and without a mythopoeic imagination Stead

writes verse that frequently lacks any sense of the mystery of life, something essential to the truest poetry. The deficiency is to some extent compensated for when he writes in the Romantic mode of the earlier part of this last volume. Besides the image of Quesada, romantic and compassionate, the book contains an admirable evocation of the South of France.

—F. M. McKay

STEPHENS, James. Irish. Born in Dublin in 1882. No formal education; self-taught. Worked as a clerk in a solicitor's office; Founder, with Padraic Colum and Thomas MacDonagh, *Irish Review*, 1911; lived as a free-lance writer, and campaigned for the creation of the Irish Free State. Recipient: Polignac Prize, 1912; Irish Tailltean Gold Medal, 1923. *Died 26 December 1950.*

PUBLICATIONS

Collections

    A Stephens Reader, edited by Lloyd Frankenberg. 1962; as *A Selection,* 1962.
    Letters, edited by Richard J. Finneran. 1974.

Verse

    Where the Demons Grin. 1908.
    Insurrections. 1909.
    The Lonely God and Other Poems. 1909.
    The Hill of Vision. 1912.
    Songs from the Clay. 1915.
    The Adventures of Seamus Beg, The Rocky Road to Dublin. 1915.
    Green Branches. 1916.
    Reincarnations. 1918.
    Little Things and Other Poems. 1924.
    A Poetry Recital. 1925.
    Collected Poems. 1926; revised edition, 1954.
    Optimist. 1929.
    Theme and Variations. 1930.
    Strict Joy. 1931.
    Kings and the Moon. 1938.

Play

    Julia Elizabeth (as *The Marriage of Julia Elizabeth,* produced 1911). 1929.

Fiction

    The Charwoman's Daughter. 1912; as *Mary, Mary,* 1912.
    The Crock of Gold. 1912.

Here Are Ladies (stories).   1913.
The Demi-Gods.   1914.
Hunger: A Dublin Story.   1918.
Deirdre.   1923.
In the Land of Youth.   1924.
Etched in Moonlight (stories).   1928.

Other

The Insurrection in Dublin.   1916.
Irish Fairy Tales (juvenile).   1920.
Arthur Griffith, Journalist and Statesman.   1924(?).
On Prose and Verse (essays).   1928.
James, Seumas, and Jacques: Unpublished Writings, edited by Lloyd Frankenberg.   1964.

Editor, *The Poetical Works of Thomas MacDonagh*.   1916.
Editor, with E. L. Beck and R. H. Snow, *Victorian and Later English Poets*.   1934.

Bibliography: *Bibliographies of Modern Authors 4* by Iolo A. Williams, 1922.

Reading List: *Stephens, Yeats, and Other Irish Concerns* by G. B. Saul, 1954; "Stephens Issue" of *Colby Library Quarterly 9*, 1961; *Stephens: His Work and an Account of His Life* by Hilary Pyle, 1965; *The Fenian Chief: A Biography of Stephens* by Desmond Ryan, 1967; *Stephens: A Critical Study* by Augustine Martin, 1977.

*   *   *

James Stephens's work as a poet may be divided into three distinct groupings. The earliest verse is one of social themes, often developed in direct speech and owing an acknowledged debt to Browning. It is very much of its period, carrying the concern of Colum and O'Sullivan for the people of contemporary Ireland into a cityscape. These realist poems are to be found in *Insurrections*, his first published book of verse. In *Insurrections* are to be found also his first visionary poems, and the beginnings of his obsession for Blake, something he derived from his older friend, the poet and painter, George Russell (AE). *The Hill of Vision* is, in fact, cloaked in Blakean imagery and ideas. It still bears, however, a vigorous Stephens imprint and a remarkable grasp of the use of satire and of humour, both of which his subsequent excursions into theosophy and Indian philosophy were to stifle. Thus the final books of verse, *Strict Joy* and *Kings and the Moon*, are composed of mystic meditations or emotional outbursts celebrating the Absolute, which are devoid of poetic tension and of the imaginative ideas and colourful idioms that characterize his earlier work. His generally most satisfying body of verse – translations from or developments of the themes of three Gaelic poets, O Bruadair, O Rahilly and Raftery, which he gathered under the heading *Reincarnations* – brings his colloquial and spiritually inspired styles together in a wealth of expressive imagery, which he uses with a triumph of economy.

The development of his prose parallels that of his poetry. *The Charwoman's Daughter*, a charmingly related idyll set in Dublin streets, marries a stern realism, with which he and his fellows were attempting to present 20th-century Ireland, with a not too rigid symbolism based on Blakean concepts. *The Crock of Gold*, his most popular book, takes his Blakean ideology a step further, moving the setting out of Dublin into rural Ireland, and perhaps excelling *The Charwoman's Daughter* in the magic and personality of its narrative. *The Demi-Gods*, not such a success, substitutes theosophical ideas for those of Blake. His two sets of short stories are self-consciously intellectual, and the medium seems to have inhibited his gift for relaxed narrative. This found further outlets, however, in his eye-witness account of the rising in 1916, *The Insurrection in Dublin*; in his retellings of Irish legends published in three volumes, of which *Irish Fairy Tales* is the most perfect; and in the series of original broadcasts which he recorded for the BBC in London during World War II.

—Hilary Pyle

STEVENS, Wallace. American. Born in Reading, Pennsylvania, 2 October 1879. Educated at Harvard University, Cambridge, Massachusetts, 1897–1900; New York University Law School, 1901–03; admitted to the New York Bar, 1904. Married Elsie V. Kachel in 1909; one daughter, Holly. Worked as a Reporter for the New York *Herald Tribune*, 1900–01; practised law in New York, 1904–16; joined the Hartford Accident and Indemnity Company, Connecticut, 1916: Vice-President, 1934–55. Recipient: Harriet Monroe Poetry Award, 1946; Bollingen Prize, 1950; National Book Award, 1951, 1955; Pulitzer Prize, 1955. Member, National Institute of Arts and Letters, 1946. *Died 2 August 1955.*

PUBLICATIONS

Collections

Letters, edited by Holly Stevens. 1967.
The Palm at the End of the Mind: Selected Poems and a Play, edited by Holly Stevens. 1971.

Verse

Harmonium. 1923; revised edition, 1931.
Ideas of Order. 1935.
Owl's Clover. 1936.
The Man with the Blue Guitar and Other Poems. 1937.
Parts of a World. 1942.
Notes Toward a Supreme Fiction. 1942.
Esthetique du Mal. 1945.
Description Without Place. 1945.
Transport to Summer. 1947.
Three Academic Pieces: The Realm of Resemblance, Someone Puts a Pineapple Together, Of Ideal Time and Choice. 1947.
A Primitive Like an Orb. 1948.
The Auroras of Autumn. 1950.
Selected Poems, edited by Dennis Williamson. 1952.
Selected Poems. 1953.
Collected Poems. 1954.

Plays

> *Carlos among the Candles* (produced 1917).   In *Opus Posthumous*, 1957.
> *Three Travelers Watch a Sunrise* (produced 1920).   In *Opus Posthumous*, 1957.
> *Bowl, Cat, and Broomstick*, in *Quarterly Review of Literature 16*, 1969.

Other

> *Two or Three Ideas.*   1951.
> *The Relations Between Poetry and Painting.*   1951.
> *The Necessary Angel: Essays on Reality and the Imagination.*   1951.
> *Raoul Dufy: A Note.*   1953.
> *Opus Posthumous* (miscellany), edited by Samuel French Morse.   1957.

Bibliography: *Stevens: A Descriptive Bibliography* by J. M. Edelstein, 1973.

Reading List: *The Shaping Spirit: A Study of Stevens* by William Van O'Connor, 1950; *The Comic Spirit of Stevens* by Daniel Fuchs, 1963; *The Clairvoyant Eye: The Poetry and Poetics of Stevens* by Joseph N. Riddel, 1965; *The Act of the Mind: Essays on the Poetry of Stevens* edited by Roy Harvey Pearce and J. Hillis Miller, 1965; *On Extended Wings: Stevens' Longer Poems* by Helen H. Vendler, 1969; *Stevens: Poetry as Life* by Samuel French Morse, 1970; *Introspective Voyager: The Poetic Development of Stevens* by A. Walton Litz, 1972; *Stevens* by Lucy Beckett, 1974; *Stevens: The Poems of Our Climate* by Harold Bloom, 1977; *Souvenirs and Prophecies: The Young Stevens* by Holly Stevens, 1977.

*   *   *

Wallace Stevens is a poet who combined a long poetic career with another career, that of a business executive. The career that concerns us here – that of poet – produced a large body of work that circles around a lifelong consideration from which all his best poems radiate. Each poem is one testimony to an encompassing vision of what Stevens judges to be the prime obligation of a modern poet. That obligation leaves its mark on comparatively brief and early poems like "Peter Quince at the Clavier," "Sunday Morning," and "Thirteen Ways of Looking at a Blackbird" and continues in later and quite extensive works like *Transport to Summer* and *Ideas of Order*. Stevens is, early and late, concerned with a purification of the human intellect and sensibility – in the first place, the intellect and sensibility of the poet who is writing, and, in the second place, the intellect and the sensibility of the reader who responds to what the poet has written.

The purification takes place as service to a set of ideas – "ideas of order" in Stevens' phrase – that are ignored or, at best, served badly and intermittently in the culture to which Stevens belongs. Our sensibility has been corrupted by habits of thought that seduce the poet and his readers from a prime duty. Poet and reader have the chance, if they but respond rightly to the world which constantly surrounds them and indeed bombards them with endless impressions, to take in special sensations (the colors of light on the sea, the taste of cheese and pineapple, a musical cadence) and set them down in words. These sensations are most pure at a special time of the year (summer) and in southern climes where light and color are most intense. The sensations are adulterated by many things, by winter and northern climes, for example. Even more crucial in Stevens' account are the betrayals that are built into human culture, the dogmas and traditions and forms of artistic expression that are conventional and hackneyed. Stevens can speak bitterly of "statues" that dominate public squares and inhibit the innocent and intense sensory responses of the people who walk there.

Implied by this emphasis is a psychology – a theory of human perception – that is basically nominalistic. What is real and worthy of reverence – the poet's reverence and his readers' – is, for example, the contact the eye makes with a certain slant of light which is never the equivalent of some past contact with a slant of light. It is a mistake to move from several such special moments to any general conception about "shades of light." Each moment of perception must be preserved in its uniqueness, and the poet must, ideally, move no farther from that moment than the carefully selected set of words that allow him to make a verbal record. Stevens – a poet quite well-informed in such matters – is aware of the traps into which other poets and other human beings have fallen. In *Harmonium*, there is an "Invective Against Swans." Stevens writes: "The soul, o ganders, flies beyond the parks/And far beyond the discords of the wind." Here the "soul" has a vertigo that takes it beyond "parks" (and their clusters of rare and unique sensations) and beyond the manifestly rich "discords of the wind." The "soul" treacherously detaches the human sensibility from its proper and health-giving ground: the never-ending moments of intense sensation. The "soul" carries the human sensibility into a context of religious and social ideas that have at best a tenuous connection with "parks" and "discords of the wind."

The positive aspect of Stevens' reiterated warning appears in such lines as the following from "Credences of Summer" in *Transport to Summer*. Here, Stevens suggests, is sound belief: "The rock cannot be broken. It is the truth./It rises from land and sea and covers them." That is, the rock is – and remains – the source of acute physical perception. It is a natural object, far removed from any piece of stone that human hands have chipped at and made into a "statue" – is a memorial of some past event or an expression of human dogmas. A few more lines refine this particular statement, one that resembles countless others in Stevens' work. The "rock of summer" (a "rock of winter" is apparently inferior) is not "A hermit's truth nor symbol in hermitage." A "hermit's truth" is what the gander soul flutters toward. Stevens continues:

> It is the visible rock, the audible,
> The brilliant mercy of a sure repose,
> On this present ground, the vividest repose,
> Things certain sustaining us in certainty.

Brief annotation – and all of Stevens' work stimulates such effort – would indicate that it is the actual rock that is esteemed, not the idea, Platonic or otherwise, of "rock." From the visible rock the errant "soul" gains a sure and not a treacherous "repose." And the rock is a "present ground" and, as such, the source of the only certainty that a poet and his reader can have confidence in.

Such lines indicate a perspective that extends throughout Stevens' work like a prairie landscape, insistent and unaltering. The lines, elegant in expression and charged with authority, invite each person to be a "center" into which are gathered separate moments of "vividest repose." Not the ersatz "repose" of some religious or political certainty. Not, even, the "repose" that some poets, retreating from politics and dogma, try to discover in personal relations, intense and unshakable. For the fierce outcry which is Matthew Arnold's only comfort on the "darkling plain" of "Dover Beach" – "Ah, love, let us be true/To one another!" – Stevens would have scarcely more patience than he has for "statues." As he observes in *Parts of a World*:

> Words are not forms of a single word.
> In the sum of the parts, there are only the parts.
> The world must be measured by eye ...

To the villainous "gander soul," the whole is always greater than the sum of its parts and testimony to principle, to some inclusive order that lies in a divine mind or, at least, at the very roots of things. The "single word" (or Word, as Christians would say) is a delusion.

Words serve the eye, and the eye takes in what aspect a "rock of summer" has at a particular moment.

As Stevens' large body of work indicates, such labor can be lifelong. It can exclude – and does – elements of existence that have counted for other poets and that, from Stevens' point of view, have corrupted them and those who read them. Stevens' "center" (the poet's awareness and perhaps his readers') is a clear crystal which sensation reaches – reaches and passes through with as little refraction as possible.

—Harold H. Watts

STEWART, Douglas (Alexander). Australian. Born in Eltham, New Zealand, 6 May 1913. Educated at New Plymouth Boys High School; Victoria University College, Wellington. Married Margaret Coen in 1946; one daughter. Literary Editor, *The Bulletin*, Sydney, 1940–61; Literary Adviser, Angus and Robertson, publishers, Sydney, 1961–73. Recipient: *Encyclopaedia Britannica* Award, 1968; Wilke Award, for non-fiction, 1975. O.B.E. (Officer, Order of the British Empire). Lives in Sydney.

PUBLICATIONS

Verse

Green Lions. 1937.
The White Cry. 1939.
Elegy for an Airman. 1940.
Sonnets to the Unknown Soldier. 1941.
The Dosser in Springtime. 1946.
Glencoe. 1947.
Sun Orchids. 1952.
The Birdsville Track and Other Poems. 1955.
Rutherford and Other Poems. 1962.
The Garden of Ships: A Poem. 1962.
(Poems). 1963; as Selected Poems, 1969, 1973.
Collected Poems, 1936–1967. 1967.

Plays

Ned Kelly (produced 1944). 1943.
The Fire on the Snow and The Golden Lover: Two Plays for Radio. 1944.
Shipwreck (produced 1948). 1947.
Four Plays (includes The Fire on the Snow, The Golden Lover, Ned Kelly, Shipwreck). 1958.
Fisher's Ghost: The Historical Comedy (produced 1961). 1960.

Radio Plays: The Fire on the Snow, 1941; The Golden Lover, 1943; The Earthquake Shakes the Land, 1944.

Fiction

A Girl with Red Hair and Other Stories.   1944.

Other

The Flesh and the Spirit: An Outlook on Literature.   1948.
The Seven Rivers (on angling).   1966.
The Broad Stream (criticism).   1975.
Norman Lindsay: A Personal Memoir.   1975.

Editor, *Coast to Coast: Australian Stories.*   1945.
Editor, with Nancy Keesing, *Australian Bush Ballads.*   1955.
Editor, with Nancy Keesing, *Old Bush Songs and Rhymes of Colonial Times, Enlarged and Revised from the Collection of A. B. Paterson.*   1957.
Editor, *Voyager Poems.*   1960.
Editor, *The Book of Bellerive,* by Joseph Tischler.   1961.
Editor, *(Poems),* by A. D. Hope.   1963.
Editor, *Modern Australian Verse: Poetry in Australia II.*   1964.
Editor, *Selected Poems,* by Hugh McCrae.   1966.
Editor, *Short Stories of Australia: The Lawson Tradition.*   1967.
Editor, with Nancy Keesing, *The Pacific Book of Bush Ballads.*   1967.
Editor, with Nancy Keesing. *Bush Songs, Ballads, and Other Verse.*   1968.
Editor, with Beatrice Davis, *Best Australian Short Stories.*   1971.
Editor, *The Wide Brown Land: A New Selection of Australian Verse.*   1971.
Editor, *Australia Fair.*   1976.

Reading List: *Stewart* by Nancy Keesing, 1965; *Stewart* by Clement Semmler, 1975.

*   *   *

Douglas Stewart is one of the most prolific and versatile of Australian writers. Well-known as a poet and radio playwright, he has also written short stories, essays, and biography. His account of the Sydney *Bulletin,* whose Red Page he edited from 1940 to 1960, is lively, informative, and graceful, and an important contribution to local literary history.

Stewart's *Collected Poems* assembled the best of his verse from 1936 onwards. Though he is a New Zealander by birth, few native Australians have developes Stewart's feeling for Australian landscape and animal life. His relationship with the natural world has been in turns egocentric, anthropomorphic, even animistic, but in the later poems it has become fraternal and non-attached. Where once he would have wished an insect to look at the world as a man would, he now tries to see the world, not merely as an insect would see it, which would be affectation, but through the eyes of an insect without surrendering the vision of a man. Courtesy is what distinguishes Stewart's attitude to the non-human world, and the reserve which is part of his own nature is scrupulously respected in other creatures, as the volume *Sun Orchids* makes clear. The mood of his verse is primarily one of good humour and well-being, and, in a darkening world living on the edge of a balance of terror, such a mood strikes many readers as superficial and evasive. The long narrative poem *Rutherford,* for instance, in spite of some fine passages, never really comes to grip with the central moral problem of post-Baconian science, while the weight of the verse suggests that the author shares the fuzzy optimism of his hero. Against this, however, should be set the magnificent ballad-sequence, *Glencoe,* with its fine structural coherence, its dramatic appropriateness and the timeless urgency of its theme: the wanton spirit of senseless faction in mankind which guarantees the suffering of the innocent. The main part of the sequence ends with one of Stewart's finest lyrics, the lament "Sigh, wind in the pine", with its grim warning:

> Oh life is fierce and wild
> And the heart of the earth is stone,
> And the hand of a murdered child
> Will not bear thinking on.
>
> Sigh, wind in the pine,
> Cover it over with snow;
> But terrible things were done
> Long, long ago.

The poem was written not long after another massacre: Hiroshima.

Those who deny Stewart the capacity for reflection must take *Glencoe* into account. They must also consider that his reflective exercises are as a rule conducted far below the surface of his poems, as the early poem "The River" makes plain: what he sees he has no objection to sharing, what he really thinks or feels, he seems to regard as largely his own business. His principal gift as a poet is the ability to transfigure the commonplace, to catch a moment of heightened experience and endow it with a history. The facility with which he seizes the poetic moment has sometimes led him into verbosity through over-exercise, and in some of his occasional verse there is a sense of strain. At times indeed he can degenerate into producing a kind of poetic "chirruping." Stewart's preoccupation with an immediate moment of intense awareness has tended to obscure the metaphysical base from which he works, expressed in paradoxical images of fire and snow, heat and cold, which perhaps hint at a struggle between the rational and the irrational in his own nature. Flame and snow come together in "Day and Night with Snow" (an early poem) and in "Flowering Place" (one of his most recent), while variants of the same image crop up in "Spider Gums," "The River," and "Flower of Winter." There is nothing static about this symbolism: fire is as much an image of destruction as it is of the continuity of life; snow, as much an image of potentiality, of steadfastness, as of death. His grasp of this archetypal imagery seems to be intuitional rather than intellectual, but for a lyrist, this is hardly a disadvantage.

The lack of intellectual rigour, however, becomes something of an obstacle in his prose work, especially in the literary criticism, in spite of its general good sense. His criticism, in *The Flesh and the Spirit* and *The Broad Stream*, belongs to the same impressionist genre, without being as captious or exhibitionist, as that of his more famous predecessor on the *Bulletin*, A. G. Stephens. It is intuitional, idiosyncratic, intensely subjective, capable of crystallising the essentials of a work under scrutiny, but liable to the temptations of large, arresting generalisations which will not stand up to close analysis because they take little account of what is extra-literary. It is never dull, always stimulating, often prejudiced, on occasions brilliant, and like much of the verse, often humorous.

Stewart's plays, written mainly for radio and all in verse, are strangely static: there is a much more genuinely dramatic element in the *Glencoe* ballads, or the poem "Terra Australis" than in *Fire on the Snow* or *Ned Kelly*. It is odd, for instance, that a dramatist should always choose situations which involve the characters in so much merely waiting around and talking. *Fire on the Snow*, about Scott's last expedition, unlike *Ned Kelly* and *Shipwreck*, is in addition devoid of human conflict; the enemy is nature, and endurance the only possible response. Written for radio, it is not a play for the theatre at all; and even *Ned Kelly*, which lends itself more easily to the stage, almost founders from excessive verbalisation. *Shipwreck* is a more shapely drama, in which the tendency to lyric expansion is kept under control. Even so, there is too much reliance at certain points on clumsy reporting of off-stage events. This play, however, is securely founded on a real moral conflict: whether a captain is justified in making a dangerous journey to bring help to his shipwrecked crew and passengers, when he must leave them on the verge of mutiny under precarious control.

Shipwreck is perhaps the strongest and most interesting of Stewart's plays. But *The Golden Lover*, on a New Zealand theme, is the most endearing. It dramatises the difficulty of choosing between dream and reality, between unearthly, intense love and domestic security; and in the Maori girl Tawhai, her lumpish husband Ruarangi, and Whana, the "golden lover" from the people of the Mist, Stewart has succeeded in creating three of his most convincing characters. As with *Ned Kelly*, however, the ending is left ambiguous; or rather it seems to be ambiguous until we reflect that the voices of commonsense have been given all the best tunes. It is difficult to avoid the conclusion, when one considers all the plays together, that the one value Stewart unequivocally endorses is sheer survival.

It is in the prose, finally, especially the biographical writing on Kenneth Slessor and Norman Lindsay, that doubts make themselves felt about Stewart's ultimate seriousness. The weight given to the superficial picturesqueness of some of the figures he admires, the flavour of old boy nostalgia for Bohemia, seem to sort ill with the realities of the life the world has known since Hiroshima. Nevertheless, it is possible that the generally light-hearted and circumspect temper of Stewart's writing may conceal a deep ineradicable pessimism, even disgust, about human nature, and that he has turned away to the natural world, content only with the surface pleasures of human society. Two passages in *Shipwreck* may crystallise his view of humanity; when Heynorick, the "observing" butler says suddenly, echoing Hamlet – "The appalling things that happen between sky and earth/Where the beast called man walks upright!" – and when Pelsart tells the condemned sailor: "I cannot pity you, prisoner; but, sometimes, my friends,/I am sorry for the race of men, trapped on this planet."

—Dorothy Green

STICKNEY, Trumbull. American. Born in Geneva, Switzerland, 20 June 1874. Spent his childhood in Europe; tutored by his father. Educated at Walton Lodge, Clevedon, Somerset, 1886; Cutler's School, New York City, 1890; Harvard University, Cambridge, Massachusetts, 1891–95 (Editor, *Harvard Monthly*), B.A. (magna cum laude) 1895; the Sorbonne, Paris, Doctorat ès Lettres, 1903. Instructor in Greek, Harvard University, 1903–04. *Died 11 October 1904.*

PUBLICATIONS

Collections

Homage to Stickney (selected verse), edited by James Reeves and Seán Haldane. 1968.
The Poems, edited by Amberys R. Whittle. 1972.

Verse

Dramatic Verses. 1902.
Poems, edited by George Cabot Lodge, John Ellerton Lodge, and William Vaughn Moody. 1905.

Other

Les Sentences dans la Poésie Grecque d'Homère à Euripide.   1903.

Translator, with Sylvain Lévi, *Bhagavadgita.*   1938

Reading List: *The Fright of Time: Stickney* by Seán Haldane, 1970; *Stickney* by Amberys R. Whittle, 1973.

*   *   *

One of that group of gifted Americans who came to early maturity in the 1890's only to have their lives snuffed out before the first decade of the new century was completed, Trumbull Stickney is memorable on several counts. As an accomplished Greek and Sanskrit scholar and one of the first intellectual cosmopolitans to attempt a career in American letters, he exhibits a cultural impulse which is to be later followed more extensively by writers like Pound and Eliot. Further, along with William Vaughn Moody and George Cabot Lodge, he aimed at resuscitating verse-drama, and his work in this genre (*Prometheus Pyrphoros* and two fragments based on the lives of the Emperor Julian and the young Benvenuto Cellini) points forward to later efforts in the century. And, powerfully under the influence of Browning, he produced a number of "dramatic scenes" ("Kalypso," "Oneiropolos," "Lodovico Martelli," "Requiescam," etc.), although his instincts for dramatic conflict and psychological subtlety seem less vigorous than his evident delight in historical reconstruction.

It is perhaps the lyrical quality of his writing that suggests the most promise in his work. Almost suffocated in the cloying rhetoric of the *fin de siècle*, heavy with twilight and rose-dust and a fatigued embrace of futility, Stickney's lyrics frequently manage a new, if wistful, vitality to the clichés of Romantic decadence. In poems like "Chestnuts in November," "At Sainte-Marguerite," "Mt. Lykaion," and in isolated passages from "Eride," Stickney's tempered musicality sustains the conventional formal structures, raising these poems above the level of similar lamentations which the Mauve Decade manufactured in wholesale lots. And in poems like "With thy two eyes look on me once again," "Leave him now quiet by the way," and, especially, "Mnemosyne," a quiet strength joins with a precise sense of rhythmical phrasing to produce verse which possesses an autonomy of statement and genuine eloquence. It is futile to speculate on what might have been, but in half a dozen poems Stickney's success was authentic and undeniable. As graceful as Santayana's verse but more concretely sensual, with an intellectual structure as sturdy as the early Robinson's but more personal and direct in tone, Stickney's achievement illustrates the highest ambitions of his generation, while implying a technique that may compensate for the weaknesses of its gentility.

—Earl Rovit

TATE, Allen.   American.   Born in Winchester, Kentucky, 19 November 1899. Educated at Georgetown Preparatory School, Washington, D.C.; Vanderbilt University, Nashville,

Tennessee, B.A. 1922. Married 1) the novelist Caroline Gordon, in 1924; 2) the poet Isabella Stewart Gardner in 1959; 3) Helen Heinz in 1966; three children. Member of the Fugitive Group of Poets: Founding Editor, with John Crowe Ransom, *The Fugitive*, Nashville, 1922–25; Editor, *Sewanee Review*, Tennessee, 1944–46; Editor, Belles Lettres series, Henry Holt and Company, New York, 1946–48. Lecturer in English, Southwestern College, Memphis, Tennessee, 1934–36; Professor of English, The Woman's College, Greensboro, North Carolina, 1938–39; Poet-in-Residence, Princeton University, New Jersey 1939–42; Lecturer in the Humanities, New York University, 1947–51. Since 1951, Professor of English, University of Minnesota, Minneapolis: Regents' Professor, 1966; Professor Emeritus, 1968. Visiting Professor in the Humanities, University of Chicago, 1949; Fulbright Lecturer, Oxford University, 1953, University of Rome, 1953–54, and Oxford and Leeds universities, 1958–59; Department of State Lecturer at the universities of Liège and Louvain, 1954, Delhi and Bombay, 1956, the Sorbonne, Paris, 1956, Nottingham, 1956, and Urbino and Florence, 1961; Visiting Professor of English, University of North Carolina, Greensboro, 1966, and Vanderbilt University, 1967. Member, Phi Beta Kappa Senate, 1951–53. Since 1948 Fellow, and since 1956 Senior Fellow, Kenyon School of English (now School of Letters, Indiana University, Bloomington). Constutant in Poetry, Library of Congress, Washington, D.C., 1943–44. Recipient: Guggenheim Fellowship, 1928, 1929; National Institute of Arts and Letters grant, 1948; Bollingen Prize, 1957; Brandeis University Creative Arts Award, 1960; Gold Medal of the Dante Society, Florence, 1962; Academy of American Poets Fellowship, 1963; Oscar Williams-Gene Derwood Award, 1975; National Medal for Literature, 1976. Litt.D.: University of Louisville, Kentucky, 1948; Coe College, Cedar Rapids, Iowa, 1955; Colgate University, Hamilton, New York, 1956; University of Kentucky, Lexington, 1960; Carleton College, Northfield, Minnesota, 1963; University of the South, Sewanee, Tennessee, 1970. Member, American Academy of Arts and Letters; President, National Institute of Arts and Letters, 1968. Since 1964, Member, Board of Chancellors, Academy of American Poets. Lives in Sewanee, Tennessee.

PUBLICATIONS

Verse

The Golden Mean and Other Poems, with Ridley Wills. 1923.
Mr. Pope and Other Poems. 1928.
Ode to the Confederate Dead, Being the Revised and Final Version of a Poem Previously Published on Several Occasions: To Which Are Added Message from Abroad and The Cross. 1930.
Three Poems. 1930.
Robert E. Lee. 1932.
Poems 1928–1931. 1932.
The Mediterranean and Other Poems. 1936.
Selected Poems. 1937.
Sonnets at Christmas. 1941.
The Winter Sea: A Book of Poems. 1944.
Poems 1920–1945: A Selection. 1947.
Poems 1922–1947. 1948.
Two Conceits for the Eye to Sing, If Possible. 1950.
Poems. 1960.
The Swimmers and Other Selected Poems. 1970.
Collected Poems 1919–1976. 1977.

Play

The Governess, with Anne Goodwin Winslow (produced 1962).

Fiction

The Fathers.   1938. revised edition, 1960.
The Fathers and Other Fiction.   1976.

Other

Stonewall Jackson: The Good Soldier: A Narrative.   1928.
Jefferson Davis: His Rise and Fall: A Biographical Narrative.   1929.
Reactionary Essays on Poetry and Ideas.   1936.
Reason in Madness: Critical Essays.   1941.
Invitation to Learning, with Huntington Cairns and Mark Van Doren.   1941.
Sixty American Poets, 1896–1944: A Preliminary Checklist.   1945.
On the Limits of Poetry: Selected Essays, 1928–1948.   1948.
The Hovering Fly and Other Essays.   1949.
The Forlorn Demon: Didactic and Critical Essays.   1953.
The Man of Letters in the Modern World: Selected Essays, 1928–1955.   1955.
Collected Essays.   1959.
Essays of Four Decades.   1968.
Modern Literature and the Lost Traveller.   1969.
The Translation of Poetry.   1972.
The Literary Correspondence of Donald Davidson and Tate, edited by John T. Fain and
    T. D. Young.   1974.
Memoirs and Opinions 1926–1974.   1975.

Editor, with others, Fugitives: An Anthology of Verse.   1928.
Editor, with Herbert Agar, Who Owns America? A New Declaration of
    Independence.   1936.
Editor, with A. Theodore Johnson, America Through the Essay: An Anthology for
    English Courses.   1938.
Editor, The Language of Poetry.   1942.
Editor, Princeton Verse Between Two Wars: An Anthology.   1942.
Editor, with John Peale Bishop, American Harvest: Twenty Years of Creative Writing in
    the United States.   1942.
Editor, Recent American Poetry and Poetic Criticism: A Selected List of
    References.   1943.
Editor, A Southern Vanguard (the John Peale Bishop memorial anthology).   1947.
Editor, The Collected Poems of John Peale Bishop.   1948.
Editor, with Caroline Gordon, The House of Fiction: An Anthology of the Short
    Story.   1950; revised edition, 1960.
Editor, with Lord David Cecil, Modern Verse in English, 1900–1950.   1958.
Editor, with John Berryman and Ralph Ross, The Arts of Learning.   1960.
Editor, Selected Poems of John Peale Bishop.   1960.
Editor, with Robert Penn Warren, Selected Poems, by Denis Devlin.   1963.
Editor, T. S. ELiot: The Man and His Work: A Critical Evaluation by Twenty-Six
    Distinguished Critics.   1966.
Editor, The Complete Poems and Selected Criticism of Edgar Allan Poe.   1968.

Editor, *Six American Poets: From Emily Dickinson to the Present: An Introduction.* 1972.
Translator, *The Vigil of Venus.* 1943.

Bibliography: *Tate: A Bibliography* by Marshall Fallwell, Jr., 1969.

Reading List: *The Last Alternatives: A Study of the Works of Tate* by M. K. Meiners, 1963; *Tate* by George Hemphill, 1964; *Tate* by Ferman Bishop, 1967; *Rumors of Morality: An Introduction to Tate* by M. E. Bradford, 1969; *Tate: A Literary Biography* by Radcliffe Squires, 1971, and *Tate and His Works: Critical Evaluations* edited by Squires, 1972.

* * *

Allen Tate is always associated with the Fugitives, the small group of Southern poets who were led by John Crowe Ransom of Vanderbilt University of Nashville during the early 1920's. But Tate was always his own man, and as a young Fugitive he found it necessary to reject much in the South; by 1924 he was living in New York City. Certainly Southern literary culture offered nothing that he could imitate directly, though his sense of the age led him to the French symbolists and hence back to Poe, about whom he was to write three of his most important essays. His best poem before 1925 is his version of Baudelaire's "Correspondences." This seems as important as his friendship with his first master, Ransom, because it allowed him access to the mainstream of modern poetry.

In New York City, married to the novelist Caroline Gordon, Tate was on close terms with many writers of his generation, especially Hart Crane, and he could easily be put among the second generation of modernists (if we put Eliot, Pound, and Joyce in the first generation). It may well be that his regional sense was sharpened by his residence in the East and then Paris for six years. At any rate, by 1926 he was writing the first version of his most ambitious early poem, "Ode to the Confederate Dead." The recently published correspondence between Tate and his Fugitive friend Donald Davidson shows him at that time occupying a kind of intermediary position between Davidson, who was writing *The Tall Men*, a long poem about Tennessee, and Crane, who was working on *The Bridge*, a visionary poem about America. Almost by instinct Tate shunned the "epical" treatment of experience. Where his Southern quality emerges most convincingly is in the elevation of tone that was characteristic of the rhetoricians of this region. In a sense the Old South was organized by the voices of the preacher and the politician, and this legacy of public speaking descended to many of the writers of the modern Southern Renascence.

The 1930's was the Agrarian period for the old Fugitive group, and Tate was frequently involved in the controversies that grew out of this movement, which coincided with an extraordinary outburst of literary achievement in the South. But his main energy went into his poetry, and his *Selected Poems* is one of the best collections of poetry in the decade. This volume contains the final version of the "Ode to the Confederate Dead," a distinguished meditative poem called "The Mediterranean," and a dozen shorter poems of great power and considerable range, such as "Emblems," "The Cross," and "The Wolves."

Meanwhile he was becoming one of the most important American critics; his first volume, *Reactionary Essays on Poetry and Ideas*, fully established his position. As critic he has always taken a large view of literary culture, but many of his influential early essays were written about such contemporaries as Crane, Archibald MacLeish, and John Peale Bishop. Certain theoretical essays have become classics of modern criticism: "Tension in Poetry," "Techniques of Fiction," "The Hovering Fly," and "A Southern Mode of the Imagination." These have generated as much discussion as anything written during the last generation in the United States. Perhaps the finest essays are two on Poe and Dante, "The Angelic Imagination" and "The Symbolic Imagination," published in 1951 at a time when he was writing some outstanding poems. Tate's criticism, in fact, is very much the work of a poet and often provides the setting for his verse.

Another work in prose that is closely related to Tate's verse of the 1930's is his novel *The Fathers*, which has been even more admired in recent years than it was when it was first published. Influenced in its technique by Ford Madox Ford's *The Good Soldier* ("the masterpiece of British fiction in this century"), the novel dramatizes with a great poetic intelligence the destruction of a Virginia family at the beginning of the Civil War. The critic Radcliffe Squires has shown the extent to which Allen Tate drew on the history of his own family for the subject.

The last phase of Tate's poetry started during the early 1940's, though it was long anticipated. It includes the splendid satire "Ode to Our Young Pro-Consuls of the Air," an attack on the modern religion of the state; his very title proposes an analogy between America and Rome. This in a sense was preparatory for the long poem "Seasons of the Soul" and a later group of poems in *terza rima*, including "The Swimmers" and "The Buried Lake," his most impressive work of all. In these late poems Tate has set his experience (his own, his family's, his region's) against a background of Christian experience represented most fully by Dante, and has "imitated" Dante's verse more closely than any other American poet has done. Brilliant and sometimes restless, Allen Tate has been more than a fine poet: he has helped to set the standards for the literary community in the United States.

—Ashley Brown

TEASDALE, Sara.   American.   Born in St. Louis, Missouri, 8 August 1884. Educated privately. Married Ernst B. Filsinger in 1914 (divorced, 1929). Lived in Europe and the Middle East, 1905–07; settled in New York City, 1916. Recipient: Pulitzer Prize, 1917; Poetry Society of American Annual Prize, 1917. *Died 29 January 1933*.

PUBLICATIONS

Collections

Collected Poems.   1937.

Verse

Sonnets to Duse and Other Poems.   1907.
Helen of Troy and Other Poems.   1911; revised edition, 1922.
Rivers to the Sea.   1915.
Love Songs.   1917.
Vignettes of Italy: A Cycle of Nine Songs for High Voice.   1919.
Flame and Shadow.   1920; revised edition, 1924.
Dark of the Moon.   1926.
Stars To-Night: Verses New and Old for Boys and Girls.   1930.
A Country House.   1932.
Strange Victory.   1933.

Other

> *Editor, The Answering Voice: One Hundred Love Lyrics by Women.* 1917; revised
> edition, 1928.
> Editor, *Rainbow Gold: Poems for Boys and Girls.* 1922.

Bibliography: by Vivian Buchan, in *Bulletin of Bibliography 25,* 1967.

Reading List: *Teasdale: A Biography* by Margaret Haley Carpenter, 1960.

*   *   *

Sara Teasdale, whose verse suggests, in her own phrase, "a delicate fabric of bird song," is one of America's most charming lyrists. Well-received and popular for some fifteen years after *Love Songs* (1917) took the Pulitzer Prize for poetry, she was posthumously, and unjustly, somewhat underrated by the time *Collected Poems* appeared in 1937.

Miss Teasdale's first book of consequence was her third, *Rivers to the Sea,* in which signs of the mature poet became clearly evident. Happily, the best of her early work was incorporated into the body of *Love Songs,* whose seemingly artless musicality informs a most lucid lyricism. *Flame and Shadow* marks, if anything, an advance in emotional depth and "natural falterings"; but *Dark of the Moon,* while gracefully competent, appears somewhat anticlimactic in its minor accents: the book of a "woman seemingly poured empty." The first posthumous collection, *Strange Victory,* has, however, some of its author's most memorable pieces – in "All That Was Mortal," "Grace Before Sleep," "Advice to a Girl," and others.

Miss Teasdale's verse, repeatedly concerned with the stars, often reflective of her travels, always simple in technique and verse form and natural in statement, dewlike and fragile in quality, and gentle in its acceptance of sorrow (though never bathetic), poses no intellectual problems. Constantly preoccupied with beauty, as idea and as evocation, it offers instead quietly ironic, but joyful, acceptance of life, exquisiteness of feminine perception, and most delicate artistry. All of which does not deny that Miss Teasdale has occasionally "reached into the black waters whose chill brings wisdom," poems like "Wood Song" and numerous others being the memorable evidence.

—George Brandon Saul

THOMAS, Dylan (Marlais).   Welsh.   Born in Swansea, Glamorganshire, 27 October 1914. Educated at Swansea Grammar School. Worked with a documentary film unit during World War II. Married Caitlin Macnamara in 1936; two sons and one daughter. Reporter, *South Wales Daily Post,* Swansea, 1931–32. Free-lance writer from 1933. Visited the United States, giving poetry readings, 1950, 1952, 1953. Recipient: Foyle Poetry Prize, 1953. *Died 9 November 1953.*

PUBLICATIONS

Collections

> *Selected Letters,* edited by Constantine FitzGibbon.   1966.
> *Collected Prose.*   1969.

Selected Writings, edited by J. P. Harries.   1970.
The Poems, edited by Daniel Jones.   1971; revised edition, 1974.
Selected Poems, edited by Walford Davies.   1974.

Verse

18 Poems.   1934.
Twenty-Five Poems.   1936.
The Map of Love: Verse and Prose.   1939.
The World I Breathe (includes stories).   1939.
New Poems.   1943.
Deaths and Entrances.   1946.
Twenty-Six Poems.   1950.
In Country Sleep and Other Poems.   1952.
Collected Poems 1934–1952.   1952; as *The Collected Poems,*1953.
Two Epigrams of Fealty.   1954.
Galsworthy and Gawsworth.   1954.

Plays

Return Journey (broadcast 1947).   In *New Directions: Five One-Act Plays in the Modern Idiom*, edited by Alan Durband, 1961.
The Doctor and the Devils, from the Story by Donald Taylor (film-script).   1953.
Under Milk Wood: A Play for Voices (produced 1953).   1954.
The Beach of Falesá (film-script).   1963.
Twenty Years A-Growing: A Film Script from the Story by Maurice O'Sullivan.   1964.
Me and My Bike: An Unfinished Film-Script.   1965.
The Doctor and the Devils and Other Scripts (includes *Twenty Years A-Growing, A Dream of Winter, The Londoner*).   1966.

Screenplays: *Balloon Site 568*, 1942; *Wales*, 1942; *New Towns for Old*, 1942; *Our Country*, 1944; *When We Build Again*, 1945; *The Three Weird Sisters*, with Louise Birt and David Evans, 1948; *No Room at the Inn*, with Ivan Foxwell, 1948.

Radio Play: *Return Journey*, 1947.

Fiction

Portrait of the Artist as a Young Dog.   1940.
A Prospect of the Sea and Other Stories and Prose Writings, edited by Daniel Jones.   1955.
Adventures in the Skin Trade.   1955; as *Adventures in the Skin Trade and Other Stories*, 1955.
Rebecca's Daughters.   1965.
Two Tales: Me and My Bike, and Rebecca's Daughters.   1968.
The Outing.   1971.
The Followers.   1976.
The Death of the King's Canary, with John Davenport.   1976.

Other

Selected Writings, edited by John L. Sweeney.   1946.
Quite Early One Morning: Broadcasts.   1954.
Conversations about Christmas.   1954.
Letters to Vernon Watkins, edited by Vernon Watkins.   1957.
Miscellany: Poems, Stories, Broadcasts.   1963.
The Colour of Saying: An Anthology of Verse Spoken by Dylan Thomas, edited by Ralph
    N. Maud and Aneirin Talfan Davies.   1963; as *Dylan Thomas's Choice: An
    Anthology of Verse Spoken by Dylan Thomas*, 1964.
Miscellany Two: A Visit to Grandpa's and Other Stories and Poems.   1966.
The Notebooks, edited by Ralph N. Maud.   1967; as *Poet in the Making: The Notebooks
    of Thomas*, 1968.
Twelve More Letters.   1970.
Early Prose Writings, edited by Walford Davies.   1971.
Living and Writing, edited by Christopher Capeman.   1972.
Miscellany Three.   1978.

Bibliography: *Thomas: A Bibliography* by J. Alexander Rolph, 1956; *Thomas in Print* by
Ralph Maud and Albert Glover, 1970, *Appendix, 1969–1971* by Walford Davies, 1972.

Reading List: *The Poetry of Thomas* by Elder Olson, 1954; *A Reader's Guide to Thomas* by
William York Tindall, 1962; *Dylan: Druid of the Broken Body* by Aneirin Talfan Davies,
1964; *The Life of Thomas* by Constantine FitzGibbon, 1965; *Thomas: A Collection of Critical
Essays* edited by C. B. Cox, 1966; *Thomas: New Critical Essays* edited by Walford Davies,
1972; *The Country of the Spirit* by Rushworth M. Kidder, 1973; *Thomas: Poet of His People*
by Andrew Sinclair, 1975, as *Thomas: No Man More Magical*, 1976; *Thomas: A Biography*
by Paul Ferris, 1977.

*   *   *

Dylan Thomas is one of the most original voices in British poetry since Yeats and Eliot.
While Thomas wrote compelling autobiographical stories and a splendid radio play, *Under
Milk Wood*, his major achievement is as a poet. He saw himself as an heir to the English
Romantic tradition, a tradition that he evoked in his poetry as an alternative to the classicism
of Eliot and the political consciousness of Auden, the other major voice to appear in the
1930's.

Critics spoke of his spontaneity as a means of explaining his difficult imagery and syntax.
However, Thomas was a craftsman who, in an obsessive quest for the meaning he sought,
rewrote every line countless times: "My lines, *all* my lines, are of the tenth intensity. They
are not the words that express what I want to express. They are the only words I can find that
come near to expressing a half" (quoted by Constantine FitzGibbon). For Thomas, poetry was
a means of self-definition and of self-discovery. Thomas's major subject was his own
emotional life; he used his poems to define his private passions and attitudes rather than to
respond to public events ("My poetry is, or should be, useful to me for one reason: it is the
record of my individual struggle from darkness towards some measure of light ..."). He also
believed that his poems about his own emotions described struggles and conflicts that readers
would recognize as their own.

Thomas's early poems are informed by a pantheistic view of the universe; God is not a
personality but a ubiquitous presence throughout the universe. In "The Force That Through
the Green Fuse Drives the Flower" (1933), Thomas defines how the destructive and
constructive forces of the natural world are in a vital relationship. In this poem, the speaker
marvels how each positive aspect is balanced by a corresponding negative aspect:

The force that through the green fuse drives the flower
Drives my green age; that blasts the roots of trees
Is my destroyer.
And I am dumb to tell the crooked rose
My youth is bent by the same wintry fever.

Thomas's early poems consist of images organized around a concept. As he wrote to his friend and fellow Welsh poet Vernon Watkins, "A poem by myself *needs* a host of images because its centre is a host of images.... Each image holds within it the seed of its own destruction, and my dialectical method, as I understand it, is a constant building up and breaking down of the images that comes out of the central seed, which is itself destructive and constructive at the same time." In his early work Thomas was intoxicated by the sound and feel of words; quite often sound partially subsumes sense and obscurity results.

Both the Welsh bardic tradition and Welsh nonconformity were important influences on Thomas. The latter shaped his concern with sin and salvation in both his religious and ostensibly secular poems. In "Vision and Prayer" and "Altarwise by Owl-light," the intense sonnet sequence that recalls seventeenth-century religious poetry, Thomas expresses his hope if not his faith in Christ's intervention on man's behalf. Thomas did much of his work as a poet between July 1931 and November 1934 in Swansea, Wales. The poems written in this period are the basis of his first two volumes, *18 Poems* and *Twenty-five Poems*; and many of his later poems were based on notebook versions of poems written then. Throughout his career he wrote about Wales and the people he knew there. The poverty and hopelessness of Swansea young men in the depression inform "I See the Boys of Summer."Among his most moving poems are "After the Funeral," his elegy for his aunt, Ann Jones, and the poem to his dying father, "Do Not Go Gentle into That Good Night."

Perhaps Thomas's masterpiece is "A Winter's Tale," a poem that is part of a great burst of creativity in 1944–45, the period when he also wrote "A Refusal to Mourn," "Fern Hill," and "Poem in October." Thomas's later poems have more of a traditional narrative shape, and are more logical, controlled, and ultimately clearer. "A Winter's Tale" is the central work in *Deaths and Entrances*, a book that established his reputation as a major figure. In this poem Thomas shows how not only the poet, but every man can achieve personal salvation through his imagination. That the creative imagination is part of each man derives from Thomas's Nonconformist upbringing. Thomas wrote of the vitality of the imagination at a time when poetry and indeed civilization seemed threatened by World War II, and when he was deeply worried about his own and his father's health in addition to his own economic situation. The man at prayer is Thomas himself who, while living through a private and historical winter, feared personal and cultural death as well as the atrophy of his poetic energies. That this lonely man becomes one with the bird – symbol of poetic creativity and the imaginative process – shows how any man can overcome self-doubt and anxiety.

Persistent lung trouble, hypochondria, and alcoholism no doubt contributed to the preoccupation with death in his poetry. His series of remarkable birthday poems, "Twenty-four Years," "Poem in October," and "Poem on his Birthday," becomes increasingly concerned with his own death which he knew was fast approaching. This obsession belies his frequent testimony within the poems that he has come to terms with death. Yet if Thomas's poems regret the inevitable passing of his vitality, they also celebrate not only his passions and joys, but the variety and splendor of God's creation. In the November 1952 note to his *Collected Poems*, Thomas wrote: "These poems, with all their crudities, doubts, and confusions, are written for the love of Man and in Praise of God, and I'd be a damn' fool if they weren't."

—Daniel R. Schwarz

THOMAS, (Philip) Edward. English. Born in London, 3 March 1878. Educated at Battersea Grammar School, London; St. Paul's School, London; Lincoln College, Oxford. Corporal in the Artists' Rifles in World War I; killed in action at Arras, 1917. Married Helen Noble in 1899; one son and two daughters. Journalist: reviewer for *Daily Chronicle* and often periodicals; encouraged by Robert Frost, began writing verse 1914, and wrote most of his poetry during acitve service. *Died 9 April 1917.*

PUBLICATIONS

Collections

The Prose (selection), edited by Roland Gant.   1948.
Poems and Last Poems, edited by Edna Longley.   1973.
Thomas on the Countryside: A Selection of His Prose and Verse, edited by Roland Gant.   1977.
Collected Poems, edited by R. George Thomas.   1978.

Verse

Six Poems.   1916.
An Annual of New Poetry, with others.   1917.
Poems by Edward Thomas – "Edward Eastaway."   1917.
Last Poems.   1918.

Fiction

The Happy-Go-Lucky Morgans.   1913.

Other

The Woodland Life.   1897.
Horae Solitariae (essays).   1902.
Oxford.   1903; revised edition, 1922.
Rose Acre Papers.   1904.
Beautiful Wales.   1905; as *Wales,* 1924.
The Heart of England.   1906.
Richard Jefferies: His Life and Work.   1909.
The South Country.   1909.
Rest and Unrest (essays).   1910.
Feminine Influence on the Poets.   1910.
Windsor Castle.   1910.
Celtic Stories.   1911.
The Isle of Wight.   1911.
Light and Twilight (essays).   1911.
Maurice Maeterlinck.   1911.
The Tenth Muse.   1911.
Swinburne: A Critical Study.   1912.
Borrow: The Man and His Books.   1912.

Lafcadio Hearn.   1912.
Norse Tales.   1912.
The Icknield Way.   1913.
The Country.   1913.
Pater: A Critical Study.   1913.
In Pursuit of Spring.   1914.
Four-and-Twenty Blackbirds (juvenile).   1915; as *The Complete Fairy Tales,* 1966.
The Life of the Duke of Marlborough.   1915.
Keats.   1916.
A Literary Pilgrim in England.   1917.
Cloud Castle and Other Papers.   1922.
The Last Sheaf.   1928.
The Childhood of Thomas: A Fragment of Autobiography.   1938.
The Friend of the Blackbird.   1938.
Letters to Gordon Bottomley, edited by R. George Thomas.   1968.
The Diary, 1st January–8th April 1917, edited by Roland Gant.   1977.

Editor, *The Poems of John Dyer.*   1903.
Editor, *The Pocket Book of Poems and Songs for the Open Air.*   1907.
Editor, *The Book of the Open Air.*   2 vols., 1907–08.
Editor, *Some British Birds.*   1908.
Editor, *British Butterflies and Other Insects.*   1908.
Editor, *The Hills and the Vale,* by Richard Jefferies.   1909.
Editor, *The Plays and Poems of Christopher Marlowe.*   1909.
Editor, *The Pocket George Borrow.*   1912.
Editor, *This England: An Anthology from Her Writers.*   1915.
Editor, *The Flowers I Love.*   1916.

Reading List: *Thomas: A Biography and a Bibliography* by R. P. Eckert, 1937; *The Life and Letters of Thomas* by John Moore, 1939; *Thomas* by Henry Coombes, 1956; *Thomas* by Vernon Scannell, 1962; *Thomas: A Critical Biography* by William Cooke, 1970; *Thomas* by R. George Thomas, 1972; *Thomas: A Poet for His Country* by Jan Marsh, 1978.

*   *   *

The diffident, tentative rhythms of Edward Thomas's poetry, full of qualification and obliquity, forever modulating into conditional and subjunctive, are the reflex of what he described in a 1908 review as "a centrifugal age, in which principles and aims are numerous, vague, uncertain, confused, and in conflict." Like his mentor, the nature-mystic Richard Jefferies, he is always "listening, lying in wait,/For what [he] should, yet never can remember," aware of the ephemeral nature of those epiphanies which endow the moment with value ("truths I had not dreamed,/And have forgotten since their beauty passed"), seeking to penetrate to some inapprehensible core of meaning contained within the shifting forms of experience, but repeatedly brought to the admission which ends "The Glory": "I cannot bite the day to the core." His poems are frequently poised – "The Signpost" or "The Bridge" – at some transit point, some "moment brief between/Two lives," in a twilight latent with forfeit possibilities. He is recurrently engaged on a journey with no clear destination, pursuing, in "The Other," his own elusive identity, or, in "Lob," a lost spontaneity symbolized by the autochthonous figure who epitomizes the threatened but irrepressible creativity of the English land, language, and people. Much of his pastoral poetry is tinged with an elegiac sadness, even when he is affirming the capacity of this England to abide, "out of the reach of change" ("Haymaking").

Thomas felt himself to be "a superfluous man," living on the margins of a society with which he could not identify, appalled by the suburbanization of that "South Country," that "Heart of England," which was his spiritual home and locale of all his writing, turning in scepticism and revulsion from the easy assurances and insistent warmongering of many of his contemporaries. At times, this leads to a sense of metaphysical dispossession and exile, as in "Home":

> I would go back home again
> Now. Yet how should I go?
>
> This is my grief. That land,
> My home, I have never seen....

But Thomas's mood is essentially that for which he praised John Davidson in 1903 – "alert, determined despair, not that comatose despair which is contented with itself, but a despair that is nervous and interested, and so strenuous that it serves some men as well as hope." Though he despised the motives that went into the Great War, he nevertheless looked to it as some kind of release from the "captivity," the "evil dream" of his life. Most of his poetry was indeed written in the two years between enlistment and his death at Arras in 1917. But, beyond this, the War seemed an answer to a dilapidated civilization, turning "young men to dung," but also replacing "the old house,/Outmoded, dignified,/Dark and untenanted" with a new one in which true community might be restored. Though Thomas acknowledged that he was a product of the old house, he affirmed, too, in "Gone, Gone Again," his hope for the new:

> I am something like that;
> Only I am not dead,
> Still breathing and interested
> In the house that is not dark....

For all his fear of becoming an "isolated, self-considering brain" there can be few collections of poetry with a higher proportion of narratives of encounter and conversation, more vocatives or simple celebrations of the unique quiddity, the richness and enigma of other lives – men, women, and children, birds, beasts, and flowers – revealing a tender and respectful affection which affirms the creatureliness of all life.

—Stan Smith

THOMAS, R(onald) S(tuart). Welsh. Born in Cardiff, in 1913. Educated at the University of Wales, B.A. in classics 1935; St. Michael's College, Llandaff. Ordained deacon, 1936, priest, 1937; Curate of Chirk, 1936–40, and of Hanmer, 1940–42; Rector of Manafon, 1942–54; Vicar of St. Michael's, Eglwysfach, 1954–67. Since 1967, Vicar of St. Hywyn, Aberdaron, with St. Mary, Bodferin. Recipient: Heinemann Award, 1955; Queen's Gold Medal for Poetry, 1964; Welsh Arts Council Award, 1968, 1976. Lives in Gwynedd, Wales.

PUBLICATIONS

Verse

The Stones of the Field.   1946.
An Acre of Land.   1952.
The Minister.   1953.
Song at the Year's Turning: Poems 1942–1954.   1955.
Poetry for Supper.   1958.
Judgement Day.   1960.
Tares.   1961.
The Bread of Truth.   1963.
Pietà.   1966.
Not That He Brought Flowers.   1968.
H'm.   1972.
Selected Poems 1946–1968.   1973.
What Is a Welshman?   1974.
Laboratories of the Spirit.   1975.
Frequencies.   1978.

Other

The Mountains.   1968.
Young and Old (juvenile).   1972.

Editor, *The Batsford Book of Country Verse.*   1961.
Editor, *The Penguin Book of Religious Verse.*   1963.
Editor, *Selected Poems,* by Edward Thomas.   1964.
Editor, *A Choice of George Herbert's Verse.*   1967.
Editor, *A Choice of Wordsworth's Verse.*   1971.

Reading List: *Thomas* by R. G. Thomas, 1964; "Thomas Issue" of *Poetry Wales,* Winter 1972.

*   *   *

Born one year before Dylan Thomas, R. S. Thomas has emerged as the most significant Anglo-Welsh poet since the death of the younger man. His concerns appear regional; there is a cyclical preoccupation throughout his career with relationships: the poet and his vocation (he is an Anglican priest), the educated man and the land-wise peasant, the poet-priest and his country. It becomes clear as one reads his work that the regional is a starting point for the universal.

His verse is, as Glyn Jones says, "lucid, sparing, austere," sometimes even bleak. There is nothing here of the nostalgic warmth of his namesake, little, it would seem, of the easy celebration that some critics affirm as the essence of Dylan Thomas. He is much more a poet of the unresolved, perhaps unresolvable, tensions with which an adult sensiblility has to cope. That he is an Anglican priest who had to learn Welsh as a second language in order to work in Welsh-speaking parishes, that he is an educated man with a care for the uneducated, an urban man amongst countrymen, that he has a wry acceptance of his own inadequacies, a fierce conscience that examines his own motives and thinks them no better than other men's – all these things make him a type of our modern dilemma. His verse, sharply focussed on the here and now, accepts without question the implications of time and eternity. His Welsh peasant is, like Alun Lewis' "landless soldier lost in war," a figure for humanity.

—John Stuart Williams

TOLSON, Melvin B(eaunorus).   American.   Born in Moberly, Missouri, 6 February 1898. Educated at Lincoln High School, Kansas City, Missouri, graduated 1918; Fisk University, Nashville, Tennessee, 1918–20; Lincoln University, Oxford, Pennsylvania, 1920–23, B.A. 1923; Columbia University, New York, M.A. 1940. Married Ruth Southall in 1922. Teacher at Wiley College, Marshall, Texas, 1924–47; Professor of English and Drama, Langston University, Oklahoma, 1947–66. Poet-in-Residence, Tuskegee Institute, 1965. Mayor of Langston after 1954. Recipient: Omega Psi Phi Award in Creative Literature, 1945; National Institute of Arts and Letters award, 1966. D.L.: Lincoln University, 1954; D.H.L.: Lincoln University, 1965. Poet Laureate of Liberia, 1947; appointed permanent Breadloaf Fellow in Poetry, 1954. *Died 29 August 1966.*

PUBLICATIONS

Verse

> *Rendezvous with America.*   1944.
> *Libretto for the Republic of Liberia.*   1953.
> *Harlem Gallery: Book I, The Curator.*   1965.

Play

> *The Fire in the Flint,* from a work by Walter White (produced 1952).

Reading List: Introduction by Karl Shapiro to *Harlem Gallery,* 1965; *Tolson* by Joy Flasch, 1972.

*   *   *

On the basis of his first volume of poetry, *Rendezvous with America,* it would hardly have been possible to predict the kind of poet Melvin Tolson was to be a decade later. A poet who writes "I gaze upon her silken loveliness/She is a passion-flower of joy and pain/On the golden bed I came back to possess" does not show particular promise. Likewise the lines "America is the Black Man's country/The Red Man's, the Yellow Man's/The Brown Man's, the White Man's" are not suggestive of the great lines yet to come.

There are, however, certain characteristics of the earlier poetry which were to be developed in such a way as to become hallmarks of the later poetry, more its essence than ornament. The second stanza, for example, of "An Ex-Judge at the Bar" is in style and content very much like a good deal of Tolson's later poetry and untypical of the rather commonplace character of much of the first volume. That stanza, "I know, Bartender, yes, I know when the Law/Should wag its tail or rip with fang and claw./When Pilate washed his hands, that neat event/Set for us judges a Caesarean precedent," is in tone typically Tolsonian. The juxtaposition of the formal and the informal, the classical and the contemporary, the familiar and the unusual accounts in large measure for the unique character of Tolson's best poetry.

Such juxtapositions are more pronounced in *Libretto for the Republic of Liberia*, where, in addition, the "gift for language" noted in Allen Tate's introduction to the volume, becomes apparent. The effect of the juxtaposition of the learned encyclopedic references and the most abstruse vocabulary with commonplace references, vocabulary, and rhyme, managed within a highly traditional form, is pyrotechnic. The occurrence in the same context of French, German, Latin, Hebrew, Swahili, Arabic, Spanish, and Sanskrit references with commonplace activities, occupations, facts, and events created a system of tensions not unlike the dynamic of forces holding an atom or a galaxy together. Each element threatens to go off on its own; yet as long as the balance of forces remains constant, the system functions. Tolson, by virtue of an extraordinary mind and intelligence, keeps a vast array of disparate elements in constant relationship. His poetry is, therefore, coherent, and the primary effect it arouses is of the containment and control of vast reserves of energy.

This bears on Karl Shapiro's controversial statement in his introduction to *Harlem Gallery*, Tolson's final volume, that "Tolson writes in Negro." It is not at bottom the language which prompted Shapiro's observation. Rather, it is the intellectual disposition of the tension between two worlds that finds its manifestation in the language. Tolson belongs (and this distinguishes him from Eliot, Pound, and Hart Crane, whom he read avidly) to an Afro-American world and an American-European world, and he knows these worlds in intricate detail. The balance he sustains between them is the source of his power. Few understand him because few know both worlds as well, and few are as totally committed as he to such a high universal standard of values.

—D. B. Gibson

VAN DOREN, Mark (Albert). American.   Born in Hope, Illinois, 13 June 1894. Educated at the University of Illinois, Urbana, A.B. 1914, A.M. 1915; Columbia University, New York, Ph.D. 1920. Served in the Army during World War I. Married Dorothy Graffe in 1922; two sons. Instructor, 1920–24, Assistant Professor, 1924–35, Associate Professor, 1935–42, and Professor of English, 1942–59, Columbia University; also, Lecturer at St. John's College, Annapolis, Maryland, 1937–57. Literary Editor, 1924–28, and Film Critic, 1935–38, *The Nation*, New York; Participant in the radio program Invitation to Learning, CBS, 1940–42. Visiting Professor of English, Harvard University, Cambridge, Massachusetts, 1963. Recipient: Pulitzer Prize, 1940; Columbia University's Alexander Hamilton Medal, 1959; Hale Award, 1960; National Conference of Christians and Jews Brotherhood Award, 1960; Huntington Hartford Creative Award, 1962; Emerson-Thoreau Award, 1963. Litt.D.: Bowdoin College, Brunswick, Maine, 1944; University of Illinois, Urbana, 1958; Columbia University, 1960; Knox College, Galesburg, Illinois, 1966; Harvard University, 1966; Jewish Theological Seminary of America, New York, 1970; L.H.D.: Adelphi University, Garden City, New York, 1957; Mount Mary College,

Milwaukee, Wisconsin, 1965; Honorary Fellow: St. John's College, 1959; Honorary M.D.: Connecticut State Medical Society, 1966. Member, American Academy of Arts and Letters. *Died 10 December 1972.*

PUBLICATIONS

Verse

>*Spring Thunder and Other Poems.* 1924.
>*7 P.M. and Other Poems.* 1926.
>*Now the Sky and Other Poems.* 1928.
>*Jonathan Gentry.* 1931.
>*A Winter Diary and Other Poems.* 1935.
>*The Last Look and Other Poems.* 1937.
>*Collected Poems 1922–1938.* 1939.
>*The Mayfield Deer.* 1941.
>*Our Lady Peace and Other War Poems.* 1942.
>*The Seven Sleepers and Other Poems.* 1944.
>*The Country Year.* 1946.
>*The Careless Clock: Poems about Children in the Family.* 1947.
>*New Poems.* 1948.
>*Humanity Unlimited: Twelve Sonnets.* 1950.
>*In That Far Land.* 1951.
>*Mortal Summer.* 1953.
>*Spring Birth and Other Poems.* 1953.
>*Selected Poems.* 1954.
>*Morning Worship.* 1960.
>*Collected and New Poems 1924–1963.* 1963.
>*The Narrative Poems.* 1964.
>*That Shining Place: New Poems.* 1969.
>*Good Morning: Last Poems.* 1973.

Plays

>*The Last Days of Lincoln* (produced 1961). 1959.
>*Never, Never Ask His Name* (produced 1965). In *Three Plays,* 1966.
>*Three Plays* (includes *Never, Never Ask His Name, A Little Night Music, The Weekend That Was*). 1966.

Fiction

>*The Transients.* 1935.
>*Windless Cabins.* 1940.
>*Tilda.* 1943.
>*The Short Stories.* 1950.
>*The Witch of Ramoth and Other Tales.* 1950.
>*Nobody Says a Word and Other Stories.* 1953.
>*Home with Hazel.* 1957.
>*Collected Stories.* 3 vols., 1962–68.

Other

Henry David Thoreau: A Critical Study.   1916.

The Poetry of John Dryden.   1920; revised edition, 1931; as *John Dryden: A Study of His Poetry,* 1946.

American and British Literature since 1890, with Carl Van Doren.   1925; revised edition, 1939.

Edwin Arlington Robinson.   1927.

Dick and Tom: Tales of Two Ponies (juvenile).   1931.

Dick and Tom in Town (juvenile).   1932.

Shakespeare.   1939.

Studies in Metaphysical Poetry: Two Essays and a Bibliography, with Theodore Spencer.   1939.

The Transparent Tree (juvenile).   1940.

Invitation to Learning, with Huntington Cairns and Allen Tate.   1941.

The New Invitation to Learning.   1942.

The Private Reader: Selected Articles and Reviews.   1942.

Liberal Education.   1943.

The Noble Voice: A Study of Ten Great Poems.   1946; as *Great Poems of Western Literature,* 1966.

Nathaniel Hawthorne.   1949.

Introduction to Poetry.   1951.

Don Quixote's Profession.   1958.

The Autobiography.   1958.

The Happy Critic and Other Essays.   1961.

The Dialogues of Archibald MacLeish and Van Doren, edited by Warren V. Busch.   1964.

In the Beginning, Love: Dialogues on the Bible, with Maurice Samuel, edited by Edith Samuel.   1973.

The Book of Praise: Dialogues on the Psalms, with Maurice Samuel, edited by Edith Samuel.   1975.

Editor, *Samuel Sewall's Diary.*   1927.

Editor, *A History of the Life and Death, Virtues and Exploits of General George Washington,* by Mason Locke Weems.   1927.

Editor, *An Anthology of World Poetry.*   1928; selection, as *An Anthology of English and American Poetry,* 1936.

Editor, *The Travels of William Bartram.*   1928.

Editor, *Nick of the Woods; or, The Jibbenainosay: A Tale of Kentucky,* by Robert Montgomery Bird.   1928.

Editor, *A Journey to the Land of Eden and Other Papers,* by William Byrd.   1928.

Editor, *An Autobiography of America.*   1929.

Editor, *Correspondence of Aaron Burr and His Daughter Theodosia.*   1929.

Editor, with Garibaldi M. Lapolla, *A Junior Anthology of World Poetry.*   1929.

Editor, *The Life of Sir William Phips,* by Cotton Mather.   1929.

Editor, with Garibaldi M. Lapolla, *The World's Best Poems.*   1932.

Editor, *American Poets, 1630–1930.*   1932; as *Masterpieces of American Poets,* 1936.

Editor, *The Oxford Book of American Prose.*   1932.

Editor, with John W. Cunliffe and Karl Young, *Century Readings in English Literature,* 5th edition.   1940.

Editor, *A Listener's Guide to Invitation to Learning, 1940–41, 1941–42.*   2 vols., 1940–42.

Editor, *The Night of the Summer Solstice and Other Stories of the Russian War.*   1943.

Editor, *Walt Whitman.*   1945.

Editor, *The Portable Emerson*. 1946.
Editor, *Selected Poetry*, by William Wordsworth. 1950.
Editor, *Introduction to Poetry*. 1951; as *Enjoying Poetry*, 1951.
Editor, with others, *Riverside Poetry: 48 New Poems by 27 Poets*. 1956.
Editor, *100 Poems*. 1967.

*   *   *

Mark Van Doren's poetry, which consists of over a thousand poems in *Collected and New Poems* and other volumes, including a posthumous collection, *Good Morning*, constitutes one of the more prolific and accomplished bodies of work by an American poet in the 20th century. While the sheer bulk has often astonished and sometimes dismayed critics, it represents, as Richard Howard has observed, "not so much an embarrassment as an embodiment of riches."

Van Doren was originally hailed by T. S. Eliot and others as a master of rural verse and conveniently placed in the tradition of Robert Frost. He soon demonstrated, however, a distinctive voice that deepened through a sustained middle period culminating in his first *Collected Poems* (1939) and which grew in variety of subject matter and range for over three more decades after he received the Pulitzer Prize in 1940. Influenced by John Dryden as a young scholar, Van Doren belongs in a group that might include Hardy, early Yeats, Graves and, in specifically American ways, Emily Dickinson, Edwin Arlington Robinson, and Frost. Allen Tate once wisely concluded, after also suggesting "a trace of William Browne (epigrams and *Britannia's Pastorals*, 1613), traces of Ben Jonson, more than a trace of Robert Herrick" that all of them might "add up to Mark Van Doren who is like nobody else."

Singularly devoid of the common French influences in modern verse, Van Doren also eschewed confessional or analytic tendencies. He treated his principal subjects, the cosmos, love, finality, family matters, and particularly children, animals, paradox, and knowledge in a lucid manner that transcends simplistic notions of modernity and personal sensibilities. There is a passionate intelligence lurking behind many of the poems that somehow never intrudes. Indeed, it is a subtle presence that calls forth different interpretations on subsequent readings, though there is never intentional obscurity.

His poetic corpus, apart from substantial accomplishments in other literary fields, contains an intricate world of pleasures, observations, and intellectual insights. As a master craftsman, Van Doren would make an excellent case study for the continuity of English lyric and narrative verse. He also personifies a humanistic and metaphysical approach that is American at its core, a kind of Emersonian individualism with contemporary concerns. Taken together, his work over a half-century illustrates the American literary presence at its best with a poetry that, as one critic observed, never having been in fashion, will never go out of fashion.

—William Claire

WALCOTT, Derek (Alton). Jamaican. Born in Castries, St. Lucia, West Indies, 23 January 1930. Educated at St. Mary's College, St. Lucia; University of the West Indies, Kingston, Jamaica, B.A. 1953. Married; three children. Taught at St. Mary's College and Jamaica College. Formerly, Feature Writer, *Public Opinion*, Kingston, and *Trinidad*

Guardian, Port-of-Spain. Since 1959, Founding Director, Trinidad Theatre Workshop. Recipient: Rockefeller Fellowship, for drama, 1957; Guinness Award, 1961; Heinemann Award, 1966; Cholmondeley Award, 1969; Order of the Humming Bird, Trinidad and Tobago, 1969; Obie Award, for drama, 1971. Lives in Trinidad.

PUBLICATIONS

Verse

> *Twenty-Five Poems.* 1948.
> *Epitaph for the Young.* 1949.
> *Poems.* 1953.
> *In a Green Night: Poems 1948–1960.* 1962.
> *Selected Poems.* 1964.
> *The Castaway and Other Poems.* 1965.
> *The Gulf and Other Poems.* 1969.
> *Another Life.* 1973.
> *Sea Grapes.* 1976.
> *Selected Poems*, edited by O. R. Dathorne. 1977.

Plays

> *Henri Christophe: A Chronicle* (produced 1950). 1950
> *Henri Dernier: A Play for Radio Production.* 1951.
> *Sea at Dauphin* (produced 1954). 1954.
> *Ione: A Play with Music* (produced 1957). 1954.
> *Drums and Colours* (produced 1958). In *Caribbean Quarterly 1* and *2*, 1961.
> *Ti-Jean and His Brothers*, music by André Tanker (produced 1958). In *The Dream on Monkey Mountain and Others Plays*, 1971.
> *Malcochon; or, Six in the Rain* (produced 1959). In *The Dream on Monkey Mountain and Other Plays*, 1971.
> *The Dream on Monkey Mountain* (produced 1967). In *The Dream on Monkey Mountain and Other Plays*, 1971.
> *In a Fine Castle* (produced 1970).
> *The Dream on Monkey Mountain and Other Plays* (includes *Ti-Jean and His Brothers, Malcochon, Sea at Dauphin*, and the essay "What the Twilight Says"). 1971.
> *The Charlatan*, music by Galt MacDermot (produced 1974).
> *The Joker of Seville, and O Babylon!* 1978.

Reading List: *Walcott: "Another Life"* by Edward Baugh, 1978.

*　　*　　*

The first and simplest pleasure offered by Derek Walcott's poetry is the sense of being alive and out-of-doors in the West Indies: sand and salt on the skin, sunlight and space and the open beach, sea-grapes and sea-almonds, liners and islands, where always "The starved eye devours the seascape for the morsel of a sail,/The horizon threads it infinitely."

Walcott was a painter before he was a poet, and as a youth set off with a friend around his native island of Santa Lucia to put it on canvas and thus create it in the imagination. Later he found he could do the work of creation better with words and metaphor, and that this too was needed:

> For no-one had yet written of this landscape
> that it was possible, though there were sounds
> given to its varieties of wood.

Walcott has kept his painter's eye, and is especially aware of effects of light. He often compares life with art ("Tables in the trees, like entering Renoir"), as indeed he often quotes or echoes lines from the English Metaphysicals, Tennyson, Eliot, Dylan Thomas, and others. These things, taken together with the high polish of his verse, have sometimes led to accusations of virtuoso artificiality and preciosity. But, though there may be some lapses which deserve such strictures, it is precisely the successful transmuting of life into art which makes Walcott's achievement so important.

At his best he fuses the outward scene with inward experience and with a form of English words, resonant within the tradition of literature in English but also appropriate to the particular occasion, all in one single act of perception. In so doing he enhances and illustrates (in the Renaissance sense of that word) the landscape and the human lives that are found on the islands. It is not surprising, perhaps, that he should be such a good love poet, for the experience of love has this same quality of enhancing places: "But islands can only exist/If we have loved in them."

Love, the creation of a centre of consciousness, and a relationship of security with the place one lives are particularly important in societies where a history of slavery, cultural deprivation, colonial dependency, and, latterly, tourism have combined to reinforce the more generalized modern feelings of alienation and contingency. Walcott's work may therefore be quite as socially important as that of more obsessively socially-orientated West Indian writers.

Walcott by no means ignores the well-known dilemmas of the West Indian situation. In "Ruins of a Great House" he works out in a complex fashion his relationship with men like Ralegh, "ancestral murderers and poets," with England and the English language, and with the earlier history of a ruined plantation house. Here and elsewhere he is aware that he has one white grandfather, who like many others "drunkenly seeded their archipelago." When the Mau Mau insurrection in Kenya occurs, he cannot give murderers on either side his blessing though "poisoned with the blood of both," and when he sees television film of the Biafran war he notes "The soldiers' helmeted shadows could have been white." In general his aim seems to be not to make rhetoric out of the past, but to transcend it: "All in compassion ends/So differently from what the heart arranged."

Walcott is also a successful and prolific playwright, the founder-director of the Trinidad Theatre Workshop, a travelling group of players who move around the Caribbean. Whereas the poetry is almost entirely in standard English, the plays are largely in the creole idiom of the West Indies. A further linguistic complication is that the popular language of Walcott's home island is a Creole French (as on Jean Rhys's home island of Dominica) and the French phrases and songs of the islands also find their way in quotation, and, with their special intonations, into his work.

In his best-known play, *Dream on Monkey Mountain*, Makak the charcoal-burner lives in utter degradation, dreams he is king of a united Africa, yet has to go on living in the everyday world. "The problem," Walcott said in an interview (*New Yorker*, 26 June 1971), "is to recognize our African origins but not to romanticize them." Generally, one feels that Walcott has little sympathy for exploitation of the past by modern ideologists, even if they are negro ideologists, and some of his bitterest lines are reserved for post-independence politicians. Against their power and rhetoric he sets out on a subtler and more revolutionary course:

I sought more power than you, more fame than yours,
I was more hermetic, I knew the commonweal,
I pretended subtly to lose myself in crowds
knowing my passage would alter their reflection

and at the same time to redeem the past

Its racial quarrels blown like smoke to sea.
From all that sorrow, beauty is our gain
Though it may not seem so
To an old fisherman rowing home in the rain.

—Ned Thomas

WARREN, Robert Penn. American. Born in Guthrie, Kentucky, 24 April 1905. Educated at Guthrie High School; Vanderbilt University, Nashville, Tennessee, B.A. (summa cum laude) 1925; University of California, Berkeley, M.A. 1927; Yale University, New Haven, Connecticut, 1927–28; Oxford University (Rhodes Scholar), B.Litt. 1930. Married 1) Emma Brescia in 1930 (divorced, 1950); 2) the writer Eleanor Clark in 1952, one son and one daughter. Member of the Fugitive Group of poets: Co-Founding Editor, *The Fugitive*, Nashville, 1922–25; Assistant Professor, Southwestern College, Memphis, Tennessee, 1930–31, and Vanderbilt University, 1931–34; Assistant and Associate Professor, Louisiana State University, Baton Rouge, 1934–42, and Founding Editor, *Southern Review*, Baton Rouge, 1935–42; Professor of English, University of Minnesota, Minneapolis, 1942–50; Professor of Playwriting, 1950–56, and Professor of English, 1962–73, Yale University; now Professor Emeritus. Consultant in Poetry, Library of Congress, Washington, D.C., 1944–45; Jefferson Lecturer, National Endowment for the Arts, 1974. Recipient: Caroline Sinkler Award, 1936, 1937, 1938; Houghton Mifflin Literary Fellowship, 1939; Guggenheim Fellowship, 1939, 1947; Shelley Memorial Award, 1943; Pulitzer Prize, for fiction, 1947, for poetry, 1958; Screenwriters Guild Robert Meltzer Award, 1949; Sidney Hillman Prize, 1957; Edna St. Vincent Millay Memorial Prize, 1958; National Book Award, for poetry, 1958; Bollingen Prize, for poetry, 1967; National Endowment for the Arts grant, 1968; Henry A. Bellaman Prize, 1970; Van Wyck Brooks Award, for poetry, 1970; National Medal for Literature, 1970; Emerson-Thoreau Medal, 1975. D.Litt.: University of Louisville, Kentucky, 1949; Kenyon College, Gambier, Ohio, 1952; University of Kentucky, Lexington, 1955; Colby College, Waterville, Maine, 1956; Swarthmore College, Pennsylvania, 1958; Yale University, 1959; Fairfield University, Connecticut, 1969; Wesleyan University, Middletown, Connecticut, 1970; Harvard University, Cambridge, Massachusetts, 1973; LL.D.: University of Bridgeport, Connecticut, 1965. Member, American Academy of Arts and Letters; Chancellor, Academy of American Poets, 1972. Lives in Fairfield, Connecticut.

PUBLICATIONS

Verse

Thirty-Six Poems. 1935.
Eleven Poems on the Same Theme. 1942.

Selected Poems 1923–1943. 1944.
Brother to Dragons: A Tale in Verse and Voices. 1953.
Promises: Poems 1954–1956. 1957.
You, Emperors and Others: Poems 1957–1960. 1960.
Selected Poems: New and Old 1923–1966. 1966.
Incarnations: Poems 1966–1968. 1968.
Audubon: A Vision. 1969.
Or Else: Poem/Poems 1968–1974. 1974.
Selected Poems 1923–1975. 1977.

Plays

Proud Flesh (in verse, produced 1947; revised [prose] version, produced 1948).
All the King's Men (produced 1959). 1960.

Fiction

Night Rider. 1939.
At Heaven's Gate. 1943.
All the King's Men. 1946.
Blackberry Winter (stories). 1946.
The Circus in the Attic and Other Stories. 1947.
World Enough and Time: A Romantic Novel. 1950.
Band of Angels. 1955.
The Cave. 1959.
Wilderness: A Tale of the Civil War. 1961.
Flood: A Romance of Our Times. 1964.
Meet Me in the Green Glen. 1971.
A Place to Come To. 1977.

Other

John Brown: The Making of a Martyr. 1929.
I'll Take My Stand: The South and the Agrarian Tradition, with others. 1930.
Understanding Poetry: An Anthology for College Students, with Cleanth Brooks. 1938; revised edition, 1950, 1960.
Understanding Fiction, with Cleanth Brooks. 1943; revised edition, 1959.
A Poem of Pure Imagination: An Experiment in Reading, in *The Rime of the Ancient Mariner,* by Samuel Taylor Coleridge. 1946.
Modern Rhetoric: With Readings, with Cleanth Brooks. 1949; revised edition, 1958.
Fundamentals of Good Writing: A Handbook of Modern Rhetoric, with Cleanth Brooks. 1950; revised edition, 1956.
Segregation: The Inner Conflict in the South. 1956.
Remember the Alamo! 1958.
Selected Essays. 1958.
The Gods of Mount Olympus. 1959.
The Legacy of the Civil War: Meditations on the Centennial. 1961.
Who Speaks for the Negro? 1965.
A Plea in Mitigation: Modern Poetry and the End of an Era. 1966.
Homage to Theodore Dreiser. 1971.
John Greenleaf Whittier's Poetry: An Appraisal and a Selection. 1971.

A Conversation with Warren, edited by Frank Gado.   1972.
Democracy and Poetry.   1975.

Editor, with Cleanth Brooks and J. T. Purser, *An Approach to Literature: A Collection of Prose and Verse with Analyses and Discussions.*   1936; revised edition, 1939, 1952.
Editor, *A Southern Harvest: Short Stories by Southern Writers.*   1937.
Editor, with Cleanth Brooks, *An Anthology of Stories from the Southern Review.*   1953.
Editor, with Albert Erskine, *Short Story Masterpieces.*   1954.
Editor, with Albert Erskine, *Six Centuries of Great Poetry.*   1955.
Editor, with Albert Erskine, *A New Southern Harvest.*   1957.
Editor, with Allen Tate, *Selected Poems,* by Denis Devlin.   1963.
Editor, *Faulkner: A Collection of Critical Essays.*   1966.
Editor, with Robert Lowell and Peter Taylor, *Randall Jarrell 1914–1965.*   1967.
Editor, *Selected Poems of Herman Melville.*   1971.
Editor, with Cleanth Brooks and R. W. B. Lewis, *American Literature: The Makers and the Making.*   2 vols., 1974.

Bibliography: *Warren: A Bibliography* by Mary Nancy Huff, 1968.

Reading List: *Warren: The Dark and Bloody Ground* by Leonard Casper, 1960; *Warren* by Paul West, 1964; *Warren: A Collection of Critical Essays* edited by John Lewis Longley, Jr., 1965; *A Colder Fire: The Poetry of Warren,* 1965, and *The Poetic Vision of Warren,* 1977, both by Victor H. Strandberg; *Web of Being: The Novels of Warren* by Barnett Guttenberg, 1975.

*   *   *

Robert Penn Warren is a distinguished American writer in at least three genres: the novel, poetry, and the essay. Although he has lived outside the South since 1942, he has so consistently written novels, essays, and poetry on southern subjects, in southern settings, and about southern themes that he must be regarded still as a southern writer. Over much of his work there is a typically southern brooding sense of darkness, evil, and human failure, and he employs a Gothicism of form and an extravagance of language and technique of a sort often associated with writing in the southeastern United States. Warren is a profoundly philosophical writer in all aspects of his work. Writing of Joseph Conrad, he once said, "The philosophical novelist, or poet, is one for whom the documentation of the world is constantly striving to rise to the level of generalization about values ... for whom the urgency of experience ... is the urgency to know the meaning of experience." The description fits him well.

In Warren's principal work in the novel and poetry, there is a persistent obsession with time and with history, a sense of man's imperfection and failure, and an awareness that innocence is always lost in the acts of achieving maturity and growth. His characters are usually men who destroy themselves through seeking an absolute in a relative universe. From John Brown, the subject of his first book, a biography, to Percy Munn, the protagonist of *Night Rider,* to Willie Stark of *All the King's Men,* to Jeremiah Beaumont of *World Enough and Time,* to Lilburn Lewis in the poem-play *Brother to Dragons,* to Jed Tewksbury in *A Place to Come To* – Warren's protagonists repeat this pattern of the obsessive and ultimately self-destructive search for the impossible ideal.

His work usually rests on actual events from history or at least on actual historical situations – *Night Rider* on the Kentucky tobacco wars, *At Heaven's Gates* on a Nashville political murder, *All the King's Men* on the career of Huey Long, *World Enough and Time* on an 1825 Kentucky murder, *Band of Angels* and *Wilderness* on the Civil War, *The Cave* on Floyd Collins's cave entombment, *Flood* on the inundating of towns by the Tennessee Valley

Authority, *A Place to Come To* to at least some extent on his own experiences as a college teacher, although the story can hardly be considered autobiographical. The poem *Brother to Dragons* is based on an atrocious crime committed by Thomas Jefferson's nephews. This concern with history and the individual implications of social and political events is also present in his non-fiction, such as *Segregation: The Inner Conflict in the South, The Legacy of the Civil War*, and *Who Speaks for the Negro?* These works, too, deal with fundamental issues of southern history.

In order to present the philosophical meaning of his novels and poems, Warren uses highly individualized narrators, such as Jack Burden in *All the King's Men*; special techniques of narrative point of view, as in *World Enough and Time*; frequently a metaphysical style; the illumination of events through contrast with enclosed and frequently recollected narratives, as in *Night Rider* and *All the King's Men*; and highly melodramatic plots which become elaborate workings out of abstract statements, as in *Band of Angels*.

His poetry reiterates essentially the same view of man. He began as an undergraduate at Vanderbilt University writing poetry with the Fugitive poetry group – John Crowe Ransom, Allen Tate, and Donald Davidson – and he continued to write a relatively fixed form, tightly constructed, ironic lyric verse until about 1943. Between 1943 and 1953 he concentrated predominantly on the novel. With *Brother to Dragons* he returned to poetic expression, and since that time has written extensively in both poetic and novelistic forms. The verse forms that he has used since 1953 have been much looser, marked by broken rhythms, clusters of lines arranged in patterns dictated by emotion, and frequent alternations in the level of diction. Behind his poetry, as behind his fiction, there is usually an implied, if not explicit, narrative pattern. This narrative pattern is often historical, as in "The Ballad of Billy Potts," *Brother to Dragons*, or *Audubon*. In his recent verse, Warren contrasts man's weaknesses and imperfections with the enduring stars, with time, and with eternity.

As a critic and teacher, Warren has had a profound influence on the study and criticism of literature. His textbook *Understanding Poetry*, written with Cleanth Brooks, a presentation of poetry in New Critical terms emphasizing the poem as an independent work of art, went a long way toward creating a revolution in how literature was taught in American colleges. He has written many other textbooks and critical studies such as his *Homage to Theodore Dreiser, John Greenleaf Whittier's Poetry*, and *Democracy and Poetry*.

Warren is still very active; during his 72nd year he published *Selected Poems 1923–1975* and a distinctive and distinguished novel, *A Place to Come To*. Warren's work in all genres is marked by a high concern with language, a depth of philosophical statement, a firm and rigorous commitment to a moral-ethical view of man, and a willingness to experiment often beyond the limits of artistic safety with the forms in which he works. Warren is a peculiarly indigenous American writer of great intelligence and of significant accomplishment. He can, with justice, be called our most distinguished living man of letters.

—C. Hugh Holman

WATKINS, Vernon (Phillips).   Welsh   Born in Maesteg, Glamorganshire, 27 June 1906. Educated at Swansea Grammar School; Repton School; Magdalene College, Cambridge, 1924–25: studied modern languages. Served in the Home Guard, 1939–41, and the Royal Air Force, 1941–45. Married Gwendolyn Mary Davies in 1944; four sons and one daughter. Clerk, Lloyds Bank, Swansea, 1925–41, 1946–65. Visiting Lecturer in Modern Poetry, University of Washington, Seattle, 1964, 1967; Calouste Gulbenkian Fellow in Poetry,

University College, Swansea, 1965–66. Recipient: Guinness Prize, 1957. D.Litt.: University of Wales, Cardiff, 1966. Fellow, Royal Society of Literature, 1951. *Died 8 October 1967.*

PUBLICATIONS

Verse

> *Ballad of Mari Lwyd and Other Poems.*   1941.
> *The Lamp and the Veil.*   1945.
> *The Lady with the Unicorn.*   1948.
> *Selected Poems.*   1948.
> *The Death Bell: Poems and Ballads.*   1954.
> *Cypress and Acacia.*   1959.
> *Affinities.*   1962.
> *Selected Poems 1930–1960.*   1967.
> *Arrival in East Shelby.*   1968.
> *Fidelities.*   1968.
> *Uncollected Poems.*   1969.
> *Ballad of the Outer Dark.*   1977.
> *The Influences.*   1977.

Other

> *Selected Verse Translations, with an Essay on the Translation of Poetry,* edited by Ruth
>   Pryor.   1977.

> Editor, *Letters to Vernon Watkins,* by Dylan Thomas.   1957.
> Editor, *Landmarks and Voyages: Poetry Supplement.*   1957.

> Translator, *The North Sea,* by Heinrich Heine.   1955.

Bibliography: *Two Swansea Poets: Dylan Thomas and Watkins,* 1969.

Reading List: *Watkins 1906–1967* edited by Leslie Norris, 1970; *Watkins* by Roland Mathias, 1974; *Watkins and the Spring of Vision* by Dora Polk, 1977; "Watkins Issue" of *Poetry Wales 12* edited by J. P. Ward, 1977.

*   *   *

Vernon Watkins has been celebrated more by fellow Welshmen than by the metropolitan critics of English literature. Yet his poetry, though rooted in the landscape of South Wales, especially the Gower peninsula, is not narrowly provincial, but has a European breadth in its range of reference. This is further reflected in fine translations of Heine's *The North Sea,* Homer, Dante, and many French and German lyrics; Hölderlin is a particular inspiration in his own poetry. Not a native Welsh-speaker (though his parents were), Watkins draws little of specifically Welsh literature into his work apart from the myth of Taliesin, the prototype of the poet-seer with the gift of inspiration and the capacity for self-transformation, who is the focus of several poems. His own metaphysical vision, shaped early by Blake and later by Yeats, is replete with visual and sensory detail. Through the verbal re-creation of a loved place or the accurate observation of, say, a hero, a foal, fruit blossom, or snow that is whiter than sea-foam, he seeks to reveal the truths of eternity mediated by the accidents of time. A sense of serene thankfulness, achieved through the conquest of grief and pain, suffuses much of his work, e.g., "Peace in the Welsh Hills":

> Here, where the earth is green, where heaven is true
> Opening the windows, touched with earliest dawn,
> In the first frost of cool September days,
> Chrysanthemum weather, presaging great birth,
> Who in his heart could murmur or complain:
> "The light we look for is not in this land"?
> That light is present, and that distant time
> Is always here, continually redeemed.

Philosophically, Watkins's poetry represents a struggle to reconcile elements of Neo-Platonism with the traditional insights of Christianity. Within these thematic limits there is a slow maturing of thought throughout his substantial published work. His poems largely lack the immediacy of contemporary allusion and fashionable subject-matter.

Watkins's attention to the craft of his verse is meticulous; many of his poems have gone through dozens of drafts before reaching their final form. In the introduction to *Dylan Thomas: Letters to Vernon Watkins* he declares his method of working to be "from music and cadence towards the density of physical shape." He experimented with a large variety of metres, rhymed and unrhymed, stanza forms, and poetic types. His diction remains generally reflective and hieratic, with some infusion of the colloquial and the plain, especially in his ballads. Although his work consists mainly of short lyric forms, several extended pieces – the "Ballad of Mari Lwyd," the rhapsodic "Sea-Music for My Sister Travelling," the transmuted chronicle of a visit to Yeats in "Yeats in Dublin," the posthumously published masque *The Influences* (Yeatsian through and through) – demonstrate a more ambitious mood, which is perhaps ultimately less successful, because too diffuse.

—David Blamires

WEBB, Francis (Charles).   Australian.   Born in Adelaide, South Australia, 8 February 1925. Educated at Christian Brothers schools, Chatswood and Lewisham; University of Sydney. Served in the Royal Australian Air Force in Canada, during World War II. Worked for various Canadian publishers. Recipient: Commonwealth Literary Fund Fellowship, 1960. *Died in 1973.*

PUBLICATIONS

Verse

A Drum for Ben Boyd.   1948.
Leichhardt in Theatre.   1952.

Birthday.   1953.
Socrates and Other Poems.   1961.
The Ghost of the Cock.   1964.
Collected Poems.   1969.

Reading List: "The World of Webb" by Sylvia Lawson, in *Australian Letters,* 1961; "The Poetry of Webb" by Vincent Buckley, in *Meanjin,* 1963.

*   *   *

Of the younger modern Australian poets of this century, Francis Webb, on the publication of his *A Drum for Ben Boyd* became one of the two leading figures, with David Campbell. Webb's early death cut his achievement short. Webb spent much of his adult life in mental hospitals and a good deal of his poetry undoubtedly attempts to convey experiences peculiar to what are called psychotic states of mind. It is inevitable, therefore, that he should have enjoyed a kind of *succès de scandale* on that account. But much of his poetry is genuinely visionary poetry, the result of a more than ordinarily lucid and energetic way of seeing, of an imagination and a sensibility of greater scope and intensity than usual.

It would be a mistake to see in Webb's early poems, written before his illness, the preoccupations with night, death, dream, eccentricity, solitude, silence, obscure terrors, and rejections that merely bespeak the alienated mind. What most characterises his verse is its immense vitality, its positiveness. Even its privacies are not egocentric. These are not poems of withdrawal, but of reaching out; in contrast to many more "normal" poets, Webb did not "live the life of monologue." Poetry for him was a means of keeping in touch with reality; his early poem, "Compliments of the Audience," is an affirmation of faith in images, which, he argues, are all that emerge to testify to reality from the blackness of memory, the blurred barrenness of thought. *A Drum for Ben Boyd*, a sequence of poems by various speakers giving their different impressions of the merchant-adventurer Boyd, was a remarkable performance for a young man of 22, especially since, in an era of historic poems, it questioned the validity of historiography. His second long poem, *Leichhardt in Theatre*, was no less challenging, and contains perhaps the central symbol of Webb's belief system: the "nomad horseman energy." Other preoccupations which bind the work as a whole together are his interest in music, in painting, and in everything to do with the sea. He gives special importance to laughter, as his last long poem, *Ghost of the Cock*, demonstrates, and the clown image is a recurrent one. Leichhardt, for instance, is presented as part-clown, part-hero.

Webb's greatest technical strength lies in his appeal to the ear. He handles the language as a musician handles tones and produces a rich concourse of sound which carries its own meaning, even if the mind is slow to interpret it. This gift is most in evidence perhaps in the volume *Socrates*, which also shows him in full possession of his visionary world. All his key experiences come together in this book: his Catholic faith, war-time flying, music, the sea, his own illness, his need for monastic solitude. There is much of the "desert father" in Webb's verse: his passionate nature made it necessary for him to turn all women into the Virgin, all children into the infant Christ. The poem "For Ethel" is the nearest we get to any sense of an earthly, particular woman. It is in a poem about a new-born child that Webb comes closest to intimate human contact, with all his senses sharpened, particularly the sense of touch: it is one of the most beautiful of all contemporary Nativity poems, as the opening stanza suggests:

> Christmas is in the air.
> You are given into my hands
> Out of quiet, loneliest lands.
> My trembling is all my prayer.
> To blown straw was given
> All the fullness of heaven.

Webb was too rich and complex a poet to yield himself to short analysis. Perhaps some glimpse of the man and the poet is revealed in his lines about Socrates, musing on the relationship between his soul and his body, as the "chains" of earthly ties are about to be loosed:

> Chains grapple with me gently, as old friends,
> The subtle iron lends its tinklings to my move.
> And it is all of love; for I see Andromeda musing,
> Given back to entire music, swathed in frail silver links:
> They chime, climb or sink with gain or fail of pulse,
> And all about, incurious hulls and the long, long flutes of the sea.

—Dorothy Green

WHEELWRIGHT, John (Brooks).   American.   Born in Boston, Massachusetts, in 1897. Educated at Harvard University, Cambridge, Massachusetts; Massachusetts Institute of Technology, Cambridge: studied architecture. Practised as an architect in Boston. Editor, *Poems for a Dime* magazine. Official of the New England Poetry Society. *Died 15 September 1940.*

PUBLICATIONS

Collections

   Collected Poems, edited by Alvin H. Rosenfeld.   1972.

Verse

   Rock and Shell: Poems 1923–1933.   1933.
   Mirrors of Venus: A Novel in Sonnets, 1914–1938.   1938.
   Political Self-Portrait.   1940.
   Selected Poems.   1941.

Other

   Editor, *A History of the New England Poetry Club.*   1932.

*   *   *

John Wheelwright published three books during his lifetime, but none received sufficient notice to give him reputation while alive. Wheelwright was not the average Socialist scribbler of the Depression era, but a "proper Bostonian" of impeccable ancestry: on his father's side, he claimed his radical blood from the first Wheelwright, an emigré from England in 1636, who preached religious tolerance until he was banished from the Bay Colony. On his mother's side, he descended from John Brooks, an early governor of Massachusetts.

The contradictions explicit in such ancestry, radicalism, and political authority, were manifest in Wheelwright's own character and poetry. He taunted Boston Brahmins with his eccentric behavior in public and declared his allegiance to the proletariat, whose Depression plight he championed in many poems. All the while he accepted his upper-class status and remained much of his life an official of the doughty New England Poetry Society.

Wheelwright was an erratic craftsman in his poems, even though he emphasized his technique in long prose commentaries that accompanied his three published books. Many poems are long-winded, prosaic, and loosely framed. But occasionally his poems spring out with unanticipated lyric genius, as in "Train Ride" (*Political Self-Portrait*). His "sonnet novel" *Mirrors of Venus*, generally over-wrought, includes his masterful elegy "Father":

> Come home. Wire a wire of warning without words.
> Come home and talk to me again, my first friend. Father,
> come home, dead man, who made your mind my home.

Wheelwright's work often takes the form of rambling poetic tracts, where he is an interpreter of what he felt to be the reshaping of America. As he wrote at the end of *Political Self-Portrait*, "The main point is not what noise poetry makes, but how it makes you think and act, – not what you make of it; but what it makes of you." Although this is unfair to the musical grace of much of his language, it is pointed and correct essentially about his intentions for his poetry.

His first book, *Rock and Shell*, shows the poet searching for some premise of unity in his experience, especially in the powerful opening poem, "North Atlantic Passage," which joins prose and poetry together. Spiritual loneliness is followed by sexual loneliness in this carefully plotted book. *Mirrors of Venus* is, as one critic described it, his *In Memoriam* to his friend Ned Couch, but sags generally from its weight of technical embellishments.

Political Self-Portrait is his best book; here he has found a balance between the wrought textures of language and loosely plotted ideological arguments. The poems are longer, more discursive, but intensely dramatic as they register a diffident, sensitive conscience faced with social unheaval and coming war. The poems are rich in imagery, raw in angry, direct language, but dignified overall by the depth of the speaker's convictions. Some of these poems have lost their edge now, but many, including "Collective Collect," "Bread-Word Giver," and "Train Ride" are lasting expressions of faith in humanity. "Dusk to Dusk," included in the recent *Collected Poems*, has an even shriller tone of indignation than *Political Self-Portrait*, and its structure seems driven to fragments by the unleashed energies of this unusual poet.

—Paul Christensen

WILBUR, Richard (Purdy). American. Born in New York City, 1 March 1921. Educated at Amherst College, Massachusetts, B.A. 1942; Harvard University, Cambridge, Massachusetts, M.A. 1947. Served in the United States Army, 1943–45. Married Charlotte Ward in 1942; one daughter and three sons. Member of the Society of Fellows, 1947–50, and Assistant Professor of English, 1950–54, Harvard University; Associate Professor of English, Wellesley College, Massachusetts, 1955–57. Since 1957, Professor of English, Wesleyan University, Middletown, Connecticut. General Editor, Laurel Poets series, Dell Publishing

Company, New York. State Department Cultural Exchange Representative to the U.S.S.R., 1961. Recipient: Guggenheim Fellowship, 1952, 1963; American Academy in Rome Fellowship, 1954; Pulitzer Prize, 1957; National Book Award 1957; Edna St. Vincent Millay Memorial Award, 1957; Ford Foundation Fellowship, for drama, 1960; Melville Cane Award, 1962; Bollingen Prize, for translation, 1963, and for verse, 1971; Sarah Josepha Hale Award, 1968; Brandeis University Creative Arts Award, 1970; Prix Henri Desfeuilles, 1971; Shelley Memorial Award, 1973. L.H.D.: Lawrence College, Appleton, Wisconsin, 1960; Washington University, St. Louis, 1964; D.Litt.: Amherst College, 1967. Member, American Academy of Arts and Sciences; since 1974, President, American Academy of Arts and Letters; Chancellor, Academy of American Poets. Lives in Cummington, Massachusetts.

PUBLICATIONS

Verse

The Beautiful Changes and Other Poems.   1947.
Ceremony and Other Poems.   1950.
Things of This World.   1956; one section reprinted as *Digging to China*, 1970.
Poems 1943–1956.   1957.
Advice to a Prophet and Other Poems.   1961.
The Poems.   1963.
Prince Souvanna Phouma: An Exchange Between Richard Wilbur and William Jay Smith.   1963.
Complaint.   1968.
Walking to Sleep: New Poems and Translations.   1969.
Seed Leaves: Homage to R. F.   1974.
The Mind-Reader: New Poems.   1976.

Plays

The Misanthrope, from the play by Molière (produced 1955).   1955; revised version, music by Margaret Pine (produced 1977).
Candide (lyrics only, with John LaTouche and Dorothy Parker), book by Lillian Hellman, music by Leonard Bernstein, from the novel by Voltaire (produced 1956).   1957.
Tartuffe. from the play by Molière (produced 1964).   1963.
School for Wives, from a play by Molière (produced 1971).   1971.
The Learned Ladies, from a play by Molière.   1978.

Other

Loudmouse (juvenile).   1963.
Opposites (juvenile), illustrated by the author.   1973.
Responses: Prose Pieces 1948–1976.   1976.

Editor, *A Bestiary* (anthology).   1955.
Editor, *Complete Poems of Poe.*   1959.
Editor, with Alfred Harbage, *Poems of Shakespeare.*   1966; revised edition, as *The Narrative Poems, and Poems of Doubtful Authenticity,*   1974.

Editor, *Selected Poems,* by Witter Bynner.   1978.

Translator, *The Funeral of Bobo,* by Joseph Brodsky.   1974.

Bibliography: *Wilbur: A Bibliographical Checklist* by John P. Field,   1971.

Reading List: *Wilbur* by Donald L. Hill, 1967; *Wilbur: A Critical Essay* by Paul F. Cummins, 1971.

*   *   *

Richard Wilbur's first volume of poems surprised its early readers in 1947: there was none of the standard theorizing about history or large "modern" issues and only occasional reflections of the poet's experiences in the war; instead, the poet of *The Beautiful Changes* spoke openly of beauty, unabashedly expressing his delight in the sights and sounds and movements of the world and demonstrating a dazzling virtuosity at recreating them in his verse. He also revealed his delight in wit, imaginative play, and even games. One of the poems was entitled simply "&," and his delights are joined in some lines from "Grace":

> One is tickled again, by the dining-car waiter's absurd
> Acrobacy – tipfingered tray like a wind-besting bird
> Plumblines his swinging shoes, the sole things sure
> In the shaken train.

In addition to the high spirits, the poems often almost exemplified elegance, poise, and good manners.

A number of those qualities and subjects came to seem even more startling in the years which followed. From the beginning up to *The Mind-Reader,* Wilbur's poetry has shown notable continuities. He has remarked that in his later poems he tends to move towards "a plainer and more straightforward" way of writing and, also, from poems that use a "single meditative voice balancing argument and counter-argument, feeling and counter-feeling" to more "dramatic" ones (such as "Two Voices in a Meadow" or "The Aspen and the Stream") that may use two opposing voices. Readers may also detect a general deepening of feeling and a clearer personal voice as well as some unpredictable developments. But most of the earlier qualities remain, and there continue to be signal exclusions: no confessional poetry and no free verse (Wilbur wrote that in the fairy story about the genie which could be summoned out of a bottle, he had always assumed that the genie gained his strength from being *in* the bottle).

It is unlikely that anyone could have predicted, however, that the poet who showed an almost Keatsian responsiveness to the sensuous should become the translator of Molière into extraordinary English couplets. In retrospect, it is clearer that Molière represents part of what Wilbur is, as well as what he admires: a humane voice of uncommonly rational common-sense; a user of language that is both familiar and chaste; a witty enemy of the pompous, the gross, and the fanatic; and a juggler, a master of poise and point. Nor could one have anticipated "Junk," the liveliest recreation of Anglo-Saxon meters and feeling since Pound, or the scathing Miltonic sonnet to Lyndon Johnson, or the tenderness of the translations from Charles d'Orléans, Voltaire, and Francis Jammes, or the effectiveness of "A Christmas Hymn," or the moving elegy for Dudley Fitts.

Neither could one have quite anticipated "Walking to Sleep," an extraordinary exploration of the paths, strategems, surprises, and terrors that lie between waking and sleep, nor "The Mind-Reader," although both long poems extend one of Wilbur's most persistent themes in his more obviously personal lyrics: the processes, reflections, and creations of the mind. Wilbur once remarked, "A good part of my work could, I suppose, be understood as a public quarrel with the aesthetics of Edgar Allan Poe." His continuous concern is evidenced by his edition of Poe's poems and a number of substantial essays on both the prose and the verse: three of the sixteen provocative and lucid essays in *Responses: Prose Pieces, 1948–1976* concern Poe. He once wrote, "There has never been a grander conception of poetry [than Poe's], nor a more impoverished one." As that sentence suggests, the quarrel continues because Wilbur finds it so difficult to make a decision once for all. His ambivalence (at the simplest level, his fascination with the intellectual, the perfectly beautiful and purely harmonious, and his almost simultaneous reaction away from such an ideal in an acceptance and love for the imperfect human and material reality that we can know here and now) is the theme of a number of his best poems. "A World Without Objects Is a Sensible Emptiness" is one of many that balances the soul's longing for purity and perfection with, almost simultaneously with the moment of ascension towards the empyrean, a counter movement as it accepts and rejoices in the body and its world. Wilbur's poetry often seems that of a natural Platonist who keeps learning to accept the Incarnation. "The Writer" movingly recognizes that the literary "flight" has its origins as well as final resting place in human suffering and love.

If Robert Frost has an authentic living heir, it is probably Wilbur – particularly as the poet of the short lyric in strict and familiar meters who speaks in the middle voice, wittily and movingly, to a wide audience. There are, however, important differences: Wilbur's voice is usually more obviously that of an urban man in contrast to the characteristic voice of the countryman which Frost so carefully crafted; and Frost never devoted such care to the attempt to translate, self-effacedly, the poetry of others, nor did he write for the public theater. But the most important difference is probably in their spirits. Frost did not share with anything like Wilbur's conviction the notion that "Love Calls Us to the Things of This World." It may have been, in part at least, that conviction which enabled Wilbur to make imaginatively convincing his "Advice to a Prophet" concerning how we might be persuaded not to destroy our earth.

—Joseph H. Summers

WILKINSON, Anne (Cochran Boyd). Canadian. Born in Toronto, Ontario, 21 September 1910. Educated privately. Married Frederik R. Wilkinson in 1932 (divorced, 1953); two sons and one daughter. Co-Founding Editor, *Tamarack Review*, Toronto, 1956. *Died 10 May 1961.*

PUBLICATIONS

Collections

Collected Poems, and a Prose Memoir, edited by A. J. M. Smith.   1968.

Verse

Counterpoint to Sleep.   1951.
The Hangman Ties the Holly.   1955.

Other

Lions in the Way: A Discursive History of the Oslers.   1956.
Swann and Daphne (juvenile).   1960.

*   *   *

Anne Wilkinson's work is beautifully of a piece, and part of the impressive effect her poetry makes on the reader is the result of the precision and firmness of her literary identity. All the poems, however varied, strike one as issuing from a single source. She brings to mind the name of Hopkins, not in any passive or imitative way but in the intensity and singularity of her sensibility. Her disinterestedness is quite pure, her eye bent without distraction upon the object, and yet the savour of inimitable individuality, of the presence of the author in every syllable, is unmistakable. She is capable of taking a single image, as in her exquisite poem "Lens," and of deriving from it a substantial poem. But all the generation is from within, so that there is no sense of the softness or accretion of pointless apposition – as there is in her weaker production. The pose in "Lens," as in all her best work, is perfect because of the clarity and force, almost the ferocity, of the vision.

She is fascinated by the variety and the continuity of sense-experience, by its blending and blurring of the physical and the psychological, by its organic relationship with the vegetable world at one end of the scale ("Still Life," "A Poet's-Eye View," "Summer Acres") and at the other by its extension into the psychic world ("The Puritan," "After Reading Kafka," "To a Psycho-Neurotic"). Such activity of the senses in the poet produces, as we see, for example, in Wordsworth's *The Prelude*, a world of exceptional presence and brilliance, the mind of the poet being in its creativity almost the opposite to the mere registering instrument advanced by Locke as a mental model. The more vital the subject in fact, the more powerful the object. Thus for Anne Wilkinson even the formless flow of time is something ferocious, "Time is tiger." The external world appears as "The striped, discerning tiger"; the poet's relations with it as dangerous and terrifying, as in "Poem of Anxiety":

> When night's at large in the jungle
> I go fearful
> Lest I kiss or claw his eye.
> Too whoo, too whit, who's who
> When all the jungle reeks?

To say that Anne Wilkinson's poetry is saturated with sense-experience is to say that she is infatuated with existence, the senses being for her the immediate and subtlest entrance into life. This is why her best work gives the reader the sense of sharing an entranced experience of pure existence. It is this model or shape of perfection she struggles to make the rest of living, and even the act of dying, conform to, just as it is the inwardness and sincerity with which the effort is made that confers on her poetry an extraordinary distinction and integrity.

There are two initiating and sustaining conceptions in Anne Wilkinson's poetry: a deep conviction about the unity of existence, which does not exclude a fine sense of its manifold distinctions; and a vibrant joy in the face of existence, which can go with the most intimate experience of grimness and pain. The first never puffs into grandiosity, the second does not slump into complacency because the poetry is marked by qualities tending constantly to work for poise and actuality, wit, continuity, palpability. It is this recovering, connecting, particularizing, palpable tradition of poetry, a line joining Robert Graves to Gerard Manley Hopkins and Keats to Donne, which Anne Wilkinson represents so strongly in Canadian literature.

If poetry as illumination of the present is the burden of the first part of the poem "Lens," poetry as the recovery of the past is that of the second. The augmentation of being becomes the rescuing of it. The imagery of eye, lens, and light turns into one of film and dark room where "the years/Lie in solution." It is because of man's unbroken connection with his own beginnings, human, animal, natural, that the poet's imagination can sharpen into needlepoint precision what lies vaguely latent in the consciousness:

> A stripe of tiger, curled
> And sleeping on the ribs of reason
> Prints as clear
> As Eve and Adam, pearled
> With sweat, staring at an applecore....

—William Walsh

WILLIAMS, William Carlos. American. Born in Rutherford, New Jersey, 17 September 1883. Educated at a school in Rutherford, 1889–96; Chateau de Lancy, near Geneva, Switzerland, and Lycée Condorcet, Paris, 1897–99; Horace Mann High School, New York, 1899–1902; University of Pennsylvania, Philadelphia, 1902–06, M.D. 1906; did two years internship at hospitals in New York City, 1906–08, and post-graduate work in paediatrics at the University of Leipzig, 1908–09. Married Florence Herman in 1912; two sons. Practised medicine in Rutherford, 1910 until he retired in the mid 1950's. Editor, *Others*, 1919; Editor, with Robert McAlmon, *Contact*, 1920–23; Editor, with Nathanael West, *Contact*, 1932. Appointed Consultant in Poetry, Library of Congress, Washington, D.C., 1952, but did not serve. Recipient: Loines Award, 1948; National Book Award, 1950; Bollingen Prize, 1952; Academy of American Poets Fellowship, 1956; Brandeis University Creative Arts Award, 1958; National Institute of Arts and Letters Gold Medal, 1963; Pulitzer Prize, 1963. LL.D.: State University of New York at Buffalo, 1956; Fairleigh Dickinson University, Teaneck, New Jersey, 1959; Litt.D.: Rutgers University, New Brunswick, New Jersey, 1948; Bard College, Annandale-on-Hudson, New York, 1948; University of Pennsylvania, 1952. Member, National Institute of Arts and Letters. *Died 4 March 1963.*

PUBLICATIONS

Collections

The Williams Reader, edited by M. L. Rosenthal. 1966.

Verse

Poems. 1909.
The Tempers. 1913.
Al Que Quiere! 1917.
Kora in Hell: Improvisations. 1920.
Sour Grapes. 1921.
Spring and All. 1923.
Go Go. 1923.

The Cod Head.   1932.
Collected Poems, 1921–1931.   1934.
An Early Martyr and Other Poems.   1935.
Adam & Eve & the City.   1936.
The Complete Collected Poems 1906–1938.   1938.
The Broken Span.   1941.
The Wedge.   1944.
Paterson, Book One.   1946; *Book Two,*1948; *Book Three,* 1949; *Book Four,* 1951; *Book Five,* 1958; *Books I–V,* 1963.
The Clouds.   1948.
The Pink Church.   1949.
Selected Poems.   1949.
The Collected Later Poems.   1950; revised edition, 1963.
The Collected Earlier Poems.   1951.
The Desert Music and Other Poems.   1954.
Journey to Love.   1955.
Pictures from Brueghel and Other Poems.   1962.

Plays

Betty Putnam (produced 1910).
A Dream of Love (produced 1949).   1948.
Many Loves (produced 1958).   In *Many Loves and Other Plays,* 1961.
Many Loves and Other Plays: The Collected Plays (includes *A Dream of Love; Tituba's Children; The First President,* music by Theodore Harris; *The Cure*).   1961.

Fiction

A Voyage to Pagany.   1928.
A Novelette and Other Prose 1921–1931.   1932.
The Knife of the Times and Other Stories.   1932.
White Mule.   1937; *In the Money: White Mule, Part II,*1940; *The Build-Up,* 1952.
Life along the Passaic River (stories).   1938.
Make Light of It: Collected Stories.   1950.
The Farmers' Daughters: The Collected Stories.   1961.

Other

The Great American Novel.   1923.
In the American Grain.   1925.
The Autobiography.   1951.
Williams' Poetry Talked About, with Eli Siegel.   1952; revised edition, edited by Martha Baird and Ellen Reiss, as *The Williams-Siegel Documentary,* 1970, 1974.
Selected Essays.   1954.
John Marin, with others.   1956.
Selected Letters, edited by John C. Thirlwall.   1957.
I Wanted to Write a Poem: The Autobiography of the Works of a Poet, edited by Edith Heal.   1958.
Yes, Mrs. Williams: A Personal Record of My Mother.   1959.
Imaginations: Collected Early Prose, edited by Webster Schott.   1970.
The Embodiment of Knowledge, edited by Ron Loewinsohn.   1974.

Interviews with Williams: Speaking Straight Ahead, edited by Linda W. Wagner. 1976.

Translator, *Last Nights of Paris,* by Philippe Soupault. 1929.
Translator, with Raquel Hélène Williams, *The Dog and the Fever,* by Francisco de Quevedo. 1954.

Bibliography: *Bibliography of Williams* by Emily Mitchell Wallace, 1968.

Reading List: *Williams* by Vivienne Koch, 1950; *Williams: A Critical Study* by John Malcolm Brinnin, 1963; *The Poems of Williams,* 1964, and *The Prose of Williams,* 1970, both by Linda W. Wagner; *The Poetic World of Williams* by Alan Ostrom, 1966; *Williams: A Collection of Critical Essays* edited by J. Hillis Miller, 1966; *An Approach to Paterson* by Walter Peter Scott, 1967; *The Music of Survival* by Sherman Paul, 1968; *Williams: The American Background* by Mike Weaver, 1971; *The Inverted Bell: Modernism and the Counterpoetics of Williams* by Joseph N. Riddell, 1974; *Williams: The Knack of Survival in America* by Robert Coles, 1975; *Williams: Poet from Jersey* by Reed Whittemore, 1975.

*   *   *

William Carlos Williams is one of the leading figures of American modernist poetry whose recent recognition critically supports the impact his poems and fiction had throughout the modern and contemporary periods. Williams was a writer's writer in that his reputation existed chiefly among other writers – Ezra Pound, H. D., Marianne Moore, Hart Crane, Wallace Stevens, John Dos Passos, Ernest Hemingway – at least until New Directions began publishing his work in the late 1930's. Most of Williams's first dozen books were privately printed or subsidized. Some were collections of poems; others were an innovative mixture of poetry and prose, or of prose-poem form. Regardless of apparent genre, Williams wrote consistently in a mode based on the rhythms of the speaking voice, complete with idiomatic language, colloquial word choice, organic form and structure, and an intense interest in locale as both setting and subject.

This most American of poets was born of mixed parentage, and part of his fascination with the identification of – even the definition of – the American character may have stemmed from his own feeling of dislocation. His short early poems as well as his collection of essays on American historical figures, *In the American Grain,* present personae and scenes germane to the United States: "a young horse with a green bed-quilt/on his withers shaking his head," "A big young bareheaded woman/in an apron," "Flowers through the window/lavender and yellow//changed by white curtains." The fact that these scenes and characters are presented with neither apology nor psychological justification emphasized the aesthetic position that the thing was its own justification. Whether echoing James Dewey, Henri Bergson, or William James, Williams's innate pragmatism led him to a concentration on the unadorned image (as a means to universal understanding, truth) that opened many new directions in modern poetry. Williams did not use the image as symbol, a substitute for a larger idea; he was content to rest with the assumption that the reader could duplicate his own sense of importance for the red wheelbarrows and green glass between hospital walls, and thereby dismiss the equivocation of symbolism. As he said so succinctly in *Paterson,* "no ideas but in things."

Allied with the notion of presentation was the corollary that the author was to be as invisible as possible, so as not to dilute the effect of the concrete object or character. Not until his later poems did Williams change that tenet, but the strikingly personal "The Desert Music" and "Asphodel, That Greeny Flower" benefit from his use of a more personal stance toward the materials. Through the writing of his five-book epic poem, *Paterson,* through the 1940's to 1958, Williams was moving toward a kind of self-revelation, albeit unevenly. The epic concerns a poet-doctor-city persona named Paterson, tracing some events of the poet-doctor's life through an intense juxtaposition of scene, image, and memory. The technique of placing one image or scene against another, often without verbal transition, resembled the montage effect in the art contemporary with Williams; troubling as it was to his readers thirty years ago, it became the *modus operandi* for many contemporary writers, a way of increasing speed, of covering more images and sources of imagery, in the context of a rapidly-moving poem.

Williams established many new principles in the writing of his poetry – his confidence that the common American was an apt source of character, his joy in re-creating natural speech, his experimentation with a structure and line that would allow the flexible and fluid pace of speech to be presented – but his prose was also influential. From the 1923 *Spring and All*, when he combined aesthetic theory with such famous poems as "The Red Wheelbarrow," "To Elsie," and "At the Ballgame," to the trilogy of a family establishing itself in American business culture (the Stetchers in *White Mule*, *In the Money*, and *The Build-Up*), Williams turned away from the established conventions in order to present sharply, idiomatically, the gist of his drama. Much of his prose is carried through dialogue that makes Hemingway's seem contrived and redundant; most of his fiction has no ostensible plot. Moving as far from artifice as possible, his prose was criticized repeatedly for being artless; but contemporary readers have found the organic emphasis on language-structure-character an important direction for their own writing. "The Burden of Loveliness," "Jean Beicke," "The Use of Force" are stories often anthologized, provocative in their presentation of convincing characters whose human conditions proceed without drama, but – in Williams's handling – always with sympathy.

That Williams was a practicing physician until the mid 1950's adds some interest to his use of apparently real people in his fiction and poetry. The authenticity of his knowledge about people is undeniable, and he speaks movingly in his autobiography about the reciprocity between being a doctor (a pediatrician by specialization, but a general practitioner for all intents) and a writer. Working from insights that a more reclusive person might not have had, Williams was able to portray accurately many elements of the American culture that had not been treated in the literature of the twentieth century (Eliot's Prufrock would not have come to Williams's New Jersey office). Disturbed as he often was about his lack of time to write, he nevertheless acknowledged that his busy life was a rich one; and his writing after his retirement (a condition which occurred chiefly because of a severe stroke) frequently returned to subjects and characters from that more active life. The stories about Williams's writing during his rushed days as physician are apocryphal: pulling his car off the road while on his way to make a house call so that he could scribble a poem on a prescription blank; equipping his office desk with a hidden typewriter so that he could flip the machine in place between patients. His production as writer in the midst of his full days as doctor is amazing, but what made that production possible was his personal intent: he considered himself primarily a poet; his aim and direction in life were toward success in writing. No hurried schedule could prevent his implementing that dream.

Williams's poems are not all affirmative pictures of American character and scene; in fact, much of his writing during the 1930's and 1940's is bleak and despairing, and the early books of *Paterson* reflect that disillusionment with what had earlier appeared to be inexhaustible American promise. The late books of *Paterson*, however, supply Williams's own hard-won answers: love, even if foolhardy; virtue; knowing oneself; doing what one can; creating. These are hardly new answers, but their lack of innovation does not lessen their impact. Like Dante traveling through the Inferno, Paterson-Williams takes us into blind alleys (his poems are realistic because we see wrong answers as well as right ones, and sometimes no answers at all), only to move up through Limbo to a kind of modern-day heaven, a place with the answers at least implied in passages like

> Through this hole
> at the bottom of the cavern

of death, the imagination
escapes intact.
It is the imagination
which cannot be fathomed.
It is through this hole
we escape....

From this resolution, it is only a step to the gentle poise of the last poems. One of the most striking poems of his Pulitzer prize-winning book, *Pictures from Brueghel*, is "Asphodel," the love poem to his wife of nearly fifty years, which speaks of "love, abiding love." "Death/is not the end of it," Williams writes, comparing love to "a garden which expands ... a love engendering/gentleness and goodness." Williams contrasts the quiet assurance of this love with "Waste, waste!/dominates the world. It is the bomb's work." And his love is broadened to include his total response to life, as he declares proudly toward the end of the poem:

Only the imagination is real!
I have declared it
            time without end.
If a man die
    it is because death
        has first
possessed his imagination....

But love and the imagination
    are of a piece
            swift as the light
to avoid destruction....

Williams's impact on modern American poetics might appear to have been largely technical, for all the discussion of his use of the local, the triadic line, the idiom; but in the last analysis readers and fellow writers probably respond as well to the pervasive optimism of the doctor-poet's view, and to the openness with which he shared his life and his reactions with his readers. One may forget the rationale for Williams's triadic line division; but one does not forget his candor and his affirmation.

—Linda W. Wagner

WINTERS, (Arthur) Yvor. American. Born in Chicago, Illinois, 17 October 1900. Educated at the University of Chicago, 1917–18; University of Colorado, Boulder, B.A., M.A. 1925; Stanford University, California, Ph.D. 1935. Married the writer Janet Lewis in 1926; one son and one daughter. Instructor in French and Spanish, University of Idaho, Pocatello, 1925–27; Instructor, 1928–37, Assistant Professor, 1937–41, Associate Professor, 1941–49, Professor of English, 1949–51, and Albert Guerard Professor of Literature, 1961–66, Stanford University. Founding Editor, *The Gyroscope*, Los Altos, California, 1929–30; Western Editor, *Hound and Horn*, 1932–34. Fellow, Kenyon School of English, Gambier, Ohio, 1948–50. Recipient: National Institute of Arts and Letters grant, 1952; Brandeis University Creative Arts Award, for poetry, 1959; Harriet Monroe Poetry Award, 1960; Guggenheim Fellowhip, 1961; Bollingen Award, 1961; National Endowment for the Arts grant, 1967. Member, American Academy of Arts and Sciences. *Died 25 January 1968.*

PUBLICATIONS

Verse

The Immobile Wind. 1921.
The Magpie's Shadow. 1922.
The Bare Hills. 1927.
The Proof. 1930.
The Journey and Other Poems. 1931.
Before Disaster. 1934.
Poems. 1940.
The Giant Weapon. 1943.
Three Poems. N.d.
To the Holy Spirit. 1947.
Collected Poems. 1952; revised edition, 1960.
The Early Poems. 1966.

Fiction

The Brink of Darkness. 1932.

Other

Notes on the Mechanics of the Poetic Image: The Testament of a Stone. 1924.
The Case of David Lamson: A Summary, with Frances Theresa Russell. 1934.
Primitivism and Decadence: A Study of American Experimental Poetry. 1937.
Maule's Curse: Seven Studies in the History of American Obscurantism. 1938.
The Anatomy of Nonsense. 1943.
Edwin Arlington Robinson. 1946; revised edition, 1971.
In Defense of Reason. 1947; revised edition, 1960.
The Function of Criticism: Problems and Exercises. 1957.
On Modern Poets. 1959.
The Poetry of W. B. Yeats. 1960.
The Poetry of J. V. Cunningham. 1961.
Forms of Discovery: Critical and Historical Essays on the Forms of the Short Poem in English. 1967.
Uncollected Essays and Reviews, edited by Francis Murphy. 1976.
Hart Crane and Winters: Their Literary Correspondence, edited by Thomas Parkinson. 1978.

Editor, Twelve Poets of the Pacific. 1937.
Editor, Selected Poems, by Elizabeth Daryush. 1948.
Editor, Poets of the Pacific, Second Series. 1949.
Editor, with Kenneth Fields, Quest for Reality: An Anthology of Short Poems in English. 1969.

Bibliography: Winters: A Bibliography by Kenneth A. Lohf and Eugene P. Sheehy, 1959.

Reading List: The Complex of Winters' Criticism by Richard Sexton, 1974; "Winters Rehearsed and Reconsidered" by René Wellek, in Denver Quarterly 10, 1975.

*   *   *

The poetry of Yvor Winters falls into two phases, the Imagist phase (1920–28), and the Post-Symbolist phase (1929–68). During the first period Winters was writing markedly cadenced, imagistic free verse under the influence of William Carlos Williams, Ezra Pound, Glenway Wescott, H.D., and American Indian poetry. The influence was technical: that is, Winters learned to write his free verse by studying carefully selected poems he admired by these authors, but his own poems were not merely imitative. He developed a style of his own of great emotional intensity, brilliantly perceptive and even hypersensitive to the point of being hallucinative. The literary and autobiographical background of these early years is described by Winters in his Introduction to *The Early Poems*, in which he states that his philosophical position at that time was solipsistic and deterministic, a position which he later rejected. Some of the most remarkable of these verses are evocative of the life and landscape of New Mexico where Winters was recuperating from tuberculosis. At the same time, Winters was studying the mechanics of the image and how it was most effectively employed not only by the Imagists but by Coleridge, Browning, Hopkins, Robinson, Stevens, Emerson, and the French Symbolists.

In his late twenties Winters became impatient with the limitations of so-called free verse; he began to suspect that he could gain a greater emotional and intellectual range by the employment of the conventional iambic line as it occurs in the heroic couplet, the sonnet, in tetrameter and pentameter quatrains, and in other forms. *The Proof*, though it opens with poems written in the imagist manner, contains in the closing pages a number of verses in traditional iambic meters. The eight poems in *The Journey* are all in heroic couplets which show the influence not only of Dryden and Pope but also of the freely run-over couplets of Charles Churchill. One of the best of these, "On a View of Pasadena from the Hills," was directly influenced by Robert Bridges's 1899 poem in iambic pentameter couplets, "Elegy: The Summer-House on the Mound."

In his early thirties Winters was re-reading the poetry of Bridges, Hardy, Robinson, Stevens, Paul Valéry, and T. Sturge Moore with increasing admiration. All these poets (including Stevens in his best poem, "Sunday Morning") wrote in conventional prosody, a fact which strengthened Winters's conviction that free verse and imagism were temporary aberrations from the main tradition of Anglo-American verse. At this time he was forming the tastes and principles to be found in his critical essays, which were to attract considerably more attention than his poetry. In *Primitivism and Decadence* he analyzed the technical innovations of the "new poetry," and, although he admired a few free verse poems by H.D., Williams, Stevens, and Marianne Moore, he concluded that on the whole the experimentalist movement had been a failure. By the time he was writing the poetry that appeared in *The Giant Weapon* and in the *Collected Poems* of 1952 he had developed his critical theory concerning the nature of poetry, applied in a series of essays eventually published under the titles *In Defense of Reason*, *The Function of Criticism*, and *Forms of Discovery*. The gist of his theory is that a successful poem is a statement in words about human experience which communicates by means of verse – as distinct from prose, which is less precisely rhythmical than verse and therefore less effective in expressing emotion – appropriate feeling motivated by an understanding of the experience. In this kind of poetry full use is made of both the denotative and connotative significance of words. This theory is obviously operating in all the poetry of Winters's mature years.

Late in his career Winters began referring to what he called the post-symbolist style of the best American poetry of the twentieth century. In his essay "Poetic Styles Old and New" (1959), after a discussion of the two major styles of the Renaissance, the plain and the ornamental, he said in describing post-symbolism, "It ought to be possible to embody our sensory experience in our poetry in an efficient way, not as ornament, and with no sacrifice of rational intelligence." Sensory experience communicated by fresh and original imagery charged with rational significance occurs in Winters's best poems from about 1930 on, including "The Slow Pacific Swell" (1931), "Sir Gawaine and the Green Knight" (1937), and "A Summer Commentary" (1938).

A few dominant and closely related themes, explored in Winters's verse from the beginning of his career until the end, give to his work a remarkable coherence and unity. Among these are a recurrent examination of the relationship between the rational mind and the poetic sensibility which may enrich it or destroy it, a theme which derives from his own experience and also from the poetry of T. Sturge Moore. In his earliest verse the sensibility is dominant to the point of rational disintegration, and even as late as 1955 Winters was writing in his "At the San Francisco Airport": "The rain of matter upon sense/Destroys me momently." Achievement of balance between intellect and sensibility is the subject of "A Summer Commentary" and "Sir Gawaine and the Green Knight"; it is implicit in his allegorical poems on Greek subjects such as "Heracles," "Theseus," "Orpheus," and others. His concern with threats to the preservation of one's identity motivated a number of poems on death and the ravages of time, the most powerful of which are "For My Father's Grave," "To the Holy Spirit," "The Cremation," "A Leave-Taking," and "Prayer for My Son."

Winters is considered one of the most intellectual of all American poets. Yet he was keenly alive to the beauties of the sensory world as well as to its dangers. His purpose was "To steep the mind in sense/Yet never lose the aim." Consequently much of his poetry is remarkable for its freshly perceived descriptive detail of the natural world as in "The California Oaks" and "Time and the Garden." Finally it should be noted that Winters is the only twentieth-century poet of consequence who mastered the technique of free verse as practised by the Imagists and then abandoned it for conventional prosody, although he did not abandon what he had learned about the effective use of imagery. His poetry and his criticism present a significant case history of revolution and counter-revolution in modern poetry.

—Donald E. Stanford

WRIGHT, Judith. Australian. Born in Armidale, New South Wales, 31 May 1915. Educated at New England Girls School, Armidale; University of Sydney, B.A. Married J. P. McKinney; one daughter. Secretary, J. Walter Thompson, advertising agency, Sydney, 1938–39; Secretary, University of Sydney, 1940–42; Clerk, Australian Universities Commission, Brisbane, 1944–46; Statistical Research Officer, University of Queensland, Brisbane, 1946–49. Since 1967, Honours Tutor in English, University of Queensland. Commonwealth Literary Fund Lecturer, Australia, 1949, 1962; Guest Delegate, World Poetry Conference, Canada, 1967; Creative Arts Fellow, Australian National University, Canberra, 1974. Co-Founder and President, Wildlife Preservation Society of Queensland, 1962–65. Recipient: Grace Leven Prize, 1949, 1972; Commonwealth Literary Fund Fellowship, 1964; *Encyclopaedia Britannica* Award, 1964; Fellowship of Australian Writers Robert Frost Medal, 1975. D.Litt.: University of Queensland, 1962; University of New England, Armidale, 1963. Fellow of the Australian Academy of the Humanities, 1970. Lives in North Tamborine, Queensland.

PUBLICATIONS

Verse

The Moving Image. 1946.
Woman to Man. 1949.

The Gateway.   1953.
The Two Fires.   1955.
Birds.   1962.
(Poems).   1963.
Five Senses: Selected Poems.   1963.
City Sunrise.   1964.
The Other Half.   1966.
Collected Poems 1942–1970.   1971.
Alive.   1973.
Fourth Quarter.   1978.
The Double Tree: Selected Poems 1942–1976.   1978.

Fiction

The Nature of Love.   1966.

Other

The Generations of Men.   1959.
King of the Dingoes (juvenile).   1959.
Range the Mountains High (juvenile).   1962.
Shaw Neilson (biography and selected verse).   1963.
Charles Harpur.   1963.
The Day the Mountains Played (juvenile).   1963.
Country Towns (juvenile).   1964.
Preoccupations in Australian Poetry.   1965.
The River and the Road (juvenile).   1966; revised edition, 1971.
Henry Lawson.   1967.
Conservation as an Emerging Concept.   1971.
Because I Was Invited (essays).   1976.

Editor, Australian Poetry 1948.   1948.
Editor, A Book of Australian Verse.   1956; revised edition, 1968.
Editor, New Land, New Language: An Anthology of Australian Verse.   1957.
Editor, with A. K. Thomson, The Poet's Pen.   1966.
Editor, Witnesses of Spring: Unpublished Poems, by Shaw Neilson.   1970.

Reading List: Critical Essays on Wright edited by A. K. Thomson, 1968; Wright by A. D. Hope, 1975.

*   *   *

Judith Wright has such an awareness of time and place that she seems to look beyond these categories. "The Cycads" (The Moving Image), whose "smooth dark flames flicker at time's own root," is a fair representative of this attitude. She sees Australia as an age-old country, but it is also her "blood's country." These poems have a firmly realised local habitation in New England, its landscape, history, and early life, particularly in her recognition of the inescapable association of man and the land where he finds himself. In her most famous poem, "Bullocky," she celebrates an early worker, compelled and driven mad by his environment, but his bones are now everlastingly part of it.

This ability for genuinely fundamental perceptions appears again in Woman to Man which records the primitive and elemental awareness of woman in several of its poems dealing with such experiences as conception, pregnancy, and parturition, what A. D. Hope has called "the continuous epic of generation." Relying much on Blake's idea of the double-vision, she grapples in *The Gateway* and in *The Two Fires* with the problem of time, the life that grows from the birth, and, beyond that, with Blakean influences, the doors of eternity, the first steps towards a later recognition of the ability of the five senses to "gather into a meaning/all acts, all presences/ ... a rhythm that dances/and is not mine."

Another influence at work in this period, and later, is T. S. Eliot, whose *Four Quartets* no doubt seemed relevant both to Wright's struggles with the problems of time and also with those which she was conscious of having – "My speech inexact, my note not right" – with language. She was wrestling with philosophical difficulties.

Birds is a return to what she calls the "reverence of the heart." She had became co-founder and president of the Wild Life Preservation Society of Queensland, and *Birds*, a book of light-weight poems, probably represents a necessary breathing-space before the next phase.

Five Senses suggests reassurance and reconciliation. The troubles of the 1950's give way to a sense of fulfilment, aptly represented by the poem "For My Daughter," growing up, growing away, the mother ready to accept the new relationship. Likewise, "Turning Fifty" (*The Other Half*) reflects a mood of acceptance; and "Shadow," the new section in *Collected Poems 1942–1970*, speaks of completeness as she elegises her husband: "Growing beyond your life into your vision,/at last you proved the circle and stepped clear." *Alive* concerns itself with her own process of ageing, but, just as in the 1950's the atomic bomb had troubled her, so in this collection and in "Shadow" she was disturbed by Vietnam and the spoliation of the Australian natural environment. Her later work, competent though it generally is, is rarely so richly satisfying as her first two collections. It does not have that intuitive metaphysical depth that characterises the earlier work.

She has written extensively in the field of literary criticism; *Preoccupations in Australian Poetry* and *Because I Was Invited* collect her best work. The latter also contains many of her articles on conservation. She also wrote short stories and novels for children. As a critic, she is no systematiser but rather a defender of what she likes; she has made a case particularly for such early Australian poets as Harpur, Baylebridge, and Shaw Neilson, who are all too easily underrated.

—Arthur Pollard

WYLIE, Elinor (Hoyt). American. Born in Somerville, New Jersey, 7 September 1885; brought up in Philadelphia and Washington, D.C. Educated at Miss Baldwin's School, Bryn Mawr, and Holton Arms School, Washington, D.C. Married Philip Hichborn in 1905 (died, 1911), one son; left her husband to elope with Horace Wylie, 1910, and moved to England with him as Mr. and Mrs. Waring; returned to the United States after Wylie's divorce, 1915, and married him, 1916 (divorced, 1923); moved to New York in 1921, and became a prominent figure in New York literary circles; married the poet William Rose Benét, *q.v.*, in 1923; thereafter lived in New York and London; Poetry Editor of *Vanity Fair*, New York, 1923–25; Editor, Literary Guild, New York, 1926–28. Recipient: Julia Ellsworth Ford Prize, 1921. *Died 16 December 1928.*

PUBLICATIONS

Collections

Collected Poems, Collected Prose, edited by William Rose Benét.   2 vols., 1932–33.

Verse

> *Incidental Numbers.* 1912.
> *Nets to Catch the Wind.* 1921.
> *Black Armour.* 1923.
> *(Poems),* edited by Laurence Jordan.   1926.
> *Trivial Breath.* 1928.
> *Angels and Earthly Creatures: A Sequence of Sonnets.* 1928.
> *Angels and Earthly Creatures* (collection). 1929.
> *Nadir.* 1937.
> *Last Poems,* edited by Jane D. Wise. 1943.

Fiction

> *Jennifer Lorn: A Sedate Extravaganza.* 1923.
> *The Venetian Glass Nephew.* 1925.
> *The Orphan Angel.* 1926; as *Mortal Image,* 1927.
> *Mr. Hodge and Mr. Hazard.* 1928.

Reading List: *Wylie: The Portrait of an Unknown Lady* by Nancy Hoyt, 1935; *Wylie* by Thomas A. Gray, 1969.

*   *   *

Elinor Wylie's prestigious social background, striking personality, beauty, elegance, and conversational gifts, with the romantic aura of her daring break with conventional society when she eloped with Horace Wylie, made her a symbolic figure to many persons caught up in the "American poetic renaissance." Consequently, judgments of her writings were for some years infused with feelings about the writer. Thomas Gray's monograph of 1969 discusses widely differing views of her achievement.

In the essay "Jewelled Bindings" (1923), Wylie saw herself and a few other contemporary lyric poets as "enchanted by a midas-touch or a colder silver madness into workers in metal and glass ... in crisp and sharp-edged forms." They choose "short lines, clear small stanzas, brilliant and compact." Such standards produced her most widely known poems: the 3-quatrain "Let No Charitable Hope" that climaxes with "In masks outrageous and austere/The years go by in single file;/But none has merited my fear,/And none has quite escaped my smile"; "The Eagle and the Mole," with its fastidious trimeter: "Avoid the reeking herd ..."; the art-for-art's-sake poem "Say not of Beauty she is good,/Or aught but beautiful"; and the exquisite "Velvet Shoes": "Let us walk in the white snow/In a soundless space...."

This preference for the delicately sensuous or even impalpable characterized many of her poems – "I love the look, austere, immaculate,/Of landscapes drawn in pearly monotones" – and her first two "novels." *Jennifer Lorn: A Sedate Extravaganza* appealed to a public that was seeking relief from the ugly realities. Set in the late 18th century in the realms of aristocracy and wealth in England and India, it is a long catalogue of lovely, delicate objects;

what plot it has concerns the fragile, fainting Jennifer and – the spine of the story – her husband Gerald, the exact, cool aesthete. It has been compared to a tapestry, and among the *mille fleurs* are many phrases and lines from 18th-century literature. Wylie's wide reading in this period showed itself also in the amusing *Venetian Glass Nephew*. Her long and perhaps abnormal admiration for Shelley brought about *The Orphan Angel*, in which the libertarian poet is rescued from drowning and accompanies a Yankee sailor to America and across the continent. This trend toward more realistic treatment continued in *Mr. Hodge and Mr. Hazard*, a satirical allegory on the stifling of the late romantics by the Victorians.

Mary Colum, who ranks Wylie as "one of the few important women poets in any literature," observes, "She seemed to write little out of a mood or out of a passing emotion ... but nearly always out of complex thought...." (*Life and the Dream*, 1947). Many found her poems cold; the fastidious speaker seeks isolation and death. A last group of sonnets, however, shows a capacity for love: "And so forget to weep, forget to grieve,/And wake, and touch each other's hands, and turn/Upon a bed of juniper and fern." H. Lüdecke (in *English Studies 20*, December 1938) finds her not a "great" poet but a "rare" poet: "Refinement is her essential characteristic as an artist."

—Alice R. Bensen

YEATS, William Butler.   Irish.   Born in Sandymount, County Dublin, 13 June 1865; son of the artist John Butler Yeats, and brother of the artist Jack Butler Yeats; lived in London, 1874–83. Educated at Godolphin School, Hammersmith, London; Erasmus Smith School, Dublin; studied art in Dublin, 1883–86; left art school to concentrate on poetry. Married Georgie Hyde-Lees in 1917; one son and one daughter. Lived mainly in London, spending part of each year in Ireland, 1890–1921: a Founder of the Rhymers Club, London, and member of the *Yellow Book* group; met Lady Gregory, 1896, and thereafter spent many of his summer holidays at her home in Sligo; Co-Founder, with Lady Gregory and Edward Martyn, Irish Literary Theatre, later Abbey Theatre, Dublin, 1899: Director of the Abbey Theatre, 1904 until his death; Editor of *Beltaine*, 1899–1900, *Samhain*, 1901–08, and *The Arrow*, 1906–09; settled with his family in Ireland, 1922: Senator of the Irish Free State, 1922–28. Recipient: Nobel Prize, 1923. D.Litt.: Oxford University, 1931; Cambridge University; University of Dublin. *Died 28 January 1939.*

PUBLICATIONS

Collections

Letters, edited by Allan Wade.   1954.
Poems, Prose, Plays, and *Criticism* (selections), edited by A. Norman Jeffares.   4 vols., 1963–64
Variorum Edition of the Plays, edited by Russell and C. C. Alspach.   1966.
Variorum Edition of the Poems, edited by Peter Allt and Russell Alspach.   1967.

Verse

Mosada: A Dramatic Poem.   1886.
The Wanderings of Oisin and Other Poems.   1889.
The Countess Kathleen and Various Legends and Lyrics.   1892.
Poems.   1895; revised edition, 1899, 1901, 1904, 1908, 1912, 1913, 1927, 1929.
The Wind among the Reeds.   1899.
In the Seven Woods, Being Poems Chiefly of the Irish Heroic Age.   1903.
Poems 1899–1905.   1906.
Poetical Works: Lyrical Poems, Dramatic Poems.   2 vols., 1906–07.
Poems, Second Series.   1909.
The Green Helmet and Other Poems.   1910; revised edition, 1912.
A Selection from the Poetry.   1913.
A Selection from the Love Poetry.   1913.
Poems Written in Discouragement 1912–13.   1913.
Nine Poems.   1914.
Responsibilities: Poems and a Play.   1914.
Responsibilities and Other Poems.   1916.
The Wild Swans at Coole, Other Verses, and a Play in Verse.   1917; revised edition, 1919.
Nine Poems.   1918.
Michael Robartes and the Dancer.   1921.
Selected Poems.   1921.
Later Poems (Collected Works 1).   1922.
Seven Poems and a Fragment.   1922.
The Cat and the Moon and Certain Poems.   1924.
October Blast.   1927.
The Tower.   1928.
Selected Poems, Lyrical and Narrative.   1929.
The Winding Stair.   1929.
Words for Music Perhaps and Other Poems.   1932.
The Winding Stair and Other Poems.   1933.
Collected Poems.   1933; revised edition, 1950.
Wheels and Butterflies.   1934.
The King of the Great Clock Tower: Commentaries and Poems.   1934.
A Full Moon in March.   1935.
Poems.   1935.
New Poems.   1938.
Last Poems and Two Plays.   1939.
Selected Poems, edited by A. Holst. 1939.
Last Poems and Plays.   1940.
The Poems.   2 vols., 1949.

Plays

The Countess Kathleen (produced 1899).   In The Countess Kathleen and Various Legends and Lyrics, 1892; revised version as The Countess Cathleen, 1912.
The Land of Heart's Desire (produced 1894).
The Shadowy Waters (produced 1904).   1900; revised version, in Poems, 1906.
Diarmuid and Grania, with George Moore (produced 1901).   1951; edited by Anthony Farrow, 1974.
Cathleen ni Hoolihan (produced 1902).   1902.
The Pot of Broth (produced 1902).   In The Hour Glass and Other Plays, 1904.

Where There Is Nothing (produced 1904).   1902; revised version, with Lady Gregory, as *The Unicorn from the Stars* (produced 1907), 1908.

The Hour Glass: A Morality (produced 1903).   1903; revised version (produced 1913), in *The Mask*, April 1913.

The King's Threshold (produced 1903).   1904; revised version (produced 1913), in *Poems*, 1906.

The Hour Glass and Other Plays, Being Volume 2 of Plays for an Irish Theatre (includes *Cathleen ni Houlihan* and *The Pot of Broth*).   1904.

On Baile's Strand (produced 1904).   In *Plays for an Irish Theatre 3*, 1904; revised version, in *Poems*, 1906.

Deirdre (produced 1906).   In *Plays for an Irish Theatre 5*, 1907.

The Golden Helmet (produced 1908).   1908; revised version, as *The Green Helmet* (produced 1910), 1910.

At the Hawk's Well; or, Waters of Immortality (produced 1916).   In *The Wild Swans at Coole*, 1917.

The Dreaming of the Bones (produced 1931).   In *Two Plays for Dancers*, 1919.

Two Plays for Dancers (includes *The Dreaming of the Bones* and *The Only Jealousy of Emer*).   1919.

The Player Queen (produced 1919).   1922.

Four Plays for Dancers (includes *At the Hawk's Well, The Only Jealousy of Emer, The Dreaming of the Bones, Calvary*).   1921.

Plays in Prose and Verse (Collected Works 2).   1922.

Plays and Controversies (Collected Works 3).   1923.

King Oedipus, from the play by Sophocles (produced 1926).   1928.

The Resurrection (produced 1934).   1927.

Oedipus at Colonus, from the play by Sophocles (produced 1927).   In *Collected Plays*, 1934.

Fighting the Waves (produced 1929).   In *Wheels and Butterflies*, 1934.

The Words upon the Window Pane.   1934.

Collected Plays.   1934; revised edition, 1952.

Nine One-Act Plays.   1937.

The Herne's Egg.   1938.

The Herne's Egg and Other Plays (includes *A Full Moon in March* and *The King of the Great Clock Tower*).   1938.

Purgatory and *The Death of Cuchulain*, in *Last Poems and Two Plays*.   1939.

Fiction

John Sherman and Dhoya.   1891.

The Secret Rose (stories).   1897.

The Tables of the Law; The Adoration of the Magi.   1897.

Stories of Red Hanrahan.   1905.

Other

The Celtic Twilight: Men and Women, Dhouls and Fairies.   1893; revised edition, 1902.

Literary Ideals in Ireland, with AE and John Eglinton.   1899.

Is the Order of R.R. and A.C. to Remain a Magical Order?   1901.

Ideas of Good and Evil.   1903.

Discoveries: A Volume of Essays.   1907.

Collected Works.   8 vols., 1908.

Poetry and Ireland: Essays, with Lionel Johnson.   1908.

Synge and the Ireland of His Time. 1911.

The Cutting of an Agate. 1912; revised edition, 1919.

Reveries over Childhood and Youth. 1915.

Per Amica Silentia Lunae. 1918.

Four Years. 1921.

The Trembling of the Veil. 1922.

Essays (Collected Works 4). 1924.

A Vision. 1925; revised edition, 1937; edited by George Mills Harper and W. K. Hood, 1978.

Early Poems and Stories (Collected Works 5). 1925.

Estrangement, Being Some Fifty Thoughts from a Diary Kept in 1909. 1926.

Autobiographies (Collected Works 6). 1926.

The Death of Synge and Other Passages from an Old Diary. 1928.

A Packet for Ezra Pound. 1929.

Stories of Michael Robartes and His Friends. 1932.

Letters to the New Islands, edited by Horace Reynolds. 1934.

Dramatis Personae. 1935.

Dramatis Personae 1896–1902. 1936.

Essays 1931 to 1936. 1937.

The Autobiography. 1938; revised edition, as *Autobiographies,* 1955.

On the Boiler (essays, includes verse). 1939.

If I Were Four-and-Twenty. 1940.

Pages from a Diary Written in 1930. 1940.

The Senate Speeches, edited by Donald Pearce. 1960.

Reflections, edited by Curtis Bradford. 1970.

Ah, Sweet Dancer: Yeats and Margaret Ruddock: A Correspondence, edited by Roger McHugh. 1970.

Uncollected Prose, edited by John F. Frayne and Colton Johnson. 2 vols., 1970–74.

Interviews and Recollections, edited by E. H. Mikhail. 1977.

The Correspondence of Robert Bridges and Yeats, edited by J. Finneran. 1977.

Editor, *Fairy and Folk Tales of the Irish Peasantry.* 1888; as *Irish Fairy and Folk Tales,* 1893.

Editor, *Stories from Carleton.* 1889.

Editor, *Representative Irish Tales.* 1891.

Editor, *Irish Fairy Tales.* 1892.

Editor, with E. Ellis, *The Works of Blake.* 3 vols., 1893.

Editor, *The Poems of Blake.* 1893.

Editor, *A Book of Irish Verse.* 1895; revised edition, 1900.

Editor, *A Book of Images Drawn by W. Horton.* 1898.

Editor, *Twenty-One Poems,* by Lionel Johnson. 1905.

Editor, *Some Essays and Passages,* by John Eglinton. 1905.

Editor, *Sixteen Poems,* by William Allingham. 1905.

Editor, *Poems of Spenser.* 1906.

Editor, *Twenty-One Poems,* by Katharine Tynan. 1907.

Editor, *Poems and Translations,* by J. M. Synge. 1909.

Editor, *Selections from the Writings of Lord Dunsany.* 1912.

Editor, with F. Higgins, *Broadsides: A Collection of Old and New Songs.* 2 vols., 1935–37.

Editor, *The Oxford Book of Modern Verse 1892–1935.* 1936.

Editor, *The Ten Principal Upanishads,* translated by Shree Purohit Swami and Yeats. 1937.

Bibliography: *A Bibliography of the Writings of Yeats* by Allan Wade, 1951, revised edition,

1958, additions by Russell Alspach, in *Irish Book 2*, 1963; *Yeats: A Classified Bibliography of Criticism* by K. P. S. Jochum, 1978.

Reading List: *The Poetry of Yeats* by Louis MacNeice, 1941; *Yeats: The Man and the Masks*, 1948, and *The Identity of Yeats*, 1954, revised edition, 1964, both by Richard Ellmann; *The Golden Nightingale: Essays on Some Principles of Poetry in the Lyrics of Yeats* by Donald Stauffer, 1949; *Yeats: The Tragic Phase: A Study of the Last Poems* by V. Koch, 1951; *Prolegomena to the Study of Yeat's Poems* and *Plays* by G. B. Saul, 2 vols., 1957–58; *Yeats the Playwright: A Commentary on Character and Design in the Major Plays* by Peter Ure, 1963; *Between the Lines: Yeats's Poetry in the Making* by Jon Stallworthy, 1963; *Yeats's Vision and the Later Poems* by Helen Vendler, 1963; *Yeats: A Collection of Critical Essays* edited by John Unterecker, 1963; *Yeats's Golden Dawn* by George Mills Harper, 1974; *A Commentary on the Collected Plays of Yeats* by A. Norman Jeffares and A. S. Knowland, 1974; *Yeats's Early Poetry: The Quest for Reconciliation* by Frank Murphy, 1975; *Yeats: The Critical Heritage* edited by A. Norman Jeffares, 1976.

*   *   *

William Butler Yeats wrote his early poetry out of a love of a particular place, Sligo, in the West of Ireland, with its folklore, its belief in the supernatural, and its legends. He found material for his own mythology in translations of the Gaelic tales into English. These tales of the Red Branch cycle and the Fenian cycle became tinged in his handling with *fin de siècle* melancholy, with what was called the Celtic twilight. His first long poem, "The Wanderings of Oisin," was founded upon Gaelic pagan legends and gave an account of Oisin visiting three islands in the other-world. In "The Rose" his poems developed this use of Gaelic material, and his Rose symbolism showed the effect of his editing Blake and his interest in the occult tradition, as well as the effect of his love for Maud Gonne. *The Wind among the Reeds* contains more elaborate poetry, intense, at times obscurely allusive, drawing upon Gaelic mythology and Rosicrucian images ("The Secret Rose"), defeatist in its romantic poems (the devotion of "He wishes for the Cloths of Heaven"), and filled with a delicate melancholic beauty.

He began to change this style; *In the Seven Woods* contains more personal, realistic poems ("The Folly of Being Comforted," "Adam's Curse"). *The Green Helmet* records the emptiness of love, now Maud Gonne had married (there is exalted celebration of her beauty in "No Second Troy" and "Words"). He reflects on how he seemed to have lost spontaneity ("All Things can tempt me from this craft of verse"). His *Collected Works* had appeared in 1908; but he found a new kind of poetic voice in *Responsibilities*; this is the antithesis of his early work; stripped of decoration and mystery it is savagely satiric in its defence of art against the philistines. He draws images of aristocratic patronage from Renaissance Italy, he contrasts contemporary Ireland with the past, filled with brave leaders ("September 1913"), he reflects on Irish ingratitude ("To a Shade"), and in his poems on beggars and hermits transmits enjoyment of coarse vitality. And yet there is still the magnificence of vision in "The Cold Heaven." "A Coat" repudiates the celtic "embroideries out of old mythologies"; now he is walking naked. *The Wild Swans at Coole* continues his praise of Maud Gonne ("The People" and "Broken Dreams"); his elegy on Major Robert Gregory and "An Irish Airman Forsees His Death" mark a new capacity for elevating the personal into heroic stature; and his three poems "Ego Dominus Tuus," "The Phases of the Moon," and "The Double Vision of Michael Robartes" reflect his interest in putting his thoughts into order, into some kind of system. This found its best poetic expression in "The Second Coming" of *Michael Robartes and the Dancer* which also contained his poems (notably "Easter 1916") on the Rising. Other poems record his marriage, and "A Prayer for My Daughter" attacks the intellectual hatred of Maud Gonne.

These two volumes showed Yeats emerging from the wintry rages of *Responsibilities* into a new appreciation of beauty balanced against tragedy. His own life had blossomed: marriage, children, his tower in the west of Ireland, the Nobel Prize for poetry, membership of the Irish Senate – and, above all, the writing of *A Vision* which gave him a "system of symbolism," a structure for his thought, and the confidence to write fully of his interests – he was now a sufficient subject for his poetry. And how superbly he wrote in *The Tower* of his ideas on life, on death. "Sailing to Byzantium," "The Tower," "Meditations in Time of Civil War," "Nineteen Hundred and Nineteen," "Leda and the Swan," "Among School Children," and "All Soul's Night" have a lofty but passionate authority about them. He was discovering his own intellectual ancestry among the eighteenth-century Anglo-Irish, expressed in "Blood and the Man" and "The Seven Sages" of *The Winding Stair*. Here, too, are the extremes of "vacillation," the contemplation of death after life in "Byzantium," and the noble poems on his friends Eva Gore-Booth and Con Markiewicz, and on Lady Gregory at Coole Park in 1929 and again in 1931 – "we were the last romantics," he cried, realising "all is changed." This note is there in *A Full Moon in March*, where "An age is the reversal of an age"; and, as Yeats grows older, the brilliant metaphysical compression of "The Four Ages of Man" strikes a note which runs through *Last Poems*, which records heroic stances in the face of coming death – of civilization and the self. There are, of course, as ever, the poems on love, the celebration of his friends ("The Municipal Galley Revisited" and "Beautiful Lofty Things"), the despairing recognition of the foul rag and bone shop of the heart, the recording of his own views on Ireland, on poetry, and on himself in "Under Ben Bulben" and, most movingly, in "The Man and the Echo."

Yeats began writing plays in his teens – heroic plays with little dramatic content. But he left conventional modes behind with *The Countess Cathleen*, written for Maud Gonne, and with the aim of blending pagan legend with Christian belief. Yeats revised this play extensively, as he did *The Shadowy Waters*, a study of the heroic gesture, carried by somewhat cryptic symbolism. He also wrote some short plays for the Irish National Dramatic Society, notably the revolutionary *Cathleen ni Houlihan*. *The King's Threshold* marks a change in Yeats's heroes from passivity to more active roles – Seanchan the poet hero in this play (founded upon a middle-Irish story) asserts the place of poetry in public life. Yeats was also deeply interested in Cuchulain, the hero of the Red Branch cycle of stories, and in *On Baile's Strand* he used the story of Cuchulain unwittingly killing his own son. In *Deirdre* he conferred a lofty dignity upon Deirdre's suicide after the heroic gesture made by her and Naoise when they realise they are doomed. In *The Golden Helmet*, rewritten in verse as *The Green Helmet*, Yeats used an old Irish tale as basis for an ironical farce, another "moment of intense life." The strangeness of Yeats's imagination and his very real capacity for farce emerged in *The Player Queen*, which is most effective on stage and extends the theories which were first elaborated in the prose work *Per Amica Silentia Lunae*.

Yeats found the Abbey Theatre was not suitable for the plays he wanted to write: his *Four Plays for Dancers* arose in part out of his interest in the Japanese Noh drama to which Ezra Pound had introduced him. He wanted to do without an orthodox theatre, and so the ritual of music and dancing aided the mysterious art he sought. *At the Hawk's Well* and *The Only Jealousy of Emer* develop the Cuchulain mythology, while *The Dreaming of the Bones* blends supernatural with political themes. *Calvary* is more complex, and depends upon *A Vision's* ideas. A later play, *Resurrection*, is far more effective, being intense and economic in its presentation of abstract ideas against a turbulent background. His versions of *King Oedipus* and *Oedipus at Colonus* capture the essence of the Greek tragedies with success, and his sense of dialogue and neat construction make *The Words upon the Window Pane* a *tour de force*, communicating via a glance the agony in Swift's spirit. After *The King of the Great Clock Tower*, *A Full Moon in March*, and *The Herne's Egg*, another examination of the limitations of the hero's role, came *Purgatory*, a brilliant evocation of the history of a ruined house and its family, bound in a murderous cycle. *The Death of Cuchulain* written just before Yeats's death in 1939 examines the proud disdain of his hero for death.

Yeats wrote a large number of articles and reviews up to the end of the century; these were mainly on Irish writing. His first extended prose work was *John Sherman and Dhoya*, fiction which gave his youthful impressions of Sligo. The essays in *The Celtic Twilight* portrayed the traditional beliefs and scenery of the West of Ireland in limpid prose, but *The Secret Rose* contained more complex stories, a mixture of symbolism and mysticism written in that "artificial elaborate English" which was popular in the 1890's. His mannered prose appeared in *The Tables of the Law* and *The Adoration of the Magi*. By the turn of the century he changed his prose style, revised *The Celtic Twilight* and some of the stories in *The Secret Rose. Ideas of Good and Evil* contained essays written earlier in his complex style. The need for propaganda for the Abbey Theatre further simplified his style, and he was influenced by Lady Gregory's use of the idiomatic language of country people in her translations from the Irish.

In his autobiographical writings Yeats created an evocative, richly patterned record of his own unique experience, and of his family and his friends. His diaries, some of which were published in *Estrangement*, show his attempts to achieve unity. And his thought, based on most diverse sources, appeared in *A Vision* which contains many witty as well as profound passages as he got "it all in order." His prose became more flexible, ranging between complexity and simplicity – "The Bounty of Sweden" is a good example. Some of his senate speeches are excellent pieces of rhetoric. His introduction to *The Words upon the Window-Pane* (1934) shows his capacity for imaginative meditation and creative criticism. The many introductions he wrote to the work of writers he admired contain a lofty generosity. On the other hand, his airing of opinions – and prejudices – in *On the Boiler* has an engaging touch of the outrageous. His intellectual curiosity, his originality, and his ability to convey his ideas attractively appears in his correspondence, notably in his youthful letters to Katharine Tynan and his later unreserved, lively letters to Mrs. Shakespeare. His criticism is beginning to be appreciated more fully as the complexity and strength of his mind are understood.

—A. Norman Jeffares

YOUNG, Andrew (John).   Scottish.   Born in Elgin, 29 April 1885. Educated at the Royal High School, Edinburgh; University of Edinburgh, M.A. 1908; New College, Edinburgh; ordained a minister of the United Free Church of Scotland. Worked with the Y.M.C.A. in France during World War I. Married Janet Green in 1914; one son and one daughter. Joined the Church of England, 1939, and after a few months at Wells Theological College became Curate of Plaistow, West Sussex, 1940; Vicar of Stonegate, Sussex, 1941 until his retirement, 1959. Canon of Chichester Cathedral, 1948–71. Recipient: Royal Society of Literature Benson Medal, 1939; Heinemann Award, 1946; Queen's Gold Medal for Poetry, 1952; Duff Cooper Memorial Prize, 1960. LL.D.: University of Edinburgh, 1951. Fellow of the Royal Society of Literature. *Died 25 November 1971.*

PUBLICATIONS

Collections

Complete Poems, edited by Leonard Clark.   1974

Verse

Songs of Night.   1910.
Cecil Barclay Simpson: A Memorial by Two Friends, with D. Baillie.   1918.

Boaz and Ruth and Other Poems.   1920.
The Death of Eli and Other Poems.   1921.
Thirty-One Poems.   1922.
The Bird-Cage.   1926.
The Cuckoo Clock.   1928.
The New Shepherd.   1931.
Winter Harvest.   1933.
The White Blackbird.   1935.
Collected Poems.   1936.
Speak to the Earth.   1939.
The Green Man.   1947.
Collected Poems.   1950.
Into Hades.   1952.
Out of the World and Back: Into Hades and A Traveller in Time.   1958.
Quiet as Moss: Thirty Six Poems (juvenile), edited by Leonard Clark.   1959.
The Collected Poems, edited by Leonard Clark.   1960.
Burning as Light: Thirty Seven Poems (juvenile), edited by Leonard Clark.   1967.

Plays

The Adversary (includes Rizpah).   1923.
Nicodemus: A Mystery, music by Imogen Holst.   1937.

Other

A Prospect of Flowers.   1945.
A Retrospect of Flowers.   1950.
A Prospect of Britain.   1956.
The Poet and the Landscape.   1962.
The New Poly-Olbion: Topographical Excursions, with an Introductory Account of the
    Poet's Early Days.   1967.
The Poetic Jesus.   1972.
Meditations on Some Poems, edited by Leonard Clark.   1977.

Reading List: Young, Prospect of a Poet: Tributes by 14 Writers edited by Leonard Clark,
1957, and Young by Clark, 1964.

*   *   *

Andrew Young belongs to that rural company of parson-poets which has included, among
others, Barnes, Crabbe, Hawker, and, in our own day, the Welsh poet R. S. Thomas. But he
differs from all these in not being mainly parochial. He takes his place as a significant nature
poet alongside Thomson, Clare, Wordsworth, and Blunden, though, again, he is different
from each of these. He had his own way of saying things.

Young is a superb miniaturist; he wrote about the natural phenomena of the British
countryside, and also about literary figures, archaeology, the Christian religion, and his
nationwide travels in search of wild flowers, with strict economy and intensity. A visionary –
as illustrated by his long poem Out of the World and Back – a scholar, and a probing
theologian, Young had the rare gift of being able to write about common things with
profundity, so that his readers are made aware of the macrocosm within the microcosm. He
packed much thought and feeling into a small space.

Although he was a writer for over 50 years, his style – with the exception of his long poem – did not greatly change. Having found what he could do best of all, he saw no reason to express himself in newer accents, so that his poems were never in, or out, of fashion. They will continue to hold our attention because of their purity, craftsmanship, imaginative content, and meditative quality. Mostly short, they are traditional in form, owing much to Tennyson, Hardy, and Housman. But they have Young's individual voice and eye, are often ironical, witty, and fanciful, with emotions controlled. Walter de la Mare said of him that he "watches words as a cat watches a mouse." He employed a concentrated technique and was himself a man of few words; his powers of observation, though, were immediate and accurate. He could shock into surprise and wonder by a few simple statements of fact, and by his skilful use of contrast and figurative language.

Young's prose writings, especially those about wild flowers and topography, are full of fascinating, out-of-the-way knowledge, but all spiced with good humour and written with a light touch. A Scot by birth and nurture, no writer was more English. No poet wrote with such enthusiasm and grace about the flora and fauna of the British countryside, the landscape and the changing scenes, and few with so mystical an awareness of the passage of the soul of man from earth to the regions beyond.

—Leonard Clark

ZUKOFSKY, Louis.   American.   Born in New York City, 23 January 1904. Educated at Columbia University, New York, M.A. in English 1924. Married Celia Thaew in 1939; one son. Teacher of English and Comparative Literature, University of Wisconsin, Madison, 1930–31; Visiting Assistant Professor, Colgate University, Hamilton, New York, 1947; Member of the Faculty, 1947–55, and Associate Professor, 1955–66, Polytechnic Institute of Brooklyn, New York. Poet-in-Residence, San Francisco State College, 1958; Guest Professor, Graduate School, University of Connecticut, Storrs, Fall 1971. Recipient: National Endowment for the Arts grant, 1966, 1968. *Died 12 May 1978.*

PUBLICATIONS

Verse

First Half of "A" – 9.   1940.
55 Poems.   1941.
Anew.   1946.
Some Time/Short Poems.   1956.
Barely and Widely.   1958.
"A" 1–12.   1959.
16 Once Published.   1962.
I's, Pronounced "Eyes".   1963.
After I's.   1964.
Found Objects 1962–1926.   1964.
Iyyob.   1965.
All: The Collected Short Poems, 1923–1958.   1965.

"A" Libretto.   1965.
All: The Collected Short Poems, 1956–1964.   1966.
Little: A Fragment for Careenagers.   1967.
"A" – 14.   1967.
"A" 13–21.   1969.
All: The Collected Shorter Poems, 1923–1964.   1971.
"A" – 24.   1972.
"A" 22 and 23.   1975.
"A."   1979.

Play

Arise, Arise.   1973.

Fiction

It Was.   1961.
Ferdinand, Including It Was.   1968.
Little.   1970.

Other

Le Style Apollinaire, translated by René Taupin.   1934.
5 Statements for Poetry.   1958.
Bottom: On Shakespeare.   1963.
Prepositions: The Collected Critical Essays.   1967.
Autobiography.   1970.

Editor, *An "Objectivists" Anthology.*   1932.
Editor, *A Test of Poetry.*   1948.

Translator, *Albert Einstein,* by Anton Reiser.   1930.
Translator, with Celia Zukofsky, *Catullus: Fragmenta,* music by Paul
    Zukofsky.   1969.
Translator, with Celia Zukofsky, *Catullus.*   1969.

Bibliography: *A Bibliography of Zukofsky* by Celia Zukofsky, 1969.

Reading List: *At: Bottom* by Cid Corman, 1966; "Zukofsky Issue" of *Grosseteste Review,*
Winter 1970, and of *Maps 5,* 1974; by Peter Quartermain, in *Open Letter Second Series,* Fall
1973; by Barry Ahearn, in *Journal of English Literary History,* Spring 1978.

*   *   *

If William Carlos Williams, by writing about roses as though no-one had written about
them before, freed the American language from its heavy dependence on English antecedents
and associations, Louis Zukofsky, by stripping words of their meaning or by overloading
them so that no single meaning comes through, showed writers like Robert Creeley and
Robert Duncan (and others) how to let the movement of words generate a play and discovery
of meaning by paying attention to their music so that the language might *sing.* It is a trick he

learned from Apollinaire (about whom he wrote a book in 1932) and from Spinoza, who insisted that a thing is said to be free if it "exists by the mere necessity of its own nature and is determined in its actions by itself alone." For Zukofsky, the poem is an object.

Here is one of his poems:

FOR
Four tubas
or
two-by-four's.

Zukofsky's Brooklyn accent emphasises the palindromic echoes of "four tubas" and "tuba-fours"; the aural rhyme of "or" with "four" and the visual rhyme of "or" with the title, and the ambiguity of the apostrophe, all reflect a mind which not only delights in puns but also takes absolutely literally Pound's dictum that poetry is made up of sight, sound, intellection, and rhythm. The complexities of meaning are established through tentative possibilities of relationship which are never fully realised in the poem: the romantic, lyric implications of the title, the mundane quality of the last line, the echoing of the final "by" back to the meaning of the "ba" of the first line, the ambiguity of the prepositions, all of whose meanings have relevance to the structure of a poem which, highly comic yet at the same time moving, draws attention to the neglected minutiae of the language: prepositions, conjunctions, articles. The poetry is in the words, rather than in the ideas.

Thus, in "A," his long poem in 24 movements which explore most traditional verse forms ("A"-7 is a sonnet-cycle, "A"-9 is a double canzone, "A"-21 is a Roman comedy), Zukofsky plays on the possibilities of the indefinite article (as, earlier – in 1926 – he had written "Poem Beginning 'The' ") while interweaving personal, political and aesthetic themes round two central figures: Bach and Shakespeare (music and poetry). If themes are stated, they are stated so that they may play against one another ("Words rangeless, melody forced by writing," in "A"-6), and much of the poem's complex play occurs as the result of pitting one specialised vocabulary or context against another – as, in "A"-9, modern physics is pitted against Marx, Cavalcanti, and Spinoza. Similarly, Zukofsky may pit one language against another, as in the opening of "A"-15 (English echoing the Hebrew sound of passages from the Book of Job), or in his "translation" of Catullus, where the English, repeating the sound of the Latin, comes to be seen, in its knotted turbulence, from "outside itself." Such work, innovative, difficult, often bewildering, and controversial, has nevertheless been influential: some readers, many of them poets, consider Zukofsky to rank with Pound and Joyce among twentieth-century writers.

—Peter Quartermain

NOTES ON CONTRIBUTORS

ALCOCK, Peter. Senior Lecturer in English, Massey University, Palmerston North, New Zealand; Associate Editor of *World Literature Written in English* and bibliographer for *Journal of Commonwealth Literature*. Member of the Executive Committee, Association for Commonwealth Literature and Language, 1968–77. **Essays:** Blanche Baughan; Denis Glover.

ALEXANDER, M. J. Lecturer in English, University of Stirling, Scotland. Author of *The Earliest English Poems*, 1966, and *Beowulf*, 1973. **Essays:** Hilaire Belloc; Rupert Brooke; Marianne Moore.

ASTLE, David. Principal Lecturer in Communication Studies, Sheffield City Polytechnic. **Essays:** Lascelles Abercrombie; Roy Fuller.

AUBERT, Alvin. Associate Professor of English, State University of New York, Fredonia; Publisher and Editor of *Obsidian: Black Literature in Review*. Author of *Against the Blues* (verse), 1972. **Essay:** James Weldon Johnson.

BENSEN, Alice R. Professor Emerita of English, Eastern Michigan University, Ypsilanti. Author of *Rose Macaulay*, 1969. **Essays:** Charlotte Mew; Elinor Wylie.

BERGONZI, Bernard. Senior Lecturer in English, University of Warwick, Coventry. Author of *Descartes and the Animals*, 1954; *The Early H. G. Wells*, 1961; *Heroes' Twilight*, 1965; *The Situation of the Novel*, 1970; *T. S. Eliot*, 1971; *Gerard Manley Hopkins*, 1977; *Reading the Thirties*, 1978. Contributor to *The Observer*, *Times Literary Supplement*, and other periodicals. **Essays:** Roy Campbell; Philip Larkin.

BERRY, Francis. Professor of English, Royal Holloway College, University of London. Author of several books of verse, the most recent being *Ghosts of Greenland*, 1966, and of critical works including *Poets' Grammar*, 1958, *Poetry and the Physical Voice*, 1962, and studies of Herbert Read, Shakespeare, and John Masefield. **Essay:** John Masefield.

BLAMIRES, David. Member of the Department of German, University of Manchester. Author of *Characterization and Individuality in Wolfram's "Parzifal,"* 1966, and *David Jones, Artist and Writer*, 1971. Co-Editor of *Studies in Medieval Literature and Languages*, 1973. **Essays:** David Jones; Vernon Watkins.

BODE, Walter. Editor in the Chemistry Department, University of California, Berkeley; Assistant Editor of *San Francisco Theatre Magazine*, and free-lance theatre and film critic. **Essay:** Ogden Nash.

BOTTRALL, Margaret. Biographer and Critic. University Lecturer, Department of Education, and Senior Tutor, Hughes Hall, Cambridge University, until 1972. Author of *George Herbert*, 1954, and *Every Man a Phoenix: Studies in Seventeenth-Century Autobiography*, 1958. Editor of *Personal Records*, 1961, and *Songs of Innocence and Experience*, by Blake, 1970. **Essay:** Edith Sitwell.

BROER, Lawrence R.   Associate Professor of English, University of South Florida, Tampa. Author of *Hemingway's Spanish Tragedy*, 1973, and of many essays and reviews in journals. Editor of *Counter Currents*, 1973, and *The Great Escape of the '20's*, 1977, and Co-Editor of *The First Time: Initial Sexual Experiences in Fiction*, 1974. **Essays:** Stephen Vincent Benét; William Rose Benét.

BROWN, Ashley.   Professor of English, University of South Carolina, Columbia; Contributor to *Sewanee Review*, *Shenandoah*, *Southern Review*, *Spectator*, and other periodicals. Editor of *The Achievement of Wallace Stevens* (with R. S. Haller), 1962, *Modes of Literature* (with John L. Kimmey), 1968, and *Satire: An Anthology* (with Kimmey), 1977. **Essays:** John Peale Bishop; Allen Tate.

BROWN, Lloyd W.   Member of the Department of Comparative Literature, University of Southern California, Los Angeles. **Essays:** Louise Bennett; Edward Brathwaite.

BROWN, Terence.   Member of the Faculty, Trinity College, Dublin. Author of *Louis MacNeice: Sceptical Vision*, 1975. Editor of *Time Was Away: The World of Louis MacNeice* (with Alec Reid), 1974. **Essays:** Padraic Colum; W. R. Rodgers.

BUTTER, P. H.   Regius Professor of English, University of Glasgow. Author of *Shelley's Idols of the Cave*, 1954; *Francis Thompson*, 1961; *Edwin Muir*, 1962; *Edwin Muir: Man and Poet*, 1966. Editor of *Alastor, Prometheus Unbound, and Other Poems*, by Shelley, 1971, and *Selected Letters of Edwin Muir*, 1974. **Essay:** Edwin Muir.

CALHOUN, Richard J.   Alumni Professor of English, Clemson University, South Carolina; Co-Editor, *South Carolina Review*. Editor of *A Tricentennial Anthology of South Carolina Literature* (with John C. Guilds), 1971, *James Dickey: The Expansive Imagination*, 1973, and *Two Decades of Change* (with E. M. Lander, Jr.), 1975. **Essay:** James Dickey.

CARPENTER, Frederic I.   Author of *Emerson and Asia*, 1930; *Emerson Handbook*, 1953; *American Literature and the Dream*, 1955; *Robinson Jeffers*, 1962; *Eugene O'Neill*, 1964; *Laurens van der Post*, 1969. Has taught at the University of Chicago, Harvard University, and the University of California, Berkeley. **Essay:** Robinson Jeffers.

CHRISTENSEN, Paul.   Assistant Professor of Modern Literature, Texas A. & M. University, College Station. Author of *Old and Lost Rivers* (verse), and *Charles Olson: Call Him Ishmael*, 1978. **Essays:** A. R. Ammons; John Ashbery; John Berryman; Robert Bly; Louise Bogan; Robert Creeley; E. E. Cummings; Stanley Kunitz; Denise Levertov; James Merrill; W. S. Merwin; Frank O'Hara; Charles Olson; Kenneth Rexroth; W. D. Snodgrass; Gary Snyder; John Wheelwright.

CLAIRE, William.   Director of the Washington Office, State University of New York. Founding Editor and Publisher, *Voyages: A National Literary Magazine*, 1967–73. Author of *Publishing in the West: Alan Swallow*, and of two books of verse, *Strange Coherence of Our Dreams* and *From a Southern France Notebook*. Contributor to many periodicals, including *Antioch Review*, *American Scholar*, *The Nation*, *New Republic*, and the *New York Times*. **Essay:** Mark Van Doren.   •

CLARK, Leonard.   Author and Editor of many books of verse, fiction, and non-fiction for children and adults, including *Collected Poems and Verses for Children*, 1975, *Winter to Winter and Other Poems*, 1977, and studies of Alfred Williams, Walter de la Mare, and Andrew Young. Inspector of Schools in Devon, Yorkshire, and London, 1936–70. Frequent contributor of verse, essays, and reviews to periodicals. **Essays:** Kathleen Raine; Andrew Young.

CLUCAS, Garth. Free-lance writer, currently engaged in research at Linacre College, Oxford. **Essays:** Geoffrey Dutton; Geoffrey Hill.

CORCORAN, Neil. Member of the Department of English, University of Sheffield. **Essays:** Conrad Aiken; Robert Lowell; Delmore Schwartz.

CROWDER, Richard H. Professor Emeritus of English, Purdue University, Lafayette, Indiana. Fulbright Lecturer, University of Bordeaux, 1963–65. Author of *Those Innocent Years* (on James Whitcomb Riley), 1957, *No Featherbed to Heaven: Michael Wigglesworth*, 1962, and *Carl Sandburg*, 1964. Joint Editor, *Frontiers of American Culture*, 1968. **Essay:** Carl Sandburg.

DAVISON, Dennis. Senior Lecturer in English, Monash University, Melbourne. Author of *The Poetry of Andrew Marvell*, 1964, *Dryden*, 1968, and *W. H. Auden*, 1970. Editor of *Selected Poetry and Prose*, by Marvell, 1952, *Restoration Comedies*, 1970, and *The Penguin Book of Eighteenth-Century Verse*, 1973. **Essay:** Guy Butler.

DOYLE, Charles. Professor of English, and Director of the Division of American and Commonwealth Literature, University of Victoria, British Columbia. Author (as Mike Doyle) of several books of poetry, the most recent being *Going On*, 1974, and of critical studies of New Zealand poetry, R. A. K. Mason, and James K. Baxter. Editor of *Recent Poetry in New Zealand*, 1965. **Essays:** James K. Baxter; R. A. K. Mason; Al Purdy.

DRAPER, R. P. Professor of English, University of Aberdeen, Scotland. Author of two books on Lawrence, and editor of *Lawrence: The Critical Heritage*, 1970, and *Hardy: The Tragic Novels: A Casebook*, 1975. **Essay:** D. H. Lawrence.

FLETCHER, Ian. Reader in English Literature, University of Reading, Berkshire. Author of plays and verse, and of *Walter Pater*, 1959 (revised, 1970); *A Catalogue of Imagist Poets*, 1966; *Beaumont and Fletcher*, 1967; *Meredith Now*, 1971; *Swinburne*, 1972. Editor of anthologies of verse and drama, and of works by Lionel Johnson, Victor Plarr, and John Gray. **Essays:** Oliver St. John Gogarty; T. Sturge Moore; Shaw Neilson.

FOSTER, John Wilson. Associate Professor of English, University of British Columbia, Vancouver; Book Review Editor of *The Canadian Journal of Irish Studies*. Author of *Forces and Themes in Ulster Fiction*, 1974. **Essays:** Margaret Atwood; Patrick Kavanagh.

FRASER, G. S. Reader in Modern English Literature, University of Leicester. Author of several books of verse, the most recent being *Conditions*, 1969; travel books; critical studies of Yeats, Dylan Thomas, Pound, Durrell and Pope; and of *The Modern Writer and His World*, 1953, *Vision and Rhetoric*, 1959, and *Metre, Rhythm, and Free Verse*, 1970. Editor of works by Keith Douglas and Robert Burns, and of verse anthologies. **Essays:** George Barker; William Empson; Ezra Pound; Sir Osbert Sitwell; Sir Sacheverell Sitwell.

GABIN, Jane S. Teaching Assistant in English, University of North Carolina, Chapel Hill. Author of an article on Dudley Buck; has directed a recital of the music and poetry of Sidney Lanier. **Essay:** John Gould Fletcher.

GALL, Sally M. Adjunct Assistant Professor of English, New York University. Distinguished Visiting Professor, Drew University, Madison, New Jersey. Author of articles on M. L. Rosenthal, Ramon Guthrie, and Sylvia Plath in *Modern Poetry Studies* and *American Poetry Review*. **Essay:** Ramon Guthrie.

GIBSON, D. B.   Professor of English, Rutgers University, New Brunswick, New Jersey. Author of *The Fiction of Stephen Crane*, 1968. Editor of *Five Black Writers*, 1970, *Black and White: Stories of American Life*, 1971, and *Modern Black Poets*, 1973. **Essay:** Melvin Tolson.

GLEN, Duncan.   Head of Graphics, Preston Polytechnic, Lancashire; Editor of *Akros*, a literary magazine. Author of several books of verse, the most recent being *Gaitherings: Poems in Scots*, 1977, and of *Hugh MacDiarmid and the Scottish Renaissance*, 1964, *The Individual and the Twentieth-Century Scottish Literary Tradition*, and other critical works. Editor of *Selected Essays of MacDiarmid*, 1969, and *MacDiarmid: A Critical Survey*, 1972. **Essay:** Hugh MacDiarmid.

GORDON, Lois.   Professor of English and Comparative Literature, Fairleigh Dickinson University, Teaneck, New Jersey. Author of *Strategems to Uncover Nakedness: The Dramas of Harold Pinter*, 1969, and of articles on Richard Eberhart, Randall Jarrell, Faulkner, T. S. Eliot, and Philip Roth. **Essays:** Richard Eberhart; Randall Jarrell.

GRAHAM, Desmond.   Lecturer in English Literature, University of Newcastle upon Tyne; Poetry Reviewer, *Stand* magazine. Author of *Introduction to Poetry*, 1968, and *Keith Douglas: A Biography*, 1974. Editor of *The Complete Poems of Keith Douglas*, 1978. **Essays:** Keith Douglas: Sidney Keyes.

GREEN, Dorothy.   Member of the Faculty, Humanities Research Centre, Australian National University, Canberra. Author of books of verse including *The Dolphin*, 1967, and of articles on Australian literature. **Essays:** Christopher Brennan; Rosemary Dobson; Robert D. FitzGerald; Mary Gilmore; Kenneth Mackenzie; Kenneth Slessor; Douglas Stewart; Francis Webb.

GRUNDY, Joan.   Reader in English Literature, Royal Holloway College, University of London. Author of *The Spenserian Poets*, 1969. Editor of *The Poems of Henry Constable*, 1960. **Essay:** Norman Nicholson.

GURR, Andrew.   Professor of English Language and Literature, University of Reading, Berkshire. Author of *The Shakespearean Stage*, 1970. Editor of several plays by Beaumont and Fletcher. **Essay:** Allen Curnow.

HARMON, Maurice.   Lecturer in Anglo-Irish Literature, University College, Dublin; Editor of *Irish University Review*. Author of *Sean O'Faolain*, 1967, *The Poetry of Thomas Kinsella*, 1974, and *Select Bibliography of Anglo-Irish Literature and Its Backgrounds*, 1977. Editor of *Irish Poetry after Yeats: Seven Poets*, 1978. **Essays:** Austin Clarke; Seamus Heaney.

HEATH-STUBBS, John.   Writer and Lecturer. Author of several books of verse, the most recent being *The Watchman's Flute*, 1978, a book of plays, and of *The Darkling Plain: A Study of the Later Fortunes of Romanticism*, 1950, *Charles Williams*, 1955, and studies of the verse satire, the ode, and the pastoral. Editor of anthologies and works by Shelley, Tennyson, Swift, and Pope; translator of works by Giacomo Leopardi, Alfred de Vigny, and others. **Essay:** Hart Crane.

HEWITT, Geof.   Poet and Editor; Contributing Editor, *New Letters*, Kansas City, Missouri. His most recent book of verse is *Stone Soup*, 1974. Editor of the poems of Alfred Starr Hamilton and of verse anthologies. **Essay:** Muriel Rukeyser.

HOFFMAN, Daniel.   Professor of English, University of Pennsylvania, Philadelphia. Author of several books of verse, the most recent being *Able Was I Ere I Saw Elba*, 1977, and of critical works including *The Poetry of Stephen Crane*, 1957; *Form and Fable in American*

Fiction, 1961; *Poe Poe Poe Poe Poe Poe Poe*, 1972; *Barbarous Knowledge: Myth in the Poetry of Yeats, Graves, and Muir*, 1973. Editor of anthologies and of works by Crane and Robert Frost. **Essay**: Robert Graves.

HOLDEN, Jonathan. Member of the English Department, Stephens College, Columbia, Missouri. Author of *Design for a House* (verse), 1972, and of poetry for *Antioch Review, North American Review*, and other periodicals. **Essay**: William Stafford.

HOLMAN, C. Hugh. Kenan Professor of English, Chairman of the Division of Humanities, and Special Assistant to the Chancellor, University of North Carolina, Chapel Hill; Editor of *Southern Literary Journal*. Author or co-author of several books, including five detective novels, *The Development of American Criticism*, 1955; *The Southerner as American*, 1960; *Thomas Wolfe*, 1960; *Seven Modern American Novelists*, 1964; *The American Novel Through Henry James: A Bibliography*, 1966; *Three Modes of Modern Southern Fiction*, 1966; *Roots of Southern Writing*, 1972; *The Loneliness at the Core*, 1975. Editor of works by Thomas Wolfe, William Gilmore Simms, and others. **Essay**: Robert Penn Warren.

JEFFARES, A. Norman. Professor of English Studies, University of Stirling, Scotland; Editor of *Ariel: A Review of International English Literature*, and General Editor of the Writers and Critics series and the New Oxford English series; Past Editor of *A Review of English Studies*. Author of *Yeats: Man and Poet*, 1949; *Seven Centuries of Poetry*, 1956; *A Commentary on the Collected Poems* (1958) and *Collected Plays* (1975) *of Yeats*. Editor of *Restoration Comedy*, 1974, and *Yeats: The Critical Heritage*, 1977. **Essay**: William Butler Yeats.

JOHNSON, Robert K. Professor of English, Suffolk University, Boston. Author of articles on Richard Wilbur, Wallace Stevens, T. S. Eliot, and William Carlos Williams. **Essays**: Robert Frost; Archibald MacLeish; Howard Nemerov.

JOYNER, Nancy C. Member of the Department of English, Western Carolina University, Cullowhee, North Carolina. **Essays**: Laura Riding; Edwin Arlington Robinson.

KELLNER, Bruce. Associate Professor of English, Millersville State College, Pennsylvania. Author of *Carl Van Vechten and the Irreverent Decades*, 1968; *The Wormwood Poems of Thomas Kinsella*, 1972; *The Poet as Translator*, 1973; *Alfred Kazin's Exquisites: An Excavation*, 1975. Editor of *Selected Writings of Van Vechten about Negro Arts and Letters*, 1978. **Essay**: Robert Service.

KEMP, Peter. Lecturer in English and American Literature, Middlesex Polytechnic, London. Author of *Muriel Spark*, 1974. **Essay**: Siegfried Sassoon.

KINNAMON, Keneth. Professor and Associate Head of the English Department, University of Illinois, Urbana-Champaign. Author of *The Emergence of Richard Wright*, 1972. Editor of *Black Writers of America: A Comprehensive Anthology* (with Richard K. Barksdale), 1972, and of *James Baldwin: A Collection of Critical Essays*, 1974. **Essay**: Langston Hughes.

LEVERNIER, James A. Assistant Professor of English, University of Arkansas, Little Rock. Contributor to *ESQ: A Journal of the American Renaissance, Research Studies, The Markham Review, Explicator*, and other periodicals. Editor of *An Essay for the Recording of Illustrious Providences* by Increase Mather, 1977, and *The Indians and Their Captives* (with Hennig Cohen), 1977. **Essay**: Kenneth Fearing.

LEWIS, Peter.   Lecturer in English, University of Durham. Author of *The Beggar's Opera* (critical study), 1976, and articles on Restoration and Augustan drama and modern poetry. Editor of *The Beggar's Opera* by John Gay, 1973, and *Poems '74* (anthology of Anglo-Welsh poetry), 1974. **Essay:** Basil Bunting.

LINDSAY, Maurice.   Director of the Scottish Civic Trust, Glasgow, and Managing Editor of *The Scottish Review*. Author of several books of verse, the most recent being *Walking Without an Overcoat*, 1977; plays; travel and historical works; and critical studies, including *Robert Burns: The Man, His Work, The Legend*, 1954 (revised, 1968), *The Burns Encyclopedia*, 1959 (revised, 1970), and *A History of Scottish Literature*, 1977. Editor of the Saltire Modern Poets series, several anthologies of Scottish writing, and works by Sir Alexander Gray, Sir David Lyndsay, Marion Angus, and John Davidson. **Essays:** Harold Monro; Sydney Goodsir Smith.

LUCAS, John.   Professor of English and Drama, Loughborough University, Leicestershire; Advisory Editor of *Victorian Studies*, *Literature and History*, and *Journal of European Studies*. Author of *Tradition and Tolerance in 19th-Century Fiction*, 1966; *The Melancholy Man: A Study of Dickens*, 1970; *Arnold Bennett*, 1975; *Egilssaga: The Poems*, 1975; *The Literature of Change*, 1977; *The 1930's: Challenge to Orthodoxy*, 1978. Editor of *Literature and Politics in the 19th Century*, 1971, and of works by George Crabbe and Jane Austen. **Essays:** Kenneth Patchen; Louis Simpson.

McKAY, F. M.   Member of the Department of English, Victoria University of Wellington, New Zealand. Author of *New Zealand Poetry: An Introduction*, 1970. Editor of *Poetry New Zealand*, 1971. **Essays:** Alistair Campbell; Eileen Duggan; C. K. Stead.

MORPURGO, J. E.   Professor of American Literature, University of Leeds. Author and editor of many books, including the *Pelican History of the United States*, 1955 (third edition, 1970), and volumes on Cooper, Lamb, Trelawny, Barnes Wallis, and on Venice, Athens, and rugby football. **Essay:** Edmund Blunden.

MUNRO, John M.   Professor of English, American University of Beirut, Lebanon. Author of *English Poetry in Transition*, 1968; *Arthur Symons*, 1969; *Decadent Poetry in the 1890's*, 1970; *The Royal Aquarium: Failure of a Victorian Compromise*, 1971; *James Elroy Flecker*, 1976; *A Mutual Concern*, 1977; and other books. Editor of *Selected Poems of Theo. Marzials*, 1973. **Essay:** James Elroy Flecker.

NESBITT, Bruce.   Member of the Department of English, Simon Fraser University, Burnaby, British Columbia. Author of *Earle Birney*, 1975. **Essays:** Dorothy Livesay; E. J. Pratt; F. R. Scott.

NIVEN, Alastair.   Member of the Department of English Studies, University of Stirling, Scotland. Author of *D. H. Lawrence: The Novels*, 1978. **Essay:** Gabriel Okara.

OLIVER-MORDEN, B. C.   Teacher at the Open University and the University of Keele. Editor of the 18th-Century section of *The Year's Work in English 1973*. **Essay:** Laurie Lee.

PERRY, Margaret.   Assistant Director for Reader Services, University of Rochester Libraries, New York; Contributing Editor, *Afro-American in New York Life and History*. Author of *A Bio-Bibliography of Countée P. Cullen*, 1971, *Silence to the Drums: A Survey of the Literature of the Harlem Renaissance*, 1976, and of several short stories published in periodicals. **Essay:** Countée Cullen.

PETERSEN, Kirsten Holst.   Member of the Commonwealth Literature Division of the

English Department, University of Aarhus, Denmark; reviewer for *Danida*. Editor of *Enigma of Values* (with Anna Rutherford), 1975. **Essay**: John Pepper Clark.

PINION, F. B.   Former Sub-Dean and Reader in English Studies, University of Sheffield; Editor of the *Thomas Hardy Society Review*. Author of *A Hardy Companion*, 1968; *A Jane Austen Companion*, 1973; *A Brontë Companion*, 1975; *A Commentary on the Poems of Hardy*, 1976; *Hardy: Art and Thought*, 1977. Editor of *Two on a Tower* by Hardy, and of Hardy's complete short stories. **Essay**: Thomas Hardy.

POLLARD, Arthur.   Professor of English, University of Hull, Yorkshire. Author of *Mrs. Gaskell, Novelist and Biographer*, 1965, and *Anthony Trollope*, 1978. Editor of *The Letters of Mrs. Gaskell* (with J. A. V. Chapple), 1966; *The Victorians* (Sphere History of Literature in English), 1970; *Crabbe: The Critical Heritage*, 1972; *Thackeray: Vanity Fair* (casebook), 1978. **Essays**: James McAuley; Judith Wright.

PRESS, John.   Area Officer, British Council, Oxford. Author of three books of verse – *Uncertainties*, 1956, *Guy Fawkes Night*, 1959, and *Troika* (with others), 1977 – and several critical books, including *Rule and Energy*, 1963, *A Map of English Verse*, 1969, *The Lengthening Shadows*, 1971, and *John Betjeman*, 1974. **Essays**: Sir John Betjeman; Donald Davie; W. H. Davies; David Gascoyne; Louis MacNeice; Charles Hamilton Sorley; Bernard Spencer.

PYLE, Hilary.   Free-lance writer. Author of *Jack B. Yeats: A Biography*, 1970. **Essay**: James Stephens.

QUARTERMAIN, Peter.   Associate Professor of English, University of British Columbia, Vancouver. Author of "Louis Zukofsky: Re Location" in *Open Letter*, 1973, and "Romantic Offensive: *Tish*" in *Canadian Literature*, 1977. **Essays**: Robert Duncan; Allen Ginsberg; Louis Zukofsky.

RAY, David.   Professor of English, University of Missouri, Kansas City; Editor of *New Letters*, Kansas City. His most recent book of verse is *Gathering Firewood: New Poems and Selected*, 1974. Editor of *The Chicago Review Anthology*, 1959, *Richard Wright: Impressions and Perspectives* (with Robert M. Farnsworth), and of verse anthologies. **Essay**: Horace Gregory.

REDEKOP, E. H.   Associate Professor of English, University of Western Ontario, London. Author of *Margaret Avison*, 1970. **Essay**: Margaret Avison.

REDSHAW, Thomas Dillon.   Associate Editor of *Eire-Ireland*, and teacher at the College of St. Thomas, St. Paul, Minnesota. Author of *Heimaey*, 1974, and of verse in periodicals. Editor of *The Collected Poems of Thomas MacGreevy*, 1971. **Essay**: John Montague.

ROVIT, Earl.   Professor of English, City College of New York. Author of *Herald to Chaos: The Novels of Elizabeth Madox Roberts*, 1960; *Ernest Hemingway*, 1963; *The Player King*, 1965; *Saul Bellow*, 1967; *A Far Cry*, 1967; *Crossings*, 1973. **Essay**: Trumbull Stickney.

RUIHLEY, Glenn Richard.   Member of the Department of English, Eastern Michigan University, Ypsilanti. Author of *The Thorn of a Rose: Amy Lowell Reconsidered*, 1975. Editor of *A Shard of Silence: Selected Poems* by Lowell, 1957. **Essays**: Amy Lowell; Edgar Lee Masters; Edna St. Vincent Millay.

SAFFIOTI, Carol Lee.   Assistant Professor of English, University of Wisconsin – Parkside, Kenosha. **Essay**: Sterling Brown.

SAUL, George Brandon.   Professor Emeritus of English, University of Connecticut, Storrs; Contributing Editor, *Journal of Irish Literature*. Author of fiction (*The Wild Queen*, 1967), verse (*Hound and Unicorn*, 1969, and *Adam Unregenerate*, 1977), and of critical works, including *Prolegomena to the Study of Yeats's Poems* (1957) and *Plays* (1958), *Traditional Irish Literature and Its Backgrounds*, 1970, and *In Praise of the Half-Forgotten: Essays*, 1976. Also a composer. **Essay:** Sara Teasdale.

SCHWARZ, Daniel R.   Associate Professor of English, Cornell University, Ithaca, New York. Author of articles on T. S. Eliot, Conrad, Hardy, and Dylan Thomas, in *Studies in the Novel*, *Modern Fiction Studies*, *Twentieth-Century Literature*, and other periodicals. **Essay:** Dylan Thomas.

SEELYE, Catherine.   Free-lance writer. **Essay:** Vachel Lindsay.

SHUCARD, Alan R.   Associate Professor of English, University of Wisconsin – Parkside, Kenosha. Author of two books of verse – *The Gorgon Bog*, 1970, and *The Louse on the Head of the Lord*, 1972. **Essays:** Gwendolyn Brooks; Robert Hayden.

SILKIN, Jon.   Founder and Joint Editor, *Stand* magazine, and Co-Founding Editor, Northern House publishers, both in Newcastle upon Tyne. Author of several books of verse, the most recent being *The Little Time-Keeper*, 1976, and of *Out of Battle: Poetry of the Great War*, 1972. Editor of several anthologies of poetry, and translator of *Against Parting* by Nathan Zach, 1968. **Essays:** Sir Herbert Read; Isaac Rosenberg.

SIMPSON, Peter.   Member of the Department of English, University of Canterbury, Christchurch, New Zealand. **Essays:** Mary Ursula Bethell; A. R. D. Fairburn.

SINGH, Amritjit.   Academic Associate, American Studies Research Centre, Hyderabad, India; Joint Editor of *The Indian Journal of American Studies*. Author of *The Novels of the Harlem Renaissance: Twelve Black Writers*, 1976, and of articles for Indian and American periodicals. Co-Editor of the bibliographies *Indian Literature in English*, 1977, and *Afro-American Poetry and Drama*, 1977. **Essay:** Claude McKay.

SIVARAMAKRISHNA, M.   Reader in the Department of English, Osmania University. Hyderabad; Editor of *Tenor* magazine. Author of many articles on English and American literature. **Essay:** Dom Moraes.

SKLOOT, Floyd.   Director of Program Services, Illinois Capital Development Board, Springfield. Author of *Vigil* (verse), 1978, and of poetry, fiction, and essays in *Shenandoah, Southern Poetry Review*, *Transatlantic Review*, *Eire-Ireland*, and *Journal of Education Finance*. **Essay:** Thomas Kinsella.

SMITH, A. J. M.   See his own entry. **Essay:** Ralph Gustafson.

SMITH, Elton E.   Professor of English and Bible, University of South Florida, Tampa. Author of *"The Two Voices": A Tennyson Study*, 1964; *William Godwin* (with Esther Marian Greenwell Smith), 1965; *Louis MacNeice*, 1970; *"The Angry Young Men" of the Thirties*, 1975; *Charles Reade*, 1977. **Essays:** C. Day Lewis; Stephen Spender.

SMITH, Stan.   Lecturer in English, University of Dundee, Scotland. Author of the forthcoming book *A Superfluous Man* (on Edward Thomas), and of articles on modern literature for *Critical Quarterly*, *Literature and History*, *Irish University Review*, *Scottish International Review*, and other periodicals. **Essays:** W. H. Auden; Ted Hughes; Alfred Noyes; Sylvia Plath; Theodore Roethke; Edward Thomas.

STALLWORTHY, Jon. James Wendell Anderson Professor of English, Cornell University, Ithaca, New York. Deputy Academic Publisher, Oxford University Press, 1974–77. Author of several books of verse, the most recent being *The Apple Barrel*, 1974, two studies of Yeats's poetry, and *Wilfred Owen*, 1974. Editor of two anthologies of verse and of a casebook on Yeats's last poems; translator of an anthology of Polish poetry and of *The Twelve and Other Poems* by Alexander Blok, 1970. **Essay:** Wilfred Owen.

STANFORD, Donald E. Professor of English, Louisiana State University, Baton Rouge; Editor of *The Southern Review*. Author of *New England Earth*, 1941, and *The Traveler*, 1955. Editor of *The Poems of Edward Taylor*, 1960; *Nine Essays in Modern Literature*, 1965; *Selected Poems of Robert Bridges*, 1974; *Selected Poems of S. Foster Damon*, 1974. **Essay:** Yvor Winters.

SUMMERS, Joseph H. Professor of English, University of Rochester, New York. Author of *George Herbert: Religion and Art*, 1954, *The Muse's Method: An Introduction to Paradise Lost*, 1962, and *The Heirs of Donne and Jonson*, 1970. Editor of *Selected Poems* by Andrew Marvell, 1961, *The Lyric and Dramatic Milton*, 1965, and *Selected Poetry* by George Herbert, 1967. **Essays:** Elizabeth Bishop; Richard Wilbur.

SWEETSER, Wesley D. Professor of English, State University of New York, Oswego. Author of *Arthur Machen*, 1964, *A Bibliography of Machen* (with A. Goldstone), 1965, and *Ralph Hodgson: A Bibliography*, 1974. **Essay:** Ralph Hodgson.

THOMAS, Ned. Lecturer in English, University College of Wales, Aberystwyth; Founding Editor of *Planet* magazine. Author of *George Orwell*, 1965, and *The Welsh Extremist: Essays on Modern Welsh Literature and Society*, 1971. **Essay:** Derek Walcott.

THWAITE, Anthony. Free-lance Writer, and Co-Editor of *Encounter* magazine, London. Author of several books of verse, the most recent being *A Portion for Foxes*, 1977; travel books; a book for children; and critical works, including *Contemporary English Poetry*, 1959 and *Poetry Today*, 1973. Co-Editor of two anthologies of English verse and translator of *The Penguin Book of Japanese Verse* (with Geoffrey Bownas), 1964. **Essay:** Stevie Smith.

TIBBLE, Anne. Free-lance Writer. Author of *African Literature*, 1964, *The Story of English Literature*, 1970, *The God Spigo* (novel), 1976, two volumes of autobiography, and books on Helen Keller, Gertrude Bell, Gordon, and John Clare. Editor of works by Clare. **Essays:** Christopher Okigbo; Okot p'Bitek.

TRAVERSI, Derek A. Professor of English Literature, Swarthmore College, Pennsylvania. Author of *An Approach to Shakespeare*, 1938 (revised, 1968); *Shakespeare: The Last Phase*, 1954; *Shakespeare: From Richard II to Henry V*, 1957; *Shakespeare: The Roman Plays*, 1963; *T. S. Eliot: The Longer Poems*, 1976. **Essay:** T. S. Eliot.

TURNER, Richard C. Assistant Professor of English, Indiana University-Purdue University, Indianapolis. **Essay:** Adrienne Rich.

WAGNER, Linda W. Professor of English, Michigan State University, East Lansing. Author of *The Poems* (1964) and *Prose* (1970) *of William Carlos Williams; Denise Levertov*, 1967; *Hemingway and Faulkner: Inventors, Masters*, 1975; *Introducing Poems*, 1976; *John Dos Passos*, 1978. **Essays:** Anne Sexton; William Carlos Williams.

WALL, Alan. Free-lance Writer. **Essays:** Thom Gunn; Edgell Rickword.

WALSH, William. Professor of Commonwealth Literature and Chairman of the School of

English, University of Leeds. Author of *Use of Imagination*, 1958; *A Human Idiom*, 1964; *Coleridge*, 1967; *A Manifold Voice*, 1970; *R. K. Narayan*, 1972; *V. S. Naipaul*, 1973; *Patrick White's Fiction*, 1978. **Essays:** Earle Birney; A. D. Hope; A. M. Klein; Anne Wilkinson.

WATTS, Harold H. Professor of English, Purdue University, Lafayette, Indiana. Author of *The Modern Reader's Guide to the Bible*, 1949; *Ezra Pound and the Cantos*, 1951; *Hound and Quarry*, 1953; *The Modern Reader's Guide to Religions*, 1964; *Aldous Huxley*, 1969. **Essays:** Hilda Doolittle; Wallace Stevens.

WILLIAMS, John Stuart. Head of the Communications Department, South Glamorgan Institute of Higher Education, Cardiff. Author of four books of verse, the most recent being *Banna Strand*, 1975. Editor of three verse anthologies. **Essays:** Alun Lewis; R. S. Thomas.

WILLY, Margaret. Free-lance Writer and Lecturer. Author of two books of verse – *The Invisible Sun*, 1946, and *Every Star a Tongue*, 1951 – and several critical works, including *Life Was Their Cry*, 1950; *Three Metaphysical Poets: Crashaw, Vaughan, Traherne*, 1961; *Three Women Diarists: Celia Fiennes, Dorothy Wordsworth, Katherine Mansfield*, 1964; *A Critical Commentary on "Wuthering Heights,"* 1966; *A Critical Commentary on Browning's "Men and Women,"* 1968. Editor of two anthologies and of works by Goldsmith. **Essay:** Walter de la Mare.

WOODCOCK, George. Free-lance Writer, Lecturer, and Editor. Author of verse (*Selected Poems*, 1967), plays, travel books, biographies, and works on history and politics; critical works include *William Godwin*, 1946; *The Incomparable Aphra*, 1948; *The Paradox of Oscar Wilde*, 1949; *The Crystal Spirit* (on Orwell), 1966; *Hugh MacLennan*, 1969; *Odysseus Ever Returning: Canadian Writers and Writing*, 1970; *Mordecai Richler*, 1970; *Dawn and the Darkest Hour* (on Aldous Huxley), 1972; *Herbert Read*, 1972; *Thomas Merton*, 1978. Editor of anthologies, and of works by Charles Lamb, Malcolm Lowry, Wyndham Lewis, and others. **Essays:** Irving Layton; P. K. Page; Duncan Campbell Scott; A. J. M. Smith; Raymond Souster.

WOODRESS, James. Professor of English, University of California, Davis; Editor of *American Literary Scholarship*. Author of *Howells and Italy*, 1952; *Booth Tarkington*, 1955; *A Yankee's Odyssey: The Life of Joel Barlow*, 1958; *Willa Cather: Her Life and Art*, 1970; *American Fiction 1900–1950*, 1974. Editor of *Voices from America's Past* (with Richard Morris), 1961, and *Eight American Authors*, 1971. **Essay:** Karl Shapiro.

YOUNG, T. D. Gertrude Conaway Vanderbilt Professor of English, Vanderbilt University, Nashville. Author of *Jack London and the Era of Social Protest*, 1950; *The Literature of the South*, 1952 (revised, 1968); *Donald Davidson: An Essay and a Bibliography* (with M. Thomas Inge), 1965; *American Literature: A Critical Survey*, 1968; *John Crowe Ransom: Critical Essays and a Bibliography*, 1968; *Ransom*, 1970; *Davidson* (with Inge), 1971. Editor of *The Literary Correspondence of Davidson and Tate* (with John T. Fain), 1974. **Essays:** Donald Davidson; John Crowe Ransom.